American Fighter-Bombers in World War II

American Fighter-Bombers in World War II

USAAF Jabos in the MTO and ETO

William Wolf

Schiffer Military History
Atglen, PA

Dedication

In the years since the end of World War II, book after book has concentrated on venerating the fighter ace, the combat pilot who shot down five or more enemy aircraft. In my previous book, *Victory Roll: The American Fighter Pilot and Aircraft in World War 2* (Schiffer, Atglen, PA, 2001) I tried to recognize not only the ace, but also the yeoman fighter pilot. In writing that book and interviewing hundreds of pilots, I came to learn from them of the importance and dangers of their transformation from fighter pilot to fighter-bomber pilot. By early 1944 the Allies had gained air superiority over the Mediterranean and then the Continent, and rendered the Luftwaffe a non-entity. This air superiority allowed the destruction from the air of the German transport and supply system, and the shattering of the morale of the German soldier. Interdiction, armored column cover, and close air support were an uncelebrated and major factor in the defeat of Germany. Strafing and low-level attacks on targets heavily defended by flak was a dangerous undertaking, and more pilots were killed or missing in action or taken prisoner than were lost in aerial combat. To these unsung heroes, I dedicate this book. I would also like to thank and dedicate this book to my wife, Nancy, who during the past four years has supported me while I spent thousands of hours writing three books and many articles on World War II air combat. For allowing her car to sit out in the Arizona sun while my library luxuriates in our air-conditioned enclosed three-car garage. And for spending four months every summer in our RV with our cat and me; hiking, biking, and kayaking the West during the days and giving me time every evening to work on my book.

Book Design by Ian Robertson.

Library of Congress Control Number: 2003108794

Printed in China.
ISBN: 0-7643-1878-0

We are interested in hearing from authors with book ideas on related topics.

Published by Schiffer Publishing Ltd.
4880 Lower Valley Road
Atglen, PA 19310
Phone: (610) 593-1777
FAX: (610) 593-2002
E-mail: Info@schifferbooks.com.
Visit our web site at: www.schifferbooks.com
Please write for a free catalog.
This book may be purchased from the publisher.
Please include $3.95 postage.
Try your bookstore first.

In Europe, Schiffer books are distributed by:
Bushwood Books
6 Marksbury Avenue
Kew Gardens
Surrey TW9 4JF
England
Phone: 44 (0) 20 8392-8585
FAX: 44 (0) 20 8392-9876
E-mail: Bushwd@aol.com.
Free postage in the UK. Europe: air mail at cost.
Try your bookstore first.

Contents

Foreword ... 7
Preface ... 8

Part One: Background, Doctrine, Aircraft, Auxiliaries, Weapons, Tactics, Targets, Enemy Defenses

Chapter 1: Introduction and Background ... 10
Chapter 2: Application of Field Manual 100-20 ... 16
First Priority: Air Superiority ... 16
Second Priority: Air Interdiction ... 17
Planned Missions ... 18
Armed Reconnaissance (Armed Recce) ... 20
8th Air Force Escorts and Targets of Opportunity ... 22
Third Priority: Close Support ... 24
Rover Joe ... 24
Close Support: Air vs. Artillery ... 26
Armored Column Cover ... 28
Night Fighters in Close Air Support and Interdiction ... 30
Chapter 3: The American Fighter Becomes a Fighter-Bomber ... 31
Early History ... 31
USAAF Fighter-Bomber Development ... 33
"Bill's Buzz Boys" ... 33
Establishment of the Tactical Air Forces ... 35
Conclusion ... 35
Chapter 4: USAAF Fighter-Bombers ... 36
P-47 Thunderbolt ... 36
P-38 Lightning ... 39
P-51 Mustang ... 40
A-36 Apache/Invader ... 42
P-39 Airacobra ... 43
P-40 Warhawk ... 44
P-61 Black Widow ... 45
Comparing the Fighter-Bomber to the Light and Medium Bomber ... 46
Shortcomings of American Fighter-Bombers ... 47
The Air-Cooled Radial vs. Liquid-Cooled Inline V Engine ... 47
Superchargers ... 51
Combat Damage and Aircraft Vulnerability ... 52
Chapter 5: Fighter-Bomber Organization ... 56
Grand Scheme ... 56
Pilots ... 57
Crew Chiefs and Ground Crews ... 58
Armorers ... 59
Casualties ... 61
Chapter 6: Airfields and Engineer and Air Service Commands ... 63
North Africa ... 63
ETO ... 64
IX Engineer Command ... 64
ALGs and IX Fighter Units (with base changes) ... 70
Air Service Command ... 71
USSTAF Air Service Command (ASC) ... 71
VIII Air Force Service Command ... 72
IX Air Service Command (IX ASC) ... 72
Chapter 7: Aircraft Armament, Ordnance and Accessories ... 76
Fighter Armament and Accessories ... 76
Machine Guns ... 76
Cannon ... 77
The Machine Gun vs. Cannon Controversy ... 77
Harmonization ... 79
American Aircraft Guns ... 79
Types of Ammunition ... 79
Gun Sights ... 81
Gun Cameras ... 82
Aircraft Ordnance ... 82
Bombs ... 82
Rockets ... 89
Napalm ("Blaze bombs," "Fireballs") ... 94
Drop Tanks ... 96
Pilot Protection and Safety ... 97
Communications ... 100
MEW Radar ... 101
Weather ... 106
Chapter 8: Enemy Targets ... 109
Claims ... 109
Strafing Attack/General Tenants
Pilot Strafing Mistakes ... 110
Enemy Targets
Transportation Network ... 110
Rail Transport ... 110
Motor Transport and the Road Network ... 114
Bridges and Tunnels ... 118
Tank Busting ... 120
Friendly River Crossings ... 122
Enemy River Crossings and Ferries ... 122
Inland Waterways, Locks and Barges ... 123
Small Naval Vessels and German Coastal Convoys ... 124
Airdromes and Strafing Claims and Aces ... 125
Tactical Attacks on Fuel ... 136
Anti-personnel Air Attacks ... 137
Communications ... 137
Ammunition Dumps ... 138
Flak Towers, Radio and Transmission Towers ... 139
V-weapon Sites ... 139
Fortifications and Gun Positions ... 140
Clean Up Missions ... 140
Chapter 9: German Counter Tactics ... 142
Aircraft ... 142
Flak - Units and Operations ... 144
German AA Guns ... 146
Sighting Apparatus ... 153
Mobile AA ... 154
Defense of Railway Trains ... 155
Evasion of Flak ... 157
Camouflage ... 159
Adapting Troop Behavior to Allied Air Superiority ... 164
Chapter 10: Fighter-Bomber Scoreboard ... 166

Part Two: Fighter-Bomber Campaigns

Chapter 11: North Africa ... 171
Operation TORCH (8 November 1942) ... 171
American Air Forces Operating from the East ... 174

Tunisia (November 1942-May 1943) ... 174
Kasserine Pass (14-22 January 1943) ... 176
Operation SUPERCHARGE (26 March 1943 and Beyond) .. 178
Operation FLAX (5 April-12 May 1943) ... 179
Final Battles (May 1943) ... 181
Results and Conclusions: North African Tactical Air Campaign ... 182
Chapter 12: Pantelleria (13 May-12 June 1943) ... 183
Chapter 13: Operation HUSKY: Invasion of Sicily (10 July-17 August 1943) ... 186
Chapter 14: The Italian Mainland Campaign: Background and Command ... 192
Chapter 15: Operation AVALANCHE, Salerno (18 August-20 September 1943) ... 194
Chapter 16: Volturno Campaign (21 September-15 November 1943) ... 199
Chapter 17: Winter Line Campaign (15 November-31 December 1943) ... 202
Chapter 18: Anzio (Operation SHINGLE)-Cassino (1 January-14 March 1944) ... 205
Chapter 19: STRANGLE (15 March-10 May 1944) ... 211
Chapter 20: DIADEM (11 May-22 June 1944) ... 215
Chapter 21: Operation ANVIL-DRAGOON (15 July-28 August 1944) The Invasion of Southern France ... 222
Chapter 22: Arno-Gothic Line (23 June-31 December 1944) 228
Operation BINGO and the Attacks on the Brenner Line ... 233
Operation BLOCKADE ... 235
Chapter 23: Po Valley (1 January-2 May 1945) ... 237
Operation HERBSTNABEL ... 239
Operation WOWSER/BOWLER ... 240
Operation BUCKLAND ... 240
Operation BOLOGNA ... 241
Chapter 24: Results and Conclusions Italian Tactical Air Campaign ... 243
Chapter 25: NW European Campaign: Background and Command ... 245
Chapter 26: D-Day/ Normandy Pre-Invasion (1 January-5 June 1944) ... 247
Pre-Invasion Fighter/Fighter-Bomber Objectives and Responsibilities ... 248
Allied Air Strategy ... 249
German Air Strategy ... 250
Air Superiority ... 251
Interdiction Missions and The Transportation Plan ... 256
Chapter 27: Normandy Landings/D-Day (5-6 June 1944-30 June 1944) ... 266
Command and Organization ... 266
Where is the Luftwaffe? ... 268
Confusion and destruction in Normandy ... 270
TACs aid the D-Day airborne troops ... 270
TACs over the beaches: D-Day to D+10 ... 271
Cherbourg (17-26 June 1944) ... 276
Results and Lessons Learned in June 1944 ... 278
Chapter 28: Breakout from the Normandy Beaches (7 July-13 August 1944) ... 281
Elle River to St. Lo Bayeux Road (7-18 July) ... 281
Operation COBRA/Falaise-St. Lo (25 July 1944) ... 283
Mortain (29 July-14 August 1944) ... 290
Chapter 29: Falaise (14 August-21 August 1944) ... 292
Chapter 30: Reduction of the French Ports (August-September 1944) ... 299
Brest (25 August-18 September 1944) ... 299
St. Malo (7-18 August 1944) ... 301
Chapter 31: The German Retreat Across Northeast France (21 August-15 September 1944) ... 303
USAAF Fighter-Bomber Campaign Against the German Transport System (15 September-15 December 1944) ... 309
Moselle River (7-12 September 1944) ... 311
Nancy (9-15 September 1944) ... 312
Activation of the XXIX TAC (14 September 1944) ... 312
Formation of the First TACAF (P) (September-November 1944) ... 313
Chapter 32: West Wall Operations (15 September-15 December 1944) ... 314
Siegfried Line (September-October 1944) ... 315
Aachen (12 September-21 October 1944) ... 316
Hurtgen Forest (September-December 1944) ... 317
Metz/Operation MADISON (17 September-20 November 1944) ... 317
Operation QUEEN (16-29 November 1944) ... 321
Roer River (16-29 November 1944) ... 322
U.S. Sixth Army Group at the Rhine (Late November 1944) ... 324
Chapter 33: Ardennes/Bulge Operations (15 December 1944-7 February 1945) ... 325
The German Build-up (Mid-November - mid-December 1944) ... 325
The Attack (16 December 1944) ... 326
American Air Reaction ... 326
Bastogne (18-31 December 1944) ... 330
Breaking the Bulge (28 December 1944-31 January 1945) ... 331
Fighter-Bomber Air Contributions ... 332
Roer River Line (19 December 1944-23 January 1945) ... 333
Retreat From the Bulge (22-26 January 1945) ... 334
Operation NORDWIND (1-26 January 1945) ... 335
Operation CHEERFUL: (20 January-12 March 1945) ... 335
Chapter 34: Attack on Germany (8 February-8 May 1945) ... 339
The Continuing Assault on German Railway System ... 339
Operation CLARION (22-23 February 1945) ... 340
Operation GRENADE (23 February 1945) ... 342
Continuing Attacks on the German Rail System (until the war's end) ... 342
Clearing the Saar-Moselle Triangle (19-23 February 1945) ... 343
Roer River (23 February 1945) ... 344
Strafing the Luftwaffe on the Ground (27 February 1945) ... 345
The TAC Situation in March 1945 ... 346
Kyll River to the Rhine (1-12 March 1945) ... 346
Rhine Bridges and the Remagen Bridgehead (9-27 March 1945) ... 346
Third Army Attacks Toward the Rhine (13-22 March 1945) ... 347
Attack on the German C-in-C, West at Ziegenberg (19 March 1945) ... 348
Rhine River Attacks (Late March 1945) ... 351
Breakout from the Rhine Bridgehead: The Ruhr Pocket (29 March-11 April 1945) ... 353
Chapter 35: Decimation of the Luftwaffe on the Ground (9-17 April 1945) ... 355
Chapter 36: Results and Conclusions ETO Tactical Air Campaign ... 366

Fighter-Bomber Aircraft in Profile ... 370
Appendices ... 378
Index ... 383

Foreword

I joined the 367th Fighter Squadron of the 355th Fighter Group of the 8th Air Force in June 1944 in time for D-Day. During my two tours over Europe I was fortunate enough to become both an ace in the air and on the ground with six aerial victories and 21 strafing victories. Over the years I have been asked more often about air combat and my air victories, but it is my strafing victories that I am equally proud. I was never really scared during air combat, as the battle was a known quantity, the German pilot against me. The two 20mm cannons on a Messerschmitt against the six .50 caliber Brownings on my Mustang. If there was air combat—which in mid-1944 wasn't too often—it was fast, and there was no time to think or be scared. But strafing sorties were another story. From mission briefing onward you knew you were going to see combat and stir up the enemy. You had too much time to worry about the mission during the long approach to the target. Would the Germans be waiting, or would the squadron be able to sneak up on them? How many flak guns would be waiting to open up? How many guns were camouflaged and not reported by the photo recon boys? You worried about the one lucky bullet fired by a soldier below hitting your vulnerable Merlin engine and bringing it to a grinding halt. You knew if you were hit on a low level strafing run you had little prospect of bailing out and would have to take your chances on a belly landing. You knew the statistics; five times as many P-51 pilots were downed by German flak as by the Luftwaffe. I became a statistic on 8 April 1945 when my Mustang was hit by flak over Ansbach Airdrome and set my engine on fire. I was lucky, as my parachute opened just before I hit the ground. After several days I was captured and shot by a SS officer and left for dead. I was saved by a compassionate German doctor and advancing American troops. Strafing was dangerous, it was exhilarating, and it was necessary. Strafing was vital to our infantry, as it made them safe from the Luftwaffe and deprived the enemy of vital supplies and reinforcements.

Bill Cullerton

Preface

My lifelong hobby has been World War II aviation, and over the years I have collected over 14,000 books and magazines, along with hundreds of reels of microfilm and videotapes on the subject. I have been told that I have the largest personal WWII aviation library in the world. My library contains nearly every book written on WWII combat aviation, and complete collections of every combat aviation magazine published since 1939. Included in the collection are many hundreds of American and other belligerent air force and unit histories, general histories, pilot narratives, parts and maintenance manuals, books on individual aircraft, etc. My microfilm collection includes vintage intelligence reports, numerous USAAF, USN, and USMC group and squadron histories, German and Japanese Monograph Series, U.S. and British Strategic Bombing Surveys, and USAAF Historical Studies. I have been fortunate in meeting many fighter aces, pilots, and fellow aviation buffs who have shared stories, sources, and photographs with me. I have made many multi-day expeditions to various military libraries, museums, and photo depositories with my copy machine and camera and copy stand, collecting literally reams of material and thousands of photos. I also have a dark room where I developed thousands of photos—many rare and unseen—from microfilm negatives. Over the years the origin of the thousands of photos I have been lent to copy and those I have copied and collected myself have become obscured or lost. Most are from military and government sources, but many are from private individuals. I apologize if some of the photos which are credited as from the "author's collection" or otherwise are in fact from individuals or other sources. Also, some of the photos are not of the best quality because of their age and source.

I would like to acknowledge the sizable and vital contribution of the brave light and medium bomber pilots and crews of the American Tactical Air Forces and the fighter-bomber pilots of the RAF 2nd Tactical Air Force, who also flew close support and interdiction missions over the MTO and ETO.

Part One

Background, Doctrine, Weapons, Tactics, Targets, Enemy Defenses

1

Introduction and Background

Introduction

In the USAAF the term "fighter-bomber" officially and unofficially was a nebulous one in World War II. There were no pure American fighter-bomber units or fighter-bomber aircraft. The fighter-bombers of the tactical air forces also flew as fighters engaged in aerial combat and escort while fighters of the strategic air forces, especially late in the war, dropped down from escort duty and dog fighting to act as fighter-bombers, strafing German airdromes and harassing targets of opportunity. The 27th and 86th Groups, flying P-40s and A-36s respectively, were officially referred to as Fighter-Bomber Groups until August 1944 when they transitioned to the P-47 and were designated Fighter Groups. Ironically, both groups probably flew even more close support and interdiction missions when redesignated as a fighter group than they did as fighter-bomber groups. The P-47, starting its career as America's best high altitude interceptor and bomber escort, ended the war as its ultimate fighter-bomber. Paradoxically, the P-51 Mustang, which was ordered by the RAF as a low-level fighter-bomber, was re-engined with the Packard-built Rolls-Royce Merlin to became America's best high-altitude escort. The USAAF always referred to the P-47 as a fighter and units flying it as fighter groups or fighter squadrons, even though the vast majority of their sorties were as fighter-bombers. Over the Mediterranean and Northwest Europe, the fighter ace and dogfighter received the praise and publicity while the strafer and dive-bomber did unheralded journeyman's work. The interceptor/escort fighter pilot flew many uneventful missions without meeting an enemy aircraft. The fighter-bomber pilot often flew one or more daily sorties against a wide range of targets extending from the frontlines to several hundred miles behind enemy lines. On every mission he flew into the teeth of the heaviest flak and small arms fire encountered in the war, often sustaining heavy losses. The measure of his effort has never been truly appreciated, but the fighter-bomber was a major player in the air war over Europe and Italy. The extensive destruction of thousands of trains and trucks and the German-run rail and road networks critically disrupted the enemy supply system, changing German battlefront strategy and reducing offensive and defensive capabilities. The fighter-bomber was constantly in the air over the front, knocking out German armor, gun positions, and troop concentrations. Nothing German could move in daylight without receiving the attention of a fighter-bomber. By 1944-45 the fighter equipped with bombs and rockets and machine guns was the most numerous component of the Allied Air Forces, and played a significant role in the defeat of the Wehrmacht.

The Germans referred to fighter-bombers as Jagdebombers, "Jabos." The term "Achtung Jabos!" translates to "Look out, Fighter-bombers!," but to the German soldier it would come to mean terror from the skies. Day after day their war became a struggle to evade air attack, to suffer hunger—as food did not arrive—and not be able to return fire on the advancing Allied armies, as ammunition was blown up on the way to the front by American Jabos that strafed German supply trucks and trains. War for the German soldier was to ride, then walk, and finally crawl to the front at night because that was safer than being strafed by persistent Jabos that seemed to be always overhead in daylight.

An officer with the U.S. Seventh Army observed the following in July 1944 near Falaise, France:

"The sun was shining as the convoy I was in made its way down this road that was hilly with many declines. There, in a defile between a wooden ridge and a ravine, a mainly horse-drawn German column had been caught in the open by Thunderbolts. For two

Halberstadt ground attack aircraft (Author)

The Sopwith Salamander was the first British purpose-built fighter-bomber but was not produced until the end of the war. This fighter-bomber provided armor protection for the pilot, engine, fuel tanks and guns. (Author)

miles along the road there was a scene of desolation almost beyond bearing. Dead horses, some disemboweled, their legs stiff in the air at angular attitudes, lined the ditches. The Americans had simply bulldozed off the road and into the ravine the shattered German armored vehicles, trucks, and wagons, with their dead. German soldiers laying dead in grotesque positions. On trees by the side of the road, signs had been posted in bold red letters: ACHTUNG JABOS."

Background

The German Army Air Corps in the First World War initiated the use of their Junkers and Fokker fighter aircraft in the close support role when they strafed Allied troops in their trenches. The technique derived its name from the German verb "strafe," translating to "to punish." In 1916 the British Royal Flying Corps used aircraft for reconnaissance, but soon entered the German verb in their aviation vocabulary when they attacked von Ludendorff's hapless troops in the trenches below by dropping small bombs by hand, albeit with little effect. By 1918 air attacks on troops began to have a significant effect on all fronts. In Palestine the Turkish Seventh and Eighth Armies attempted to retreat along a road cut into the side of a cliff and were pounded for four hours from the air by nine tons of small bombs and grenades and 50,000 rounds of machine gun ammunition. The dazed and beaten Turks abandoned their trucks, carts, artillery, and supplies in a total rout. These devastating air attacks were repeated in Macedonia when the Second Bulgarian Army was decimated. The British DH4s, SE5s, FK8s, and RE8s were fragile conventional fighters modified to carry weapons and were vulnerable to ground fire and suffered heavy losses. The Germans manufactured the first planned fighter-bombers and created the first specially trained "Schlachstaffeln" (Battle Squadrons), which flew in close coordination with ground forces. Their aircraft were all metal, such as the Ju J-1 "Flying Tank" built by the new Junkers company formed in 1917, and the Halberstadt two-seat ground attack aircraft fitted with bomb racks at the side of the cockpit. However, it was not until the end of the war that the first British purpose-built fighter-bomber was produced, the Sopwith Salamander. This fighter-bomber provided armor protection for the pilot, engine, fuel tanks, and guns.

During March 1918 the British Army was in retreat after being battered by Ludendorff's offensive north of the Somme. In an effort to slow the German advance Maj.Gen. Sir John Salmond, C-in-C of the RFC, ordered: "Squadrons are to bomb and shoot up everything they can see in the enemy lines. Very low flying is essential." All types of British aircraft were deployed and the front was stabilized. On 8 August 1918, the RAF formed only four months previously, supported the Allied offensive by mounting the largest and most coordinated air assault of the war. First they gained complete air superiority preventing German reconnaissance aircraft from discovering the build up and then used the noise of their engines to hide the massing of tanks. Once the attack began, eight squadrons supported ground forces up to four miles in advance of the front. Other squadrons were assigned to attack German infantry, cavalry, and artillery. Still others were to support British tanks and artillery through observation and laying smoke screens.

In World War I, America's air arm was stepchild of an army that believed wars were won with infantry and artillery, and a navy that believed battleships and big guns won the day. American airmen flew English or French-built aircraft and were merely considered a sideshow, but afterward would become fodder for heroic stories for pulp magazines and Hollywood movies.

Between the wars the Germans developed the "Blitzkrieg," fast-moving, powerful armored attacks, which required air support because their artillery was unable to follow the armor. During the Spanish Civil War the Luftwaffe developed their aircraft and tactics, and became a tactical rather than a strategic air force, a move that was to have dire consequences during the Battle of Britain.

In the Second World War the Germans again were the first to utilize their fighter aircraft in the bomber role. By late summer 1940, during the Battle of Britain, Luftwaffe dive-bombers and medium bombers suffered acute losses and were removed from daytime operations over Britain. To fill the void, the Luftwaffe formed a Jabo Staffel, or fighter-bomber squadron, equipped with the Messerschmitt Me-109E, which was capable of carrying one 550lb. or four 110lb. bombs. The fighter-bombers raced across the English Channel and dropped their bombs by diving at a 45-degree angle, aiming their bombs using their Revi gun sight. This stopgap measure caused minimal damage, but the raids were very difficult to defend against and led to the employment of the Me-109 and, later, the Focke-Wulf-190 as "Jabos" in a close support role over the Eastern Front and Mediterranean.

In the 1930s the RAF Air Ministry had rejected the dive-bomber concept, and at the start of the war had no dedicated ground-attack aircraft. Once the war began, the RAF realized that its fighter aircraft needed to be equipped with bombs to attack ground targets. The Hurricane IIA was equipped with underwing attachments to carry external fuel tanks that could be adapted to carry 250lb. bombs, and were used against the Italians over Libya in late 1940. Later in 1941, the Hurricane IIA was outfitted with twelve .303 cal. machine guns and the IIB with four 20mm cannon, and both marks were designed with underwing bomb attachments. By 1943, the RAF had developed the Hawker Typhoon, which would become the premier RAF fighter-bomber of the war.

Pre-World War I American tactical aviation began with the earliest aircraft assigned to the Army Signal Corps Aeronautical Division, where pilots or observers fired hand-held guns and dropped bombs by hand. The Aviation Section succeeded the Aeronautical Division, and when America entered World War I it became the Air Service. The Air Service function was described as "attack and pursuit aviation," which attacked enemy infantry and pursued enemy aircraft. It supported ground troops and operated as an integral part of the ground echelon.

After World War I the Air Service Tactical School was established, and a debate raged between Army air and ground officers that became public in the infamous Billy Mitchell vs. the Navy case. Generally, ground leaders touted the conventional notion that a ground army was essential in order to defeat an enemy army and capture its homeland, and that the air force was principally a supporting force to aid the army in this undertaking. On 2 July 1926, the Air Service became the Army Air Corps (AAC), but remained under the control of the Army. Until the mid-1930s Army ground officers held the advantage of tenure and dominated the General Staff. Few of these General Staff officers understood or cared to understand the changes in aviation. They controlled and limited the publication of air doctrine that would have been included in the education of ground officers at a time when the role of air power was becoming more important in European military thinking.

During the pre-war 1930s the Army Air Corps emphasized the strategic bombing philosophy, but it was realized that the achievement of air superiority was the pre-requisite objective of air power theory. On 1 March 1935 this policy gave air officers increased internal command and control through the formation of a General Headquarters (GHQ). GHQ was based at Langley Field, VA, and was comprised of three wings. The First Wing, based at March Field, CA, was made up of two bomb groups, one attack group and two reconnaissance squadrons. The Second Wing, also based at Langley Field, consisted of two bomb groups, two pursuit groups, and a reconnaissance squadron. The Third Wing, located at Barksdale Field, LA, had two pursuit groups and two attack groups. Ground officers continued in their desire to have control of "their" air arm, and thus AAC GHQ independence and control did not compare to that of Britain's RAF, as AAC GHQ was subordinate to the Army Chief of Staff. Training Regulation, *TR 440-15, The Employment of the Air Forces of the Army, 15 October 1935*, which not only stated the AAC mission, but acknowledged the compromise between the opposing air and ground positions on AAC operational independence. The AAC was allowed to direct air operations independently against an invading enemy force until ground forces became operational. But *TR 440-15* confirmed the Army doctrine that the AAC would "further the mission" of the Army commander to which they were assigned. *TR 440-15* did concede the validity of the concepts of the close air support air doctrine developed by the AAC Tactical School. These principles included: the emphasis on offensive action; the establishment of air superiority; aerial operations preceding ground armies into battle; and that the air force

In January 1929 this crew of flyers set a record for refueling when their aircraft, The *Question Mark* stayed in the air for almost 151 hours. Four flyers would become influential in later years (left to right): Sgt. Roy Hooe, Lt. Elwood "Pete" Quesada (CG IX TAC), Lt. Harry Halverson (led first Ploesti raid), Capt. Ira Eaker (CG 8th Air Force and C-in-C MAAF) and Maj. Carl "Tooey" Spaatz (CG 12 Air Force and CG USSTAF). (USAF)

Chief of Staff, Gen. George C. Marshall meets with Generals (left to right) Gerow, Wheeler, Miles, Arnold, Haislip, Twaddle and Bryden in 1941. At the time the Air Force was considered an adjunct to the infantry. (US Army)

would be concentrated against a significant target and "not dispersed or dissipated in minor or secondary operations."

Despite *TR 440-15*, tactical operations were subordinated to strategic bomber air doctrine and its pre-requisite, the establishment of air superiority. This opposition to close support missions went so far as to prohibit the installation of bomb racks on pursuit aircraft from 1936 to 1938! The successes of the Luftwaffe in the Spanish Civil War, along with Italian and Japanese use of their air forces in Ethiopia and China changed America's thinking on its aerial doctrine.

By 1938, Hitler's rise to power and subsequent revitalization of the German military had alarmed European nations, particularly Britain and France, who looked to America and President Roosevelt to supply them with additional aircraft. In mid-November 1938, FDR met with Army Chief of Staff, Gen. Malin Craig, Deputy Chief of Staff, Gen. George C. Marshall, and Air Corps Chief, Gen. Henry H. Arnold, to discuss the protection of the Western Hemisphere against the potential threat from Germany and Italy. The President wished to expand and modernize the Air Corps, and by doing so American industry could manufacture enough aircraft to supply itself and Europe. Congress deliberated for several months, and in early 1939 endowed the Air Corps with its first in a number of sizable budget grants. The special interest shown by the President and Congress to the Air Corps gave it a new stature within the Army in asserting its independence and views of ground support aviation. When the Second World War broke out in September, Hitler's remarkable use of close air support in his Blitzkrieg in Poland and France impressed American Army ground force leaders, and they petitioned for air support and suitable aircraft.

At the start of the war in 1939 USAAC inventory had very few modern combat aircraft of any type available, in particular for close support role, and by 1940-41 air and ground officers became increasingly anxious over this deficiency. In the inter-war years, limited government funding had diminished aircraft research and development, but in 1939, FDR and Congress granted vast funding for aircraft procurement. The three to five year time lag from drawing board to combat aircraft would be too long, but fortunately American industry had entered the international commercial and military markets prior to 1939 and had a number of light and medium bomber types and designs available. Gen. Arnold decided, in light of the successes and high regard that European air forces held the light and medium bomber, to order twin-engine light and medium bombers for use in both interdiction bombing and close support. These bombers, while superlative in their interdiction role, were unsuited for accurately hitting targets in close proximity to friendly infantry. The ideal ground support aircraft was one which could carry a large number of guns and droppable ordnance, have heavy armor protection against ground fire, sufficient range to enable it to remain over the target area, and speed to be able to meet or retreat from enemy fighters. Into late 1941, the Plans Division of the AAC rejected any modification of existing fighter aircraft for ground support purposes. Also, there were no such designs available or on the drawing boards, and such an aircraft would not be available until after the war.

Impressed by Luftwaffe Stuka dive-bomber successes, Gen. Marshall uncharacteristically interfered with more knowledgable AAC heads and requested the Air Corps to study the dive-bomber concept and purchase models for study. Gen. Arnold informed Marshall that the dive-bomber concept was tested years earlier and was found wanting. Nonetheless, Marshall insisted, and Arnold was obliged to comply. The AAC had no dive-bombers in inventory and none on the drawing boards. Conscious of certain failure, Arnold's dive-bomber program was half-hearted. He ordered only small numbers of modified Navy dive-bombers and had the first production P-51s modified with dive brakes and wing racks and designated as the A-36.

In September 1939, Gen. Marshall was appointed Army Chief of Staff. Marshall had long studied air power and was considered a friend of the AAC. He posted many air officers to positions on the Army General Staff and worked hard to resolve the differences between the ground and air factions in the Army. Marshall had previously worked successfully with AAC Chief, Gen. Arnold, and gave Arnold and the AAC as much autonomy as possible. In 1940, the world military situation was such that to split the AAC from the Army was too extreme and complicated that both men agreed that the AAC could not become an independent arm, as was the Royal Air Force. Arnold agreed not to push for AAC independence during the war and Marshall rewarded him. The American Air Force was ultimately permitted to fully develop its strategic and tactical tenets, and was supplied with the best aircraft and pilots in the world. But in 1940 a disagreement over air doctrine continued within the AAC.

The AAC Tactical School had long stressed the traditional importance of long-range bombers, independent strike forces, and the bombing of industrial targets and pre-war canon described close air support as "aviation in support of ground forces." The German military threat in 1939 led to the downgrading of offensive air doctrine and instead planned for the defense of the American continent. Secretary of War, Harry H. Pickering, instructed Gen. Arnold to appoint a board of officers from all Army branches to plan the future role of the Air Corps. Their conclusions were issued in September 1939 as the Air Board Report. Soon, Gen. Marshall asked for a new statement of American air doctrine using this report. The result was *Air Corps Field Manual 1-5, Employment of Aviation of the Army, 15 April 1940*, and did little to promote support aviation. It rejected support aviation as unsuited for direct attacks in the "hostile rear area." It stated that support aviation was "not to be employed against objectives which can be effectively engaged by available ground weapons," and "was poorly suited for direct attacks against small detachments or troops which are well entrenched or disposed." However, the manual did describe contemporary air support theory, emphasized "centralized control" for maximum success, and that the "combined operations of air and ground forces must be closely coordinated by the commander of the combined force and all operations conducted in accordance with a well-defined plan." *War Department Training Circular, The Army Air Force Basic Doctrine, 24 July 1941* continued to downgrade close support aviation, stating that operations in close cooperation with the other sections of the mobile Army were secondary to interdiction and air superiority missions.

After Pearl Harbor and America's initial combat efforts, organizational deficiencies were exposed. In March 1942, Gen. Marshall reorganized the General Staff General Headquarters into the Army Ground Forces and Army Air Corps (AAC). The result of the reorganization was that the AAC achieved more independence of action. Ground officers were worried that the AAC would adopt RAF-type ground support in which the air units were not attached to ground officers at any echelon, and the air officer made all decisions on the use of air support. The reorganization of air units into air forces led to increased centralized, overall control by air officers, but in turn led to the division of units formerly designated to close air support and other ground support duties. To rectify this, specialized air support commands were organized to merge units affording close air support for ground troops and by creating a HQ staff committed to air support and interaction between the air and ground arms. By and large, this reorganization gave more independence and importance to the role of the air arm in close support. But even so, there were dissenters, such as John J. McCoy, the Assistant Secretary of War, who stated in early 1942:

"It is my firm belief that the Air Forces are not interested in this type work (close air support), think it is unsound, and are very much concerned lest it result in control of air units by ground forces. Their interest, enthusiasm, and energy is directed to different fields."

In March 1942, *Army Training Regulation 52* stated that all types of aviation—pursuit, bombardment, and reconnaissance—were to engage in close support work. *TR 52* did not provide for an organization under which air support could be united. It was not a part of either the Air Force Combat Command or the component air support commands. *Army Field Manual 31-35 "Aviation in Support of Ground Forces,"* which succeeded *TR 52* in April 1942, was a collection of tactical doctrine put together by the Air Support Section of the Air Force Command. *FM 31-35* stated that air support aviation was "normally constituted into air support commands which ordinarily are parts of air forces." These air support commands were attached to or supported an army in a theater and were under ground force command. Even though the Air Force Combat Command had been phased out earlier on 9 March, *FM 31-35* remained the only reference that could be used in actual combat to answer the many procedural questions that arose. Operation TORCH in November 1942 was the first field test of tactical organization and doctrine. The Twelfth Air Force that had been activated on 20 August 1942 was assigned to provide air support. The XII Air Support Command (ASC), formed in September 1942, was to be the tactical component, but did not have any fighters, as all fighters were placed under the XII Fighter Command that was to support strategic operations. There was also a major division of command between the USAAC and the RAF in the early Tunisian campaign. This division of command led to the minimal effectiveness of close support during TORCH. The Allied Air Support Command was formed on 7 February 1943 under Air Marshal Sir Arthur Coningham and his American deputy, Brig.Gen. Laurence Kuter. The results of this reorganization in combat will be discussed in detail in the North African Campaign section.

In February 1943, Gen. Eisenhower in a report to the Combined Chiefs of Staff stated:

"To a large extent in our experience the creation of separate Strategic and Tactical forces resolved the conflict between the immediate needs of the commander for direct air support and the equally compelling necessity of knocking out the enemy's war potential far behind the lines; but, perhaps the greatest advantage of our new organization was its flexibility."

In a Pentagon press conference on 22 May 1943, Brig.Gen. Laurence Kuter, discussing his North African experience, stated:

"The Tactical Air Force is a completely new idea in the organization of an air force fighting in the field along side an army. The idea was not evolved from book study or by theorists. Its conception, together with the details of its organization, grew gradually and as a direct result of long and bitter battles stemming back to the air-ground efforts of the British crossing the Western Desert.... In the Tactical Air Force we combined the desirable features learned in the Western Desert and believe we have eliminated the errors that had previously been made.... In a modern battlefield we put two strong powers (e.g. the Air Force and Army, ed.), each working in its own element towards the same goal, each helping the other."

However, this Air Force-Army coordination was on an upper echelon basis that only took into account the broad objective of the battle, but did not take into account the often immediate needs of local ground commanders. In North Africa the true success was that the tactical air force was no longer a supporting force of the Army, but proved and then asserted itself as an equal and independent partner. In June 1943, Gen. Arnold announced:

"The Tactical Air Force, as the Air Force to work on a coequal basis with the Ground Forces in the battle are, has been accepted by the War Department and is now being prepared in Field Service Regulation form."

A slim booklet was published by the War Department on 21 July 1943, entitled *Field Manual 100-20, Command and Employment of Air Power*, which laid the foundation for American tactical air power at a time when it had only limited battle experience in North Africa, no training scheme, inadequate fighter-bomber aircraft, and few experienced pilots for such an undertaking. The authors of *FM 100-20* were academics who formulated three priorities for waging tactical warfare and affirmed air power to be an equal and independent entity commanded by a senior air commander who was to be responsible only to the theater commander. Throughout the war USAAF leadership was committed to maximum autonomy in the War Department with the intention of gaining post war independence, but had to settle for the autonomy given to them by *FM 100-20*. Nonetheless, it was the Emancipation Proclamation for air power.

Much of this doctrine was taken from the British experience in North Africa. Parts of *FM 100-20* were based on a pamphlet written by Gen. Montgomery in January 1943 entitled Some Notes on High Command in War. Vice Air Marshall Sir Arthur Coningham, whose air units supported Montgomery in North Africa, influenced Montgomery's thinking on the application of tactical air power. In *Ideas, Concepts, Doctrine: A History of Basic Thinking in the United States Air Force, 1907-1964* (Air University, AL, 1974), Robert Futrell quoted Gen. Robert Candee as saying the Air Force "...had swallowed the RAF solution of a local situation in Africa hook, line, and sinker, without analyzing it or report it in 'Americanese' instead of British speech."

As the Allies took the offensive in the air and on the ground in the ETO and MTO in 1943, *FM 100-20* prioritized an air plan in which to conduct the war. Their first priority was to win air superiority:

"The primary aim of the tactical air force is to obtain and maintain air superiority in the theater.... Without this air supremacy the initiative passes to the enemy. Air supremacy is best obtained by attack on hostile airdromes, the destruction of aircraft at rest and by fighter action in the air. This is much more effective than any attempt to furnish an umbrella of fighter aviation over our troops. At most an air umbrella is prohibitively expensive and could be provided over a small area for a brief period of time."

The second priority was:

"The disruption of hostile lines of communication, the destruction of supply dumps, installations and the attack on hostile troop concentrations in rear areas will cause the enemy great damage and may decide the battle. This accomplishes 'isolation of the battlefield.' If the hostile force is denied food, ammunition and reinforcements, aggressive action on the part of our ground forces will cause him to retire and the immediate objective will be gained. Massed air action on those targets should turn the retirement into a rout."

In general the second priority could be summed up as "behind the lines attacks." The third priority was:

"The destruction of selected objectives in the battle area in furtherance of the combined air-ground effort.... Teamwork, mutual understanding and cooperation are essential for this success of the combined effort in the battle area. In order to obtain the necessary teamwork, the command posts of the Tactical Air Force and of the ground force concerned should be adjacent or common, at least during this phase of operations. Air and ground commanders profit greatly from the other's successes. Airplanes destroyed on an enemy airdrome and in the air can never attack our troops. The advance of ground troops often makes available new airdromes needed by the air force. Massed air action on the immediate front will pave the way for an advance. However, in the zone of contact, missions against hostile units are difficult to control, are most expensive and are, in general, least effective. Targets are small, well dispersed and difficult to locate. In addition, there is always a considerable chance of striking friendly forces, due to errors in target designation, errors in navigation, or to the fluidity of the situation. Such missions must be controlled by phase lines, or bomb safety lines, which are set up and rigidly adhered to by both ground and air units. Only at critical times are contact zone missions profitable." The third priority then was "battle front attack/close support."

At the end of the war the air campaign had demonstrated that ground direction of fighter-bombers to targets was very effective and did not cause loss of Air Force control or flexibility. Attacks on Second and Third Priority targets were most effective when the objective and method of the attack was jointly selected and planned by both air and ground staffs.

2

Application of *Field Manual 100-20*

To meet the three air priorities set forth in *FM 100-20* changes were made. In the MTO the Twelfth Air Force was divided in November 1943 with the purpose of creating a tactical and a strategic air force. The Fifteenth Air Force was created to be the strategic component, leaving the Twelfth as the tactical component. In the ETO the Ninth Air Force was reconstituted on 19 October 1943 as a tactical air force. Thus, the USAAF fighter airplane was to become the fighter-bomber; a multi-tasked aerial weapon that was able to conduct close air support, short- and long-range armed reconnaissance, deep- and shallow-interdiction missions, and also provide escort for light and medium bombers. *FM 100-20* was field tested in September 1943, as the invasion of the Italian mainland began. Its concepts withstood the test of combat, as the air campaign was successfully carried out without any revision.

All six fighter-bomber combat missions are included in the three priorities:

First: Escort and Fighter Sweep
Second: Interdiction/Planned Mission and Armed Reconnaissance
Third: Close Support and Armed Column Cover

First Priority: Air Superiority

The first priority was the attainment of air superiority. Invasion, first in Sicily, then on the Italian mainland, and finally in Normandy, was the primary reason for securing air superiority; it was essential to prevent the Luftwaffe from disrupting the invasion so later the full impact of Allied air power could be used against German ground forces as the Allied armies fought their way from the invasion beaches. The attainment of air superiority was achieved by:

1) Strategic attacks against German aircraft production
2) Strategic attacks against German gasoline and oil production
3) Tactical attacks against Luftwaffe airdromes, aircraft on the ground, and supply centers
4) Tactical superiority in air combat

Strategic bombardment initiated the campaign for air superiority. In April 1943, the 8th Air Force began to fly its first deep penetrations of Germany, and continued with impressive but sporadic large-scale raids on the fighter assembly factories at Regensburg and Wiener Neustadt in August, and then the raid on

FM 100-20

COMMAND AND EMPLOYMENT OF AIR POWER

WAR DEPARTMENT • 21 JULY 1943

United States Government Printing Office
Washington : 1944

Right: *FM 100-20*, the primer for American tactical airpower doctrine. (USAF)

Marienburg in October 1943. The Reichs Luftfahrtministerium responded to the bombing offensive by increasing fighter production from 600 to 1,200 fighters per month. By early 1944 the Allied bomber forces had reached capacity, an efficient long-range fighter escort (P-51 Mustang) had been developed, and the winter weather gave way to long periods of clearing. These factors allowed the methodical devastation of German aircraft factories. The last week in February saw six consecutive days of bombing followed by two months of judicious repeat attacks that dropped German fighter production to 400 per month. These attacks continued, and by the D-Day invasion aircraft production remained low and the Luftwaffe was absent over the Normandy beaches. On 1 March 1944, the production of fighter aircraft was transferred to the Speer ministry from the Luftwaffe. Albert Speer, the brilliant architect turned Armaments Minister, had Hitler's ear and launched his Jaegerstab Program that approved the money, manpower, and machinery to restore the aircraft industry. By October 1944 Speer accomplished the impossible and succeeded in his ambitious plan by producing 2,400 fighters per month, including revolutionary jet and rocket aircraft. Ironically, once this impressive fighter production was realized strategic bombing had devastated German gasoline production. Hundreds of new German fighters sat idle without fuel on airfields and assembly points, fodder for marauding Allied fighter-bombers.

Fighter-Bombers Maintain Air Superiority: The nonstop flying of second and third priority missions by fighter-bombers assured the continuous maintenance of air superiority without the loss of ground support. As the name fighter-bomber implies, if the Luftwaffe should appear, bombs were jettisoned and the fighter would intercept the German aircraft.

Escort missions to Fighter Sweeps: After air superiority over the Luftwaffe had been achieved and American bombers were no longer being harassed, the fighter escorts were given freedom to attack targets of opportunity, especially Luftwaffe airfields, on their way home. Then in spring 1945, in order to utilize their massive fighter force, the 8th Air Force introduced freelance and coordinated strafing missions against the grounded Luftwaffe. In strafing these targets, the flight leader needed to devise an impromptu plan of attack as he circled the target. He assessed a number of factors: cloud cover; sun position; terrain; and enemy defenses. The flight leaders were instructed to exercise good judgment and to take into account the anticipated results as weighed against possible losses. Huge numbers of Luftwaffe aircraft were destroyed on the ground for lack of fuel during the last months of the war.

Air superiority benefited both Allied air and ground forces. With command of the skies Allied air forces could operate with maximum flexibility and effectiveness against enemy ground forces. Allied air power greatly limited the combat effectiveness and supply of enemy ground forces. The Germans were forced to expend a great amount of resources and effort to cope with the relentless attacks from the air that could have been devoted to fighting Allied ground forces. Only the extensive use of AA fire and camouflage could ameliorate the lack of air superiority. On the other hand, amply supplied Allied troops, with the Luftwaffe a non-entity, were not hampered by air attacks and were able to concentrate on attacking the beleaguered Germans.

On 24 June 1944, Ike's son, 1Lt. John D. Eisenhower, a recent West Point graduate, was riding along the crowded roads in Normandy with his father and had the following discussion:

"The roads we traversed were dusty and crowded. Vehicles moving slowly, bumper to bumper. Fresh out of West Point I was offended at this jamming up of traffic. It wasn't according to the book. Leaning over Dad's shoulder, I remarked, 'You'd never get away with this if you didn't have air supremacy.' I received an impatient snort, "If I didn't have air supremacy I wouldn't be here."

Second Priority: Air Interdiction

Second priority missions, referred to as interdiction missions, were behind the lines attacks intended to isolate the battlefield. After D-Day, armies engaged in the ground campaigns across Europe moved rapidly over great distances, exerting continual pressure on the enemy. One of the decisive weapons was air power that blockaded and isolated the battlefield and limited movement of personnel and weapons to and within the battle area. Tactical light and medium bombers played the major role in second priority missions, but fighter-bombers also played a large part in the Allied interdiction program and took a heavy toll on the German supply system.

Requirements of an interdiction program were that tactically it needed to be developed from a ground plan, either offensive or defensive, and be closely tied to its objectives. The air program must have a high priority in order to be completed in a timely and effective manner, and the plan must be within the capabilities of the air units involved.

Two weeks after D-Day Ike's son, 1Lt. John D. Eisenhower, a recent West Point graduate, was riding along Normandy roads jammed with Allied vehicles and remarked to his father, "You'd never get away with this if you didn't have air supremacy." Ike replied, "If I didn't have air supremacy I wouldn't be here." (USAF)

Planned Missions

The USAAF tactical air support scheme was generally comparable to that of the RAF. The U.S. Tactical Air Force was an organization of several Tactical Air Commands (TACs) consisting of fighter, fighter-bomber, and reconnaissance squadrons. The 9th Air Force consisted of the IX, XIX, and XXIX Tactical Air Commands.

Each TAC general was in direct command of the air immediately in front of and to the limit of his aircraft's range over the army he was to support. He cooperated with the Army not as a supporting force, but as defined by the War Department, "as a co-equal and interdependent force." He had the Air Defense Command (ADC) to protect his bases, the Air Service Command (ASC) for supply and aircraft service, and the Engineering Command (EC) to build and maintain airfields.

Each TAC supported an Army within an Army group, with the Headquarters of each TAF and Army Group and TAC and Army placed together. If this were not possible then the TACs dispatched a small mobile command echelon at the advanced HQ of the Army they were to support. Air Force HQ deployed the TACs, controlled their movements and logistics, and planned operations.

Each TAC planned and coordinated the daily air support of its designated Army from a Combined Operations Center at TAC/Army HQ staffed by Air Force and Army personnel. The 9th Air Force held "Evening Target Conferences" during which the next day's operations were discussed. The Army G-3 (Operations) Section maintained a complete, updated situation map. Initially 1:100,000 situation maps were used, but advances on the ground became so rapid and the battlefronts so widespread that spearheads were continually running off the map, even though they were plotted on boards 16 feet long by eight feet high. Finally 1:200,000 maps were used to keep up with the advances. The G-3 would review the ground operations planned for the next day and brief the air force on these operations. Jointly, with air operations personnel, it would request TAC missions in support of these operations and coordinate the bomb line. The bomb line was a line to protect friendly forces, in front of which aircraft could operate freely on any target. The bomb line was marked with puffs of white smoke made and maintained by artillery shells. They were to be placed 3,000 yards in front of the forward troops and periodically moved forward, usually every 15 minutes and placed about a mile apart and extended across the entire front, conforming as closely as possible to the natural contours of the terrain. An air controller would relay the ground situation to the Ground Liaison Officers (GLOs) at the airbases and provide them with the necessary information to brief the pilots. It was the responsibility of G-3 to supply ground and air units with the essential operational information to coordinate the tactical action of the two. The Army G-2 (Intelligence) Section presented the enemy situation, submitted requests for air reconnaissance, and gathered and distributed air recon data. G-2 maintained comprehensive target intelligence collected from ground force sources. The A-2 (Air Intelligence Officer), together with G-3 and the A-3 (Air Combat Operations Officer), would plan the attacks on suitable targets. The A-2 would discuss the latest air intelligence, and the A-2 Target Officer discussed prospective targets. The weather officer would present his prediction for the next day. The minimum weather for close air support over the target was 5,000 feet with broken cloud and 3,500 feet and broken cloud for armed recce. For take off the minimum was 1,000 feet and three miles visibility. Plans for large-scale air support operations were prepared at TAC HQ and submitted to TAF HQ, where they were reviewed and completed by combined Army and Air staff.

Following this conference the A-3 determined the units available for TAC operations. Some units would be required for bomber escort, some for special targets requested by TAF HQ, some for armed recon, and there always were units undergoing maintenance. The remaining units were available for the pre-planned air support missions. Orders were issued, assigning these missions to Air Groups, which then assigned missions to its squadrons.

Often, air support requests were made after the evening conference or during the next day. These requests were assessed by the Army G-3 according to priority and the consequence to the ground unit making the request and were handled in turn. It took about a quarter hour for the potential mission to be plotted on a continually updated situation map and a bomb line assessed. After the G-3 approved the request it was passed to the nearby A-3, who would approve the mission if feasible and if aircraft were available. He would inform group HQ by telephone or teletype of his approval and of the aircraft to be deployed and their mission. The ground unit that had made the request was informed of the approval or the refusal. If the mission was approved the ground unit was given the ETA of the aircraft, and if the mission was refused the reason was given. The A-3 could divert aircraft from pre-planned missions for particularly urgent requests for immediate support. Most of these requests were responded to by diverting fighter-bombers from armed recon missions.

The fighter-bomber pilot needed not only to locate and identify the specific target requested by ground troops, but also needed to know the exact location of these ground troops so as not to subject them to attack. Initially, infantry or armored personnel were utilized as forward observers, but were inadequate, as they were unable to locate or visualize the target, as they were unfamiliar with the pilot's viewpoint of the target from the air. To remedy the problem the TAC liaison with the Army units was assumed by fighter pilots who had completed their combat tour and were designated Air Liaison Officers (ALOs). There were several Air Liaison Officer titles depending on the TAC to which they were attached: Tactical Air Party Officers (TAPOs) or Air Support Party Officers (ASPOs) or Tactical Air Liaison Officers (TALOs). They were attached to the headquarters of corps, divisions, and armored commands for 90 days as air advisors and to assess targets submitted by the G-3 (Air). The TAPOS were in VHF and UHF radio communication with the TAC HQ to convey air support requests. TAPOs functioned as forward air controllers to direct air strikes from the combat area. There was no provision for the air liaison officer for assignment to corps or divisions in any of the Tables of Organization within any TAC. They were carried as overages, and were as such unable to be promoted. After D-Day every division and corps had a TAC air liaison officer (usually a Lt. Colonel) assigned to it with a crew of seven air force enlisted men. One operated the VHF out of a jeep driven by a driver/mechanic; four to operate the other large radio out of a half-track, and the seventh was a weather observer who drove a jeep for the ALO.

Provisions were made for the possibility of a forward observer and his radio being captured, or if the Germans interfered with instructions to the fighter-bomber pilot. The Germans tried to use intercepted American call signs; broadcasting as an American headquarters or armored column command, they would try to lure the fighter-bombers into traps or send them off on wild goose chases. It was not long before U.S. pilots would easily recognize the German linguist's awkward attempts to use our vernacular and confront him to authenticate. A letter and/or number code called an "authenticator" was devised. Anytime a pilot became suspicious of the ground instructions he was receiving, the pilot would radio his half of the authenticator and wait for the other half from the ground. Once used on a mission it would be invalid for the remainder of the day and was changed daily.

On scheduled missions the pilots were briefed at a specified time, but on stand-by missions they waited in the ready random. The standard dress was a flying suit over shirt and pants and leather flying jacket. Most carried a .45 in a shoulder holster and a knife strapped to their leg.

The pilot briefings were an informal but methodical affair held in a tent with the situation map pinned to the canvas wall. The operations officer, a pilot, discussed the nature and location of the primary target and method of attack. Armaments to be used were discussed, and pilots were reminded to call their targets so there would be no duplication or wasted effort. They were told not to bomb targets that could be destroyed by strafing. Top cover was instructed to come in and destroy undamaged targets if the flak was not dangerous. If the primary target was neutralized, the squadron was to be turned over to ground control for further targets. If ground control could not assign targets after 15 minutes, the squadron was released to hunt for targets of opportunity. The Intelligence Officer, a non-pilot, briefed anticipated flak concentrations and evasion. The

373rd Fighter Group ALG Woodchurch (UK) mission briefing in early July 1944. The 373rd arrived late in the UK in April 1944 and flew B-26 escort missions from England until it moved to France (Tour-en-Bessin) at the end of July. From then it took on a fighter-bomber role following American armies across France and into Germany and took part in the Battle of the Bulge. (USAF)

squadron was directed around identified flak batteries. Radio discipline and codes were set. Bail out and escape and evasion procedures were gone over, and escape kits distributed and zipped into the shin pocket of their flight suit. The Weather Officer briefed the weather to and over the target. Army G-3 (Air) and G-2 (Air/Intelligence) were attached to TAC HQ as liaisons/advisors. Ground Liaison Officers (GLOs) were attached to air groups and squadrons to keep these units up to date on the battlefield status and to update unit battlefield situation maps. The GLO assisted in pre-mission pilot briefings. He would brief the pilots on the situation the infantry was facing, such as: "The infantry is advancing here but has been under heavy fire from a pillbox and has suffered heavy casualties and are running low on ammunition." The GLO would describe the target area and make certain that the pilots were familiar with the bomb line to protect friendly troops. They also assisted in post mission debriefings, gathering information through pilot interrogation that was passed on to the ground units via the G-3 and G-2. These daily briefings by the GLO made the pilot aware of the plight of the ground soldier and connected the two.

Upon leaving the briefing the pilot put his wallet and personal belongings in a small cloth bag for safe keeping with his name on it and proceeded by jeep to the equipment tent that was near the flight line. Here he picked up his parachute and helmet. The oxygen mask, goggles, and built-in microphone and headset were attached to the helmet. He strapped on his parachute and made sure that the extra knife was on the chest strap. If, in a bail out, the pilot got hung up in a tree and was unable to reach his leg knife, he could cut himself free. Once the pilot reached his fighter, the Crew Chief greeted him and assured him that everything was fine with the plane. The pilot reached up for the handhold and lifted his leg to get a toe in the foothold of the huge P-47 to get onto the wing and into the cockpit. He usually needed a boost from the Crew Chief. Once in the cockpit the CC helped with the shoulder harness and seat belt while the Assistant Crew Chief checked the parachute. If the mission were a daily planned mission on a designated target the engine start time, taxi time, and takeoff time were assigned at the briefing. However, for a target called by a ground controller, the pilot usually received his instructions over the cockpit radio or from ground signals, but sometimes the flight leader improvised. Since the P-47 was a "tail dragger" powered by a huge radial engine, the pilot had no forward vision and had difficulty in seeing the taxiway. On the wide taxiways on English bases the pilot had enough room to S-turn to see out the side of his cockpit, but on the temporary fields in France there was no room to maneuver. Here the Crew Chief had to lay on the wing with one arm clinging to the leading edge of the wing so as not to be bounced off on the rough strip and the other relaying hand signals to direct the pilot. At the takeoff area the CC slid off the wing and the launch officer took over and directed the fighters into line for takeoff. The pilot would run up the engine, check his seat harness and canopy (to open/locked), check the magneto, throttle back to fast idle, and push the flap control to full flaps. Watching the launch officer, he would roll and then brake the large Thunderbolt into takeoff position. The interval between takeoffs was about half a minute. Once next in line for takeoff the pilot would apply full brakes, lock the tail wheel, pull the stick back into his stomach, and watch the launch officer's flag that motioned in larger and faster circles as his arm rose. Throttle was increased; matching the increased flag motion until full throttle on the 2,300-horse power Pratt & Whitney was reached. The fighter was noisily vibrating and shuddering ferociously, ready to hurdle into the sky. The launch officer abruptly dropped his flag for takeoff. The pilot released his brakes, but instead of leaping into the sky, the fighter slowly accelerated down the runway, the pilot seeing only the sky in front of him. Finally at 75 mph the tail began to feel lighter and the pilot put the stick forward to bring it up. Engine torque increased, and the pilot compensated with some right rudder. The heavy fighter increased its speed, 100-110-120-130, and as the end of the runway quickly approached the pilot pulled back on the stick to force the brute into the air. He retracted the landing gear as soon as the wheels left the ground, slowly raised the flaps, and finally, at 180mph, the plane began to fly itself. The pilot closed the canopy, checked the temperature gauges, and closed the cowl flaps. At 200mph and 100 feet off the ground the pilot began his turn to climb into formation, adjusting the prop pitch control, fuel mixture, and throttle. The formation was joined and climbed steadily to 10,000 feet, spaced about 30 feet apart and with 150 feet between flights. Once approaching the target area the formations spread out to 100 feet between aircraft and 500 feet between flights to give the flak gunners below a less concentrated target. The most dangerous position in a formation was the rear-most spot, called "Blue Four." The responsibility of this "tail-end Charlie" was to protect the flight from surprise attack from Luftwaffe fighters that favored attack from the rear and was their first target of an attack. During bombing and strafing attacks Blue Four was the last man in, and German AA gunners were able to recover from the momentary surprise of the attack and adjusted their range and elevation to deadly effect on him.

The ground controller contacted the mission leader, and the flights began to circle the target area. A flight was assigned to provide cover and guard against a Luftwaffe bounce that probably would not happen. The squadron commander either went in alone to assess the target or led the first flight down on the target, diving in line and increasing speed. If there was return fire the pilot skidded the aircraft. At 3,000 feet he banked the plane slightly and opened fire with his eight .50s to suppress AA and small arms fire. At 1,000 feet and 400mph the bombs were released and the attackers climbed, feeling the G-forces push them into the seat. After the attack the squadron leader climbed to 5,000 feet to access the results. He often needed to send the other two flights in to finish the job. Once the primary targets were destroyed the formation reassembled at 10,000 feet. If they had any bombs or ammunition remaining, the ground controller would inform the squadron leader of other targets and locate them on a special grid map carried by the squadron leader. Often the squadron was released to freelance, to seek out targets of opportunity behind the enemy lines. After leaving the target area and returning to base the squadron leader asked if anyone had been hit or was running low on fuel. Those aircraft with battle damage would land last so as not to crash and block the runway. Those aircraft low on fuel would be given priority to land. The flights came in fast and low over the field, breaking into a semi-loop, each aircraft following the other in a widening turn. The pilots would lock their harness, and at the top of the loop drop the landing gear and lower flaps, open and lock the canopy, and ease into a landing. The CC was waiting just off the runway and climbed on the wing to guide the pilot into the parking area. Once parked, the brakes were locked and the engine shut down. A jeep transported the pilots to the equipment tent to drop off their parachutes and helmets and then to debriefing. Debriefing was done according to seniority and rank. Each pilot gave an assessment of his part in the mission and reported any intelligence information he may have seen. The clerk collected the escape kits and returned the personal belongings. The mission was over for the pilots.

The average frequency of operation was two group missions or six squadron missions per day. The initial 16-plane squadron was later reduced to 12 for added flexibility, and was found to be sufficient for any mission type. Two daily group missions meant that 72 aircraft needed to be put into the air day after day without affecting maintenance. It was also found that two missions with 12-plane squadrons were the maximum that could be sustained to keep pace with the arrival of replacement aircraft and pilots. The group was permitted a day off every seven to ten days for aircraft maintenance.

Once based on the Continent a TAC was moved from base to base and was dependent on their air service and aviation engineer commands to move service personnel, equipment, and supplies. Special Airdrome Squadrons were formed to maintain tactical operations by refueling and rearming air units on advanced airfields, especially at newly operational fields, while the unit's personnel were being transported to the new base.

Armed Reconnaissance (Armed Recce)

Col. Gilbert Meyers, a former West Point All-American football player and 9th Air Force combat operations chief, is given credit for developing armed reconnaissance missions in response to the large demand for fighter-bomber missions by the infantry after D-Day. Armed Reconnaissance was the long-term and continuous application of airpower to targets far behind enemy lines as part of a concerted air offensive to prevent reinforcements and supplies from reaching the battlefield. Pilots flying armed reconnaissance, usually referred to as armed recce, were assigned to a large area some distance behind enemy lines to seek out and attack tactical targets at their discretion. Included in these targets were airfields, trains and motor transport, ships and barges, roads and bridges, fuel dumps and supply depots, troops and barracks, etc. Armed recce was an interdiction campaign requiring a ceaseless commitment of men and material to fly a continual air offensive. Although armed recce was more armed than recce, there was a component of reconnaissance involved. Pilots were instructed to collect intelligence regarding enemy ground status, transportation, communication, and supply.

In the ETO more armed recce sorties were flown than close air sorties. According to the *Statistical Summary of Ninth Air Force Operations* between mid-October 1943 and the end of the war, the 9th Air Force flew 73,123 armed recce sorties as compared to 55,983 close support missions. From November 1944 to May 1945, the First TAF *Summary of Operations* records 14,479 armed recce sorties versus 5,563 close air support missions by its P-47s in supporting the Sixth Army Group. The intensity of armed recce missions depended on the status of the battlefront, but was highest when there was little activity at the front and the need for close air support was reduced. The level of armed recce rose after an Allied ground offensive had achieved a breakout and the Germans were in retreat. Withdrawal meant a large number of targets for the fighter-bombers. It also meant that there was a significant reduction in the call for close air sorties. However, in the several days of the initial ground offensive there was a significant rise in close air missions and a concomitant reduction in armed recce sorties, but not to the extent that they were abridged so as to lessen the constant pressure on rear area German psyche. Despite the fact that more armed recce sorties were flown there were no problems in the TACs regarding allocation of fighter-bombers for the two types of missions. The TACs possessed large numbers of fighter-bombers and pilots, and a continuous supply of replacements for each. Also, the TACs were able to requisition air superiority fighters into the fighter-bomber role. As the Allies gained complete air superiority and the Luftwaffe became insignificant, more and more fighters and their pilots were converted to fighter-bombers. Also, the TACs had the ability to temporarily deploy fighter-bomber units from quiet areas and concentrate them in hot spots.

The typical armed recce mission had each squadron fly an assigned, specific area to reconnoiter, usually after a primary or secondary bombing mission was completed or not completed. The squadron leader and his Red Flight would fly a weaving pattern at low altitude, moving from deck to 1,000 feet looking for hidden targets. White and Yellow Flights would stack up behind at 1,000 to 3,000 feet, while Blue Fight (and sometimes Yellow Flight) flew top cover at 5,000 feet or more. When a target was found Red flight would drop to attack, followed by White and Yellow Flights. Toward the end of the war, when the Luftwaffe had all but disappeared from the sky, the Blue top cover flight could be called down to partake in the attack when one of the attacking flights ran low on ammunition.

Due to the defense of armed recce targets by heavy concentrations of flak, studies showed that the armed recce loss rates were much higher than those of close-support and increased in proportion to the distance the attacks took place behind enemy lines. Airfields, communication centers, headquarters and barracks, supply dumps, and concentrations of reserve infantry and armor were the targets subject to armed recce attack and were heavily defended by flak. Close air support targets were comparatively small, and the Germans defended only a few of the more important targets near the front lines. The justification for deeper armed recce penetrations was that more targets of quantity and quality were available. Losses sometimes became so high that headquarters limited armed recce missions and increased the number of participating aircraft when they were to be flown.

In an attempt to maintain a continual armed reconnaissance offensive there often were extended periods when the battlefront was stable and there were few targets available. Since target selection by armed recce pilots was visual, it was only in times of German offensive or retreat that abundant targets presented themselves. Most armed recce sorties did not consistently destroy large numbers of tactical targets and thus reduce the ability of German armies to fight effectively. Despite the fact that German armor and infantry was required to move at night, a significant percentage of them did arrive at the front and had time to reorganize.

As was the case of close air support missions, the armed recce threat was often more important than the actual damage inflicted. The menace of armed recce attack paralyzed German movement and thinking from the battlefront to the rear echelons. The German rear areas remained in a state of neutralization, threatened by eternal air attacks both figuratively and literally. The effect on German tactics and planned operations can never be calculated. Field Marshal Erwin Rommel, commander of Army Group B in Normandy, reported that he had to leave his staff car 30 times and seek cover from marauding fighter-bombers while driving to the front. German infantry units marching in daylight placed special air sentries in the front and rear of their column to watch for air attacks. Infantry marched with a separation of 1,500-2,000 feet between companies, and a separation of 50-75 feet between personnel. Stops for rest or meals were made under cover and were widely dispersed, with a constant eye and ear alert for air attack. Motorized units moved only at night, and then at 30-minute intervals and with widely spaced vehicles. Poor weather brought a reprieve from daylight air attack. There were occasions when it was critical for the Germans to move in daylight, when an offensive was to be prepared or an Allied breakthrough thwarted. It was at these times the fighter-bomber exacted its toll on German units, decimating them and leaving the survivors devastated, dazed, and confused.

The high level of armed recce missions being conducted in 1944-45, at a time when armies demanded a high level of close support sorties, was due to the extravagant amount of air resources available to the TACs during the period. The armed reconnaissance offensive never took such precedence that close air support requests were denied. At times there was also an integration of the two missions. Often, in 1944-45, armed recce sorties were diverted to respond to meet unanticipated situations at the front. By 1945 it had become SOP of U.S. Army units to call in immediate close support from armed recce missions instead of relying on the pre-briefed close air strikes. Conversely, if there were no frontline targets or the pre-briefed target was no longer available or a menace, the close air fighter-bombers in their briefings would be assigned a pre-arranged armed recce alternate target behind the lines, or would be directed to one by the army unit at the front.

Fighter-bombers were more effective against targets attacked behind enemy lines. Particularly vulnerable to air attack were German motor and rail transport and supply, fuel, and ammunition dumps. Concerted attacks against buildings used as headquarters or strong points were carried out. Attacks on transportation and the loss of supplies it carried had a greater effect than attacks on supply installations that were generally protected and dispersed. Destruction of gasoline and oil supplies had the most detrimental consequences on the Wehrmacht, followed by the loss of ammunition and general ordnance. The great losses of every kind of vital military equipment suffered by the Germans ultimately depleted all reserves and necessitated the delivery of replacements directly from

Two of America's greatest fighter-bomber commanders and innovators. Maj.Gen. Elwood "Pete" Quesada, IX TAC CO, and Brig. Gen. Otto P. "Opie" Weyland, XIX TAC CO. (USAF)

the factories to the front, instead of being routed through the normal logistic conduit. These en route equipment replacements were vulnerable to fighter-bomber attacks, and their destruction and delay had an immediate effect on the troops awaiting them. The Germans dispersed critical industries and installations to offset the effects of strategic bombing on them, but in doing so increased the area of responsibility on the transportation system, making it a more vulnerable and valuable target. The delay caused by each air attack accumulated and increased delivery time to the battlefield.

The rapid advances of army groups left their flanks exposed, and the TACs were assigned the task of protecting these flanks by preventing the concentration of enemy forces that might counterattack. The classic aerial protection of an army's flank was conducted by Gen. O.P. Weyland's XIX TAC for Patton's Third Army during the breakout from Normandy. There was extensive use of photo and tactical reconnaissance that alerted fighter-bombers to attack enemy troops and transport and interdict road and rail movement to prevent any threatening enemy build up.

In his report, *The Effect of Air Power on Military Operations/ Western Europe* (12th Army Group, Germany, 1945), Gen. Omar Bradley credited armed recce missions as being "one of the outstanding developments of the tactical air force supporting our armies."

8th Air Force Escorts and Targets of Opportunity

In January 1944 the 8th Air Force and its new commander, General James Doolittle, changed its escort policy. Previously, the fighter pilots were instructed to first safeguard the bombers by shooting down attacking Luftwaffe fighters. The escorts were under no circumstances to pursue attacking enemy fighters, and consequently many damaged German aircraft and pilots escaped to fight again. Doolittle decreed that Luftwaffe fighters could be hunted in the air whenever and wherever they were encountered. In February, Gen. Arnold issued his "Down to Earth" edict. The escorts were to stay with their assigned bombers until relieved, and then were encouraged to use their remaining fuel and ammunition on targets of opportunity on the way back to base. Targets of opportunity had a wide definition, and airfields, trains, motor transport, staff cars, and even horses from that time on were constantly harassed in a free for all over northwestern Europe.

Col. Avelin Tacon, a P-51 pilot for the 359th Fighter Group, described targets of opportunity (Eighth Fighter Command; *Down to the Deck: VIII Fighter Command Strafing Tactics FAC 39* (May 1944):

"Targets of opportunity fall into two categories: those you find in assigned areas and those you spot returning from escort missions. On the former we brief on the area in general. The topography is covered, main roads, marshaling yards, etc. We do not like to comb an area right on the deck. We feel this method has two disadvantages. First, when you do run into a target you're past it before you can identify it and draw a bead. This means that you've got to circle back to attack it and thus you lose the element of surprise as well as speed. Secondly, you're being fired at constantly, particularly in western France. Our method is to fly as a group with the low squadron that is the initial striking force, flying at about 4,000 feet, medium squadron at about 5,000 feet and top cover at about 8,000 feet. From 4,000 feet the low squadron can spot their targets, dive and attack with speed, which is like money in the bank. By flying at 4,000 feet if you are fired on by light flak it isn't very accurate and if it should become accurate you can dive, pick up speed and get the hell out of there. When the low squadron attacks the other two orbit and cover it. We rotate the squadron if the expenditure of ammunition warrants it. When attacking targets whose defense is unknown the lead flight goes in first while the others in the squadron holds back. We don't like to commit a whole squadron until we know what we're up against.

In strafing targets of opportunity returning from escort missions the formation leader has to plan his attack as he circles the target. Every advantage has to be taken of: sun, cloud cover, terrain and speed. It is usually impossible to achieve surprise on a target of

Col. Avelin Tacon, a P-51 pilot for the 359th Fighter Group (USAF)

this type so we like speed, around 450 on the clock. It isn't too easy to hit an aircraft going that fast. There is one point we insist on and that is that the flight leader must use good judgment and consider the results he expects to gain is commensurate with the expected losses. This is particularly true of airdromes in western France. Those things are poison. As a rule of thumb on airdromes in that area we estimate a loss of one pilot out of every four pilots. Seems high? Check the casualties on attacking those airdromes. In Germany our favorite targets are those little grass auxiliary airdromes that are scattered about. They're usually either undefended at all or very lightly and have from 10 to 15 single engine fighters on them. However, we attacked one of these one day with FW 190s on it and the dirty Hun had drained all the gasoline from the ships. Although they were pretty well hit they just wouldn't burn."

Col. John Henry, P-51 pilot for the 339th Fighter Group, discussed targets of opportunity and strafing (*Down to the Deck*, ibid.):

"Ground strafing tactics of this organization are based on the principle that maximum damage to ground installations must be accomplished during the shortest possible time, during which our airplanes are in the range of light flak. Because of the extreme vulnerability of the P-51 airplane to any kind of damage, it is considered by most of our pilots that attacks on ground targets are not worth the risk unless those targets are poorly defended and are extremely vulnerable to .50 caliber fire.

Most of our ground strafing objectives are targets of opportunity and tactics are varied somewhat to suit circumstances of the attack. It is considered that good air discipline and solid understanding of the basic principles of strafing are the most important explanations of our light losses while "on the deck."

Col. John Henry, P-51 pilot for the 339th Fighter Group (USAF)

While searching for targets we prefer to cruise at from 12,000 to 14,000 feet with all flights line abreast. When a desirable target is called in, a squadron splits in two sections. One section conducts the attack while the other provides the air cover. The first pass is made across the target is made at a speed of 400 miles per hour, if there is reason to suppose that ground fire will be encountered.

Flights making the attack are spread astern at intervals of 3,000 feet or more. This interval is large enough to allow each man in the flight to pick out his target and study it before opening fire. The interval is also large enough to prevent damage to preceding flights from ricochets and to allow breaking of the attack at any moment. Men flying astern always cover the flights which have immediately preceded them across the target in an effort to reduce the ground fire when it is encountered but flights not already committed to attack, break away as soon as ground flak is called in and the order is passed out by the squadron leader.

Most of our ground strafing has been done by individual squadrons acting independently. However when two or more squadrons are acting together, one squadron is always left for top cover.

Flights in trail, with individual airplanes flying several hundred feet apart, is the preferred formation for ground strafing. However, when the target does not have sufficient horizontal length, we often break off into two sip elements. For dive-bombing we use a string formation of individual airplanes. Each pilot must be allowed to give his entire effort toward gaining the utmost accuracy, whether it is in firing guns or dropping a bomb. The interval between airplanes is large enough so that no attention need to given toward avoiding a collision.

From the moment the first airplane crosses the target every effort is made to keep waves of flights on the target without interruption until satisfactory damage is done, flak has been called in or until all but reserve ammunition has been expended. On some targets the top cover has been called in to make a few attacks and the flights that are low on ammunition replace them.

A very strong effort has been made to get pilots 'accuracy conscious' in ground strafing. Motion pictures showed the typical burst starting a few hundred feet in front of the target and crossing through the target to a few hundred feet on either side, without a pause. At the present we try to fire one or 'two sighting-in' bursts at long range so that at 1,200 feet or so the pilot can be all set to open up with a long burst, down to 500 to 600 feet without a break. Pilots are told to apply slight forward pressure to the stick during the entire pass to correct for bullet drop and to cease firing the moment their sights went off the target....

It is well and good to say that one pass is enough for any airfield but we find that 400 miles per hour is too fast (for much damage to be done). So, unless ground fire has been encountered, before the last flight passes we have the first flight in position for another attack. After the first pass the flights start coming in from different directions but always remain in mutual support of each other. The pattern is at a very low altitude....

By flying past a ground target we usually are able to position ourselves for the attack, either out of the sun or downwind. In the late afternoon, when the sun is low on the horizon, we prefer the 'out of the sun' attack if the ground defenses are unknown. However, for the most part, we try to attack downwind so the smoke from the target will not obstruct the vision of the pilots following. Cross wind targets are avoided when possible because of the excessive drift which sets in during the long burst. Incidentally, these long bursts are a "must" since most of our airplanes (P-51s) have only four guns and usually at least one or two are jammed and useless. One of our "pet peeves" against this airplane is its lack of firepower in combat models prior to the "D" series.

Briefing for ground strafing missions has been of very little value. Information on the nature of the target and its defenses has never proven correct for us. When ordered on a ground-strafing mission, it would be of great value to know the location of light flak positions and heavy flak positions within radius of 50 miles. By knowing heavy flak positions in the area we could ascertain the best course to take in climbing back up to safe altitude. As it is we usually leave the target area, then climb back in a series of turns to avoid cities. During the attack, the squadron leader pulls about 40 inches of manifold pressure and maintains the highest possible airspeed."

Third Priority: Close Support

Both the U.S. Army Air Corps and RAF had learned and practiced close support in World War I, and also realized the need to gain air superiority in order to successfully conduct close support. Despite their tactical air successes in World War I, the RAF justified and maintained its independence on strategic bombing, while the U.S. Air Corps remained part of the Army and bridled for its independence for the next three decades. It took the German Blitzkrieg in Poland and France to reawake the RAF to the necessity for close air support in modern warfare. The RAF formed the Army Cooperation Command in response. The need for a close air policy was driven home in the Western Desert of Egypt. In an army-air conference in Cairo in July 1941, ACM Arthur Tedder, AOC-in-C (Air Officer Commanding-in-Chief) Middle East, defined close air support and proscribed procedures of conduct. AVM Arthur Coningham, AOC Western Desert Air Force, placed army and air headquarters side by side, and the result was cooperation and efficiency. When Lt.Gen. Bernard Montgomery took command of the Eighth Army he embraced and enhanced the close air support philosophy:

"The first and great principle of war is that you must first win your air battle before you fight your land or sea battle....

The second great principle is that the Army plus the Air has to be so knitted that the two together form one entity. If you do thatÖnothing will be able to stand against it....

The next principle is there are not two plans, Army and Air, but one plan, Army-Air.

Next the Army and Air Staff must sit together at the same headquarters. There must be between them complete mutual confidence and trust...."

Senior commanders who felt little commitment to it controlled close air support in 1943-45. Only in 1945, did the 9th Air Force deem the term "support" inappropriate and substituted "cooperation." Fortunately, the integration of ground and air forces on the operational level was surprisingly effective, particularly because the AAF was part of the Army. The two armed forces exchanged thousands of personnel as counterparts in ground and air units. Pilots saw ground combat first hand, while army personnel became involved in air operations, each becoming aware of the other's responsibilities and problems. Enlightened junior air officers, such as Maj.Gen. Elwood "Pete" Quesada, helped the situation operationally.

Close air support was "the short-term application of aerial firepower at a key time and place to aid infantry and/or armor to attain fixed objectives immediately after application." Its success was contingent on quick response and its capacity to destroy or neutralize targets. However, close air fighter-bomber response was inherently slow. Requests had to be passed from the battlefield through the air support control unit that usually consisted of three officers and ten enlisted men and their communications. This unit evaluated the mass of incoming information and passed on what was important to the ground commander, who expedited the plans formulated for fighter-bomber deployment. Orders were sent to the fighter-bomber airbase, where time was needed to brief the pilots and then to man their aircraft, taxi, takeoff, form up, and continue to the target area. Even if the fighter-bomber squadron were at readiness it would take an hour for the aircraft to attack. Timeliness was of the essence, because if a request was made during an advance in which a German strongpoint was encountered, to minimize casualties the German position needed to be reduced ASAP. Calling in artillery was a solution, as their fire control coordination could not be matched by the fighter-bombers, but often artillery was out of range.

Rover Joe

A method to decrease response time was to maintain standing patrols of fighter-bombers over the battlefront. Pilots could be fully briefed on the battlefield situation and positions of the opposing forces in the air by ground controllers. They were able to respond as quickly as artillery, and be guided to ground targets as they appeared by ground controllers. The RAF in North Africa developed this method. There the responsibility for close air support fell on ground-based air liaison officers at all wing and group headquarters, and with the mobile operations room. Targets were radioed to and accepted by Desert Air Force and Area Army HQs and forwarded to the air liaison officer, who briefed the assigned squadrons. While this procedure worked well in the flat open deserts, quicker, more accurate air responses were necessary in the valleys and mountains of Italy, where combat was at much closer quarters. W/C David Heysham, Operations Commander at DAF HQ, devised the mobile observation post located in a truck or jeep with a trailer. The mobile observation post was stationed with the forward troops at brigade HQ and was in direct VHF communication with overhead aircraft. Both controllers and pilots had the same photographic map with a superimposed grid. A "cab rank" of 6, 12, or 18 fighter-bombers would be patrolling in line astern for 15-20 minutes, and if they were not contacted they would attack a pre-selected target. If the army requested an attack, one or more aircraft from the cab rank would dive to bomb and/or strafe the requested target. Permanent or moving targets could be attacked within minutes. A large number of aircraft were required to maintain the cab rank, especially by short-ranged fighter aircraft. It was only effective if complete air superiority were attained so the cab could be maintained. This system, known as "Rover David" after its originator, was known as "Rover Joe" by U.S. personnel.

Rover Joe was a "network of direct ground army force to air force liaison through which air power could be delivered in close cooperation with ground operations." It consisted of radio and telephone communications from Rover Joe to the aircraft making the attack. Usually three to four radio jeeps were deployed to the regiments making the ground attack. The regiments were in constant voice communication with Rover Joe. Over and above this voice net, a carrier wave net was maintained with the Air Support Control, Army Group, and the Divisions in the coordinated ground attack.

The mechanism of Rover Joe: Ground units requested that ground control liaison officer authorize an attack on a given target. Once the request was made, the ground controller screened it for priority. If the target was accepted it was forwarded to the Rover Joe, who notified the ground unit of the expected time of the attack and was kept posted of any changes of plan. Pilots flew in continuous patrols near the battlefield and were briefed while in the air and directed to the target by Joe, and were sometimes aided by artillery smoke shells to lead them to the target.

Experienced Squadron COs with the rank of Major or above took turns as Rover Joes for ten days, and another pilot, who was usually an experienced flight leader, accompanied him as an assistant. It took several days for the new controller to learn his new duties from the outgoing controller. Ground officers who provided the necessary liaison and technical support and managed the administration of the unit aided the pilot controllers. Soon these ground liaison officers became so proficient in air cooperation that they were able to eliminate attacks on targets too close to friendly troops or otherwise unsuited for air attack. A typical mission for the controller involved a request from the liaison officer for the attack on a selected target. Using maps and photographs and taking into account the position of friendly troops, weather conditions, and ordnance carried by the aircraft, the controller accepted or rejected the target. Once the target was accepted, he further studied the maps and photos and used his "air knowledge" to determine how the terrain would look to the pilots flying over it. The controller chose checkpoints to draw the pilot's attention and tried to locate prominent terrain features that could not be confused with similar features in friendly territory. If this were not possible the controller would arrange for artillery to fire smoke shells to indicate the target at the time the aircraft were to attack. Pilots often questioned why they needed to attack a target that could be indicated and hit by artillery. But the damage done by an artillery shell could not compare to that done by 500lb. bombs. While this frequent rotation insured that experienced pilots served as controllers and did not permanently withdraw pilots from combat, ten days was found to be inadequate, as several days were lost in training each new Joe.

"Rover Joe" in a jeep radio installation. The ALO is looking up into the air directing a flight to a target while another flight provides top cover waiting to attack. (USAF)

Fighter-bombers were rotated every 30 minutes or more, depending on the amount of fuel the fighter-bomber had remaining on arrival and if they arrived on schedule. Missions were not scheduled closer than 30 minutes, as delays and the time it took to brief the pilot in the air required at least that amount of time without causing confusion and subsequent danger to friendly forces. When the fighter-bombers arrived in the area they reported to the controller and were informed of the target. The flight leader was given the map coordinates of the target, and the characteristics of the surrounding terrain were described, as were useful check points and any smoke signals if used. Under ideal conditions the controller was in position for direct observation and positive identification of the target. Usually Rover Joe missions were carried out in flights of four. As with other air-to-ground missions, the axis of attack was not flown towards friendly troops to avoid the danger of over flights, ricochets, and hung bombs.

The Rover Joe procedure required a large number of pilots and aircraft and could not be continued over long periods, despite the TAC's seemingly unlimited quantities of both. Many aircraft in standing patrols often were not required for close support and were regularly redirected to attack pre-briefed alternative targets or to fly armed recce attacks directly behind German lines. While these standing patrols may have immobilized German defenses, the Germans made certain that they presented these air patrols with few obvious targets when preparing their defenses. These extra fighter-bombers could have been utilized more constructively on deep penetration armed recce or against more obvious interdiction targets behind enemy lines.

Fighter-bomber units on alert at their bases needed to decrease their response time to attack a target, and Rover Joe required numerous fighter-bombers to maintain the cab rank. Another solution was to contact airborne aircraft, usually armed recce, in or near the frontlines and divert them from their assigned sortie and order them to respond to the request. Time would be needed for them to alter course and continue to the new target, where they would contact the ground controller at the forward command post or vehicle. The ground controller would brief the pilots on their target and the attack would proceed. The problems with this procedure were that the incoming pilot was not as familiar with the battlefield and combat situation, and was not as thoroughly briefed on the disposition of friendly and enemy troops.

Close air support never was able to achieve the destruction of intended targets that was hypothetically required of it. Fighter-bomber pilots, flying at high speed over an often smoke shrouded battlefield, had only a few seconds to identify their target, aim, and release their bombs and rockets, which were intrinsically inaccurate. Near misses had little or no effect on prepared defenses or even basic, quickly prepared defenses. Strafing was more accurate than bombs or rockets and could exact substantial damage to troops and equipment if large numbers of fighter-bombers were involved over an area of concentrated men and equipment. Close air support operations were successful because the Allies had achieved air superiority by 1943 and possessed numerous aircraft for close air support. Any weaknesses in the system were shrouded by their enormous quantitative superiority in fighter-bomber numbers. Nonetheless, these weaknesses were often evident in unsuccessful individual daily operations to the detriment of many soldiers and airmen.

In the third priority of *FM 100-20*, the writers were concerned "with the considerable chance of striking friendly forces" and considered close air support ("contact zone missions") "difficult to control, are most expensive and are, in general, least effective." They cautioned that they should be used "only at critical times (to be) profitable." They did not foresee the degree and proficiency to which air-ground "teamwork" would develop. Initially fighter-bomber attacks were not called on targets closer than 1,000 yards to friendly troops, but as experience was gained, seasoned troops had the confidence to call in strikes as close as 300 yards to their position.

Gen. George Patton commented on his first impression of close air support in *War as I Knew It*:

> "I asked General Weyland, commanding general of the XIX Tactical Air Command, to send some fighter-bombers to stop it (a column of enemy tanks).... The planes did do some very effective work knocking out enemy resistance ahead of the 4th Armored Division and this was the precursor of many such other jobs. It was love at first sight between the XIX Tactical Air Command and the Third Army."

This admiration between ground commanders and the TAC fighter-bombers continued throughout the war.

Close Support: Air vs. Artillery

As the war progressed, both air and artillery close support saw comparable advances in communications and responsiveness. By 1944 U.S. artillery had become accomplished in delivering immediate and concentrated firepower in the close support of infantry and armor. The use of specially trained forward observers, both on the ground and flying over the front in light observation aircraft, further enhanced the effectiveness of artillery. The most important advantage of artillery over close air support was that it was able to operate in all weather and both day and night. The post D-Day weather, June and to mid-July, was more or less normal but had more wind and cloud. After a period of good weather from mid-July through October the weather turned bad in November, which allowed the Germans to build up for their Ardennes Offensive ("Battle of the Bulge"). They launched their surprise attack in bad weather in mid-December. In December there were ten days in which there were no operational missions, and a further eleven in which operations were restricted. Fortunately, the poor weather broke for a few days in late December for large fighter-bomber operations, and the first medium bomber operations since the start of the attack. In January there were seven days of no operational flying and three restricted days. The USAAF night fighter force was always a minimal factor in its close air support role.

The range of artillery was such that it could control an area of 30 square miles behind enemy lines. The 105mm howitzer could

AVM Arthur Coningham, AOC Western Desert Air Force, was considered the "Father of Air-Ground Cooperation" as in North Africa he placed army and air headquarters side by side and the result was cooperation and efficiency. (Author/West)

fire four rounds/minute seven miles, the 155mm howitzer could fire two rounds/minute nine miles, and the 155mm gun could fire one round/minute 14.5 miles behind enemy lines. An infantry division had three battalions of field artillery, each with 12 105mm howitzers, and one battalion of 12 155mm howitzers. Self-propelled armor added to the artillery battalion's effectiveness. Near the battlefront artillery held an advantage over the slower reacting fighter-bomber. The Allied breakout from Normandy and the push across France caused problems for artillery and fighter-bombers. Artillery battalions could not be moved up fast enough to aid the rapidly advancing armor and infantry when it encountered enemy strong points. Fighter-bomber bases fell some distance from the advancing battlefield and could not supply rapid support. It was found that the average response time was about 75-90 minutes: nine minutes for the request to arrive at Army/Air HQ; 12 minutes for a decision to be made on deployment; 30 minutes for pilot briefing and aircraft readiness and to man their aircraft; and 20-40 minutes to reach the target area. But in the breakout the fighter-bomber became the best alternative for close support despite the long response time. As discussed, to decrease air response time continuous Rover Joe patrols were flown over the battlefield, and close air attacks were called down via radio. However, after the close air support mission there was a substantial turn around time to get the squadron airworthy for its next mission, as the aircraft needed to be rearmed and refueled.

If an intended air target could be marked for attack with an artillery smoke shell, then reasonably it should have been an artillery target in the first place, and this logic should have effectively discontinued close air support. The reason this did not happen was that there was not enough artillery and ammunition available, terrain and logistical factors hindered artillery deployment, and artillery neutralization took longer and required vast quantities of shells when compared to a fighter-bomber attack. During the advance across France there was a chronic shortage of artillery ammunition. Many infantry commanders felt that the weight of firepower of 500lb. GP bombs or 260lb. fragmentation bombs delivered at close range to their forward positions had a far greater destructive effect on enemy personnel, material, and morale than an artillery attack, but only if immediately followed by a resolute infantry attack.

Artillery smoke shell fired to identify a target. (USAF)

In close support of infantry and armor attacks it was important for the air attack to be on a scale sufficient to neutralize the target and to disorient and demoralize the enemy for a sufficient length of time. In both the MTO and ETO it was seen that the effect of an air attack or artillery barrage on morale was of short term and needed to be exploited immediately by the ground forces. Fighter-bombers possessed several advantages over artillery. Air attacks could achieve a demoralizing effect quicker than artillery, and the effect was of longer duration, allowing a somewhat longer time for the infantry to attack.

Their attacks allowed troops to advance closer to their objective than during an artillery bombardment. Air strikes could neutralize an enemy position more rapidly and for longer periods of time than artillery. Time, not dead Germans, was imperative, as time cost American lives. It was only a matter of minutes after the air attack before shocked German troops would recover from the effects of the attack and begin to function. The closer to the end of the close air attack that the infantry attacked, the more quickly they were able to exploit the German confusion and were able to take the enemy position with fewer casualties.

On the other hand, artillery could furnish support day and night, and in good weather and bad. The fighter-bomber was operational only in daylight and good weather. Artillery batteries were able to provide rapid response that could only be matched by standing Rover Joe patrols of aircraft that utilized many pilots and aircraft, often without result. As for destructive effect, close air support was considered somewhat more effective against dug-in troops, being able to saturate the target area with a heavier weight of firepower. However, artillery was more often in range against dug-in troops and could deliver a sustained bombardment against them. Both artillery and close air attacks were extremely deadly against German troops unlucky enough to be caught in the open.

Close air targets were comparatively small, and it was impossible for the Germans to defend such targets as trenches, gun positions, and troop positions with AA, but this does not suppose that there was no flak defending German frontlines. The effectiveness of fighter-bomber and medium bomber attacks on close air support targets could be augmented by the coordinated counter flak artillery fire. With a TALO and G-3 Air of the ground unit cooperating before the air attack the ground force artillery fired on all known enemy flak positions within range. A light liaison "Cub" was put into the air during the attack to direct and adjust artillery fire on known and newly discovered flak positions. U.S. artillery was able to suppress and destroy frontline German AA positions within their firing range. U.S. artillery gunners became proficient in counter-battery fire and could bring German AA gun positions under air burst shelling very quickly when German flak revealed its positions when firing on fighter-bombers flying close air attacks.

Conclusion: The profitable use of the fighter-bomber on close support targets was found to depend on the type of target and the availability and proximity of friendly artillery. Except in circumstances where artillery was unavailable or its ammunition in short supply, close air support presented no clear advantages and could have been put to better use in other priority attacks.

Armored Column Cover

In a technique, adopted by the IX TAC under Maj.Gen. Pete Quesada, named "Armored Column Cover," TACs were able to integrate their fighter-bombers with armor to provide continuous air support during armored operations.

In the First World War, Britain's armor tactics pioneer, Col. J.F.C. Fuller, had seen the aeroplane as an anti-tank weapon to protect his own tanks from attack. In the next world war, the British had developed the technique in Italy when they used "contact cars' that were mobile air-ground control posts assigned to leading armored units so that tactical air units would know the position of friendly and enemy forces. The contact cars were in close contact with tactical reconnaissance aircraft in order to reduce the time required to call in immediate ground support air attacks. AVM Harry Broadhurst of the 2nd TAF's 8rd Group adapted the procedure in Normandy. Broadhurst and Quesada had a close working relationship stemming from D-Day when control of 2nd TAF and IX TAC tactical aircraft passed from shipboard control centers to the individual land-based control centers of the two tactical air forces. The American and British centers cooperated to such an extent that AEAF CO, AM Arthur Coningham, commented on their "excellent teamwork." Quesada adapted the contact car system for IX TAC use.

In July 1944 combat experience during the initial phases of OVERLORD had shown the need for improved air-armor communications. Previously, requests for air support went from the requesting ground component to signal interchanges in the rear, to the tactical air command, and finally to a fighter-bomber group. This system functioned fairly well early in the invasion when the battles were individualized and slow moving, and when the ground troops and armor could wait at least an hour or more for the fighter-bombers to appear. Once the Allies consolidated their beachhead and the advance became fast moving this air-ground communications system was totally lacking. Quesada realized from experience in North Africa something needed to be done to improve communications between armor and aircraft. Quesada and Gen. Omar Bradley, then CO of the U.S. First Army, had a close professional relationship and their headquarters were in walking distance of each other. In July 1944, Bradley was unwilling to concentrate his armored units because of the size of the German defensive forces facing him. Quesada proposed to place a SCR-522 ground-to-air radio set in the lead tank to direct XI TAC fighter-bombers that would be patrolling over Bradley's tank column from sunrise to sunset. Bradley sent two Sherman M4 tanks to Quesada's signals command for compatible radio installation and testing. It was found that the pilot in the air could not find targets or landmarks as de-

Armored Column Cover was directed by an experienced pilot assigned on TDY (temporary duty) to be a ALO (Air Liaison Officer). The ALOs were placed in a command tank equipped with a ground-to-air VHF SCR-522 radio set to contact flights of P-47s flying in cab rank rotation overhead and direct them to targets. (USAF)

Maj.Gen. Elwood "Pete" Quesada was the commander of the IX Fighter Command and the IX Tactical Air Command. Quesada is considered the "Father of Armored Column Cover", a technique where TACs were able to integrate their fighter-bombers with armor to provide continuous air support during armored operations. (USAF)

scribed by a tank commander. To remedy the situation an experienced pilot, the Forward Air Controller (FAC), was placed in the tank replacing the armorer to talk "pilotese" in directing the fighter-bomber overhead. Regular flights of four aircraft flew overhead to ensure that the armored column was always covered. It would seem that this easy solution could have been implemented earlier, but the Air Force's ongoing fear of ground commanders controlling aircraft was the overruling factor.

Flights of four P-47 fighter-bombers relieved by another flight every half-hour would collaborate closely with spearhead armored units at each phase of an attack. FACs traveling in a VHF-equipped lead tank called down strikes or requested searches of the roads ahead of the armored column. The leader of the relieving flight would contact the FAC on the ground and the flight leader on station for a situation report. Any targets under attack or surveillance could be attacked at once, and incoming pilots were warned of any German opposition. If no resistance was being met and the column was advancing rapidly, the flight would patrol up to 35 miles in advance of the column, seeking enemy troops, armor, or strong points.

Prior to the St. Lo breakout, from ten to 14 tanks of every armored division carried the SCR-522 ground to air radio sets to contact the fighter-bomber flight leaders. The amount of armored column cover depended on the situation on the ground: how fast the front was moving; whether the armor was spearheading in front of the infantry; and the type and strength of enemy opposition. The technique also provided protection to the armor from enemy air attack. The number of fighter-bombers and their weapons load varied with the number and type of opposing enemy armor and the possibility of encountering enemy aircraft. Flights of four to twelve aircraft were usually flown. When enemy air opposition was expected 12 plane flights were flown, with four aircraft assigned top cover and eight aircraft bombed up. Flights of four or eight fighter-bombers circled over the lead tanks of the armored columns waiting for requests to attack, to recon hidden or moving enemy units, and to destroy enemy delaying actions. Four plane flights were used if there was a shortage of aircraft, and if little ground and air opposition was expected. If only a few enemy tanks supported by infantry were to be encountered then bombs could be dispensed with, and the sortie could be successfully dispatched as a strafing mission. To protect American tanks from friendly attack, the white stars on all U.S. tanks were repainted, and the tankers were supplied with red and yellow identity panels.

The use of one fighter-bomber group to provide continuous cover over one armored column during daylight worked well in the relatively static battles in Normandy in June. Groups were ordered to fly 8 to 12 aircraft over the tank columns. As the flight neared its patrol area its leader called the leader of the flight and told him he was relieved, and with the air cooperation party on the ground. Available targets were assigned to the relieving flight. SOP was for flights to patrol up to 35 miles ahead, searching for enemy strong points that could slow down the advance. It became evident in the initial phase of rapid advances by army divisions that one air support party per armored division was insufficient. Armored divisions moved in two or three columns, each a combat command. Because each column moved rapidly and were separated from one another, each required an individual air support party, complete with equipment and personnel. By the end of July the 2nd Armored Division had three air support parties: one with the division commander and one each with each of its Combat Commands.

On 26 July 1944, the second day of COBRA, the first effective use of mass armored column cover took place. American armor broke through the German front and moved in three columns to drive toward Coutances, Granville, and Villedieu. The retreating Germans put up an improvised defense of strong points, anti-tank positions, and occasional armor. Fighter-bomber flights armed with bombs flew in 30-minute relays over their assigned armored column, supplying constant air cover and air support. Air-ground communications from flight leaders was by aircraft VHF radio to tank commanders by the IX Air Service Command equipped air force SCR-522 sets in the tanks. When the armored column ran into difficulties it called for air support that was only minutes away, and then designated what action should be taken. FAC pilots were attached to the armored command to consult about the feasibility of the fighter-bombers to attack the desired target and how best to direct the flights to the target. The flight leader also was able to initiate attacks on targets he discovered from his aerial vantage point. Often fighter-bombers neutralized German positions, allowing American armor to bypass them, but the German troops in these positions would recover from the air attack in time to resist the following U.S. infantry.

The TACs gave a high priority to armored column cover in a rapid moving situation from the breakout from the Normandy beachhead to the final drive across France, Belgium, and Germany, enabling infantry supported armor to break through and encircle German armies. Brig.Gen. O.P. Weyland of the XIX TAC pressed the air attack when:

"The Third Army would run these armored columns into the Germans and I would violate what used to be a principle of tactical air power, 'Don't use airpower against something that the artillery can hit.' Well, time was of the essence. So I said to hell with that. Here, they were moving, so by the time they had stopped the col-

Armored Column Cover. Here a P-47 flies over an American tank column (far right) with their turrets showing over a wall along side the road. (USAF)

umn and deployed their artillery and what not, hell it might take them an hour or two. I'd had fighter-bombers out in front and we would try to take care of anything out there." (post war interview USAFHRA)

The policy of rotating fighter-bomber pilots in the forward VHF equipped tanks every ten days was not efficient, as it took several days for a new pilot to become familiar with his new position. An armored division required six pilots for air controllers, two for each of the three combat commands in a division. In each combat command one pilot was stationed with HQ and the other with the task force frontline combat command. It was recommended that detached pilots be assigned to the armored command for two to three month periods, but FACs who were veteran pilots resisted such a long period away from the more exciting action in the air.

Conclusion: The main drawback of armored column cover was that it required a large portion of TAC resources. The post war USAAF Evaluation Board in the ETO determined that a TAC could only cover three armored columns that utilized 30 to 60% of the TAC's available air power, the equivalent of one fighter group per armored division. *The Effect of Air Power on Military Operations*, written by Gen. Omar Bradley in the post war, and the Air Effects Committee of the 12th Army Group both determined that the 9th Air Force's decision to assign significant fighter-bomber resources to armored column cover was a major factor in the various armored breakouts following D-Day through France and into Germany at the end of the war. They went on to credit armored column cover with solving the inherent problems of close air support during various phases of mobile warfare, and recognized it as one of the major successes of tactical air warfare.

Night Fighters in Close Air Support and Interdiction

The USAAF night fighter force in the ETO consisted of relatively few aircraft. It is questionable whether increasing their number would have had any effect on German movement at night that was forced by their inability to move in daylight due to the constant harassment of armed recce fighter-bombers. The Allies had not yet developed radar able to detect movement on the roads or rails at night. Night operations utilizing dropped flares met with only partial success. To compensate for the lack of night fighters, delayed-action bombs were dropped during daylight and timed to explode at night, especially at key road junctions and concentration points. Although supplies and reinforcements reached the front, movement at night was no substitute for 24-hour logistics, especially in the summer when there were more hours of daylight. In the post war interrogation of Gen. Fritz Beyerlein, commander of the Panzer Lehr Division, he stated that it took 36 hours for his division to reach the front in Normandy, when it would have taken 12 hours had he been able to move unmolested in daylight.

The USAAF never pursued night intruder or patrol missions during the winter of 1944-45, while the Luftwaffe operated almost nightly, conducting visual and photo reconnaissance, bombing and strafing sorties, and dropped parachutists and agents behind Allied lines. There also was an interval between daylight and darkness when the few U.S. night fighters and the great numbers of day fighter-bombers were on the ground. Luftwaffe aircraft usually used these times at dusk and dawn to operate with relative impunity. Although under total domination by Allied fighter-bombers in daytime, German troops were able to move freely at night and were able to mount the Ardennes counter-offensive undetected and unhindered. A large Allied night fighter force equipped with effective radar could have limited both Luftwaffe and Wehrmacht nighttime activity. Adequate Allied nighttime reconnaissance could have detected and prevented German Army counter-attacks and withdrawals.

By their uncontested daytime air superiority, the Allies forced the Germans to limit much of their tactical and operational troop actions and replacement and supply movements to nighttime. It would have been reasonable for the Allies to aggressively pursue the development of effective night fighter-bombers, tactics, and target detection. By not doing so they lost the opportunity to increase the damaging effects of daylight attacks. The full effect and outstanding contribution of the daytime fighter-bomber was diminished by the lack of effective nightly reconnaissance, interdiction, and intruder missions.

3

The American Fighter Becomes a Fighter-Bomber

Early History

After the First World War the U.S. Congress ruthlessly slashed military appropriations; from what little was doled out, a disparity of funds was allotted to the Navy. Gen. William "Billy" Mitchell challenged the accepted military doctrine of the day that the navy ruled the waves. Mitchell, a well-known pilot in WW-I and an air power activist, declared that the next war would be won by air power and would sink navy warships. In 1921, a test was scheduled in which Army bombers sunk captured German capital ships. The Navy saw Mitchell's success as an affront and decided any future air attacks on naval targets would be the sole province of the navy. Meanwhile the Army also saw Mitchell's success as an affront. Mitchell had the audacity to question his superiors and then, when put to the test, demonstrated he was right. But in being right, he had committed the intolerable—he had proven Senior Staff wrong. Instead of receiving promotions and decorations Mitchell was relieved of command, court-martialed, reduced in rank, and expelled from the Army for five years. Mitchell resigned from the service and was vindicated when the next war did break out. There were a few, but fortunately influential, protests in Congress that prompted the Army to separate its air arm and establish the Army Air Corps in 1926. Despite this independence, the Air Corps remained a non-entity for the next decade. In a weakened Army, Senior Staff Officers could only attain star rank in the time-honored branches of the Army: the infantry, the artillery and, in those days, even the cavalry.

By the mid-1930s, Army thinking on the role of air power changed and decided that the airplane's primary role in the next war would be to support the infantry. The Air Corp's Tactical School at Maxwell Field, Alabama, ordered Army infantry and the command of close air support elements to be directed by a ground commander as if it were artillery or armor. AAC generals did not concede, but it was a moot point, as there were no aircraft or trained pilots for close air support, no matter who was in command.

Meanwhile, by the mid-30s the Navy developed and perfected the dive-bomber. Trained pilots using newly establish tactics made their Douglas SBD Dauntless or Curtis SB2C Helldivers effective weapons. The AAC was not impressed, but German chief of the

Gen. William "Billy" Mitchell was a well-known pilot in WW-I and an air power activist, who challenged accepted military doctrine of the day that the navy ruled the waves. He declared that the next war would be won by air power and would sink navy warships. In 1921, a test was scheduled in which Army bombers sunk captured German capital ships. Instead of receiving promotions and decorations Mitchell was relieved of command, court-martialed, reduced in rank and expelled from the Army. (USAF)

The AAC was not impressed with Navy dive-bombing developments in the mid-30s, but Luftwaffe Gen. Ernst Udet (shown here in Los Angeles) saw a demonstration and returned to Germany to develop the Junkers Ju-87 Stuka dive-bomber and dive-bombing tactics and techniques taken from the U.S. Navy. German air doctrine consigned the Luftwaffe to a tactical air force supporting the Wehrmacht, rather than a strategic and air superiority air force. (Author)

technical bureau of the Luftwaffe, Gen. Ernst Udet, saw a demonstration and returned to Germany to develop the Junkers Ju-87 Stuka dive-bomber and dive-bombing tactics and techniques taken from the U.S. Navy. German air doctrine consigned the Luftwaffe to a tactical air force supporting the Wehrmacht, rather than a strategic and air superiority air force.

The stunning defeat of Poland in less than a month by German Panzer columns supported by ruthless Stuka dive-bombers was seen as the definitive use of a coordinated assault by air and ground units, and put a new term in the military dictionary, "Blitzkrieg." The defeat of Poland and then the Blitzkrieg in France alarmed the senior American commanders who had developed no close support aircraft, and now insisted on a Stuka-type dive-bomber. Gen. H.H. Arnold, Commander of the AAC, countered their choice with orders to utilize the twin-engine light bomber, the Douglas A-20 Havoc, which was already in production for export to England. By this time the Luftwaffe had found the Stuka to be vulnerable and had turned to the twin-engine light bomber, the Junkers Ju-88. The ACC dive-bomber faction persisted, and in early 1941 U.S. Army Chief of Staff, Gen. George C. Marshall, ordered Arnold to develop an Army Air Corps dive-bomber. The product was a hybrid. The North American Aviation Company had developed and was producing a single-Allison V-1710 engine close support fighter, the Mustang I, for the English. To make it a dive-bomber it was modified to Navy dive-bomber specifications, with dive brakes and bomb

Above: Marshall and Arnold meet at Randolph Field, TX, in 1940. Arnold and the Army Air Force wanted autonomy similar to the RAF. Marshall thought the world military situation was such that to split the AAC from the Army was too extreme and complicated that both men agreed that the AAC could not become an independent arm, as was the Royal Air Force. Arnold agreed not push for AAC independence during the war and Marshall rewarded him. The American Air Force was ultimately permitted to fully develop its strategic and tactical tenets and was supplied with the best aircraft and pilots in the world. (USAF) Right: 1Lt. Quince Brown of the 78th Fighter Group/84th Fighter Squadron conducted the first strafing in the ETO since the early rhubarb missions. Brown lost altitude and was heading back to England on deck west of Rotterdam and decided to expend his remaining ammunition on a locomotive and assorted gun positions. Ironically, on 6 September 1944, Brown's P-47, *"Okie"*, was shot down by flak while strafing and was captured. A SS officer, prodded by irate German citizens, murdered Brown. (USAF)

racks, and designated the A-36. The A=Attack designation could not make it more than a mediocre dive-bomber. In March 1943 a conference was held at Wright Field, Ohio, to finally determine whether to use the dive-bomber or fighter-bomber in the ground support role. It was decided that the fighter-bomber was to be employed operationally, as its fighter capabilities allowed it to establish the absolute air superiority that needed to be achieved before first-line fighters could be consigned to the fighter-bomber role. The fighter-bomber also enjoyed the tactical flexibility that the dive-bomber did not possess; it was not restricted to attack a singular target. It was able to strafe, drop bombs, and launch rockets in high-speed, low-level passes, which gave it the element of surprise and a degree of protection from AA fire. A fighter-bomber squadron was able to perform multiple duties on the same mission, such as flying a close air support mission and then move on to an interdiction mission. The fighter-bomber squadron also was able to respond to sudden changes of target and be re-briefed by radio to the changes.

Development of USAAF Fighter-Bomber Tactics

On 30 July 1943, the P-47s of the 78th Fighter Group crossed the German border to rendezvous with returning B-17s near Haldern. The group's P-47s had been using belly auxiliary fuel tanks for a short time and found them to be cumbersome, leaky, often refusing to draw fuel, and at times to unrepentantly fall off! Nonetheless, on this mission the 78th surprised the Luftwaffe by penetrating into German territory many more miles than usual. After engaging German fighters, 1Lt. Quince L. Brown of the 84th Fighter Squadron lost altitude and was heading back to England on deck west of Rotterdam. On the way Brown decided to expend his remaining ammunition on a locomotive and assorted gun positions. Brown's attack was the first strafing in the ETO since the early rhubarb missions. Strafing was done only sporadically, and usually for the fun of it in the ETO for the remainder of 1943. Ironically, on 6 September 1944, Brown's P-47, "*Okie*," was shot down by flak while strafing near Schleiden. Brown was captured, and a SS officer, prodded by irate German citizens, murdered Brown.

"Bill's Buzz Boys"

In early 1944, the Luftwaffe was reluctant to engage the fighters of the VIII Fighter Command, as it was saving its aircraft for advantageous tactical situations. Gen. H.H. Arnold's 1944 New Year's message had emphasized the importance of defeating the Luftwaffe both "in the air, and on the ground." Engineering advances, such as water injection and the installation of paddle blade propellers enhanced the low-altitude performance of the P-47. The introduction of drop tanks increased its range, making it more suited for ground strafing duties. Eighth Air Force Lt.Gen. James Doolittle had commanded the 12th Air Force in North Africa and had seen the fruitful results of ground strafing in the MTO. Doolittle and Maj.Gen. Carl Spaatz were instrumental in the decision to have the VIII Fighter Command move from the defensive to an offensive posture against the Luftwaffe. The decision was made to allow withdrawing escort fighters to attack German airdromes (A/D) on the way back to base. To encourage pilots to engage in this dangerous endeavor, the 8th Air Force decided to credit ground victories towards total victories. This practice was also adopted by Gen. Clair Chennault of the 14th Air Force in the CBI Theater, and earlier by the American Volunteer Group—the Flying Tigers—over China, also commanded by Chennault.

On 22 February 1944 the 353rd Fighter Group, after being released from bomber escort duty, was led by Col. Glenn Duncan on a strafing run on FW-190s on Ostheim A/D. Following Duncan, Walt Beckham led the next flight in. The second strafing attack was always more dangerous, as the enemy AA defenses were alerted. The German gunners hit Beckham's P-47, "*Little Demon*," forcing him to pull up and bail out. The leading ace in the ETO at the time with 18 victories was captured and made a POW for the duration.

The first planned pure strafing mission was flown on 11 March, when Duncan's 353rd Fighter Group conducted a low-level sweep over a Luftwaffe A/D in the Pas de Calais area. Small arms and light flak claimed two P-47s, while a third crashed on its return to base. These losses were unacceptable, and Duncan wanted to maxi-

On 7 July Col. Glenn Duncan led the 351st Fighter Squadron of the 353rd Fighter Group on Wesendorf A/D, getting a parked He-111 on his first pass. Duncan decided on another injudicious run and flak hit his oil line, causing his engine to overheat on the way home. He was forced to belly land behind enemy lines, and after setting his fighter on fire became an evader and spent nine months with the Dutch Underground, returning to England in April 1945. (USAF)

mize the rewards and minimize the risks of strafing. Duncan presented Maj.Gen. William Kepner, CG of the VIII Fighter Command, with the idea of organizing a unit of strafing specialists. The group was to develop ground-strafing tactics, and the pilots were to pass their knowledge on to their respective units after disbanding. Kepner agreed, and four pilots each from the 353rd, 355th, 359th, and 361st Fighter Groups volunteered, forming a unit to be known as "Bill's Buzz Boys" after Kepner, who eagerly lent his name to the group. The pilots were put on detached service to the 353rd "C" Fighter Group. The pilots in this group were from:

353rd Fighter Group
Lt. Kenneth Chetwood
Lt. Charles Durant
Lt. Francis Edwards
Lt. John Sullivan

359th Fighter Group
Capt. Charles Ettleson
Lt. Clifford Carter
Lt. John Oliphint
Lt. Robert Thacker

355th Fighter Group
Capt. Albert Starr
Lt. Norman Fortier
Lt. Kenneth Williams
Lt. Gilbert Wright

361st Fighter Group
Lt. Eugene Kinnaird
Lt. Martin Johnson
Lt. Joseph Kelly
Lt. Johnny Wright

On 15 March, the 16 pilots from the four fighter groups began training at Metfield, England, the home of the 353rd Fighter Group. "C" Group was equipped with rugged P-47s, all fitted with paddle blade propellers and water injection, which greatly enhanced its low altitude capabilities. They practiced and refined their strafing techniques on targets at Metfield Airfield. The first combat mission flown by the unit came on the afternoon of 26 March, when 12 P-47s, each carrying two M-4 fragmentation cluster bombs, were led by Capt. Albert Starr to strafe and bomb five different German A/Ds. Attacking five airfields gave the group the opportunity to vary their approach and presented different terrain, landmarks, natural hazards, and AA defenses. On the first field attacked (Chateaudun), claims were made for one aircraft destroyed, one probably destroyed, and two damaged by the fragmentation bombs. Once the bombs were dropped, the group went on to strafe hangers, buildings, and AA defenses on the other fields. At Chartres two aircraft were damaged. One P-47 pilot (Lt. Kenneth Williams) was shot down and taken prisoner, and five aircraft were damaged by flak. The mission determined that the P-47's .50 caliber machine guns were more destructive than the fragmentation bombs, but that these bombs did tend to discourage enemy AA gunners.

The mission on 29 March was probably the unit's most successful when Duncan led 12 P-47s against four airfields in the Dummer Lake/Rheine area in northwest Germany. The group preceded a scheduled heavy bomber mission and found an ideal 6/10th to 8/10th, 5,000-foot cloud layer over the target. Duncan's flight of four dove from 10,000 feet out of the sun to deck level about two miles from Vechta Airdrome. At the edge of the field they pulled up to 150 feet, looking to strafe parked e/a, but found none. A flak tower at the corner of the field put out a lot of return fire but was unable to get proper deflection on the low flying, 400mph Thunderbolts. The group passed over the end of the field, pulled up to 5,000 feet, and watched as Duncan attacked the other side of the A/D, which was loaded with parked aircraft. Duncan dove and lined-up two twin-engine aircraft, hitting them with machine gun fire. He then proceeded onto a line of fighters, putting a few rounds into each while avoiding some flak. Following Duncan in, the group knocked out the flak positions, which had revealed themselves on Duncan's run, and destroyed more parked aircraft. A crash landed 8th Air Force B-17 was intact in an open field, and Duncan deprived the Germans of their trophy by setting it on fire. The group reassembled at 5,000 feet to attack Twenthe A/D. Duncan had run out of ammunition, but four P-47s flying line abreast destroyed more parked aircraft there, along with a speeding staff car. Rail and river targets of opportunity were harassed on the return to base. Total claims were 7 destroyed and 13 damaged aircraft on the ground and 8/3 locomotives, in addition to damage to two hangars, six flak towers, and several barges. Duncan was credited with two destroyed and seven damaged for the day. One P-47 was lost (Lt. Francis Edwards' P-47 took a hit in the fuel tank and ran out of gas over the Channel, and he was picked up by ASR) and four received minor damage.

Left: Maj.Gen. William Kepner, CG of the VIII Fighter Command, was instrumental in implementing Gen. Arnold's "Down to Earth" edit of February 1944 which allowed escort fighters to seek out the Luftwaffe on the ground. Kepner ordered a study of strafing techniques. (USAF)

Mission Four was flown on 1 April against targets in northwestern Germany. The "Buzz Boys" shot up a number of parked aircraft, locomotives, and rolling stock and river traffic. Four Ju-88s were destroyed at Guterloh A/D. Poor weather aborted Mission Five in route. Mission Six on 8 April was only moderately successful, but 1Lt. Clifford Carter was lost. Mission Seven was flown on 10 April in the Paris area in target support of the 55th Fighter Group, and then went on to harass Luftwaffe airdromes in the area. Two Me-110s were destroyed on the ground and hangars and buildings strafed at Villaroche. On 12 April Mission Eight concluded the experiment, achieving minor damage to rail transportation and facilities.

A total of eight missions were flown (two uneventful), in which 90 P-47s were dispatched with 83 making effective sorties. Three aircraft and two pilots were lost, and 13 were damaged. Claims were 16 aircraft destroyed and 18 damaged on the ground, one air probable, 9 hangars, 9 flak towers, 35/3 locomotives, and 9 barges. It was noted that a parked aircraft could be shot full of holes and not catch fire, as the Germans learned not to fill the fuel tanks of parked aircraft. The results demonstrated that strafing could be effective, but also that the two pilots lost and the 3/16 cost in aircraft made strafing a dangerous activity.

On 12 April Kepner disbanded the group, thanking them for their work and returning them to their stations. Their mission resulted in the formulation of basic strafing tenants:

Preparation: Obtaining as many photographs and information about an A/D in pre-planned attacks allowed the unit leader to plan the approach, the attack, and the withdrawal using all the local terrain features to his advantage. For impromptu attacks a quick assessment, based on the skills learned in prepared missions, was a requirement for the mission's safety and success.

Surprise! Attack and knockout the German before he can react.

"Bill's Buzz Boys" were a group of 16 pilots, four each from the 353rd, 355th, 359th, and 361st Fighter Groups, that were formed in mid-March 1944 by Gen. William "Bill" Kepner. (USAF)

Plan one pass: Always go into a strafing pass considering the target to be heavily defended. Pick a target. High speed/stay low. Make every round count. Get out low and quickly.

Consider risk/reward: A parked enemy aircraft destroyed is not worth our fighter and its pilot. How many trucks equal a fighter? In equal numbers ground attack was found to be four times more dangerous than air-to-air combat.

Establishment of the Tactical Air Forces

By the end of 1943 the worth of close air support had been firmly demonstrated by both the Germans and Russians on the Eastern Front, and by the Allies over North Africa. In November 1943 the Allies established tactical air forces for the impending invasion of Europe. The RAF established the 2nd Tactical Air Force from experienced personnel from the Mediterranean. The USAAF transferred the entire 9th Air Force HQ from the MTO to England. However, initially the 9th Air Force operated under the control of Fighter Command in a fighter escort role. It was not until April 1944 that two Tactical Air Commands were instituted to support the two U.S. Armies slated to take part in the D-Day invasion. The IX TAC (7 P-47 groups/21 squadrons and 3 P-38 groups/9 squadrons) was to support the First U.S. Army, while the XIX TAC (5 P-47 groups/15 squadrons and 2 P-38 groups/6 squadrons) was to support the Third U.S. Army. In early October 1944 the XXIX TAC was established from the merger of the 303rd and 84th Fighter Wings of the 9th Air Force. During the same month the First Tactical Air Force (Provisional) was established to provide tactical air support for the Franco-American Army group over the southern ETO. The mission of these TAC Air Forces was threefold:

1) Gain air superiority by attacking enemy airfields, destruction of E/A on the ground and in the air.
2) Isolate the battlefield by destroying enemy motor and rail transportation, cutting rails and bridges, and attacking supply depots and troop concentrations in the rear to prevent or delay their movement to the battlefront.
3) Give direct support to ground forces by hitting troop concentrations, strong points, armor and gun positions.

Conclusion

The increasing effectiveness of 9th Air Force TACs can be illustrated by comparing the monthly, June 1944, performance figures to a one-day figure, 25 March 1945, when the Allies pushed across the Rhine:

TARGET (Destroyed/Damaged)	June 1944	25 March 1945
E/A Air	180/96	3/0
E/A Ground	33/15	15/26
Locomotives	91/55	76/26
RR Cars	427/513	858/1351
Tanks/Armored Vehicles	22/24	118/76
Motor Transport	1288/583	742/649
Guns	14/10	27/16

4

USAAF Fighter-Bombers

P-47 Thunderbolt

It was ironic that the P-47 that was originally designed as a high-altitude escort became the premier fighter-bomber, while the P-51, designed as a ground support fighter as the Mustang I for the RAF, would become the premier bomber escort. Alexander Kartveli designed the XP-47 for Alexander Seversky's Republic Aviation, and a prototype was ordered on 6 September 1940. The massive fighter, powered by Pratt & Whitney's new XR-2800 18 cylinder, 2 row air-cooled engine, first flew on 6 May 1941. After a troubled development production of the P-47B began in March 1942. Production of the celebrated -D model was ordered on 13 October 1941, and the first —Ds rolled off the assembly line in early 1943. The P-47D production run of 12,602 was the largest total for any fighter subtype in history. At the end of 1943, General H.H. Arnold declared war on the Luftwaffe both in the air and on the ground in his "Down to earth" edict. Eighth Air Force Jugs returning from their escort missions dropped to the deck to expend their remaining ammo strafing ground targets of opportunity. The fuselage shackle could be used for a 500lb. bomb, but was used to carry a drop tank for the escort mission. Republic consequently redesigned the wing after the so-called "universal" British wing by strengthening the mainplane and adding several external ventral pylons. The Thunderbolt could carry a variety of armament: either two underwing 1,000lb. bombs or three 500lb. bombs (two underwing and one on the fuselage shackle) or a variety of bombs, drop tanks, and rocket clusters. Meanwhile, the 9th Air Force had been reformed as a tactical air force to support the invasion and subsequent land battles. P-47 production peaked at 660 aircraft per month at the two Republic plants. The 9th Air Force was assigned 18 fighter groups in the first three months of 1944, with 13 being equipped with the Thunderbolt. The 8th Air Force had received its full complement of ten P-47 groups at the end of 1943. 8th AF P-47 pilots were led by those of Hub Zemke's 56th Fighter Group: "Gabby' Gabreski, Robert Johnson, Dave Schilling, and Bud Mahurin had mastered the huge fighter, and were taking their toll of Luftwaffe aircraft in the air. But the 8th was beginning to transition its P-47 units to the P-51s, which were considered the better long-range escort, and by March 1944 its P-47s were being mentioned in official reports as fighter-bombers.

A 404th Fighter Group P-47 armed with a potent load of three 500lb. bombs and four 5-inch HVAR rockets is parked on PSP at St.Trond, Belgium (A-92) in the late fall of 1944.The 404th under Col. Leo Moon played an important role in CLARION in late February 1945 attacking and destroying locomotives and rolling stock. (USAF)

The T-bolt weighed almost seven tons, which was almost three tons more than a fully loaded FW-190A. Despite its size it was able to roll with and was faster at all altitudes than either the Me-109 or FW-190, and its diving prowess was renowned. The aircraft was easy to fly and to land and had a roomy cockpit. The Thunderbolt was a stable gun platform for its awesome eight .50 caliber machine guns, and was able to carry and deliver prodigious amounts of ordnance. Its airframe's and air-cooled radial engine's ability to absorb punishment is legendary.

The Air Proving Grounds Command (APGC) at Eglin Field, Florida, supervised extensive tests using various combinations of bombs and drop tanks that changed the P-47 from a fighter to a fighter-bomber. In late 1943 several technical developments were introduced to enhance the P-47's lackluster low altitude performance. The first was water injection, which increased the horsepower of the Pratt & Whitney by 15%, horsepower from 2,300 to 2,535, and its top speed from 406 to 433mph. A 15-gallon tank containing a water/alcohol mixture was located on the bulkhead just to the rear of the engine and was connected to the fuel intake. A switch on top of the throttle control activated the water/alcohol mixture to enter the cylinders at a gallon per minute to produce short emergency spurts of power. It was found that at lower altitudes water injection gave the P-47 a considerable increase in performance when compared to other fighters, Luftwaffe or Allied. On the P-47D-11 models water injection was initiated automatically when the throttle reached the final eighth inch of movement. Conversion kits were available for the P&W R-2800-21 engines installed on P-47C and D models. The R-2800-59 and-63 engine had water injection factory installed.

The so-called "paddle-blade" or "high-activity" 13ft. Curtiss Electric or Hamilton Standard Constant Speed replaced the 12ft. 2in. Curtiss Electric 4-Blade standard, constant speed propeller. The new broad-bladed prop increased the rate of climb 600ft per minute, and the speed as much as 10mph.

The attachment of under wing shackles to carry bombs or drop tanks gave the P-47 new flexibility in its missions. The first shackle installation was a flush-fitting type designed to carry the impregnated, compressed paper four-point 200-gallon external belly tank. Installation problems, and the fact that these tanks could only be filled to 100 gallons (above 20,000ft atmospheric changes prevented the withdrawal of fuel) led to their abandonment of both. The two-point suspension bomb rack/drop tank with sway braces proved more effective. The B-10 shackles were mounted on small pylons extending from the under wing which, in the first types, decreased maximum speed by as much as 45mph. Subsequent pylons were streamlined to reduce the speed loss by two-thirds. The installation of the complicated fuel lines and control mechanisms were labor-intensive, and several months were required to outfit all the P-47s of the 8th and 9th Air Forces. A P-47 C or D without a drop tank could fly for about one and three quarter to two hours, while the addition of a 108-gallon drop tank increased its duration to three to three and a quarter hours. In the 8th Air Force the P-47 escort's range was increased 150 miles by attaching two 108-gallon drop tanks, while in the 9th Air Force the P-47 fighter-bomber could carry two 500lb bombs and a 75-gallon centerline fuel tank. The use of two 108-gallon drop tanks was optimal, as it extended flying time to five and a half hours. Lt.Col. Cass Hough of the VIII FC Air Technical Section at Bovington first adapted 75-gallon metal drop tanks originally intended for the P-39. He then adapted the 108-gallon glue and pressed paper pressurized drop tanks manufactured by the English company, Bowwater-Lloyd, that was in limited use by the RAF. To pressurize the tanks he utilized the exhaust from the vacuum pump. Although it had been approved in June 1943, it was not until early December that these tanks and the standard U.S. 75-gallon, 108-gallon, and 150-gallon tanks had been improved and were ready in large numbers.

A P-47 of the 353rd Fighter Group poses with a full fighter-bomber load: two 500lb. bombs, a M-10 triple tube "Bazooka-type" rocket launcher, six .50 cal. machine guns and a belly drop tank. (USAF)

The configuration of ordnance and fuel tanks varied to fit the mission. A short mission allowed the use of maximum armament: two-underwing 500lb. bombs; one belly-mounted 260lb. fragmentation bomb; eight rockets; and eight .50 caliber machine guns. A longer mission required more fuel than the 305 gallons carried internally, so external fuel tanks replaced some or all three bombs. A 200-gallon external fuel tank would replace the belly fragmentation bomb, or the two underwing 500lb. bombs would be replaced by 150 gallon auxiliary tanks and a 500lb. bomb would carried on belly shackle.

Initially six wing-mounted .50 caliber machine guns with 267-500rpg were specified for the P-47, but its eight guns were soon standard. Ninth Air Force pilots preferred to carry 425rpg that fired for 34.5 seconds each. The bomb loading corresponded to the target type and distance. The Thunderbolt could carry two 1,000lb. bombs or ten 4.5-inch rockets and three 500lb. bombs, or ten 4.5-inch rockets and two 1,000lb. bombs. For short range sorties the P-47 could carry two 1,000lb. bombs on the wing pylons and a 500lb. bomb on the centerline shackle. Initially the M series triple cluster rocket launchers were fitted, but were very inaccurate and slowed the fighter significantly. Later the 5-inch HVAR using zero-length launchers were fitted with better results. Rockets were not used in the ETO to the extent of the RAF 2nd TAF.

In the fall of 1943, the VII FC was evaluating the role of the Thunderbolt as a fighter-bomber. Maj. Loren McCollom, CO of the 353rd Fighter Group, tested the P-47's dive-bombing capabilities flying training sorties over the 353rd base at Metfield. On 25 November the first 8th Air Force dive-bombing mission of the war was scheduled for St. Omer-Fort Rouge airdrome. McCollom led four bomb-carrying flights of the 351st Squadron escorted by the 350th and 352nd Squadrons and some fighters from the 78th Fighter Group. The plan was to dive from 15,000ft. following McCollom down in flights of four, dropping their 500lb. bombs at the altitude McCollom determined best for accuracy. However, five miles south of the airdrome the initial point was passed and heavy AA fire began. As McCollom rolled to approach the target a flak burst hit his fuel tank, engulfing his fighter in flames. McCollom bailed out, suffering serious burns, and was captured by Luftwaffe personnel on the ground. The remaining P-47s dropped their bombs from 8-

10,000ft., scoring only three hits on the target, and AA fire damaged six more P-47s.

The same day 56th Fighter Group CO, Capt. Hubert Zemke, decided to try another approach. As the P-47 was not equipped with a bombsight he decided to have a B-24 navigate the fighters to the target, where his P-47 pilots would release their bombs horizontally on a signal from the Liberator bombardier. Lt.Col. David Schilling led the mission with the 62nd Squadron to the right rear of the Liberator, the 61st to left rear, and the 63rd astern. The mission failed when the B-24 released its bombs late, and consequently all bombs missed the German airdrome at St. Omer-Longunesse.

The size and toughness of the P-47 is best described by its pilots, who said that the P-47 was built by the "Republic Locomotive Works and Iron Foundry." Stories of the toughness of the P-47 are legend. 1Lt. Robert Goff of the 366th Fighter Group had his turbo-supercharger malfunction after being damaged in a dogfight, increasing the manifold pressure and obliterating several cylinders. Oil covered the windshield, and Goff could only navigate by cracking his canopy to see his wingman, who escorted him back to friendly territory. While he was preparing for a crash landing he collided with the second floor of a brick building. He was helped out of the wreckage, taken to a field hospital, released, and returned to his base.

The Republic P-47 was the preeminent fighter-bomber in the USAAF, and probably of WWII, because of its firepower and bomb-carrying capacity and ruggedness. The P-47 was sturdily built and could withstand the cannon hits from Luftwaffe fighters. It was particularly indestructible from the standard rear attack, and Luftwaffe victories over the P-47 were usually by deflection shots. Its ability to withstand damage from the heaviest and most accurate AA defenses of WWII made it a superlative fighter-bomber. Between March 1943 and V-J Day the P-47 flew 546,000 sorties with a loss rate of 0.7%. All top-ten P-47 ETO aces survived the war, even though six were shot down:

Name	Cause	Date	Outcome
Francis Gabreski	AA	7/20/45	POW
Walker Mahurin	Combat	3/27/44	E&E
Glenn Duncan	AA	7/7/44	E&E
Walter Beckham	AA	2/22/44	POW
Gerald W. Johnson	AA	3/27/44	POW
Hubert Zemke	Engine*	10/30/44	POW

POW = Prisoner of War
E&E = Escape and evasion
*In P-51

The P-38 has been described as a jack-of-all-trades; master of none. In the early stages of the war in the ETO and MTO the P-38 performed adequately as a bomber escort and fighter aircraft but the transformation of the P-38 to an effective fighter-bomber/dive-bomber came about as its previous escort responsibility was taken away. The nose compartment mounted four .50 caliber machine guns and a 20mm Hispano-Suiza cannon. The ordnance carried could be two 500 or 1,000lb. bombs or ten 4.5-inch rockets or ten 4.5-inch rockets with two 500lb. bombs or up to a 4,000lb. load of external stores. (USAF)

Left: In the fall of 1943, the VII FC was evaluating the role of the Thunderbolt as a fighter-bomber. Maj. Loren McCollom, CO of the 353rd Fighter Group, tested the P-47's dive-bombing capabilities flying training sorties over the 353rd base at Metfield. On 25 November he led the first 8th Air Force dive-bombing mission of the war. (USAF)

Between June 1944 and the end of the war against Germany T-bolts destroyed 9,000 locomotives, 86,000 railway cars, 6,000 armored vehicles, and 68,000 road vehicles, and had an air combat kill ratio of 4.6 to 1.

P-38 Lightning

The P-38 was Lockheed's first military project and had many innovative features. First design work began in 1937 under Clarence "Kelly" Johnson and H.L. Hibbard to meet the USAAC specifications for a high-altitude interceptor that also spawned the P-40 and P-39. The first USAAC twin-engine, single seat interceptor was the first to have a turbo-supercharger, the first to exceed 400mph, and the first to use the twin boom configuration, and it also was to be powered by the 12 cylinder Allison V-1710, which had recently passed its 150 hour approval tests. These innovations conspired to delay the development of the fighter and caused problems throughout its Mediterranean and European combat career. Early in its career it was plagued by a compressibility problem that was eventually overcome by re-engineering. It was claimed that every P-38 in the ETO had at least one unscheduled complete engine change. The turbo-superchargers were difficult and required attentive handling by experienced pilots. The AAF just did not have the time to train newly arrived pilots to overcome the Lightning's peculiarities in combat. Most P-38 pilots were happy to transition to the less demanding P-47s and P-51s when they became available. Winston Churchill facetiously remarked that the P-38 was a blessing "quite effectively disguised."

The P-38 has been described as a jack-of-all-trades; master of none. In the early stages of the war in the ETO and MTO the P-38 performed adequately as a bomber escort and fighter aircraft, but the transformation of the P-38 to an effective fighter-bomber/dive-bomber came about as its previous escort responsibility was taken away. Early in its career in the ETO its Allison engine limited its effectiveness as both a fighter and escort. However, because the twin-Allisons were located in two outboard nacelles, the fighter was a very stable gun platform, and heavy armament could be concentrated in the nose of the fighter without the need of a synchronizing gear. The nose compartment mounted four .50 caliber machine guns with 500rpg firing for 41.5 seconds and a 20mm Hispano-Suiza cannon with 150 rounds that fired for 13.5 seconds. The ordnance carried could be two 500 or 1,000lb. bombs or ten 4.5-inch rockets, or ten 4.5-inch rockets with two 500lb. bombs, or up to a 4,000lb. load of external stores

In the ETO as P-47s then P-51s took over escort duties the 8th Air Force decided to use the P-38 in ground attack and short-range escort missions. After D-Day P-38 units were flying escort and attacking targets of opportunity. As the Luftwaffe was driven from the air, the Lightning's role moved more and more to the fighter-bomber role. When Gen. James Doolittle assumed command of the 8th Air Force in mid-1944 he decided that P-47 and P-38 groups would be equipped with the P-51 for both escort and ground attack missions. P-47 commanders did not agree with the decision, as they felt the Thunderbolt's great diving speed, heavy armament, and rugged airframe gave it an advantage over the Mustang. ETO P-38 commanders, on the other hand, felt that their J-models were not yet an effective aircraft, and that the P-51 had more potential. Since the Italian campaign had become a secondary theater, 15th Air Force Commander Nathan Twining and MAAF commander, ACM Sir Arthur Tedder, were happy to receive the P-38s down-graded in the ETO. So was Gen. George Kenney, commander of the Fifth Air Force in the Pacific, where the P-38's long-range capability, high altitude performance, and speed made it the ideal fighter against Japanese fighters in the widespread and warmer Pacific island-hopping campaign.

Droopsnoots:

An interesting P-38 development was the "Droopsnoot." The Droopsnoot was a modified P-38J having its nose guns and metal nose gun fairing removed and replaced by a Plexiglas nose fairing with a flat bomb-aiming window on its underside. Entry and exit was through a hatch located on the top of the nose, and an escape hatch was provided at the bottom. Two additional windows on each

A bombardier laid prone in the "droopsnoot" of this P-38J lead ship guided other conventional Lightnings to the target. When the bombardier dropped his bombs the other pilots also jettisoned their bombs. The aircraft dubbed the "B-38" had mediocre success and was not used to a great extent. (USAF)

Droopsnoot pilot and bombardier. The bombardier is standing in the entrance hatch of the "snoot." Bombardiers had served a tour with a bomb group before being assigned to the specialized P-38. (USAF)

side behind the Plexiglas nose fairing furnished additional light. The bombardier who had previously completed a tour in bombers "sat" in a reclining seat in the cramped compartment. The shorter time of the short-range missions flown by the Droopsnoot compensated for this discomfort. Crammed into the front of the snoot was a Norden Bombsight with a PDI (Pilot's Directional Indicator). A panel on the lower left side contained bomb indicator lights and arming and selector switches. Forward of this panel was an altimeter, airspeed indicator, ree air temperature gauge, and clock. The bombardier had an interphone connection with the pilot and was able to transmit on the radio if the pilot's radio was set to do so. The snoot had its own independent oxygen system with a demand-type regulator and flow meter. For the bombardier's comfort there was a relief tube and a heating duct and bombing window defroster. For the bombardier's safety there was armor-plated seat and floor, crash pad, and a bombing window defroster. A K-24 camera was mounted in the 20mm cannon shell ejector chute to take bomb strike photos.

The Droopsnoot led eight conventional P-38s carrying bombs. Droopsnoot "B-38," mission bomb loads varied according to target distance. External fuel tanks were carried on longer missions that decreased the bomb load. The mission was flown in a normal fighter formation until ten minutes from the initial point, at which time the formation closed up to the tight, wing tip to wing tip bombing formation. On the way to the target the formation cruised at an altitude about 2,000 to 3,000 feet above the bombing altitude. On the turn at the bomb run, altitude was lost at a rate of 1,000 feet per minute until the desired bombing altitude was attained. The bombardier took over at the bomb run turn and a 30-second bomb run at 210 to 270 mph at 10,000 to 20,000 feet. Several methods of bomb release were used. While lining up the target on the Norden Bombsight the bombardier counted down from ten on the radio to all P-38s for bomb release or, on sight the formation would simultaneously release their bombs when the bombardier released. Or by connecting the automatic release on the Norden to the VHF radios of the formation so that when the Norden bombsight indices crossed the target all bombs in the formation were released by radio signal.

In April, the 20th and 55th Fighter Groups were equipped with several "Droopsnoot" P-38s. On 10 April the first Droopsnoot mission was sent out to Florennes Airdrome, but bad weather obscured the target and the bombs were jettisoned in the English Channel. Later that day a Droopsnoot mission was dispatched by the 55th Fighter Group, and 16 P-38s dropped 17 tons of bombs on the Coulommiers Airdrome, which was a secondary target. Two P-38s were lost to heavy flak, including 55th CO, Col. Jack Jenkins, who became a POW. The 20th flew a second test mission that day when 27 P-38s escorted by 46 359th Fighter Group P-47s attacked Gutersloh Airdrome. The 13 tons of bombs dropped caused minor damage, and one P-38 was lost to flak. Further Droopsnoot missions were flown on 23 April when they flew bombing missions, the 55th to Laon and Tours and the 20th to Chateaudun Airdromes. 78th Fighter Group P-38s and 352nd Group P-51s escorted them. On 30 April, Droopsnoot missions continued with a mission to Tours airdrome. The 20th Fighter Group's 44 P-38s carried four 500lb. bombs and were escorted by 55th Group P-38s. The Droopsnoots bombed from higher altitudes than previously, and the escorting P-38s swept the airdrome after the bombing. That afternoon 22 20th Group Droopsnoots escorted by 364th Group fighter-bombers attacked the Orleans/Bricy airdrome.

The 15th Air Force flew 21 Droop Missions between 1 August 1944 and 21 January 1945. Eighteen of these missions were flown by the 82nd Fighter Group, and three by the 14th Fighter Group. From three to 53 P-38s flew on these missions with mixed results. A 15th Air Force report rated the results of one mission as excellent, 11 as good, four as fair, one as fair to poor, one missed the target, and two had no rating, as there was no photo recon available. The three plane raid dropped 1.75 tons of bombs, while the largest attack dropped 41.25 tons (*Report of Employment of Droopsnoot P-38 Aircraft in the 15th Air Force*).

The Droopsnoots had some success against large military and industrial installations, airfields, and marshaling yards. Post strike analysis showed the Droopsnoot to have comparable results against these targets as heavy and medium bombers. The fighter-bombers did more damage to airdromes when they dropped several tons of fragmentation bombs on the runway and facilities. They were ineffective against pinpoint targets, such as bridges and buildings, as the bomb patterns were too dispersed. The reason for its lack of success was attributed to the lack of training of the fighter pilot in flying the tight, wing tip to wing tip formations necessary to attain a good bombing pattern. Another factor was the inability of the lead pilot to make corrections as given by the bombardier from the PDI. Also, the P-38's design as a fighter and its speed made it difficult to be a stable bombing platform and maintain formation when making the corrections indicated by the PDI. Another drawback of the Droopsnoot was that it carried fewer bombs and had a shorter range than a medium bomber, and certainly a heavy bomber. The ideal target for the Droopsnoot formation was one having light AA defenses, whose destruction did not require a heavy bomb tonnage, was relatively large, and was within 500 miles. It was determined that the P-38 could be better employed as a dive-bomber.

P-51 Mustang

In April 1940, the British approached North American Aviation to build the Curtiss P-40 for the RAF. However, North American had other ideas, and proposed that it would build a better fighter using the P-40 Allison V-1710 engine. The British agreed, stipulating that

A P-51B of the 355th Fighter Squadron/354th Fighter Group carrying two 500lb. bombs for one of the early dive-bombing sorties. (USAF)

due to the grave war situation in Europe the prototype had to be completed in 120 days. North American president, J.H. "Dutch" Kindelberger, and his design team, Raymond Rice and Edgar Schmued, incredibly completed the NA-73 in 117 days, although the engine was not ready for an additional six weeks. The NP-73 flew for the first time on 26 October 1941, and it demonstrated notable performance due to its innovative laminar flow wing that was to become the standard for most future high-speed fighter designs. The USAAF and test pilot, Robert Chilton, tested two NA-73s designated as the XP-51, and the USAAF was impressed enough to order 150. The RAF ordered 620 as the Mustang I, with deliveries starting in November 1941, and another 150 were ordered as the Mustang II (55 were repossessed by the USAAF to be converted to the F-6A photo recon aircraft). The low altitude Allison engine made the Mustang I unsuited for air to air combat that took place at higher altitudes in the ETO, and these models were relegated to ground attack by the RAF. In England the Rolls Royce Merlin 60 was fitted to the Mustang I airframe and was to establish the Mustang as the "Cadillac of the Air" and ultimate long-range escort fighter, relegating the P-47 to ground support missions. In England the Rolls Royce Merlin 60 was fitted to the Mustang I airframe, which was to define the Mustang as one of, if not the elite fighter of the war. In the meantime the Air Force had accepted 500 Allison-powered A-36s, the ground attack version of the P-51, and 310 Allison-powered P-51As. The RAF received 50 Allison Mustangs as the Mustang II, and 35 others to be modified to F-6Bs. The A-36 was briefly named the "Invader" and the first P-51s the "Apache," but the RAF designation "Mustang" was the adopted name for all P-51 models. The first Merlin-powered Mustangs were the P-51B and C (RAF Mustang III). The American-built Merlins were licensed to Packard, and the USAAF ordered 2,200 before its Merlin Mustang had ever flown. The B and C models were identical, with the B being built in Inglewood and the C in Dallas, and both began operations in December 1943. A combined total of 3,749 (1,999 Bs and 1,750 Cs) were built, of which 910 were shipped to the RAF and 91 were converted to the F-6C (a total of 482 F, photo recon, versions were completed to F-6A/B/C/D/K from P-51/51A/C/D/K, respectively). The P-51D was the first major design change that was to give the Mustang its classic lines. The fuselage cockpit fairing was cut down to the tail plane to permit the elegant teardrop canopy to be fitted, and thus eliminate the blind spot created by the faired cockpit. A dorsal fin was added to compensate for keel loss. The D carried six .50 machine guns instead of four, moved the wing slightly forward, and provided rocket launchers. The D was the most numerous P-51 model, with 7,956 being produced, including 876 Mustang IVs for the RAF. The 1,337 K models were similar to the Ds. The H was the last production model (555 built) and was the fastest, with a speed of 487 mph. Neither the K nor H saw operational service, as the war ended in the Pacific and contracts for an additional 3000 were canceled. Some 15,367 Mustangs were built and helped to change the course of the war in the ETO, allowing American bombers to penetrate into German-held territory under continuous escort protection.

Armed to the teeth. A P-51D carrying two 1,000lb. bombs and six 5-inch HVAR rockets. (USAF)

The Luftwaffe had been virtually driven from European skies, and an VIII Fighter Command HQ decision was made to allow its pilots to drop to the deck to strafe targets of opportunity after their escort duties ended. The P-51s lacked the massive firepower of the P-47, as the P-51D was armed with six .50 caliber wing guns carrying 1780 total rounds: 350rpg (32 seconds) for each inboard gun and 270rpg (22 seconds) for each center and outboard gun. The Mustang could carry two 1,000lb. bombs or ten 4.5-inch rockets, or six 4.5-inch rockets and two 1,000lb. bombs.

The Mustangs did considerable damage to Luftwaffe airdromes and targets of opportunity, but suffered about four times the losses in ground attack than they did in aerial combat. If the pilot closed to 250 yards or less on his target the six MGs were sufficient, but at that range the pilot had to duck the AA and flying debris during the attack. P-51 pilots would fly seven to eight hours of tedious and tiring bomber escort duty and then drop down to spend a dangerous hour as a fighter-bomber. Later when more Mustangs reached the ETO, P-51s were sent on longer-range (than the P-47) pure fighter-bomber sorties against Luftwaffe airfields strongly protected by experienced Luftwaffe AA batteries. The Mustang's liquid-cooled Merlin engine, its radiator, and web of coolant-carrying hoses and pipes were vulnerable to even small arms fire. A pilot whose Mustang received a hit in the cooling system had only a short time to convert his 400mph diving speed into enough altitude to bail out. Although many P-51s returned to base with considerable damage, many crashed into the ground at 400mph when the aircraft's control surfaces or control mechanisms were damaged by AA fire. The P-47 and P-38 were much better suited for ground attack than the Mustang. Again, it was ironic that the Mustang that was ordered by the RAF as a ground attack fighter would become a superlative high altitude escort, and the Thunderbolt that was designed as a high altitude escort would become the superlative ground attack fighter!

The Mustang was an amazing aircraft from the time of its inspired creation until the end of the war, when it was probably the best piston-engined fighter of WW II. In its 13 months of combat the Mustang recorded the destruction of nearly 5,000 Axis aircraft in the air. Although its superb interceptor and escort qualities precluded it from becoming an equally superb fighter-bomber, through sheer numbers it did destroy an additional 4,000 Axis aircraft on the ground which, when combined with its aerial victories accounted for more than half of the aircraft destroyed by all AAF units in Europe in 1944-45.

The Tally: 8th and 9th Air Force P-47s, P-51s, and P-38s

Aircraft Type	Sorties	Air Victories	Ground Victories	Losses
P-47	423,435	3,082	3,202	3,077
P-51	213,873	4,950	4,131	2,520
P-38	129,849	1,771	749	1,758
Total	767,157	9,803	8,082	7,355

A-36 Apache/Invader

The A-36 was a by-product of P-51 Mustang development. Even before Louis Wait made the first flight in the XP-51 on 29 May 1942, funding for fighter aircraft had been expended for the fiscal year June 1942. But there was money in the budget for attack aircraft, and to get the P-51 in production, North American Aircraft Company designer, Dutch Kindelberger, added bomb racks and dive brakes to the P-51 Apache (the RAF designation "Mustang" was substituted in July) airframe and designated it as an attack bomber, the A-36. The installation of the bomb racks (which also could carry external fuel tanks) and dive brakes required a total redesign of the wing. The racks were located outboard, close to the landing gear strut to minimize structural load during taxiing and takeoff. The bomb rack placement permitted prop clearance when releasing the bombs. The high diving speed of the A-36 presented a particular problem for the North American engineers, but the solution was literally next door. The Vultee factory, which produced the A-31 Vengeance dive-bomber, was located next to the North American factory, and visiting NAA engineers took the hydraulic dive brake system of the A-31 and adapted its design for the A-36. Four cast aluminum alloy lattice-shaped brakes were installed outboard of the ammunition bays in the wing panels. A selector lever to extend and retract the dive brake was located on the left side of the cockpit behind the throttle lever. A selector valve and hydraulic actuators that, upon activation, extended the brakes out of the top and bottom of each wing controlled the dive brakes. The retracted brakes were housed in a faired recessed well in the wing contour. The diving speed with the dive brakes deployed was about 300 mph.

The .50 caliber machine gun nose armament of the NA-73 was preserved, but two .50 caliber guns were mounted in the wing to provide six machine guns for ground support duties with 1,200 rounds/200rpg. A N-3B gun sight and N-1 gun camera were installed.

The engine was the liquid-cooled Allison V-1710-87 that developed 1,325hp at 3,000ft. The location of the engine coolant and after-cooler radiator under the fuselage, aft of the cockpit, made it vulnerable to ground fire. At 5,000ft. a clean A-36A had a maximum speed of 365mph, and carrying two 550lb. bombs its speed was 310mph and cruised at 250mph. Due to the lack of a turbosupercharger and high altitude pressurized ignition system the Allison's performance fell off markedly above 12,000ft. Its maximum performance was at 5,500ft.

Bomb Loading and Range Characteristics

Load/Range	Mission Type
2 x 500lb. bombs 150 miles	To target, bomb, patrol 30 min., return to base
2 x 500lb. bombs 225 miles	To target, bomb, return to base
1 x 500lb. bomb + 75 gal. tank 250 miles	Fly to target, bomb, patrol 30 min., return to base
1 x 500lb. bomb + 75 gal. tank 300 miles	Fly to target, bomb, return to base

On 16 April 1942 an order for 500 A-36s was placed, and on 23 June 310 P-51As were ordered. On 21 September 1942 test pilot Bob Chilton flew the first A-36, and on 3 February 1943 he flew

The A-36 could carry two 500lb. bombs 150 miles to the target, bomb and then patrol for 30 minutes and then return to base or carry two 500lb. bombs 225 miles to the target, bomb, return immediately to base. The A=Attack designation couldn't make it more than a mediocre dive-bomber but it did play a yeoman's role over Italy in that role. (USAF)

North American Aviation transformed the P-51 into a dive-bomber by modifying it to Navy dive-bomber specifications with dive brakes and bomb racks (see photo) and designated it the A-36. (USAF)

the first P-51A fighter. The production models of the A-36 were designated the A-36A-1NA. Original testing at Eglin Proving Grounds resulted in the recommendation that the A-36A's angle of descent be reduced to 70 degrees and, because of inconsistencies in deployment, that the air brakes not be used. However, true testing came in combat, as the 27th Fighter-Bomber Group found maximum dive-bombing accuracy could only be achieved in a 90-degree dive, and that modifications to the dive brakes made them reliable.

NAAF Tactical Bulletin No. 23 (1 July 1943) evaluated the A-36 in light of the 27th's combat experience:

"It became an excellent fighter-bomber, capable of delivering its bomb load with extreme accuracy. Its high speed and maneuverability make it an excellent aircraft for either glide or dive-bombing but it must be noted that the accuracy obtained in glide bombing is much less than that obtained by using the dive brakes to secure vertical dives on the target.

Because of the excellent range characteristics, the A-36 may be used to good advantage against strategic, pinpoint targets and could complement the work of the strategic bombers very effectively within reasonable range. Dive-bombing accuracy greatly increases the accuracy now realized by our other fighter-bombers. With its high speed, fighter-bomber support calls can be answered more quickly. The A-36 carries a greater bomb load than any other tactical fighter-bomber in use at present. It is only exceeded by the P-38 fighter which is now used only strategically."

The report continued to describe the technique of a dive bombing attack. In combat it was found that bombing accuracy varied directly with the angle of the dive; the more perpendicular, the more accurate. Any dive of less than 72 degrees was a glide-bombing attack. It was determined that best results were produced by a 12 aircraft line abreast formation, with its leader on the flank toward the sun. Over the target the leader rolled over and dove, followed closely as possible in the dive by the other aircraft, and then reforming after the attack to a normal fighter defensive formation. The second formation used was the echelon of flights back and away from the target:

"For well-defended targets, an altitude of 12,000ft. is obtained before the bomb run. The formation loses altitude to 10,000ft. for the beginning of the dive and recovery is made between 4,000 and 5,000ft. For lightly defended targets, the altitude at the start of the dive is from 6,000 to 8,000 feet with recovery on the deck. A higher degree of accuracy is obtained by the latter but at the expense of greater danger to the flight from ground fire. The rollover method is much preferred to the pushover method for obtaining a vertical dive. The dive brakes are opened immediately before the rollover signal from the flight leader. Strafing with all guns is possible with individuals of the flight during the dive."

The 500 A-36s built gave good account of themselves in Italy and the CBI, dropping 8,014 tons of bombs and destroying 84 enemy aircraft in the air and 17 on the ground. In 23,373 combat sorties 177 were lost in combat (0.8% loss rate per sortie), mostly to ground and AA fire. Their effectiveness was due to the air superiority around them that did not make them vulnerable, as was the German Stuka, which fell prey to enemy fighters.

The 27th Fighter Bomber Group under Lt.Col. John Stevenson started off as an A-20 Havoc unit. Its aircraft were taken from it to replace losses in the 47th Bombardment Group that had seen action in North Africa. The 27th's three squadrons, the 16th, 17th, and 91st (redesignated 8 September to the 522nd, 523rd , and 524th, respectively) flew their first action on 6 June 1943 when 34 of its Invaders swept German airfields on Pantelleria. The 86th Fighter-Bomber Group had received its A-36s at Key Field, Mississippi, in late 1942, and was trained and shipped to North Africa in March 1943 and first saw action in July 1943 over Sicily. The 86th's three groups were the 309th, 310th, and 311th (redesignated the 525th, 526th, and 527th respectively on September 1943). Both groups supported the landings and operated over the central and western areas of the front. From 1-18 July they flew 1,238 sorties, losing 20 aircraft to AA fire.

During the Italian campaign the 27th Fighter-Bomber Group claimed 45 aerial victories (26 by the 522nd Fighter Squadron and five by 1Lt. Michael Russo of the 522nd, the only A-36 ace), and 21 by the 86th Fighter-Bomber Group.

P-39 Airacobra

Bell Aircraft's art-deco P-39 Airacobra has a place in World War II aviation history as a symbol of America's being unprepared for war and its overconfidence in its aircraft designs. The P-39 possessed two unique features that were dictated by its heavy nose armament, the most unusual of which was the placement of the engine behind the pilot. The second was that it was the first USAAC fighter with retractable tricycle landing gear. From the onset of the design, the Bell people were enamored with the American Armaments Corporation's T-9 37mm cannon that was to be fired through the propeller hub. To do so meant that the engine needed to be placed in the fuselage, directly above the rear of the wing. A ten-foot drive

P-39 The D model was equipped with self-sealing fuel tanks, extra armor plate and a shackle for a 500lb. bomb or drop tank. The armament on the D-2 was a 37mm cannon, two .50 machine guns in the nose and four .30 caliber machine guns in the wing. The D-1 was armed with a 20mm cannon in place of the 37mm. The D-3 and –4 models were special ground attack models with extra armor plate. (USAF)

shaft passed under the cockpit floor to couple the engine to the propeller reduction gear.

The power plant was the Allison liquid-cooled, 12-cylinder inline V-1710 with an integral single-stage, single-speed supercharger that produced 1,100 to 1,300hp. The deletion of the turbo-supercharger on the early Allisons has always been brought into question. At the time of its development America had no reliable turbo-supercharger, and P-39 wind tunnel testing showed it to have numerous aerodynamic and technical problems that precluded it from becoming an interceptor without expensive and time-consuming changes. During its production run the P-39's performance remained constant, as Bell engineers checked the weight increases which beset other fighter designs. The Q model was only 200lbs. heavier (empty) than the D.

With the development of other fighter types, the AAF decided to banish the P-39 to an advanced training role, and many pilots remembered its performance as a trainer. The Airacobra did see limited AAF combat in North Africa and Italy, and more so in the Pacific, but was generally held in low regard. There were 2,150 Airacobras in inventory in early 1944, and these were released for sale or lend-lease. However, the Soviets commended their Lend-Lease P-39s (and P-63 Kingcobras) that they used in large numbers (4,743 P-39s and 2,400 P-63s) to great effect in its proper role as a low-level attack aircraft against German Panzer columns.

The P-39 Ds (923 built) and Ns (2,095 built) were the versions most used by the AAF (there were 4,905 Q models built, but the majority went to Russia; 75 went to the AAF). The P-39D-1 and P-400 equipped the 81st and 350th Fighter Groups in North Africa and Italy, where they saw considerable action as they supported the Allied advance up the Italian boot, attacking German infantry, armor, transport, and supply depots. The 322nd Fighter Group, the black "Tuskegee Airmen" unit, flew the P-39Q models while flying routine patrol missions over Italy during the first months of 1944. The D model was equipped with self-sealing fuel tanks, extra armor plate, and a shackle for a 500lb. bomb or drop tank. The armament on the D-2 was a 37mm cannon, two .50 machine guns in the nose, and four .30 caliber machine guns in the wing. The D-1 was armed with a 20mm cannon in place of the 37mm. The D-3 and -4 models were special ground attack models with extra armor plate. The Q model retained the nose 37mm cannon and two .50 caliber machine guns in the nose, but deleted all wing guns, which were sometimes replaced by a pod under each wing that held one .50 caliber machine gun. The P-39 was originally designed to be America's principal fighter, capable of intercepting any enemy fighter, but developed into an overweight, underpowered, high maintenance fighter that was useless over 12,000ft. and needed to be protected on its ground support missions by medium and high cover fighters.

The 81st Fighter Group equipped its 91st and 92nd Squadrons with the P-39 Airacobra, but the aircraft was to play only a minor role in the air fighting in the MTO, as there was a shortage of spare parts and their mechanics had no training in P-39 maintenance. At the end of January 1943, there were no more than 25 P-39s combat ready between the two squadrons.

P-40 Warhawk

Because it appeared there was little chance that high-altitude bombers could attack the continental U.S., 1930s AAC strategy was influenced by the theoretical need for long-range bombers, while pursuits (fighters) were to meet the need for ground attack and coastal defense. Pursuit aviation was characterized by low-altitude performance and rugged construction. When the war broke out for America on 7 December 1941, the P-40, which dated back to early 1937, was already obsolete, but implausibly remained in production until December 1944, by which time over 14,000 were produced. Throughout the war the design was continuously upgraded and improved, and the production numbers and longevity of the P-40 reveal that Donovan Berlin's design had something going for it. But the weight increases associated with these changes kept P-40 performance below that of the P-38, P-47, and P-51. The Curtiss P-40 and the P-39 design, both under the "bombardment over pursuit" concept, were to make up over half of AAF overseas fighter strength until July 1943. By July 1945 one P-40 group was still operational, but the P-39 had seen very little combat anywhere. Throughout the war, from Chennault's Flying Tigers onward, P-40 pilots were able to utilize the fighter's strengths to advantage against superior performance, maneuverability, and firepower. With the introduction of the P-38, P-47, and P-51, the P-40 was not needed as a fighter, but the strength of its airframe and firepower and armament load allowed it to continue as a journeyman fighter-bomber in secondary theaters, such as Italy and the CBI.

Like the P-39, the P-40 languished in the poor performance of its Allison engine above 12,000ft., and its lack of a supercharger consigned the fighter to low and medium altitude operations. It could not climb or run, and its range was limited, but it could dive and turn with a Me-109. The cockpit was cramped and noisy, but did offer good visibility. To maintain a straight and level course the rudder needed constant attention. The fighter was a stable gun platform, and its six .50 caliber machines guns were more than adequate. The P-40 was the only fighter available at the time, and its

Armorers of the 57th Fighter Group bomb up a P-40F on a Libyan base with a 500lb.hung on the belly and 40lb. anti-personnel bombs under the wings. The RAF Desert Air Force utilized the good low-level performance of their export P-40E Kittyhawks and Tomahawks to good advantage in North Africa hitting Rommel's critical fuel and supply depots, infantry and even Panzers. The 57th Fighter Group went into combat in North Africa and adopted the successful ground attack tactics used by the RAF. (USAF)

virtues kept it flying with the Allied air forces in all theaters, in a variety of roles until the end of the war.

The installation of the Packard-built Rolls-Royce Merlin in the P-40Fs did increase performance, but not as much as it did for the P-51 Mustang, as the Warhawk's mid-1930s engineering prevented modifications to increase performance. The RAF Desert Air Force utilized the good low-level performance of their export P-40E Kittyhawks and Tomahawks to good advantage in North Africa, hitting Rommel's critical fuel and supply depots, infantry, and even Panzers. They fitted a centerline bomb shackle that could carry a 500lb. bomb, and some versions carried a wing rack that could carry four 50lb. bombs. On USAAF models nose guns were deleted in the D-model, but four .50 caliber machine guns were mounted in the wing. The E-model carried six. .50 caliber machine guns in the wing with 280rpg at 24 seconds duration, the centerline bomb shackle could mount a 500lb. bomb, and external stores could be carried on the underwing racks. The USAAC 57th Fighter Group went into combat in North Africa and adopted the successful ground attack tactics used by the RAF. To maintain that any other fighter-bomber could have performed better than the P-40 over North Africa and Italy has no meaning, because the aircraft and its pilots were available when they were needed and did the job required of them until the better fighter-bomber came along.

There are very few photos of a P-61 loaded for interdiction missions. Pictured is a 425th NFS Black Widow with napalm in drop tanks and a five rocket 5-inch HVAR mounting in place. (USAF)

P-61 Black Widow

After the war began in Europe and the Luftwaffe was bombing English cities at night, American military planners envisioned enemy long-range bombers attacking U.S. coastal cities at night. The Emmon Board of the USAAC drew up a preliminary proposal in late 1940 for a twin-engine aircraft to operate at night, manned by a pilot and an "operator of a device to detect aircraft in the dark" (the designers were not told any details about radar). On 21 October Northrop was presented the proposal, and on 17 December, less than two years after the company's founding, Northrop Aircraft designers John Northrop and Walter Cerny had their design proposal for a USAAC design specification for a large radar-carrying, long range, high performance night fighter approved. Northrop's reputation led to a contract for two XP-61 prototypes on 11 January 1941. Even before the XP-61's first flight, the necessity for the development of an operational night fighter led to the order of 13 YP-61s on 10 March, 150 more on 1 September, and 410 on 12 February 1942. Finally, on 21 May 1942, test pilot Vance Breese flew the XP-61 on a successful initial flight. The XP-61 was a twin boomed, cantilever mid-wing fighter powered by two Pratt & Whitney R-2800 radial engines and armed with four fixed ventral 20mm cannons and a dorsal GE turret with four .50 cal. machine guns. The twin engines were housed in twin nacelles that tapered towards the vertical tailplanes, which were connected by a horizontal tailplane with control flaps. It was crewed by three: the pilot; the radar operator in the nose; and the observer/gunner situated above the pilot. At 25,000 lbs. it was as large as a medium bomber, but had fighter speed and maneuverability. The aileron surfaces were very small, and were mounted at the wing tip to give the necessary roll for a turn. A small set of retractable spoilers located forward of the flaps performed as ailerons so the P 61 was able to quickly reverse direction. The test fighters were painted black, and hence the name "Black Widow." The first of 200 P-61As were delivered in November 1943. The first 37 had dorsal turrets and the remain-

The P-61 was ineffective in its nighttime interdiction role as radar to detect transport movement on the ground had not been developed and flare and searchlight mission were ineffective. It was unfortunate that the Allies never developed a large night fighter force and radar to harass the German transportation system around the clock. (USAF)

der was delivered without, as they caused buffeting (the observer/gunner position was deleted). The buffeting problem was solved, and all P-61s from 201 onward had the dorsal turret. Throughout its operational life the P-61 maintained its original appearance with little external change. The Pratt & Whitney R-2800 engines were minimally upgraded in the A and B models, and the supercharged -73 increased the maximum speed from 370 to 430 mph in the P-61C models. The first operational P-61s were delivered in the Pacific in early 1944 and in the ETO in May 1944. The P-61 was a successful night fighter design, but it entered service too late to have any serious effect on the outcome of the air war, as neither the Luftwaffe nor Japanese were able to raise any night attacks. Of the 706 Black Widows produced there were 200 P-61As, 450 P-61Bs, and 517 P-61Cs, of which only 41 were produced before the contract for the remaining 476 was terminated as the Pacific war ended. The P-61 was the forerunner for post war all-weather fighters and remained in front line service until the early 1950s.

Medium bombers, principally the B-26 Marauder and B-25 Mitchell, played an important part in the tactical air campaigns but in terms of damage caused for effort expended the fighter-bomber was more efficient than light or medium bombers and was able to attack most targets with more accuracy. The fighter-bomber was particularly effective against targets such as motor vehicles, armor, rail transport and strong points but was less effective against targets requiring pattern bombing such as heavily defended positions. (USAF)

In March 1944 the 9th Air Force was in the process of building up to full strength when it was assigned the 422nd Night Fighter Squadron (NFS), followed by the 423rd and 425th. It was not until July that any of the squadrons became operational because of delays in receiving the fighter from America, getting its crews ready for operations, and also due to a much belated controversy about its superiority to the Mosquito. Its first missions were chasing V-1 Buzz Bombs. It was not until the Black Widow units moved to the Continent in late July that they would operate primarily against Luftwaffe night intruders and take part in some nighttime interdiction sorties against road and rail movement. Since the Allies ruled the daytime skies the Germans were forced to move troops and supplies at night. The P-61 was ineffective in its nighttime interdiction role, as radar to detect transport movement on the ground had not been developed and flare and searchlight mission were ineffective. It was unfortunate that the Allies never developed a large nightfighter force and radar to harass German transportation around the clock.

Comparing the Fighter-Bomber to the Light and Medium Bomber

In addition to its strafing/ground attack role, the adaptable fighter-bomber was able to carry out a number of tasks: light and medium bomber escort; short and long range interdiction missions; short and long range fighter sweeps; and anti-shipping sorties. In contrast to light and medium bombers, the fighter-bombers were mission-adaptable and not confined to one target. They could go from an interdiction target and proceed to a ground support target on the same mission. The fighter-bomber could be rearmed, refueled, and its pilot briefed more quickly than a bomber crew, which enabled fighter-bomber units to carry out three or four missions per day as compared to the usual two for light and medium bombers. The fighter-bomber boasted imposing firepower and ordnance, and compared to medium bombers could deliver more ordnance per day and inflict more damage for effort expended. The fighter-bomber was able to attack targets with more precision than medium bombers, with the exception of targets requiring pattern bombing, such as extensively prepared positions or gun areas. Being able to deliver their ordnance at lower altitudes they were less vulnerable to heavy enemy AA than the higher flying bombers. Enemy fighters were of little consequence at this stage of the war, but small-caliber flak was a major concern, as it was effective to 3,000 feet and not visible.

When comparing the number of missions that could be flown in a day, the weight of bombs delivered per mission, and the number of aircrew and ground crew required per mission, the fighter-bomber was more efficient than the medium bomber. A 12-plane Mustang squadron carrying a maximum 2,000lbs. of bombs per aircraft was able to fly three squadron missions per day and deliver 72,000lbs. of bombs. To achieve this tonnage delivered approximately 300 officers and men were required, giving a tonnage/personnel factor of 240. A 6-plane B-26 Marauder squadron carrying 4,000lbs. per aircraft could fly two missions per day and deliver 48,000lbs. of bombs, requiring approximately 600 personnel, for a tonnage/personnel factor of 80. The fighter-bomber could be refueled and armed and pilot briefed more quickly than the medium bomber. After D-Day, fighter-bomber and light/medium bomber squadrons moved to forward airfields on the Continent. These fields were newly constructed or quickly repaired former Luftwaffe fields, and therefore had small dispersal areas and narrow taxiways, which favored the fighter-bomber.

In terms of damage caused for effort expended the fighter-bomber was more efficient than light or medium bombers and was able to attack most targets with more accuracy. The fighter-bomber was particularly effective against targets such as motor vehicles, armor, rail transport, and strong points, but was less effective against targets requiring pattern bombing, such as heavily defended positions. The fighter-bomber formation was less vulnerable to heavy-flak. The major threat to the fighter-bomber was not the Luftwaffe, which rarely appeared over the battlefield in daylight, but German flak. Fighter-bomber squadrons needed slightly more maintenance than the pure fighter squadron. More armorers were needed for the fusing and maintenance of bombs. The bomb racks, fusing, and release apparatus required only regular maintenance and were mostly trouble-free.

Shortcomings of American Fighter-Bombers

The significant drawback of USAAF fighter-bombers was their combat radius. The major shortcoming for the fighter-bomber was its lack of combat range. With 2x500lb. bombs (thus unable to carry external fuel tanks) the P-38 and P-47 had a combat range of 260 miles, while the P-51 had a range of 325 miles. The short-range factor necessitated that fighter-bomber airfields be located near the battlefront.

The P-51 had the lowest fuel consumption of the three main USAAF fighters: P-51B>65gph, P-47D>140gph, and the P-38J>144gph

The Air-Cooled Radial vs. Liquid-Cooled Inline V Engine

The WWII aircraft engine was a reciprocating engine. Reciprocating described the movement of the engine's pistons, as they provided power by moving up and down in the cylinders. The piston movement was converted to rotary motion to move the propeller via the connecting rods and crankshaft. Aircraft engine manufacturers were constantly looking for ways to increase power, and the way to accomplish this was to increase the number of cylinders. The increase in cylinder number also had the advantage of providing a smoother power supply and increased number of power strokes per revolution of the crankshaft. To accommodate a number of cylinders in an engine there are several different engine designs. The standard method of classifying engines is by their cylinder arrangement.

During WWI rotary and in-line engines powered aircraft, as the radial engine was still under development. As the war ended the rotary was phased out and the in-line was the engine of choice. Radial development proceeded rapidly, and soon the in-line vs. radial controversy developed and continued into WWII. The controversy centered on their cooling systems: air-cooled radial vs. liquid-cooled in-line.

The internal combustion engine converts heat into mechanical energy. An efficient engine only converts 30-35% of generated heat into mechanical energy. About 40% is expelled on the piston's ex-

Radius of Action: P-51, P-47, and P-38*

Aircraft	Take-off Weight (lb.)	Bomb Weight (lb.)	Fuel (US gal.) Internal	External	Radius (mi.)
P-38L	19,500	1x1,000 (uw)	410	1x165 (uw)	400
	18,500	2x500 (uw)	410	-	260
	19,500	2x1,000 (uw)	410	-	250
	19,500	-	410	2x165 (uw)	600
	17,500	-	410	-	290
P-47D	14,500	-	370	-	280
	15,150	-	370	1x108 (cl)	400
	16,150	2x500 (uw)	370	1x108 (cl)	360
	15,500	2x500 (uw)	370	-	260
	16,500	2x1,000 (uw)	370	-	230
	16,400	-	370	2x150 (uw)	575
P-51B/C/D	9,800	-	269	-	350
	10,800	2x500 (uw)	269	-	325
	10,800	-	269	2x75 (uw)	650
	11,200	-	269	2x108 (uw)	750

* Conditions (from AAF Proving Ground at Eglin data)
(a) Warm-up and take-off at 10 minutes at normal power
(b) Climb to 10,000ft. at normal rated power
(c) Cruise to target at 10,000ft. at 200mph (P-47) 220mph (P-38 & P-51)
(d) Jettison drop tanks at target
(e) 5 minute combat at war emergency power and 15 minute combat at military power
(f) Cruise back to base at 10,000ft. at 210mph (P-47) and 230mph (P-38 & P-51)
(g) No account taken for decreased fuel consumption during descent
(h) Allowance made for 30 minute reserve fuel at minimum cruising power
(i) No allowance made for formation flight or evasive action other than 20 minutes combat
(uw) = underwing (cl) = centerline

haust stroke, while another 5-10% is lost through friction. This means another 20-25% must be released to continue efficient operation and prevent damage. A cooling system dissipates this excess heat. To prevent the generation of even more heat, all moving parts require lubrication to reduce friction, prevent deterioration of engine parts that rub together, and increase efficiency. There are two ways to cool an engine: air-cooled (radial) and liquid-cooled (in-line).

Radial Engine

The radial engine had its cylinders arranged in a circle around the crankshaft, like spokes on a wheel. All the connecting rods were connected to a single master rod on the crankshaft. The engine could have only one row of cylinders, or they could be arranged in two or more banks. Each bank had its own master connecting rod. Radial engines always had an odd number of cylinders, usually seven or nine in each bank. The cylinders usually exhausted into an exhaust collector ring with one or two outlets.

Radial engines were air-cooled. This made this engine more lightweight, because no radiator and its associated plumbing was required, but this necessitated a large frontal area. Radial twin-row, or "twin-bank" engines were developed to gain more power without increasing frontal area. The two rows of seven or nine cylinders each were mounted on an elongated crankcase, like two engines one behind the other. In the twin- row version the problem was to get enough cooling air to the rear cylinders. The rear cylinders were placed behind the openings behind each pair of front cylinders to increase cooling. Baffle plates kept the hot air from coming off the front cylinders away from the back cylinders, and also slowed down the circulating air to its best cooling speed. Cooling was also accomplished by cast or machined cooling fins on the cylinder heads and along the cylinder barrel. The improvement of design and manufacturing procedures and of materials yielded an increase in cooling area, as horsepower per cylinder increased due to higher cylinder head temperatures. Air coming through the cowling from the outside swept away the heat of combustion. The pilot controlled the opening or closing of cowling flaps according to conditions and engine temperatures. On the ground these flaps were opened, as only the propeller provided air for cooling. At high altitudes the air is very cold and more air is provided over the engine through forward motion, and the engine could possibly run too cold for efficient operation. Airflow could be further increased by an augmenter tube that created a pressure differential between air inlet and outlet that caused a suction, speeding airflow when necessary (venturi effect).

The radial engine was shorter, lighter, and more compact than the in-line engine per cubic inch displacement. The radial, however, was not lighter for equivalent horsepower. The installation was larger in diameter than the in-line and increased drag. Radial fighters, such as the Navy Grummans and the Thunderbolt, were pug-nosed when compared to the sleek in-line Mustangs and Spitfires.

Pratt & Whitney

Frederick Rentschler, who had resigned as president of Wright Aeronautical, established Pratt & Whitney in Hartford CT in 1925. Rentschler had set up his new aircraft engine company in an unused factory owned by machine tool company Pratt & Whitney, from which his company received its name. His first engine was the venerable nine cylinder air-cooled Wasp radial.

The R-1830 Twin Wasp, two-row radial was designed in 1931 by a team headed by Luke Hobbs. The 14 cylinder was the largest aircraft engine being built in the United States in the 1930s. Produced in the greatest numbers of any U.S. piston engine in WWII, a total of 178,000 of this great engine were built, not only by P&W, but also by Buick and Chevrolet. Most of these engines powered the 19,000 B-24s, along with PBYs and C-47s. Almost all (98%) American transport aircraft were powered by P&W engines. The engine was fitted in the Seversky P-35, Curtiss P-36, and Republic P-43 fighters, but the Grumman F4F Wildcat and later FM-1 were the most famous of the R-1830 powered fighters. The R-1830-76 was the world's first two-stage supercharged engine. However, as a fighter power plant it lacked the necessary horsepower and displacement to match Japanese aircraft, but for American bombers and transports it was the perfect engine.

Arguably the most important American engine of WWII was the P&W R-2800 Double Wasp. The R-2800 was a development of the 1936 R-2600 and was ready for production in 1940. P&W built

Pratt & Whitney Double Wasp R-2800 (2-stage).

P&W Double Wasp engine being changed in a P-47. (USAF)

a manufacturing plant in Kansas City to build the R-2800 C-series. Chevrolet and Nash also built the R-2800, but Ford was the biggest sub-contractor. In fact, Ford built an exact duplicate of P&W's Hartford plant in Dearborn to manufacture its R-2800 B model. During its long production life the engine saw extensive development and increase in power. The 18 (air-cooled) cylinder, two row, geared drive supercharged, 4-cycle engine digressed from earlier P&W twin radial engine design. The crankshafts and cylinder heads were not only of unique design, but required the development of new manufacturing methods. The R-2800 was not a world-beater in any one area of performance, but the dependable engine was powerful, relatively small, and of low weight, had low fuel consumption, and was extremely tough and could sustain enormous battle damage and return to base. The supercharger was constantly improved, and toward the end of the war became almost as large as the engine itself. Water/methanol injection for war emergency power (WEP) gave the engine significant increases in power for a recommended maximum of five minutes, although this was often exceeded in combat.

Besides the Douglas A-26 and Martin B-26 bombers, the R-2800 powered America's great fighters of the Second World War: the Grumman F6F Hellcat; Chance-Vought F4U; the Northrop P-61 Black Widow; and the Republic P-47 Thunderbolt, which was the epitome of radial-powered WWII fighters.

In-line Engines

An in-line engine had all its cylinders in a straight line in either a vertical or inverted position. The family automobile has an in-line engine. The V in-line engine had two straight lines, or banks, of cylinders set like the letter V. The V-engine was compact and had the advantage of being easily streamlined, because it had little frontal area. An upright V in-line engine had its cylinders located above the crankshaft. The inverted V in-line engine had the crankshaft above the cylinders. The opposed engine had its cylinders arranged in two parallel rows, one row on each side of the crankcase. The opposed type was most frequently used on low-powered four or six cylinder engines.

In-line engines were more efficiently cooled with liquids because air could not be easily directed over all cylinder heads, especially the ones in the rear. Liquid systems cooled more evenly and could be built with less frontal area opposing the air stream. They were also heavier and more expensive to manufacture, difficult to maintain, and in combat were more vulnerable to damage from enemy fire. Liquid-cooled engines actually had a significant problem of the cooling agent actually freezing in the cold of high altitudes.

In-line engines were liquid-cooled, and radiator construction and placement were always the preeminent design consideration for cooling. The internal cores of the radiator improved in the 1930s, and as war broke out automobile radiator producers, with no automobiles being manufactured, turned their attention to aircraft radiators. Fin and tube cores were developed that reduced drag and weight, and were much more efficient and less expensive to manufacture. Also there were advances in coolant development, with 30-50% glycol to water finally being used. Radiator placement varied with the aircraft: the P-51, British Hurricane, and Japanese Ki-61 in an aerodynamic duct in the fuselage belly; the P-40, Typhoon, and Tempest under the engine; the Spitfire and Me-109 under the wing; and the Mosquito on the wing leading edge.

Even though they were longer, in-line engines had much less frontal area than radials with equivalent displacement. Because of its better cooling, the horsepower (weight per horsepower) of the in-line was higher, and high and war emergency power could also be sustained longer. Liquid-cooled were notably more vulnerable to battle damage. One bullet penetrating a radiator would mean loss of coolant, and the engine would rapidly overheat and seize. Stories abound of entire cylinder heads of radial engines being shot off and the engine continuing to run for hours.

Allison

During World War II only one American company, Allison, a division of General Motors, produced an American designed liquid-cooled aircraft engine. James A. Allison founded the company in 1915 in Indianapolis IN. During WWI the company designed and produced 20,000 water-cooled V-12 Liberty engines. The Liberty was a poor design and suffered through numerous problems, and the post-war reduction in demand meant lean years for Allison. After Allison suddenly died in 1929, Fischer & Co. of Detroit purchased the company. After three months Fischer sold the company to General Motors, which kept the company going during the Depression by supplying dirigible and blimp engines.

In 1928 the company looked into the development of the family aircraft business. The Depression killed the idea, but its six-cylinder engine became the basis in 1930 for the 12 cylinder V-1710 that was to be known as the 1710, or "Allison". The design was a combination of the conventional and the innovative, and thus suffered developmental and production problems that were not resolved until the late 1930s and early 1940s. The major criticism leveled against the engine was its lack of high altitude performance, as it was only driven by a single-stage, engine-driven supercharger. The AAC insisted that all Allisons utilize the General Electric supercharger, which was to be succeeded by the GE turbo-supercharger. Because tooling was in place for mass production of the V-1710, trade-offs needed to be made so as not to disrupt vital production at this critical stage of the war. So the addition of the turbo-

Allison V-1710-F

supercharger was neglected, as the engine continued to suffer developmental and production problems that needed to be resolved first to meet contract demands. When Rolls Royce developed its superior two-speed, two-stage inter-cooled/after-cooled supercharger, Allison did not add it to the V-1710.

The lack of altitude performance was to penalize Allison's bottom line. The Allison-powered P-51A was to be re-engined with the Rolls Royce Merlin licensed to Packard. The P-38 would have also been re-equipped with the Merlin but for persuasive lobbying by General Motors. Royal Air Force orders for the P-40, P-38, and P-39 may also have continued at a higher level. The P-38 suffered many problems serving with the Eighth Air Force, where missions were flown at high altitudes, and by October 1944 the Eighth abandoned the Lightning. Fortunately the Pacific, with its milder climate and lower operational altitudes, proved to be more suited to the P-38's attributes.

Among the fighter aircraft powered by the Allison were the P-39, P-40, P-38, P-51A, and P-63. The P-40, P-39, and Allison P-51s served America well early in the war. All were sold as export models to augment the RAF early in the war. The unwanted P-39 and P-63 were given to a desperate Soviet Union throughout the war. The Allison's success story was the P-38, which was the top USAAF scorer in the Pacific and boosted America's two top aces, Dick Bong (40v.) and Tom Maguire (38v.).

Factory V-1710 engine installation in P-38. (Lockheed)

Packard V-1650-7.

Rolls Royce

Before his death in 1933, Sir Henry Royce initiated an engine design to replace the aging Kestrel. Rolls Royce was forced to develop the new engine, the PV-12 (PV = private venture), without government funding. When the government funded the project the engine was named the Merlin after a bird of prey, as were most RR engines. The design was similar to the Kestrel, being a 60-degree, V-12 mono-block, pressure water-cooled, gear driven, supercharged 4-cycle. Like the Allison, it suffered many design and developmental problems. But unlike the Allison, RR was able to constantly resolve problems and improve the design throughout the late 1930s and during the war. The development of the Supermarine Spitfire and the Merlin were synonymous. The Spitfire's success and that of the Hawker Hurricane led the RAF to try the two-stage Merlin in the North American Aviation Company's Mustang I (P-51A). The Mustang II (P-51B) was the first Merlin-powered Mustang. The result was perhaps the war's best fighter aircraft. Because the Merlin was more fuel economical, yielding more miles per gallon, and the fighter was able to carry auxiliary fuel tanks it was able to escort bombers deep into Germany. The Merlin was a flexible engine design, and changes doubled its power output over the years without increasing bore or stroke size. The frontal area stayed the same, and the length increased only a matter of a few inches. The two-speed, two-stage inter-cooler/after-cooler supercharger gave the fighter superior altitude capabilities for escort and interceptor duty. This supercharger was the cornerstone of RR Merlin performance.

At VJ-Day Pratt & Whitney and its licensees had manufactured 49% of all horsepower (fighter and bomber) used by combined American air forces, and a significant portion of England's air power. Wright Aeronautical and its licensees provided 27% (mostly bomber), and the remaining 24% was divided between Packard as the Rolls Royce Merlin licensee and Allison.

Engines

Manufacturer	Allison	Rolls Royce/Packard	Pratt & Whitney
Model	V-1710	Merlin	R-2800
Type	In-lineV/60 Degrees	In-line V/60 Degrees	Radial/2 Row
Cylinders	12	12	18
Cooling	Ethylene glycol	Pressure water	Air
Displacement (cu.in.)	1710	1649	2804
Width (in.)	29.3	29.8	52.5 (diameter)
Height (in.)	37.6	41.2	52.5 (diameter)
Length (in.)	85.8	70.6	88.5
Frontal Area (sq.ft.)	6.1	5.8	15.0
Weight (lbs.)	1395	1450	2480
Wt./hp (lb/hp)	0.95	0.98	1.24
Fuel Consumption (lbs./hp/hr.)	0.54	0.52	0.48
Max. HP	1475	1480	2000
Normal HP	1100	1210	1675
Supercharger	Gear driven/1-speed	Gear driven/2-speed	Gear driven/2-stage

Superchargers

The need to increase power output at high altitudes where atmospheric pressure is lower led to the development of the supercharger. At sea level the weight of the earth's atmosphere is 14.7 pounds per square inch, but at 25,000 feet it decreases to 5.5 pounds. The greater the air pressure the greater the air weight (density = pounds per cubic foot) and vice versa. As an aircraft flies higher the pressure becomes less and the density becomes less. If an engine is to maintain its power at higher altitudes, it has to take in a higher volume of air from the outside to keep the weight flow of air from decreasing. By using a supercharger the weight of airflow can be maintained at the rated power output of the aircraft. This is done mechanically by pumping air into the engine carburetor at the required pressure, causing the carburetor to add more fuel to keep the air/fuel mixture at the proper ratio. This increased amount of fuel and air, under greater than normal pressure, goes through the intake manifold and provides a greater charge to the cylinder, thus increasing the force of the piston's power stroke. The mean effective pressure in the cylinder determines horsepower. There are two types of superchargers: external and internal.

Internal Supercharger

The internal supercharger is one that is located between the carburetor and the intake manifold, and forces a charged mixture into the cylinder. The internal supercharger provides a uniform distribution of the fuel/air charge to the cylinder and increases the density of the charge. It is built into the engine and obtains its power by being geared to the crankshaft.

External Supercharger

The external supercharger is one that is located between the outside air and the carburetor, and forces an increased amount of air or compressed air into the carburetor. The external supercharger is a turbine (turbo supercharger) that is turned by the engine's exhaust gases.

Intercoolers and After Coolers

In using a supercharger with sufficient compression capacity to provide the full weight of air at high altitudes it is necessary to cool off the air or mixture after it has been compressed. This is accomplished by using special radiators called intercoolers or after coolers, de-

Packard Rolls Royce V-1650 installation in the P-51 Mustang. (USAF)

The ruggedness of the P-47 was legend. Here a T-bolt of the 367th Fighter Group demonstrates its ability to take punishment. (USAF)

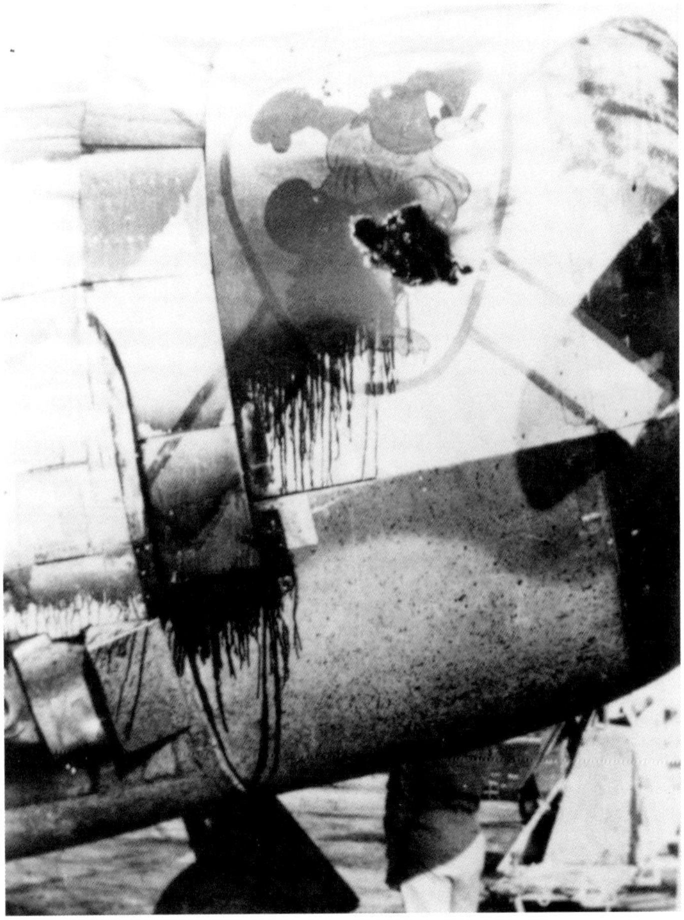

Despite what looks like a fatal hit to its engine this 57th Fighter Group P-47 made it back home. (USAF)

The liquid-cooled Packard Rolls Royce V-1650 was very vulnerable. A small arms bullet hit the coolant system of this 355th Fighter Group P-51D, causing its engine to seize. (USAF)

pending on their location in relation to the carburetor. Both methods, with their large radiator equipment, not only increase weight and drag, but also increase aircraft vulnerability, as it adds another vital system that could be hit by enemy fire.

Combat Damage and Aircraft Vulnerability

Fighter-bombers often returned from missions perforated with jagged flak holes varying in size and number that required repair to stringent specifications. Initially, in the field, the irregular flak hole was hand cut into a square or rectangular shape. Patches were hand cut from stock aluminum sheets, and rivet holes were hand drilled and fastened over the hole. The repair took about an hour to complete. Later, a self-centering saw was used to cut out a clean, round hole larger in diameter than the flak hole. Circular patches of various sizes were pre-fabricated and pre-drilled. The proper patch was selected and placed in about five minutes.

In 1950, the "Think Tank" at the Rand Corporation of Santa Monica, California, conducted an extensive investigation of aircraft vulnerability (*RM 402: Aircraft Vulnerability in WWII*) for Air Force and Navy aircraft in WWI using the above determinates.

The twin engines of the P-38 were thought to give the Lightning an advantage but suffered the worst loss rate of any frontline American fighter. Here a P-38H of the 364th Fighter Group made a successful—for the pilot—wheels up landing. (USAF)

Vulnerability by Aircraft Type

USAAF

Three principal fighter types were studied: P-47, P-38, and P-51. The P-47 mounted an air-cooled Pratt & Whitney engine. The P-38 was powered by twin Allison liquid-cooled engines. The Mustang initially had an Allison engine, but later became a great fighter when it converted to the liquid-cooled Packard/Rolls Royce. The engines of the P-38 and P-51 were liquid-cooled and caught fire when damaged, while the air-cooled Pratt & Whitney of the P-47 was less vulnerable to damage. The ruggedness of P-47 airframe and engine during the war is legend. Approximately eight of ten P-47s hit returned, as compared to seven of ten P-38s and six of ten P-51s.

Because a fighter was able to continue flying after it had been damaged, distance to base became a major factor. Holed oil or coolant systems would allow about 10 to 20 minutes flight time. If friendly territory were within this radius the aircraft was damaged, otherwise it was lost. The P-51 had the longest range of the three and was used as a long-range bomber escort. This assignment contributed to the Mustang's higher loss rate when hit far from base. The P-47, because of its lesser fuel capacity, was assigned shorter missions that would tend to reduce its loss rate. Contrary to the belief that the second engine of the P-38 increased its chances to return safely, less than 10% of damaged P-38s returned to base on one engine; the disablement of one engine generally led to the loss of the fighter. A rough measure of the degree of exposure to enemy action is the number of claims vs. enemy aircraft. While the loss rate for the P-51 was three times that of the P-47 per 1,000 sorties, its claim rate was approximately four times that of the P 47. In contrast, the P 38 loss rate was about the same as the P-51, but its claim rate was lower than both the P-51 and P-47. In the latter stages of the war the Luftwaffe was decimated and anti-aircraft fire became the major cause for damage and loss. With no air opposition the Air Force concentrated on flak-intensive ground support and strafing sorties. An interesting finding was that bombers hit by enemy aircraft fire were about ten times more likely to be lost as those hit by AA fire, whereas fighters hit by enemy aircraft fire were only two times as likely to be lost as those hit by AA fire. Almost all AA fire causing loss to bombers was of large caliber (75mm to 120mm)/ large fragmentation type fired to the high altitudes at which bombers operated. However, for fighters most of the hits from AA weapons were small caliber, consisting of armor-piercing, incendiary, and cannon shells. These types of hits were sustained mostly on strafing missions. Comparing hits from enemy aerial machine guns and cannon showed the following. Hits from .50 caliber were about 2.4 times as lethal as .30 caliber, while 20mm cannon hits were 5.4 times more lethal as .30 caliber and 2.2 times as .50 caliber.

Vulnerability to Anti-Aircraft
(A/C lost:A/C hit)

A/C	%	A/C	%
P-51	29%	F4U	26%
P-38	25%	F6F	25%
P-47	10%	F4F	22%

F4F includes FM-2

Vulnerability to Enemy Aircraft
(A/C lost:A/C hit)

A/C	%	A/C	%
P-38	49%	F4U	46%
P-51	46%	F6F	36%
P-47	37%	F4F	25%

F4F includes FM-2

Between August 1943 and May 1944, the Eighth Fighter Command recorded a summary of the causes for damaged (1,330A/C) and lost (659 A/C).

Causes of Damaged and Lost Aircraft

Causes	% Damaged	% Lost
AA Fire	63%	27%
E/A Fire	22%	39%
Unknown	6%	12%
Collision (with ground or A/C)	7%	6%
Mechanical failure	1%	12%
Others	1%	4%

Causes of Damaged and Lost Aircraft

	Damaged			Lost		
A/C	E/A	AA	Other	E/A	AA	Other
P-47	22%	63%	15%	40%	20%	40%
P-38	16%	70%	14%	40%	28%	32%
P-51	25%	59%	16%	37%	35%	28%

The Evaluation Section, Air Branch, Office of Naval Intelligence studied 1,202 Navy aircraft lost to AA fire and 234 lost to enemy aircraft. The study determined the aircraft component that was damaged, thus causing the loss.

Component Damage

Component	AA Fire	E/A Fire
Engine	23%	16%
Flight controls	8%}>	6%}>
Pilot	4%} >25%	2%} > 34%
Pilot or flight controls	13%}>	26%}>
Fuel system	16%	12%
Oil system	13%	11%
Airframe	13%	13%
Hydraulic system	7%	11%
Other	3%	3%

The Navy study also determined how often a component, when hit, failed and caused the aircraft to be lost:

Component	AA Fire	E/A Fire
Oil system	74%	85%
Engine	70%	62%
Pilot &/or Flight controls	67%	76%
Fuel system	61%	80%
Hydraulic system	44%	60%
Airframe	7%	12%

Of the aircraft which went down immediately, 54%, were due to hits on the pilot and/or flight controls, and 25% to hits to the fuel system. Hits on the engine or oil system caused the loss of 68% of those aircraft forced to make a controlled water landing or bailout near target. Damaged airframe and hydraulic systems accounted for 73% of the aircraft, which were able to make a landing at base, but were written off.

The aircraft component hit by enemy fire causing damage to a returning aircraft was:

By AA Fire	Airframe	60%	Surface Controls	14%
By E/A Fire	Airframe	60%	Surface Controls	10%

The VIII Fighter Command conducted a study assessing damage and loss as to mission type due to the changing character of the war.

Loss Rate of Fighters Hit by Enemy Fire

A/C	Avg.Hrs/ Sortie	A/C Damaged/ 1,000 Sorties	A/C Lost/ 1,000 Sorties	% A/C Lost/Hit
		8/24/43 to 5/31/44		
P-47	3.2	18	6	25%
P-38	4.2	22	17	44%
P-51	4.4	27	19	41%
		6/1/44 to 8/31/44		
P-47	3.7	28	7	19%
P-38	3.9	16	7	30%
P-51	4.3	16	11	41%

Damage/Loss by Mission Type

Mission Type	# Sorties	A/C Damaged /1,000 Sorties	A/C Lost/ 1,000 Sorties	%A/C Lost/Hit
		March - May 1944		
Bomber Support	31,688	23	10	30%
Sweeps	1,999	35	13	27%
Strafing	1,723	80	36	31%
Fighter-bombing	1,722	49	9	16%
		June - August 1944		
Bomber Support	39,675	13	6	35%
Strafing, sweeps	17,488	34	14	29%
Fighter-bombing	1,669	32	16	33%
Fighter-bomber escort	370	24	3	11%

Escort of bombers in both periods was the safest mission for fighters (despite the high loss/hit ratio due to the long distances involved), with only 16.5 and 9.5 hits/1,000 missions respectively. Fighter-bombing became similar to sweeps and strafing in the latter period because of low level bombing of tactical targets during the period before and after D-Day. While the loss and damage rates for this type of mission were very high in the first period compared to the second (37avg./1,000 sorties vs. 20.5 avg./1,000 sorties), the return rates if hit in each period were similar when looking at the % A/C lost figures. Fighter-bombers in the earlier period tried to remain above the light AA fire that is reflected in the 16% to 33% figures in the two periods.

Changing Character of Operations

Period	Damaged % Due to AA	Damaged % Due to E/A	Lost % Due to AA	Lost % Due to E/A
8/43-5/44	63%	21%	27%	39%
6/44-5/45	69%*	5%	32%	13%

* Includes 14% small arms and ground fire

The decreased and selective Luftwaffe fighter opposition after mid-1944 is shown in the decreased losses due to E/A (25% fewer damaged and 33% fewer lost). AA fire continued to be the dominant cause for loss and steadily increased form 2.5 to 5.5 to 1 times the losses due to E/A by February 1945, despite the contribution of flak maps to fighter pilots in August 1944 to aid them in avoiding known AA concentrations.

In a paper prepared for the Secretary of Defense and Institute of Defense Analysis in 1966, Joseph Reinberg researched in part a quantitative comparison of various American fighter types in Europe and the Pacific (*see chart opposite page*).

ETO summary

In all, operational periods surveyed of air-to-air combat the sturdy P-47 had the lowest loss rate, followed by the P-51, and then in a poor third place was the P-38. The P-61 night fighter had a very low loss rate because it was virtually unopposed. In all operational periods surveyed of air-to-ground sorties the legendary ruggedness of the P-47 again proved itself, as it far surpassed the P-51 and P-38 in this dangerous undertaking, primarily due to its air-cooled Pratt & Whitney engine and sturdy airframe.

USAAF Fighter Combat Losses by Theater and Cause

Fighter Combat Losses

Theater/Cause of Loss	Total	1942	1943	1944	1945
ETO		*			*
Total Losses	5,324	10	178	3,765	1,371
Enemy Aircraft	1,691	10	161	1,293	227
Anti-aircraft Fire	2,449	-	1	1,611	837
Other Causes	1,184	-	16	861	307
MTO		**			**
Total Losses	3,157	54	1,088	1,571	444
Enemy Aircraft	1,357	46	816	441	24
Anti-aircraft Fire	822	8	115	493	206
Other Causes	1,008	-	157	637	214

* August-December 1942 & January-May 1945

** June-December 1942 & January-May 1945

Fighter Comparison by Type
ETO & PTO USAAF

A/C Type	Sorties A/T/A	Sorties A/T/G	Loss % E/A	Losses % AA	Losses % Ops	Loss % All
			6 April to 5 June 1944			
P-51	24,000		.66		.15	.48
		6,000	.25	.83	.32	1.53
P-47	25,000		.53		.11	.24
		25,000	.17	.38	.14	.70
P-38	19,000		.41		.36	.77
		1,000	.90	1.50	.90	3.30
			6 June to 5 Sept. 1944			
P-51	59,200		.29	.02	.22	.53
		2,000	.74	4.74	.40	5.88
P-47	41,900		.11	.02	.22	.35
		72,300	.09	.25	.23	.57
P-38	13,600		.41	.03	.25	.69
		1,600	.31	4.18	.31	4.80
P-61	26,200		.02	.02	.10	.14
			6 Sept. 1944 to 7 May 1945			
P-51	152,100		.26	.06	.12	.44
		16,500	.49	1.87	1.19	3.55
P-47	140,000		.32	.11	.12	.55
		113,500	.14	1.90	.12	2.15
P-38	9,300		.77	.11	.42	1.29
P-61	38,200		.04	.05	.25	.34

(A/T/A = Air-to-air A/T/G = Air-to-ground)

5

Fighter-Bomber Organization

Grand Scheme

The 9th Air Force had four Major Generals, 20 Brigadier Generals, 150 full Colonels, and nearly 20,000 other officers and 160,000 enlisted men. The three TACs each had 12,000 personnel, including 1,800 officers. Each TAC had 15-18 fighter-bomber groups; each group had three squadrons with 36 (normal) to 48 (maximum effort) operational aircraft per group. Each TAC had a Photo and Tactical Reconnaissance Group, while the XIX and IX TAC each had night fighter squadrons, and the XXIX had the only night Photo Recon Squadron.

A pilot was assigned to a group, then to one of its three squadrons, and then to one of the three flights of each squadron. A squadron was self-contained, with its own Officer and Enlisted messes, PX, supply, vehicles, drivers, vehicle mechanics, communications men, clerks, drivers, cooks, medics, etc. The fighter-bombers were serviced by aircraft mechanics, armament and ordnance men, aircraft maintenance and repairmen, radio men, oxygen men, parachute men, fuelers, etc. Each squadron normally had at least 36 pilots and 25 plus fighters, with about 225 men to support these pilots and aircraft. The Group and its Headquarters numbered in excess of 850 officers and men.

A group mission involved 36 fighters (3 squadrons of 3 flights x 4 aircraft), and a squadron mission involved 12 fighters (3 flights of four planes). When a squadron flew a mission, three flights of four fighters were sent up. Each of the 36 pilots would fly every third mission. While flying from England a pilot would ideally receive a 3-day pass every two weeks. Squadron missions were usually flown, as few targets justified a group effort.

Group and Squadron Formations

Before D-Day fighters flew in Group missions of 45 aircraft, 16-plane squadrons of four flights flew in two sections, one flying 300 yards behind the other and from 500 to 1,000 feet higher. In a 12-plane squadron the flights usually flew in a loose, shallow V, with 200-300 yards between them. Two extra fighters also took off to replace any aborts, and would return to base after flying to about halfway across the English channel. The group climbed to 20,000 feet heading for the French coast. The flights were assigned color codes: Red, lead; White second (stacked down sun); Yellow, third (stacked up sun); and Blue, top cover (usually stacked up sun and to the rear). Blue Four was the most vulnerable position to both enemy fighter attack and AA fire that was intended for the three other flights. Yellow Four was the equivalent of Blue Four in a 12-plane formation. Group missions worked fine for pre-day fighter sweeps and escort missions, but once interdiction missions were assigned squadron missions became SOP for close support, armed recce, targets of opportunity, and armored column cover. Squadron missions consisted of three or four flights, with one flight assigned

ORGANIZATIONAL CHART (GENERALIZED) OF A FIGHTER GROUP and SQUADRONS

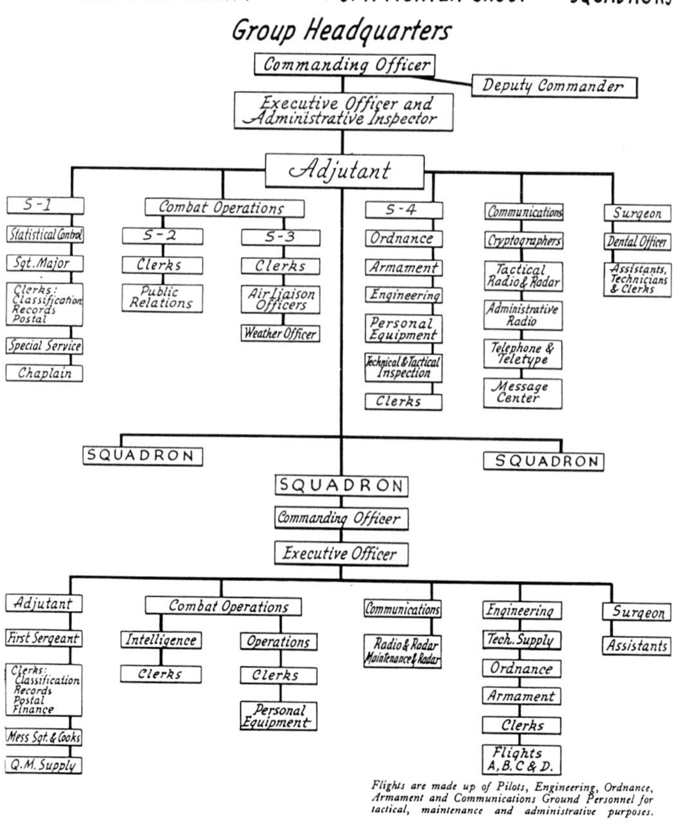

Flights are made up of Pilots, Engineering, Ordnance, Armament and Communications Ground Personnel for tactical, maintenance and administrative purposes.

to top cover. The top cover flights carried only light bomb loads, usually fragmentation bombs or extra drop tanks. The other flights carried two 500lb. bombs, usually with delayed fusing to escape the detonation during low level bombing attacks. After the primary target had been attacked the squadron would be free to seek out targets of opportunity.

Attacking in trail: The squadron flew in a large circle over the target area. As each aircraft reached an assigned position, each peeled off at ten-second intervals from the same compass point and headed for the target at the same angle. This allowed time for the bombs from the preceding aircraft to explode before the next fighter was over the target and released its bombs. Attack in trail was the ideal mode of attack if the target was not heavily defended, but could lead to heavy losses if it was defended, especially by quad mount 20mm flak.

Moving figure-8 (offset): Each aircraft converged on the target at a slightly different angle in line astern. This technique made it difficult for AA gunners to cope with different firing angles at each successive incoming aircraft. It also increased the damage to the target on the ground, as it assured constant fire on the target as the firing fighter broke quickly, allowing the following fighter approaching at an offsetting angle to start firing with minimum danger to the lead fighter. This offset attack protected the following aircraft from expended shell casings and belt links from the lead fighter.

Col. Thomas Christian, P-51 pilot for the 361st Fighter Group (USAF)

Pilots

After D-Day the First Priority, Air Superiority, had been achieved, and the Luftwaffe had been swept from the skies. The Second and Third Priorities then took precedence, and fighter aircraft became fighter-bombers. Pilots realized the inherent dangers of strafing. and low-level bombing. If enough sorties were flown the eventuality was sustaining combat damage resulting in death, a bailout, or crash landing, hopefully in friendly territory. Pilots saw the value of the fighter-bomber in the enormous quantity of men and materiel that did not reach the front, as they devastated the German road and rail system and destroyed the Luftwaffe in the air and on the ground.

Col. Thomas Christian, P-51 pilot for the 361st Fighter Group, in *Down to the Deck* (ibid.), described the prerequsites:

"...qualifications for a successful strafing pilot are plenty of daring, the ability to size up a situation and to arrive at a plan of attack quickly and on the spot, and, of course, he must be a cool shot. He must know when not to attack as when to attack. Many pilots enjoy ground strafing much more than escort work due to the certainty of action when they start out."

Lt.Col. William Bailey, a P-47 pilot in the 353rd Fighter Group, discussed the new pilot (*Down to the Deck*, ibid.):

"The first few times a new pilot goes down on a ground attack he is probably just plain scared. He feels there are hundreds of hidden guns that will open up on him at any moment. Naturally, this mental attitude will reflect on the firing accuracy of the individual concerned. He will invariably come in too fast, too high, or too low, slipping and skidding without much thought of hitting the target until he is closing so fast he has only the briefest interval to fire.

The first step in overcoming these errors is to instill in the pilot a sense of security. This is done by proper briefing, giving him an accurate knowledge of the existing flak installations, making ar-

Lt.Col. William Bailey (far left), a P-47 pilot in the 353rd Fighter Group, leads a briefing of the 352nd Fighter Squadron in June 1944. (USAF)

rangements for flak spotters, whose job it was to neutralize the flak and to assign adequate top cover for the operation."

Capt. Leslie Cles, P-47 pilot for the 353rd Fighter Group, discussed the pilot's fear of hitting the ground with his plane in a strafing attack (*Down to the Deck*, ibid.):

"One of the greatest failures in what should have been a successful attack is that the pilot made his approach too steep or too shallow. Both almost give almost the same results. That is, your mind is half occupied with the fear of hitting something with your plane rather than full concentration being placed on the target. When you are too steep, the tendency is to open fire at long range and stop firing at your best range. If the pass, however, is too low the tendency is to fire short, snap bursts that are very ineffective. You always have to pull up to avoid some object, when you could be doing your best firing. A good pass on most targets will be one that is as low as a good safety margin will allow. This will clear the plane of all ground obstacles and give the best possible allowance for the pull out. The fire can be held to a close and deadly range."

Capt. William Maguire, P-47 pilot of the 353rd Fighter Group, in *Down to the Deck* (ibid.) stated:

"Many of our pilots today think that ground strafing is just a simple matter of putting the plane into a dive and squeezing of the tit. He must stop this type of attack and take into consideration the type of target that he is going after, his angle of dive, his air speed, the position of the sun and just what evasive action he is going to take from ground fire. There are just as many factors to consider, if not more, than attacks on E/A in the air."

AAF psychologists recommended a five-minute quiet time for reflection and to relax just before take off. Arthur Davis of the 362nd Fighter Group commented on this quiet time (*Color of War: P-47*, History Channel video):

"It was approximately five minutes long and was a very important thing as it enabled each and everyone of us strapped in our aircraft to get ready for the task at hand. The first time I did it, I thought it was rather foolish. 'Let's get up and go,' that was my attitude. Then after experiencing this quiet time once or twice I realized how important it was and my whole attitude changed in that five minutes. I imagine that it leaked over to the flight crews, mechanics, armorers and they felt the same. It was a feeling of peace." However, Davis went on to say: "I felt I was taught to hate the German army in my service schooling. Most of it was subtle but I just wanted to kill them."

Robert Brulle (*Angels Zero*, Smithsonian, Wash, DC, 2000) gave insight into the fighter-bomber pilot's psyche:

"After our bombing, our air/ground controller reported that enemy activity was reported east of Grosshau. Investigating, we discovered a column of German horse-drawn vehicles hiding along side a hilly and wooded country road. What happened next gave me a taste of the gory business of war. As I pulled up from making a strafing pass on a parked wagon, I caught sight of a large gun being pulled by a double team of horses. The horses had bolted from the gunfire noise and roaring of our aircraft and were galloping down the road. I banked around, keeping my eye on them, but when I lined up in my gunsight I had second thoughts. I didn't want to kill the horses, but how else could I destroy the gun? I gave them a short burst and as I banked over them saw the gory sight of horses and gun all tangled in a big ball, tumbling down the road. I was glad to be fighting the war in the air where was usually spared such sights.... It may seem strange that I would be concerned about killing some horses, while every mission I went on had a high probability that I killed or wounded some humans. I never had any reservations about shooting anything or anybody in Germany.... Nazi Germany was an evil place that plunged the world into a conflagration of unprecedented proportions and they deserved to reap what they started."

Although fighter-bomber pilots accepted their lot, they always considered themselves fighter pilots first and foremost. Their training prepared them for air-to-air combat. Interdiction and strafing sorties gave them very little opportunity to dogfight the Luftwaffe, and the only missions that encountered the Luftwaffe were fighter sweeps. The 9th Air Force was assigned fighter sweeps only once or twice a month, so there was a long line of potential aces wanting to be placed on the mission roster for these sweeps. Ranking squadron, group officers, and experienced pilots had priority on these missions.

Crew Chiefs and Ground Crew

Each fighter had its own ground crew. The crews usually consisted of three mechanics, the Crew Chief (CC) and Assistant Crew Chief, and an armorer who was shared by two other crews. For each four aircraft there was a maintenance coordinator, the flight chief. Two hangar crews, each working a 12 hour shift, took care of maintenance which could not be accomplished on the line, such as engine changes and repair of battle damage. At many bases, ground crews lived a mile or two from the base and bicycles, jeeps, or trucks were the transport to the hardstand. To provide refuge from the fickle English weather, most crews set up tents or constructed more elaborate shelter from the wooden drop tank crates near their aircraft. The tour of duty of a ground crew was usually for the duration. They were assigned the responsibility for a single fighter during its service life. The importance of the crew to the pilot was seen by the frequency their names were stenciled below the pilot's name on the cockpit. Crew Chiefs were usually "older" men, being in their mid to late twenties, while their assistant CCs were youngsters in their late teens or early twenties. They often filled in on other aircraft that were shorthanded due to illness or leave.

After wake up, often one of the two crew would head to the aircraft while the other went to breakfast. That way someone would be present to remove the covers from the Plexiglas and engine air intakes and begin the pre-flight inspection. An external walk around visual inspection was done, checking the canopy, gun camera, panel fastenings, control surfaces, undercarriage, and tire inflation. Any puddles developing overnight were given the taste test. Coolant had a very bitter taste. The propeller was pulled through five or six blades to clear the cylinder of accumulated oil or gasoline. The battery cart was connected, and the CC climbed into the cockpit to prime and start the engine and run it up to high power. The damp English weather played havoc with the spark plugs and electrical system. A thorough pre-takeoff check of oil pressure, fuel, hydraulics, temperature, and mag drop were made. The fuel selector was switched to the right and left tanks to draw fuel into the lines.

The fuel service tanker, or "gas wagon," arrived to fill the external drop tanks and top off the internal fuel tanks, which were diminished somewhat during the CC's pre-flight check. The ground crew checked fuel leaks, especially on the drop tanks. After fueling, the jeep-drawn oxygen cart delivered new oxygen bottles to be installed in the fuselage behind the cockpit. This concluded the ground crew's work, but usually the CC stayed until the pilot arrived, taking care of last minute details, such as polishing the last smudges off the windshield and canopy. Soon the pilots would arrive.

The armorers had a labor intensive and sometimes dangerous job. The bombs had to be delivered from the dump that was usually located some distance from the field. Here an armorer moves a 500lb. HE bomb into positioned under a 353rd Fighter Group P-47D. This mobile trolley had a jacking device to raise the bomb into the shackle. (USAF)

Pilots were close to their crew chiefs as their lives depended on the efficiency of the CC. Capt. Robert Johnson (27 victories/56th Fighter Group) and his CC SSgt. J.C. Penrod inspect the bite of the P-47. (USAF)

Armorers
Training

After basic military training the fledgling armorer received 3 months of training in technical school. Classes consisted of two 3.5-hour sessions per day. Classes were:

(1) Weaponry: .30 and .50 caliber machine guns and 20 and 37mm cannons (Armorers were required to be able to assemble and disassemble them)
(2) Ammunition: high explosive, incendiary, tracer and training rounds

Armorers throughout all theaters of war engaged in public relations photos, such as this of armorers of the 365th Fighter Group, the *Hell Hawks*. Note the bomb dolly. (USAF)

Mobile ordnance and armament shops. (USAF)

(3) Gun sights
(4) Gun cameras
(5) Bombs (hang and fuse) and bomb shackles
(6) Rockets

Preparing a fighter-bomber for a mission

After a mission the CC and the armorers met the returning fighter. After every mission the armorers removed the guns from their bays and took them to the armament hut for cleaning, lubrication, and inspection for wear and damage. If more than 25 rounds had been fired, all the rounds were changed to avoid mixing two ammunition issue lots. All ammo was drawn from the squadron dump, and even if it were new, it was run through the repositioning machine to insure it would be correctly aligned in the metal clipbelts.. The number of rounds for each gun varied on group requirements, but usually were set at the maximum. As a warning to the pilot that he was running low on ammo, five rounds of tracers were belted before the final 25 rounds. The magazine bays were filled with the help of the CC so that the belt (linked rounds) would stay in alignment. To complete the armorer's post-mission work, the gun muzzles were retaped to keep out dirt and moisture on the ground and in the air.

In England there were 14 ground crew per Nissen Hut, led by a hut chief and assistant hut chief. Their cots were at the front and rear doors, and they were responsible to wake and get the men ready to go to the flight to prepare their aircraft for a mission. On the Continent the Nissen gave way to tents and mobile ordnance trucks and trailers. The Staff Sergeants rotated for Charge of Quarters duty. The CQ began his tour at 6PM in the Orderly Room. He was to stay awake throughout the night to take care of any emergencies. He was to awake the officers and enlisted men at a predetermined time, usually at 6-6:30AM, to be at the flight line for the day's mission. After breakfast the armorer went back to his hut to finish personal duties and then proceeded to the armaments shop and flight line to begin the 30-45 minute pre-flight. At this time his was essentially an inspection, as the majority of his duties were done after the previous mission. There were three "armament flights" in each squadron, and each flight chief had nine or ten armorers to attend to the eight fighters in each flight. Guns were checked to determine if the solenoids were activated when the trigger was depressed. The guns were made "hot" by inserting a round in each chamber, permitting the pilot to begin to fire as soon as he switched his guns on. A strip of tape was placed over each gun muzzle to keep out dirt and moisture. The gun camera film had been removed as soon as the fighter reached the hardstand after a mission and fresh film was installed. A photo shop man took the exposed film to be processed immediately so it was ready for viewing for intelligence and the next morning's briefing. A piece of protective cloth tape was placed over the clear Plexiglas camera aperture located on the leading edge of the wing.

On the morning of the next mission, the armorer did a preflight inspection of two or three fighters. The inspection included gunsight, gunmount seating, opening of the gun bay doors to check ammo feeds and chutes, solenoid and firing circuit testing, and finally gun charging. The gun camera was checked to determine if it was activated when the trigger was depressed and if the film was loaded properly. The bomb shackle release that carried either bombs or wing fuel tanks was checked for release. If the mission were to use bombs, an armorer would take a bomb loader to the ordnance department bomb storage dump to pick up the required bombs. A specialized lift raised the bomb to the shackle for attachment. After attachment, a predetermined fuse (e.g. delayed or instantaneous) was placed in the nose and tail of the bomb. An arming wire was attached to the shackle and run through a hole in the fuse from which the tagged safety pin had been removed. The tagged pins were given to the pilot. When the bombs were released from the shackle by the bomb release inside the cockpit the arming wires were pulled away from the fuses, and the arming vanes or propellers rotated loose and fell away after a few hundred feet—the bombs were now "hot" (armed). Armorers were instructed to grasp the fuse with their fingertips instead of the full palm, as the sensitive fuse could be accidentally set off by body heat. When the innovative K-14 gunsight was introduced, an armorer from each of the three squadrons was sent to learn of its maintenance at a school in Blackpool, England. The gunsight alignment had to be inspected in the pre-flight, as there was a tendency for the pilot to use it as a handhold when entering and leaving the cockpit. The armorer frequently helped the Crew Chief in his pre-flight inspection of his aircraft. The armorers and radiomen remained on call in case of last minute problems.

An experienced ground crew could turn around an aircraft in 30 minutes, refueling and rearming with bombs and ammunition. As soon as a returning fighter-bomber landed and taxied to the hardstand, armorers and ordnance men, radiomen, mechanics, and the fuelers would pounce on the aircraft. Two teams of armorers hung bombs and were followed by ordnance men, who would wire and fuse the bombs. Other armament men would replenish the ammunition bays. When their aircraft left, ground crews would often help other crews to get their fighter off the ground.

Casualties

The squadron mission board was displayed in the operations hut. Every pilot who ever served with the squadron was listed in chronological order, with the number and type of missions flown in bar graph format. At the far right was a blank space for the next mission. If a pilot were MIA (missing in action) or KIA (killed in action), an hourglass was placed in that space, and there was a prevalence of hourglasses that stopped at three to five missions. The board had a number of experienced veteran pilots with 10, 15, and 20 or more mission bars, but even many of these had hourglasses following them. Squadron and group commanders suffered heavy casualties. While the line pilots flew every third mission on average, the squadron commanders led most missions. The group commander not only led group missions, but also took part in squadron missions when group missions were not being flown. The effects of MIA pilots were put into special boxes and stored for six months, and if the pilot had not returned by then, his effects were sent to his next of kin in the States.

A P-47 crashes in flames (upper top center) after being caught in its own bomb burst after attacking Italian rail tracks. (USAF)

By mid-1944 flak became more of a danger than being shot down by enemy aircraft. When a pilot was hit by flak it was usually at low altitude, and he had to either try to climb to bail out or find a flat area to crash land. If the P-51's liquid-cooled Packard Merlin was hit, its pilot had to make a quick decision on what to do next for self- preservation, let alone becoming a POW. The P-47 pilot with a damaged air-cooled Pratt & Whitney usually had more flying time and was often able to limp back to friendly territory.

In late December 1944 1Lt. William Cullerton of the 355th Fighter Group/357th Squadron returned to the group for a second tour. He had scored big on 2 November when he shot down two Luftwaffe fighters in the air and then added six more on the ground for a record 8th Air Force eight combined daily kills. On 8 April 1945 he was leading a flight on a strafing run on Ansbach Airdrome when flak hit his Mustang's fuel tank and set it on fire. He tried to gain some altitude, then jettisoned his bombs and bailed out. Cullerton pulled the ripcord immediately, which saved his life, as he hit the ground just after the chute opened. He landed heavily, bruised and banged up, but mobile. He released his parachute and dragged it into a nearby wood, where he hid it and crawled into thick brush, just as a German patrol appeared. Cullerton contemplated surrendering or shooting it out with his .45 automatic if he was discovered, but the patrol passed within feet of him and left. He waited until dark and headed west toward advancing American lines. He traveled west for several days, digging out newly planted potatoes for food and trying to sleep in the cold spring nights. As he traveled west he heard artillery fire and decided to hide in a wood until the Americans arrived. Without warning, a shell exploded in the trees over him and he moved toward the safety of another nearby woods. As he did he ran into a counter-attacking Waffen SS unit and was captured. A SS officer took the American's .45 and stuck into the prisoner's stomach and said, "For you the war is over" and pulled the trigger. The round passed through Cullerton's body and he was left to die, as the Germans were not taking prisoners. He was found several days later by a passing German farmer who thought he was a downed Luftwaffe pilot and took him to a hospital in a donkey-drawn cart. Cullerton awoke in an operating room and was told he had been shot through the liver and had lost a lot of blood. The Germans had wanted to move him, but the compassionate doctor refused, saying that the move would kill the patient. Cullerton became stronger over the next several weeks, but the German counter-attack had been broken and the SS was in retreat and would take him with them. That night, with the help of the doctor and his staff, he escaped and hid in a culvert with German Panzers moving over him. In severe pain and with his internal bleeding starting again he heard more tanks moving over the culvert, but soon English-speaking voices were also heard. He crawled out of hiding and was rescued by members of the 14th Armored Division and taken to a hospital for treatment and then back to Stateside hospitals.

Top-scoring 12-15th Air Force 12-victory ace, 2Lt. Michael Brezas, of the 14th Fighter Group was hit by flak on a fighter sweep over Vienna on 2 April 1945. His P-38 had its right engine and rudder shot out, and its left engine was streaming coolant as Brezas headed toward the safety of advancing Russian troops who were occupying Hungary. Brezas crash-landed safely behind the Russian lines and expected to be transferred to American lines. But instead he was made a prisoner of war and treated very badly by the Soviets until his release on 9 May. After the war Brezas was very bitter and outspoken about his treatment by the Soviets.

The infantry always looked at the airman as having a comfortable and safe tour of duty. But total air casualties in the ETO and MTO were 96,565 KIA, WIA, MIA, and POW; a quarter of airmen engaged had become casualties. On the ground more soldiers were wounded than killed, while in the air fatalities prevailed. Heavy bomber crew and fighter pilots had about a one-third chance of becoming a casualty, while light and medium aircrew had a 22% chance. Experience added longevity, as during a 25-mission heavy bomber tour the loss rate for the first five missions was 5.4%, while during the last five missions it dropped to 1.2%. Rotation for fighter pilots required 200 hours of combat, and the number of missions depended on this time. A P-47 pilot flying short-range tactical missions might have to fly a 100 or more missions, while a P-51 flying long-range bomber escort missions might have to fly 40 or so missions.

6

Airfields and Engineer and Air Service Commands

Part of the third objective of *FM 100-20* stated that the aiding of "the advance of ground troops often makes available new airdromes needed by the air force." In reality the taking of an airdrome was never an infantry objective. The writers of the Field Manual could not predict how efficiently and rapidly the Engineering Command units of the TACs would become in the preparation of almost any nearly flat area, and in the lying of prefabricated surface material to construct an airfield.

North Africa

After TORCH the North Africa rainy season arrived, and the Tunisian airfields became virtually inoperable. There was a shortage of pierced steel planking (PSP) because the rail and motor transport system was overtaxed carrying the necessary military supplies, ordnance, and personnel to the ground forces. Troop carrier air transport was used in the emergency to bring in critical freight and supplies. An airfield in North Africa usually was a level area near a roadway with a windsock set in the ground and gasoline drums at each end to mark off the runway. Everything; aircraft, food, water, gasoline, ammunition, and personnel was dispersed to protect it from complete loss from Luftwaffe raids. The aircraft were dispersed over a wide area with a tent close by each aircraft. Each tent housed two ground crewmen who would maintain the aircraft. Motor transport was particularly valuable in the desert, as everything needed to be brought in by truck from supply dumps miles away. The Americans adopted the simple RAF "two party system," which permitted fighter units to keep up with the fast moving and constantly changing front lines that were common in desert warfare. Each squadron was split into two, with equal numbers of ground crew, armorers, technicians, truck drivers, etc. in each half, or "party." The party which moved forward toward the advancing front was designated the "A" Party, while the rear echelon was the "B" Party. As soon as the infantry secured a location suitable for a forward landing ground, "A" Party would immediately move forward, transporting half the squadron's equipment and supplies to establish servicing facilities on the new field. Meanwhile "B" Party continued to service flight operations from the now rear base. As soon as "A" Party was ready to begin flight operations from the new

Building advanced airfields in Tunisia. Although the area in the photo is dry, these fields became bogs during the November-March rainy season and had to be evacuated back west toward the Algerian-Tunisian border. (USAF)

At Youks pilots moved from their "pup" tents and lived in tarp-covered underground dugouts to escape the cold and rains of December to March. Here is a luxurious abode constructed of ground-filled five-gallon fuel cans. (USAF)

field the fighters would fly in to begin operations. "B" Party would also move up to join "A" Party in operations, or if the front had moved ahead it would leapfrog "A" and set up a new forward base.

In November 1943 U.S. fighters of the 14th and later the 1st Fighter Groups had been based at Youks les Bains, which had a 4,500ft. runway and was situated in a narrow valley in northeast Algeria. It had 4,000ft. foothills on either side and a deep wash at one end, and this geography funneled the rains into the area and turned the fields into quagmires. Since it was a forward base all supplies had to delivered by the C-47s of the 60th Troop Carrier Group. The XII Fighter Command moved to Thelepte, an airbase 40 miles southeast of Tebessa, in early December 1943. Thelepte was in the Tunisian semi-desert and was a good all-weather base. Base personnel lived in a ravine about three-quarters of an hour walk from the field. At Youks they moved from their "pup" tents and lived in tarp-covered underground dugouts to escape the cold and rains of December to March. Thelepte was plagued by high, cold winds, and only the Biskra airdrome was located in the stereotypical African desert oasis.

1Lt. Jack Ilfrey of the 1st Fighter Group, 94th "Hat in the Ring," Fighter Squadron, describes a base at Constantine, Tunisia, North Africa (*Happy Jack's Go-Buggy*, Exposition Press, NY, 1979):

"At Constantine we got back into tents with four to six officers living in one pyramidal tent. It was early February and still pretty cold in the mountains. We had our homemade stove which we had concocted by cutting the bottom out and placing it over a little pile of rocks. For a chimney we took smaller (empty) cans of beans, peas, etc., and cutting out the tops and bottoms, we had our chimney. Outside the tent we placed a can of gasoline at a higher level than the stove and the gasoline was fed by pipes (small copper tubing) that led to the stove. The gasoline dripped on the rocks, burned, and we had fire. We produced lights in the tents by means of a small portable generator and by connecting a speaker to our tent, which was attached to our big communications radio, we were still able to hear Sally and Pete and their Nazi nonsense.

Brig.Gen. James Newman's IX Engineering Command on D-Day had 16 active Engineer Aviation Battalions most of which were experienced having built heavy bomber bases in the UK over the previous year. With the construction of ALGs Allied tactical ground planners no longer needed to make the capture of permanent airdromes part of their objective. (USAF)

We now had heat, lights and music and with our stove we could have hot water helmet baths instead of cold water wash offs we avoided. Eggs were plentiful in Constantine and whenever we received our ration of British cheese we made zouffl̀Es, now and then we had French toast. Once in a while an Arab goat would accidentally get in front of a jeep and that night we would have barbecued goat. It was only coincidental that it always turned out to be a young and tender goat."

ETO

The unsung heroes of the success of the TACs were the Engineer Command (EC) that built the airfields and the Air Service Command (ASC) that supplied them.

IX Engineer Command

An aviation engineer division was planned to be formed within the VIII Air Support Command, but when a minimum of 20,000 engineers were required for the ETO, it was decided to create an independent Engineer Command. The Engineer HQ was established at the end of 1943 to train personnel and to plan for its part in OVERLORD. Despite not becoming a full-fledged Command, Engineer HQ had completed the training of four battalions and was assigned another four. Materials and equipment had arrived, and a communications system was put in place. On 30 March 1944 the IX EC was provisionally activated under Brig.Gen. James Newman. It was comprised of 17,000 officers and enlisted men (23,000 peak strength), whose task after D-Day was to build and maintain airfields in France, then closely follow the advancing Armies and build more airfields and restore any captured enemy airfields. The composition of the IX Engineer Command was:

Headquarters and a HQ squadron
1 Camouflage battalion
3 Airborne aviation battalions
4 Aviation regiment HQs
16 Engineer aviation battalions
4 Combat communications teams
and Support units
IX EC Engineer Aviation Brigades, Regiments and Battalions
Brigades (3)
1st, 2nd and 3rd
Regiments (5)
922nd, 923rd, 924th, 925th and 926th
Battalions (25)
816th, 818th, 819th, 820th, 825th, 826th, 826th, 830th, 832nd, 833rd, 834th, 837th, 840th, 843rd, 846th, 847th, 850th, 851st, 852nd, 859th, 861st, 862nd, 876th, 877th, 878th

In May 1944 the IX Fighter Command received seven new fighter groups, raising its total to 18. IX TAC had three Wings (the 70th, 71st, and 84th) of 11 groups stationed at ten bases in Hampshire, and one in Dorset (474th Fighter Group). Three of the Hampshire bases were Advanced Landing Grounds (ALGs): Lymington (50th Fighter Group), Bisterne (371st Fighter Group), and Winkton (404th). The XIX TAC, with two Wings (the 100th and 303rd) of seven groups, was based at seven fields, all ALGs, in Kent near the English Channel. Of the 100th Wing groups, the 354th Fighter Group was based at Lashenden, the 358th at High Halden, the 362nd at Headcorn, and the 363rd at Staplehurst. Of the 303rd wing, the 36th was based Kingsnorth, the 373rd at Woodchurch, and the 406th at Ashford. The ALGs were temporary airfields, often quickly built on farmlands or cow pastures.

On D-Day Brig.Gen. James Newman's IX EC had 16 active Engineer Aviation Battalions, most of which were experienced, having built heavy bomber bases in the UK over the previous year. The IX EC battalions benefited from the experience of other theaters and had been provided with enough men and equipment for maximum efficiency.

Three types of airbases were planned to be constructed on the Continent for the invasion:

ELS: Emergency Landing Strips, a rough, graded strip, 2,000ft. long, where damaged planes could land or belly-in for emergencies

R & R: Refueling and Rearming Strips near the front lines, with a runway and marshaling area on each end of the runway, designed for the use of aircraft based in the UK.

ALG: Advanced Landing Ground, primary-operating fields with better runways and stores of armament and fuel and personnel billets. With the construction of ALGs Allied tactical ground planners no longer needed to make the capture of permanent airdromes part of their objective.

The airfield construction schedule had been programmed carefully for the first six weeks of the campaign. Until 10 June (D+4) tactical air support was scheduled to be provided from bases in England. The 8th Air Force was stationed around Ipswich, Norwich, Cambridge, and Bedford. The RAF 2nd TAF and the 9th Air Force were stationed on the south coast to be as close to the French invasion beaches as possible, to be able to conduct air cover and close support with as much fuel and air time as possible. In March 1944, ACM Leigh-Mallory had pushed for the early capture of airfield construction sites on the Continent. Most of the suitable sites were in the British sector, but Montgomery declined to obligate his army to give priority to ground attacks for the capture of airfield sites. Invasion plans called for the construction of two Emergency Landing Strips (ELS) on D-Day; two Refuel and Rearm airstrips (R&R) to be operational by noon D+3; five Advanced Landing Grounds (ALG) to be operational at 0600 on D+8; and three more ALGs to be completed on D+14. Detachments of the IX Engineering Corps landed with the first troops on D-Day and were quickly reinforced by others and Quartermaster truck companies. These initial R&R bases were available for refueling and rearming, but as the Allies established the beachhead these bases became semi-permanent bases for squadrons. Some fighter-bomber squadrons were to attack targets only a mile or so from the field and had to fly out over the Channel to gain altitude and stay clear of ground fire from the front lines.

An emergency landing airstrip (ELS) cut in the Normandy hedgerows. Two of these 2,000 foot ELS were scheduled to be built on D-Day to accommodate damaged aircraft. (USAF)

The 819th Battalion landed on UTAH beach on the morning of D-Day as the first engineers to land. They reconnoitered a location at Hegert while it was under fire, and as soon as the battle lines moved inland they completed a grass emergency strip at 2115. Casualties from German artillery or Luftwaffe attacks were negligible, but land mines and booby traps did take a number of lives. Comprehensive training in England had alerted the engineers to the dangers from mines and booby traps.

However, on OMAHA beach the schedule could not be met, as the 834th Battalion was unable to get ashore until the next day because of the heavy fighting and beach obstacles. When they finally were able to land they were without much of their equipment, none of its building materials, and the proposed sites were still in enemy hands. They chose a new site near the beach at St.-Laurent-sur-Mer and completed the 3,500-foot emergency field by 2100 hours on 8 June. Hundreds of mines and booby traps plagued construction, but E-1 accepted its first C-47s, which landed critical supplies and evacuated the wounded. Quesada was one of the first 9th Air Force personnel to land on E-1. On D+3 construction of A-1 at St. Pierre du Mont began when German defenders in the area were subdued. Work was done day and night utilizing floodlights. Sniper fire caused a few casualties, but the shrapnel from falling friendly AA fire caused more, mainly bad cuts. The 834th leveled hedgerows and tried to lay down rolled Marston matting that tried to reroll when the tethering stakes constantly popped loose. A-1 was completed on D+12 (18 June), and the 366th Fighter Group became fully operational the next day. The 834th went on to build three more ALGs in Normandy, and renovated many captured Luftwaffe airfields during the next months. Captured and repaired established Luftwaffe airfields such as Rennes, St. Dizier, and Chateaudun were ideal, as both fighters and bombers had used them. These fields had extensive runways, large dispersal areas, and could accommodate two groups. But the Luftwaffe fighter airdromes used by agile Me-109 and FW-190 interceptors were often significantly shorter than that required for safe takeoffs by American fighter-bombers carrying full interdiction loads of 1,000lb. bombs and a fuselage drop tank.

The 816th EAB landed at Omaha Beach on 14 June and moved to Cardonville to build A-3. Survey crews immediately began to lay out the runway. The next day bulldozers began to clear the area, followed by graders the next day. By daylight on the 17th the grading was completed, the runway half surfaced, and the taxiways completed; the first P-47 of the 368th Fighter Group landed that afternoon. The 5,000-foot steel mesh surface runway, 2.5 miles of taxiway, and 75 hardstands were completed on the 20th. A maintenance unit was left behind as the 816th moved to Deux Jumeaux to start A-4. On 30 June the 3,600-foot runway was completed, and in the late afternoon the 48th Fighter Group landed. The Battalion left for Colleville-Sur-Mer to build A-22, a terminal field for transport aircraft. Upon its completion the 816th returned to Deux Jumeaux to maintain A-3 and A-4 in August 1944.

Two-thirds of the fields in the original plans were to be 3,600-foot fields for pure fighter aircraft. But as total air superiority had been achieved and the Luftwaffe did not attack the invasion beaches, the 9th Air Force could utilize its fighters as fighter-bombers. But a fully loaded Thunderbolt fighter-bomber with two 500lb. bombs, ammunition for eight machine guns, and maximum internal and external fuel could barely manage to take off in this distance. To accommodate the fighter-bombers the runways were extended to 5,000ft., and stronger surface material ("tracking") to support the heavier loads carried by the fighter-bombers was installed. Since there was a shortage of surface material, the first 3,600 feet of the 5,000 feet were constructed with surfacing material, and the remaining 1,400 feet were either grass or earth until better material would become available. The temporary "summer" fields used 750 tons of tracking, while the fields built to semi-permanent specifications used 3,500 tons of tracking and large quantities of local materials, such as asphalt and gravel. During the campaign the twenty-five 9th Air Force Engineer Aviation Battalions rebuilt captured airdromes, but mostly constructed new temporary airfields on any nearly level piece of captured terrain. The engineering battalions utilized more than a hundred men to build a field. As construction began, a pool was dug near the future runway and filled with water,

PHS, Hessian surface was a type of waterproof tarpaper (asphalt impregnated burlap). The future airfield surface was first heavily packed and then special machines laid the 300-foot by three-foot rolls after which a fine gravel top surface was laid over the tarpaper. This was the least permanent surface and was quickly turn up with heavy use and poor weather. (USAF)

SMT overlaying Hessian matting. The underlying tarpaper strips and lightweight wire mesh covering the rain-soaked field (seen in the background) proved to be insufficient in anything but a temporary role. The rolled SMT had to be held down as it had a habit of re-rolling. (USAF)

Rolls of Square Mesh Track (SMT) wire mesh being unloaded at the beaches for shipment by truck to forward landing fields. (USAF)

Engineers lay down rolls of wire mesh (SMP) on the A-10 advanced landing ground at Carentan which was occupied by the 50th Fighter Group on 25 June 1944. (USAF)

A P-47 takes off from an ALG under construction. Note SMT rolls laying on runway. (USAF)

PSP (Pierced Steel Plank, or Marston Mat) was interlocking rectangular planks with small holes and was the all-weather airfield surface of choice. Shortage of PSP led to its early use for medium bomber fields on the Continent. As more became available it was used to "winterize" fighter-bomber fields in late 1944. (USAF)

The dust and rough runways caused increased maintenance problems on ALGs in France. The 368th Fighter Group required 23 engine changes in July 1944, all but one due to dusty fields causing excessive oil use. Here a P-47 of the 48th Fighter Group taxis through the dust at A-4 at Deux Jumeaux, Normandy in mid-June 1944. (USAF)

A tracked tow vehicle moves a P-47 onto a snow covered runway. The tractor was probably used to prevent a white out from all the whirling propellers of taxiing aircraft that made gathering for take off difficult. (USAF)

Snow on PSP presented a problem as it caused a whiteout for taxiing aircraft. Here a 368th Fighter Group P-47 clears the runways at Metz/Frascaty (Y-34) by taxiing in tight circles to blow the snow away (January 1945). (USAF)

The soft ground of a Hessian surfaced runway caused this P-47 to flip upside down on take off. The pilot survived but had to have a hole dug out next to the cockpit to escape. Note that the bombs somehow remained attached to their shackles. (USAF)

and truckloads of straw were dumped into the pool to form muck. Bulldozers and graders leveled the field, and the straw/muck was spread as a surface hardener and rolled flat. Then truckloads of gravel or cinders were dumped and spread over the field, and the field was again rolled. The engineers then rolled out the Hessian tarpaper (PHS) and/or Square Mesh Track (SMT), also called Sommerfield Track by the British, or laid Pierced Steel Planking (PSP), known as Marston Mat—named after Marston, NC, where it was first tested. More straw was used to cover the gravel/cinders for (PSP) installation, as the straw kept the gravel/cinders and soil from washing up through the holes in the PSP. SMT was a heavy wire welded in three-inch squares and was nicknamed chicken wire. It was troublesome to work with, as it was difficult to lay flat. It came in rolls, and the ends had to be staked down to reel out the roll. The stakes would often pull out, usually after a large length had been rolled out, and the end would begin to rewind. The first Hessian waterproof material (PHS), a type of tarpaper (asphalt impregnated burlap), was used by the 816th EAB in July at Colleville-Sur-Mer. First the surface was heavily packed, and then special machines laid the 300-foot by three-foot rolls, after which a fine gravel top surface was laid over the Hessian tarpaper. PHS was intended to keep water from seeping through, which it did initially, but heavy use quickly tore up the surface. Both PHS and SMT were light and easily transported, and were often used in combination with the SMT laid on top the PHS. Pierced Steel Plank (PSP) were interlocking steel planks with small holes in the surface and were used mainly on medium and light bomber fields. PSP allowed operations to continue regardless of the weather and was used to "winterize" fighter-bomber fields. PSP was slippery under the best conditions, and in cold weather was often covered with ice. But the surface was so flexible that the ice would crack under the weight of the taxiing aircraft, and the prop wash would blow it off the runway. During periods of snowfall take offs had to be made by instruments, as the prop wash from the preceding aircraft would create a blizzard, blinding the fighter behind. During the first three months in France the IX EC shipped 700 tons of track per day from the UK and used 62,034 rolls of steel mesh track (SMT), 723,510 pierced steel planks (PSP), and 42,561 rolls of Hessian matting (PHS). As the war progressed PSP became the surface material of choice, as it was more durable and made for a better surface. The engineers also set up their camps, water supplies, and built and repaired roads.

By 5 August all but one of the 16 original engineer battalions were in Normandy, and by working 15-17 hours a day, seven days a week they had built 17 fighter fields surfaced with SMT or PHS and two medium bomber fields with PSP. Seven more fields were under construction, which when completed would reach the saturation point for airfield construction. Units then were withdrawn from construction and given R&R, which meant "only" ten to twelve hour days maintaining completed fields! It should be noted that the British airfield engineers were also very efficient, constructing four fields, and had two more in the process for the RAF 2nd TAF by 11 June. The plan was for 35 ALGs to be constructed by D+40 within 60 miles of the front. But this goal was not achieved because of the Allies' failure to breakout through the Bocage, and therefore did not have a 60-mile beachhead to build the 35 fields. Many engineer battalions were also landed behind schedule when heavy seas delayed the unloading of men, equipment, and material. Fortunately for the Allies, the weather was blustery but was not extremely wet, and the fair-weather fields constructed of PHS, SMT, or grass held up for the first several weeks. But the PHS and SMT strips were not designed for prolonged use and deteriorated. Most fields had a dip or roll, and acceleration was not as quick as on a hard surfaced runway. On landing the pilot needed to hit his wheels at the very end of the runway and apply the brakes, quick and hard. A flak-damaged aircraft or a rookie pilot made landings extra dicey. The dust and rough runways caused increased maintenance problems. Fighter-bombers carrying heavy bomb loads from these fields suffered warped wings and engine problems. The 368th Fighter Group required 23 engine changes in July 1944, all but one due to dusty fields that caused excessive oil use. The maintenance problem became so severe that Quesada reduced his squadron strength from 16 to 12. By the first week in August the mission mechanical abort rate reached its highest point of the war, and Quesada ordered two groups a day to be stood down for maintenance.

After the Normandy breakout, the IX TAC moved to the Continent in a continuous succession of base movements. The routine of these movements was the two-stage "A" Party "B" Party" movements that had been pioneered in the North African Desert. Operations were up and running in a short time through the great efforts of the ground and supporting units. The accommodations on the ALGs were tents with six cots, wooden floors, and a stove. Slit trenches were dug nearby in case the Luftwaffe made an appearance. Fighter-bombers had been based on the coastal fields in late June and early July during the static ground fighting, but after the breakout had to remain close to the front lines for rapid deployment. Many fields had too many squadrons based on them, which led to serious congestion problems that were exacerbated when British and American units were based together. To alleviate the problem aircraft were allowed to take off and land in either direction to shorten taxiing distances and bring them as close to their dispersal areas as possible. The over-worked Aviation Engineer Corps built over 60 bases in August and September, moving from one area to another behind the advancing infantry preparing bases for waiting fighter-bomber groups. From mid-July General Quesada moved his command post five times in six weeks. Most fighter-bomber groups moved three times, but one relocated five times. The average move was 100 miles or less, but there were several moves of 200 miles. Fighter-bomber groups were intended and trained for mobility, and each move involved 173 distinct, planned procedures, moving 2,000 personnel and 67 tons of ground equipment.

The breakout and rapid advance across France and Belgium in late July was timely, as there were no sites available for development and the heavily used fields required constant maintenance, especially the PHS and SMT surfaced fields. Half of the engineer battalions that were originally assigned to the IX Air Force Service Command were being utilized for field maintenance duties. On 8 August the IX EC organized the 1st Airfield Maintenance Regiment from its command and transferred it to the IX AFSC to maintain rear area fields and free up engineer battalions for construction.

While in the confines of the beachhead EC HQ was able to monitor and control its command, but after the breakout it became evident that operational control would have to be decentralized, as the IX EC lines of communication from the UK to the beaches to the front became overextended. To deal with the situation and decentralize command, two Engineer Aviation Brigades (EAB) were formed on 1 August 1944 to be positioned behind the TACs and armies they were to support. They had four regiments that were divided equally between them. The 1st Engineer Brigade, commanded by Col. Karl Schilling, was to build fields for the First Army, and the 2nd Engineer Brigade, under Col. Rudolph Smyser, constructed fields for the XIX TAC and the U.S. Third Army that began operations on 1 August. A third EAB was formed in September from units of the 1st EAB and 2nd EAB and units stationed in the UK. The 3rd EAB moved to the Continent in March 1945 and was assigned to help in the rear areas, and also employed a large number of civilians. Later the rd EAB maintained airbases west of the Rhine.

After the breakout fields were constructed in groups of four or five, called "clutches," to provide for the requirements of a TAC group or medium bombardment wing and their attendant Air Depot Group. In August and September the responsibilities of the engineers increased when they were assigned to build supply and evacuation strips immediately behind the fast-moving frontlines. The 9th Air Force also wanted its light and medium bombers to be based in France ASAP, and in July four fields were built. Their construction used all the PSP in France ear-marked for the "winterization' of fighter-bomber strips and bomber fields near Paris. As a remedy, the rehabilitation of captured Luftwaffe hard-surfaced fields was prioritized, but ALG construction continued to be required. In early August the 1st and 2nd Brigades moved into the LeMans area and developed a clutch of fighter-bomber fields. A combination of bad weather, poor soil, and the shortage of surfacing materials and transport delayed their completion until early September. By this time the front had moved so far east that these bases were beyond the effective combat radius of their fighter-bombers. The destruction of the French rail net and the unavailability of Communications Zone trucks, which were being used to supply the ground armies, caused the EC to use its own inadequate truck fleet and any trucks that could be begged and borrowed from the IX AFSC to transport surface materials. The shortage of surfacing material and truck transport would be a chronic EC problem throughout the war in the ETO.

French civilians were often employed by both the German and Allied forces for repair work. Here they repair a bomb crater on a former Luftwaffe base now used by the 32rd Medium Bomber Group flying B-26 Marauders. (USAF)

New fields in the Chartres area were planned, but the advance through the area was also so rapid that the plans were abandoned. Fields in the Paris area were reconnoitered while the Germans still occupied the city. After the Germans withdrew, six fields were completed in the Paris-Orleans area for supply and evacuation, and later to feed the Parisian population. The 2nd Brigade followed the Third Army and built fields in their wake, but often had to pass up good sites to keep up with the advance. By 19 September the Third Army had outrun its supplies and stopped in the Nancy-Toul-Verdun area. The 1st Brigade followed the First Army to the German border to Aachen, where it was stopped. Along the way it rehabilitated as many captured German fields as possible, which was quicker than building new fields.

During the rapid advance from Normandy to the German border the IX EC built or put into operational condition 60 airfields. As of 15 September the RAF had built 76 airfields, of which 49 remained operational. The EC encountered increasing problems during the advance. Some Engineer Aviation Battalions had to move as much as 200 miles from one assignment to another. Supply lines lengthened, and the number of trucks was spread more thinly among the Battalions, and the amount and timeliness of supplies and materiel became more critical. Fortunately, communication lines kept pace with the advance and were able to keep contact with the supply depots on the beachhead, and thus IX EC trucks could at least bring critical material from the beaches and ports. Throughout the summer the IX EC operated on a daily need basis. PSP was in particularly short supply, and the IX EC truckers made exceptional efforts to deliver it. Asphalt and other building materials were procured locally and civilian labor was employed. Later in 1944 the Allies were able to repair some of the immense damage they had inflicted on the French rail system, and each Engineer Aviation Brigade was finally able to start to establish forward supply dumps using rail facilities.

From the autumn of 1944 to the spring of 1945, the Allied advance stalled and the aviation engineers no longer were under the demand to keep pace and build new fields and refurbish captured fields. However, they needed to enlarge and winterize existing fields, a process that required large quantities of PSP, which was the only surface material, other than concrete, that could stand up to winter conditions. Maintenance was increased during the winter. The 1st Brigade was assigned to prepare airfields in Belgium, Luxembourg, and Holland ready for fighter-bombers. But despite their work there were not enough fields available, and several fields housed two fighter-bomber groups. The 2nd Brigade prepared fields in their area, and also was to develop fields for the First TACAF.

Engineer battalions from Italy built fields for the XII TAC, which was following its Armies during the invasion of southern France. These battalions were returned to Italy in October, and their place was taken by the IX EC to build and maintain fields for the new First Tactical Air Force. The 92rd EAR was sent from the UK and was made the Engineer Command for the First TAF, which took some of the burden off the 2nd Brigade. The IX Troop Carrier Command and the 302nd Transport Wing also demanded new airfields, and Gen. Knerr formed the Engineer Command (Prov.) in October to construct and maintain airfields in the rear areas, where the troop carrier, transport, and light and medium bomber groups were concentrated. These two new engineer commands were small, and were dependent on the IX EC for supply and administration. The IX EC also had to coordinate the operation of its three engineer commands. So in February 1945, the system was reorganized by disbanding these two smaller commands and transferring the IX EC from the 9th Air Force to the USSTAF. By doing so all American aviation engineer units were placed under one command, and made the construction and maintenance of airfields the responsibility of the theater air force instead of the 9th Air Force. In March the 3rd Engineer Aviation Brigade (Prov.) was assigned to build and maintain airfields in the rear areas. In April, the IX EC and the 3rd Brigade were reunited, with the EC of the USSTAF (Prov.) as a component of the operational command. The IX EC and its two brigades were responsible for all 9th Air Force and First TAF construction in forward areas. The 3rd Brigade did all construction in the rear areas west of the Rhine.

The winter of 1945 gave the engineers time to catch their breath and reorganize. The German Ardennes Offensive caused the demolition of only one American airfield, and none were overrun. With the crossing of the Rhine in March 1945 the aviation engineers again found themselves trying to keep up with the rapidly advancing armies. The first airfield in German territory was built at Trier on 10 March. Many strips were required and built for supply and evacuation immediately behind the lines. By mid-April aviation engineers had constructed 52 operational fields in Germany, 39 east of the Rhine. Thirteen engineer battalions operated east of the Rhine, and five were in Germany west of the Rhine. There continued to be a shortage of surfacing material, which had to be brought up by engineer trucking, but the good spring weather allowed grass fields to be used.

The IX EC command underwent changes and modifications throughout the campaign that put an excessive burden on it that it was generally able to meet. The following is a reiteration of the convoluted changes in the IX EC command. The IX EC HQ was located near Paris, and an Advanced HQ 9th Air Force and its Brigades were set up in the field. But as the Allied armies advanced IX EC HQ and the field HQ found it difficult to maintain contact with the movement of its units and the development of airfields. In October an advanced and rear HQ were established. Engineer Commands were set up in the USSTAF and First TAF, but in November these new commands were shifted to the IX EC for supply and administration. In February 1945 the USSTAF took command of all aviation engineer personnel in Europe. The IX EC's rear HQ assumed control of this new organization, and its advanced HQ became the central HQ and was to control the construction and repair of airfields for all three 9th Air Force TACs and those of the First TAF. The USSTAF EC was the administrative head, but the IX EC was the operational entity, and this arrangement continued until the end of the war.

On VE Day there were 182 operational American airfields of all types on the Continent of a total 274 built or rehabilitated during the campaign. The IX EC had constructed or rehabilitated a total of 241 fields, engineer units from Italy built 32, and the U.S. Navy one. A total of 295,000 tons of prefabricated surfacing material were used, of which 190,000 tons was PSP. Some 125 fields were grass and earth and did not use any surfacing material. Another 30 fields were constructed entirely of PSP that was always in short supply. Many fields used one or a combination of SMT and PHS surfacing materials. Light and medium bombers used the 32 captured concrete fields. About 20 airfields were built or rehabilitated for the use of the aircraft of the IX ASC and its air depot groups. The IX EC Engineer Aviation Regiments were eminently successful in building airfields. The 926th Engineer Aviation Regiment (EAR) landed in France on D+5 and built 76 airfields from Cherbourg to Pilsen, Czechoslovakia. The 925th EAR landed in France on 2 July 1944 and built 77 airstrips in ten months. The 924th EAR landed in France on 8 July 1944 and built or rebuilt 47 airfields.

The ALGs and IX Fighter Units (with base changes) were: 1944*

Date Completed	Field	IX FG	Location
19 June	A-3	368	Cardonville
20 June	A-1	366	St. Pierre du Mont
23 June	A-6	371	Beuzeville
23 June	A-2	354	Criqueville
25 June	A-10	50	Carentan
28 June	A-4	48	Deux Jumeaux
29 June	A-7	365	Azeville/Beauchamps
1 July	A-8	405	Picauville
2 July	A-9	67	Le Molay (TRG)
2 July	A-12	362	Lignerolles
5 July	A-15	363	Maupertus
6 July	A-5	404	Chippelle
16 July	A-14	358	Cretteville
17 July	A-16	36	Brucheville
19 July	A-13	373	Tour en Bessin
22 July	A-6	367	Beuzeville
24 July	A-3	370	Cardonville
31 July	A-13	406	Tour en Bessin
6 August	A-11	474	St. Lambert
10 August	A-27	362	Rennes
11 August	A-31	354	Gael
14 August	A-2	367	Criqueville
14 August	A-28	358	Pontorson
15 August	A-19	370	La Vielle
15 August	A-12	365	Lignrolles
16 August	A-17	50	Meautis
17 August	A-14	406	Cretteville
19 August	A-29	373	St. James
23 August	A-35	36	Le Mans
23 August	A-40	368	Chartes
24 August	A-41	366	Dreux/Vermouillet
29 August	A-42	48	Villacoublay

29 August	A-48	404	Bretigny
29 August	A-43	474	St. Marceau
? August	A-7	363	Azeville
? August	A-46	67	Toussus le Noble
3 September	A-48	365	Bretigny
4 September	A-35	406	Le Mans
4 September	A-47	50	Orly
6 September	A-72	474	Perrone
8 September	A-70	366	Laon/Couvron
8 September	A-71	367	Clastres
11 September	A-73	370	Roye/Amy
11 September	A-69	368	Laon
13 September	A-68	404	Juvincourt
14 September	A-64	405	St. Dizier
14 September	A-67	358	Vity-le-Francois
15 September	A-69	50	Laon
15 September	A-74	48	Cambrai/Niegnies
15 September	A-68	365	Juvincourt
17 September	A-66	354	Orconte
18 September	A-65	371	Perthes
19 September	A-79	362	Prosnes
19 September	A-62	373	Reims
22 September	A-80	406	Mourmelon-le-Grand
23 September	A-76	36	Athis
26 September	A-78	370	Florennes/Juzaine (Belgium)
28 September	Y-6	50	Lyons/Bron
? September	A-35	363	Le Mans
? September	A-87	67	Charleroi
1 October	A-68	36	Juvincourt
1 October	A-97	363	Luxembourg
1 October	Y-7 3	71	Dole/Tavaux
1 October	A-92	404	St. Trond (Belgium)
1 October	A-78	474	Florennes/Juzaine (Belgium)
2 October	A-84	368	Chievres (Belgium)
4 October	A-84	365	Chievres (Belgium)
22 October	A-89	373	Le Culot (Belgium)
23 October	A-89	36	Le Culot (Belgium)
23 October	A-92	50	St. Trond (Belgium)
28 October	A-68	367	Juvincourt
29 October	Y-10	363	Le Culot East (Belgium)
5 November	A-82	362	Rouves (Belgium)
19 November	Y-29	366	Asche (Belgium)
1 December	A-98	354	Roiseres-en-Haye
27 December	Y-34	365	Metz/Frescaty
27 December	A-68	368	Juvincourt

1945**

5 January	Y-34	368	Metz/ Frescaty (France)
27 January	Y-32	370	Ophoven (Belgium)
30 January	A-78	365	Florennes/Juzaine (Belgium)
1 February	A-64	367	St. Dizier (France)
2 February	Y-34	406	Metz/Frescaty (France)
8 February	Y-29	406	Asche (Belgium)
9 February	Y-32	405	Ophoven (Belgium)
15 February	Y-34	371	Metz/Frescaty (France)
11 March	Y-55	373	Venlo (Holland)
14 March	A-94	367	Conflans
16 March	Y-46	365	Aschen
22 March	Y-59	474	Strassfeld
26 March	Y-54	48	Kelz
28 March	Y-46	36	Aschen
30 March	Y-54	404	Kelz
? March	Y-51	67	Vogelsang
2 April	Y-83	67	Limberg
7 April	Y-74	371	Frankfurt Eschborn
8 April	Y-62	36	Neidermendig
8 April	Y-64	354	Ober Olm
8 April	Y-63	362	Frankfurt-Rhein-Main
10 April	Y-74	367	Frankfurt Eschborn
10 April	R-11	67	Eschwege
11 April	Y-94	366	Munster/Handorf
12 April	Y-86	404	Fritzlar
13 April	Y-86	365	Fritzlar
15 April	Y-73	368	Frankfurt-Rhein-Main
15 April	Y-94	406	Munster/Handorf
17 April	Y-96	48	Kassel
20 April	Y-99	370	Guterloh
20 April	Y-98	373	Lippstadt
21 April	R-12	48	Kassel/Rothwesten
22 April	R-2	474	Langensalza
29 April	R-10	48	Illesheim
30 April	R-30	362	Furth
30 April	R-6	405	Kitzingen
3 May	R-30	362	Illesheim
5 May	R-30	371	Furth

Note:

A: USAAF usage

Y: Airfields captured by U.S. and French troops advancing from southern France

R: Airfields captured in Germany and used by the USAAF

B: Airfields used by the RAF)

* All bases in France unless noted

** All bases in Germany unless noted

IX Medium Bomb Groups also used ALGs

Only two fighter groups of the VIII Fighter Command used the ALGs. The 352nd moved to Asch, Belgium (Y-29), from their long time base at Bodney, England, on 23 December 1944 and stayed there until 26 January 1945, when they moved to Chievres, Belgium (A-84). They moved back to Bodney on 13 April 1945. The 361st moved to St. Dizier, France (A-64), on 23 December 1944, moving on to Chievres on 1 February 1945, and then moved back to Little Walden, England, on 10 April.

Air Service Command

USSTAF Air Service Command (ASC)

Lt.Gen. Carl Spaatz of the USSTAF established the Air Service Command (ASC) on 6 January 1944 at Bushy Park outside London. It was formed to have operational control of the U.S. 8th and 15th Air Forces and administrative control of the U.S. 8th and 9th Air

Forces. The 9th Air Force was under the operational control of the AEAF. Brig.Gen. Hugh Knerr was named commander of the ASC, USSTAF, and also was named the deputy administrative general, which gave him authority over all USAAF logistics. Both the VIII and IX ASC operated under the control of the USSTAF, ASC, and by D-Day supplied all base services for both commands. Knerr was a good choice, as he demonstrated an aptitude for supply and logistics. Early in the war putting operational units in the air took precedence over support units. USSTAF HQ realized that administration was instrumental in conducting efficient modern air warfare and placed logistics and operations as equals. The USSTAF ASC was a buffer between the 8th and 9th Air Forces, preventing competition between the two by establishing supply priorities, and procured the supplies for both, reducing wastage and duplication. Under the USSTAF ASC both air forces were to become huge, effective forces. The 9th Air Force was subordinated to the USSTAF ASC, and thus Spaatz was able to prevent the AEAF and Leigh-Mallory from controlling the 9th Air Force, allowing the 9th Air Force to become more independent.

VIII Air Force Service Command (VIII AFSC)

The VIII AFSC was established in July 1942 under Maj.Gen. Walter "Tony" Frank at Bushy Park, which also was 8th Air Force HQ. Frank reached an agreement with the SOS (U.S. Army Services of Supply) that divided the important control of construction, maintenance, and supply between the Army and Air Force. The VIII ASC was able to control its own supply and maintenance, thus allowing it to grow at an expanded rate. Maj.Gen. Henry Miller succeeded Frank in November 1942, and then he was succeeded by Brig.Gen. Henry Knerr in October 1943. When Knerr became the head of the new Air Service Command he absorbed the VIII AFSC into his new command and created the new VIII AFSC from the 8th Strategic Air Depot Area, HQ, with Col. Donald Goodrich as its commander. For the duration of the war the VIII AFSC supplied, maintained, and repaired 8th Air Force bombers and fighters.

IX Air Service Command (IX ASC)

The IX ASC operated with the 9th Air Force in Egypt, but was reformed in the UK on 16 October 1943 from 8th Air Force service units, VIII AFSC, and VIII Tactical Air Service Area Command. Maj.Gen. J.F. Miller was put in command at Sunninghill House, near Ascot. The original cadre numbered only 6,300 men, and the Army Personnel Command in the States did not have enough complete units to send overseas to expand the IX ASC.. The individual soldiers who were sent were partially trained, and the IX ASC had to train thousands of men in its own and RAF technical schools. On 6 May 1944 Brig.Gen. Myron R. Wood took command of the IX ASC. In January 1944 there were 2,964 officers and nearly 42,000 enlisted men in the IX ASC. At a peak strength of 62,000 officers and enlisted men in 439 units, the Air Service Command was the largest element in the 9th Air Force. It was as complex as a huge business conglomerate, with over 50 types of units located in 13 air depot groups or the 23 service groups. It transported, supplied, fed, housed, armed, maintained, and repaired the entire air force. Unlike the VIII AFSC that was permanently based in England, IX air support units needed to be mobile to supply and maintain air groups operating from advanced air fields, and were constantly moving to support the advancing ground armies. The ASC maintained a constant stream of supplies that came from England, crossed the Channel to damaged ports, and then were transported across war-ravaged France on damaged roads in bad weather. A testimony to its efficiency was that no combat missions were canceled or delayed because of a shortage of supplies. Advanced air depots were set up immediately and efficiently behind the front lines. Before D-Day in England, the units of the ASC had practiced packing up, moving, unpacking, and setting up air depots from color-coded or code-numbered prepackaged and prefabricated elements.

ASC Units (August 1944):

AADA (Advanced Air Depot Area)

TADs (Tactical Air Depots)	**ASGs (Air Service Groups)**
2 ADGs (Air Depot Groups)	2 ASTs (Air Service Teams)

Six TADs were formed in November 1943. A TAD was in name only a method of defining two ADGs. A TAD had no CO and each of its ADGs was independent.

IX Air Force Service Command
1st Advanced Air Depot Area
1 Tactical Air Depot (North Witham)
2 Tactical Air Depot (Stansted)
3 Tactical Air Depot (Grove)
2nd Advanced Air Depot Area
4 Tactical Air Depot Kingston Bagpuize)
5 Tactical Air Depot (Chilbolton)
6 Tactical Air Depot (Membury)
Transport Wing
31st Air Transport Group (Grove)
Quarter Master Truck Regiment (2)
6 Battalions
A typical Tactical Air Depot (TAD) was made up of:
2 HQs and HQ Squadrons
2 Supply Squadrons
2 Repair Squadrons
2 QM Platoons
2 QM Truck Companies
2 Mobile Repair and Reclamation Squadrons
2 Ordnance Medium Maintenance Companies
1 Signal Company (Aviation)
1 Ordnance Depot Company
1 Medical Supply Platoon
1 Station Complement Company
1 MP Company
Each Service Group (SG) was made up of:
2 Service Squadrons for Aircraft Maintenance
2 Ordnance Supply and Maintenance Companies
1 QM Company (for general supply and salvage)
1 QM Truck Company
1 Chemical Company
1 Signal Company (for maintenance of airborne radio)

The Base Air Depot Area (BADA) was formed in late October 1943 and located at Baverstock. BADA was to receive all 9th Air Force supplies and serve as the command HQ for Intransit Depot Groups (IDG), Base Air Depots (BAD), aircraft assembly depots, and the ammunition depot at Grovely Wood. On 17 May 1944, after playing a vital role in the D-Day supply build up, the BADA was discontinued and its components were assigned to other organizations in the IX ASC.

The primary element of the Air Service Command was an Air Service Group, one of which was assigned to and supported every bomber and fighter-bomber group. It consisted of individual companies from Ordnance, Chemical Warfare, Quartermaster, and a detachment of Finance and Signal Corps personnel. A Service Group was divided into two teams that served two tactical groups. Since the battlefield was ever mobile the components of the service teams moved in specially modified trailers that transported the equipment and materials of their specialty.

The first ASC personnel to land in France were the Intransit Depot Group (IDG) Beach Squadrons, who were attached to the Army Engineer Special Brigades. It was the duty of the IDGs to identify and separate their supplies, fuel, and ordnance that landed on the beaches. Quarter Master Truck companies were landed next to carry these materials to the R&R strips built by the IX EC. Airdrome Squadrons would then be landed equipped with the minimum essentials to man these strips until the better-equipped Service Squadron units arrived. By the end of July seven Service Groups and three Air Depot Groups under the 2nd AADA had arrived in France.

Airdrome Squadrons were instrumental in maintaining tactical operations by refueling and rearming aircraft at advanced landing grounds. The Airdrome Squadrons were utilized in temporarily servicing aircraft at new airfields while the Group's personnel were being moved forward from their previous base. Three Airdrome Squadrons went ashore during the first week of the Invasion and moved to the landing strips being built by the engineers, setting up fuel and ammunition dumps for the use of fighter-bombers. The first operational squadrons began to use French strips on 13-14 June on a regular basis and were serviced by Airdrome Squadrons. On 19 June, the first Advanced Landing Ground (ALG) on the European Continent, A-3 at Cardonville, landed its first P-47s of the 395th Fighter Squadron of the 368th Fighter Group to become the first permanently based squadron on the Continent. Soon after A-4 at Deux, Jumeaux, and five other ALGs were completed. In July the 404th Fighter Group operated from Chapelle, the 36th Fighter Group from Brucheville, and the 373rd Fighter Group from Tour-en-Bessin. Ground crews at the ALGs were able to carry out everything from minor servicing to major overhauls. The ground mechanics were supplied with good quality and an adequate supply of tools, jacks, work stands, and spare parts. As more and more aircraft came into the theater and more combat damage and wear and tear was sustained, a shortage of spare parts occurred and continued. Engine changes were due after 200 hours of flying, and removal and reinstallation could be accomplished literally in the field in three hours. Even though the "book" called for a ten-hour run in of a new engine at the ALGs this was done in two hours. The shortage of spare parts led to the cannibalization of written off aircraft, which greatly aided the repair of damaged aircraft, especially aircraft wings, which were frequently damaged by flak. The civilian representatives of various companies; Republic Aviation (P-47); Pratt & Whitney engines; and Curtiss and Hamilton-Standard propellers were on hand to solve difficult problems. In dry weather the thick dust caused problems with the in-line engines of the Mustang, Spitfire, and Typhoon, while the Pratt & Whitney radial engine of the P-47 prevailed.

Air Service Command mechanics. On 6 May 1944 Brig. Gen. Myron R. Wood took command of the IX ASC. In January 1944 there were 2,964 officers and nearly 42,000 enlisted men in the IX ASC. At a peak strength of 62,000 officers and enlisted men in 439 units, the Air Service Command was the largest element in the 9th Air Force. It transported, supplied, fed, housed, armed, maintained and repaired the entire air force. (USAF)

The USSTAF decided to establish a base depot in France to supply the great number of American air groups on the Continent. But it was not until December 1944 that the Continental Air Depot Area (CADA, later redesignated the Central Air Depot Area in early February) was established with headquarters at Compiegne. The CADA was to become the Continental equivalent of the BADA in the UK, and Brig.Gen. Isaac Ott, former head of BADA, was transferred to command the CADA. The CADA controlled supplies for all the air forces on the Continent. Due to the continuous movement of its air groups and the difficulty in supplying and serving them, the IX ASC needed to alter its organization in the Fall of 1944. It created "clutches" of air bases occupied by fighter-bomber and medium bomber groups. The 9th Air Force moved its own Advanced Air Depots on the Continent into the airfield clutches, and these AADs were responsible for the service of all groups in the area. Soon they replaced the Advanced Air Depots and Service Groups that already had been substantially decreased by transfers to the IX TCC and First TAF.

The Communications Zone (CZ) controlled the movement of men and supplies by water and land. It was responsible for movement across the Atlantic to the UK, and then across the English Channel. The utilization of the European rail system was initially delayed by the very efficient Allied interdiction campaign that destroyed a large portion of the rail networks in France and Belgium. The CZ operated the largest fleet of trucks on the Continent, and operated the depots from which the air force depots drew basic supplies. In August 1944, the CZ began to transport supplies to air force dumps and depots to within 40 miles of airfields, from which the air force was required to complete the hauling. The rapid ground army advance that lengthened supply lines and the inactive, damaged rail system hampered the planned delivery volume By the fall, the French and Belgian rail systems were becoming functional, and the large quantities of supplies were being hauled, but mainly to the ground armies and secondarily to the air forces. As a result the USSTAF ASC and the IX ASC had to take care of its own needs. The air service command was vital to the mobile tactical air force, but even the pooling of motor transport often left the air service command unable to adequately supply or transport tactical units. Gen. Weyland of the XIX TAC, in particular, concentrated in equipping his ASC with adequate motor transport to move and supply his tactical units over distances of 300 miles.

The key to the 9th Air Force's success was transport. As the rail systems in France and Belgium had been destroyed during the Transportation Plan attacks and the CZ was unable to provide adequate transport, the 9th Air Force had to utilize its own air and motor transport. The central pool truck companies were assigned to transport supplies from depots and dumps to airfields in the combat zones. The first 9th Air Force truck companies arrived on D+1 and were adequate until the Allies broke out of the beachhead. The advance of the armies extended transport miles and time between the beachhead and ports to the airfields at the front. However, the ground forces were even more pressed for transport and supplies, and at times some 9th Air Force transport was commandeered. Gasoline was in short supply until pipelines could be built, and 9th Air Force trucks needed to haul gasoline over long distances. As the ground breakout and rapid advance continued in August, the distances of moving supplies from the central pool was increased even more. This caused fighter-bomber groups and their service teams to move as much as a hundred miles using their own transport, which was limited. Air transport was used to move critical personnel and supplies, but was limited when compared to road transport. The 302nd Air Transport Wing was created in July 1944 to assume command of the 31st Air Transport Group, which carried the 9th Air Force's personnel and cargo and was to control all air transport of the command. Three airstrips in France were assigned to the 302nd, and one, Colleville (A-23C), at one point was busier than La Guardia in New York City. The rehabilitation of the French rail system after its devastation relieved the supply situation.

The need for replacement aircraft was increased immediately after the invasion. It was not only due to increased combat losses as the number of operations increased, but also to a lower level of maintenance forced by the use of mobile field maintenance units on the Continent. Fighter-bombers that often flew up to three or four missions per day literally wore out. Hard landings on deteriorating runways, dusty conditions, and the chronic shortage of spare parts added to the dilemma. AAF HQ increased the replacement rate for fighters from 20 to 30% per month in the summer of 1944, but these figures were inadequate. The USSTAF allocated the P-51 to the 8th Air Force because of its long-range escort qualities. The 8th Air Force increased its P-51 Groups from seven to 14 by converting its seven P-38 and P-47 groups between June and December 1944. The 9th Air Force's two P-51 groups had problems in procuring replacement aircraft, as replacements went to the 8th Air Force. Many of the surplus 8th Air Force P-38s and P-47s were sent to the 9th Air Force as replacement aircraft, and not a few were in very poor condition, and some were unserviceable. Several 9th Air Force fighter-bomber groups had to transition from one type of aircraft to another in order to take advantage of the flow of aircraft from the States or 8th Air Force. As a rule First TAF and 9th Air Force fighter groups were usually under strength during the war.

The initial stocks of gasoline and oil landed during the first three weeks after D-Day were pre-packaged and could be easily transported by truck to the nearby airfields. Bulk fuel delivery was to begin on D+15 by the Communications Zone. The CZ was unable to deliver the promised fuel stocks, but there was no shortage

The initial stocks of gasoline and oil landed during the first three weeks after D-Day were pre-packaged and could be easily transported by truck to the near-by airfields. Bulk fuel delivery was to begin on D+15 by the Communications Zone. Ninth Air Force personnel transfer gasoline from a tanker truck to Jerry Cans for transport to front line ALGs. (USAF)

The IX ASC received its bulk truck units from the UK and collected additional transport to haul fuel from depots and pipeline termini. A 2-1/2 ton GMC 6x6 gasoline tanker pulling an oil tank trailer provided fuel and oil to the P-47s along the flight lines. Note the uneven Hessian/SMT surface. (USAF)

in June, as the number of airfields in service was less than projected, as were the number of sorties flown. With the increased number of airfields and sorties in July it became apparent that the delivery of bulk fuel had became vital. The CZ allocated the Normandy port of Port-en-Bessin to accept bulk fuel and erected handling and storage facilities there. IX Engineer Command built storage facilities on their airfields. Small collapsible Mareng tanks that held from 750 to 3,000 gallons were used until more permanent and larger facilities could be erected. Transportation of fuel to the airfields was a problem, as the 9th Air Force did not have any of its bulk gasoline trucks on the Continent. The CZ was assigned to haul the fuel, and was able to comply initially because the level of operations remained low. Gasoline consumption increased as operations from Continental bases increased, but remained below anticipated levels through D+19 when 350,000 gallons had been used. By the third week in July 90,000 gallons were used daily, and by early August daily consumption rose to 180,000 gallons. To solve the bulk fuel delivery problem a fuel pipeline was built from Cherbourg, and the partially repaired rail system became more significant. After a while the Cherbourg-based pipeline extended to St. Lo, but it and the inadequate numbers of trucks and rail tank cars could not keep up with the rapid ground advance and the concomitant movement of the airfields. The more advanced fields needed to be supplied with packaged fuel delivered by truck and air transport. By early September the rail system was further repaired and operating tank cars to the Paris area. By October the newly captured ports of Le Havre and Ostende were opened and accepted bulk fuel. The Cherbourg pipeline was extended to Chartres by the end of September, and to its final length to Chalons, 80 miles east of Paris, by early 1945. Antwerp was opened in November and the construction of aviation pipelines began at once, and by February reached Maastricht. Distribution of bulk fuel from the ports and from the end of the pipelines was a problem throughout the war. The Allied interdiction campaign destroyed many of the tank cars of the French and Belgian rail system, so tank cars were brought in from the UK and from America. The IX ASC received its bulk truck units from the UK, and collected additional transport to haul fuel from depots and pipeline termini. It also called on the CZ when it needed additional supplies of fuel. A fuel transportation system was set up by the early winter, but only supplied adequate fuel to the forward airfields. The advance into Germany in spring 1945 further stretched the fuel supply situation, and truck transport was often augmented by air transport. The ASC supply system was always able to just keep ahead of the demand. By April 1945, the fuel distribution scheme could theoretically transport 6,300,000 gallons of gasoline per day.

Aircraft maintenance increased as operations increased from primitive bases on the Continent after D-Day. The IX ASC repair and maintenance units serviced 1,029 aircraft in May 1944 and then 1,842 in June. They repaired 154 battle-damaged aircraft in May and 744 in June. Repair rates continued to be high throughout the summer and fell in the fall when 9th Air Force operations fell and

During 1944, except for July, serviceability rates for the 9th Air Force at forward combat fields surpassed its 80% average in the UK before D-Day. The rates increased steadily after November, and by April 1945 reached 90%. A P-47 is maintained in the open almost in the shadow of a damaged French chateau. (USAF)

then rose again in the spring of 1945 during the final push into Germany. Over 1,600 aircraft were repaired in March 1945. In the months after D-Day, maintenance and repair was difficult from the ALGS due to poor working conditions, lack of materials and spare parts, and increased damage and repair rates. The service teams did yeoman duty, as there was a lack of base depot repair facilities on the Continent, and most of the service was done at the airfields. Airfields were temporary, without hangars and with widespread, open-air dispersal areas that required maintenance and repair to be done in the open. In July, losses and write-offs exceeded replacement aircraft. To cope the IX ASC received more service units from the UK, and specialists were flown in when needed. Mobile reclamation and repair squadrons from the air depot groups aided the service teams. By October the IX ASC had received all its service units from the UK.

Except for July, serviceability rates for the 9th Air Force at forward combat fields surpassed its 80% average in the UK before D-Day. The rates increased steadily after November, and by April 1945 reached 90%. The First TAF did not achieve as high rates because initially it did not have enough service units, and its forward bases were more widespread. With time and experience First TAF fighter serviceability rates increased from 65% in December 1944 to 77% in April 1945. The 8th Air Force had the best facilities and bases in the ETO, centered in the friendly UK, but actually had a lower serviceability rate than the 9th, averaging slightly less at 80%.

Throughout the campaign in Northwest Europe the IX ASC supplied 9th Air Force units on the Continent with a massive volume of fuel and ammunition. During the first two months of the campaign the IX ASC supplied over 200,000 gallons of fuel per day, and a staggering 241 million gallons from D-day until the end of the war. IX ASC maintenance units kept over 80% of 9th Air Force aircraft operational during the war, a difficult task on the primitive advanced airfields. By the end of October 1944, 92% of IX ASC personnel were based on the Continent, contributing to the success of the 9th Air Force.

7

Aircraft Armament, Ordnance, and Accessories

Fighter Armament and Accessories

Machine Guns

The American air services adopted the .50 caliber M2 Browning Machine Gun derived from the .50 caliber ground service heavy machine gun as its standard fighter weapon during WWII. It was a recoil-operated, air-cooled, belt-fed gun that weighed 52 pounds and was 57 inches long (barrel 36 inches). Its rate of automatic fire (shots per second) averaged 700 to 750 rounds per minute depending on attachments, such as a flash suppresser or muzzle booster. Its muzzle velocity was 2,700 to 2,850 feet per second. Its extreme range (extent of forward travel) was 20,000 to 21,500 feet, and its effective range (round able to penetrate airframe or engine to cause damage) was 3,400 to 3,500 feet. All of the above performance figures varied in the field due to internal (e.g. age and condition of the mechanism and barrel, age of the ammunition, feed and type) and external (e.g. temperature) conditions.

The M2 was either engine, nose, or wing-mounted. When engine-mounted it was synchronized to fire through the propeller by a mechanical trigger motor attached to the gun receiver, causing the gun to fire semi-automatically. When the gun was wing-mounted, firing was attained through a remote control solenoid attached to the receiver causing it to fire automatically. To assure that a fighter's gunfire would exact the maximum damage to an enemy aircraft, the guns were harmonized so that their fire would converge at the optimum combat range. Harmonization range was often the personal preference of the individual pilot, but it is well known that most aces preferred very short ranges.

Though the .50 caliber bullet lacked the punch of a 20mm cannon shell, the concentrated firepower from six or eight machine guns had a devastating effect. There were four basic types of .50 caliber ammunition: armor piercing (distinguished by a painted black tip); tracer (red tip); incendiary (blue); and armor piercing incendi-

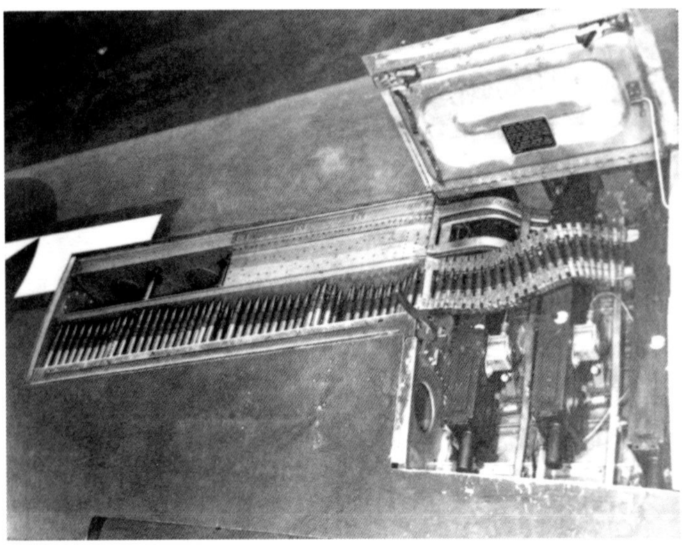

Browning M2 .50 caliber machine gun installation in the wing of P-51 was the standard American aircraft weapon in WW-2. It was a recoil-operated, air-cooled, belt-fed gun. It fired 700 to 750 rounds per minute at 2700 to 2850 feet per second to an effective range of 3400 to 3500 feet. The P-51 carried four to six M2s with 400 rounds per gun. (USAF)

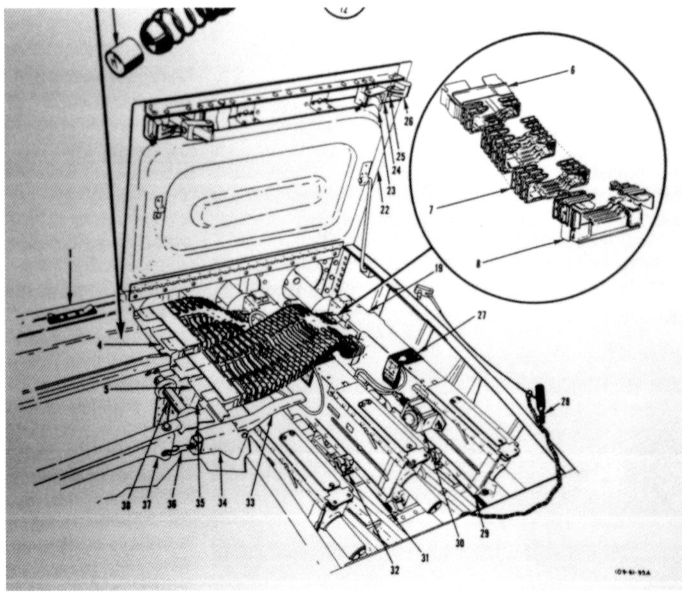

P-51D M-2 .50 caliber machine gun installation. Earlier the guns were canted but had frequent feed and jamming problems caused the conversion to an upright installation. (USAF)

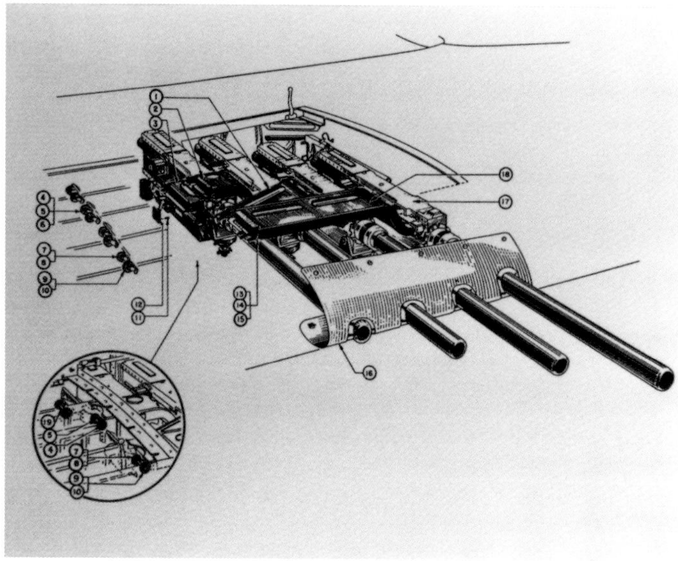

P-47 .50 caliber M-2 machine installation. (USAF)

Left: Armorers loading .50 belts into the ammunition bays on ETO top ace (28 victories) Gabby Gabreski's P 47. (USAF)

ary (silver). The bullet weighed about 1.6 ounces and was about 5.5 inches long. Between 267 and 500 rounds of ammunition could be stowed per gun (rpg). The P-47 carried eight guns with 425 rpg, the F6F and F4U mounted six guns with 400 rpg, and the P-51 carried four or six guns with 400 rpg. The expression "the whole nine yards" is attributed to Dick Bong. The ammunition belts of the P-38's .50 caliber machine guns measured 27 feet when laid out full length. As he pre-flighted his P-38, he made sure it was topped with fuel, oil, and had the "full nine yards" of ammo.

Cannon

The U.S. dabbled with cannon armament in early fighters. The P-39 Aircobra was equipped with a 30 round Oldsmobile 37 mm T-9 or M-4 cannon. Because of its inherent inaccuracy and low rate of fire it was abandoned in favor of the .50 caliber machine gun. The P-38 carried the Hispano-Suiza 20mm cannon, and late in the war several fighter-bombers were fitted with 20-mm cannon, as was the P-61 night fighter. But because no Axis fighter could withstand the pounding of multiple .50s the cannon was reserved for special purposes.

The Machine Gun vs. Cannon Controversy

The difference between a machine gun and cannon was that a machine gun fired a solid slug, while a cannon fired rounds called shells that could be solid, but were often hollow and filled with detonation or incendiary material. The solid machine gun round did its damage through kinetic energy that is the function of projectile weight times its velocity squared. The .50 caliber slug weighed about 1.6 ounces, while the 20-mm projectile weighed 4.6 ounces, and the 37-mm projectile weighed almost 17.6 ounces. The machine gun had a somewhat higher muzzle velocity (the speed at which the projectile leaves the barrel). Thus the machine gun round's kinetic energy was higher, as its higher muzzle velocity was squared.

The P-38 was armed with four Browning .50 cal. M2 machine guns and a 20mm Hispano-Suiza cannon. (USAF)

It also had a higher rate of fire than the cannon, which meant it could fire more rounds per minute—or more correctly, per second—to do damage. The muzzle velocity affected the round's kinetic energy and the flight time to the target. The shorter the time to the target gave the target less time to maneuver. Guns with higher muzzle velocities were more likely to hit a target, could be fired at longer ranges, and caused more damage.

A cannon shell, depending on its design, would explode on contact or penetrate and then explode or set a fire. A solid machine gun slug would penetrate and depended on its kinetic energy to cause damage. The aircraft cannon was a more deadly weapon due to their heavier explosive shells. But they were heavier than a machine gun, often weighing more each than two machine guns depending on the caliber (a 37mm cannon weighed 135lbs. and a 20mm cannon weighed 118lbs. vs. a .50 cal. machine gun that weighed 52lbs. and a .30 cal. machine gun that weighed 24lbs.). Therefore the equal weight of two machine guns could fire many more rounds per second than a cannon. Also, cannon shells weighed more and were larger than machine gun rounds, so a cannon-equipped fighter could carry far fewer rounds than a machine gun-equipped fighter could. The 37mm gun (P-39) could carry 30 rounds per gun (rpg), the 20mm (P-38) 150rpg, the .50 cal. (P-47 or P-51) between 400-450rpg, and the .30 caliber (P-39) 1,000rpg. Fewer cannon shells meant a shorter firing time at a lower rate of fire. The 30 rounds of 37mm shells fired by a P-39 had a duration of fire of 11.8 seconds, while its four-.30 cal. machines with 1,000rpg fired for 67 seconds per gun. The P-38's 20mm cannon fired 150 rounds at 11.2 rounds per second in 13.4 seconds. The .50 cal. machine gun fired 12 rounds per second for a duration of 35 seconds (425 rounds). A cannon shell caused more damage per hit, but there were less potential hits when compared to the higher rate of fire and more rounds found in machine gun equipped fighters. Many British and Luftwaffe fighters carried a combination of machine guns and cannon, with the machine guns being used to find range and attain hits and the cannon to deliver the lethal blow. The RAF replaced its Browning .303 caliber machine guns with the Hispano-Suiza 20mm cannon, as one 20mm shell did much more damage than four .303 hits, which were ineffective against armor plate and self-sealing fuel tanks. The 20mm cannon, with its explosive shell, would leave a large hole upon impact. The American fighter aircraft .30 cal. machine gun was replaced with the .50 cal. Both projectiles left small, clean entrance holes in the metal fuselage surface, but after they hit they would be deflected and begin to tumble end over end. The larger .50 cal. slug would cause a substantially larger exit, or secondary, hole than the .30 cal.

The American fighter carried six or eight .50 cal. machine guns that concentrated enough firepower to cope with Axis fighters, especially against the fragile Japanese fighters in the Pacific, particu-

Harmonization, commonly called bore sighting, aligned the path of rounds fired from all guns. Here armorers of the 41st Fighter Squadron of the 39th Fighter Group set up boresighting apparatus 1000 inches in front of a P-51D at Clark Field, Philippines late in the war. P-51 guns, gun cameras and gun sights were generally harmonized at 300 yards. (USAF)

Left: The P-39 was equipped with a 30 round Oldsmobile 37mm T-9 or M-4 cannon which was fired through the propeller hub. The inaccurate cannon had a low rate of fire and was abandoned for the .50 machine gun. (USAF)

larly when using the API round. Also, the major Axis bombers (He-111, Do-17, and G4M3 Betty) were usually of medium bomber size and not well armed or armored. Thus, the six or eight machine guns mounted in the superior P-51, P-47, P-38, or F4U and F6F gave the American fighter pilot a good chance of achieving a high probability shot, firing out the most number of rounds in the shortest amount of time.

American aircraft ammunition: .50 caliber belted AP (top), .30 caliber belted tracer (left center), 37mm cannon (right center) and 20mm cannon (bottom) (from Author's equipment collection)

Harmonization

Harmonization, commonly called bore sighting, was aligning the path of the rounds fired from all guns. It was accomplished by one of two methods. One was to converge the four, six, or eight machine guns to a point 250 to 300 yards ahead of the fighter. At a three mil gunsight setting the convergence pattern at 300 yards was about three feet in diameter, which was difficult for the average pilot/marksman and resulted in excessive dispersion at most ranges. A remedy to gain wider bullet dispersion was to bore sight each gun at different ranges, generally 250, 300, and 350 yards for outboard, middle, and inboard guns respectively. Called "pattern harmonization," it was innately less damaging than a tighter cone of fire, but the greater dispersion of bullets made the probability of obtaining a hit more likely.

American Aircraft Guns

GUN/AMMO	Gun Wt. (lbs.)	Muzzle Velocity (ft./sec.)	Rounds per Gun	Projectile Weight (lbs.)	Rate of Fire (rps)	Duration of Fire (sec.)	Weight of Fire (lbs/sec)
Browning .30 cal. Machine Gun	24	2,600	1,000	0.025	15.0	66.5	0.40
Browning .50 cal. Machine Gun	52	2,800	425	0.100	10.2	19.6	0.90
Hispano-Suiza 20mm Cannon	118	2,800	150	0.290	11.2	13.4	3.20
American Armament	135	1,800	30	1.100	1.5	11.8	1.65

Types of Ammunition

Type	Use	Color of Tip	How It Works
Ball	Against personnel and light material targets	Unpainted; plain copper	The outer jacket point contains a lead and antimony filler that covers the tip of the underlying steel core. When the projectile hits a target, the soft outer jacket and filler smears, giving the steel core a grip. The core then penetrates the surface instead of being turned aside.
Armor-Piercing	Against armored aircraft and vehicles, concrete shelters and other bullet-resisting targets	Black	The projectile is the same as the ball cartridge, except that the core is made of very hard tungsten-chrome steel to give it greater penetrating power.
Tracer	For observing fire, it makes a streak of light easily seen at night and usually is visible in daylight	Red	Inside the outer metal jacket is a slug of lead and antimony. Behind it is a pocket of tracer composition that is set afire by the propelling charge as the projectile leaves the cartridge case.
Incendiary	Used to set fire to explosive or very inflammable targets	Light blue	In front of the jacket is an incendiary composition that is sealed by plugs of an alloy that easily melts. As the bullet goes through the barrel, the heat melts the plugs and the incendiary composition is set on fire as it meets the air.
Dummy	Training	Unpainted (hole in side of case)	Has no priming or propelling charge.
Armor-Piercing Incendiary	Used to set fire to armor-plated inflammable objects.	Black with small blue tip on the nose.	Similar to the armor-piercing projectile, except that there is incendiary compound behind the steel core.

Ammunition lot numbers were assigned at the time of manufacture to all types of service ammunition, and were the means by which all service ammunition was identified. Production orders and specifications called for the manufacture of lots for specific weapons. It was of utmost importance to armament officers and armorers, as mistakes in recording could result in accidents or the condemnation of large stocks of usable ammunition. The use of the wrong grade of ammunition in synchronized or remote-controlled aircraft machine guns could result in a propeller being shot off, or jamming that could not be corrected in the air. Aircraft ammunition required more precise uniformity in dimension and weight, and minimum variations in the rate of ignition than for ground use machine guns. Grade designations did not denote that one grade was better than another, but that it was designed for a particular weapon. The grades were:

R=For use in rifles
AC= For use in aircraft machine guns
MG=For use in ground machine guns
Grade 3=Not to be used in any weapon

Early in the war the ammunition belts contained a mixture of tracers, ball, and armor piercing rounds. Tracers were used to let the pilot know where the bullets were going, but after a while it was found that all tracer rounds did not have the same trajectory as the incendiary material, which gave the tracer its distinctive color burned at different rates. The tracer round burned in flight that changed its center of gravity, causing it to diverge from a true flight path. Also, when tracers hit they ricocheted and led the pilot to think he was flying into his own fire. Pulling every fifth round and replacing it with tracer rounds was tedious, and they were difficult to load. Also, each tracer linked meant the loss of one effective round. At first pilots did not care for armor piercing rounds, as they made smaller holes than the blunter ball rounds, but the AP could penetrate the armor plate surrounding the enemy pilot. Later armor-piercing incendiary (API) ammunition was introduced and shown to be more effective than the standard mixed loading of two armor-piercing, two incendiary, and one tracer. The API round allowed the pilot to see hits on his target, as the incendiary part of the shell would cause small puffs of white smoke on hits and the inner steel core would pierce aircraft armor. Also, API was easy to load, as it linked straight. Several tracer rounds were used before the last 20-25 rounds to let the pilot know he was almost out of ammunition. Toward the end of the war T-48 ammunition was developed that had a higher muzzle velocity and incendiary quotient and destroyed an extraordinary number of parked German aircraft in April 1945. The T-48 round had been developed to set the low-grade aviation fuel used for the Me-262 on fire. The "jet" ammunition was so incendiary that it set the grass on fire during strafing attacks. The six or eight .50 machine guns arming American fighter-bombers was the most effective weapon against motorized and horse-drawn transport, locomotives, and rolling stock, light armor, fuel, ammunition and supply dumps, troops, and other personnel.

In late March 1945, when there were many targets available as the Allied armies were driving into the heart of Germany, a shortage of .50 caliber ammunition occurred for many fighter-bomber units. The 405th Fighter Group scoured the surrounding countryside in every available vehicle looking for downed U.S. aircraft. They found a downed B-25 and two B-17s to salvage 18,000 rounds. They went to AA units begging .50 rounds and got another 10,000 rounds from units who had not encountered too many Luftwaffe aircraft of late. They removed the ammunition from aircraft in repair shops and somehow found enough for a day's missions. The crisis was only alleviated when C-46s, C-47s, and even B-17s flew ammo in from England.

Capt. Leslie Cles, P-47 pilot for the 353rd Fighter Group, discussed a firing run (*Down to the Deck*, ibid.):

"Somewhere around 500 yards is a good range to open fire, if you are on your target. Firing at a greater range than this will give you only a very few scattered hits. Then more than likely you will be off target, when the range is correct. Spend the time up to the opening range in centering the needle and ball and your sight steady on the target.

By closing to less than 500 yards to fire you will run up against this: You are doing about 400 miles per hour which will give you about a 2.7 second burst from 500 yards to the target/ You may need all this to get to your target. It is not good enough to just hit anywhere on the target. Almost every type of target will have a more vulnerable area somewhere on it. Know these areas and aim for them.

In sighting use a little thought as to where your sighting point will be. Your guns are bore sighted for around 300 yards, therefore, there will be more bullet drop in the opening ranges. You are also traveling at a speed in which the angle of attack will be on the negative side. These combined factors will require more than the usual amount of sight elevation. The sight will have to be placed at least on top of the target and in some cases slightly higher. The "G" pull on the bullet stream in a turn will require an additional lead, if you must fire in turn. This, however, should be avoided if possible.

When the range is correct and you are on target, then fire a good steady burst. You won't have time to take several short bursts. Neither will you be able to fire, see where your bullets go, and fire again. You must use and trust your sight. Then make full use of the few seconds you have.

Never spray bullets around, pick one target and hold it. One destroyed target is far better than several damaged. Then, when you are no longer on target, stop firing. It's a pure waste of ammunition to keep firing as you pull out. If you are fortunate to have an undefended target, set up a flying school gunnery pattern and go to it but make your passes count."

It was recommended that pilots should save about 50 rounds per gun during strafing missions to engage in aerial combat, if necessary, on the way home. In the P-51D a pilot could expend all the ammunition in his outboard guns and have enough left in reserve in the two inboard guns.

Gun Sights

The simple ring and bead gun sight of the interwar years was no longer sufficient with the increasing performance and combat ranges seen in the newer monoplane fighters of the mid-1930s.

The N-2, N3A, L3-B, N-9, and MK VIII series of reflector sights were basically a refined ring and bead sight, with the latter two eventually becoming the standard. They were characterized by a center dot, or "pipper" (bead), surrounded by 50- and 100- mil radii rings that aided in the calculation of deflection. The retile image of this sight, although it was only a few inches from the pilot's eye, was made to look as if it were at a distance in front of the fighter. There was no need to readjust focus, the sight could be viewed with both eyes open, and the pilot could move his head without changing the alignment of the target. The image of the ring(s) and pipper was superimposed onto a special glass in front of the pilot's eyes in such a way that they were visible only if the pilot were looking along the longitudinal axis of the fighter (convergence of the guns). The pilot had only to track the target and get it into the center of the sight. The sight was accurate when closing on an enemy at the same speed and course, but deflection shooting ("lead-shooting," e.g. bird hunting) continued to be the province of the gifted pilot.

The AAF K-14 series and Navy Mark 18 were introduced in July 1944 and were a development of the British gyroscopic Mk IIC and Mk IID sights. It was originally developed for bomber turrets, but engineers adapted it as the standard U.S. fighter gunsight. The new sight provided much improved deflection shooting from the average pilot, as it computed the correct lead angle for a target crossing speed at ranges of 200 to 800 yards. The K-14 was based on the reflector sight, but was combined with a gyroscope. Below the reflecting glass was a panel with a control calibrated to the wingspan of the intended victim. The pilot dialed in the enemy's wingspan (pre-marked on the controls as Me-109, FW-190, etc.), and the sighting reticle on the reflector glass then adjusted itself to the size of the enemy wingspan. The pilot would fly the fighter so that the target appeared in the gyro reticle circle and rotate a throttle twist grip until the diameter of the gyro reticle circle matched the aircraft. The gyro apparatus in the sight produced the correct deflection for the range and rate of turn corresponding to the target size. The pilot would frame the target with the twist grip as the range changed, track the target for at least one second, and then fire. Initially, it was not well received because of its size and apparent intricacy, but soon earned the nickname "No Miss Um." It allowed shooting at twice the previous maximum range, and more

MK-8 Illuminated Optical Reflector Sight. The pilot leaned forward and looked into the glass with both eyes open to superimpose the sight and target and then fired. Note protective pad under glass. (Author's equipment collection)

Sperry K-13 Gyroscopic Lead-Computing Optical Sight (LCOS) (Author's equipment collection)

importantly greatly improved deflection shooting, which with the N-9/MK VIII sights was a combination of guesswork and individual ability. The K-14 made even 90-degree deflection as easy as that from dead astern. Though the new sight required some additional manual coordination, it greatly increased the number of kills at long range (500+ yards) and at large deflection angles (45+ degrees).

Gun Cameras

The utilization of the Type N-4 or N-6 gun camera greatly aided in authenticated victory claims. The gun camera, officially titled the Gun Sight Aiming Point Camera, was manufactured by the Fairchild Camera and Instrument Company of Jamaica, NY, and the Morse Instrument Company of Hudson, OH. The gun camera was mounted in the leading edge of the inboard port wing, or inside the leading edge of the starboard outer wing panel behind curved laminated glass faired into the wing. It was accessible for loading and adjustment from the wheel well. A small, spring-loaded metal plate covered the camera aperture in the wing and remained open during flight; it was closed by a mechanical cable linkage when the landing gear was extended, protecting the lens from blown sand and pebbles. A small, self-contained heater warmed the camera bay. The electrically operated 16mm camera could be set for 16, 32, or 64 frames per second. The diaphragm stops were marked "B" (bright), "H" (hazy), and "D" (dull) to allow for various light conditions, but in practice the camera was unable to adjust to light conditions, and footage would be lost or inconclusive. Each unit did its own evaluation of combat film, and would forward conclusive film to higher echelons for confirmation.

355th Fighter Group armorer removing gun camera film magazine for processing from its heated compartment on the leading edge of a P-47 wing. The 16mm-film magazine can be seen in his right hand.The Plexiglas covered window is above the access panel. (USAF)

Guns and camera were controlled by a three-way toggle switch (guns, camera, and sight). The bore sight adapter focused the camera on the convergence point. When the trigger on the stick was pressed the guns fired, and the cameras operated if the toggle was in gun position. The camera and sight positions on the toggle took motion pictures when the trigger was pressed but did not fire the guns. The camera was sighted a little below the gun sight line so that the camera remained on the target for a longer period after the pullout from the gunnery run.

Aircraft Ordnance

Bombs

A bomb is defined by the Ordnance Department as "a missile intended to be dropped by an airplane."

Parts of a bomb:
Casing
Suspension lugs
Anti-ricochet device
Tail fins
Side pocket for fuses
Nose fuse (there could be a separate arming device in the tail which may also be combined with a nose fuse)
Adapter-booster
Primer detonator (fit in the adapter-booster)

The explosive train is a series of actions that cause the bomb to detonate. It is made up of a fuse or fuses (nose, tail, or both), which act on a primer detonator, the detonation of which actually sets the explosive train in action. The primer detonator's action is transmitted to an adapter booster that sets off the main explosive charge. The sensitivity of the train begins with the primer detonator, which is extremely sensitive, since it must react to the comparatively weak blow from the firing pin, while the main explosive charge is more insensitive and must be detonated by an intermediate charge contained in the booster.

The most common fighter-bomber bomb loading was two 500lb. general-purpose bombs with instantaneous fusing. It could be filled with various compositions:

Explosive:	Ingredients:
RDX (Cyclonite, Hexogen)	Cyclotrimethylene trinitranmine
TNT (Trinitrotoluene)	Toluene, nitric acid
Torpex	TNT, RDX, aluminum
Amatol	TNT, ammonium nitrate

Note: RDX (tritonal) was a new, more powerful explosive used against bunkers and concrete fortifications.

Bomb Types

Demolition	Practice
Fragmentation	Drill and gauge
Chemical	

Only the first three are used in combat.

A beautifully composed photo of a 373rd Fighter Group P-47 framed by 500lb. bomb storage racks. (USAF)

500lb. GP bomb bundled with 24 20lb. fragmentation bombs. (USAF)

Demolition Bomb

A demolition bomb was a package of high explosive carried in an aerodynamic bomb body or casing that needed to be light yet strong. Between 50 and 60% of the weight of the bomb was high explosive, and the remainder steel. The bomb needed to remain in one piece until it detonated, generally inside the target instead of breaking up on first impact. In order to achieve the penetration necessary for different targets and still contain the maximum amount of explosive, demolition bombs were constructed of several different metals of varying hardness and thickness:

Type	% of Explosive
General purpose (GP)	50-55%
Semi-armor piercing (SAP)	32%
Armor piercing (AP)	5-12%
Light case (LC)	77%
Depth bomb (DB)	70-75%

A new range of GP bomb became available in late 1943 in five sizes:

100lb. - Would demolish a two-story building, destroy a gun position, locomotive, motor transport, or aircraft on the ground (damage it at 75 feet) if exploded within ten feet of the target. Generally were considered uneconomical, as a fighter-bomber could carry two or three versus two or three 500lb. bombs.

250lb. - Would destroy the walls and floors of most buildings, and sink or severely damage shipping up to cruiser size within 20 feet. Replaced the M31 300lb. bomb.

500lb. - Would destroy steel bridges, underground defenses, most tanks, and light cruiser-type shipping within 25 feet. Fighter-bomber bomb of choice.

1,000lb. - Would destroy or severely damage light concrete fortifications and displace piers and the spans of the heaviest bridges.

2,000lb. - Would destroy heavy concrete fortifications and crack or burst a large hole in dams, or sink a heavy cruiser or battleship with a direct hit or nearby explosion in the water.

For air attacks on railways, roads, bridges, and roads through built up areas demolition bombs were used. Unlike fragmentation bombs, demolition bombs caused deep craters and caused long-term damage to roads. In Italy road attacks were particularly effective, as the hilly or mountainous nature of the terrain made it difficult to detour around the steep slopes on which the roads were constructed. Demolition bombs caused critical damage to the surface and sub-surface foundation of the rail bed, and to the intricate switch and signal installations at rail junctions and marshaling yards. Demolition bombs were the only air weapon that could have an effect on

1,000lb. GP bomb packaged with four clusters of three incendiary bombs. (USAF)

the support structures of a bridge to close it to traffic. Demolition bombs were effective against roads through built up areas. The rubble from bombed buildings fell into the streets and blocked them for long periods of time. These attacks were less effective on towns and cities located on the plains, where houses tended to be farther apart and traffic could be detoured. Demolition bombs were very effective in the hilly and mountainous towns and villages of Italy, where the houses were tightly packed together and only one or two roads ran through them.

On the early ALGs 1,000lb. bombs could not be carried as the runways were too short and too rough to carry bombs on the wings, and the fin on the center line bomb would hit the ground. Landing with bombs still attached was normal, as often targets could not be located. Hung up bombs were also a fairly common occurrence, and one that was feared by pilots. It was essential that the touch down be made as gently as possible so the bomb would not be jarred loose, which was difficult on the bumpy Advanced Landing Grounds on the Continent. If the bomb jarred loose the pilot had to hope that the tail fin would not come loose and arm the bomb.

In the ETO, more than 80% of the bombs dropped by P-47s were 500lb and less than 10% were 1,000lb. with the remaining 10% consisting of fragmentation bombs, rockets, and napalm.

A P-51 is fitted with 12x30lb. anti-personnel fragmentation bombs which were utilized at the end of the war with devastating effect against enemy troops. (USAF)

Major U.S. Demolition Bombs (Post -1943)

Type	Weight	HE Weight
AN-M30 GP	100lbs.	54lbs.
AN-M57 GP	250lbs.	123lbs.
AN-M64 GP	500lbs.	262lbs.
AN-M65 GP	1,000lbs.	530lbs.
AN-M66 GP	2,000lbs.	1,051lbs.

Major U.S. Demolition Bombs (Pre-1943)

Type	Weight
M30	100lbs.
M31	300lbs.
M32	600lbs.
M33	1,100lbs.
M34	2,000lbs.
M43	500lbs.
M44	1,000lbs.

Fragmentation Bombs

The destructive power of fragmentation bombs resulted entirely from the fragmentation of the bomb case, whose scored casings had been designed to break into 1,000 to 1,500 pieces weighing about 3 ounces and projected at up to 4,000 feet per second. There were two types of fragmentation bombs:

Anti-personnel: - Designed to burst on contact with the ground and spray fragments the size and speed of a .30 caliber bullet, or a finned model designed to explode in the air.

Anti-material: - Designed to burst on the ground or above parked aircraft or light-skinned motor transport.

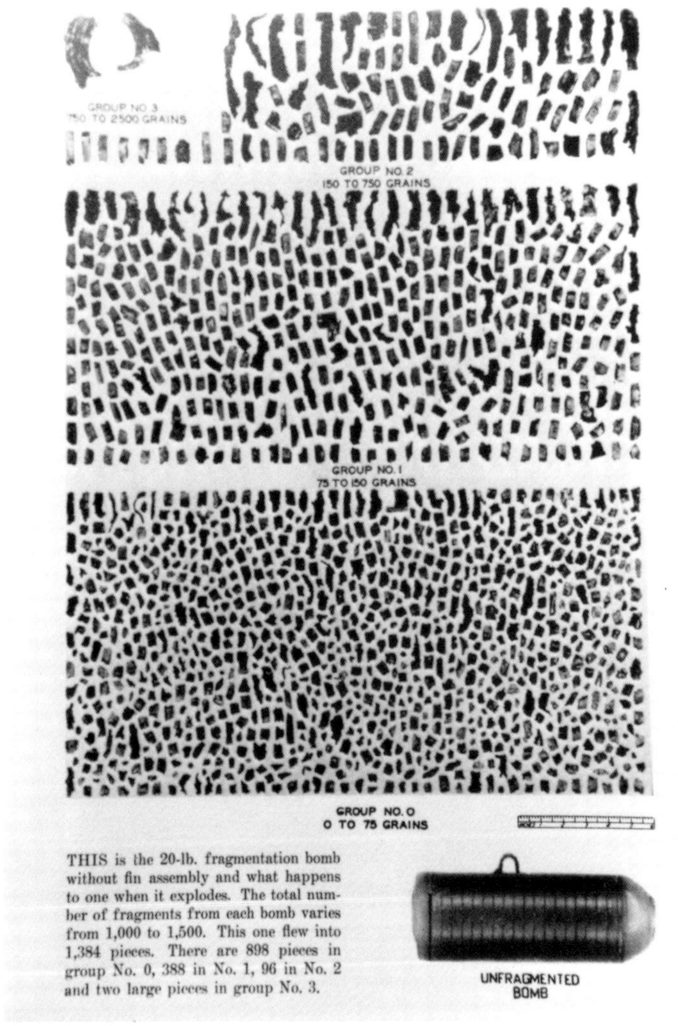

The 1,384 pieces from an exploded 20lb. fragmentation bomb tore holes into anything near its explosion. (USAF)

The trajectories of the GP and fragmentation bombs were different and required different aiming techniques.

In general fighter-bombers attacked German armored and troop concentrations, artillery positions, and positions in open areas with fragmentation bombs. Anti-personnel frags were satisfactory against enemy troops if they were not dug in, or while they were advancing over terrain that had little cover. Anti-material frags dropped on aircraft, exploding at 200ft., had the fragments penetrate wings or fuselage, fuel tanks, tires and control wires, and perforate radiators and intercoolers. Ground crews needed 25 to 30 hours to repair aircraft damaged by fragments of bombs hitting 90ft. or less from the aircraft.

Fragmentation bombs were not utilized as extensively in the ETO, as there were fewer opportunities than in Italy, since they needed to be dropped on concentrated troops to be effective. The exception was their use in air attacks in the Falaise Gap, where M41 frag clusters and the 260lb. anti-personnel fragmentation bombs wrecked havoc on retreating German troops and thin-skinned vehicles. Various combinations were carried on the wing pylons or under the fuselage, depending on the weight. They were carried in clusters of 12 to 24 20lb. bombs with two tandem bomb rows. A release vane began to operate after the cluster was dropped to scatter the bombs. Eight frags could be wrapped around a 500lb. bomb. Pilots preferred to carry these bombs on the wing pylons rather than the belly shackle, as a takeoff crash or a hung up (unjettisoned) of these sensitive bombs could detonate on landing.

Armorer tail-fusing a 500 lb. bomb. (USAF)

Armorer nose fusing a 500lb. that has been hung on its shackle. (USAF)

Fuses

Fuses on bombs were timed to give the attacking aircraft the ability to escape the explosion and allow the bomb to penetrate deeper, making the explosion more effective. Before a mission bombs were mounted to the underside of the wing by a shackle. The bomb was then pre-armed by screwing a fuse into the nose, or sometimes the tail of the bomb. All bomb fuses were unarmed before their release. While unarmed a mechanical restraint prevented the firing pin from moving and firing the primer. Both nose and tail fuses were armed after the bombs were hung on the shackles. An arming wire was secured to the shackles and was run through a hole in the fuse, from which the tagged safety pin had been removed. The tagged pins

A 358th Fighter Group plane lays burned out on the runway as fragmentation bombs exploded when the aircraft's wheels collapsed on a soft area on a grass field. (USAF)

from each bomb fuse were given to the pilot. When the bomb was released the arming wire was withdrawn from the fuse, making the bomb "live." As the bombs fell away from the aircraft the arming wire was pulled from the fuse(s), and the arming vanes or propellers began to rotate loose and fell away after a few hundred feet, arming the bomb. If the need to release a bomb over friendly territory arose the mechanical arming wire was released with the bomb, preventing fusing.

Simply, the fuse of a bomb consisted of two parts: the firing pin and detonator. The detonator, usually fulminate of mercury, exploded when struck by the firing pin. Lying between the detonating charge and the firing pin were safety devices that prevented the firing pin from hitting the detonator during shipment and handling. An intermediary charge between the fuse and the main charge was used to produce the maximum explosive effect. Multiple fuses were sometimes fitted to insure detonation. These could be in the nose, tail, or center body.

Fuses were classified according to their position on the bomb and their operating principle. The type of fuse installed depended on the type of target, the method of attack, and the type of explosive used. Bomb fuses were classified according to arming method:

Arming vane type
Arming vane type with mechanical delay
Arming pin type
Arming pin type with time delay
Time

Any of these types could be used in the nose or tail of a bomb. Nose fuses, except time, functioned on impact by direct action, e.g. the firing pin was driven into the primer at the instant the nose of the bomb hit the target. Tail fuses functioned by inertia, e.g. the plunger, which carried the firing pin, continued its forward motion as the bomb was slowed or stopped by the resistance of the target. Thus, the nose fuse was slightly faster than the tail fuse.

The 500lb. GP bomb with an instantaneous fuse was effective against most military installations not protected by reinforced concrete or masonry. When fused with eight to eleven second delayed fusing it was used to cut railway lines by driving the bomb into an embankment on a minimum altitude skip-bombing attack. With six to twelve hour delayed fusing the bomb was dropped on roads to discourage nighttime road movement, or in rivers to frustrate barge traffic.

Bomb Markings

GP-TNT:	Olive with yellow nose and tail bands. Marked on nose: G.P. 500lb./AN-M64A1/TNT/ S1HTA
GP-COMP B:	Olive with double yellow nose and tail bands with inner bands marked COMP. B: Marked on nose: G.P. /500lb./AN-M64A1/COMP./ B/ S1HWA
GP-TRITONAL:	Olive with triple yellow nose and tail bands with inner bands marked TRITONAL: Marked on nose: G.P./500lb./AN-M64A1/ TRITONAL/ S1ICA
INCENDIARY:	Silver-white with three red bands: top middle and bottom Marked on nose: INCENDIARY/ 500lb./AN M 76/PT 4
CHEMICAL:	Silver-gray with green band(s): One green band: non-persistent gas Two green bands: persistent gas Marked on nose: C.G. GAS/thlb./AN M 78

Bomb Effects on Targets

Target	Bomb Weight	Fuse	Point to Hit on Target Effective Radius	Expected Results
Parked Aircraft	100lb.	Instant.	Within 75-100 feet of aircraft	Serious structural damage
	250lb.	"	Within 100-125 feet	"
Bridge*	1,000lb.	Delay	Piers & approach spans	Displacement of piers & span Collapse of 1+ span
Railway tracks	100lb.	Instant.	Within 7ft. of track	Cut rails
			Center of rail yard	Destroy 20ft. of track
	250lb.	"	Within 9ft. of track	Cut rails
				Destroy 30ft. of track
Buildings**	500lb.	Delay	Building itself	Penetrate floors, major structural damage, fires
Underground	250lb	Delay	15ft. either side	Cave in or penetrate walls
fortified positions	500lb.	"	above	
***	1,000lb.	"		

* Concrete reinforced and supported by piers
** Brick, steel concrete composite
*** Bomb weight depends on type of reinforcement

All these bombs had dark lettering and the lot number marked on mid-section, and all but the chemical bomb had the arsenal named on the mid-section.

LEAFLET:	Olive with no stripes Marked on long axis: BOMB LEAFLET/thlbs. Size M 105A1/LOT #
23lb.FRAGMENTATION:	Olive with yellow bands on the top of the first segment Marked on first segment: FRAG/AN M 81/Lot #
4lb. FRAGMENTATION:	Olive with yellow band on each side Marked on side M83
PWP SMOKE:	Silver-gray with yellow band on middle and bottom section Marked in yellow lettering: 100lb./M47A4

The D-22 bomb pylon with sway braces and B-10 shackle exposed. (USAF)

The D-22 bomb pylon with its streamlined fairing in place when not in use. (USAF)

D-22 bomb pylon with shackle sway brace screws in place to hold a 500lb. bomb. (USAF)

Bomb pylons and shackles

In January 1944 D-15 and D-16 pylon adapter kits were sent to P-47 units to be installed in the field, and were installed on all production aircraft. The streamlined pylon containing the B-10 shackle was positioned outboard of each wheel well, and the pylon was capped by a fairing when no bombs were attached. Later, a smaller pylon, the D-22 with anti-sway braces, was introduced. The Interstate Bomb Shackle was rated at 2,000 pound capacity.

Bomb Loading

A special bomb hoist mounted on a trailer or the bed of a truck was used to transport the bombs from the dump to the aircraft. A small trailer carried bombs and lifted the bomb into position with a hydraulic jack, called the Fighter Aircraft Bomb Loading Device.

Bomb-hoist truck delivers a 500lb. bomb to a bomb dolly that will be pushed under the wing of a waiting P-47 of the 358th Fighter Group. (USAF)

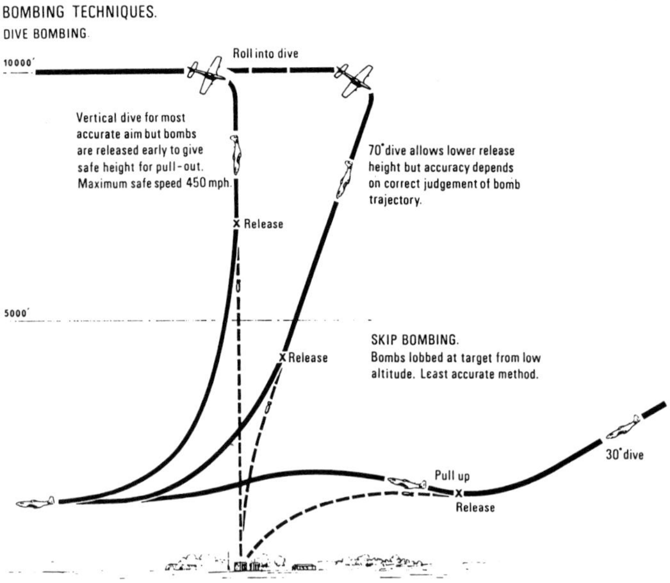

Bombing Techniques:

Dive-Bombing

Dive-bombing was an attack from 8,000 to 15,000 feet, at angles of 20 to 50 degrees, with the bombs being released from 6,000 to 1,500 feet. Since the bomb release was over 1,000 feet instantaneous fuses were used. Dive-bombing tactics were determined by target type, AA concentration, and weather/wind. High-level dive-bombing attacks were made at steep angles, usually between 60 and 70 degrees, which were imperative for accuracy. It was difficult for the pilot to see straight down to the target without tipping the wing. Target identification needed to be precise but was difficult, and often the leader would use the R/T to ID the target to his pilots. As he was about to dive the leader would R/T "Bomb switches on," followed by "Diving in 10 seconds" and "Diving now." The dive was braked by dropping the main gear, whose fairing acted as a dive brake. This would allow the pilot time to line up the target before releasing his bombs. Following their leader into the attack, the pilots released their bombs at 2,000 to 3,000 feet. After releasing the bombs an intense evasive turn was made in a predetermined direction before reforming in line abreast. If the target were heavily defended, the attack would be made out of the sun and/or from two directions in order to reduce AA proficiency.

Col. F.C. Gray of the 78th Fighter Group described diving angles (*Down to the Deck*, ibid.):

"Dive, skip and glide-bombing when first attempted in the Group gave some pretty poor results. However, due to the many such missions we have had lately. Our efforts have begun to bear fruit. This has solely been due to the intensive practice and experience of each individual pilot. It is my belief that efficient fighter-bombing depends upon practice and more practice with supervision. The most accuracy results from steep dives. By that I mean dives in excess of 60 degrees. The average pilot will swear that he has made an attack from 60-70 degrees, when in reality he has been diving at 30-40 degrees. I have personally stooged around near the target on several occasions and observed this tendency among my own pilots. We try to impress on them the fact that they are not approaching a 60-70 degree dive until they seem to be going straight down. I personally approach the target from 180 degrees to my intended direction of attack and when it has passed under my wing halfway as nearly as I can judge, ease back slightly on the throttle, give my rudder tab two twists left and split-S to the attack. I prefer starting at about 8-9,000 feet and releasing at 3,000. When cloud bases have caused lower approaches however, I generally attack from 90 degrees, flying very close on to the target on the approach in order to make the dive steep. My best results have been on this type attack rolling down from 5-6,000 feet and releasing at 2,000 feet or lower. The P-47 comes around nicely at low release altitudes, even when shackle failure leaves one with two 500 pounders."

Low level attacks were usually at 20 to 30 degrees, with the bombs being released at 800 feet at high speed and short range in order to evade small arms and light flak and the burst and debris from their bomb explosions. Minimum altitude bombing was attacking on the level and on deck. It was the most accurate, but also

Col. F.C. Gray of the 78th Fighter Group. (USAF)

Capt. Wayne Blickenstaff, P-47 pilot for the 353rd Fighter Group. (USAF)

the most dangerous unless AA was not present, or had been suppressed by an artillery anti-flak barrage.

Col. Joe Mason, CO of the 352nd Fighter Group discusses dive-bombing (*Down to the Deck*, ibid.):

"Bombing with a fighter aircraft is 100% personal skill and it's just like playing basketball, the more you practice, the more baskets you can sink. We, in the VIII Fighter Command have not had the time, ranges or equipment to practice fighter-bombing to even approach the degree that could be obtained. But we are basically an escort outfit and in that we have had sufficient practice to come closer to perfection. The score board shows that."

Capt. Wayne Blickenstaff, P-47 pilot for the 353rd Fighter Group, describes dive-bombing in *Down to the Deck*, ibid.):

"In my opinion any consideration of air to ground firing would not be complete without touching on dive-bombing. Being a member of the group that pioneered in dive-bombing in this theater, I am particularly interested in it. After experimenting both in practice and operational dive-bombing missions, we soon found certain principles that were essential to success. For instance, vertical dive-bombing requires individual aiming and release from an altitude of not more than 10,000 feet. Without these essentials accuracy is sacrificed. Coordinated flying is of course necessary and without that old ball in the center one can not reasonably to do accurate dive-bombing. It is to be emphasized that the plane must be properly trimmed. In this connection, it is well to remember that aileron as well as rudder trim must constantly be used. This means a well-planned run without having to hurry through it. For the average pilot tenseness due to flak encountered is the main cause for haste and sloppy flying. Thus provisions should be made to neutralize flak as soon as possible. For this purpose we carry a flight with frags or 250 pound general-purpose bombs to take care of the flak positions. Another effective means of neutralizing the ground fire is to detail a flight to observe for and strafe any fire encountered.

After D-Day the type of targets and the bad weather prohibited the use of vertical dive-bombing. As a consequence glide bombing and skip bombing were used. It was soon found by operational experience that glide bombing had to be at least 30 degrees, otherwise, even the 1,000 pounders will fail to stick. This likewise required coordinated flying during the dive. Proper briefing to include thorough study of contour and flak maps pays dividends. Contour maps are especially necessary for planning attacks on bridges. Glide bombing allows us to release within 2,000 feet of the target with the result that greater accuracy is accomplished. In this connection, it is well to warn against releasing to close to the target when instantaneous are used. Sad experience taught us that 500 feet was needed for 250 pounders, 800 feet for 500 pounders and 1,500 feet for 1,000 pounders. These are minimum altitudes."

Skip-Bombing/Glide-Bombing

Skip-bombing was a variation of minimum bombing, but the attacking aircraft went into a 10-20 degree dive, releasing at altitudes of 100 to 500 feet and pulling out just over the target. This method gave the pilot more visibility, but also made him even more vulnerable to flak. Glide-bombing was a high speed, accelerating attack delivered at 30 to 55 degrees without the use of dive brakes. The initial element of surprise and the built up speed made the attacker a difficult target going in and out.

Col. Thomas Christian, P-51 pilot for the 361st Fighter Group, discussed skip-bombing and glide-bombing (*Down to the Deck*, ibid.):

"We are in favor of bombing with fighter aircraft but recommend that nothing less than a 500lb. bomb be used. The average bridge encountered in occupied territory can usually be damaged but not readily destroyed by fighter-bombers. It can be more easily damaged by skip-bombing with a 500lb. bomb and a delay fuse. Dive-bombing is much too inaccurate for pinpoint targets. Our fighter-bombers have been very accurate in cutting railways by glide-bombing with 500lb. bombs, four second delayed fuses. Marshaling yards, having a concentration of Freight cars have been dive-bombed successfully. We still believe that a flight of B-24's can do more damage by bombing than a group of fighters can do by dive-bombing. It must be remembered that, in skip-bombing, the bomb must be skipped into something solid. There have been a few instances in this Group (361st) where 250 pound and 500 pound bombs were skipped into locomotives and freight cars but due to the speed and weight of the bombs they went through the target and exploded harmlessly in adjacent fields. After releasing their bombs, pilots must take immediate evasive action by turning sharply to the left or right; otherwise, they will stand a chance of being blown up by their own bombs which may skip along underneath the plane."

Rockets

Basics

The rocket incorporated a warhead and a motor that was a propellant powder. Rocket warheads included high explosive in thin and thick-walled heads, solid shot, incendiary, smoke, and chemical. Depending on the target, the rocket was nose and sometimes base-fused. In most rockets the motor comprised most of the length. The rocket motor was comprised of the propellant charge, motor tube, nozzles, and powder trap or grid. The motor propellant was a smokeless powder composed of nitrocellulose and ingredients to generate high-pressure gases rapidly. The mass of smokeless powder used in a rocket motor was called a grain no matter its size. The exhaust of high-pressure gases released by the burning of the powder propelled the rocket body. The rate at which gases were generated by the burning of the propellant depended on the amount of the exposed surface of the grain. Even burning was best achieved by manufacturing the grain in the shape of a tube. The grain was contained in the motor tube, which had to withstand the gas pressure exerted equally in all directions. The motor tube was open at the rear end, through which the gases escaped, providing about 70% of the thrust. The gases passed through the nozzle, expanding to a lower pressure with increased velocity, and by pushing against the outward flaring part of the nozzle provided the remaining 30% of the thrust.

Rockets had several advantages. The rocket was very simple in construction and employment. Because the rocket motor caused no recoil, the warhead could be much heavier and of a larger caliber than the airborne cannon shell. The rocket was self-propelled, and so would have a much greater impact velocity. As with dive-bombing, rocket tactics were determined by target type, AA concentration, and weather/wind. The rocket was difficult to fire accurately and demanded a high degree of skill. In operations, the distraction of having to identify an often camouflaged or moving target under AA fire was reason enough to diminish accuracy. The rocket's weight and weight distribution caused it to have a curved trajectory, therefore it needed to be fired at a range of 1,000 to 2,000 yards, which put the pilot in jeopardy from AA and ground fire. Beyond that range the trajectory became too pronounced for any hope of accurate fire. The fighter-bomber needed to remain stable as it launched the rocket. If the pilot skidded or turned the aircraft at launch, the rocket's low launching speed would cause a large error in aiming it at a target. Pilots were likely to undershoot their targets either because they launched their rockets at too long a range, or flew too slowly at the lower dive angles. Wind also needed to be considered accurately, as a 10mph wind could cause a 15 foot miss in line and a 9 foot miss in range, which was the difference in scoring a hit or a near miss, as in the case of a tank or gun position. The modification of the gyroscopic gunsight in late 1944 compensated for the gravity drop of the rocket, and also for the effect of the wind and target movement. Against heavily defended targets pilots were advised to make a steep 60 degree dive at 7-8,000 feet and fire all rockets in salvo at about 4,000 feet at a range of 5,000 feet. On these strongly defended targets, doctrine stated that they should only be attacked once. If the target were lightly defended, the pilots were to make a shallow dive of 20-30 degrees at 3-4,000 feet and to fire them in pairs from 1,500 feet at a range of 3,000 feet. However, in practice the pilots disregarded the prescribed tactics and developed their own tactics.

It was estimated that the salvo of all eight rockets would result in a one-in-twenty chance of hitting a target the size of a Panzer tank. Despite their inaccuracy the rocket was more accurate than the free-fall bomb, but much less than strafing with machine gun or cannon, which, in turn, had much less striking power to inflict significant damage when hitting the target. The HVAR had the explosive effect of a 155mm shell. A rule of thumb on rocket targets stated that any target suitable for artillery fire was a suitable rocket target. Rocket attacks created a morale problem for the enemy that was more of a factor than the actual destructive damage they caused. Scuttlebutt spread among German troops that exaggerated the effect of the rocket attack. The noise and the sight of the diving fighter-bomber and then of the launched rockets unnerved the German troops on the receiving end of the attack.

Development

In 1941 British and American scientists exchanged information on developing the rocket as a modern military weapon. Contracts for research and development were let at various universities and industrial companies. Labs at Cal Tech (CIT) and George Washington were engaged in all aspects of rocket R&D, while Duke, the Universities of Wisconsin and Minnesota, and Hercules Powder Co. researched propellants. Budd Induction Heating Co. and Bell Telephone Labs concentrated on the engineering design of rocket components and equipment. The major breakthrough was the adaptation of the British dry-extrusion process for manufacturing high performance large grain propellant. As the U.S. had no rocket designed for aircraft use, in June 1942 the AAF began to adapt rockets developed under these R&D contracts for aircraft use at the Material Center at Wright Field. U.S. Army Ordnance had designed the M-8, a 37lb, three-foot, 4.5-inch diameter rocket for use by ground forces as the "Bazooka." The 4.5-inch RP had an explosive filling of 5lb., a launching speed of 800-850fps, and a maximum range of 4,600 yards. The first M-8s were fired from the original "Bazooka-type" metal launching tubes (M-14) that were found to be too unwieldy at 10ft. and too heavy at 190lbs. Lightweight tubes manufactured from flameproof plastic (M-10) soon replaced the M-14. Initially lightweight metals, such as magnesium and aluminum, were in short supply, and General Electric and the Ordnance Department developed a special paper impregnated with a plastic compound and fabricated the 80lb. "Launcher, Rocket, 3-tube, 4.5-inch Aircraft, M-10." However, the flaming rocket exhaust limited the life of these composite plastic tubes, and when light metals became available the 3-tube interchangeable M-15 magnesium tubes of comparable weight (86lbs.) replaced them. The rockets were fired from three or four (per wing) six-foot underwing tubes mounted either in M-10 or M-15 clusters, and had an effective range of 800 to a 1,000 yards. Individual electrical circuits fired the rockets. The rocket had folded fins attached to the rear of the motor that opened when it left the tube to stabilize it in flight. Although the tubes could be dropped after use, field trials revealed that the launching apparatus severely decreased performance and further development was necessary. The first American aircraft to fire rockets (M-8s in tubular cluster launchers) in combat were B-25s of the 10th Air Force in Burma in early 1944. The final report on these tests and field trials was dated 28 February 1944. It concluded that the 4.5-inch, M-8/M-10 rocket and launcher combination was effective in frontal attacks against area targets, but was not suitable for use against point targets, such as armor or pillboxes due to the wide dispersion of fired rockets. Positive aspects of the tests were the

Good photo of a loaded 4.5-inch bazooka-type triple rocket launcher and a 500lb. bomb hung on a wing pylon with sway braces clearly evident. (USAF)

Armorers aligning the "Bazooka-type" rocket launching tubes on a 57th Fighter Group P-47 in Italy. (USAF)

P-51D armed with triple bazooka-type rocket tubes. (USAF)

selection of the P-47D as the rocket fighter of choice and the replacement of the launching tubes by slightly modified British MK rail launchers under the supervision of RAF personnel in December 1943. These British launchers were the prototypes for later American RP launchers. In tests the harmonization of the rockets was accomplished by aligning the rails with the wing guns, with the pilot using an MK VIII gunsight for both weapons. Between December 1943 and July 1944 there were seven P-47D groups stationed in Italy, but none used the rocket.

American Rockets

3.5-inch Rocket

The 3.5-inch AR consisted of a motor 3.5-inches in diameter, hence the designation. The motor was attached to a 20lb. solid steel head, giving the projectile a 65-inch length and 54lb. weight. Its maximum velocity was 1,175fps. (plus the speed of the carrying aircraft), and its accurate range was 1,000 yards. The primary use of this rocket was against submarines, as the solid steel head could easily penetrate the hull of a sub even if it was traveling at periscope depth.

4.5-inch Rocket

The first combat aerial rocket was the 4.5 inch M-8 or M-10 types, that was 4.5 inches in diameter, about three feet long, and weighed 40lbs. The forward (head) portion contained a nose fuse and five pounds of HE. The aft portion consisted of the motor, which contained the propellant charge that was a solvent base, wet extruded grain with zone charges. The charge was a rapid-burning type, lasting about one-tenth second, and gave it excellent acceleration characteristics, making it an ideal medium range weapon (800 yards). Its accurate range was about 750 yards at a maximum velocity of 865fps. (plus the speed of the firing aircraft). At this range the 4.5-inch rocket could penetrate one inch of homogenized face-hardened steel and about one foot of reinforced concrete. The rocket was carried in three launcher tubes clustered together and suspended under each wing, so as not to interfere with the normal bomb load or external fuel tanks. The launcher tubes were bore-sighted to harmonize the rockets with the machine guns, so one gunsight setting could be used for both. Each rocket carried a nose fuse that could only be adjusted on the ground for a .015 second delay or for instantaneous setting. The round was placed in the tube from the rear and fastened in face, and then the electrical firing connections were made. The rocket was fired electrically through a small cockpit control box and intervalometer. This allowed selective firing or salvo firing with a one-tenth interval. Contact was made with the ignition circuit through two metal rings on the closure at the back end of the motor on the early type rockets. Later models had a double contact, single prong plug attached to the rear end. The plug was inserted in jacks on the launchers.

Operations

In early 1944, under the ATSC, the AAF Army Ordnance established a rocket-testing center at the Army Air Field at Dover, DE, with 200 rocket scientists and technicians under Col. Donald B. Diehl. The Navy and NDRC also did further work. Rockets were tested, launching installations and methods were developed and refined, and the effectiveness of rockets against various targets was evaluated. The aircraft best suited for rocket attacks was one with good maneuverability at high speed: fighters, then dive-bombers and torpedo bombers. It was found that rocket accuracy depended on pilot aiming error, altitude, and rocket dispersion after launching. Inaccuracies decreased as the speed of the firing aircraft increased. The AAF claimed that at 250mph a trained pilot was able to put half of his rockets within a 16-foot circle at 400 yards!

By February 1944, only four months before D-Day, the "rocket question" remained unresolved in the USAAF. On 5 May 1944 the 9th Air Force finally began trials using the P-47 equipped with prototype MK V rocket projectors. These jettisonable installations were attached to standard bomb shackles and could carry four M-8 or M-10 rockets on each carrier. There was not enough time to conduct effective trials, standardize the fittings, or train pilots before D-Day, so the 9th Air Force's P-47s carried no rockets into combat on D-Day.

In August, four 8th Air Force fighter groups were supplied with four sets of 4.5-inch triple-tube rocket installations with 60 M-8/M-10 rocket installations. The 56th and 353rd Fighter Groups were immediately equipped with trial installations, but the 78th and 356th met delays due to lack of installation tools. All four 8th Air Groups participated in a few lackluster, half-hearted ground attack rocket missions. First and foremost, 8th Air Force pilots thought of themselves as fighter pilots, and if they had to be ground attack pilots they preferred strafing and the 500lb. bomb, which was easier to use and had a lower AA fire risk. On 17 August the 56th Fighter Group, led by deputy group CO, Lt.Col. David Schilling, attacked the Braine-le-Compt area firing M-10 rockets with mixed results. Schilling was able to destroy four rail cars, but he only proved that a highly experienced pilot could achieve good results. The P-47s had no special sight to aim the rockets, but needed to use machine gun fire to aim the rockets. Success was correlated to combat experience and pilot skill, and 8th Air Force bomber escort pilots had received no training for ground attack. Again, despite the potential of the rocket, by mid-September the rocket tubes were removed from 8th Air Force P-47s. The inevitable disagreements within the USAAF high command occurred. XIX TAC commander, O.P. Weyland, correctly favored saving the rockets for use against tanks and armored targets, but throughout the summer of 1944 the limited rocket supply was wasted haphazardly.

Despite this moderate success that was as good as bombing results, American pilots preferred bombing targets to "rocketeering." The rockets were found to be inaccurate on pinpoint targets, and the tubes reduced the Thunderbolt's performance after the rockets were salvoed. Pilots found other faults with the rocket. When the pilots received their new rockets they were given a chart that listed the sight settings as a function of dive angle, air speed, and distance to the target. Pilots found it very difficult to correlate all these factors during a firing pass. The P-47 rocket installation had a serious disadvantage, as the machine guns could not be fired until the rockets were salvoed. The rockets were located under the chutes that ejected the machine gun belt links and shell casings that would break the rocket firing wire. Probably the biggest fault was that a rocket had to be fired within a 1,000 yards of the target to attain any accuracy, and this range exposed the fighter-bomber to accurate AA and ground fire.

However, the RAF 2nd TAF was equipped with RP-equipped (RP=Rocket Projectile) Typhoons, which were instrumental in preventing German tanks from reaching the front. Studies of the 2nd TAF's rocket-equipped 124 Squadron show that it only destroyed 12 tanks in June using 3,700 rockets for an immense expenditure of 308 rockets per tank destroyed! The RAF used long rails to give the rocket its initial accuracy, but experience found that the fixed fin rocket tended to align itself with the air stream, much like a weathervane. Tests showed comparable accuracy could be obtained with shorter rails. The term "zero-rail" referred to the lack of guide rails, as the rail actually guided the rocket for only about an inch. With these posts the top speed of the fighter was only decreased six to nine miles per hour. The rockets were aligned parallel to both the centerline of the fuselage and the aircraft's line of thrust. Rockets were fired in pairs, one from each wing, to maintain equal wing loads. The zero-rail launcher went into U.S. service in the spring of 1944.

In spring 1943 the California Institute of Technology and the U.S. Navy, under a contract to the Office of Scientific Research and Development, actively pursued an aerial rocket development program. Their research quickly produced a number of rockets and launching techniques. The three rocket types were: the 3.5-inch aircraft rocket (AR); the 5-inch aircraft rocket (AR); and the 5-inch high velocity aircraft rocket (HVAR), which were all fin-stabilized and intended for a assortment of different targets. A few P-47 squadrons were equipped with eight HVARs, and were particularly effective against the Germans at St. Lo. During this period the HVAR was produced by CIT, and about 100 rockets per day were airshipped from California to the east coast, then to USAAF airfields in France. So it was that civilian scientists and Navy developers and testers would have the Air Force use the HVAR in combat.

5-inch AR and HVAR Rocket

The same motor in the 3.5-inch rocket propelled the 5-inch AR. The 5-inch AR had a 5-inch diameter warhead that increased its weight to 80lbs., but was about the same length as the 3.5-inch AR. The larger head slowed the weapon to about 850fps. This rocket was intended for use against targets where high explosive effect, not penetration was important. The celebrated 5-inch HVAR was developed from the 5-inch AR, employing the warhead of the 5-inch AR attached to the 5-inch diameter motor. The rocket's length was standardized at six feet and weighed 140lbs., which included eight pounds of HE in the warhead. The propellant was a non-solvent base, dry extruded grain. It had a comparatively slow burning time (1.2 seconds) that gave it a slower acceleration with a higher maximum velocity (1,375fps plus the speed of the firing aircraft) and greater accurate range (1,000 yards) than the 4.5-inch rocket.

5-inch HVAR Rockets are being unloaded from a bomb trailer. (USAF)

The 406th Fighter Group combat tested the 5-inch HVAR rocket fired from zero-length launchers. Three 500lb. bombs added to the P-47's punch. (USAF)

AAF Public relations drawing of a 5-inch HVAR rocket test attack near Marigny, France. The US P-47 was flown by GC H.W. Dean of the RAF and knocked out two German Mark V Panther tanks. (USAF)

At 1,000 yards it was able to penetrate 1.75 inches of homogenized face-hardened steel and three feet of reinforced concrete. The armor-piercing plug in its head was capable of penetrating reinforced concrete and armor, and could be replaced with a nose fuse set for instantaneous detonation on impact. A lightweight (15lb. for a six rocket installation) zero-rail launcher was developed to launch these rockets, and was made up of two streamlined posts attached to the underside of the wing. The Mark 5 rocket launcher consisted of four posts mounted on a forward plate, and four on a rear plate attached by screws on the outer wing surface. Lugs attached to bands encircling the rocket and fitted into slotted plates on the bottom of the posts, one at the forward end of the rocket and the other at the rear. The zero-rail slung the projectile about six inches below the wing surface, parallel to the long axis of the aircraft. The HVAR's forward mounting lug fit into a slot on the bottom of the Mark 5's forward post. The rocket's rear section mounting lug fit into the lower front of the post. An aft-facing socket in the rear post accom modated the rocket ignition wire that connected to the rocket motor for electrical ignition similar to that firing the 4.5 inch rocket. The launcher fixed the initial direction of the rocket's flight by limiting the motion of its center of gravity until it left the launcher. The fin-stabilized rocket fired from the zero rail launcher flew a "line of flight" attitude, and its trajectory could not be harmonized with the guns. A different sight setting was required for firing guns and rockets. There was no danger if both machine guns and rockets were fired at the same time.

The Ordnance Department of the USAAF had done tests and trials using the rocket for nearly two years, but rocket accuracy was inconsistent, and the bulky launching tubes so reduced aircraft performance even after rocket launch that P-47 pilots preferred dive-bombing attacks. Once a bomb was released the shackles had little effect on aircraft performance. It was decided that operational trials could resolve the "rocket issue." Col. H.L. Donicht of the AAF, Drs. C.C. Lauritsen and Carl Anderson of CIT, and RAF GC H.W. Dean flew to England to supervise the installation and combat tests. In July 1944, several P-47Ds of the "rocketeer" 513th Fighter Squadron of the 406th Fighter Group were equipped to carry four HVAR 5-inch rockets, two under each wing. On 17 July American HVAR rockets were used for the first time in the ETO when Col. Anthony Grossetta led three flights of four P-47s from their base at Ashland, England, to attack marshaling yards (Tiger-Quail) near Nevers, France. The first pass was made on a flak tower protecting the yards that suffered a direct hit, putting it out of commission. The Thunderbolts dove on a concentration of over 50 locomotives, firing 48 rockets, 38 of them hitting 25 valuable locomotives. Three repair shops and a roundhouse were also damaged. On the 26th the first American rocket attacks against German armor were made with nine tanks destroyed (four by rockets, three by strafing, and two by bombs) and three damaged (all by rockets). On the next day three rocket-equipped flights attacked the German airdrome at Coulommiers. A total of 37 rockets were fired at 1,000 yards at a 30-degree dive. Moderate damage was done, as one large hangar,

A photo of the first of the German Mark V tanks that was stopped by the rocket attack and finished off by .50 cal. machine gun strafing. (USAF)

four small hangars, a fuel dump, and one Me-110 were hit. A rail bridge at Montford was claimed destroyed by seven rockets. In a later mission several Luftwaffe FW-190s attacked rocket-carrying P-47s, and four Thunderbolts were shot down. On 13 August, the 513th attacked four heavy and one light German tank and destroyed all five. The attack was against German Mark V Panther tanks moving along a road near Marigny, France. It was led by Group Captain H.W. Dean, who had been a RAF Typhoon rocket expert. By September the 513th Squadron had flown 323 sorties, firing 1,117 rockets and claimed:

Target	Destroyed	Damaged	Totals
Tanks	85	29	114
Armored Cars	15	1	16
Motor Vehicles	164	23	187

The 79th Fighter Group was the first group to use rockets in Italy on an 86th Squadron armed recce led by Col. Melvin Neilsen along the east Italian coast. It was assigned to use three 4.5-inch bazooka tube rockets mounted under each wing on a combat trial basis. Initial missions were ineffective, as these rockets were found to be generally unreliable, since their fins would not always deploy. The HE explosive warheads were ineffective against the heavy armor of the German Panzer. Aiming was difficult, and took time and skill to accomplish. A hit could easily destroy M/T, railway rolling stock, locomotives, and gun positions. But against larger targets, such as buildings, they could be very effective. The first effective use was on 6 November 1944 during an attack on the Brenner Rail Line at Verona and claimed 18 direct hits on the main buildings and 23 hits on the transformer stations in a combined attack with bomb-carrying DAF P-40s. On the 9th the 86th and 87th Squadrons attacked the German stronghold at Forli, where the British 4th Infantry Division was being stymied. The attack hit the fortress with 26 rockets, and it was taken a few hours later. However, a diving P-47 had its rocket tubes fouled in its ailerons, turning the fighter over on its back and then crashing into the ground. During the trials the group fired 444 rockets with 97 claimed as direct hits. The group continued to use rockets increasingly throughout the remainder of the war.

A 9th Air Force Report (No. 59) entitled *Rocket Status in the 9th Air Force* (19 Sept. 1944) concluded that rockets could be fired at longer range than .50 machine guns, reducing the threat from AA fire. Rockets had more penetration capability than machine gun rounds or general-purpose bombs, which tended to break up upon contact with the target, and were more accurate than dive-bombing. The report advocated further use of rockets, but nonetheless, the 9th Air Force never made large-scale use of the rocket despite its potential. In the MTO and ETO U.S. fighter-bombers never adopted rockets on a large scale. The 9th Air Force utilized only 13,959 during the war, as compared to 222,515 used by the RAF 2nd TAF, which preferred the rocket as its primary anti-tank and ground support weapon.

A photo of the second tank that was disabled by a HVAR and abandoned by its crew. (USAF)

U.S. Rockets

Characteristic	**4.5-inch M8**	**5-inch HVAR**
Maximum velocity (fps)	860	1,350
Burning time (sec.)	0.20	0.88
Weight (lb.)	38.4	136.5
HE weight (lb.)	5.3	8.2
HE wt. as % total wt.	13.8	6.2
Diameter (in.)	4.5	5.0
Length (in.)	34	28
# carried by aircraft	6	4
Total wt. of all rockets (lb.)	230	546
Total HE wt. (lb.)	31.8	32.8

Napalm ("Blaze bombs," "Fireballs")

Napalm is a powder that thickens gasoline to a gel. It was named so because it is made from the aluminum salts of naphennic and palmitic acids. A white phosphorous igniter ignited napalm. A 150-gallon tank could burn out a 90x150-foot area and were extremely difficult to extinguish. A fighter-bomber could carry three napalm tanks: 160 gallon on the centerline pylon and two 150 gallon on each wing pylon. The pilot used the engine cowl as a sighting device, releasing the tanks when the end of the cowl came over the target. Initially napalm was considered most effective for the incineration of entrenched enemy troops, but it was also used to destroy enemy camouflage and expose the target prior to rocket and bombing attacks. For this reason napalm tank(s) were mixed with bombs or rockets in attacks.

Napalm tanks were hung on the fighter empty and then filled with petroleum jelly, usually pumped from 50-gallon drums or a special fuel bowser. Various containers were tested, and the 108-

Napalm gel being hand-pumped from 55-gallon drums to drop tanks that used as napalm bombs by the 86th Fighter Group. (USAF)

Pumping cart used to pump napalm gel from 55-gallon drum into drop tank bombs. (USAF)

Napalm drop tank bomb with external igniter attached and the fuse of the internal igniter protruding through the gas cap. (USAF)

gallon paper composition tank was preferred and fused with an igniter. For best effect, the napalm tanks were to be tumbled onto the target. Officially named the "Class C-Fire Bomb," in the ETO they were usually referred to as "blaze bombs." Napalm tanks were usually painted flat yellow, although dark red and natural metal were common.

Napalm tanks were used in the ETO and MTO on a limited basis, but much more extensively in the PTO. In attacking hilly or mountainous areas, the fighter-bomber pilot dropped the napalm tank from a shallow angle, tumbling the tanks into enemy positions, which produced concentrated oval areas of fire on the ground. On flat terrain napalm was dropped from level flight at minimal altitude and produced long swaths of fire that engulfed the selected target, such as trenches, foxholes, or gun positions. Napalm exploded with a large, intense fireball that was fueled by the gelled gasoline mixture and would adhere to anything it touched as it spread forward upon impact. Dropped napalm spread and rushed into the trenches and foxholes, causing horrific casualties. Napalm attacks on defensive positions made up of rubble and shattered buildings drove enemy troops into the open. Until napalm was introduced German troops in wooded areas were attacked with fragmentation bombs, but their trenches and foxholes afforded them good cover. Concrete, stone, and steel-reinforced buildings and pillboxes were relatively immune to napalm, unless it engulfed the ventilation systems. It had a significant demoralizing effect on the troops defending the area around these fortifications, and they were forced to take refuge inside them to escape the napalm. This allowed U.S. infantry to flank the fortifications and get to their rear to utilize satchel charges, pole charges, or grenades to neutralize them.

In March 1944 the IX TAC conducted experiments on methods of dropping and exploding napalm. The napalm burned off too quickly on contact, and the tests were discontinued. In the Pacific flame-throwers were achieving surprising successes against heavily fortified Japanese positions, and Bradley's First Army was supplied with these flame-throwers with the improved napalm. General Pete Quesada requisitioned some of this new napalm and directed the 370th Fighter Group to carry out operational trials. By 16 July the aerial napalm bombs were ready for operations. Unfortunately, before the first test, one of the tanks exploded while a ground crew was hanging it to a P-38; one man was killed and another badly burned, and the Lightning was fused into a molten lump. Very late in the afternoon of the next day Col. Howard Nichols led three flights of 402nd Fighter Squadron napalm-carrying P-38s to buildings in a rail supply area near Coutances, France. Two droop snoot P-38s carrying HQ Brass accompanied the mission to observe the results. The P-38s, flying in tail, dropped to 3,500 feet about a mile from the target in a shallow 300mph dive and released their napalm at about 1,000 feet. Nine P-38s dropped 18 blaze bombs, while three stayed above for top cover. The 165-gallon tanks were not streamlined and tumbled onto the target, but the results were good, as eight bombs hit the buildings and set them on fire. the Lightnings then strafed the area, causing more damage.

In late 1944 the 12th Air Force fighter-bombers in Italy began to use "home-made" napalm bombs called "fuel tank incendiary bombs" on targets on the Gothic Line. They were constructed from

Napalm was introduced in Italy in early October 1944 where it was very efficient against German positions during the static ground fighting. (USAF)

external fuel tanks filled with thickened gasoline. They were intended to explode on impact with the ground by two igniters modified from an infantry hand grenade. In March 1945 there was a shortage of bombs, as the Allies outpaced their supply lines as they neared the Rhine. The 404th Fighter Group had captured a stock of German auxiliary fuel tanks, which they filled with napalm and then used a small incendiary bomb as an igniter. Although they worked well, spreading concentrated flame, these German tanks tumbled when dropped and thus could not be accurately aimed.

Drop Tanks

Of the developments in air power that affected the course of the war, the jettisonable auxiliary fuel tank was one of the most consequential. The "belly" or "drop" tank gave the fighter extended range to allow it to provide continuous escort to bomber formations, or reach deeper into enemy territory on fighter-bomber missions. During 1942 it became evident that the P-47 did not have sufficient range for bomber escort duties. Various wing-mounted tanks were tried, including two 75-gallon steel tanks, two 108-gallon metal or composition paper tanks, and two 150-gallon steel tanks. Single centerline fuselage paper or steel 108 gallon tanks, steel 150 gallon tank, and paper or steel 200-gallon tanks were used. Early tanks had glass connectors to the tank that were susceptible to breakage during taxiing. So-called "quick fix" crews were positioned near the ends of the runways to repair broken connectors. The P-51, which had very good range without tanks, used two wing-mounted 108-gallon paper tanks, nicknamed "babies," as more or less the standard drop tank. These large tanks were equipped with external sway braces to keep them from swinging and breaking loose in flight. Steel bands were wrapped around the middle of the tank for added strength. These paper tanks had flat, reinforced indentations where fuel and air connections and filler caps were located. At high altitudes the drop tanks needed to be pressurized by a vacuum pump so that the fuel could be drawn. The P-38 generally used two 165-

The 110-gallon metal tank was used mainly in the Pacific and Italian campaigns. (USAF)

Classic photo of a 375th Fighter Squadron/361st Fighter Group crew chief at Bottisham waiting for "his" Mustang to return from a mission on D-Day. The two tanks on the ground on the right are 108-gallon paper while the others are 75-gallon steel tanks. (USAF)

gallon steel tanks. The 110-gallon metal tank produced in 1944 was a development of the 75-gallon metal tank, and was mostly used in the Pacific and Italy with a few going to the ETO.

The lighter paper tanks were preferred to steel tanks by ground crews because they were easier to manhandle, and by pilots because they had less effect on flight characteristics. The auxiliary tank was attached behind the center of gravity, or in tandem under each wing, which affected aircraft handling characteristics. To remedy this situation; after using the main wing tank for takeoff the pilot switched to the fuselage tank and used it until there was about 30 gallons remaining. He then switched to and alternated between the external drop tanks, changing from one to another about every three quarters of an hour to an hour, and when empty jettisoned them. The routine for jettisoning the drop tanks was to switch to internal fuel first so as not to interrupt the flow of fuel to the engine. Upon entering combat the pilot jettisoned his drop tanks, but in the excitement more than a few pilots forgot to switch over to internal fuel and found their engine would stop in mid-dive. After jettison the pilot had the 30 gallons of fuselage fuel and a large amount of wing tank fuel left for combat and/or to return to base. But, if a drop tank did not deliver fuel to the engine or did not release, the sortie needed to be aborted, not only for the troubled fighter, but also for another pilot to escort him back to base. Both the Allies and Luftwaffe caused unknown amounts of collateral damage when they jettisoned thousands of drop tanks over the European countryside.

As discussed earlier, the addition of drop tanks on the P-51 supplanted the P-47 as an escort fighter and made it a fighter-bomber.

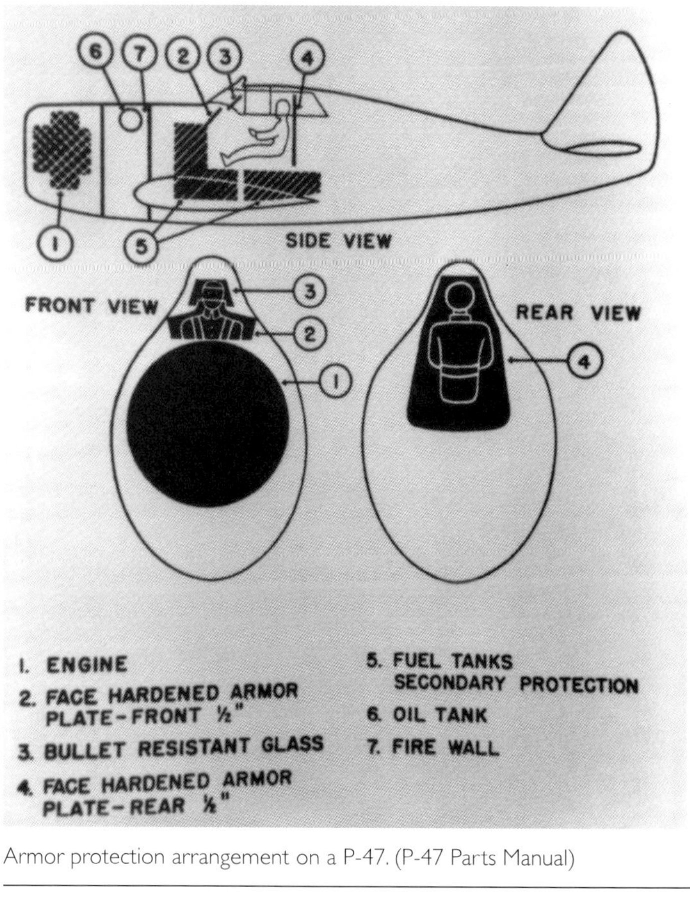

Armor protection arrangement on a P-47. (P-47 Parts Manual)

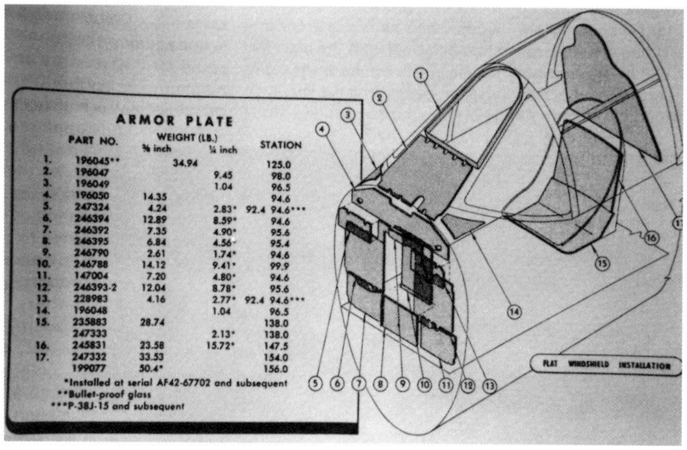

ARMOR PLATE

	PART NO.	WEIGHT (LB.) ⅜ inch	¼ inch	STATION
1.	196045**	34.94		125.0
2.	196047		9.45	98.0
3.	196049		1.04	96.5
4.	196050	14.35		94.6
5.	247324	4.24	2.83*	92.4 94.6***
6.	246394	12.89	8.59*	94.6
7.	246392	7.35	4.90*	95.6
8.	246395	6.84	4.56*	95.4
9.	246790	2.61	1.74*	94.6
10.	246788	14.12	9.41*	99.9
11.	147004	7.20	4.80*	94.6
12.	246393-2	12.04	8.78*	95.6
13.	228983	4.16	2.77*	92.4 94.6***
14.	196048		1.04	96.5
15.	235883	28.74		138.0
	247333		2.13*	138.0
16.	245831	23.58	15.72*	147.5
17.	247332	33.53		154.0
	199077	50.4*		156.0

*Installed at serial AF42-67702 and subsequent
**Bullet-proof glass
***P-38J-15 and subsequent

Pilot protection on a P-38. Armor plate parts are rated for weight and thickness. (P-38 Parts Manual)

The 9th Air Force adopted the use of the jettisonable drop tank, but the 8th Air Force had priority for its long-range escort duties. There was a shortage of tanks during the summer of 1944, as 108-gallon drop tank production in the UK could not keep pace with the needs of the 8th Air Force. By October the IX Air Service Command limited each of its depots to a maximum of 150 tanks. Ninth Air Force fighter-bomber operations were little affected by the lack of drop tanks, as their fighter-bombers, mostly P-47s, flew from ALGs close to the front and normally flew missions within internal fuel tank range. The longer armed recce missions were supplied with drop tanks. Eighth Air Force fighters used the drop tanks to range far into Germany on its "targets of opportunity" agenda after dropping off its bomber escort duty.

Pilot Protection and Safety

Armor

Theoretically, the ideal means to protect the pilot would be to armor the entire aircraft so that there would be no vulnerable areas. Of course, this aircraft probably would be so heavy that it would be unable to fly. So aircraft designers attempted to find a compromise between the "maximum protection/minimum weight" formulas in their designs. The ever-increasing speeds of the fighter during the war meant that the 400 mph+ fighter flew so fast as compared to rate of fire of machine guns and cannon that bullet holes were four inches or more apart. So, unless the pilot or a vital area of the fighter were hit, the wide dispersal of bullet strikes gave the aircraft a protection to hits. Aircraft speed not only dispersed the hits, but also brought about changes in the angles the bullets hit the rapidly moving aircraft. Knowing the angles from which enemy attack was most probable designers were able to locate the armor plate most strategically. Stopping and deflecting the bullet were two ways to protect a pilot. To stop frontal bullets a heavy armored plate was placed behind the propeller hub. Another plate was placed in front of the cockpit to stop bullets not stopped by the engine and hub plate. A heavy armored bulkhead was placed behind the pilot's seat to stop bullets from the rear. When ground strafing became more prevalent a floor plate was fitted. To save weight, these bulkheads were placed as close to the pilot as possible so he could hide directly behind them, and thus they could be made smaller than if they were placed

The pilot seat armor on a P-51A. The armor, designated X-7440, was manufactured from a nickel-alloy steel and was either face-hardened or homogeneous. (USAF)

further away. This armor plate was nickel-alloy steel, known as X-7440, and was either face-hardened or homogeneous. Face-hardened, as its name indicates, had the front face of the plate hardened, while the homogeneous was uniformly hard throughout. The face-hardened plate was preferred, as when a bullet struck it only a small coin-size piece fell off the plate, while the homogeneous tended to shatter. Also, in plate thicker than 3/8th's of inch, face-hardened was lighter and had a higher ballistic limit (e.g. bullet resistance). But face-hardened was less adaptable to mass production methods and required complex heat treatment, and therefore cost more.

Another method of protecting the pilot while reducing weight was to fit the fighter with aluminum alloy deflector plates to protect the cockpit and engine. The engine was protected by curved aluminum plates on top and under the cowling to protect the engine and pilot from bullets from a head on attack. Deflector plates were placed at the left and right sides of the cockpit to deflect bullets fired at angles from the rear. All armor needed to be accessible, and was bolted for easy removal and repair in case of hits.

Armored glass stopped a bullet by breaking it up and absorbing the pieces between the layers of glass. As seen on the P-47 windscreen, the glass powdered, starred and cracked three inches around the point of impact. (USAF)

Bullet-proof windscreens

Windscreens presented a particular problem, because laminated glass needed to be very thick and thus heavy because of its low ballistic limit. A one-foot piece, 1.5 inches thick, weighed 30 pounds. This thickness stopped the penetration of a .30 caliber bullet, while twice that thickness was required to stop a .50 bullet (1/2 inch of armor plate could do the same). Armored glass was manufactured by taking sections of highly polished glass and sandwiching them between sheets of transparent plastic and bonding them under very high heat and pressure. Because laminated glass does not resist bullets at right angles it was set at deflection angles as close as possible to the pilot's eyes. Armored glass stopped a bullet by breaking it up and absorbing the pieces between the layers of glass. At the point of impact the glass powdered, starred, and cracked three inches around impact.

Self-sealing Fuel Tanks. The fuel cell was constructed of hard, thick formed rubber in two layers. A gel-like substance was sandwiched between the inner and outer layers of rubber. The gel expanded when it contacted gasoline so when a bullet penetrated the tank, gasoline leaked into the gel which expanded to close the hole. When the fighter returned to base the hole could be easily repaired by placing a piece of rubber in the hole. (USAF)

Self-sealing Fuel Tanks

The fuel cell was constructed of hard, thick-formed rubber in two layers. A gel-like substance was sandwiched between the inner and outer layers of rubber. The gel expanded when it contacted gasoline, so when a bullet penetrated the tank gasoline leaked into the gel, which expanded to close the hole. When the fighter returned to base the hole could be easily repaired by placing a piece of rubber in the hole.

Life Vests

The B-3 and B-4 life vest was dubbed the "Mae West" by the British after the buxom 1930s Hollywood star. It was constructed from rubber and bright yellow canvas and worn over all flight clothing. Two small CO2 cylinders inflated each of the two inflatable bladders in the chest compartments and were supplemented by mouth tubes to each bladder. The vest weighed about four pounds. In early 1944, the B-4 was designated as AN6519-1.

Parachutes

The standard U.S. fighter parachute was the Type S-1, or AN6510 seat type with cushion. The ripcord handle was located on the left side. It had snap fasteners for the three-point harness release, one on the chest and one on each leg strap. The Type S-1 had a 24-foot nylon canopy, while the S-2, with a 28-foot nylon canopy, was designed for pilots weighing over 180 pounds. The harness was constructed of flexible or nylon webbing. The primary element was the main lift web, which passed from the connector links at the hips in slings around each leg connecting to the shoulder straps, which were secured by a fastener across the chest and criss-crossed the back. The rip cord assembly was a 31 inch metal cord that attached to a "D" ring. The S-1 was replaced by the AN6510, and the S-2 by the AN6511 in mid-June 1942, and were almost identical to their predecessors, except for minor differences in cushions, chest straps, and fasteners. The B-7 was standardized in October 1940 and had featured the standard 24-foot canopy with a three-point harness re-

B-4 (AN6519) life vest was dubbed the "Mae West" by the English after buxom 1930's Hollywood film star. Nine-victory ace, Capt. Virgil Merony, of the 352nd Fighter Group is shown here. (USAF)

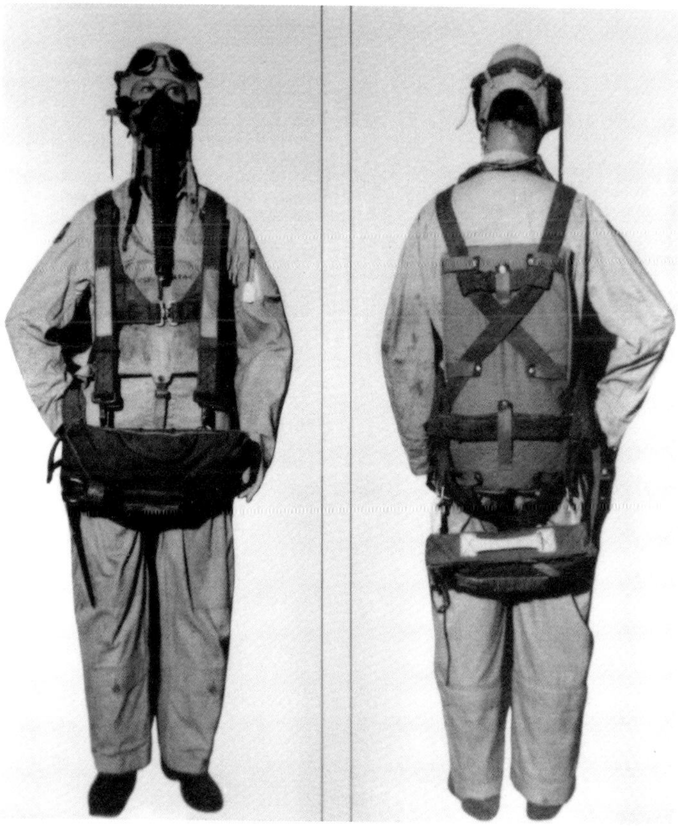

S-1 AN6510 backpack parachute was used by P-47, F4F, F6F and F4U pilots. The AN designation indicated A=Army and N=Navy. (USAF)

lease with a waistband to hold it close to the body. In June 1942 the B-7 was standardized for Army/Navy use as the AN6512. The AN designation stood for ArmyNavy. P-47 pilots wore the S-1 or AN6510 with the C-type dinghy backpack, while P-51 pilots wore the B-8 backpack parachute and the dinghy pack as the cushion. Navy and Marine F4U, F6F, and F4F pilots used S-1 or AN6510 seat packs with attached C-type dinghy. The pilots carried a sheafed ankle knife to cut away the heavy parachute/dinghy pack in case it was necessary, such as in a ditching.

One Man Dinghy

The AN6520-1 one man parachute type pneumatic life raft was widely used by Army and Navy fighter pilots. The raft fit into a parachute pack, which was stowed on the pilot's seat or fastened to his parachute harness by snap rings. Its weight with accessories was 16 pounds, and inflated dimensions were 66x40x12. The accessory pack contained a CO2 cylinder, sail, sea anchor, bailing cup, pair of hand paddles, can of drinking water, first aid kit, repair kit, bullet hole plugs, three cotton cord, and a can of sea marker. The VIII FC widely used the RAF one man K type dinghy in a C type pack until the AN6520-1 was available.

Communications

In 1942 and early 1943 ground-air communications were in the exploratory and developmental stage. The panel system used ground markers that required time to put out, were susceptible to weather, could be clouded by smoke from the battle, and were vulnerable to enemy deception. The use of radio and wire equipment required the exploration of multiple combinations of wires, receivers, transmitters, and antennae. Of course, radio was the only means to contact an airplane in flight if plans needed to be changed after takeoff, and to relay requests from the ground, but the early VHF radio sets were unreliable and short-ranged. Basic communications from headquarters to air bases was by telephone or teletype.

In 1940 the AAF saw the success of the German Stuka-Panzer radio coordinated attacks. Reliable and continuous ground-air and air-ground communications was the keystone to successful ground-air cooperation. Early WWII radios were susceptible to overheating, vibration, and dirt. Maintenance was difficult, and spare parts were in short supply. The channels on ground and aircraft VHF radio sets were lettered differently, causing confusion. Early AAF air-ground communications were a problem, as ground units went into combat without VHF radios, which were the only means of communication with SCR-274 VHF command radios used in air-

Ninth Air Force HQ radio center. Brig.Gen. Pete Quesada developed the most efficient radio communications network in the Air Force as he purchased FM equipment from civilian sources. (USAF)

The IX TAC routed and maintained over 10,000 miles of wire from its HQ to the various infantry and armored units it supported. The numerous times IX HQ moved necessitated a prodigious effort in rerouting the wire. (USAF)

craft. A snafu occurred, as the AAF was responsible to propose and develop a companion ground VHS radio and so none was developed. In early 1943, in North Africa, the field-developed "Veep" set, the AN/VRC-1, came into use. The unit was a HF/VHF composite, consisting of a jeep-mounted HF, SCR-193, and aircraft-mounted VHF, the new SCR-522. During 1943 VHF radios were allotted to divisions at random; some Armies or Corps were able to supply one to each infantry division, while others had so few as to be able to supply only the Combat Commands. The Veep setup was able to provide only the infantry with air-ground liaison. The armored forces utilized FM radios, and the Veep SCR-193 was an AM set. So if a tank commander was to call for air support he would need to call HQ on his FM set and HQ, in turn, would communicate with AAF control centers via wire lines or AM radio. AAF controllers would then direct aircraft via their VHF system. The SCR-506 for use by armored units was under development in 1941, but was delayed until 1943. But by this time the aircraft SCR-274 was replaced by the SCR-522, whose megacycle range was far above that of the SCR-506 to be used in tanks. After D-Day American tankers took matters into their own hands and mounted SCR-522 sets, initially developed for aircraft, in their tanks. By July every armored division had VHF sets installed, which were used to great advantage in the St. Lo/Falaise slaughter of the retreating German armies. However, the standard SCR-522 radio set was unreliable and not durable enough to withstand use on the ground. It was ultimately replaced by the tougher SCR-624. In late 1943, the AAF belatedly requested the first specific air-ground set to be developed. The result was the small VHF, AN.TRC-7, which could be used by paratroopers. It was tested in the summer of 1944 and put into production late in the year.

It was the IX Fighter Command that developed efficient and reliable communications that made the fighter-bomber a success. Col. Blair Garland became the Signals Officer for the IX TAC. Garland had served with the 8th Air Force, where he was instrumental in developing the H2S, H2X, and OBOE radar bombing systems. By 1943 he was responsible for all USAF signal planning for OVERLORD, but for some unexplained reason he was deposed as the top 8th Air Force communications officer and called Pete Quesada at the IX TAC for a job. Garland brought along a MIT radar expert and two AT&T telephone experts. Quesada understood that without reliable communications fighters and fighter-bombers could not function, and he recognized Garland's genius and gave him free reign to establish a communications system. He set up five Signal Aircraft Warning Battalions along England's south coast, six Fighter Control Squadrons at air bases, and four Tactical Communications Squadrons on ships to direct OVERLORD air traffic. Air Support Parties supplied with air and ground radios were assigned to accompany infantry units onto the landing beaches. As a back up, a visual signaling system using large red, orange, and yellow ground panels was devised to inform pilots to start, resume, or cease their attacks. To connect this widespread communications network, 53 radio and telephone channels were distributed across southern England. Quesada was unable to obtain efficient FM radio equipment through AAF sources and sent a communications aide to New York to purchase the equipment in the civilian market. The transmitters and receivers were shipped to England and assembled into the best FM military communications network anywhere. A fundamental rule in communications was the allotment of separate channels for transmitting only air-ground cooperation information and requests. The C-channel was in early use for all communications between aircraft and ground units. After the Invasion the channel became seriously overcrowded. The problem was overcome by assigning frequencies as follows: Button A- Group frequency and homing; Button B-air-ground communication with ground force (Corps); Button C-fighter-bomber communication; and Button D-air-ground communication with additional ground forces (Corps). All air co-operation communication was considered as "Operational Priority" or "Urgent" and could not be processed routinely through the standard staff and command channels.

Tactical Air Liaison Officers (TALO) on the ground were provided with radio and wire lines to the combined operations center. Air Force and Army telephone and teleprinter lines supplemented the air force radio channels to ground units. In static situations the telephone and teleprinter were used to both forward ground units and to airfields. In rapidly moving situations the radio became necessary, as the wire lines to ground units could not be maintained. However, in this fluid situation the use of armored column cover precluded the need for radio communication between forward ground units and the combined operations center. In a rapid advance the wire communication for the Command, and control between the various constituents of a TAC were found to be unsatisfactory. This was due to long lines of communication, shortages of wire, and repeater and carrier equipment and shortages of maintenance, construction, and operating personnel and the cutting of lines by saboteurs. By September 1944 IX TAC communications center received over 500 Teletype, 200 radio, and 5,000 telephone messages each day. Despite a new relay station atop the Eiffel Tower, IX TAC's communications system was so overloaded and understaffed that secret messages were sometimes sent uncoded or over non-secure lines. The use of radio teletypes and telephones remedied the situation when introduced,

Careful radio discipline was maintained, as the Germans monitored the four radio channels of the U.S. fighter aircraft. For inter-fighter group communications, code letters were used rather than the names of the towns for checkpoints. Formation changes were made with visual hand signals. Once in the area, R/T discipline and courtesy on targets of opportunity missions was important. Pilots calling out targets of opportunity or other important information needed to be clear, specific, and identify themselves. Pilots reported hearing the continuous hum of German radar monitoring their flight.

In contrast to the sophistication of the new communications systems being developed for D-Day was the so-called "Pigeon Officer" of the IX Fighter Command, who was in charge of routing and care of the feathered messengers!

Microwave Early Warning Radar (MEW)

Radar was probably the one most significant development in the tactical air war, and allowed the fighter-bombers to operate in conditions that normally would have grounded them, and aided them in locating otherwise invisible targets.

The Microwave Early Warning system (MEW) was a development of the Radiation Laboratory that designed it as the AN/CPS-1 to replace the long-wave SCRs (270, 271, 527, and 588). The Radiation Laboratory rushed a pre-production set to test at the AAF School of Applied Tactics in the summer of 1943. Initially the MEW prototype could provide target range and azimuth but not altitude. Despite this drawback, Lt.Col. George Metcalf, Chief Signals Officer, coordinated MEW development to meet AAF requirements. The AAF ordered 25 sets for 1943 and another 75 for 1944. Development of the 60-ton giant, with its large horizontal rotating double concave antenna was complicated, and progress lagged before production could be initiated. Finally in November 1943, a laboratory-built set was ready for testing. The set demonstrated was able to ascertain altitude and demonstrated the ability to direct friendly aircraft and detect enemy aircraft. During testing the set was improved with additional and larger oscilloscopes. In early 1944 five laboratory-built MEWs were sent to England. Until early 1944 radar had been used in a defensive manner, but the shorter frequencies used by MEW could now accurately identify individual aircraft. In early 1944 there were only a few of the cumbersome sets available. One was located in southern England and was used by RAF Coastal Command to locate Allied aircraft in trouble over the Bay of Biscay and guide them back to base. Col. Blair Garland, IX Signals Officer, convinced Quesada of MEW's potential to direct fighter pilots to targets. Quesada traded two conventional radar sets for the MEW set. It required eight trucks to carry the dismantled MEW set and associated equipment. Only ten days before D-Day Quesada somehow managed to place the set onboard an invasion transport ship, and the set was in France soon after the invasion. MEW took a while for its operators to set it up, calibrate, and then learn how to use. By 15 July MEW had guided only five aircraft to targets, but did perform well as a flight control station around the busy French airfields.

The integral part of Allied air control was ground-based radar. Gen. Quesada used Microwave Early Warning (MEW) and SCR-584 anti-aircraft radar in new and innovative ways, constructing a complete command and control network combining this new technology. MEW operators coordinated with SCR-584 operators to furnish navigation and precise control for fighter-bombers. The wide-band MEW was used for long-range and area control, while the narrow-band SRC-584 was used for close-range, precision missions. Radio intercept stations (Y-Service) were combined with MEW and radio controllers. The Y-Service was developed by the British to monitor Luftwaffe ground-to-air communications, enabling them to intrude on Luftwaffe operations. Quesada's MEW radar controllers used the Y-Service intercepts to direct fighter-bombers to attack Luftwaffe airfields when their fighters (especially the Me-262 jets) were at their most vulnerable; landing, and low on fuel and ammunition. In December 1944, MEW controlled intercepts were credited with 161 Luftwaffe aircraft destroyed and 72 damaged.

MEW was able to locate fighters in the air with great accuracy, but could not relate each aircraft's position to the ground with enough accuracy for bombing. Heavy bombers had surmounted this problem with airborne radar and the Norden Bombsight. Fighter-bombers did not have enough space or load capacity for either, and in any event required more accuracy for their work than could be provided by H2X, OBOE, or GEE. Garland and his chief aid, Lt.Col. William Cowart, were, in modern parlance, techno-geeks, and worked relentlessly on finding an answer to the fighter-bomber size limitation problem. Earlier, Cowart had wangled a Signal Corps Radio 584 (SCR-584) from an artillery unit and foraged a Norden bombsight from a downed B-17. The SCR-584 was designed to direct anti-aircraft radar and was the most accurate American radar at the time. The Norden bombsight was a rudimentary computer that bombardiers used to compute the variables of wind, speed, and altitude. In mid-July the two had combined the two pieces of equipment into an improvised system to direct a small aircraft through the worst of weather.

Cowart connected the SCR-584 to the MEW in a way that combined the great accuracy of the SCR 584 and the long range of the MEW. He then designed a X-Y axis 1:1,000,000 scale map table that used detailed area maps that was combined with the Norden Bombsight, mounted upside down and backwards, to duplicate the system used by bombardiers. The bombsight projected a light beam that represented the tracked lead fighter-bomber along the map table. The fighter-bomber pilot would fly a course directed by the radar and would radio his airspeed, altitude, and wind velocity to the radar station. The ground controller ("bombardier") would dial the information into the Norden computer. As the aircraft flew toward the target the ground controller would move the Norden bombsight over the appropriate map mounted on the map table, and once over the target would release the bombs by radio. The pilot did nothing but fly his aircraft. Bombing was done from target to aircraft and not aircraft to target. The accuracy of the system put the bombs within 300 yards on a ground target located over 30 miles distant. In these blind bombing "SCR-584 missions" the squadron flew in tight formation about 200 feet behind a lead aircraft, whose radar IFF (Identification Friend or Foe) transponder was turned on to give the ground radar operator a fix for guidance on the bomb run. A constant 220mph indicated air speed and specified altitude was maintained, ground radar instructions were followed, and the bombs were salvoed on command.

The large mobile MEW concave "snowplow" antenna rotated to locate aircraft, friend or foe. The MEW apparatus was located in a van or on a Jamesway hut, which was dominated by a large gridded plotting board. Originally designed for early warning and ground control of fighter interception of enemy aircraft, MEW was adapted to control fighter-bomber missions. MEW was able to take complete control using its radar and VHF radio, but the MEW usually transferred this to one of its SCR-584 units, which had greater accuracy. The SCR-584 Forward Director Post (FDP) had early warning, filter, and control equipment (e.g. the SRC-584). The FDP followed the flight on radar and maintained VHS radio contact (the MEW had more VHS radio channels). Each FDP had plotting tables with a map of the target area in relation to the radar's position. The controller followed the line of flight that showed through the map as an illuminated moving dot. While the controller guided his aircraft to their targets the FDPs and MEWs watched for enemy aircraft, relieving the pilots of this worry. After the bombs were dropped

Fighter Control Center (FCC) of TAC HQ set up the mission and then turned over control to radar by teletype to the Signal Aircraft Warning battalion's MEW station. (USAF)

Operations Room of a SCR-527 Radar Van. The MEW display incorporated four round scopes that could be adjusted to show nearby areas or areas several hundred miles away. The range of the radar depended on the altitude of the aircraft being followed as radar display was limited by the curvature of the earth. (USAF)

Filter Room of the Control Center. The Chief Controller sat in a balcony overlooking the operations board and had radio control on all VHF channels. (USAF)

64th Wing control center in Loudres, France with Wing CO, Brig.Gen. Glenn Barcus (standing center, pipe in hand) watching the MEW controllers. (USAF)

A MEW rotating antenna mounted on a steel frame platform. (USAF)

A MEW station of the XIX TAC located in Luxembourg. The concave antenna were called "snowplows" which may have been appropriate in this case. The truck-mounted SCR-584 antenna can be seen on the left of the MEW antenna. (USAF)

MEW vertical plotting board in operations room.The lighted display showed targets in relation to radar sited position. (USAF)

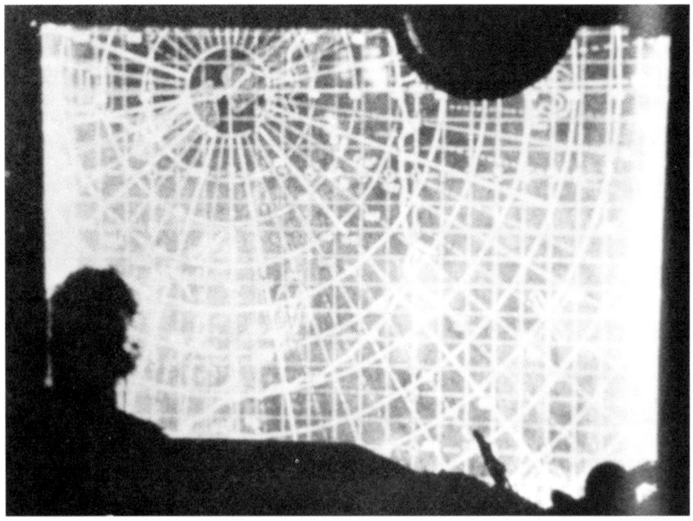

The vertical plotting board of the operations room of a MEW station. (USAF)

the fighter-bombers were released and the SCR-584s picked another mission. The released fighter-bombers were picked up by other units in the radar network to lead these aircraft home.

In times of limited visibility, especially in the winter, there was extensive use of the MEW and SCR-584 radar sets by forward controllers who were posted close to the front. The fighter-bombers were directed to the target area by radar and radio control, flying above the overcast on the correct approach and then led through the overcast to the target, at which time the pilot made the final alterations for the attack. The results were generally effective and denied the Germans the use of poor weather to move troops and supplies near the front.

The system was first tested on 16 July by the 404th Fighter Group, led by Col. Carroll McColpin, who was the top scorer in the RAF American Eagle Squadron with eight Spitfire victories, and had added three more with the 404th. Despite weather that would normally ground the group a briefing was called for 0900. The remote radio-controlled bomb releases had been installed on the P-47s, and by 1220 the other modifications were ready, and four flights took off from their new base near La Chapelle. From his radar station named "Sweepstakes" Cowart controlled the P-47s after take off and directed them toward a prominent ridge east of St. Lo. The Thunderbolt squadron, carrying 16 500lb. bombs, flew through the overcast and was instructed to begin their blind dives. Watching their altimeters spin down, the pilots anxiously waited for the radio command to automatically drop their bombs. Finally at 700 feet the command was given, the bombs dropped, and the pilots pulled up. Post mission reconnaissance showed poor results, with only one bomb causing damage to the intended target and the majority hitting a farm, killing nine cows, two horses, and a number of chickens.

The next day more radar-directed missions were dispatched. The 366th Fighter Group suffered an electronic problem and failed to hit the target. A squadron of the 404th Fighter Group had better results in its attack on a Seine River bridge near Rouen, as five of twenty 1,000lb. bombs scored direct hits and knocked out two of the bridge's four lanes. On the 18th, escorts had missed their ren-

The Forward Director Post (FDP) of a SCR-584 unit followed the flight on radar and kept in contact by VHS radio. (USAF)

SCR-584 Control Station with radar antenna on top of the control trailer. (USAF)

Interior of a SCR-584 station with controllers over the plotting table. The plotting table had a map of the target area in relation to the radar's position and allowed the controller to follow the flight's line of flight that showed through the map as an illuminated moving dot. (USAF)

dezvous with IX Bomber Command medium bombers, and SCR 584/MEW equipped P-47s on patrol were directed to the mediums, and for the first time aircraft in the air were directed to an objective.

By the fall of 1944 IX TAC communications system between ground and air extended with great efficiency from forward director posts to radar centers, to fighter control stations, to a combat command post, and finally to a fighter-bomber group. Each TAC had a Tactical Control Center (TCC, also called a Fighter Control Center) sited near the Combined Operations Center. This was a radar control group using MEW radar that was sited 10 to 30 miles from the front. The MEW was supported by Forward Director Posts (usually three) and three to four SCR-584 Close Control Units, and finally by four Direction Finding stations, called "Fixer" stations. MEW directed aircraft to and from targets, united bombers with their fighter escorts, and detected the few aircraft the Luftwaffe sent out. In the fall of 1944, MEW consisted of several large ground radar sets (usually four round scopes individually manned), on which every aircraft or formation of aircraft in the sky would show up as a dot of light. The scope could be adjusted to concentrate on an area only a few miles away, or to areas several hundred miles away depending on the altitude of the aircraft being tracked, as radar can only track on line-of-sight and cannot follow an aircraft around the curvature of the earth. The MEW operator was able to follow the movement of his assigned aircraft and directly communicate with it via radio. If a TAC R pilot spotted a target he would send a radio direction fix to the controller, who would notify fighter-bombers. Once the fighter-bombers came into the range of his radarscope the operator would vector them directly to the fix. If the fighter-bombers were unable to locate the target the radar operator would recall the TAC R fighter to guide them to the target. The controller also advised the fighter-bombers if there were other aircraft, friend or foe, in the area, and could give them directions back to base if needed. The SCR-584 radar set came into wide use at this time. It was highly accurate with a range of 30 miles, and the controller was able to vector a single fighter-bomber or a group of fighter-bombers to within a few hundred yards of a suspected target. Often the fighter-bomber would lose sight of a small target and the controller could easily redirect it back to the target area. A F-5 photo aircraft shooting strip photo reconnaissance could be kept on course to assure no gaps in coverage.

Operations Room of a SCR-584 Radar Van. The MEW display incorporated four round scopes that could be adjusted to show nearby areas or areas several hundred miles away. The range of the radar depended on the altitude of the aircraft being followed as radar display was limited by the curvature of the earth. (USAF)

During the Battle of the Bulge the battlefield was obscured by thick, low clouds, which along with the shifting battle situation made navigation and ground target identification very difficult. Quesada's

Mobile weather unit of the 358th Fighter Group. Initially on the Continent the Weather Officer (WO) set up in the Group Operations tent and usually had an enlisted assistant. Later better equipped mobile weather units made their way to the Continent to advise several fighter and bomber groups. It was his duty to brief pilots of the anticipated weather conditions along their route, at the target and on their return flight to base. (USAF)

radar operators directed the fighter-bombers to fly under and through the weather both to the target and back to base. Targets were fixed by correlating the known ground positions and vectoring the fighters by SCR-584 into the target area. Friendly vehicles on the ground would notify the radar controller as the fighter-bombers flew over. The radar operator, knowing the fighter position and the location of friendly positions on his X-Y table, could direct the fighter-bombers to the target.

There were ongoing problems using the MEW/SCR-584 radars to direct fighter-bombers in blind bombing. Slight variations in temperature and humidity in the radar huts could distort the readings from complex instruments by as much as a quarter of an inch. An inaccuracy as little as an eighth of an inch on a radar map could mean an error of a half-mile on actual terrain. To provide the altitude, airspeed, wind velocity, and atmospheric pressure to the Norden Bombsight required a long time, and pilots in flight had little time to change altitude or course once the radar controllers had plotted their bomb runs. There always was a lack of skilled radar operators, and Garland knew that there was little likelihood of getting any. So he determined that improved coordination between the radar stations and the directing positions was the answer. In mid-February 1945 he began to train pilots of the 70th Fighter Wing in six-week rotations as flight controllers. These pilots not only eased the manpower problem, but when they returned to their units they had an understanding of the workings and limitations of the radar setup.

At the time of the Battle of the Bulge there were only six MEW sets in operation, and if German intelligence had been alerted to this weakness, Allied air power could have been crippled by attacks on the system.

Weather

Pre-war American air training seldom discussed the weather, and after America entered the war the Air Corps was too preoccupied with getting as many pilots into the air as quickly as possible to give anything but a fleeting mention of weather problems. Of all the factors affecting air action, weather, although somewhat predictable, was the most uncontrollable. Whereas ground operations could continue tactical combat in any but the harshest weather conditions, air operations were limited to good weather unless pilots and aircraft were to be put into jeopardy. From D-Day to V-E Day in the ETO it was estimated that about a quarter of USAAF air capacity was put down by weather, and poor flying weather averaged one in three days. Officers and personnel from Eisenhower down chronically complained about it. However, the lost flying time in the ETO was not due to atypical weather, as is often stated, but to weather that fell within the "very good-very bad" range of long-term weather records, and Allied weathermen's failure to discover what should have been an obvious fact. In the MTO, long-term weather records also revealed that "sunny Italy" was not so sunny. That air planners did not anticipate periods of poor and even extreme weather is remarkable, as air operations are particularly de-

Weathermen release a weather balloon at 9th Air Force HQ in France. (USAAF)

pendent on good weather. The summer months of 1944 saw exceptionally good flying weather that suddenly changed in late September to normal October rains, decreasing fighter-bomber operations. November had 30% more rain than normal; the infamous weather that hid the German's Ardennes Offensive build up and shielded German operations was more or less normal. After the Battle of the Bulge was won, aided by a few days of good weather, more snow fell in January 1945 than any January for 175 years. Although weather conditions were generally worse than normal from September through January, the sum of fighter-bomber operations from D-Day matched or surpassed the number of possible flying days, as was calculated from an eight-year pre-war average; despite the November rains, poor "normal" December weather, and January record snows. During the 337 days of the war after D-Day, some medium bombers flew operations on 228 days (67%) and some fighter-bombers flew 289 operational days (86%). Of the 337 days only 138 days (41%) were considered optimal.

Air support was at best intermittent, and its use had to be planned to take full advantage of good weather. Since weather changed quickly, the planning of daily ground operations had to be flexible enough to recognize that close air support may not be available. Often ground troops had to attack without depending on close air support. However, the planning of a major ground offensive included air power as a fundamental component, so the fixing of the date and hour of the offensive depended on fair weather. Built into the plan was flexibility in both the ground and air forces, so that weather delays would not jeopardize the opening stages and final objective of the plan. In any case, ground attacks could not be delayed until the weather improved, allowing air power to come into play. To neutralize the weather factor, planners needed to accurately assess its possible effects and compensate for them by allowing for alternative plans of action.

There were periods, often extended, when poor weather disrupted planning and operations. It is well documented that weather affected D-Day's planning and start date. It also delayed the start of Operation QUEEN, the U.S. First and Ninth Armies' offensive to wards the Roer River, in mid-November 1944. Flying time in fall and winter was curtailed by shortened hours of daylight. To allow more flying time bases were built closer to the front. But the rains in November hampered the building of new fields and forced the abandonment of bases that were "dry weather" bases, as well as slowed the "winterization" of existing bases. In November and December, when the Germans were assembling their forces for the Ardennes Offensive, there were a number of non-flying days and abortive missions at a time when air disruption of supply and transport would have been decisive. Once the German offensive began, poor weather prevented fighter-bomber operations from obstructing its progress. In Italy Field Marshal Albert Kesselring used the chronic poor weather that restricted or postponed Allied air action to time and again skillfully regroup or withdraw German troops, and to transport supplies, making the Italian Campaign slow and costly for the Allies.

Poor weather restricted both Allied and German air power, but not equally. Priority One (air superiority) missions were suspended, but the point was moot, as the Luftwaffe was a non-entity much of the time after D-Day. In poor weather, Priority Two and Three missions were not flown, so blockade of the battlefield could not be maintained, and ground forces and supplies were able to move openly without fear of air attack. Again, it was the Germans who benefited from bad weather, as they were able to escape the continual Allied air attacks, a problem that Allied troops never had to worry about from the Luftwaffe, as it was incapable of conducting sustained Priority Two or Three operations. In poor weather Allied ground forces lost the added striking power from the air on close support missions that the Germans were masters of in the first Blitzkrieg years of the war.

The fighter-bomber pilot had to be concerned about good weather three times during a mission. The weather had to be reasonably good at take off and assembly, good at the target area, and then good when returning back to base for landing. The infantryman waiting desperately in clear weather for air support to arrive often complained about the comfortable life of the flyboy when told that support would not be coming because of bad weather. But the fighter-bomber groups, stationed miles away, were socked in by the weather and unable to take off. Nonetheless, there were many missions that took off in clear weather and returned to zero-zero conditions that resulted in many dicey successful landings and crash landings.

The Weather Officer (WO) of a fighter group usually had obtained a BS in a science on the university level. After the standard basic training regimen he was sent for nine months of Weather Officer training (Massachusetts's Institute of Technology offered this course). Initially on the Continent the Weather Officer set up in the Group Operations tent, and usually had an enlisted assistant. Later better-equipped mobile weather units made their way to the Continent to advise several fighter and bomber groups. It was his duty to brief pilots of the anticipated weather conditions along their route, at the target, and on their return flight to base. Cloud layers in route and over target, target visibility, and home base ceiling and visibility were briefed. Icing conditions and frontal zones were indicated. Alternate landing fields were chosen in case of poor weather. To accomplish this he would mainly rely on weather information from the Weather Squadron at Wing HQ, which gathered pertinent Continental information on weather conditions, but he would also take into account pilot reports from debriefings from earlier missions and his own experience and intuition. The Wing Weather Section kept group Weather Officers current on changes that could affect operations. The WO could forward the latest weather information to the pilots in the air. Weather detachments were posted among the fighter-bomber units, and they sent out F-5 (P-38) weather reconnaissance aircraft to the intended target area to radio back reports to waiting fighter-bomber pilots. As the Allied advance moved across France the 9th Air Force established mobile weather units to armies and corps. Weather forecasts were prepared for use by ground and air staffs for daily planning, and to warn of the possibility of the unavailability of air support.

Minimum weather for take off was 1,000ft. ceiling and three miles visibility. Visibility needed to be at least 6,000 feet, and the cloud base no lower than 5,000 feet for dive-bombing, 3,500 feet for armed recce, and 3,000 feet for strafing. For rocket attacks and dive-bombing the wind could impose the direction of approach. When adverse weather conditions persisted and the tactical situation became critical, fighter-bombers would fly when ceilings over the target were 1,000 or 1,500 feet. The terrain of Northwest Europe and, particularly, Italy complicated winter flying operations. Snow-covered deep valleys and hills shrouded in fog and low cloud limited visibility, making navigation and target identification difficult, and more conscientious ground control and briefing was required. When the landing fields were socked in pilots used the radio direction finder (RDF) located on the field. The RDF operator would listen for the fighters flying over the field and would inform them to turn to a heading of 240 degrees. The pilots would drop in trail, ten seconds apart, through the overcast at a specific air speed and rate of descent. A procedure turn was made when half the altitude was lost, and they continued to let down on a reciprocal heading of 60 degrees. At 500 feet the overcast was usually penetrated, and the gear and flaps could be dropped and the final approach made on visual. When the overcast was ground level landings were made "by guess and by gosh."

During late 1944 the weather became particularly bad along the front in northeastern France. To keep air commanders informed of the weather and to update forecasters the 9th Weather Reconnaissance Squadron (Provisional) of the 9th Air Force was formed. The unit was equipped with P-51s and flew frequent missions to investigate and report the weather conditions over the front lines. From 8 to 18 December the Squadron flew 19 hazardous low-level missions over the Roer Dam area, flying under the ceiling that was often under 100 feet, dodging enemy AA fire and barrage balloons. Through their effort, information to aid ground operations against this vital objective was obtained. For these missions and 62 others in December the 9th WRS (P) was awarded the Distinguished Unit Citation (DUC).

Poor weather not only restricted air operations. In the XIX TAC aircraft maintenance increased from 20 to 30% due to additional inspections and winterization procedures on aircraft. Winter conditions reduced the efficiency of ground crews and further added to the time aircraft were not in operations. Poor winter weather closed the replacement aircraft assembly areas for periods of weeks, and affected the ferrying and delivery of replacement aircraft to maintain tactical units at full strength. When the limited number of good weather days did arrive and a maximum effort was required, the tactical units were under strength.

The weather in Italy was atrocious and legend, and the 79th Fighter Group based at Madna, a newly constructed gash in the coastal lowlands, suffered in the late autumn rains. Don Woerpel described their predicament in *The 79th Fighter Group in World War 2* (Schiffer, PA, 2001):

"It was a lousy place, the worst they had ever encountered. Everyone sort of came apart. By the end of December, morale was the worst since leaving for overseas; men rarely washed—it was too cold—and most of the food was canned and dreary.The runway which ran uphill (take-offs were downhill, landings uphill, regardless of wind direction) had been covered with a narrow strip of PSP matting, but dispersal areas were still knee-deep in a sea of sticky gumbo."

8

Enemy Targets

Claims

Bombing or strafing claims by pilots were made from observations made at high speeds, sometimes under fire and always under duress. To receive credit for destroying a tank, motor vehicle, locomotive, or rail rolling stock, the pilot needed to see "visible disintegration" or "visible flames." Intelligence surveys of air damage inflicted closing the Falaise-Argentan pocket revealed that a small percentage of the claimed motor vehicle destruction by bombs and rockets was valid. Later damage assessment by bombs and rockets was made more accurate and immediate by the installation of under wing cameras. Strafing damage claims were much more accurate, as the pilot could see the target as he attacked and hit it, and were also verified by gun cameras. The results of close support missions were verified by ground controllers or other ground observers.

Strafing Attack/General Tenants

Every scheduled strafing attack required thorough planning, compelling the pilots to become totally familiar with the geography around the target area and the layout of the target itself, particularly the location of AA guns. Landmarks in a five-mile radius of the target needed to be memorized, and the best approach and withdrawal routes selected.

An altitude of 15,000 feet was maintained on the way to the target area. The leader located the target and dropped to the deck with or without his wingman to check the target, particularly AA. The formation then turned 180 degrees, setting course on the target, flights dropping line astern at about 1,000 yard intervals. The approach was made at normal cruising speed at as low altitude as possible, trying to use a road or other landmarks to stay on target. About one mile from target the first flight pulled up to 1,000 feet, correcting their heading if necessary, and gave full RPM and throttle. The flight and element leaders concentrated on shooting up the target itself, while the wingmen acted as "anti-flak" aircraft, picking out gun positions and knocking them out. It was important to pick an aimed target, rather than "hosing" the area. The pilot had to have his aircraft properly trimmed and know where his machine guns were harmonized to fire at correct range, putting as many rounds into the target while firing on it. Succeeding flights utilized similar tactics. Once past the target all aircraft stayed on deck until the formation leader gave the signal to climb, usually five to ten miles away.

Another method of attack had the formation come around on the target at 4,000 feet, dive at high speed, shoot up the target, stay low and get away. It was a matter of the leader's preference on which method was used, but the on deck method was most common. A minimum airspeed of 250 mph was advised because of the constant possibility of passing over unexpected AA positions while on deck, as well as the possibility of being bounced.

The guns of the fighter were harmonized for rounds to converge at a point ahead of the aircraft so that the rounds would impact the target together. The harmonization point was set for air-to-air combat at 250 yards, which was acceptable when strafing individual targets, such as soft or armored vehicles. Low-level strafing attacks at this harmonization range were risky to the pilot, as apart from the danger from AA and small arms fire, a small miscalculation or target-fixation could cause the fighter to crash into the target or into trees or obstructions just beyond it. Also, if the target were carrying ammunition or explosives it could explode in the path of the attacker and damage it. The most accurate of all fighter bomber armament was the machine gun or cannon, as the great number of rounds fired assured more hits in an area, but the striking power of each round inflicted much less damage to the target than a hit or near miss by heavier ordnance, such as bombs or rockets, which were much less accurate. It was advised that pilots save about 50 rounds per gun during strafing missions. In the P-51, a pilot could expend all the ammo in his outboard guns and have enough left in the two inboard guns to engage in combat, if necessary.

If heavy AA fire was encountered only one pass was made, but if the target were undefended the formation leader detailed at least one flight to fly top cover, while the remainder of the formation flew another pass on the target. Top cover circled at 2,000 feet above the target in the opposite direction to the attacking aircraft to be able to intercede without delay if enemy aircraft attacked. The attacking formation often was disrupted after the first pass, and afterward all aircraft had to beware of other aircraft and stay out of their fire and flight paths.

If AA fire was heavy (in line astern attacks) the pilot needed to take evasive action in all but the last part of his attack, the firing run. On the way in, a slight pumping of the stick and small turns could confuse enemy gunners in determining the direction of the attacker's flight path. Once the pilot sighted the target he needed to end his evasive maneuvers and forget the AA fire until he finished his pass.

Pilot Strafing Mistakes

In combat the fighter-bomber pilot needed to apply the same general principles that he first learned in gunnery school and OTU: be prudent in choosing, attacking, and destroying the target.

Often the inexperienced pilot sighted the target through the gunsight pipper and then tried to correct his firing error by watching his strikes. The consequence was that at the start of his firing pass he would shoot below the target, and then trying to correct would spray the rounds above and around the target. The pilot could correct this fault by leaving the pipper above the target at the start of his run, and as the range decreased to allow the pip to drop on the target.

If the approach was too steep or too shallow it caused the pilot to split his concentration between hitting the ground with his fighter and hitting the target with his bullets. If the pass was too steep the tendency was to open fire at too long range and to pull up at the optimum firing range, when the concern about crashing into the target appeared. If the pass was too shallow the tendency was to open fire too close to the target, snapping off quick, ineffective bursts, then pulling up too soon, again to avoid flying into the intended target. Instead of choosing one target and hitting it with a continual burst to destroy it, pilots tended to spray bullets at several targets in their view, missing or only slightly damaging them. Pilots also tended to continue firing as they pulled up past the target, wasting ammunition. In any attack the pilot would always have to pull up to avoid the target or its surroundings. After a while the pilot developed the instinct to determine a good safety margin to clear his fighter of all ground obstacles in order to hold his fire until reaching a close and lethal range.

Enemy Targets

Transportation Network

Combat surveys and postwar interrogations of German military officers and civilian officials firmly established that the persistent aerial assault on the transportation network precluded the enemy from massing troops, weapons, and supplies at crucial points and times at the front lines. The transport system was the Achilles' heel of the German logistics organization, and its continual harassment and subsequent destruction was to prove to be the obvious cause of the failure of the supply system, and accordingly was a key reason for the destruction of the German Army.

In order of consequence, German commanders considered the following air attacks on the supply network the most important (*US Bombing Survey: Post War Interrogations*):

1) The attacks on and the destruction of the rail network; locomotives, rolling stock, track, and bridges that prevented the delivery of supplies to the front.
2) The attacks on and the destruction of primary supply roads and traffic in the army area.
3) Attacks on and the destruction of army forward railheads.
4) Attacks on and the destruction of army supply installations: dumps, depots, pools, parks, and other collection sites.
5) Attacks on and the destruction of division supply installations.

The losses of supplies in shipment by rail and road transport from home depots to the front were far greater than the losses suffered once these supplies were unloaded into Army depots, dumps, and reserve pools, which were dispersed and camouflaged so that attacks on them caused insignificant damage and losses. It was the failure to receive supplies (in order of importance: fuel, ammunition, and motorized vehicles) from home depots that had the most decisive effect on combat operations.

Rail Transport

The rail system in northwest France SNCF (French National Railway) and Belgium SNCB (Belgium National Railway) was large and interconnected, and from mid-1942 the Reich Transportation Ministry coordinated this system with the complex and well-developed Deutsch Reichsbahn (German National Railway) in the Rhineland and Saar industrial areas of western Germany. In February 1944 Sir Solly Zuckerman developed the "Transportation Plan," to attack the French and Belgian rail marshaling yards to isolate the battlefield. Zuckerman maintained that the destruction of 101 rail centers and maintenance facilities over a three-month period with 45,000 tons of bombs would paralyze the French rail system. The USAAF endorsed an "Interdiction" plan to block German military movements close to the battlefield by destroying critical transportation targets, such as bridges, roads, and railways, and the transport on them. The "Transportation Plan" will be discussed later in detail. From the end of summer 1944 to the end of the war the major effort of the USAAF was allocated to attacks on the well-developed rail network (Deutsch Reichsbahn) inside Germany, upon

A common scene in the French and Belgium countryside as over 4,000 locomotives were destroyed as part of the transportation plan. (USAF)

which its military and industry was dependent for supply. Armor, fuel, troops, raw material, and heavy and bulky cargo was moved more rapidly and efficiently on the rail system than the road system.

The Western European rail system was far ranging and highly developed, which made it difficult to interdict. In Eastern Europe and Asia there were few railroads, and concentrated attacks and even local destruction dealt a heavy blow to the military effort there. While the Western European rail system offered too many targets and alternative routes, it also offered a number of choke points, which if prudently selected could effectively damage the rail net. Tracks, small bridges, and switches could be repaired or replaced relatively easily, but large bridges, as well as large and complex electrical circuits and switching and signal systems were much more difficult to repair and replace.

After the war the AAF Evaluation Board published an extensive report that concluded that rail bridge destruction, track cuts, and air attacks on moving locomotives and rail cars were the foremost transportation problems faced by the Germans. But rolling stock and equipment, and especially the difficult to replace locomotives, were the choice targets for the eager fighter-bomber pilots. A carefully camouflaged, stationary train on a remote siding could escape detection by a fast-flying fighter-bomber, but a moving train was extremely apparent. It was not only the steam and smoke of the locomotive, but the movement of the train along the rail bed that could be seen from miles away. Tactical attacks on rail transportation included strafing attacks and level-, glide-, and dive-bombing of railheads, rail yards, repair installations and stations, bridges and trestles, tracks and sidings, locomotives and freight cars, and enemy equipment located in freight cars and near rail installations, and against moving rail stock. In an attack, a locomotive and its rolling stock could be derailed, damaged, or completely destroyed, but any attack delayed schedules, increased the burden on rail repair facilities, and depleted vital manpower and material (a locomotive required 24,000 manpower hours to build).

The recommended mode of air attack on rail traffic was at right angles to the length of the train. Little or no firing lead was necessary, and moving trains were considered a stationary target. To stop the train and make it an easier target the engine was the initial target. Attacks on the engine were made from 90 degrees by the No.1 and, if necessary, No. 2 of a flight. Long, methodical bursts caused the most damage and minimized return AA and small arms fire. Fighter-bomber .50 caliber bullets could readily penetrate the locomotive's boiler, stopping the entire train. A bomb hit on the locomotive would blow it off the tracks, derail the following cars, and destroy track, making clearing, salvage, and repair more difficult. Once the train was stopped, 10 to 15 degree deflection passes were made by Nos. 2, 3, and 4 to destroy as many cars as possible with a minimum number of attacks. Each pilot would attack in a relatively slow (under 300 mph), shallow dive and make a climbing turn to about 500 feet, then circle to make another attack. Air traffic discipline was essential, with each pilot following in trail the aircraft ahead of him to avoid mid-air collisions and shooting at other squadron aircraft. If a target had the possibility of exploding pilots fired a short burst from a long distance away, aiming high, in an attempt to explode it and be able to evade the debris. If this failed, a long burst was fired somewhat high from a long distance on the next run. The pilot watched for hits and then led fire into the target. These attacks were to be broken off at a distance to insure safety from an explosion, but all too often strafing fighters were lost to explosions.

In December 1944 the Ordnance Section of the 12th Air Force, using 57th Fighter Group fighter-bombers, conducted a study of attacks on a static Italian steam locomotive. Strafing damage was found to stall a locomotive and cause repairs ranging from one to 35 days, and that strafing was much more likely to achieve hits

Classic strafing run on a locomotive with the .50 caliber bullets hitting the cab and boiler. (USAF)

The standard method for attacking marshaling yards near or in sizable towns or cities was to dispatch three squadrons; two to carry two 500lb. bombs and a belly tank or, if the target was in range, three 500lb. bombs and a third squadron to furnish top cover. (USAF)

than bombing or rockets. It was suggested that strafing using a .50 belting of four armor piercing incendiary (API) rounds to one tracer was ideal (as opposed to the previous API-Incendiary-API-Incendiary-Tracer belting). Strafing from 90-degree beam was suggested over an attack from a shallower angle, as these perpendicular strikes were more likely to perforate the locomotive's boiler and less likely to ricochet.

The standard method for attacking marshaling yards near or in sizable towns or cities was to dispatch three squadrons; two to carry two 500lb. bombs and a belly tank or, if the target was in range; three 500lb. bombs and a third squadron to furnish top cover. The group would climb to 25-30,000 feet and, because of the heavy flak associated with this target, bomb in a four plane Vic. The group leader would have the squadrons and their flights form in trail, with each flight in close right echelon making a shallow diving turn toward the target to gain speed. The flight leader No.1 would half-roll left with his wingman No.2 rolling on his starboard wing. The No.3 and No.4 would each half-roll left, in place, and the flight would end up in a close finger four formation in a near vertical dive. Three or four flights would dive simultaneously, with the lead flight firing its guns to suppress AA fire. The formation would gain speed to 400 to 500mph in the dive and release its bombs on the lead flight. The aircraft would either pull up in loose formation and zoom climb to about 20,000 feet or pull out at the deck and head for a predetermined rendezvous. The two attacking squadrons would be rejoined with the top cover squadron and return home. This method was also used to bomb airfields.

Rail-cutting sorties were used extensively before and following D-Day, but assessment of the results was difficult due to the large number of bomb craters found everywhere, mostly misses, aimed not only at the rail lines but at adjacent targets. After the St. Lo breakout rail cutting missions were greatly limited to preserve the rail system for Allied use. In late 1944, when the battlefront was stabilizing at the German frontier, rail-cutting operations were resumed to isolate the battlefield. Using attacks on the eight rail lines carrying east-west traffic west of the Rhine for its analysis, *Operational Assessment of Rail Interdiction by Fighter-bombers Attacking Open Rail Lines* (IX TAC Report No. 67, Operational Research Section) determined that systematic air attacks were required to destroy all the rail lines supplying a specific battle area in order to isolate it. A network of rail lines leading to a battle area could carry five to ten times the required military traffic. Cutting one track only inconvenienced the enemy, and only meant that there was one less track to cut to make isolation total. One track left uncut continued to allow traffic to carry the necessary supplies to the front. It was found that three sorties were required to cut one line. A force of four flights was necessary to give 90% probability to cut one rail line. To cut eight rail lines leading to the front, at 90% probability, 260 fighter-bombers were required. With perfect pre-attack reconnaissance the 90% probability of cutting all eight lines required 100 fighter-bomber sorties. Rail-cutting was made using a dive-bombing attack with the 500 lb. GP bomb armed with an 8-15 second delay fuse. The object of the 500 lb. bomb was to create as large a crater as possible. No reliance was given to pilot's post-mission assessment that their particular assigned rail line had been cut, as dive-bombing bomb bursts were not observed by the pilot at close range. It was reported that it took only five to eight hours to repair even a direct hit on a line by non-essential (e.g. POW or civilian) labor. With these apparently mediocre results, rail cutting was used as a stopgap to other, more effective, and longer term isolation operations, such as against bridges. IX TAC Report No. 67 found:

A rail cut behind the Normandy beaches. Rail cuts were easily repaired but needed to be completed quickly so rail traffic could be restored. (USAF)

"With the present number of fighter-bomber aircraft available, the bombing accuracy, weapon effectiveness, and nature of the German rail network, it is impossible to achieve isolation or paralyzation over a period of time by the sole use of F/B attacks against open rail lines.... The results of these attacks then were of a harassing nature, for isolation was probably never attained."

Most rail-cutting missions were made near large cities or on congested areas of trackage for maximum results. Fighter-bomber pilots in Italy particularly hated to cut rail tracks around the Bologna area, where the Germans had placed heavy concentrations of both light and heavy flak. Near the end of the war many experts, including the AEAF staff, believed that track cutting had been more costly in aircraft and ordnance than attacks on bridges. However, their postwar study showed that track cuts required a lower bomb ton per cut than anticipated, and the cuts accounted for a larger than anticipated decrease in traffic. If the attacks had been more systematic and determined much better results could have been achieved for less bomb tonnage. This conclusion was supported by the IX TAC ORS (Operational Research Section) report (*USAFHRA 505.78-3 July 22, 1944*), which stated:

"...that the tactic (rail-cutting) was productive if not sufficient unto itself. The enemy was forced to revamp procedures and reroute traffic over circuitous routes. The resulting disruptions often lead to bottlenecks and traffic congestion which could be exploited by fighter-bombers."

The ORS Study found that rail-cutting was more effective and economical than bridge busting, especially when it was done away from populated areas where it took longer to reach and repair the cuts. Rail cuts on tracks in open areas could be made safely and effectively by dropping bombs at the minimum altitude for the best accuracy, as AA fire was not a concern. Much more time and effort had to be expended on bridge attacks which, when successful, required longer repair time than track cuts and created major rerouting and rescheduling problems. However, bridges tended to be more heavily defended by AA fire.

Because of Zuckerman's "Transportation Plan," rail marshaling yards in France and Belgium received an inordinate amount of attention from air attack and should have been considered to be damaged beyond the point necessary to continue rail interdiction attacks. Attacks on marshaling yards extensively damaged track and rail beds, but traffic on through lines was only interrupted, and troops and supplies reached their destinations through rerouting, rescheduling, and detrainings, although not by the shortest and most direct route. Extensive delays became necessary, and local civilian traffic was curtailed, as the military traffic had priority. Locomotives/rolling stock and coal supplies stored in the yards were destroyed and caused the Germans to disperse them, causing further delays and rescheduling. The German rail system, unlike the British, American, and French systems, depended on the working of marshaling yards for movement of goods and services, and so had more and better equipped yards, especially in the Ruhr. Because of the number and size of these yards attacks by heavy and medium bombers, which had other priorities (e.g. oil and the aircraft industry), were largely ineffective from a military standpoint in 1944, when the battlefield was in France. Once the front neared the Rhine, fighter-bomber attacks on these yards began to have a direct effect on daily German operations by reducing and delaying the delivery of supplies.

Bombing and strafing of the water tanks along the right of way or in the marshaling yards caused problems for the steam locomotives of the German rail system. Unfortunately, fighter-bomber pilots ignored these unglamorous targets until other targets became scarce later in the war. Repair was difficult, and water had to be hauled and stored in trucks to rail centers and then laboriously transferred to the locomotives.

The Germans had anticipated large-scale attacks on their rail system and developed a large repair organization, supported by

Both the Allies and Germans made use, voluntary and involuntary, of French civilians in repairing damaged rail lines. (USAF)

skilled repair crews supplemented by civilian and prisoner of war labor and stockpiled with essential repair materials. The efficient system quickly repaired damage, and targets had to be attacked frequently to keep them out of operation. The determining factor in reopening railway lines was the repair of bridges, which was a lengthy labor and material intensive process. Numerous rail-cuts were irritating and consumed time and resources, and further added to delays. Substantial quantities of rolling stock were destroyed in the marshaling yards, but the Germans always had enough to meet their requirements by bringing in replacements from Germany. The main problem the Germans had with their rolling stock was that it was often loaded or waiting in areas that had been cut off from the main line by air attacks and could not move until substantial lengths of track had been repaired. This immobile stock presented choice targets for marauding fighter-bombers. If the wait was to be too long troops and equipment would be unloaded and moved toward the front by motor transport or on foot.

As Allied strafing attacks increased in 1944, the Germans armed many of their important trains with specially-built flak cars. These flak cars will be described later. To minimize the risk from these guns strafing attacks were made at 90 degrees in line abreast to the target and in a 20 to 30 degree dive from 2,000 to 500 feet, concentrating fire from the .50s. A trick the Germans used was to move a badly damaged locomotive to a siding or spur to entice fighter-bombers into an unnecessary attack, or into the fire of camouflaged AA guns set up nearby.

Capt. Marvin Bledsoe, a P-47 pilot with the 350th Fighter Group, described his first attack an a train in his book *Thunderbolt: Memoirs of a World War II Fighter Pilot* (Van Nordstrand Reinhold, NY, 1982):

"It was the first time I had ever shot at a train and it really had me excited. The train was traveling at top speed and I thought I should lead the engine a little. I estimated the distance and squeezed the trigger and was disappointed to see my bullets kicking up the dirt in front of the engine. I had led it too much. I tried to lead a burst of bullets into the engine by kicking rudder but got only a few hits, a little steam came spewing out as I passed over.

The Chief (Col. Ben Rimmerman) came in right behind me and blew the hell out of the locomotive. The train skidded to a stop with the engine pouring geysers of steam high into the air.

We made a circle back over the train but it was full of civilian passengers and we didn't shoot. People jumped off the train even before it came to a halt. They ran into the fields, diving onto the ground and flattening to hide from our expected bullets. Even though we saw soldiers in uniform mixed in with the women and children, we held our fire."

Later in the mission Bledsoe came upon another train:

"This time I corrected my mistake of leading the engine. I zeroed in to aim at the nose of the huge locomotive as it raced down the railroad track. I squeezed the trigger and the *Little Princess* (his P-47 ed.) bucked as her machine guns went into action. Hurrah!

The stream of bullets struck the engine. Smoke and steam billowed into the sky as I pressed the attack to make sure the locomotive would be destroyed. Just as I passed over the train, it blew up. The smoke momentarily blinded me and I could feel the surge of my ship as the explosion knocked me into the air. I learned a lesson. Hereafter, I would shoot and skirt around the engine."

Col. Hubert "Hub" Zemke discussed damage to locomotives (*The Hub, Fighter Leader*, Airlife, UK, 1988):

"Blocking enemy railways to prevent movement of troops and materials was a frequent task. We had a field day in the Strasbourg area on 3 August (1944), shooting up 31 locomotives in the course of a near five-hour mission; 'Ajax' (VIII Fighter Command HQ-ed.) liked us to classify locomotives as destroyed or damaged. In my view very few were destroyed because perforating a boiler and firebox to bring one to a spectacular steam cloud halt didn't destroy the loco. I'm sure most were soon towed away and repaired."

There are no complete Allied records available as to the loss of locomotives, but German records indicate that between August 1944 and the end of that year an average of 600 per month were lost. However, in 1945 the Allies increased their attacks, and in January 800 were lost, and February 1,700 more.

The post war *US Strategic Bombing Survey* gave the following report on fighter-bomber effect on the German rail system:

"Intensive fighter-bomber activity against small stations, main trackage outside the stations, bridges, etc. permits much more complete paralysis of the enemy rail transportation than the activities of heavy bombers against yards. The work of heavy bombers is, however, a valuable preliminary to such fighter-bomber activity. Successful line cutting is, moreover, the only effective method of reducing the movements of troops and supplies in complete trains and the more moderate volume of commercial traffic, which is suitable to similar handling. Strafing was of some significance as a supplement to other methods since it added to the general confusion, was partly responsible for the disruption of communications and forced much traffic into the night hours. The destruction of locomotives and rolling stock by this method was not, however, important. By the time strafing had reached large proportions this equipment was in surplus. Moreover the damage usually resulting from strafing was transitory and the capacity of repair shops had not been impaired."

Motor Transport (M/T) and the Road Network

German Soft-skinned Vehicles

In the late 1920s the German Waffenamt (Ordnance Department) issued a specification for a 4x6, three-ton design, and a number of companies manufactured the type. In 1933 Germany began her re-armament program, and a 6x4 and 6x6 specification was issued. The 6x4 and 6x6 chassis arrangement was also used by Britain and America, as it allowed rear wheel drive, and the long, high chassis could be adapted to a number of configurations. By the late 1930s 113 truck, 52 automobile, and 150 motorcycle types were in German inventory, making maintenance and stocking of spare parts difficult. To deal with the situation Oberst Adolf von Schell, the Director of Mechanization, reduced the number to 30 truck, 19 automobile, and 30 motorcycle basic models in the so-called "Schell Program," which placed German manufacturers under military direction. Load-carrying vehicles were of four types: 1.5 tons; 3 tons; 4.5 tons; and 6.5 tons, and in each type there was a Standard Type (S-type) with 4x2, 4x4, and 6x4 drive. There were all-wheel drive (Allradantrieb) cross-country versions designated the A-type. German vehicle nomenclature was:

Kfz. = Kraftfahrzeug or Motor Vehicle
Kom. = Kraftomnibus or (Motor) Bus
Krkw. = Krankenkraftwagen or Ambulance
Kw. = Kraftwagen or (Motor) Vehicle
Lkw. = Lastkraftwagen or Truck
Pkw. = Personenkraftwagen or Passenger Car
Schlp. = Schlepper or Tractor
Sd.Kfz. = Sonderkraftfahrzeug or Special Motor Vehicle
Zgkw. = Zugkraftwagen or Prime Mover

The standard truck of the German Army was the high quality 3-ton "Blitz" 34 4x4 manufactured by Opel, the German subsidiary of General Motors. There were two versions built: 95,000 "S" and 25,000 "A" (off-road). (US Army)

The 12 ton half-track SdKfz 8 towing a 88mm mounted on an Anger SdAh 201 trailer was a prime mover in the German army. (US Army)

The Germans used relatively few diesel engines in their trucks, as the German synthetic oil industry could produce gasoline more readily and economically than diesel fuel. The major truck was the 3-ton "Blitz" that was manufactured by Opel, the German subsidiary of General Motors. In 1931, the production of the 1.5- and 3-ton Opel Blitz built to American standards began. These high quality trucks carried a large load for a low net weight. The license-built 75-horse power Buick engine was a straight six cylinder, 3.6 litre gasoline engine. The truck was very reliable, and Opel maintained an excellent spare parts supply and distribution. The Opel Blitz was the primary German military truck in WWII, and a total of 95,000 Blitz-S were built until production stopped in August 1944. Although the S was rated as off-road, an improved Blitz-A with all-wheel drive was produced in 1940 and 25,000 were built. The A had the same motor as the S, and all parts were interchangeable. In 1943 Daimler-Benz dropped its similar design to build 3,500 Blitz-S under license. About 4,000 half-tracked Maultier versions were built, most with open bodies. There were over a hundred special-purpose Blitz variants built, the most important of which was the "Einheitskofferansbau," which was distinguished by its box-type body that could be adapted for a number of functions. The box was constructed of wood and pressed card to save on steel, and the cab was later similarly constructed. The so-called "Wehrmacht Bus" was a Blitz chassis fitted with a bus body that could carry 26 seated soldiers or 23 stretchers as an ambulance, or be used as a command vehicle. Blitz construction resumed after the war, and the S-type became the major post-war German commercial truck. Daimler-Benz, Henschel, Krupp, Bussig-NAG, Magrirus, and Borgward manufactured medium 6x4 and 6x6 trucks in smaller numbers. In 1937, to standardize the manufacture of a light truck, the "Uniform Diesel" was designed under the direction of the Wehrmacht Weapons Office. The 6x6 had outstanding off-road capabilities and several companies built 10,000, but it was found to be very expensive to manufacture and was discontinued.

The most recognizable vehicle in the German Army was the Volkswagen Type 82 "leichter Personenkraftwagen" or better known as the Kubelwagen (German for "bucket car") designed by Ferdinand Porsche. Over 52,000 Kubelwagens were built and used on all fronts with its air-cooled, four-cylinder engine adaptable to the hot North African desert and the cold Russian steppes. In the background is a Bussig Nag 8-ton 4x2 truck. (US Army)

Automobiles

The most recognizable vehicle in the German Army was the Volkswagen Type 82 "Leichter Personenkraftwagen," better known as the Kubelwagen (German for "bucket car"), designed by Ferdinand Porsche. Over 52,000 of the ubiquitous Kubelwagens were built and used on all fronts, with its air-cooled, four-cylinder engine adaptable to the hot North African desert and the cold Russian steppes. German Chiefs of Staffs and Field Marshals used the Mercedes 540 K as a staff car, which is well-known today from war movies made after the war. Intended for civilian use, the five speed, 180hp, straight eight was well appointed and known for its comfort and prestige.

Only the elite divisions of the German army were equipped with front-line tactical vehicles, and to a large extent it used captured or confiscated civilian vehicles or those manufactured in occupied countries. Once the war began, the automobile industries in the newly occupied countries France (Renault, Latil, Citroen, Peugeot), Austria (Saurer, OAF, Steyr), and particularly Czechoslovakia (Tatra, Skoda), were utilized by the Germans to build vehicles. The Italian auto industry (Fiat, Alfa Romeo) also built vehicles for the Wehrmacht. By spring 1945 civilian-type vehicles and horses were commandeered by the military and vastly outnumbered military vehicles. Probably the softest-skinned vehicle was the horse, and thousands were used throughout the war, usually behind the front lines and in occupied countries.

In 1939, of the 2.74 million men in the field armies, 191,000 (7%) belonged to the supply or administrative services. By 1943 350,000 (12.2%) supply troops were numbered in the field army of 4.27 million. Wehrmacht and SS divisions required 300 to 500 tons of supplies each day. The lower echelons made wide use of horse-drawn transport, but the main armies were supplied by motor transport, and railheads were extended to as close as ten miles of the front. The rail and road network of Western Europe was modern and widespread, increasing the Armies' ability to transport the required quantity of supplies. The road system was so dense that destroying it from the air was impossible. There were obvious choke points that were vulnerable to air attack, such as bridges, tunnels, or roads in narrow passes or valleys. Most air damage to the road net was not locally extensive and could be easily repaired or bypassed by driving around it, or by using an alternate route. It was considered useless to try to camouflage or hide key road points, such as bridges, tunnels, and junctions, as they were well-known in the pre-war and the surrounding environment made them obvious (e.g. a river runs under a bridge). Bridges and key road junctions were often heavily protected by AA positions and barrage balloons. Until 1945 road traffic was secondary to rail traffic in cargo volume. There was very little civilian transport on the roads, and any vehicle on a road was considered military or hauling military-related cargo. Anything moving on or parked along a road was attacked. The daylight attacks by fighter-bombers caused the Germans to move at night, and the efficiency of the transport system was decreased. From D-Day the time available for night movement was decreased by shorter summer nights, and German supply suffered the consequences. Also, night movement was slower and required blackout driving that exhausted drivers, causing delays and accidents that upset delivery schedules. The "Kfz.-Nachtmarschgerat," designed and built by Nova-Technik GmbH, was a standard item on German military vehicles. It consisted of a detachable "Tarnschienwerfer," or blackout lamp, on the left front fender, and a specially designed distance/stop/tail light. The taillight had two pairs of two square openings in a row with a hinged lid that could cover the lights. The configuration of taillights allowed the driver to judge the distance from the vehicle ahead of him. If four squares appeared as one light then the driver was too far behind (125 to 1,000 feet), if it appeared as two lights then the distance was correct (75 to 125 feet), and if it appeared as four squares then the driver was too close.

German soft-skinned vehicles suffered enormous damage from fighter-bombers. Strafing by machine gun and cannon fire was much more accurate than rockets and bombs, as their rounds could be aimed accurately with the gunsight or "walked" up to the target. In strafing road convoys a flight would attack in line abreast, perpendicular to the road. Each pilot chose a target and concentrated on it. The front and rear vehicles were taken out first to immobilize the convoy and make it an easier target on succeeding attacks. The .50 cal. round could easily penetrate vehicle bodies, hitting engines, fuel tanks, and occupants. The most vulnerable area of a truck was the fuel tank or radiator, and since trucks and half-tracks carried their own fuel supply in Jerry cans they often exploded when hit. Bombs and rockets did not have to hit vehicles to destroy or badly damage them, as they were vulnerable to the blast or shrapnel of a near miss. The Germans used light motorcycles and bicycles, many horse and ox-drawn wagons, and widespread use of towing, which was more satisfactory in Italy, where the battlefront was static for long periods, but not so during the constant retreats in France. The fighter-bomber was most effective against German armor by destroying the soft-skinned vehicles that supplied them with fuel and ammunition.

The attack on the road network was enhanced by the systematic and permanent destruction of supply roads at vulnerable points, such as bridges, tunnels, swampy and marshy areas, narrow and precipitous areas (e.g. along cliffs), and closely built up areas (e.g. narrow streets in cities, towns, and villages). Road transport was persistently attacked between the railheads and the front lines, creating "traffic deserts" that prevented the enemy from concentrating troops and supplies at decisive times and places. The use of GP bombs against M/T caused craters on the roads that were a particu-

An ammo and fuel convoy under attack. (USAF)

Three-frame gun camera sequence of a 15th Air Force P-38 exploding a German ammunition truck. The Lightning had its starboard engine knocked out and upon landing the pilot found pieces of uniform, a cigarette pack and shell casings in the fighter's air scoops. (USAF)

lar problem in rainy weather. Bomb cratering could cause traffic jams in constricted areas, such as narrow valleys, at road junctions, and on streets in cities and towns. Air attacks prevented the delivery of supplies to the front, and also hampered empty trucks from returning to the rear to pick up more supplies. Attacks on communication centers along the road network did result in local reduction in road traffic. But, by and large, the attacking points of congestion, such as towns and bridges, in the road system was ineffective as the European road network was so extensive that these areas could be readily detoured. Despite the extensive and constant air effort in both Italy and France the Allies failed to completely incapacitate Axis motor transport.

Capt. Leslie Cles, P-47 pilot for the 353rd Fighter Group, gave tips on attacking motor convoys (*Down to the Deck*, ibid.):

"In a truck convoy, size it up for types of trucks and what defense it carries. Most of the enemy's trucks and half-tracks carry their own supply of gasoline. If you can explode this, you destroy the truck. Don't waste our fire on the gun the half-track or truck might be pulling. Hit the vehicle. An immobile gun is useless on the roadside. When the truck convoy has its own anti-aircraft defenses, it may be safer to work from the ends toward the middle in passes that cross at right angles to the roadway. You'll find, however, that many times you can see your truck only by coming straight down the road."

The Germans formed special "Arrow Flash" truck convoys, much like the famed American "Red Ball Express," to cope with the confusion, congestion, and destruction wrought by American bombing of their road system. The "Red Ball Express" was successful, as it was not under constant attack by Luftwaffe Jabos. Pilots debated whether a strafing attack on a single truck could be justified in the expenditure of ammunition. But the brass felt that single trucks needed to be attacked, because if they were not the Germans would split their convoys into single trucks and send one down the road every five to ten minutes, allowing a large amount of supplies to get through. Single trucks were usually safe to attack,

In spite of its Blitzkrieg reputation, the German Army was largely dependent on horse-drawn supply and artillery. When fighter-bombers attacked, horses became terrified and tried to escape the pandemonium, falling or overturning their carriages. Mixed horse and motor transport column before fighter-bomber attack in north Italy. (USAF)

as they generally transported cargo instead of troops that could put up small arms fire.

In spite of its Blitzkrieg reputation, the German Army was largely dependent on horse-drawn supply and artillery. When fighter-bombers attacked, horses became terrified and tried to escape the pandemonium, falling or overturning their carriages. During the German retreat from the Falaise pocket horse-drawn vehicles suffered heavy losses. Days afterward, pilots flying over the area claimed to be able to smell the stench from bloated horse carcasses, rigid legs directed skyward at their killers. When Allied troops moved into the recently bombed and strafed areas they came upon horses that had been horribly wounded and were bellowing in pain, and were forced to put them out of their misery. From the Ste. Eugenie Road to the Mesnil-Laird Road, 82 dead horses and their vehicles blocked the road for over a mile, where they rotted in the sun until the end of October. So many dead horses polluted the Dives Plain it was declared an "unhealthy zone" for two months, and Allied troops were ordered to stay out. When post battle analysts came into the area to determine the extent of the destruction the stench of the dead, bloated horses drove them off. The French population living there had to be supplied with fresh water trucked in from Caen.

In order to preserve the road net for later Allied use it was felt that the bombing of it should be restricted. But because the Germans would probably destroy them when faced with their loss in retreat Lt.Gen. J. Lawton Collins, VII Corps commander, stated:

"I believe the destruction of enemy signal communications is of such great importance to us that it should be done irrespective of any delay that might be caused in our subsequent use of this system."

However, many times when Allied forces were moving rapidly, they requested that the air forces discontinue bombing road bridges along the direction of the advance, as the Germans had no time for demolition in their harried retreat.

Although the German soft-skinned vehicle industry was a secondary strategic bombing target, these attacks produced a significant decrease in production. These production losses could not begin to keep pace with the miles of wrecks that lined the roads of France, Belgium, and Germany caused by fighter-bombers. One German source estimated that more than 30,000 trucks were destroyed in Northern France alone. Also, large numbers of trucks were unavailable at all times for two or three weeks, as they were being converted from gasoline to alternate power. From mid-1944 the Germans converted their vehicles to burn methane gas, coal, and wood, which decreased engine performance, but that did not matter, as the continual air attacks had slowed the pace of transport to a virtual crawl at night. The conversion was slow and labor-intensive, but in Italy the Germans had converted 2,800 vehicles by the end of the war. The Germans also diluted their gasoline with alcohol derived from sugar beet molasses and grape pressings. The Allies then bombed sugar beet refineries, compelling the Germans to conserve their diluted gasoline for combat vehicles. The loss of M/T was combined with the shortage of gasoline, lack of spare parts, and the regularity of breakdowns from overuse and poor maintenance. The sum was the cost to German mobility and supply in the field.

Miscellaneous transport included horse-drawn vehicles and bicycles. It was estimated that the annual horse replacement requirement of the German army was 500,000. It was estimated that in late 1944 horses moved two-thirds of the supplies of some divisions. Late in the war, after the destruction of the rail system and the shortage of fuel and M/T, horse-drawn vehicles carried a large proportion of necessary supplies.

The Allied Jabos became so destructive, the August 1944 issue of the *"Panzer News Bulletin" (Nachrichtenblatt der Panzertruppen)* that was published by the General Inspector of the Panzertruppen spoke to the combat experience of Panzers after D-Day and instructed troops and vehicles on counter measures:

> "I) Marches
> It is impossible to conduct marches without enemy aerial observation. Therefore, marches can be conducted only at night. Pulling into cover must be completed by dawn, especially if the day's objective has not been reached. Never use lights during night marches.
> Conduct marches only in small groups. Maintain air defenses intervals within the groups, even at night. The enemy fighters illuminate the road with searchlights.
> The pre-requisite for a smoothly flowing march is well-organized route scouting and guiding. When halts occur, the vehicles must be prevented from closing up.
> When enemy aircraft attack, each vehicle is to independently drive into cover. The entire march movement halts. Single vehicles must halt from time to time, turn off the engine and listen. Aircraft are often heard at longer range than they can be seen.
> Fighters continue to attack until there are signs that the vehicles are burning. In such attacks, which are also directed against single vehicles, throwing out smoke pots or smoke grenades can successfully fool the opponent.
> II) Bivouacs
> Avoid towns because they are increasingly selected for air attack and the bivouacked units (headquarters) are reported to the enemy by civilians.
> Move into woods, maintaining large intervals, and prohibit civilians from entering the bivouac areas.
> Dig in wheeled vehicles. Wheels and engines must be protected against fragments.
> In all cases, forbid the use of radio communication even for tuning in. This also applies to assembly areas. Several times units behind the front were covered by carpet bombing after sending a few messages."

Authors notes:
1) Careless exposure of tracks and tires was the most frequent method of detecting armor or motor transport.
2) Towards the end of the war many German vehicles were equipped with a metal seat attached to the right front fender to seat an aircraft spotter.
3) Drive-in dug outs or shelters were placed at intervals along the main roads so an entire vehicle could be driven into it to hide during the daytime in case of air attack.

The unrelenting attacks and destruction of forward rail facilities (railheads, bridges, and crossing points) increased the demand for motor vehicles for transport, which increased the demand for fuel that, in turn, needed to be brought from Germany by rail. To make matters worse the German oil industry was under strategic bombing attack, causing shortages. Air attacks pushed railheads further back from the fronts, causing the motor columns to use more fuel on the longer runs, exposing them to air attacks for longer periods and increasing the delay in deliveries to the front. The fact that regular railway traffic all but ceased in 1945 caused the whole burden of transport to fall on road vehicles that had to travel at night. The maneuverability of the Wehrmacht in the field was largely dependent upon motor transport, and the damage or destruction of the motor transport system had immediate and direct effect on the battlefront in terms of casualties and ground lost. From D-Day to the end of the war the three 9th Air Force TACs destroyed 53,811 motor vehicles destroyed and 22,546 damaged for loss of 1,374 P-47s.

Bridges

Bridges were difficult to destroy, as the span was narrow, the abutments were reinforced concrete, and they were often defended by flak. Fighter-bombers were more effective against bridges than

Bridges were difficult to destroy as the span was narrow, the abutments were reinforced concrete and they were often defended by flak The Narni highway bridge was hit by 1,000lb. GP .01 second delay fused bombs that destroyed the masonry supports and collapsed the trusses into the river. (USAF)

The fuse and bomb type needed to destroy a bridge determined the type of aircraft assigned to attack it. The P-47 could carry 1,000lb. bombs but many bridges required heavier bombs and the mission went to light and medium and occasionally heavy units. The Acquasparta highway overpass was destroyed by two 1,000lb GP .025 second delay fused bombs. The non-reinforced concrete was vulnerable to bombing. (USAF)

medium bombers. The bombers dropped their bombs in a walking pattern across the bridge and usually missed it altogether. After an extensive briefing and study of the reconnaissance photos fighter-bomber pilots determined the direction of approach and dive angle that would put their bombs on the bridge's supporting structures. Since traditional dive-bombing was generally ineffective a new technique, a type of skip-bombing called "drive-bombing," was developed using 500lb. bombs that were fused with 8-11 second delayed fuses. The pilot began his diving approach from about a mile away and then leveled out at about a third of a mile from the bridge at about 400mph. Flying just above the water, below the span of the bridge, the pilot aimed and dropped his bomb at the abutment, pulling up at the last split second. The 400mph bomb drove itself deep into the abutment area, and when it exploded, the buried bomb collapsed the abutment and the span it supported.

The German engineer corps became very efficient in repairing and building bridges, nearly as quickly as the Allies attacked them. The German repair organization also used impressed French and Italian civilian labor, POWs and German troops that were waiting for repairs to be done so they could proceed to the front. (US Army)

German engineers were very resourceful in trying to confine bridge destruction from the air. As, one-by-one, the permanent bridges in the ETO and MTO were being so badly damaged or destroyed as to make repair futile the Germans resorted to pontoon bridges. These bridges could be placed overnight, and fighter-bombers had a constant battle to keep them from being used. As soon as reconnaissance missions discovered new pontoon bridges, fighter-bombers were scheduled to attack them. As these bridges were placed in vital areas of transport movement they were often heavily defended by flak. The method of attack was to first dive-bomb the pontoon bridge to break it apart and then strafe the pieces that were floating downstream. In other attempts to keep ahead of Jabo bridge destruction, the German engineers would construct a bridge just under the surface of the water to fool aerial photo-reconnaissance. The "night-operational bridge" was a bridge that would be repaired just short of completion, leaving one span missing so that photo recon would classify it as impassable. At night a specially built movable span would be put in place and then removed before dawn. The engineers would also take advantage of the transition from day-night/night-day (dusk/dawn) attacks to frantically work on repairs. The efficient German repair organization used impressed French and Italian civilian labor, POWs, and German troops that were waiting for repairs to be done so they could proceed to the front. Partisan groups in Italy and France constantly harassed the repair organization and were instrumental in causing further delays.

On 6 May 1944 the AEAF directed the 365th Fighter Group to conduct bridge bombing trials on a steel bridge at Vernon, two concrete bridges at Mantes-Gassicort, and "further attacks were to await studies of the results obtained." (The trials are discussed later in the Campaigns/Pre-invasion section.) After the trials, full combat attacks were made on the Seine, Meuse, and Liore River Bridges (also discussed in the Campaigns/Pre-Invasion section). After the liberation of France, IX TAC Operational Research Service (ORS) visited the Seine bridges that had been attacked and issued a report (*IX TAC ORS #90*). In its introduction Quesada stated that many of the IX TAC's attacks were ill planned and poorly executed. He stated that there was only one best method of attack for each bridge, and that could be determined only by careful study. He derided the AEAF for not developing procedures for planning and executing bridge-busting attacks and stated: "Instructions related to attacks on the Seine bridges were issued often from hour to hour." The ORS investigated 13 bridges of the "through types" (steel lattice work main structure) that required instantaneous fusing, and that of 1,401 bombs dropped on them only 232 had the correct fusing. The fuse and bomb type needed to destroy a bridge determined the type of aircraft assigned to attack it. The P-47 could carry 1,000lb. bombs, but many bridges required heavier bombs, and the mission went to light and medium, and occasionally heavy bomber units. The long distance to the Loire bridges made it necessary for heavy bombers to attack them due to their range and bomb capacity. The AAF Evaluation Board also examined the bridge damage and found that fusing and bomb sizes were often wrong. The AAFEB report found to achieve maximum effect the bomb needed to detonate as close to the vital supporting structure as possible, and the selection of the fuse that determined the point of detonation was very important.

Delayed fused bombs hitting the "through type" bridge penetrated before detonation, and the explosion was dissipated in the air under the span, causing no damage. It was found that instantaneous nose or non-delay tail bomb was most effective against the "through" bridge.

The average bridge encountered in occupied territory could usually be damaged but not readily destroyed by fighter-bombers. Drive-bombing with a 500lb. bomb and a delay fuse could more easily damage it than dive-bombing, which was much too inaccurate for pinpoint targets. Successful attacks on bridges caused the maximum delay on the movement of German reinforcements and supplies, and increased the fuel shortage in the battle area by imposing long detours, and causing more wear and tear and maintenance on vehicles and armor. The construction and repair of bridges blocked traffic and created choice targets for fighter-bombers.

Tunnels

A direct against a tunnel was preferred but difficult to achieve, as tunnels were often located in difficult hilly or mountainous terrain. A near miss was nearly as good as a direct hit, as it would collapse and seal the entrance.

Tank Busting

U.S. fighter-bombers were not equipped with a specifically designed anti-tank weapon; gun, bomb, or rocket. The rocket was the RAF anti-tank weapon of choice and made the Hawker Typhoon the premier Allied "tank buster." When U.S. infantry came upon concentrations of German armor, RAF rocket Typhoons were called in to engage them. The rocket was inherently inaccurate but did not lack punch. A well aimed, or more likely, a lucky hit, could penetrate all but the frontal armor of a German heavy tank hull. A near miss was of no value, as the explosion and flying debris caused no damage. It was extremely difficult for a fighter-bomber pilot to hit individual tanks on the battlefield, as the tanks were either moving targets or took cover as soon as the attacking aircraft was spotted. Also, the tanks were often camouflaged and protected by mobile flak. Congregations of armor along a road or in attack formation presented better targets. The fighter-bomber flights went into a vertical dive, salvoing all their rockets to saturate the area, hoping to score a hit. When armored columns were discovered moving along a road the fighter-bombers tried to seal the escape by destroying the vehicles in the front and rear of the column and then destroying the tanks and vehicles between with rockets, bombs, and bullets.

The USAAF decided to utilize fighter-bombers for ground support, interdiction, armed recce, and armored column cover, and not develop an aircraft or airborne gun specifically designed to combat enemy tanks. AAF fighter-bombers relied on general-purpose high explosive or armor-piercing bombs and .50 cal. machine guns to attack German armor. A 45-degree dive-bombing attack was normally used to attack tanks, but required a great measure of skill that was beyond the training and ability of the average pilot. Often, with a direct hit, the GP bomb would glance off or break up ineffectively against the tank's armored hull. Accurately aimed AP bombs were the most effective weapon against a tank if they obtained a high velocity and hit on a vulnerable area, such as the bogey wheel tracks, engine compartment, or any hull area that had ventilation louvers. The loss of a wheel or the unhinging of the tracks could be quickly repaired if field maintenance crews were close by. The maintenance and recovery unit was an important part of the German Panzer Division, as they salvaged numerous tanks damaged by air attacks to fight another day.

Strafing with six or eight .50 cal. machine guns was much more accurate than rockets or bombs, and many hits could be scored. Even though the .50 caliber round fired from a fighter flying at 300-400mph had high momentum that could penetrate several inches of soft steel, such as on a locomotive boiler, and could be devastating to soft-skinned vehicles or light armor; it only dinged the hardened steel plate of a Panzer. The Germans had three main battle tanks in service in 1944: the Mark IV; the Panther Mark V; and the Tiger Mark VI. Of the three only the Mark IV was vulnerable to strafing, and then only by hits on its lightly armored rear deck that covered the engine. Strafing the Panther or Tiger would cause the

The US did not develop an aircraft or airborne gun specifically designed for the anti-tank role. The development of effective dive-bombing techniques and rockets proved this decision to be correct. The P-47 was the AAF anti-tank aircraft of choice. Here a StuGIII was destroyed by P-47s outside Daleiden, Germany in February 1945. (US Army)

The maintenance and recovery unit was an important part of the German Panzer Division as they salvaged numerous tanks damaged by air attacks to fight another day. Here a Sd.Kfz9/1 and a Sd.Kfz 8 tow a Tiger tank. (Author)

Tiger tank (US Army)

Panzer III and IV (US Army)

Panther tank (US Army)

crew to button up and wait out the attack, or head toward cover and hope that the fighter-bombers were not equipped with bombs or rockets. But remaining confined in the small compartment while .50 cal. slugs dinged off the armor and not knowing whether a bomb or rocket would come next was sure to have a psychological effect on a tank crew. There was a story spread among fighter-bomber pilots of an attack on the German Tiger tank. A Tiger was caught out in an open field heading toward a woods by three flights of P-47s on an armed recce. All 12 fighter-bombers made a low strafing run, aiming at the bogey wheels and hoping to knock off a track. Failing this, on their next run, at a steeper angle, they concentrated on the rear engine compartment, hoping to stop the engine, and failed again. On their final pass they attempted to ricochet API and ball into the underside of the tank to penetrate the thinner armor there, or to get a lucky bounce into a vent or louver, but to no avail, as the Tiger disappeared into the trees.

No matter how skilled and experienced the pilot, there was no such thing as accurately aiming and hitting a specific area of a tank. Pilots considered the top of the turret and the rear engine deck as the most vulnerable part of a tank, having the thinnest armor, but .50 caliber AP bullets would bounce off these areas. To stop a tank, lucky hits needed to be made on vulnerable points such as sighting or steering ports or engine louvers. Pilots thought that AP rounds hitting the tracks could disable a tank, but in reality the tracks were manufactured of very hard steel, and .50 caliber hits bounced off; it took a lucky hit to cause a thrown track. If the tank with a thrown track were on road it could get to safety or repair on its road wheels. When tanks traveling on hard surfaces were attacked, pilots attacked from the rear and attempted to ricochet bullets into the more lightly armored Panzer undersides, where exhaust or cooling vents were located. Due to a design flaw in the placement of the air vents in Tiger tanks, .50 caliber machine bullets could enter the crew compartment and ricochet repeatedly, killing or severely wounding the crew. When traveling long distances, when gasoline supplies and ammunition were scarce due to air attacks, German Panzer crews carried ammunition and extra cans of fuel on the sides or rear of their tanks. Armed reconnaissance fighter-bombers hoped to find such a vulnerable Panzer which, if hit by the bullets of strafing P-47s, could meet disaster. Napalm could be effective against German armor, as it could incinerate the crew with a direct hit or near miss, but was not used against tanks to any extent.

From D-Day to VE Day 9th Air Force TACs claimed to have destroyed 4,509 tanks and other armored vehicles and damaged 22,546 others. Despite large number of claims, the fighter-bomber pilot did not destroy as many German tanks as credited. The high number of claims for the destruction of armor was due to pilots often misjudging the effect of their attacks. In a few seconds a section of road could be left burning and smoking under rocket, bomb, and machine gun fire. Claims assessment was divided between damaged ("smokers") and destroyed ("flamers"). Of course, much of the smoke and flame was not the consequence of only tanks being hit. With the pilot diving across the burning and smoking vehicles at high speed it was difficult to distinguish between the types of vehicles: soft-skinned; armored artillery; tank destroyers; and assault guns or tanks. Target duplication was another reason for excessive claims, as more than one pilot would attack the same burning or smoking tank. Burned out and abandoned tanks were often attacked several times. Ace German tank commander of the 101st SS Heavy Panzer Battalion, Michael Wittmann, described the extreme means his unit had to use to evade the constant threat of Allied fighter-bomber attack. When lookouts on top of a tank detected an approaching fighter-bomber the tank stopped, depressed, and traversed the gun to the side, opened all hatches, and released smoke so the tank looked destroyed and abandoned.

The British analyzed 110 captured German tanks between 6 June to 7 August 1944 and found that 70 were destroyed by artillery or anti-tank projectiles, only ten were destroyed by aircraft, and 11 were destroyed or abandoned by their crews. From 8 to 31 August the British examined 223 captured Panzers and found 29 were destroyed by artillery or anti-tank projectiles, ten by aircraft, and 171 were either abandoned or destroyed by their crews. Since the Panzer attrition rate was high there were many new, inexperienced crews, which would explain the high percentage of abandoned tanks.

Ace German tank commander of the 101st SS Heavy Panzer Battalion, Michael Wittmann. (Author/West)

Although anti-tank air attacks could be considered ineffective in the number of Panzers actually destroyed, the weight of firepower these attacks were able to concentrate on their targets caused considerable chaos and subsequent demoralization of tank crews during the constant retreat after the Normandy landings until the end of the war. Even a fully armed and fueled tank was useless if its crew were cowering in a ditch seeking shelter from an air attack, or were constantly searching the skies and for cover for their tank in anticipation of an air attack. German armored movement needed to be carried out at night, and any daytime movement or operations was immediately attacked and immobilized by swarms of Allied fighter-bombers. The wholesale abandonment or scuttling by Panzer crews was due to lack of fuel and ammunition (due to air attacks), mechanical breakdowns (especially among the Panther tanks), and demoralization due to the constant threat and actuality of air attack. Battlefield tanks did not have to be destroyed in order to neutralize them. The effective attacks on their vulnerable soft-skinned motorized supply transport deprived them of gasoline and ammunition.

Anti-tank footnote: Necessity on the Russian Front motivated the Germans into perfecting tank busting into an art form. The greatest tank buster of all time was Hans-Ulrich Rudel, who flew a mind-boggling 2,530 missions in the Ju-87 Stuka on the Eastern front from the 22 June 1941 Invasion of Russia to VE-Day. He destroyed 519 tanks (17 on 22 March 1944 and 12 on 8 February 1945); 800 vehicles; four armored trains; 150 artillery; anti-tank and AA positions; one battleship (Marat); a cruiser; a destroyer; and 70 landing craft. He was also an air ace with nine victories, but was shot down 30 times by ground fire and wounded five times, losing a leg on 8 February 1945. Leading Soviet tank buster was A. N. Yefimov, who flew 222 missions in the Shturmovik Il-2, knocking out 126 tanks and 85 Luftwaffe aircraft on the ground.

Friendly River Crossings

Air superiority was imperative for a crossing of a defended river line to protect vulnerable crossing troops from enemy air attacks. The fighter-bomber was ideally fitted for close support in river crossings. The river itself provided a well-defined bomb line, and enemy targets on the opposite side could be easily identified and attacked effectively and safely. The enemy was forced to move his mobile and infantry reinforcements directly toward the crossing points, exposing them to air attack. The fighter-bomber was also assigned to suppress enemy artillery fire and to blunt enemy counterattacks.

Enemy River Crossings and Ferries

The Germans used purpose and makeshift ferries to cross rivers that had their bridges destroyed. In Italy the Po River bridges, and in France the Liore and Seine bridges had been destroyed, resulting in a desperate scramble for troops to cross. Crossing in the daytime was impossible without devastating fighter-bomber attacks. In many cases the ferry crossings were disorganized, and personnel and material backed up and then presented daylight targets. As a result large quantities of first to arrive, first to cross, non-essential material was transported across the river, leaving armor, trucks, artillery, and other weapons behind to be destroyed by retreating troops.

A canal lock defended a little too late by two twin Flak 38s mounted on a tracked chassis. (US Army)

A string of barges towed by a tug is strafed by P-47s of the 78th Fighter Group. (USAF)

Inland Waterways, Locks and Barges

Europe possessed a well-developed and complex system of canals and inland waterways. They linked major mining and industrial regions and ports, providing slow but economical movement of a high volume of bulk cargo, such as coal, ore, and steel. The most vulnerable points of canals were areas where the bulk of their water could flow out. Locks often limited the amount of lost water to the entire system, but a few well placed attacks could cause damage that required lengthy repair. Aqueducts were the primary choke point, as they were structures where canals crossed rivers, valleys, roads, rail lines, etc. Damaging or destroying an aqueduct not only disabled that section of the canal, but was difficult and expensive to repair, and needed to be completely repaired before the canal was back in operation.

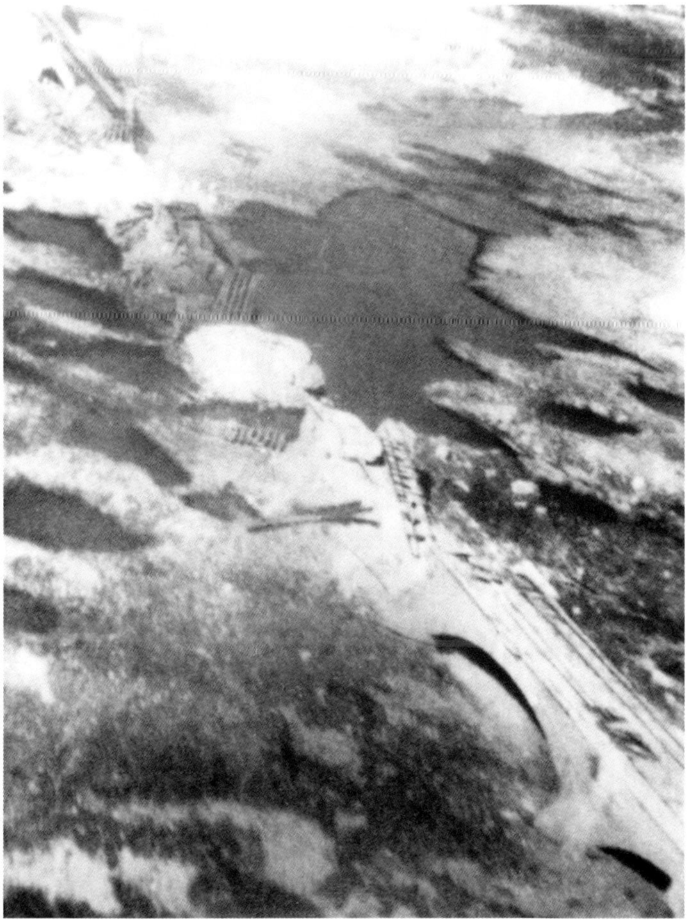

Viaduct at Lavis, Italy, destroyed by fighter-bombers in February 1945. (USAF)

The heart of the German waterway system was the Rhine River in Germany and Holland, and the Danube in southeastern Europe, along with the Weser, Oder, Elbe, and numerous canals. In 1939, Germany possessed 6,000 steam and motor-powered vessels and 14,000 unpowered barges with a capacity of six million tons. Over 50% of the cargo transported on the Rhine was ore (37% coal), mainly to the Ruhr. The Danube carried the oil and agricultural products from Rumania and Hungary to be handled among the 38 major ports on the Danube. After the annexation of Austria in 1938 the Danube Flotilla was formed of minesweepers and escorts ships that were heavily armed with AA guns. River flotillas were formed on other major rivers to protect river traffic.

The nature of river and canal traffic made it conducive to fighter-bomber attack. Although many barges were destroyed by air attack, the Germans had sufficient numbers to continue night movement. Destroyed barges could easily be removed from blocking the waterway. Effective air attacks damaged locks and bridges that spanned canals (whose center sections needed to be movable to allow the passage of barges), and the repair of both was labor intensive. After Allied interdiction had destroyed the rail and road net in northern Italy, Armaments Minister Albert Speer extended and reorganized the northern Italian inland waterway system. So-called "Speer barges" of the Transportflotte carried essential materials and armaments.

German trawler is being strafed in the English Channel. (USAF)

A Kriegsmarine Schnellboot carried a 20mm Flak gun on a pedestal mount. The gunner aimed the gun with the help of two curved shoulder braces. Note the mesh basket to catch spent shell cases. (Author)

Small Naval Vessels and German Coastal Convoys

The French coastal ports were filled with small Kriegsmarine vessels of all types, ranging from S-bootes (Schnellbootes), T-bootes (Torpedobootes), R-bootes (Raumbootes), M-bootes (Minensuchboote), VP-bootes (Vorpostenbootes) and assorted supply ships, repair ships, escort ships, training ships, tugs, harbor defense launches, etc. By the end of 1943 they were unable to operate in daylight for fear of air attack.

The British Admiralty named the 90-95-ton German S-boote, fast torpedo boat the "E-boat," meaning enemy torpedo boat. It was unlikely that the Kriegsmarine, of all the world's navies, would develop the best fast torpedo boat of the war. They manned them with talented, young, aggressive officers and men. The S-bootes were the most important naval weapon in coastal waters, sinking over 40 enemy warships and 100 merchantmen in all theaters, including the Mediterranean and Black Sea. The rugged hulls of the Schnellbootes were constructed of inner and outer wooden planking built over a light alloy frame. The typical S-boote's defensive armament in 1944 consisted of a 20mm AA cannon located forward on a retractable mount between the torpedo tubes, a 40mm Bofors or a rapid-firing 37mm AA cannon on the stern, and a twin 20mm AA cannon amidships. A few S-bootes mounted a quadmount 20mm Verling on the stern and removable light machine guns on the bridge. The S-bootes were crewed by 20-23 men and powered by three fuel guzzling Daimler Benz engines that drove it to a top speed of 35-40 knots. About 200 were built during the war. The S-bootes cruised in flotillas of eight to ten boats, moving in line astern formation, which made them a menacing target for strafing air attacks, which was the most effective method of attacking them. P-47 fighter-bombers attacked in a high speed (400+mph), low-level (10-20ft) run, pulling up about a 1,000 yards from their targets, away from the bristling AA fire. Fragmentation bombs were utilized but were ineffective, as they were dropped from too high altitudes. By early 1944, because of Allied air superiority and naval dominance, the S-bootes operated only in darkness that in June meant leaving port after 2200 hours and returning at 0430. While in port during daylight hours, they were attacked by fighter-bombers and finally had to be moved into the concrete pens along the Channel Coast, particularly Boulogne, LeHavre, Cherbourg, and Calais. Late in the war S-boote use was restricted by fuel shortages.

Initial German minesweeper design was based on WWI types, but as the war progressed they were continually improved and enlarged. They were armed with two 105mm, two 37mm AA guns, and six to eight 20mm AA guns, and were referred to by the Allies as "Channel Destroyers" due to this heavy armament. The Types M35 and M-40 were crewed by 76 to 104 men and had a top speed of 18 knots. Over 300 minesweepers were built during the war.

As Allied anti-shipping aircraft became more plentiful and effective, especially after the introduction of aerial rockets, the Germans increased AA defense for their coastal convoys. The merchantmen were more heavily armed, and the Germans added the Vorpostenboote (Outpost or Patrol boats), which were armed trawlers, and Sperrbrecher (Barrier Breaker or Auxiliary Minesweepers), which were heavily armed (105mm and 88mm) ex-merchantmen, to their convoys. Minensuchboote (Minesweepers) swept the

The strafing of German airdromes was probably the most dangerous ground attack undertaking as they were usually heavily defended by AA positions. 8th Air Force fighters drop down to attack a Luftwaffe airdrome near Leipzig on 27 February 1945 as they claimed 81 aircraft destroyed on the ground. A P-51 is seen flying lower center of photo. (USAF)

The low level of the strafing attack is demonstrated by the P-47 (upper right) attacking a sitting Potez bomber. (USAF)

waters ahead of the convoy, and for close escort Raumbootes were employed. The R-bootes were also used for coastal protection, coastal minesweeping, mine laying, and rescue of downed aircrews. The 140-ton R-bootes initially carried one 37mm and three 20mm AA guns and were upgraded to three more 20mm guns. They were crewed by 34-38 men and had a top speed of 21 knots. S-bootes protected the flanks of the convoys. The convoys along the French and Low Country coasts were abandoned in early 1944, but continued on the Baltic and Norwegian coasts until the end of the war.

Occasionally German ships shot shells to a 1,000ft. that deployed parachutes that had cables suspended vertically. When these cables were used the attack was altered to a longitudinal approach in a 30-degree dive.

Airdromes

Of all strafing sorties, attacks on airdromes were the most dangerous and feared. Chet Borek, P-47 pilot for the 362nd Fighter Group, commented (*Color of War: P-47*, History Channel video):

"The times you really didn't want to go on a mission was when they would announce at a briefing that you were going to hit an airdrome today. Some pilots would back out of the mission saying they were sick. Many pilots had gone through an awful lot and knew they were going to get hit. It was not a guess but an assumption. How severe you didn't know but you just knew."

Planned Attacks

Planned airdrome attacks had the primary objective of surprise. They were flown by four aircraft in line abreast within flights, and flights in close trail and firing individually. No more than two eight-ship sections were considered safe for these attacks. The sections were to make their passes from different directions and timed as close together as possible. If a pilot did not have a target in front of him he was discouraged from turning toward another target, as that interfered with the adjacent pilot's run and was dangerous for both. Because valuable airdromes were usually heavily defended by flak the flights stayed as close to the deck as possible. Well defended airdromes were often attacked by an anti-flak flight detailed to attack ground defenses before the actual attack. The flight opened fire at 300 to 400 yards and fired as long as possible. Pilots were urged not to cross the middle of the airdrome. Flying close to the edges was safer because the flak positions were situated there. By flying close to the guns the aircraft presented a target moving at a high angular speed that made it difficult for the gunners to track. Also, hangars containing enemy aircraft were most likely to be found close to the perimeter of the field. On withdrawal evasive action was continued on deck, skidding and keeping up airspeed for five to ten miles beyond target, when altitude was regained and sections reformed.

P-51 strafer walks bullets to an aircraft parked outside an armored camouflaged hanger. Note another P-51 at upper left of photo (arrow). (USAF)

If the A/D were heavily defended a pre-planned strafing attack could be carried out in conjunction with medium bombers. The bombing units would fly at medium altitude followed by the strafers. About 20 miles from target the bomber squadron leader would waggle his wings. Acting on this signal, the strafers turned 360∞, losing altitude to ground level on the original course and speed. This maneuver allowed the strafers to arrive at the A/D shortly after the bombers struck, which caused the base to be in a state of confusion and the AA gunners under cover.

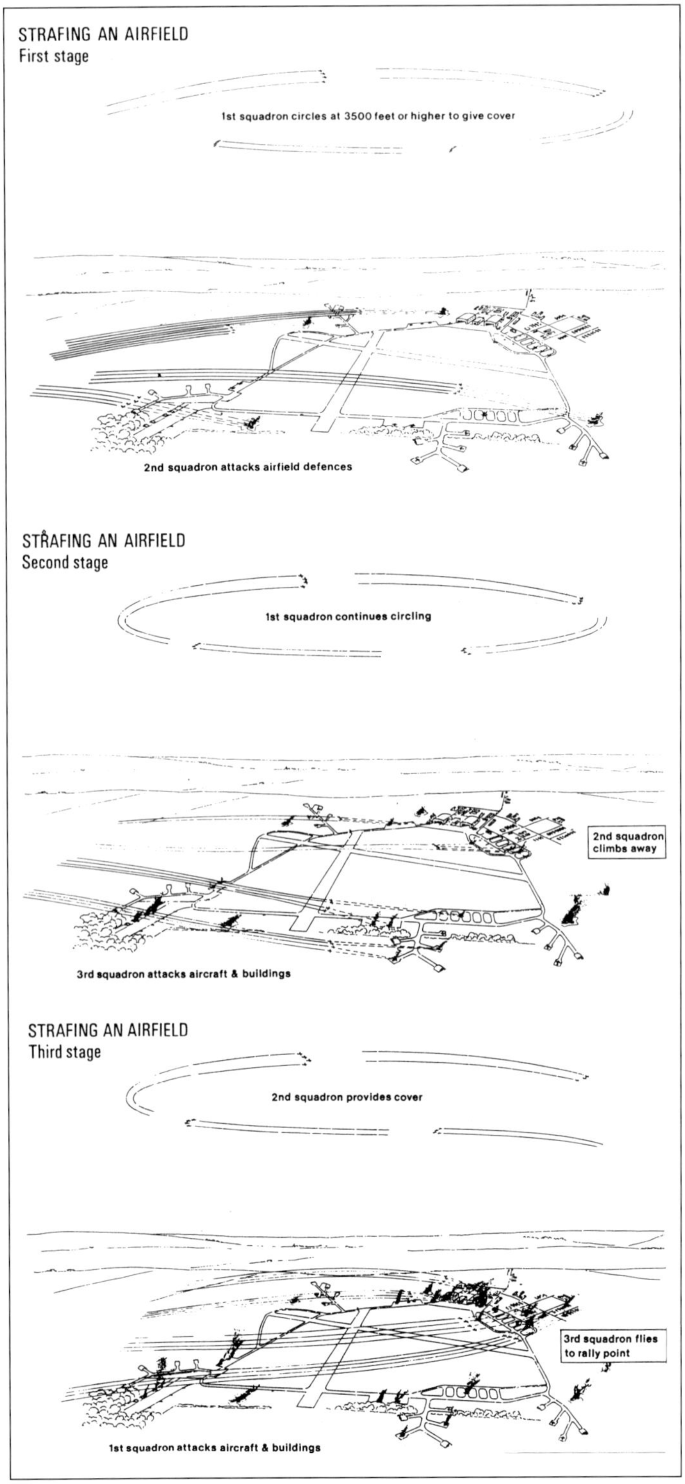

Targets of Opportunity

A/D attacks as targets of opportunity after an escort mission had the disadvantage of having airdromes in line with the bomber's track being alerted as to the possibility of attack from withdrawing escort fighters strafing. The impromptu A/D mission in mid-1944 had the group's squadrons separated by a few miles. They flew at 12-15,000 feet in order to detect enemy aircraft parked on the airfields and moving transport: trucks, trains, etc. Once a A/D was spotted part of the squadron was left out of the target's sight for top cover, while the remainder flew 10 to 20 miles beyond the objective, appearing to be headed home. The fighters would descend in a shallow 180∞ dive back toward the target. The direction of the approach was sometimes determined by wind direction and strength. Attacking downwind was desirable so that smoke from the aircraft damaged in the first pass would not conceal targets for the next strafers. Also, attacking across a strong wind could cause the aircraft to drift and influence accuracy. A low morning or afternoon sun in a clear, revealing sky or cloud cover could be used to conceal the attack. Each flight attacked line abreast or staggered line astern. The line abreast formation exposed all attackers at once for a short period of time, while the line astern exposed each flight in turn to all the defensive fire. The staggered astern mode required 1,000-yard intervals to prevent ricochet damage to the flight ahead from those following. The line astern mode did allow the trailing aircraft to spot ground AA positions, firing at those ahead and to then attack these AA positions. A reference several miles from the A/D was chosen while at altitude to aid navigation to the target once on deck. One flight was assigned to patrol at medium altitude as top cover. The lead flight(s) came in at 300-350 mph, as higher speeds interfered with gunnery. If heavy AA fire were encountered the leader would radio off the remainder of his unit. If opposition were light then the next wave of attackers was able to come in at lower speeds, improving their accuracy. The remaining flights would be quickly briefed as to what courses and area of the target they would attack. The approach was made on deck, with a bounce up to 30 to 70 feet on sighting the objective, each member of the flight selecting a target on his run. About 500 to 750 yards from the target, with a slight pull on the control column to correct for bullet drop (e.g. G-pull on the fired round), long two to three second fringe bursts were made. It was important for the pilot to have his aircraft properly trimmed and know the characteristics of his gun sight. The fighter continued to fly low once beyond the end of the A/D for a half mile or more to escape airfield defenses. But if no flak were encountered then a climbing turn could be made and a textbook, flying school gunnery pattern would be initiated on the following passes. If the last flight remained behind to finish off the target, the squadron leader would not get too far ahead before he started his orbit to wait for the trailing flights.

On 13 April 1945 the 356th Fighter Group, led by Maj. Donald Carlson, flew a Ramrod to Wismar and strafed Schwerin Airdrome. Lt. Herbert Rutland of the 360th Fighter Squadron had a close call that day as he described (*Aces and Wingmen II*, Danny Morris, USK Publishing, WA, 1989):

"I am flying number four in the lead flight of the 360th Squadron as our leader dives toward the enemy airfield below. As I watch, my airspeed indicator climbs toward the 400mph mark. I think to myself that this is not at all like the Stateside gunnery patterns that we were taught with their well-defined targets. I concentrate on holding position and trimming PI-R to fly a straight course. I recall a previous mission and the hole shot in my wing by someone who was in a following flight when he skidded behind me in a firing pass. As the field approaches, I try to pick out a suitable target. There is very little room for changing direction, so my line of attack will determine what I will be able to shoot at. As usual, the flight leaders will focus on the most promising targets on the ground. Wingmen will stay with them and take the leftovers, if any. Just as we scream over the edge of the field I glimpse a German aircraft directly in front of me. It seems to have been hit before, as one wing dangles down at an odd angle, presenting me with a large black cross to center in my gunsight. I decide to give it a good burst just for luck and press the trigger.

Just as my bullets start to strike, my eye catches the ominous flashes of ground fire pointed at me from a spot on the ground between me and the damaged Jerry aircraft. I dropped the nose on my Mustang down enough to spray the source of the aggravating muzzle flashes. We were so low that this action is regretted immediately, as I fly through a wall of dirt, muck, rocks and debris that my six fifties have sent skywards in a cloud. It is with disbelief that I find myself safely past the field and climbing to join my leader. That we will not make another pass on the field bothers me not in the least.

We are heading west and the clouds now cover all the land below. We have a long way to go when I see that my oil pressure has dropped to 20 pounds which is bad news. I radio this fact to my leader and he slides over to look at my ship. Aside from several dents in the leading edge of my wings, he finds that everything is where it ought to be and so we continue on our way. The Packard Merlin continues to churn away without protest while I keep an eye on the gauges. I am cautioned to set in high manifold pressure and low revs so as to lessen the strain on the engine. I am warned not to try to let down through the overcast if the engine quits altogether but to bail out. No engine, no gauges I go over the bail out procedure in my mind; disconnect all hoses and wires that connect me to the cockpit before stepping over the side. Ground control advises us that we are near Bremen and at that time there id fighting going on and that is definitely a no-no. Then comes the welcome message that we have crossed the Rhine.

My squadron leader takes us down through a hole in the cloud base that sweet Providence has provided and points to a small, flat field below us. I saw a short, temporary runway that had been laid out and on it were several light reconnaissance planes wit US insignia in their wings. I thank Mr. Rolls and Mr. Royce and the Merlin, chop the throttle and touch down on the pierced steel planking that had not been fully secured down into place. I am on the ground examining the dents in my wings and the scrapes put in the Mustang's belly by the loose PSP when an American jeep arrived."

Airdrome Strafing Takes its Toll

Airdrome strafing was the most hazardous form of ground attack. Permanent German air bases were usually well defended. The impromptu solo attack on the way home was especially dangerous. A bored pilot, seeing no combat and having a full load of ammunition, would inevitably be tempted to go on deck to carry out an exhilarating high- speed sweep of an airfield, often with disastrous consequences. The list of pilots lost on strafing missions reads like an ace's who's who: Beeson; Beckham; Gerald Johnson; Jucheim; Hofer; Goodson; Schreiber; Millikin; Carpenter; Mahurin; Gabreski; and on and on. On 7 July after an escort penetration, Glenn Duncan led the 351st Fighter Squadron on Wesendorf A/D, getting a parked He-111 on his first pass. Duncan decided on another injudicious run and flak hit his oil line, causing his engine to overheat on the way home. A quarter hour later he was forced to belly land behind enemy lines, and after setting his fighter on fire became an evader. He spent nine months with the Dutch Underground and returned to England in April 1945.

On 20 July 1944, Lt.Col. Francis "Gabby" Gabreski, CO of the premiere 61st Fighter Squadron and top American ace with 28 victories, decided to tempt fate and flew one last mission. (USAF)

On 20 July Francis "Gabby" Gabreski had achieved everything a young man from a Pennsylvania coal-mining town could hope. He was a Lt. Colonel, CO of the premiere 61st Fighter Squadron, top American ace with 28 victories, and was about to take his 30-day leave for home that day to be married to his fiancé, Kay. Before he left he checked the field order for the day's mission and found it was a ramrod escort to Russelheim, near Frankfurt. The mission was to be flown in good weather and was guaranteed to bring up the Luftwaffe. Hoping to add a few victories to his total, Gabreski asked Lt.Col. Dave Schilling to add him to the flying roster. Gabreski hurried over to the transport that was leaving to take him back to the States and told his friend, Capt. Jim Carter, of the combat opportunity, and asked him to delay the trip for a day to come along. Carter declined, handed Gabreski back his packed bag, and told him he would see him in the States. Gabreski dashed to his P-47 and took off on his 166th mission. He led the 61st across the Belgian coast, rendezvoused with B-24s, and flew in clear weather toward Frankfurt. The bombers dropped their loads on marshaling yards, and the fighter squadrons began to search for targets of opportunity to attack on the way home. Gabreski saw an airfield near Koblenz and called for Yellow Flight under Lt. Praeger Neyland to check it out. Neyland reported that there were He-111 and Me-110 bombers and only light flak. Gabreski sent Capt. Don Smith's Blue Flight down while his White Flight flew top cover. When Neyland's Flight finished it took over top cover and Gabreski led White down to the deck several miles northeast of the airfield, picking up speed and hoping to surprise the aroused Germans. He saw several intact He-111s and chose one, firing a trail of rounds toward the Heinkel, which exploded as he passed over. Gabreski pressed his luck and, against the one pass and out policy, he decided to make another pass. He hugged the ground and swung his P-47 in a 180° turn and came in low over the field in the opposite direction. He picked out another -111, but the German AA gunners were waiting for him. Gabreski's machine gun rounds were high and over the target. To compensate he dropped the nose, and as he did he heard a thump as his propeller tips hit the ground. The prop control mechanism was stripped and oil showered his windscreen. The engine began to vibrate, and Gabreski decreased the throttle to minimize the vibration. His Thunderbolt did not have enough power to climb to bail out, so he decided to belly-in at the first good location he saw. In this part of Germany open fields were infrequent, but Gabreski saw a small wheat field through his oil spattered windscreen and headed toward it. He hit the wheat at about 160-mph and began his skid through it, holding the stick forward trying to maintain some rudder and elevator control. As he neared the end of the field, a row of trees was closing rapidly and he hit the right rudder pedal violently and continued his slide with the left wing cutting a swath in the wheat. To protect himself from hitting the gunsight Gabreski covered his face with crossed arms and waited for the wing to smash into something and stop the fighter's motion. Nothing happened, as the wing and nose dug into the ground and almost flipped the Thunderbolt over on its back. The tail came back down and Gabreski found himself sitting at the edge of the field. It took him a few seconds to recover from the shock and realize that he was unharmed. His fighter was smoking, and he had to get out before it caught fire. The canopy would not open, and he braced his feet against the instrument panel and pulled the canopy release bar as hard as possible, and somehow the adrenaline rush opened it far enough for him to squeeze out. He began to run but heard bullets whiz past his head. He turned and saw two German soldiers firing at him. When they stopped to fire at him he would drop to the ground and then get up to run again. He made it to a wooded area where he hid as the soldiers ran past. He heard his flight come down to strafe his downed fighter so it would not fall into German hands intact. It was about midday, and Gabreski continued to hide until dark, when he left the woods. He came to a village, where he was discovered and pursued by some farmers. He hid in a cornfield, and the farmers gave up the search. Gabreski continued his escape and ran into a man and boy who were Polish forced laborers working on a farm. He called to them in Polish learned from his parents and asked for food and water. They left and returned several hours later with some bread and water. Gabreski headed west at night for four days and was discovered by a German farmer and his son. He had no choice but to accompany them to their farm, where they turned him in to the local police. They turned him over to the Luftwaffe, and he spent the rest of the war as a POW at Stalag Luft I to join Colonel Hub Zemke, who was the senior officer there.

Maj. John Godfrey, 16.3 victory P-51 ace for the 4th Fighter Group (USAF)

Maj. John Godfrey, 16.3 victory P-51 ace for the 4th Fighter Group, described strafing a German airdrome in his biography, *Look of Eagles* (Random House, NY, 1958):

"Did I have any premonition of my fate on that mission of August 24? (1944-ed.) No, there was no dream to forewarn me. Even the wobble pump which I now used to prime my engine before starting was just another instrument on the panel.... Everything was the same-the takeoff, the joining of squadron and group, the climb over the channel, the constant whine of the Germans trying to jam our RT. The flak, which always plagued us when we entered over the enemy coast, still had a terrifying effect and we dodged in and out of the black explosions.

So many things could have happened to make me turn back. My radio could have gone dead; the motor could have easily started spitting; my belly tanks could not have dropped; my oxygen could have run low-all or any of these mishaps had forced me back on previous missions.

I had no reason to ask the squadron leader to break formation, since there were no enemy fighters in sight; but I wanted to leave the many fighters who were protecting the bombers, to see if there was more action near the ground.

Two boys in my section found a marshaling yard with trains in abundance-not good enough targets for me. I wanted bigger game and left them with their little set of trains. Up ahead I suddenly saw an enemy airfield. And there they were-eight juicy fat Ju-52s, sitting peacefully at the edge of the field. One pass, I promised myself; there's no harm in that. Down I went, building up speed in my dive to the ground. One Ju-52 loomed bigger in my ring sight. Now, I said and pressed the tit to watch the fat Ju-52 wither in a shroud of machine gun fire. Pulling up I waited; no flak. Then-down again, this time joined by my wingman. Another Ju-52 melted into the ground.

Why didn't I leave now? What was I trying to prove?

I heard the crunch of a shell as it exploded near my wing. But down again I flew, to ensure the destruction of the last two planes on the field. The light tattoo of machine gun fire raked my plane from the hub of the propeller to the tail assembly. Not one struck the cockpit. My motor was suddenly sluggish but there was one last plane-and I dove once more for my final kill.

But there was no fast pull up now. As I flew over the burning wreck; my engine began to falter badly but my momentum carried me up to 1,500 feet before the 1,200 horses gave their last gasp. I aimed the nose of the plane at a small clearing I could see ahead. And as my plane started its downward plunge, I felt a strange sense of relief-there were no flashbacks of my life, no self-pity for what was happening. For I was tired, dead tired of the struggle. As I pulled back on the stick to ease the crash, I felt the plane slide into the soft earth. My head shot forward and hit the gun sight as the plane crunched to a stop."

Godfrey scrambled out of the Thunderbolt and began to run, but realized that he had forgotten his escape kit and had not destroyed the IFF (Identification Friend or Foe) apparatus on the aircraft. He ran back and pressed the IFF button, which caused an explosion in the fuselage, and grabbed the escape and first aid kit. He had a large gash on his temple and injected a morphine vile to relieve the pain and fell asleep. Once awake he began to walk west, but needed more morphine to relieve the pain. He continued on, using five vials of morpine, but after five days he was captured by a German farmer who pinned him down with a pitch fork. He was handed over to the Luftwaffe and became a POW. After a failed escape attempt in December 1944 he was successful on 3 April 1945.

As the Third Reich was shrunk by the onslaught of Allied troops in 1945, the Luftwaffe was able to concentrate more AA guns around its shrinking number of airbases. As a result enemy gunners were constantly on the alert for the inevitable strafer, who had no foe in the air, only on the ground. Without the element of surprise losses to strafers mounted. In January 1945 Bill Cullerton, with 21 strafing victories, was taken prisoner. On 16 April Elwyn Righetti, top ETO strafer with 27, crash landed his damaged P-51, and the next day the second leading strafing ace, Joe Thury with 25.5 ground claims, barely limped back to base in his damaged fighter.

Conclusion

Fundamental rules of airdrome strafing:

Surprise was the most important element for the success of the airdrome attack, whether it was a planned attack or target of opportunity. No two ground targets were the same, but they presented similar problems, so it was important for the pilot to plan his attack. An experienced pilot would have had a good mental picture of the complete pass in his mind before attacking. He determined how he would make the pass, its speed and altitude, the AA defenses, and where and when to break it off. Any valuable target was well defended, and only a fast pass provided safety, but also every effort had to be made to make the pass accurate. The pilot had to navigate to achieve the element of surprise; pick a reference point several miles from the airdrome and drop to the deck, a few feet off the ground, and fly to it. Once at the target, he pulled up to 50 feet and selected a target. He did not fly over the center of the field, as enemy aircraft were most likely to be found near the perimeter of the field. Also, flying close to the edges of the field was much safer because enemy gun positions were situated there. By flying close to the guns the fighter presented a target moving at a high angular speed that was very difficult for the gunner to hit. After the run the pilot dropped back to the deck until he was out of range of the flak. The pilot was instructed to make only one pass on a heavily defended field. If an airdrome was known to be defended by flak an additional anti-aircraft flight would be sent to suppress ground fire before the main attack.

Strafing Victories

8th Air Force Strafing Aces

On 8 February 1944 Gen. H.H. "Hap" Arnold issued Field Order No. 237, the "Down to Earth" edict, directing the American air effort in the ETO "to destroy the Luftwaffe in the air and on the ground." F.O. No. 237 stated:

"If bombers are not being attacked, groups will detach one or two squadrons to range out searching for enemy aircraft. Upon withdrawal, if the endurance permits, groups will search for and destroy enemy aircraft in the air and on the ground."

To make the prospect of dangerous ground strafing more appealing the 8th Air Force decided to allow ground victory claims toward total victory credits and ace status. Previously Gen. Claire Chennault, Air Commander of the CBI Air Forces, stated:

"I don't care if we get them in the air or on the ground—as long as we get them. It's better to get the enemy on the ground before he has a chance to cause any damage."

While leading the AVG, Chennault had allowed bonus payments for strafed aircraft destroyed on the ground. So it is not surprising that the 10th and 14th Air Forces under his command also allowed strafing victories as part of a pilot's victory total.

The 9th Air Force not only did not allow ground victory credits toward victory totals, but also made it difficult for their pilots to claim aerial victories. Ninth Air Force pilots were trained for ground attack, but once in combat, as with any fighter pilot, were looking to engage in aerial combat and to claim air-to-air victories. But the tactical air force leaders issued orders that their pilots were not to strike back unless attacked by the enemy. The 9th also implemented the vague "unconfirmed destroyed" category that denied ace status for a large number of 9th Air Force pilots.

First "Down to Earth" Strafing Missions

On 22 February 1944 the 353rd Fighter Group, after being released from bomber escort duty, was led by Col. Glenn Duncan on a strafing run on FW-190s on Ostheim A/D. Following Duncan, Walt Beckham led the next flight in. The second strafing attack was always more dangerous, as the enemy AA defenses were alerted. The

On his 30th birthday, Lt.Col. Righetti led his 55th Fighter Group to strafe the Reiss/Canitz A/D where there were a large number of FW-190s parked on the runway and in the hanger area. Righetti's P-51 was hit by flak as he destroyed nine German aircraft on the Ground. He crash-landed and post war investigation showed he was possibly killed by either by his civilian or military captors. (USAF)

German gunners hit Beckham's P-47 "Little Demon," forcing him to pull up and bail out. The leading ace in the ETO at the time with 18 victories was captured and made a POW for the duration.

The first planned pure strafing mission was flown on 11 March, when Duncan's 353rd Fighter Group conducted a low-level sweep over a Luftwaffe A/D in the Pas de Calais area. Small arms and light flak claimed two P-47s, while a third crashed on its return to base.

On 19 May the 339th Fighter Group provided escort for bombers attacking the Berlin/Brunswick area. They rendezvoused at Havel and took them to Berlin, and after they passed off the bombers they headed for the deck to look for ground targets. During their hunt they shot down three aircraft, destroyed three on the ground, and damaged ten more for the first strafing victories of the war. Lt. James Crockett of the 50rd Squadron destroyed two Ju-52 transport aircraft on the ground near Ludwiglust, and went on to strafe a locomotive in the area. Observers saw Crockett's fighter "mush into the train or misjudge and flew into it." The 339th was to become one of the top-strafing units in the ETO.

Lt.Col. Elwyn Righetti: Top Strafing Ace in Europe.

As one of the first groups to receive the P-38, the 55th Fighter Group based at Wormington took heavy losses, most of which could be blamed on the inadequacies of the Lightning in the ETO. Once re-equipped with the P-51 the group was more successful, but was considered only average at best. In October 1944 the 66th Fighter Wing appointed an outsider to take a command position with the group, by-passing the unit's experienced officers. To make the situation worse the new man was not an experienced officer from another group, but came directly from the States without any combat experience.

Lt.Col. Elwyn Guido Righetti was assigned to 55th HQ and flew with the 338th Squadron to acquire combat experience. Righetti enlisted in late 1939 and was assigned to Kelly field as an instructor, and then to Randolph Field, where he became the CO of an advanced instructors training unit. By the time he entered combat he was at the relatively old age of 29. When he came to the UK he was assigned a personal P-51, which he named *Katydid* after his wife Cathryn, who was known as Katy. After a week of familiarization with the administration and operational side of his post he flew his first combat mission on 2 November. During this mission he flew as wingman to Capt. Darrell Cramer, who led the 338th Squadron, to hunt Luftwaffe aircraft. After an unsuccessful search, Cramer took the squadron down to follow rail tracks to find trains to strafe southwest of Leipzig. Suddenly a Me-109 appeared heading toward and slightly above them. Cramer pulled up into the attack, and as he fired hitting the Messerschmitt, it banked to his starboard. Righetti, who had overrun Cramer, banked left and was now in firing position, getting two short bursts and finishing off the German for a shared victory. During the next several weeks Righetti participated in more missions, and on 21 November led the 338th for the first time, on the 26th was appointed its CO, and in early December he led his first group mission. Pickings in the sky were slim, but on Christmas Eve he claimed three FW-190s destroyed and two damaged near Munster. By the end of the year Righetti had become known as "Eager El" because of his aggressive style, especially against the German rail system, on which he had inflicted the destruction of 21 locomotives. During the first month of the new year the 55th became the top group in the 66th Wing, shooting down 55 aircraft and destroying 157 locomotives, with Righetti scoring four more air victories (including two Mistel Ju-88 mother ships and one FW-190 pick aback destroyed and one FW-190 pick aback probable) and ten locomotives. On 22 January Righetti became Air Exec at group HQ, and on 22 February became Group CO. Righetti continued to lead missions, and personally went down to test enemy defenses on airdromes and rail targets at a time when experienced commanders were commanded not to expose themselves to danger. During February the 55th became the premier rail strafers when they claimed 354 locomotives, with 170 being destroyed on the 19th and 20th, but at the cost of a dozen P-51s.

On 21 March Righetti led the group on an attack on Hopstein Airdrome that was thought to base Me-262 jet fighters. The operational plans called for B-17s to bomb the base and be followed by 55th Mustangs, each carrying a 500lb. fragmentation bomb. After the bombers left Righetti and his wingman dropped down to make two low-level orbits of the field to draw enemy fire so the location of the gun positions could be identified and attacked. Despite the heavy bombing the Germans threw up heavy AA fire. The tail of Righetti's fighter was hit, and his wingman took a direct hit and crashed. Righetti dove over the field and strafed and burned the only two undamaged aircraft he could find, one through a wooden shed. He radioed the Group to stay put until he rejoined them.

By April the 55th had claimed 940 locomotives, but as Allied armies were advancing rapidly into Germany the strafing of rail and road targets was curtailed, as it would slow Allied ground progress and endanger them. Allied air reconnaissance found that the Luftwaffe had massed large numbers of aircraft on fields throughout Germany. Although it was suspected that the Germans had no fuel to fly these aircraft the order was given to take no chances and attack these fields. On the 9th the 55th attacked fields between Munich and Salzburg, getting 54 on the ground and one in the air. Righetti claimed six, with three being Me-262 jets. Although other groups were getting large scores on the ground it was not until the 16th that the 55th returned to the Munich area and strafed a large number of aircraft parked at Bad Aibling, Neubiberg, and on the autobahn at Brunnthal. The total for the day was 52 with Righetti getting six. The cost, however, was four P-51s lost to flak.

The next day Righetti celebrated his 30th birthday by leading 54 Mustangs 400 miles on a B-17 escort to Dresden. After flying for two hours the 55th R/V'd with the bombers near Freiburg and escorted them to the target. After passing off the bombers to another group on their way home, Righetti led his group through a hole in the clouds over the Riesa/Canitz Airdrome, on which many single engine aircraft were parked. Righetti and his wingman, Lt. Carroll Henry, circled the field and dropped down for a test pass. The two approached from the east, and as they neared the field through the haze they saw a FW-190 with its undercarriage down, trying to land. Righetti dispatched Henry to attack the unsuspecting Focke Wulf that was only 50 feet above the ground when he hit it with a long burst. Henry over ran his victim and turned to make another pass when he saw that it had crashed and was burning. Righetti made a pass on the field, setting three Me-109s on fire. Henry then made a north to south strafing pass, shooting up aircraft on the northwest side of the field. As he pulled up from this pass he noticed Righetti's P-51 making a third pass and seven aircraft burning on the field. Henry pulled in behind his leader and noticed that the fighter had a white stream trailing from it. Righetti radioed that he had been hit and that his oil pressure was dropping quickly, and his aircraft could not fly much further. He said he had enough ammunition for one more pass and was going in. Henry covered his leader and watched him strafe and hit two more parked aircraft. Righetti then pulled up slightly, leveled off, and headed west toward Allied lines. Righetti radioed that he had crash-landed and that he had broken his nose but was OK, and would see them later.

Three weeks later the war ended and Righetti did not show up when the POWs were repatriated. The area where he crashed was in the Russian Zone of Occupation, and the investigation by American officers was thwarted by the Soviets. There was some speculation that he had been killed by angry German civilians who had been upset over the daily destruction done by Allied fighters and bombers. No grave was ever found, and his fate would never be known for certain. Righetti's nine ground credits on his last flight gave him 27, tops for the 8th Air Force. Along with his 7.5 air victories and over 30 locomotives and other ground targets, "Eager El" reigned as the "King of the Ground Strafers."

Many pilots found strafing more exciting and rewarding than aerial combat. One of them was William Cullerton of the 357th Fighter Squadron/355th Fighter Group, who was a legitimate ace with five or six aerial victories, but also had 21 ground victories. Some sources credit him with 13 on the ground, but 355th Group records credit him with 21. On 2 November 1944 Cullerton's squadron was escorting B-17s, and on the mission he shot down a Me-109 while it was landing. The squadron proceeded to strafe the same field, destroying 26 Luftwaffe aircraft, of which Cullerton accounted for six. In April 1945 Cullerton's P-51, "*Miss Steve*," was shot down while strafing. He was taken prisoner but escaped to survive the war.

The highest scoring American strafing ace was Maj. Thomas Reynolds of the little known Chinese American Composite Wing

1Lt. Bill Cullerton of the 357th Fighter Squadron/355th Fighter Group preferred strafing and had 21 ground claims to go with his five air victories. In April 1945, Cullerton's *"Miss Steve"* was shot down and he was a POW until the end of the war. (Author/Cullerton)

(CACW), operating with the 14th Air Force in China. Reynolds was credited with 38.5 ground victories flying P-40s and P51s for the Fifth Fighter Group. He and 1Lt. James Moore each destroyed ten Japanese aircraft on 10 February 1945 at Tsingtao, China.

8th Air Force Strafing Aces

Pilot Name	**Rank**	**Ground Victories**	**Aerial Victories**	**Group**
Righetti Elwyn	Lt.Col.	27	7.5	55
Thury, Joseph	Lt.Col.	25.5	2.5	339
Cullerton, William	1Lt.	21 (or 15)	6	355
Landers, John	Lt.Col.	20	8.5 (+6)	55,78,357
Godfrey, John	Capt.	18 (or 12.7)	18	4
Tower, Archie	Maj.	18	1.5	339
Kinnard, Claiborne	Col.	17	8	4,355,356
McKennon, Pierce	Maj.	16.5	5.5	4
Heller, Edwin	Capt.	16.5	5.5	352
Compton, Gordon	Maj.	15	6.5	353
Brown, Henry	Capt.	14.5	17.5	355
Montgomery, Gerald	Maj.	14.5	3	4
Hightshoe, Melville	1Lt.	14.5	0	353
Kolb, Herbert	Capt.	14.5	0	353
Hofer, Ralph	1Lt.	14	16.5	4
Meyer, John	Lt.Col.	13	24	352
Goodson, James	Maj.	13 (or15)	15	4
Littage, Raymond	Capt.	13	10.5	352
Elder, John	Lt.Col.	13	8	355
Everson, Kirke	Capt.	13	1.5	339
Godfrey, John	Maj.	12.66	14	4
Glover, Frederick	Maj.	12.5	10.33	4
Boone, Walker	Maj.	12.17	2.67	353
Welch, Robert	Capt.	12	6	55
Biggs, Oscar	1Lt.	11.5	0.5	339
Olds, Robin	Maj.	11	13	479
Ammon, Robert	Capt.	11 (or 9)	5	339
Corey, Harry	Capt.	11	1	339
Lanoue, Roland	1Lt.	11	1	353
Miller, Gerald	2Lt.	11	0	353
Schilling, David	Col.	10.5	22.5	56
Gustke, Richard	F/O	10.5 (or 12.5)	0	353
Ceuleers, George	Lt.Col.	10.5	0	364
Morris, Ray	1Lt.	10	3.5	355
Murphy, Randall	2Lt.	10	2	56
Pattillo, Charles	1Lt.	10	1	352
Burch, Harold	1Lt.	10	0	339
McMullen, Joseph	1Lt.	10 (or 11)	0	353
Blickenstaff, Wayne	1Lt.	10	0	353
Broadhead, Joseph	Maj.	10 (or 8)	0	357
Lines, Ted	1Lt.	10	0	4
Meroney, Virgil	Capt.	10 (or 9)	0	352
Rankin, Robert	1Lt.	10	0	56
McKennon, Pierce	Maj.	9.67	11	4
Graham, Gordon	Lt.Col.	9.5	7	355
Gilbert, Olin	Lt.Col.	9.5	2	78
Olson, Thomas	1Lt.	9.5	1	479
Lowell, John	Lt.Col.	9	7.5	364
Duffy, James	Capt.	9	5.2	355
Anderson, Woodrow	Capt.	9	4.5	352
Johnson, Martin	Capt.	9	1	361
McCormick, Arthur	Capt.	9	1	364
Greenwood, Ray	1Lt.	9	0	353
Marvel, Thomas	1Lt.	9	0	339
Orcutt, Leon	1Lt.	9	0	339
Taylor, Clyde	2Lt.	9	0	78
Rimmerman, Ben	Lt.Col.	8.5	7	353
Duffie, Claire	Maj.	8.5	3	479
Pierce, Don	Capt.	8.5	0	4, 479
Zemke, Hub	Col.	8	19.5	56, 479
Bankey, Ernest	Capt.	8	9.5	364

Maj. Thomas Reynolds of the CACW was the top American strafing ace of the war with 38.5 ground victories in the CBI. (USAF)

Harrington. Francis	1Lt.	8	4	78
Mellen, Joseph	Capt.	8	2	355
Peal, Joseph	Capt.	8	2	78
Clark, William	Lt.Col.	8	1	357, 339
Hermansen, Cephas	1Lt.	8 (or 5)	0	339
Josey, Danford,	2Lt.	8	0	78
Jurgens, Fred	F/O	8	0	20
MacClarence, Wm.	1Lt.	8	0	339
Messinger, Richard	1Lt.	8	0	78
Palson, Richard	2Lt.	8	0	479
Duncan, Glenn	Col.	7.8	19	353
Waggoner, Horace	Capt.	7.5	5	353
Munson, Norman	Maj.	7.5	0	78
Gentile, Don	Capt.	7	21.83	4
Luksic, Carl	1Lt.	7	8.5	352
Malmsten, Donald	Capt.	7	3.5	4
Mansker, Joseph	1Lt.	7	3	20
Waldron. Karl	1Lt.	7	3	352
Cunnick, John	1Lt.	7	2	55
Kyler, Russell	1Lt.	7	3	56
Emory, Frank	Capt.	7 (or 10)	2	353
Gevorkian. Sam	Capt.	7	2	55
Kier, Edward	1Lt.	7	2	20
Slack, Henry	1Lt.	7	1.5	78
Ayers, James	1Lt.	7	1	4
Zettler, Vincent	1Lt.	7	1	357
Antonides7, William	2Lt.	7	0	4
Caywood, Herbert	1Lt.	7	0	339
Chinn, Claude	1Lt.	7	0	56
Elmgren, Charles	1Lt.	7	0	479
Hepner, Neal	2Lt.	7	0	78
Hollingsworth, Jas.	Capt.	7	0	479
Hopcroft, Ernest	1Lt.	7	0	479
Kulik, Edward	Capt.	7	0	78
Mahany, Howard	2Lt.	7	0	55
Murphy, Jerome	1Lt.	7	0	339

Lt.Col. Joseph Thury (right) of the 339th Fighter Group ended the war with the second highest total of ground kills in the ETO with 25.5 (2.5 aerial victories). (USAF)

Weber, Carl	1Lt.	7	0	352
Witzell, George	1Lt.	7	0	479
Duncan, Glenn	Col.	6.83	19.5	353
Andrew, Stephen	Maj.	6.5	9	352
Starnes, James	Capt.	6.5 (or 6)	6	339
Sowerby, Theodore	Capt.	6.5	2	479
Swift, Ben	1Lt.	6.5	1	56, 353
Falvey, Harold	F/O	6.5	1	355
Boring, Lloyd	1Lt.	6.5	0.5	55
Garlich, Robert	1Lt.	6.5	0	355
Leslie, Charles	Capt.	6.5	0	?
Truett, Jesse	Capt.	6.5	0	364
Gentile, John	Capt.	6	21.8	4
Jucheim, Alwyn	Capt.	6	10	78
Haviland, Fred	Capt.	6	6	355
Bostwick, George	Maj.	6	9	56
Dade, Lucian	Lt.Col.	3	6	56
Biel, Hippolitus	1Lt.	6	5.33	4
Cole, Charles	Capt.	6	5	20
McElroy, James	Capt.	6	5	355
Merritt, George	Maj.	6	5	361
Jacobson, Gail	1Lt.	6	4.5	479
Duncan, John	1Lt.	6	4	357
Kirk, John	1Lt.	6	4	78
Giller, Edward	Maj.	6	3	55
Hatter, Robert	1Lt.	6	3	359
Hunter, John	Capt.	6	3	364
Johnson, Clarence	Capt.	6	2	479, 352
Alexander, Fred	1Lt.	6	2	20
Flagg, Walter	Capt.	6	3	56
McGinnis, Keith	1Lt.	6	2	55
Mudge, William	1Lt.	6	2	339
Chetneky, Steve	1Lt.	6	1	339
Diamond, Brack	1Lt.	6	1	4
Silva, Stanley	Capt.	6	1	355
Smith, Robert	Capt.	6	1	78
Jones, Thomas	1Lt.	6	0.5	353
Barger, Clarence	2Lt.	6	0.33	355
Apple, George	2Lt.	6	0	55
Blizzard, Robert	1Lt.	6	0	339
Bowers, Arthur	2Lt.	6	0	4
Bryan, Gillespie	Maj.	6	0	78
Chenez, Gordon	1Lt.	6	0	?
Clifton, Frank	1Lt.	6	0	339
DeAnda, Louis	2Lt.	6	0	78
DeVilliers, Don	1Lt.	6	0	78
Einhaus, Lowell	Capt.	6	0	20
Frisch, Robert	1Lt.	6	0	339
Frum. Rollin	F/O	6	0	?
Gordon, Ray	1Lt.	6	0	353
Horner, Kenneth	1Lt.	6	0	364
Jennings, Loton	1Lt.	6	0	4
Pattillo, Cuthbert	1Lt.	6	0	352
Poage, Charles	F/O	6	0	4
Pederson, Douglas	1Lt.	6	0	4

Poage, Charles	1Lt.	6	0	4
Paul, Robert	1Lt.	6	0	339
Shope, Herbert	1Lt.	6	0	78
Stewart, David	1Lt.	6	0	20
Rogue, Edward	1lt.	6	0	20
Tracey, Richard	Capt.	6	0	20
Uttenweiler, ?	Capt.	6	0	?
Williams, Gene	Capt.	6	0	?
Woolery, James	1Lt.	6	0	339
Jackson, Michael	Maj.	5.5	8	56
Anderson. Charles	1Lt.	5.5	10.5	4
Johnson, Michael	Maj.	5.5	8	56
Miklajiyk, Henry	Capt.	5.5	7.5	352
Dregne, Irwin	Col.	5.5	5	357
Fortier, Norman	Maj.	5.5	5.83	355
Jones, Frank	Capt.	5.5	5	4
Jabara, James	1Lt.	5.5	1.5	355
Malstrom, Einer	Col.	5 .5	1	356
Golden, John	1Lt.	5.5	1	479
McMahan, Bruce	2Lt.	5.5	0.5	353
Bell, Thomas	Capt.	5.5	0	4
Bledsol, Norman	Capt.	5.5	0	353
Cooper, Randolph	2Lt.	5.5	0	355
Preddy, George	Maj.	5	26.83	352
Norley, Louis	Maj.	5	10.33	4
Quirk, Michael	Capt.	5	11	56
Schlegal, Albert	Capt.	5	8.5	4
Jones, Cyril	1Lt.	5	6	359
Sykes, William	1Lt.	5	5	361
McDuffie, Duncan	1Lt.	5	4	78
Visconte, Romildo	Capt.	5	4	364
Webb, Roy	Lt.Col.	5	4	361
Alfred, Carl	Capt.	5	3	?
Jones, Reps	1Lt.	5	2	20
Farmer, Owen	Capt.	5	2	339
Jones, William	1Lt.	5 (or 4)	2	339
Kier, Edward	Capt.	5 (or 7)	2	20
Shupe, Joseph	1Lt.	5	2	359

Strafing aces of the 353rd Fighter Group: (left to right): Col. Ben Rimmerman, Maj. Loren McCollom and Col. Glenn Duncan (USAF)

Henry, Carroll	Capt.	5	1.5	55
Olander, Richard	Capt.	5	1.5	339
Rich, George	Capt.	5	1.5	339
Bosworth, Richard	1Lt.	5	1	78
Brasher, G.E.	1Lt.	5	1	78
Colletti, Anthony	1Lt.	5	1	78
Dissette, Lawrence	Capt.	5	1	355
Gould, Clifford	1Lt.	5	1	55
Irion, Robert	1Lt.	5	1	339
Kirby, Henry	Maj.	5	1	355
Nelson, Robert	1Lt.	5	1	4
Reynolds, Garth	Maj.	5	1	20
Speer, Frank	2Lt.	5	1	4
Whinnem, Donald	1Lt.	5	1	352
Carter, Joseph	1Lt.	5	0.5	352
Kurtz, Robert	Capt.	5	0.5	355
Loveless, Philip	Capt.	5	0.5	339
Morgan, Frank	Capt.	5	0.5	356
Peel, Eugene	1Lt.	5	0.5	78
Ramm, Albert	Capt.	5	0.5	55
Baugh, Donald	F/O	5	0	4
Best, Donald	1Lt.	5	0	55
Birtciel. Frank	Capt.	5	0	55
Blodgett, Burton	1Lt.	5	0	56
Byers, John	1Lt.	5	0	339
Denson, Gordon	2Lt.	5	0	4
Demars, R.E.	1Lt.	5	0	?
DeWitt, Charles	Capt.	5	0	78
Dickey, Melvin	1Lt.	5	0	4
Doss, Gene	1Lt.	5	0	78
Fletcher, Jack	1Lt.	5	0	355
Fussell, Roscoe	1Lt.	5	0	?
Galer, Donald	1Lt.	5	0	355
Guyton, William	1Lt.	5	0	339
Hanson, Kenneth	1Lt.	5	0	479
Helfrecht, Kenneth	1Lt.	5	0	4
Hendrickson, Robt.	1Lt.	5	0	?
Hunt, Harlan	1Lt.	5	0	339
Jackson, Boyd	1Lt.	5	0	339
John, Leedom	1Lt.	5	0	55
Kerr, Warren	Capt.	5	0	56
Kesler, Gilbert	1Lt.	5	0	4
Kissell, William	1Lt.	5	0	364
Lynch, William	2Lt.	5	0	355
MacKean, Robert	Capt.	5	0	352
Maloney, John	1Lt.	5	0	55
Marsh, Halbert	2Lt.	5	0	355
McClure, James	1Lt.	5	0	353
McCollom, Frances	1Lt.	5	0	355
McFadden, Jack	1Lt.	5	0	4
McHugh, Philip	1Lt.	5	0	355
Peterburs, Joseph	1Lt.	5	0	20
Phaneuf, Richard	1Lt.	5	0	78
Pryor, Thomas	1Lt.	5	0	353
Queen, Thomas	2Lt.	5	0	56

Reinhardt, Edwin	1Lt.	5	0	353
Rice, John	F/O	5	0	339
Rose, Robert	1Lt.	5	0	353
Shane, Presson	Capt.	5	0	479
Smigel, Alfred	1Lt.	5	0	479
Smith, Vernon	2Lt.	5	0	56
Sweat, Dale	1Lt.	5	0	78
Sykes, Henry	1Lt.	5	0	352
Vickery, Daran	1Lt.	5	0	355

Combined Air-Ground Aces in a Day

Name	Rank	Ground Victories	Air Victories	Date	Group
Bankey, Ernest	Maj.	4	2	4/16/45	364
Jones, Cyril	1Lt.	2	4	9/12/44	359
Peters, Robert	1Lt.	2	3	7/20/44	355

Judgment of ground victory claims as either destroyed or damaged was determined by gun camera evidence. "Destroyed" was an aircraft left burning or exploded, while a "damaged" was an e/a holed by machine gun fire. Combat film confirmation was subjective, much like football instant replays, and there was a lot of give and take between group and wing assessments

On 17 April Capt. Robert Ammon destroyed 11 aircraft on the ground: four Me-109s, three Ju-88s, two FW-190s, and two He-111s breaking Randal Murphy's record of 10 set three days earlier with the 56th Fighter Group. Ammon also damaged four aircraft. (USAF)

Ground Aces in a Day

#V	Pilot	Rank	Grp	Date
11	Ammon, Robert	Capt.	339	4/16/45
10	Murphy, Randall	Lt.	56	4/13/45
9.5	Kolb, Herbert	Capt.	353	4/16/45
9	Landers, John	Lt.Col	78	4/16/45
9	Miller, Gerald	Lt.	353	4/16/45
9	Orcutt, Leon	Lt.	339	4/17/45
9	Righetti, Elwyn	Lt.Col.	55	4/17/45
8	Jurgens, Frederick	F/O	20	4/10/45
8	Taylor, Clyde	Lt.	78	4/16/45
8	Tower, Archie	Maj.	339	4/10/45
7	Cullerton, William	Lt.	355	9/12/44
7	Everson, Kirke	Capt.	339	4/17/45
7	Heller, Edwin	Capt.	352	4/16/45
7	Kulik, Edward	Capt.	78	4/16/45
7	Stewart, David	Lt.	20	4/10/45
7	Boone, Walker	Maj.	353	2/27/45
6.5	Gilbert, Olin	Lt.Col.	78	4/16/45
6	Cole, Charles	Capt.	20	2/9/45
6	Chetneky, Steven	Lt.	339	4/16/45
6	Clark, William	Lt.Col.	339	4/16/45
6	Cullerton, William	Lt.	355	11/2/44
6	Einhaus, Lowell	Capt.	20	2/8/45
6	Hatter, Robert	Capt.	359	5/21/44
6	Hunter, John	Capt.	364	4/13/45
6	Littge, Raymond	Capt.	352	4/17/45
6	Malmsten, Donald	Capt.	4	2/27/45
6	Pattillo, Cuthbert	Lt.	352	4/16/45
6	Righetti. Elwyn	Lt.Col.	55	4/9/45
6	Righetti, Elwyn	Lt.Col.	55	4/16/45
6	Rimmerman, Benjamin	Col.	353	4/16/45
5.5	Goodson, James	Maj.	4	4/10/45
5.5	Alexander, Frederick	Lt.	20	4/10/45
5	Antonides, William	Lt.	4	4/16/45
5	Baugh, Donald	F/O	4	4/16/45
5	Benjamin, Swift	Lt.	353	8/29/44
5	Birtciel, Franklin	Capt.	55	4/9/45
5	Byers, John	Lt.	339	4/16/45
5	Carter, Joseph	Lt.	352	4/17/45
5	Colletti, Anthony	Lt.	78	4/16/45
5	DeVilliers, Donald	Lt.	78	4/16/45
5	Doss, Gene	Lt.	78	4/16/45
5	Elder, John	Maj.	355	11/2/44
5	Gentile, Donald	Capt.	4	4/5/44
5	Gustke, Richard	F/O	353	3/21/45
5	Gustke, Richard	F/O	353	4/16/45
5	Helfrecht, Kenneth	Lt.	4	4/16/45
5	Hepper, Neal	Lt.	78	4/16/45
5	Hightshoe, Melville	Capt.	353	4/16/45
5	Johnson, Clarence	Capt.	352	9/10/44
5	Jones, Reps	Lt.	20	2/9/45
5	Josey, Danford	Lt.	78	4/16/45
5	Kepner, Neal	Lt.	78	4/16/45
5	Kier, Richard	Lt.	20	4/10/45

5 Kolb, Herbert	Capt.	353	2/27/45
5 Kyler, Russell	Lt.	56	4/13/45
5 Lanoue, Roland	Lt.	353	2/27/45
5 Mahany, Howard	Lt.	55	4/17/45
5 Marsh, Halbert	Lt.	355	4/16/45
5 McClure, James	Lt.	353	4/16/45
5 McElroy, James	Capt.	355	4/15/45
5 McDuffie, Duncan	Lt.	78	4/16/45
5 McMullen, Joseph	Lt.	353	4/13/45
5 Mellen, Joseph	Capt.	355	4/13/45
5 Morgan, Franklin	Capt.	356	2/20/45
5 Murphy, Jerome	Lt.	339	4/10/45
5 Olds, Robin	Maj.	479	4/16/45
5 Paul, Robert	Lt.	339	4/10/45
5 Pederson, Douglas	Lt.	4	4/16/45
5 Peterburs, Joseph	Lt.	20	4/10/45
5 Pierce, Donald	Capt.	479	4/16/45
5 Swett, Dale	Lt.	78	4/16/45
5 Sykes, Henry	Lt.	352	4/16/45
5 Thury, Joseph	Lt.Col.	339	4/17/45
5 Truett, Jesse	Capt.	364	4/13/45
5 Vickery, Duran	1Lt.	355	4/13/45
5 Waldron, Karl	Lt.	352	4/17/45
5 Webb, Roy Lt.	Col.	361	6/29/44

1Lt. R. B. Hatter of the 359th Fighter Group described the mission in which he became an ace-in-a-day (*Down to the Deck*, ibid.):

"This particular mission was a briefed Chattanooga mission (special attack on rail targets), our area being NW of Berlin. I was flying No.2 in White Flight. When we reached the SW corner of our area we dropped our external tanks and hit the deck and preceded to look for suitable targets. After about five minutes we came upon a small town with some railroad cars sitting in a siding. White leader circled around to make a pass and I fell in trail. On making my pass, the target did not seem worthwhile so I held my fire. Coming away from the town we turned to the left and observed several planes making passes at a square grass field. There were about 25 planes parked on the field with one long row of planes and the rest parked around the edges. There was no enemy ground fire and we started making passes too. We made numerous passes setting fire to many of the planes. On one pass I strafed the row of planes but found it was better to pick out and certain plane and concentrate on it. We finally had to leave because of gas and ammunition. I claimed six enemy aircraft destroyed and three damaged."

Tactical Attacks on Fuel

Fighter-bomber attacks on forward oil stores and rail and truck transport carrying fuel began to have an effect on the German ground operations after the St. Lo breakout in late July. The German move from Caen to Mortain was hindered by fuel shortages; the German counter-attack at Mortain was delayed while the Panzers waited on fuel, and the planned counter-attack on Patton's flank was abandoned for lack of fuel. The increased lack of fuel during the closing of the Falaise-Argentan Gap and the subsequent race across France and Belgium caused the Germans to destroy thousands of their own fuel-starved vehicles, or made them sitting ducks for fighter-bombers. One of the primary objectives of the German's Ardennes Offensive was the capture of Allied fuel dumps. The Allied breakouts east of the Rhine in February 1945 across the Rhine in March and into Germany in April could not be contained due to the lack of fuel caused by fighter-bombers. German supply trucks and wrecked tanks and trucks were drained of gasoline to fuel undamaged fighting vehicles.

Under Minister of Armaments, Albert Speer, the expansion of synthetic fuel production increased German fuel stocks to an all-time high of 574,000 tons in April 1944. In May the Allies began their bombing campaign against the German oil industry, and soon these fuel stocks declined precipitously: 195,000 tons in May; 52,000 tons in June; 35,000 tons in July; and 16,000 tons in August. A brief respite in the bombing during the summer allowed a slight increase in oil production in October at 19,000 tons and November at 39,000 tons, but that was not nearly sufficient to fuel the German war machine. The destruction of German fuel supplies being transported

Young, 40 year old Albert Speer, was Hitler's Minister of Armaments and increased German production to wartime highs: fuel (April 1944) and aircraft (October 1944). (Author/West)

to the front and at the front added to the German fuel dilemma. The Germans instituted austere fuel conservation measures that affected Luftwaffe operations. Most importantly training flights were limited, and the lack of gasoline for training became more and more critical, as the Luftwaffe lost their veterans pilots in the war from attrition in the air. In November Göring cut air operations by ordering them to take place only when weather and tactical and strategic considerations insured success. He discontinued night ground attack operations and transport flights, and most bomber operations were virtually eliminated, as bombers used too much gasoline. Synthetic fuels cost about four times as much to produce as to refine crude oil. Also, synthetic gasoline was rated at 89 octane (with 16% aromatics) maximum, while U.S. aviation fuel rated at 100 octane and gave a much higher performance. In 1944, to raise the octane number to 96 the Germans added 40% aromatics that helped to decrease overall fuel production, but the aromatics were damaging to aircraft engines over the long run. The fuel situation became so perilous that the world's most advanced aircraft, the Me-262 jet fighter, was being "taxied" to the runway pulled by horses!

The German organization of delivering fuel to both the civilian economy and the military was especially susceptible to disruption by air attack on the fuel transportation system. Strategic bombing disrupted the supply of raw oil to refineries, destroyed the refineries—particularly the hydrogenation plants—and destroyed reserve stocks. Tactical bombing disrupted the supply from the refineries to depots, and then to the front. The combination of these air attacks prevented the German fuel conduit, from wells to the front, from being filled. However, the destruction of fuel supplies near the front lines was felt more by troops on the divisional level and below than was the loss of fuel production inside Germany by strategic bombing. German field commanders considered the destruction of army and division level fuel dumps as the most important supply loss, followed by ammunition and general ordnance. The destruction of enemy fuel supplies (dumps) close behind the front, fuel supply lines, and motorized and rail fuel transport by fighter-bombers was more apparent operationally at the front than the loss of production caused by strategic bombing of the synthetic oil plants in Germany and the Ploesti oil fields in Rumania. The attacks by fighter-bombers on fuel supply dumps near the battlefront caused the Germans to disperse these depots to insure that sufficient supply could be made to frontline fighting vehicles. Dispersion was difficult, as reduced production and fuel reserves made it necessary to ship what fuel that was available directly to the battlefield, where fighter-bombers disrupted distribution of fuel to vehicles on the battlefield. Since there were large numbers of German motor transport and aircraft destroyed the decrease in fuel supplies was somewhat alleviated, as the Germans had fewer vehicles and aircraft to fuel.

Anti-personnel Air Attacks

Armies on the move were very visible and vulnerable to air attack. Even with the addition of mobile AA guns there was no effective answer to the problem. The most common defense was to cut brush or branches for personal camouflage, or to just run as fast and far as possible from the attack of the onrushing Jabo. If observers heard or saw approaching aircraft the column was alerted to hide under any trees or hedges, hoping to escape detection and, if not, provide some cover against attack.

Allied infantry grew used to the generous amount of air support against enemy troops, but did not exploit its demoralizing effects by immediately pursuing a ground offensive on the dazed German soldier. The recommended method for attacking ground troops was for flights to fly abreast, firing 32 .50 caliber machine guns simultaneously, followed by attacks by two or more flights of the attacking squadron and repeat attacks by the initial flights until their ammunition ran out. It was found that an air attack on enemy infantry would realize a demoralizing effect more rapidly than artillery, and that it would be of longer duration. It would be imperative that the infantry exploit air attacks as soon as possible after delivery, as the effect lasted about 20 minutes depending on the quality of the German troops and their amount of protection from the attack. If fighter-bombers remained in the area after their initial attack, making feints toward enemy positions, the ploy would keep them pinned down while infantry and/or armor closed in.

Field Marshal Walther Model, CO of *Herresgruppen B*, distributed a leaflet to German soldiers encouraging them to fire at strafing fighter-bombers with their weapons. The propaganda leaflet described how a non-com had shot down a Thunderbolt with his machine pistol. Successful gunners and units were given "special favors," and soldiers who shot down a strafer with his infantry weapon were promised a ten-day furlough. The German soldier was well trained in small arms anti aircraft defense. It was best to combine bombing/rocket and gunnery runs in attacking troops. Allied air supremacy had a distinct effect on the morale of German ground troops from the High Command to the lowest private. A number of German commanders, including Rommel, were either killed or wounded by strafing attacks on staff cars and headquarters. The diary entries of German soldiers were dominated by their fears of Allied Jabos that ruled the battlefront and effective, resolute small arms return fire was forgotten in favor of self-preservation. After D-Day Allied air power had an overwhelming and completely paralyzing influence on German conduct of the battlefront. Whenever the weather permitted, Allied fighter-bombers appeared from sunrise to sunset over the front lines to a depth of 10 to 12 miles. Anything that moved was attacked with rockets, bombs, and machine guns. Men and vehicles were hidden in dense vegetation or in barns until nightfall. No one dared to show himself in the open, and the skies were constantly searched.

German *Intelligence Summary No.299S, 6 January 1945*, to all troops that gave suggestions for behavior in the face of fighter-bombers:

"The Chief Enemy in the West is the All-Around Fighter

On the way up to the front behave as though you are already there! Fighters attack at all points. Therefore, have all air defense weapons manned and ready for action even during hours of darkness.

Never put troops in the (railroad) car immediately behind the engine. Ammunition wagons at the end of the train. Fuel well away from ammunition.

During an air raid alert or in case of the train stopping, alight only when ordered to do so. Panicky movement often provokes new attacks.

Camouflage: Use all available cover, trees, shadows, foxholes. Each vehicle must have air observers with a clear view in all directions. The more the better. Observation from a closed vehicle in not sufficient.

March discipline: Arms always with the men. Pistol belt fastened. Distance between men at least 100 meters. Keep distances when halted. Stop only when cover is available. Road must remain clear.

When column halts have traffic control established at once in front and behind the column. Tactical commanders must get traffic moving again after jams At once and regardless of all else.

Columns may be passed only by single staff cars. Right of way to be given to vehicles going to the front.

Send reconnaissance ahead when you come to narrow passages, bridges, bombed out cities. Rush vehicles through; do not jam up. Appoint traffic officers.

Fire at fighters.

Stop at a place offering the best cover if a fighter attack is heavy. Proceed at short bursts at opportune moments. Cut engine, listen. By the time you see the enemy aircraft it is too late. Avoid wide roads, second class roads get you there more quickly.

Drive without lights at night.

If the road is lighted up by chandelier flares, stop under cover. Be on your guard when short light signals are used. Bombs will be used immediately after.

Any movement made in the light is clearly obvious.

A lighted cigarette can be seen up to 1,000 meters altitude at night. Therefore be careful. Smoking while driving is prohibited.

Remember: Each soldier and each vehicle is irreplaceable and may decide the fate of the war.

Classic photo of a P-47 flying through the enormous explosion of an ammunition truck. If a target had a possibility of exploding, pilots fired a short burst from a distance away, aiming high to explode it before they got too close. This explosion was so bright that it reversed the film exposure making it appear that it was taken at night. (USAF)

Thoughtlessness, carelessness, 'showing off' lead to avoidable losses and therefore will be prosecuted by court martial.

(Signed) General of the Armored Forces West."

Ammunition Dumps

Usually ammunition dumps were well camouflaged or part of other storage facilities. When ammunition dumps were attacked the result often surprised the attacker, as described by Bill Colgan in *Fighter-Bomber Pilot* (TAB Books, PA, 1985):

"Strafing ammo dumps could always provide some real fireworks. We had a classic mission in that regard. Not more than a few rounds had hit the target when there was a blinding flash across the countryside of Bavaria. Then, with ungodly speed, an enormous fireball, dust, smoke, earth, trees and ammo rushed skyward. As the monstrous explosion rose towards the attacking aircraft, many rounds of ammo being carried aloft were set off, sending them out like sky rockets in advance of the main body of the oncoming disaster. The airplanes were engulfed as the deadly cloud and debris carried on up to 15,000 feet or higher.

Now these pilots face a very demanding task—flying on instruments through an aerial explosion. They all got out OK. And they all made it back to base even though each airplane suffered

Although this photo is spectacular, flak towers were generally off limits as they could outgun and out range the attacking fighters. (USAF)

German early warning radar station under attack (USAF)

Air attacks frequently damaged communications lines and temporarily disrupted communications between battlefield units. German troops were well disciplined and disruption of communications between commands did not cause serious problems as the individual German officer's ability to lead an attack as well as to maintain an organized defense was outstanding. Command post destroyed at Calderare di Reno on 15 April 1945 by the 350th Fighter Group. (USAF)

damaged. The planes of the leader and his wingman, who were closest to the brunt of the blast, were stripped clean of paint and markings. Their wind shields were so pitted and marred that they had to fly home with their canopies open in order to see."

Flak Towers, Radio and Transmission Towers

While these structures are very visible from the ground with the sky in the background, they are not as visible from the air, particularly if they are painted with one or two dull colors to match with their surroundings. Low flying fighter-bombers were better able to recognize these structures and to attack them than high-flying bombers. Shadows gave away the structure, and care was taken to distort the shape of the shadow with plantings surrounding the structure.

Pilots were hesitant to attack flak towers, as these defenses could outgun and out range fighters. The only time they were attacked was if they were causing a problem to heavy bomber attacks in the area. Also, many towers reported as flak towers were actually water towers!

Communications and Command Posts

Air attacks frequently damaged communication lines and temporarily disrupted communications between battlefield units. German troops were well disciplined, and disruption of communications between commands did not cause serious problems, as the individual German officer's ability to lead an attack as well as to maintain an organized defense was outstanding. The destruction of communications between transportation HQ and rail centers made the location and routing of trains difficult.

During the first weeks of the Normandy invasion Allied fighter-bombers wrecked havoc on the rail system in northern France. Due to damage to marshaling yards and tracks, trains needed to be rerouted and the repair organization dispatched. The destruction of telephone lines complicated the German rail problem, and it became necessary to send messengers with information and orders concerning train movement and repair.

V-weapon Sites (CROSSBOW Operations)

As D-Day neared the Allies discovered the V-1 sites ("ski sites," or NOBALLs) just inland on the northwest coast of France. The location was made up of a launching ramp and three missile assembly and checkout buildings. The checkout buildings were unique in that they had curved entrances looking like skis lying on their sides, giving the sites their name. The Germans tried to disguise these buildings by adding false roofs and making them look like farm buildings, but their best concealment was to position the buildings so that their characteristic lines would not be apparent after the addition of camouflage netting. Allied photo-reconnaissance put a high priority on discovering the sites, and multiple dangerous low-level missions discovered the first site on 24 October 1943, as well as most of 75 completed or near completed sites thereafter. The British had followed the German V-weapon program for years and were concerned about the threat. On 24 December 1943 the 8th Air Force sent 722 heavy bombers to bomb 23 sites. The relatively small, well-concealed concrete and steel buildings escaped the bombing mostly intact. Arnold and Spaatz had doubted that heavy bombers would be effective against the sites. In January 1944 Arnold ordered the AAF Proving Ground Command to conduct a priority program to determine the best way to destroy the sites. Construction crews built a simulated V-site at the AAF Proving Ground at Eglin Field, Florida. These tests showed that minimum altitude attacks by fighter-bombers did the most damage to the sites compared to heavy and medium bombers. However, British leaders ignored the findings and continued to demand that USSTAF heavy bombers and 9th Air Force medium bombers attack the V-sites, despite their diversion from POINTBLANK operations.

Gen. Tooey Spaatz ordered the 365th Fighter Group to fly experimental attacks against V-weapon "ski sites." On 3 May 1944

Col. Lance Hall led three squadrons on four sites. Each plane carried two 1,000lb. bombs with eight to eleven second delay fuses. At about three miles from the target the fighter-bombers went into a steep dive to the deck and approached the sites at ground level at full throttle. The pilot and his wingman struck the target simultaneously, releasing their bombs at point blank range. The mission achieved good results on the sites and no losses were suffered.

Most of the fighter-bomber CROSSBOW attacks on the V-1 sites were in conjunction with medium bomber attacks on the sites located on the French coast. On 9 May 9th Air Force P-47 groups were briefed on AA gun positions guarding the "Buzz Bomb" sites that had been taking a heavy toll on attacking USAAF medium bombers. The fighters were waiting off the coast and attacked on a broad front simultaneously with the B-26 and A-20 bombers. German AA fire would open up on the bombers, and the Thunderbolts would choose a gun position and hit it with a dive-bombing run, dropping a 500lb. bomb and strafing.

Generally air attacks on the initial V-weapon sites were ineffective, and later German resourcefulness developed small, easily transported and assembled sites that were simple to hide and camouflage and difficult to find. The Germans increased flak defenses and camouflage, and added dummy sites and smoke screens to confuse the attackers. A large portion of the attacks were made on the abandoned original ski sites. An enormous outlay of ordnance was expended to stop the V-weapons, but on the night of 12/13 June the V-1 offensive began from these smaller ski sites.

Fortifications and Gun Positions

Fighter-bomber attacks on concrete pillboxes and casemated guns were found to be ineffectual, except for the blast effect on the morale of the occupants. The 250 and 500 lb. bombs carried by fighter-bombers were too light to crack the concrete and steel reinforced fortifications. The 1,000lb. bombs could take out these fortifications with a lucky direct hit. Gun positions were difficult to detect until they opened fire. It was suggested that American pilots observe friendly (e.g. known) gun positions, as they were similar to the enemy's, to help them identify enemy positions.

Clean Up Missions

After the bombers attacked an objective, fighter-bombers were dispatched to clean up lightly or undamaged targets that remained in the general area of destruction within the bomber raid. For instance, after a bomber attack on a marshaling yard there were often locomotives, rail cars, and switching machinery left intact that required attention.

Friendly Fire

Between 8 to 17 June 1944, fighter-bombers of the IX TAC supporting the D-Day Invasion attacked U.S. troops on nine separate instances. The result was that troops would fire on any aircraft in their vicinity. The problem became so bad that troops began displaying recognition panels when they were not on the front lines.

A Wehrmacht light field artillery battery in action in December 1944. The necessity of mobility didn't give these batteries time to pay attention to camouflage made them vulnerable to air attack. (USAF)

Smoke shells indicate the enemy position for attacking fighter-bombers. (USAF)

Low-tech communications. To delineate the front lines during large scale air attacks, ground force would lay out canvas panels such as these during Operation QUEEN in November 1944. (USAF)

The consequence was pilots assumed that any troops in front of these panels were the enemy and attacked them. Col. E. L. Johnson, G-3 of the U.S. First Army, stated that a pilot reported he had seen panels stretching from the frontlines back to Corps HQ!

Much of the problem can be attributed to insufficient air support training of both the ground and air personnel before D-Day. Until May 1944 the 9th Air Force was allocated to supporting the 8th Air Force and did not train for their tactical role. By the time the invasion ground forces had been trained they were quarantined in the pre-embarkation port areas and were inaccessible for any training in coordinating ground support attacks. Fighter-bomber pilots were inexperienced in dive-bombing and strafing battlefield targets, as they had been trained in the States as air-to-air combat pilots.

Smoke shells and colored identification panels were employed to identify enemy targets and friendly troops, respectively. Smoke shells were fired by American artillery to designate enemy positions for incoming fighter-bombers. There were some early attacks on friendly troops when the Germans intercepted radio messages requesting that smoke shells be fired on German targets to identify their position. The Germans had their artillery fire smoke shells on American positions that were then attacked. This ploy was countered by using colored smoke shells. After the smoke shells were fired the ground controller would report to the circling fighter-bombers that smoke shells had been fired, and as they hit he would report their colors. Troops would display 3x5 foot colored oilskin recognition panels to identify their position. To prevent the Germans from using similar panels to deceive the pilots a daily color scheme was used to mark the front line position.

In close air support it was inevitable that accidents would happen. This was particularly true in the close quarters of the Normandy hedgerows. The 112th Regiment was hit four times, experiencing 30 deaths and over 100 casualties. After a while some units had become so anxious about being hit by friendly fire that they refused to call in close air support. Friendly fire accidents were common and extremely demoralizing. Armored column cover, particularly after a breakthrough, was responsible for preventing friendly fire accidents because of the direct communications between the tankers and pilots.

Friendly fire worked two ways: friendly AA fire also was responsible for losses of friendly aircraft. On Christmas Day 1944, Maj. George Preddy, leading the 328th Squadron of the 352nd Fighter Group, took off from Y-29 to patrol over the Battle of the Bulge. The squadron got into a short dogfight in which Preddy shot down two Me-109s to put him at 26.83 victories. Preddy and two P-51s were vectored toward Leige, where several bandits were reported on deck. Preddy dove on a FW-190 flying just above a wooded area. Part way through the pursuit, Preddy ran into potent light flak and small arms fire. American AA units were to be informed of friendly aircraft in the area and were to hold their fire. Instead the 12th AA Group was given a red alert for enemy aircraft approaching. As the Mustangs flew over, a gunner on a .50 quad machine gun opened fire briefly before he realized that they were friendly aircraft. Preddy's fighter was hit, and he broke off the attack in a chandelle to the left. As he reached 700 feet his canopy flew off and the Mustang, *Cripes A'Mighty*, nosed into the ground. Preddy was hit by one of the .50 caliber rounds, killing the leading active ace in the ETO.

On Christmas Day, George Preddy, top 8th Air Force ace at the time with 27 victories, was leading the 328th Fighter Squadron of the 352nd Fighter Group and was shot down by a nervous US AA battery after BODENPLATTE. (USAF)

9

German Counter Tactics

Aircraft

To counter American fighter-bombers on interdiction missions the Luftwaffe would send out a few fighters. The fighter-bombers were at a disadvantage, carrying bombs and perhaps a belly tank, and their first inclination would be to jettison their bombs and chase the Germans. Since the German's intentions were to save the target from bombing they would race away untouched, saving valuable aircraft and pilots. The Americans countered this tactic by retaining their bombs and faking attacks towards the Luftwaffe fighters, but continuing on to bomb the target. If the German attack was too tenacious or in force, the Americans would then jettison their bombs and concentrate on the German fighters.

Flak

Bill Colgan, flying P-47s for the 86th Fighter Group, discussed flak in his book *Fighter-Bomber Pilot* (ibid.):

"Fighter-bomber pilots were well aware of the pounding taken by bombers by flak and their losses to both flak and enemy fighters. I would never have wanted to trade places with any of the bomber crewsÖ.Still, the intensity of German flak and other gunfire (in both tracking and barrage fire) and combinations thereof gave the low-altitude combat skies of World War II a very violent and deadly reputation. Those particular skies are the domain of fighter-bomber pilots on the great majority of their missions."

RAF 609 Squadron CO Charles Demoulin, a 2nd TAF (RAF) Typhoon pilot, stated in his book *Firebirds, Flying the Typhoon in Action* (Airlife, UK, 1987), that in Normandy the Germans possessed 20,000 AA guns (this figure seems somewhat high and may include AA machine guns-author). This figure would give the Germans a 4 to 1 gun to attacking aircraft superiority, and upwards of 20 or 30 to 1 in highly defended areas. Nearly 95 percent of losses sustained in attacks on ground targets were due to flak, and only 5 percent to the Luftwaffe. The reason for the high loss rate to flak was that it was concentrated to defend the typical armed recce targets: airfields; communication centers; bridges; radar sites; supply dumps; and HQ buildings. Near the battlefield, except for the defense of vital points, it was improbable that the Germans would invest flak guns to defend such dispersed close-support targets as gun positions, pillboxes, and armor. Also, U.S. artillery was often in range to fire and suppress enemy flak. Against heavily defended armed recce targets, flak suppression fighter-bombers were dispatched to deal with the flak but suffered a high casualty rate.

German Flak Units

The word "flak" is derived from the German nomenclature for their anti-aircraft weapons, *Fliegerabwehrkanonen*, whose length demanded abbreviation. *Flieger* = to fly, *abwehr* = to protect, and *kanonen* = guns. With a few exceptions, German AA units were a part of the Luftwaffe. While operating with the army AA units they were under command of the army, but administratively they were under the control of the parent Luftwaffe ground unit. The distribution of AA units to the Army varied depending on its predicted operational requirements. Generally, an Army Corps had one or more individual AA battalions permanently attached to it, and at least one mixed battalion attached to a Panzer division. In 1943, the fundamental combat AA component was the Abteilung, or battalion, that was divided into three types: heavy, mixed, and light.

Heavy Battalion: This unit was uncommon and usually operated in static positions in the defense of Germany. It was equipped with either 88mm or 105mm AA guns or both. Its organization consisted of a headquarters with three batterein (batteries) equipped with four or sometimes six guns.

Mixed Battalion: This was the typical battalion, using either four or, preferably, if available, six 88mm guns per battery. The organization of the mixed battalion was:

(1) Three heavy batteries of four or six 88mm guns and two 20mm guns for close support
(2) Two light batteries of twelve 20mm guns and four 60cm search lights (a medium battery of nine 37mm guns and four 60cm searchlights at times replaced one of the light batteries)

Light Battalion: There were two types of light gun battalions:
(1) Headquarters:
- (a) Three light batteries each equipped with twelve 20mm guns
- (b) One searchlight battery with sixteen 60cm searchlights

(2) Headquarters:
- (a) Two light batteries each equipped with twelve 20mm guns
- (b) One medium battery equipped with nine 37mm guns
- (c) One searchlight battery equipped with sixteen 60cm search lights

The batterie (battery) was the standard AA unit, and in the mixed battalion consisted of:

(1) Heavy battery:
- (a) Combat echelon:
  - Battery HQ
  - Gun, searchlight and instrument detachments
  - Communication detachments
  - Light flak section
  - Ammunition detachment
  - Combat train
- (b) Ration transport
- (c) Baggage transport

(2) Light and medium batteries each with:
- (a) Combat echelon:
  - Battery HQ
  - Gun and searchlight detachments
  - Communication detachment
  - Ammunition detachment
  - Combat train
- (b) Ration transport
- (c) Baggage transport

(3) Searchlight battery

Zug: Was the smallest operational German AA unit exceeding one gun and usually applied to light and medium units of three guns.

AA Personnel: 7 man Gun Detachment
- Detachment Commander
  - No.1: Gun Layer
  - No.2: Range-setter
  - No.3: Course-setter
  - No.4: Loader
  - No.5: Ranger-taker
- Vehicle Driver

Railway Flak Units

Luftwaffe railway flak units were divided into regiments, battalions, and batteries, and were under the administration of the Luftwaffe, but under the operational control of the transport authority. Panzer divisions had their own flak units that consisted of:

AA battalion staff
One heavy AA battery (6 heavy and 2 light guns) Luftwaffe
One light AA battery (12 light guns) Luftwaffe
One light AA battery (9 light guns less a gun section) Luftwaffe
One AA company (12 light guns) Heeresflak (organic Panzer)

Moving Panzer units were directed to maintain a considerable distance between separate units and groups, and where possible a division was to move in several columns along parallel routes. The majority of its AA guns were positioned well forward of the columns, with all defiles, bridges, and resting places well defended by AA units. Panzer columns usually stopped for 20 minutes rest after two hours on the move, and after four or five hours of movement needed to stop for three hours. When attacked along roads the Panzer column was supposed to continue moving, and its AA crews and infantry machine gunners and riflemen were to lay a concentrated mass of fire on the attacking low flying fighters. If the Panzers were caught in the open the tanks were to deploy in a "V" formation and move on while protected by their AA units.

By early 1944 the Wehrmacht, in response to Allied air superiority, increased their light automatic anti-aircraft firepower. An infantry division was equipped with a minimum of 84 20mm AA guns, while a panzer division at D-Day was equipped with 21 self-propelled, 55 towed, and 32 truck and half-track mounted AA guns of the 20mm or 37mm variety. Attacks on transport and supply often limited the amount of German AA ammunition reaching the front. At times flak batteries curtailed firing, as they often had a very limited number (10-20) of rounds available.

For the AA defense of rear area installations there were no set principles laid down for the deployment of AA. The major factors were the importance of the target, the amount of AA available, the amount of enemy fighter-bomber activity in the area, and which side had attained air superiority. In battle situations not only did the moving columns require AA protection, but also semi-permanent installations, such as supply depots and motor parks, and permanent installations, such as airdromes, rails/roads, and their bridges.

Note: As the war progressed German battle experience developed the mobile and multi-purpose use of AA guns in the field. The Polish and French Campaigns, and finally Rommel in North Africa demonstrated the use of AA guns, particularly the 88mm, in an anti-tank role. Light and medium German AA gun positions were usually disposed in zugs of three guns. A triangular layout was common, with guns anywhere from 200-450ft. apart. Due to their light weight, mobility, high rate of fire, and the AP shell these guns were also used extensively in an anti-tank role, though without the success of the 88mm. They also were used particularly in emergencies against light fortifications, machine gun nests, and buildings in towns and villages. In built up rear areas light and medium guns were used on specially constructed towers on airdromes, supply depots, and the like, and they were also mounted on the roofs of buildings.

Operational Use of AA Against Fighter-Bombers

Obviously, the re-establishment of air superiority, or at least, air parity, would have been the answer to German supply and transport problems caused by Allied air interdiction. But by the end of 1943 the Luftwaffe was stretched thin, not only over the Mediterranean and Russia, but also it was obligated to defend the Reich against the escalating Allied strategic bombing attacks. In addition, decreased German aircraft production, pilot training capability, and fuel production made this impossible. The Germans did not appreciate the value of battlefield air defense. Since the Luftwaffe could not regain air superiority, an effort should have been made to institute a strong anti-aircraft artillery force at the front. Some German Army commanders who had experience in North Africa and Italy and were leading well-trained units, were able to counter escalating Allied air superiority and maintain operations by revising German pre-1942 combat doctrine and employing light AA. However, at D-Day many unit commanders in Western Europe had either commanded occupation forces or had transferred from Russia or the Balkans, where enemy air superiority was not a problem. Their inexperience in employing AA doctrine led to the slow destruction and apathy of their forces and supply system. After the breakout from the Normandy beaches, the absence of the Luftwaffe, and complete Allied air superiority, all the Germans had left was their formidable AA defense. The September 1944 issue of Impact discussed the change in German air defense strategy: "The Luftwaffe, with its back to the wall, is fighting the world's greatest concentration of air power with the world's greatest concentration of flak." In October 1944 the Luftwaffe Flak arm had 600,000 soldiers and 520,000 auxiliaries. These auxiliaries were German youth and women, foreign volunteers, and wounded soldiers unable to return to frontline duties. Battlefield AA defenders were able-bodied soldiers. The Waffen SS had its own flak defense units that usually were used in ground action against tanks and troops. The Kriegsmarine flak units served on shipping, but also in coastal defense.

The major threat to the fighter-bomber was not the Luftwaffe that had all but disappeared over the battlefront during daytime, but was German flak that dictated fighter-bomber tactics on the way to the target and during the attack. Light and medium caliber AA cannon was effective up to 6,000 slant feet. Heavy AA fire was not considered effective against fighters flying directly over the battery at altitude of less than 1,200ft. For this reason each heavy AA battery was supported by two 20mm. Heavy caliber automatic flak (20mm-40mm) was effective up to 6,000 feet, and the pilots easily saw its explosions. Pilots were briefed to fly at 7,500-8,000 feet, an altitude that was out of range of automatic flak, and where heavy non-automatic (e.g. 88mm) was inaccurate. Small caliber 20-37mm automatic anti-aircraft fire was effective up to 3,000 feet and its explosions were not visible. Pilots were briefed not to drop below 3,000 feet except during their bombing run, at which time they would come in as low as possible and at as high a speed as to effect accurate fire, as enemy gunners had less time to track and lay down a large quantity of fire. The German soldier was trained to use his weapon against attacking fighters, and concentrated fire by rifles and semi-automatic weapons was very effective up to slant ranges of 1,500ft. and machine gun fire up to 2,400ft. On a strafing run enemy gunners tended to underestimate the attacker's speed.

Bill Colgan (P-47/79th Fighter Group), in his book *Fighter-Bomber Pilot*, discussed flak guns:

"Most pilots did not concern themselves to any great extent in the technical aspects of flak guns, such as the exact sizes or German nomenclature (Flak 18, Flak 30, Flak 41 etc.). While we had seen automatic flak guns listed from 15mm to 37mm, some of us still talked in terms of 20mm to 40mm sizes. Any of them could do a fighter-bomber in with a good hit. Of greater importance was knowing the general capabilities and where and how they might be installed, carried, mounted and encountered. (On the other hand, some pilots said there was a simple answer to all that: 'If the Germans are there, the automatic weapon flak will be there.') There was one aspect of flak capabilities that pilots and intelligence officers could never did see eye to eye on. That was the effective range of the German guns. Of course, anything larger than 37mm could effectively reach above the altitude that fighter-bombers flew on most missions. It was the automatic-weapon flak where the differences of opinion existed. For example, if pilots were told that the "effective range" of certain of the guns was 5,000 feet and then saw rounds from those guns at 9,000 feet or so, many of them said to hell with whether they are 'scientifically effective' up here; more important was the simple fact that they could shoot this high. Other pilots discounted the entire business of studying the facts and fig-

Capt. Marvin Bledsoe, a P-47 pilot with the 350th Fighter Group (USAF)

ures on flak guns, their theory being where we flew much of the time, a kid could throw a rock and reach us."

Capt. Marvin Bledsoe of the 350th Fighter Group described his encounter with the heavy flak in the Ruhr Valley, which was nicknamed "Flak Valley" *(Thunderbolt: Memoirs of a World War II Fighter Pilot*, ibid.):

"Then suddenly the sky fell in on us!

Unknowingly we had worked our way to the outskirts of a city. Flak of all descriptions came up from all directions-tracer bullets from machine guns, tiny white puffs of exploding 20-millimeters and large black blossoms from the heavy guns. Flak was flying everywhere. The flak gunners who were not shooting directly at us were laying up a barrage of steel over our heads. In every direction the wall of bullets and shrapnel had us hemmed in. We seemed to be trapped.

Jonah here," Rimmerman (Colonel and CO) yelled excitedly. "Everybody out!" Jesus Christ, we're right in the middle of the Ruhr Valley. You guys get the hell out of here the best you can."

We made a tight turn on the deck and headed away from the industrial section ahead. Rimmerman was going like a bat out of hell, so low to the ground that the trees and bushes swayed back and forth as he passed over them. I poured water injection to my ship to get maximum emergency power and stay with Rimmerman.

The sky was full of death for miles around. It was impossible to dodge the flak. Our only escape route seemed to be through the overcast. The thousand feet to the comparative safety of the clouds was going to be like a thousand miles. As soon as we headed upstairs every gunner in the area would be after us.

I stayed on Rimmerman's tail, my throttle wide open, calling on every ounce of power I could drain from the 2,000-horsepower engine. Rimmerman twisted and turned as he made for the overcast. I could see where the flak was hitting his ship. At the same time I could feel *The Little Princess* (his P-47) shudder at the impact of exploding shells. My heart was beating wildly in my throat as we leaped into the clouds.

I had been able to pull up on Rimmerman's wing and stuck with him as he made his way through the overcast. I was still able to feel and hear the concussion of exploding flak in the darkness of the clouds. Rimmerman and I were alone. Although we were out of sight of the flak gunners below, we were not out of range. We continued to climb and take evasive action. The flak was still bursting in our direction, controlled by radar.

Above the clouds the flak was even more intense, the higher we climbed, the better the opportunity for the long-range heavy guns to work on us. Our only consolation was that we finally escaped the deadly aim of the light stuff, the scourge of al fighter pilots.

Just as we thought we were getting away, a large burst of flak exploded between us. Those gunners seemed to have us zeroed in. Holes suddenly appeared in my left wing. Rimmerman peeled off in a wingover in a twisting dive. I yanked my stick over and wheeled after him. We were diving at more than five hundred miles per hour, but we still barely managed to keep one jump ahead of the flak.

Rimmerman and I kept zooming, diving, twisting and turning, trying to get away. The black smoke pods of exploding flak kept burst all around us.

For a moment when the flak became extremely heavy I lost Rimmerman. 'Are you okay, Bledsoe?' Rimmerman called almost immediately. 'How bad have you been hit?'

I'm okay, Jonah. A couple of good-sized holes in my left wing that I can see. I've been hit at least a dozen times but this baby is still flying. I've got you in sight and will try to cut you off in a second. I'm still trying to shake these damn flak gunners.

'*The Little Princess*' must look like a sieve. Thank God, she's still flying right and responding. Good baby.

A minute later we were in the clear. The flak had disappeared. We were over Holland and it wouldn't be long and we'd make the English Channel."

Flak in Italy

In November 1944 the German flak in northern Italy was probably the most concentrated of any theater of the war. Its 2,500 guns were divided into three sectors controlled by Luftwaffe Colonel Eduard Neumann: Western, Central, and Eastern. The rd Flak Brigade covered the Western Section, the 25th Flak Division covered the Central Section that extended to the northern border, including Brenner, and the 22nd Flak Brigade covered the Eastern Section over the Venetian Plain. Even though the Germans lost many AA guns in their summer retreat north of Rome they actually had more guns protecting critical targets because there had been a decrease in the area to be protected. Axis informers behind the lines radioed the takeoffs of Allied bomber and fighter formations and German long-range, and 190 mile Wassermann radar and Freya 100 mile surveillance radar transmitted information to air defense HQ in Verona. HQ, in turn, advised the appropriate section Flakf¸hrer to have his heavy batteries, medium and light AA guns, and mobile radar on standby.

Flak batteries were composed of four to 12 guns manned by 60-70% German and 30-40% Italian crews (Verona flak, however, was manned by all-Italian crews). When a battery detected a target it was tracked by radar for range and tracked optically for direction. Each battery defended a sector and fired on any enemy aircraft entering the sector. The Flakf¸hrer alone could order any sector to fire into another sector. While this flak detection/direction method was effective against bombers, it was not nearly as effective against low-flying fighter-bombers. These fixed flak units and the mobile units protecting the targets had to maintain constant observation to detect their surprise attacks. P-47 units, armed with machine guns, rockets, and napalm would swoop in at low-level against German AA batteries that were busy concentrating on a concurrent bomber raid above. It was found that reducing the number of the standard P-47 formation from 12 to eight or four fighter-bombers gave greater maneuverability and better accuracy, and also drew less AA fire.

German AA Guns

The Germans divided their flak guns into three classifications:

(1) Light (20mm referred to as "machine cannon"): Light AA was to be used against targets flying from ground level to an effective range of 7,200ft., and thus needed to be on a flexible mounting, have a high rate of fire, and fired with sights, requiring only brief firing time calculations.
(2) Medium (37 to 50mm): Medium AA also was used against low-flying aircraft, but had an effective maximum altitude of about 14,000ft.
(3) Heavy (75mm+): AA guns were intended for use against bombers flying above 20,000ft.

Wehrmacht infantry were well trained in anti-Jabo small arms defense. Any soldier who knocked down a fighter-bomber was awarded a 10-day furlough. (US Army)

German Light and Medium AA Guns

AA Gun Type	Maximum Elevation (Degrees)	Rate of Fire (Rds/min)	Maximum Vertical Range(Feet)
20mm Flak 20	90	280	12,500*
20mm Flak 38	90	450	12,500*
20mm Flakvierling	100	1,800 (4 barrel)	12,500*
37mm Flak 18	85	160	15700**
37mm Flak 36 & 37	85	160	15700**
37mm Flak 43	90	250	15700**
37mm Flakzwilling 43	90	500 (2 barrel)	15700**

*Maximum effective ceiling 7,200 feet

** Maximum effective ceiling 13,800 feet

Note: The Germans used centimeters rather than millimeters in their classification (i.e. the 20mm Flak 38 AA gun was designated the 2cm Flak 38 AA gun).

AA shells were to explode automatically after a predetermined distance, so as not to fall to earth as a whole shell.

A MG 34 on an AA mount with a 50 round belt linked to 250 rounds. (US Army)

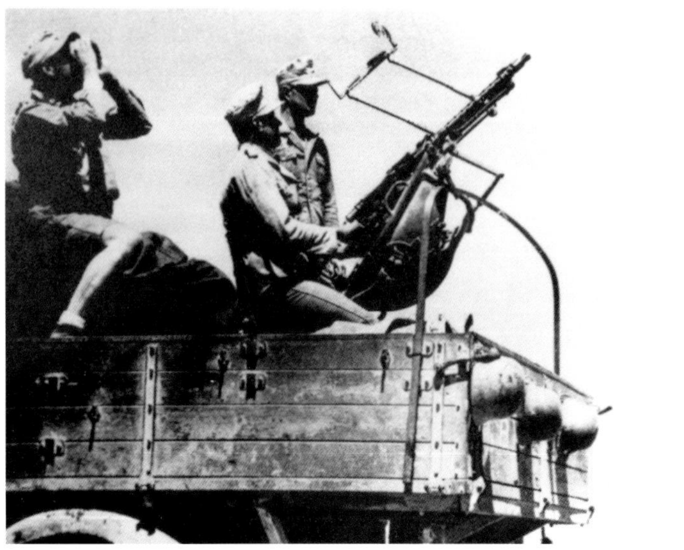

Twin MG 34 AA gun (Zwillingslafette 34) mounted on the back of a truck of the 21st Panzer Division. (US Army)

Infantry

Along with his rifle, the German infantryman used the standard, air-cooled 7.92mm MG 34, MG 34/41, and MG-42 light 7.92mm machine gun in the AA role for local protection against low-flying aircraft. As AA guns they were fitted with special single and dual mounts on special bipod or tripods with adjustable legs. Special belt drums containing a 50 round belt (and multiples) coiled inside were fed into the left side of the gun. The simple fast-change barrels needed to be replaced after firing 150 rounds. The MG 34s had an aperture rear sight for use with an AA "cartwheel" front sight. The MG 34 was used early in the war by the Afrika Korps as an open sight twin installation called the Zwillingslafette 34 and mounted on a truck or light vehicle. Introduced in mid-1942, the MG 42 was the easily and cheaply mass-produced successor to the MG 34/41, and mounted types increased throughout the war. The MG 42 had a "speed" ring sight (concentric circles around center post) on the barrel jacket and a hinged rear AA sight. The high cyclic rate, approximately 1,250rpm, ran through the 50 round (and multiples) very quickly and was very inaccurate.

Ex-Aircraft AA Machine Guns and Cannon

Towards the end of the war the production of 20mm Flak 38s could not keep up with the demand, and aircraft machine guns were taken from abandoned Luftwaffe bombers and placed on airfields, patrol boats, and rail cars. These ex-aircraft guns were mounted on free-standing socket mounts or installed on light flak mounts:

MG 81 (7.92mm) on a twin mount
MG 151/15 (15mm) on a triple mount
MG 151/20 (20mm) on a triple mount

The mount could rotate 360°, but had no traversing and elevating mechanisms. It had to be aimed manually, which reduced their efficiency in shooting down enemy aircraft. However, their high rate of fire and the number of tracer shells dissuaded low-flying aircraft from pressing their attacks. A horizontal tube linked the guns, with grips at each end linked to the trigger mechanism. The right grip fired the two outside guns, while the left grip fired the middle gun. The high rate of fire (720rpm) made manual aiming very difficult. The 3-ton Sd.Kfz.251/21 half-track armored troop carrier mounted the Mauser MG 151s primarily for ground combat, and secondarily for AA defense against low-flying aircraft.

German Light and Medium Automatic Flak Guns

The 20 to 37mm AA guns were characterized by their rapid rate of fire, filling the air within their range with a very high volume of small projectiles. This feature made them very effective against fast, low-flying aircraft that were taking evasive action on their approach. The design and construction of these guns and their mounts emphasized light weight and the ability to traverse quickly through arcs of fire against aircraft that would be within their range for only brief periods. Automatic flak guns did not have great range, even though they had high muzzle velocities. The effective vertical range was limited, as the curving path of their trajectory did not provide great accuracy over the entire length of their flight.

There are two considerations regarding rates of fire. The "cyclical" rate is the theoretical maximum rate of fire for one minute that a weapon can achieve. Cyclical rate of fire is only a useful reference for comparative purposes, as it cannot be maintained for any long period of time due to overheating and the subsequent risk of failure. The "practical" rate of fire is the rate of fire that could be sustained over shorter periods of time without danger of damaging the guns.

Hand-held 20mm cannon protected Luftwaffe airdromes. These guns were adapted from former aircraft guns. (US Army)

Mauser MG 151s mounted in a 3-ton Sd.Kfz.251/21 half-track armored troop carrier was used primarily for ground combat and secondarily for AA defense against low-flying aircraft. The high rate of fire (720rpm) made manual aiming very difficult. (US Army)

20mm Flak 30 with a Flak Sight 35 with the K1 (target aimer) turning the elevation hand-wheel with his right hand. Note four victory rings on the barrel. (US Army)

The Gun Aimer of a 20mm Flak 30 battery looks through the hole of the rear ring sight as he tries to keep the target inside the large front circle and line it up with the small suspended target ball in the center of the circle. (US Army)

20mm Flak Guns

In 1932 the Geneva Disarmament Conference allowed Germany to develop self-defense weapons; the 20mm Flak 30 was ready to equip the German Army against low-flying aircraft in 1933, and by 1934 twelve units were in force. On 1 April 1935 Hermann Göring appropriated all Flak units for the Luftwaffe, but in 1938 the Army was allowed a twelve gun 20mm Flak company for every machine gun battalion.

There were three 20mm German Flak guns: the Model 30 and 38, and the most feared of all AA guns by fighter-bomber pilots, the quadmount Flakvierling 38. These were considered light flak guns.

20mm Model 30

The 20mm (.79 inch) Flak 30 was manufactured by Rheinmetall-Borsig, developed from the Solothurn S5-100, and was introduced into the Kriegsmarine in 1930 and the Luftwaffe in 1935. It was used in large numbers by all branches of the German services and was the primary gun of light AA units. It was used in an anti-tank role with a special AP40 round, and were employed on U-boats using a special twin mount. The barrel gas cylinder plug and breech mechanisms were locked together until after the projectile left the barrel. Loading, delivery of the next round, and ejection of the empty casing were accomplished through the pressure of the spent powder gases. A flat box magazine containing 20 rounds weighing 21lbs. fed the gun. It was recoil operated in single and automatic modes with a pedal-operated trigger mechanism and had a detachable barrel. The normal crew for the Flak 30 was the Detachment commander and five men: No.1-Layer for bearing and elevation; No.2-Range setter; No.3-Loader; No.4 Ammunition loader; and No.5-Rangetaker (eliminated after August 1944), plus the vehicle driver. Sighting was by the Lineavisier (Linear Sight) 21 operated by two men. The primary Flak 30 mount was a triangular platform leveled by three adjustable feet. The gun carriage revolved on ball bearings that had a cradle adjustable for elevation by a hand wheel located on the right side and a traversing wheel at the back. The gun was transported on a light single axle two-wheel carriage (Sonder Anhanger 51) that could be either horse-drawn or pulled by a motor vehicle. It was also mounted on a variety of self-propelled carriages and trains. The cyclical rate of fire was rated at 280rpm, but in practice was 120rpm, as the magazine needed to be changed after its 20 round capacity was fired. At about 160∞F. the barrel needed to be changed. To change the hot barrel asbestos gloves were used. This 120rpm rate of fire was considered too low for effective defense against fast-flying fighter-bombers. The gun also had a tendency to jam on occasion.

20mm Flak 38 and 20mm Quadmount Flakvierling 38

The low rate of fire of the 20mm Flak 30 led to a contract with Mauser that produced the Flak 38 in 1939. Mauser preserved the Flak 30 feed mechanism, but modified the breech mechanism to produce a cyclical rate of fire of 420-480 rpm (e.g. 2.5 seconds for a 20 round magazine), but the practical rate continued to be a rather low 180-220rpm. The ballistics were the same as the Flak 30 since the same ammunition was used. Cartridges were fed from a curved box magazine hinged on the left side of the gun. A mesh net was

The low rate of fire of the 20mm Flak 30 led to a contract with Mauser that produced the Flak 38 in 1939. A 20mm Flak 38 being towed by a the small NSU *Kettenkrad* tracked tow vehicle in North Africa in mid-1942. (US Army)

The 1-Meter-Base Range Finder operator calls the measured target distance to the gun aimer of a well-camouflaged 20mm Flakverling 38. This range finder was widely used and effective in the hands of an experienced operator. (US Army)

attached to the right side of the gun to catch spent cartridges. Its maximum effective ceiling was 7,200 feet. The rate of elevation and traverse was improved by the use of an overdrive mechanism. The gun layer sat on the right side of the weapon. He operated the vertically mounted elevation hand wheel located on the right side of the gun mount with his right hand and the horizontal hand wheel of the traversing mechanism with his left hand. The gun layer activated the trigger mechanism by a foot pedal. A lever on the right side of the breech allowed him to select semi-automatic or full-automatic fire, and to employ the safety. The carriage and trailer remained the same as used by the Flak 30, but it was also mounted on half-track vehicles and trains. The sight was the Flakvisier 38 or 39A, and the Schweberkrevisier 38 was introduced in November 1944. The 3x8 degree telescopic sight was used against ground targets. The single Flak 30 was preferred over the Flak 38, as it was quieter, and due to its weight more stable when firing. While its lower rate of fire was a disadvantage against aircraft, it did allow the gunners to make more corrections when firing against land targets. As flak guns were often used against ground targets a 260lb. shield was provided to cover the barrel and extended to protect the gunners.

The German AA gun most feared by fighter-bomber pilots was the 20mm Quadmount Flakverling 38. The high rate of practical fire of the combined four guns (800rpm) put up a virtual wall of fire, which tracer ammunition made visible to the enemy fighter pilot. This weapon was originally produced for use by the Kriegsmarine in 1940. It was then installed on the mounting pedestal of railway cars, the mounting ring with levelers of self-propelled vehicles, and there was a static version for use in flak towers, coastal defenses, and aboard shipping. It was transported by a special trailer,

20mm Quadruple Flakverling 38 mounted on a Sonder Anhanger 52, Special Trailer. This was the AA gun most feared by Allied fighter-bomber pilots as it could put up 800 rounds per minute. As flak guns were often used against ground targets a shield was provided to cover the barrel and extended to protect the gunners. (US Army)

Two 20mm Quads mounted on self-propelled 8 ton half-tracks. (US Army)

the single-axle Sonder Anhanger 52, which was towed behind motor transport in which personnel and stores were carried. The trailer was a wishbone-shaped, welded quarter-inch steel plate frame supported by pneumatic tires. The Flak 38 could be fired from the trailer in emergencies, but otherwise the gun and mount could be quickly and conveniently deployed for action. The mount consisted of a triangular base that had a jack at each apex for leveling the gun. The weapon weighed nearly 3,000lbs:, and its trailer 1,800lbs. The gun had folding seats and handles and built-in ammunition racks. A shield could be fitted to the carriage and folded back for transport. It was also mounted on the self-propelled Flakpanzer IV Mobelwagen or the Wirbelwind. As the gun mounted four barrels the number of crew increased to a commander and seven men: No.1-Layer for bearing and elevation; No.2-Rangesetter; No.3 and 4-Loading crew; No.5 Rangetaker (eliminated after August 1944); and No.6 and 7-Ammunition loaders. In an emergency the commander, No.1, and two ammunition loaders could operate the gun. The Flakvisier 40 and 40A that succeeded the 38 was used as a sighting apparatus, and as the war ended radar lying was about to be introduced. The mount was traversed and elevated manually by No. 2, who had the two hand wheels in easy reach. Two foot-levers operated the trigger mechanism, with each lever actuating two diametrically opposed guns (e.g. the top left and bottom right and the top right and bottom left). This arrangement provided uninterrupted continuous fire. While two guns were firing the magazines of the other two were being changed. When both firing levers operated, all four guns fired simultaneously. If there was a stoppage on one or more guns the remaining guns could continue to fire. Each gun could be fired in a single shot or continuous mode. The mount stored 16 boxes (320 rounds), and loading was via flat 20 round box magazines in two staggered rows. Spent shells were ejected toward the center of the gun into chutes leading to a collection box that held 500 shell cases. The barrels could be easily and quickly replaced. In August 1944 the Luftwaffe had 17,589 Flak 30 and 38 guns and 3,605 Flakvierling 38 guns in service.

The 37mm Flak 18 gun used standard 37mm ammunition in eight round frame (clip) weighing 66lbs.The clips were fed horizontally from the left from a fixed loading tray and was operated by the recoil of the gun itself. It fired 150 to 180 rounds per minute. (US Army)

The 37mm Flak 36 was a widely used AA gun with over 4,200 being manufactured.This successful gun crew has claimed 15 aircraft.The range finder is a Flakvisier 38. (US Army)

37mm Flak Guns

There were four types of German 37mm flak guns: the Flak 18; the Flak 36 and 37; the Flak 43; and its twinmount version, the Flakzwilling 43. These were the smallest caliber medium flak guns.

37mm Flak 18

The Flak 18 was originally a Rheinmetall-Borsig design as the ST 10, but was further developed as the Solothurn S10-100, and again further developed by Rheinmetall, who put it into production. It entered service in 1935, but had a number of problems with the gun and its carriage, and only a few were produced until production ended a year later. The four-wheeled carriage was large and heavy, the gun experienced many stoppages, and traverse was slow. The gun required a well-trained crew of eight to cope with its idiosyncrasies, but the 18s remained in use into 1945.

37mm Flak 36/37

The Flak 36 was essentially an improved Flak 18 on a new two-wheel carriage, the Sonder Anhanger 52 (see 20mm Flakvierling 38), and was lighter and more mobile. This 3,600 lb. gun was also found on self-propelled half-tracks, railway mounts, flak towers, and U-boats. The ballistics of the Flak 36 were the same as the Flak 18, and in 1940 new ammunition was introduced with a single driving band instead of two. The chamber of the Flak 36 was shortened to accommodate this ammunition (the Flak 18 was not modified for this ammunition and continued to use up remaining stocks of two band ammo). The gun was automatic and recoil-operated. The firing mechanism could be set for single or automatic fire as required. The ammunition was loaded in clips holding six rounds. Its theoretical rate of fire was 150rpm, but its practical rate was 60rpm. Its maximum effective ceiling was 13,800 feet. It was operated by 12 men: (1) Detachment Commander; (2) No.1-Layer; (3) No.2-Range-Layer; (4) No.3-Course-setter; (5) No.4-Loader; (6) No. 5-Range-taker; (7-8) No.6 and 7-Ammunition loaders; (9) Vehicle driver; (10) Vehicle driver relief; and (11-12) Spotters. In August 1944 the Luftwaffe had 4,211 of these guns in service.

A 37mm Flak 36 protecting canal ship traffic and the nearby bridge. (US Army)

37mm Flak 43

The 37mm Flak 43 was a completely new Rheinmetall design that decreased production time from 4,320 hours to about 1,000. The breech mechanism was a completely new gas-operated type, and there were numerous detail changes. The gun was light, fully automatic, and gas-operated. The gun used the standard 37mm ammunition in an eight round frame (clip) weighing 66lbs., and the barrel remained the same as those of the 37mm Flak 18 and 36/37. The practical rate of fire was increased from 60rpm to 150-180rpm over the Flak 36/37, and elevation and traverse speeds were increased. It was fed horizontally from the left in clips of eight rounds from a fixed loading tray and was operated by the recoil of the gun itself. The gun could be statically placed on a pedestal mount, mounted on a self-propelled chassis, or transported on a mobile trailer, either the single axle Sonder Anhanger 58 or the twin axle Sonder Anhanger 104 or 206. The sight was the Flakvisier 43 that was the successor of the Flakvisier 37. An armored shield protected the front of the gun. In February 1945 there were 1,032 Flak 43 guns in service.

37mm Flakzwilling 43

Rheinmetall increased the firepower of the Flak 43 by mounting one gun vertically over another. Eight round clips fed the gun. It was transported by the Sonder Anhanger 106, but was difficult to emplace due to its height. The Flakzwilling 43 with horizontally mounted 37mm guns reached the prototype stage, and plans were drawn for a quadmount. The gun was a very successful and effective AA weapon, but only 390 were in service in February 1944.

88mm Flak

Medium and heavy bomber pilots feared the 88mm flak gun, but its rate of fire was too low against fast, low-flying aircraft. Heavy caliber radar-controlled flak was only rarely experienced by fighter-bomber pilots, and then usually on fighter formation flights. Air planners attempted to route attacks around known flak. German radar could follow the flight path and altitude of an aircraft if it flew on a fixed course over a period of time. Calculations were made to predict with accuracy where an aircraft would be when the AA shell reached its target. It took an AA projectile one second to gain 1,000 feet in altitude. To evade flak the fighter pilot would not keep the same course for more than one second for every 1,000 feet of altitude above the ground before he would change course. Direct hits on fighter aircraft were infrequent, but near misses could cause a fighter to be lost. Pilots claimed to hear a buzzing sound in their headphones when their aircraft was being tracked by radar. Kemal Saied of the 404th Fighter Group describes an encounter with radar-controlled flak (*Thunderbolt Odyssey*, Stonewood, 1995):

The 37mm Flak 43 was a completely new Rheinmetall design. With the 37mm Flakzwilling 43 Rheinmetall increased the firepower of the Flak 43 by mounting one gun vertically over another. (US Army)

The 88mm gun was the best gun of World War Two excelling as an anti-aircraft and anti-tank gun. Medium and heavy bomber pilots feared the 88mm flak gun but its rate of fire was too low against fast, low-flying aircraft. Heavy caliber radar-controlled flak was only rarely experienced by fighter-bomber pilots and usually on fighter formation flights. (US Army)

The feared 88mm used in its anti-aircraft configuration. This particular gun seems to have been very successful as the number of victory rings on its barrel. (USAF)

"Suddenly while looking behind me I saw three puffs of black smoke following my flight path, bursting at about one second intervals. Knowing that their ack-ack was shot in bursts of four in a straight line I immediately pulled my plane hard to the right, escaping the fourth burst that exploded precisely where my plane would have been in a straight line."

Due to its characteristics heavy AA was best suited against aircraft operating above 10,000 feet. These characteristics were:

1) Slow rates of fire as there was no automatic handling mechanism to load shells weighing between 12 and 90 pounds and therefore the rate of fire depended on human efficiency. To average heavy battery rate of fire was about 15 rpm but some skilled batteries were able to attain rates of fire of over 30rpm.
2) Shells needed to be fused for different times of flight (altitudes) and to different slant ranges (points in the sky).

Heavy flak damage by 88mm guns could tear gapping holes in an aircraft, as to the wing of this P-47 (USAF)

3) These guns needed to be large, as they were required to fire large shells to great altitudes. The equilibrators and other shock-absorbing mechanisms, along with the heavy mounting, traversing, and elevating apparatus gave these guns great weight and naturally slowed motion and performance when compared to automatic AA guns.

AA Projectiles and Fusing

Two types of ammunition were used: the HE (High Explosive) tracer with a percussion fuse and AP (Armor Piercing) tracer. Because only a small amount of high explosive could be contained in the 20 or 37mm projectile, and if it were detonated on contact with the outer surfaces of the attacking aircraft much of the explosive force would be lost in the air. Therefore a degree of "insensitivity" was engineered into an AA shell to ensure its passage through the relatively thin skin of the aircraft and require impact with a more solid structural component inside the aircraft before detonation occurred. AA shells were engineered with a self-destroying fuse to explode after a specified time or altitude time so they would not fall to the ground intact and explode.

The Flakvisier 38 was an electric automatic sight consisting of illuminated crossing wires and was automatically controlled in terms of elevation and deflection. It was used by 20mm and 37mm AA detachments. This instrument was strapped to the range-takers shoulders on a small tripod and its light source was contained in a small backpack. The instrument was delicate and difficult to handle and to master but was very effective in the hands of an experienced operator. (USAF)

A 37mm flak gun mounted on a Sd Kfz 251 half-track on alert outside San Angelo Castle in early June 1944. (US Army)

AA Sighting Apparatus

1-Meter-Base Range-Finder

This sight was used by 20mm and 37mm AA detachments. This instrument was usually handheld, but could be strapped to the range-taker's shoulders on a small tripod. It was manufactured by Carl Zeiss, Jena factory, and had a six-fold magnification and a range of 250 to 8,000m. It estimated distance by means of two reticles, one in each eyepiece, which when "fused" stereoscopically appear superimposed upon the image in depth. The operator, No.5 range-taker, called the measured target distance to the gun aimers; No.2 the range-setter and No.3 the course-setter. The instrument was difficult to handle and to master, but was very effective in the hands of an experienced operator.

The Lineavisier 21

The Lineavisier (Linear Sight) 21 was operated by two men and was a direct AA sight, providing course, speed, and range adjustment. It was a horizontal bar that was graduated from 0 to 1,600 meters. Range was set by turning a cylindrical range knob on the runner of a rotating ring foresight that increased the lead as the range increased and enabled the course of the target to be set. A movable bar showing the speeds from 11 to 150 meters per second was mounted on the ring foresight. The speed bar could also be adjusted for the angle of dive or climb.

Flakvisier 38 and 39A

The Flakvisier 38 or 39A was an electric automatic sight consisting of illuminated crossing wires, and was automatically controlled in terms of elevation and deflection. The elevating and traversing gears were coupled to elevating and traversing tachometer-dynamos in such a way that the voltages generated by them varied with the speed of the laying. The layer kept the cross wires on the object glass coincident with the target, thus obtaining the angle of sight and azimuth. Range was estimated or called out by the range-setter. The Flakvisier 38 was complicated, fragile, and expensive, and was gradually supplanted by the open sight Linealvisier 38 Ring Sight. This sight was a direct AA sight giving speed, course, and range adjustment. It consisted of a horizontal bar that was graduated from 0 to 1,600 meters. Turning a hand screw on the runner of a ring-type foresight increased the lead set range as the range was increased. The ring foresight could be rotated, enabling the target's course to be set. A movable bar indicating speed from 11 to 150 meters per second was mounted on the foresight. This speed bar could also be adjusted for the angle of climb or dive. The light source was carried in a small pack on the operator's back. This range finder was delicate and difficult to use, but was very effective once mastered. It was succeeded by the Flakvisier 43, and then the Schweberkrevisier 38 introduced in November 1944.

A Kfz 81 light AA vehicle, obviously of the Afrika Korps, mounting a 20mm Flak 38 duel purpose gun, being shown here in its anti-tank role. (US Army)

Quad-mount 20mm AA gun mounted on a medium tank chassis. (US Army)

Mobile AA

Battlefield anti-aircraft was to provide troops protection against low-flying enemy aircraft. To accomplish this the AA needed to be mobile and armored against light weapons and shrapnel. However, out of necessity the Germans used their flak guns against ground targets, particularly in the role of tank destroyers in North Africa and Russia. Once the Allies had established air superiority in late 1943 the Germans introduced AA half-tracks, and later flakpanzers.

In late 1943 German Panzer columns were being decimated by Allied air attacks. The anti-aircraft units of the Panzer Grenadiers were supplied with more anti-aircraft half-track and flakpanzers that were interspersed in armored columns, whose tanks were separated by 150 feet. Usually the initial fighter-bomber attack was too sudden to effectively deploy the AA panzers, but the second wave met with a solid wall of 20mm fire that discouraged the others. The categories of self-propelled flak guns were:

1) On wheeled vehicles
2) On unarmored half-tracks
3) On armored half-tracks
4) On SPW half-tracks
5) On full track vehicles
6) On tanks

Flakpanzer IV "Mobelwagen" was the first flakpanzer on a PanzerIV chassis to be assigned to armored units. The Mobelwagen or "furniture van" (e.g. Moving Van), mounted a single 37mm Flak 43 or 20mm Flakvierling that were interchangeable. The weapon and crew were housed in a four-sided rectangular hinged open turret. In combat the armored sides had to be dropped, exposing the gun crew. (US Army)

Wheeled Vehicles

The Germans mounted 20 and 37mm flak on a variety of German and captured trucks and Kubelwagen chassis.

Half-tracks

8-ton Sd.Kfz.7/6: The 20mm Flakvierling 38 and the 37mm Flak 36 were both mounted on the 8-ton half-track Krauss-Maffei Sd.Kfz.7, which was considered the most notable and versatile prime mover in the Wehrmacht. This medium prime mover (Mittlerer Zugkraftwagen 8) was, like all German half-tracks, very maneuverable and easy to steer and shift. It was powered by a 6-cylinder, 140hp Maybach gasoline engine with a range of 155 miles on a 50-gallon tank. The cab was open, but some later versions were equipped with armored steel plates to cover the cab. A six-man crew manned them: (1) squad leader; (2) gunner; (3) range finder; (4-5) loaders; and (6) driver. The 8t Sd.Kfz.7 carried 600 rounds of ammunition, and an ammunition trailer was often pulled behind. They were generally assigned to the AA companies of Panzergrenadier regiments to provide protection for their tanks and armored personnel carriers.

1-Ton Sd.Kfz.10/4: The 1-ton Leichter Zugkraftwagen began production in 1939; 25,000 were produced during the war, and a number were converted to carry the 20mm Flak 38 and five man crew. It was powered by a 90hp, 6 cylinder Maybach engine with a top speed of 30mph, and 115 gallons of gasoline gave it a range of 180 miles on the road and 105 miles cross-country. The Flak 38 was mounted on the rear cargo compartment, and ammunition boxes containing two magazines were attached to the sides of the gun compartment. A trailer containing ammunition and the crew's personal belongings was towed behind. The gun was used in both AA and ground operations against enemy troops and light armor, particularly in Russia.

3-ton Sd.Kfz.11: This Borgward-built light half-track was powered by a 6-cylinder, 100hp Maybach engine that produced road speeds of 42mph. Some 25,000 chassis were built, with 16,000 converted to the medium Sd.Kfz.251 armored personnel carrier. The 251 mounted the Mauser MG 151 twin machine guns, primarily for ground combat and secondarily for AA defense against low-flying aircraft. The guns were set side-by-side in the same plane in standard aircraft cradles that were bolted to a common block on the top bracket of the pedestal, pivoting on trunnions for elevation and de-

Flakpanzer IV "Wirbelwind" (Whirlwind) mounted the 20mm Flakvierling 38 quadmount. The gun and crew were sheltered in a rotating open topped, multi-faced sloping armored turret. (US Army)

pression. They were cocked manually, percussion fired, and sighted with the cartwheel-type AA sight. The belt-fed guns fired 700rpm from steel boxes to each gun. Each vehicle carried 3,000 rounds.

Flakpanzers

Flakpanzer 38(t) aus M

In response to the call for a special purpose, self-propelled AA vehicle, the 38(t) was a simple transition built on a Pz Kw 38(t) M chassis built by BMW. The engine was moved forward, and the full traverse 20mm Flak 38 gun was mounted in an open-topped armored superstructure at the rear that afforded the four or five man crew little protection. The top half of this superstructure was hinged and could be dropped to give the crew more room and allow the gun to be depressed. 140 to 162 were built and used in small numbers in 1943 with AA platoons of tank battalions. The one 37mm Flak 38 was insufficient and no match for marauding Typhoons and Thunderbolts, and were often the target and victim of the aircraft they were supposed to destroy. The Flakpanzer IV succeeded them.

Flakpanzer IV

The Flakpanzer IV was SP AA mounted on the basic Pz Kw IV chassis and served with AA platoons in tank regiments from 1944. Although they provided poor armor protection for the crew the designs were effective transitional designs that also could be used against ground targets. The variants were:

Flakpanzer IV (37cm) "Mobelwagen" auf Fgst IV was the first flakpanzer on a PanzerIV chassis to be assigned to armored units. The Mobelwagen, or "furniture van," mounted a single 37mm Flak 43 or 20mm Flakvierling that were interchangeable. The weapon and crew were housed in a four-sided rectangular hinged open turret. In combat the armored sides had to be dropped, exposing the gun crew.

Flakpanzer IV (2cm) "Wirbelwind" auf Fgst Pz IV (Whirlwind) mounted the 20mm Flakvierling 38 quadmount. The gun and crew were sheltered in a rotating open topped, multi-faced sloping armored turret. The laying speed of the turret was inadequate due to the increased weight. 150 were built and served with AA platoons of tank battalions from 1944.

Flakpanzer IV (3.7cm) "Ostwind" auf Fgst IV (Westwind) that mounted a single 37mm Flak 43 AA gun in an open-topped, multi-faced sloping turret similar to the Wirbelwind. 40 were built and served with AA platoons of tank battalions from 1945.

The "Kugelblitz" (Ball Lightning) was built as a prototype at the end of the war. It mounted triple 30mm MK 103 aircraft machine guns, as the standard German flak guns were too big to fit in the closed turret.

The Defense of Railway Trains

The Germans were dependent on Europe's rail net to carry men and materiel to battlefields, first on the Eastern Front and then in the West. The Germans had three types of railway flak battalions: the Heavy Railway Flak Battalions, which acted as mobile reserves that could be moved to wherever they were needed; the Light Rail-

Light Flak Rail Car II mounting a Quad 20mm Flakverling 38 on a gun platform.The gun crew lived in the car below and ammunition and extra barrels were stored directly below the gun platform. (US Army)

Left: Flakpanzer IV "Ostwind" (Westwind) that mounted a single 37mm Flak 43 AA gun in an open-topped, multi-faced sloping turret similar to the Wirbelwind. (US Army)

A 20mm Twin Flak 38 gun mounted on an armored train. (US Army)

way Flak Battalions, which were to protect trains from air attack; and Light Railway Transport Protection Flak Battalions.

As the war progressed the Germans were forced to become very proficient at protecting their railroad stock by mounting AA guns on rolling stock, primarily twin-axle open flat cars. The Reichsbahn (German State Railway) converted conventional freight cars into Light Flak Gun Cars I and II by removing part of the upper sides and building superstructures to house the guns. In addition to the gun platform both cars included lower living quarters, toilet facilities, and storage. Gun barrel deflectors protected the engine and other cars from being hit. Gun Car II had four foot splinter-proof walls filled with iron reinforced concrete that could be lowered The primary AA gun used was the 20mm single or quadmount, and secondly the 37mm, although some 88mm guns were used. These guns were mounted on their triangular bases or on fixed mounts. The 20mm was mounted on one end of a "R-Wagen" flatcar, with the crew carried in shelter with a removable roof on the other end. A German manual prescribed three methods for protecting trains:

1) Three cars with machine guns on AA mounts located one-quarter, one-half, and three-quarters the length of the train.
2) Three cars carrying 20mm flak guns: one on the end; one in the middle; and one directly behind the locomotive, which usually is not manned, being a spare to allow for reversing the train without shunting the gun car.
3) Important trains also had an additional gun car in front of the locomotive.

On the move the guns were continuously manned, and all AA personnel were on constant alert for air attacks. Two specialized aircraft watchers were assigned to watch 180∞ in the front and rear of the train and were relieved often. During an attack tracer ammunition was used, as the train's motion prevented accurate sighting. Sectors of fire, or "safe fire zones," were set up. The conventional method of positioning flak guns was to place a flatcar before and after the gun car so as not to obstruct vision and to provide room for firing. When not firing the guns were pointed upward to the front or rear depending on their sector of fire. Care had to be taken for

20mm Flakverling 38 quadmount on an armored train. (US Army)

A heavily-armed Siebel Ferry with a twin and two single Flak 38s. These ferries were instrumental in the evacuation of Axis troops from Sicily across the Strait of Messina during July 1943. (US Navy)

the gunners not to shoot up signal posts and signs and other installations along the tracks.

Fighter-bombers attacking a train had to assume that the train contained flak cars. The tactics used to confront the surprise use of flak railway cars had the committed flight or element leaders turn on the exposed flak cars and try to out shoot them while their wingmen knocked out and stopped the locomotive. The attack was perpendicular to the train so that the flak cars could not concentrate their fire on each attacking aircraft as they could if the attackers strafed the train down the length of the track. The Germans equipped certain trains with a number of flak cars and ran the train in the open so as to lure fighter-bombers into attacking. It became critical to distinguish a train hauling cargo from a flak trap.

Battle and Transport Flak Ferries

Flak and battle ferries were organized in early 1942 as special units and were used on Lake Ladoga during the siege of Leningrad, between North Africa and Sicily, and during the evacuation of Sicily to the Italian mainland. The 50-ton purpose-built anti-aircraft Flak Battle Ferries had a large deck platform mounted on large, shallow-draft pontoons. The armament varied and could be a mix of 88mm Flak 18 or 36 guns and 20mm Flak 30 or 38 light AA guns.

The Flak Battle and Transport Ferries provided AA defense for the transport of troops and supplies. These ferries were called "Siebel Ferries" after their designer. The guns were sited on raised platforms, main permanent and secondary movable, along with bow and stern mounts. The usual armament deployment was 20mm Flak 30 or 38, 37mm Flak 36, and one or two 88mm Flak 18 or 36 in many different combinations on main and secondary platforms. The ferry's guns were inaccurate, as they did not have the leveling mechanism standard on navy guns that compensated for the rolling from waves.

Evasion of Flak

The obvious method of evading flak was to lead flights around or above previously identified automatic weapons batteries, but that was not possible once the target was being attacked. In a dive, glide or low level attack over or through automatic AA batteries speed and surprise were considered the most important factors in getting safely through the relatively small effective area of fire, as the range of the automatic small caliber AA weapon was short. The enemy gunner had only seconds to take advantage of his gun's high rate and density of fire. Approaching directly across the AA guns, although it offered the gunners a no deflection shot, also gave the attacker the shortest possible exposure time. An aircraft flying at 300-350mph would only be in range for a very short time before the gunner had elevated to 90∞ and had to swing his gun to resight and engage the aircraft on its exit. A plane flying at 500 feet per second was only in the gunner's sights very briefly no matter how quick the gun's traverse. Evasive actions tended to cause the loss of speed and only lengthened the time exposed to AA fire. The pilot was encouraged to confuse the enemy AA gunner by taking advantage of terrain features (water, trees, low-lying hills), which caused visual confusion in the gunner's mind between the oncoming aircraft and the background. The gunner's estimation of the attacking aircraft's speed and direction of approach would be faulty and too slow for accurate firing in the short time the aircraft was in range.

Siebel Ferry with a 37mm Flak 38 mounted on the main platform the two auxiliary stern platforms mount 20mm Flak 30 guns. (US Navy)

The means of achieving surprise was either by means of a thorough briefing for planned attacks or by the flight leader's ability to appraise the tactical situation upon arriving for an impromptu attack. Basically surprise could be achieved by:

1) Use of terrain especially hills and mountains.
2) Use of the sun or clouds.
3) Staying low on deck
4) Coordinated attacks. A multiple attack converging from different directions not only achieved surprise, but also divided the enemy firepower. An attack by part of the force was used to draw attention to that force while a larger force would sneak in to bomb and strafe from another direction.
5) Timed attacks used the surprise of the first attacking element to draw fire on the receding aircraft. A second element would immediately attack from the same direction. Enemy gunners would have to swing their guns around to meet the newly arrived fighter-bombers.

Lt.Col. Kenneth Gallup, a P-47 pilot for the 353rd Fighter Group, described flying into heavy areas of flak in *Down to the Deck*, (ibid.):

"In heavily defended areas the element of surprise is one of the most important factors to be considered. Personally, I like to come in on the deck at a very high speed, bounce up just high enough before I get to the target, so I will be able to make a good pass at it and yet not too high so as to offer a good target for the defending gunner; then, bounce down to the deck again and get away before the enemy is able to get well organized. Good navigation for this type of pass is essential, however, and a prominent landmark, preferably very close to the target, should be selected while the pilot has altitude. To get the most out of the element of surprise it is necessary to stay right on the deck until the last possible second."

Legendary fighter tactician Col. Hubert "Hub" Zemke, flying P-47s for the 56th Fighter Group, described flak evasion (*The Hub, Fighter Leader*, Airlife, UK, 1988):

"The volume of light flak and small arms fire we encountered seemed to grow with each passing day. To survive you learned to keep high enough for it not to reach you or low enough so they didn't see you coming in time to draw an accurate bead. More often it was the latter. Several times Thunderbolts came back to Dogday (base) with damage caused by trees. Fred McIntosh must have flown through a forest judging by the branches embedded in both wings. After jumping down from my plane one day I noticed slashes in the fuselage and found a considerable length of telephone wire wound around my prop boss. But we couldn't escape all the fire and more than once I heard the clunk, clunk of shell splinters of bullets smashing into my P-47.

A Surprised Enemy Gunner is an Unprepared Enemy Gunner. Every target had certain favorable approaches and the enemy set up his defenses to defend them. These approaches usually could not be avoided but surprise lessened their effect."

Col. Don Blakeslee gave the following description of airdrome attack and flak evasion in the Intelligence Summary of the First Fighter Command, No. 412, of 9 December 1944:

"A) Thorough Briefing Aids Surprise

I consider surprise as one of the chief factors in a successful strafe. When my Group (4th Fighter Group) is assigned to strafe a particular airdrome, I ask for all the photographs available. I want to know what the target looks like before I get there. I want the intelligence officer to get the best information he can on the target, the pin-point positions of the flak posts if possible. I want to know what kind and how many aircraft are reported to be on the field and just where on the field I can expect to find them parked. I want to know what the terrain is around the target. With this I can plan the approach best calculated to achieve surprise.

B) Coming in on the Deck

I use hills, gullies and trees for cover; and such airdrome installations as hangers, etc. to screen my approach. I never come right in on an airdrome if I can help it. If I have planned to attack the airdrome beforehand, I pick up an I.P. some ten miles away-some easily recognizable place. I have my course from the drome worked out. Once in the air, I take my boys right past the airdrome as if I had no intention of attacking it at all. At my I.P. I let down and swing back flat on the deck. I usually try to have another checkpoint on the course from my I.P. not far from the airdrome and

Col. Don Blakeslee, 4th Fighter Group CO, shown here with Maj.Gen. William Kepner. (USAF)

Left: Col. Hubert "Hub" Zemke flew P-47s for the 56th Fighter Group (USAF)

which I pass that I know that I am definitely coming in on the right field. I don't like to end up on an airdrome before I realize I am even coming to one. But once I hit the drome I really get down on deck. I don't mean five feet up; I mean so low the ground is brushing the bottom of my plane.

C) The Getaway

After the attack on the field, stay low on the deck for a good mile beyond the drome before pulling up. The break should consist of rudder yawing. Never cock a wing up. If you must turn on the drome, do flat skidding turns. Don't give the enemy a better target to shoot at.

D) Speed Reduces Risk

When hitting an airdrome, it's important to go in full bore. You want all the speed you can muster. The aircraft should be trimmed for high speed before you go in and not for cruising speed, at which speed you first go by the field.

In general, my pilots and I realize that ground strafing involves a greater risk than shooting down the enemy in the air. But it seems to be quite as important. Besides we get more fun out of strafing ground targets.

(Signed) Col. Donald Blakeslee"

Camouflage

The general term camouflage is defined as the passive method of protecting targets by disguise, concealment, and deception. Disguise is the distortion of recognizable target shapes and their characteristics to make them disappear or merge into the background. Concealment was the hiding of the target so it could not be seen directly (e.g. hiding a target in a tunnel or under a net). Deception was the placement or imitation of things or activities to mislead the enemy as to their location or purpose, or to conceal some impending course of action (use of decoys). Camouflage and deception was always in competition with intelligence. In WWII intelligence combined the airplane and aerial camera and the art and science of photo interpretation into a very effective tool against the art and science of camouflage. The fighter bomber pilot was usually well briefed with aerial photographs and maps of his target, but once near the target visual identification of the target and surrounding landmarks became necessary. Therefore any method to reduce visibility or confuse the identity of the target was desirable. Even a reduction of 10 to 25% could confuse the rapidly approaching fighter-bomber pilot to release his bombs too late and overshoot his target. As German camouflage discipline was usually excellent, it took pilots 15 to 20 missions to become adept at camouflaged target detection.

Early in the war when the Germans had aerial superiority they did not pay too much attention to camouflage or other passive defensive applications. But that luxury changed once Allied bombers and fighter-bombers roved the enemy skies. In *The Fighting Grasshoppers* (Ken Wakefield, Midland, UK, 1990) Lt. John Hayden, a liaison pilot for the 339th Field Artillery Battalion/88th Infantry (Italy), noted:

"The Germans were masters of camouflage. During the winter (1944) when the front was static, we would fly all over German territory and not see a thing. After a snow storm we would be looking for tracks in the snow but seldom saw any. On the American side there were tanks, trucks and men all over the place but on the German side nothing."

Of course, the American Army did not have to be concerned with German air reconnaissance or air attacks.

Methods of Camouflage

Nets and Screens

The basic principal of the effectiveness of the camouflage net can be compared to the common window screen. In the daytime it is easy to see from the inside looking out, but almost impossible to see inside from the outside looking in. Camouflage net was usually made from rope, string, or wire. The fishnet type was used on smaller installations or mobile targets. The net was festooned with long (3 to 6 foot), narrow (3 to 6 inch) cloth strips. Wire net was of the "chicken wire" type that could be pulled out and stretched lengthwise without being pulled out of shape, which was important when covering large distances. This wire net was also garnished (covered) with any number of different materials that were appropriate to the surrounding area. There was no rule of thumb as to the density of the garnishing, which could range from 25% to 75% coverage depending on the size, location, and visibility of the target being covered. The average concealment provided by garnishing was about 33%. The effectiveness of the net depended on the textured

Recon photo of camouflage netting at a German airdrome. Note that the netting, especially over the hanger on the left is transparent to the aerial camera. (USAF)

surface (net and garnishing) and the broken appearance of the irregular shadows cast by the net on the surface under it. The entrance openings and the edges of the net needed to be invisible from the air. The garnishing material had to be thinned out irregularly toward the edges so it blended into the background. Nets needed to be parallel to the ground (e.g. flat or horizontal). If the nets hung on or touched the target, shadows were created that were easy to detect from the air.

Aircraft and Airfields

Dispersed parking was the main method of protecting aircraft. In urban settings with long taxiways they were spaced some distance apart along the perimeter of the field or in revetments. In open fields the aircraft were parked some distance apart or in trees and forests. The easiest and quickest method of camouflaging an aircraft was to push it into a line of trees or brushes and then cover it with natural vegetation. Of course too much vegetation would draw attention from the photo interpreters and make it difficult to service the aircraft and get it into the air quickly. In the open an aircraft with properly painted camouflage scheme and with a few branches could escape detection by fast, low-flying fighter-bombers. Before any camouflage was begun all glass, plastic, and shiny metal surfaces had to be covered, as even low light could cause glinting.

Aircraft camouflage netting was usually easily detected by photo recon, but fast-moving attacking aircraft, knowing there were camouflaged aircraft on the field, had difficulty in detecting their location, and when detected the camouflage made aiming more difficult. Aircraft netting needed to be uncomplicated. Aircraft had to be easily serviced under it and quickly moved in and out of it. Most importantly, netting needed to break up shadows and straight lines. Netting came in plain, painted, strip, and garnished styles. Plain or painted mesh net only negated shadows but were widely used, as they were light and easy to remove quickly for take off. They were slung from poles on four corners to cover aircraft parked in the open or in revetments. These lightweight nets only cut shadows, were transparent to photo recon, and semi-effective against low-flying attacks. Strip net allowed the use of a light net or mesh to obtain a dense camouflage pattern. Strip netting was fabricated by attaching short strips of colored cloth into fishnet in a regular or irregular pattern, or attaching long bands of cloth to bands of fishnet. It was good for disrupting the lines or shadow of the aircraft, particularly if it was consistent with the background. Strip netting was easy to put on and take off and added to the disruption of both the aircraft's lines and shadows, and was very effective if its pattern was consistent with the surroundings. Garnish net was a mesh or fishnet with small pieces or tufts of cloth or natural material added to form random patterns. Lightweight garnish netting cut shadows, but the outline of the aircraft could be seen underneath by reconnaissance. Well-done heavily garnished nets were probably the most effective of aircraft netting, particularly against strafers, as it blended into its surroundings, such as perimeter tree lines. At permanent, well known air bases it was easier to cover the revetments or hardstands with garnished netting and move the aircraft under them. Heavy garnished netting was particularly useful covering aircraft based on temporary airstrips, but it took time to remove and quick scrambles were impractical. The Germans used it especially effectively late in the war when they were constantly retreating and moving airfields and needed to hide their harried aircraft from fighter-bomber attacks. The major disadvantage of garnished netting was that it was heavy and took a long time to remove for takeoff and made maintenance difficult.

A Me-109 hidden in a wood along the German Autobahn. (USAF)

Pattern painting of aircraft helped a parked aircraft blend in with its surroundings by distorting the characteristic aircraft shape, minimizing color contrast, and reducing shine. Pattern panting was not effective in itself, as low and medium flying aircraft could easily spot them by their shape and shadows. Pattern painting also required good dispersal, wheel track concealment, and effective use of artificial camouflage materials.

Runways were a particular problem to conceal, as they were straight, level areas stretching long distances, with intersections that stood out from natural shapes. The color of the runway usually contrasted with the rest of the field and could be stained to match the surroundings so attackers would have trouble dropping bombs accurately on it. Simple darkening of the runway edges masked the straight lines if it were the same color as the adjacent areas. The addition of a few parallel lines and irregular shapes disrupted intersection patterns. If the surrounding area was farmland then the airfield could be plowed, have planted crops or even orchards, areas of erosion, dummy roads, ditches, etc. Large forests of simulated trees on nets were used to hide large buildings, such as aircraft hangars, but the attempt was often wasted, as the "forest" did not extend beyond the hangar and the light colored concrete apron gave away the hangar. Hangars disguised as houses were also betrayed by being out of place, and by the large amount of concrete around them. Gasoline and bomb storage areas were usually placed a distance away from the airfield to protect them and were carefully camouflaged

In *Berlin Diary* (Alfred Knopf, Bonanza, NY, 1984), William L. Shirer described Luftwaffe airfields:

"The camouflage of this field (Ghent) is worth noting. From the air I noticed it looked just like any other place on the landscape, with paths cutting across it irregularly as though it were farmland.

Each warplane on the ground had its own temporary hanger made of mats plastered with grass. Tent poles support the mats. So skillfully are these hangers constructed that I doubt if you could distinguish them from above a 1,000 feet.

How wonderfully the Germans have camouflaged their temporary airfields! We drove by at least three between Calais and Boulogne. They have established them not only in pasture, as I expected, but in wheat fields. The shocks of wheat are left in the field, with only narrow lanes left free across the fields for the planes to take off from and land on. Each plane is hidden under a hanger made of rope netting over which sheaves of wheat have been tied. Workshops and oil dumps are also under the same kind of netting."

Shirer's observations were made early in the war when the Germans had time to do the necessary work on their camouflage. However, late in the war, temporary airfields were quickly constructed as the Germans retreated across the Continent.

If an airfield could not be easily camouflaged then the Germans tried to make it appear that it was damaged beyond use. Unfilled runway bomb craters made the airfield seem unused. The Germans tried fake bomb craters, but with little success. Even the best of the fake painted craters were not realistic, as even the ones with painted shadows had the shadows on cloudy days! These paintings lacked the patterns of a blasted hole in concrete and were easily distinguished from the nearby real bomb craters. Decoy airfields might fool high-flying bombers, but not fighter-bombers.

The most perfect of all German airfield camouflage occurred in 1945 when Allied fighter-bombers were everywhere over Germany and no airfield was safe. The Luftwaffe began to operate fighters, including the Me-262 jet, from long stretches of the autobahn. The median strip was paved over to make the runway wide enough and then painted green and camouflaged to make it look like it was still in place.

Roads, Rails, and Bridges

The modern day passenger looking out the window of an airliner at 20,000ft. is struck at how clearly visible roads and highways and rail lines appear. Transportation systems were difficult to hide or disguise, as they were usually straight lines and obvious in their surrounding environment, crossing rivers and valleys and leading from one population center to another. Since it was impossible to cover Germany with netting or smoke, the easiest but ultimately ineffective solution was to make major transportation targets more difficult to find, identify, and then to attack. But a bridge could not be hidden, as the road or track leading to it and the river over which it ran could not be hidden. These points were in known locations and easily found by using a map. To effectively interdict a transportation system its choke points, such as bridges and tunnels, were attacked, along with the trucks, trains, and barges moving on the system. For this reason many motor vehicles and a few trains were camouflaged with paint or natural material, but these means were only effective if the vehicle was stopped. Motor vehicles were more often camouflaged, as opposed to a train, because individual vehicles could easily stop and pull off the road. The best that could be done to protect transportation choke points was to surround them by AA fire and barrage balloons and cover them with smoke.

Long, straight roads were more visible than curved or winding ones. It was impractical in labor and materials to try to conceal portions of major highways, although some critical areas of concrete were top-covered with an inexpensive emulsion of pigmented bituminous emulsion. Black top roads were less visible than white concrete highways of the same width. Dirt and gravel surfaces were equally visible, but were more difficult to locate from the air because such roads were usually narrower, winding, and in backcountry areas. Railways were easily recognized by their long parallel lines, gradual curves, and the shine from the tracks. The most visible feature of a railway line was the roadbed, and ties that were usually darker than the surrounding lighter ground directly adjacent. The problem with roads and railway tracks was that they led to towns and cities and served as checkpoints to aid in navigation. Traffic circles and intersections served as excellent waypoints just as they would for the motorist. The Germans tried to camouflage these areas if they were close to a target.

Bridges were almost impossible to camouflage because of their location over rivers and their high structure. By altering the approaches, which were usually long, straight roads or rail beds, the attacker's visibility could be reduced and delay his identification of the location. On a partially damaged but useable bridge additional damage could be simulated by painting decoy craters and removing guard rails. Decoy vehicles or actual damaged vehicles could be placed at the entrance of the bridge to simulate a blockage of traffic from an earlier attack and removed at night to allow crossings. To further the effect a nearby alternate crossing could appear like it was being prepared. Smoke was found to be an effective method to hide a bridge during an attack.

Installations

The Germans tried to erase the signs left during and after construction of supply depots and installations. Netting and site selection were important in protecting them from air attack. Tread and tire track activity to these sites needed to be erased, and then the inhabitants of the site had to take care not to leave paths to and near the site during its use. The access roads leading to important installations were camouflaged. These access roads were often rerouted past the installation and a dummy installation built at its end. To camouflage supplies it was important to arrange their storage. Boxes and crates of non-hazardous material were usually stacked in compact piles for ease of handling. Because of their hazardous nature ammunition, fuel drums, and other hazardous materials were stored in separate small stocks.

Vehicles

A poorly concealed vehicle could mean not only the loss of that vehicle, but the discovery and loss of the entire column, and perhaps the disclosure of a tactical plan, such as a counter-attack. Camouflage of a vehicle did not only depend on the concealment of the

This well-camouflaged German tank needed to pull off to the side of the road and stop to make its camouflage effective. (US Army)

vehicles themselves, but also on considering their shadows, shapes, and shimmer, and on preventing and concealing their all-revealing tracks. The telltale signs of military activity are called signatures, and vehicle tracks were the most important and obvious signs of military activity and could easily be differentiated from similar civilian activity. Tracks indicated the type, location, strength, and even the intentions of the motorized unit. The gradual turns of wheeled vehicles could be distinguished from the skidding turns of a tracked vehicle. The track of a single vehicle in an area of low vegetation could often be clearly visible, especially when there was early morning dew. New tracks were to closely follow existing paths and roads, and were to follow and be parallel to hedges, fences, cultivated fields, or natural lines in the terrain pattern. Exposed routes were not to end at a position, but needed to extend to another logical terminal point. If practical, exposed tracks needed to be camouflaged by brushing out of covering. Of course, in order to deceive the enemy and give the appearance of greater strength extra or simulated tracks could be created. Tracks could be made to areas of cover and the vehicle then moved to another area, and its tracks there concealed in hopes the enemy aircraft would attack the oroginal area.

The chart at the bottom of this page describes track characteristics including foot traffic (*US Army FM5-20*).

In some German units a party was sent out in advance to scout out areas of concealment, considering the size of the unit, duration of occupancy, enemy activity on the ground and in the air, and the effect of the weather on visibility at the time. But prior reconnaissance was usually not possible in the chaotic German retreats of mid-1944 and thereafter. It was through their training and experience that the drivers automatically followed the terrain features and utilized overhead cover and shadows. There are two types of shadows that were taken into account in camouflage. The concealing shadow was the one cast by another larger object and a vehicle parked in them virtually could not be seen from the air. The north side of the shadow of a higher object was the best side to park whereas the east and west sides were ineffective for half a day. The other kind of shadow is that of the one cast by the vehicle itself, called the revealing shadow. This shadow had to be hidden by park-

	TYPE OF TRACK		
	FOOT	WHEELED	CATERPILLAR
GENERAL APPEARANCE	NARROW WITH MANY FILAMENTS AND UNTRODDEN PATCHES. i. e. 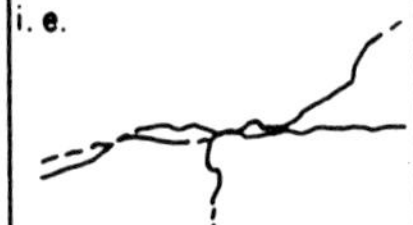	BROAD TRACK WHICH GRADUALLY COVERS AN AREA WITH A UNIFORM TONE.  EACH TRACK A SINGLE LINE	A NUMBER OF INDEPENDENT DOUBLE TRACKS CROSSING AND RECROSSING. i. e. 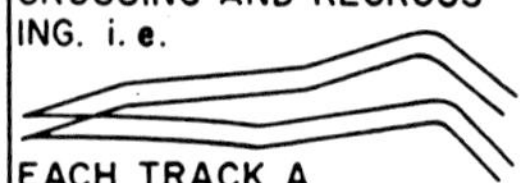 EACH TRACK A SINGLE LINE
STRAIGHTNESS	NEVER STRAIGHT.	STRAIGHT FOR SHORT DISTANCES.	WAVY BUT ALSO RUNS IN STRAIGHT STRETCHES.
BENDS AND TURNS	GOES AROUND SHARP BENDS AND ANGLES; NO SPECIAL MARK AT BENDS.	USUALLY AT LEAST A 20 FOOT RADIUS ON CURVES. CURVES EVEN.	MOST TURNS ANGULAR, CAN TURN AS SHARP AS 90°. U-TURNS CHARACTERIZED BY DEEP RUTS AT CURVE AND NOT AS EVEN AS WHEELED VEHICLE U-TURN.
HILLS	GOES STRAIGHT UP HILLS.	ZIG-ZAGS UP ALL BUT SLIGHT INCLINES.	MAY WIND UP A STEEP HILL — OTHERWISE GOES STRAIGHT UP.
CROSS COUNTRY	AVOIDS MINOR HUMPS AND DAMP SPOTS BUT GENERALLY NOT AFFECTED BY TERRAIN.	MUST HAVE GOOD GOING WITH EASY GRADES.	CANNOT GO OVER ROCK AND USUALLY FOLLOWS EASY GRADES IN EVEN TERRAIN.

NOTE: ALL TRACKS ARE IRREGULAR IN OUTLINE AND ARE MOST VISIBLE WHERE MANY TRACKS CONVERGE, SUCH AS AT GAPS IN WIRE OR MINE FIELDS OR TURN-OFFS INTO BIVOUAC AREAS.

ing in the shadow of another larger object, or by parking close to another object's sunny side so the vehicle's shadow was only cast against the object and not elongated. In the open a vehicle could be parked into or away from the sun to reduce the shadow. Care had to be taken to prevent shine from windshields and windows, headlights, or a wet vehicle body that could be reflected into the air even by low light. Pattern painting of the vehicle could disrupt the square lines of the vehicle from different angles but needed to be combined with the background and positioning of the vehicle. Nets draping over the vehicle could be quickly deployed and removed. When properly suspended and supported a net could conceal the vehicle from observation, or at least conceal the identity of the vehicle under it. However, nets were usually detected by photographic recon.

Col. Thomas Christian, P-51 pilot of the 361st Fighter Group, discussed German road transport camouflage (*Down to the Deck*, ibid.):

"The enemy is making use of shadows cast by trees which line almost all French roads. He is using the smaller side roads, the cover of darkness and such camouflage techniques as painting his vehicle to resemble civilian trucks and piling hay over his equipment. We discovered half-track personnel carriers and gun carriers camouflaged by the means of a canvas cover framework. They were painted red or green and had signs on the sides. The half-tracks showed below the canvas cover."

Renown German camouflage discipline is certainly lacking in this photo of Panzers in full retreat in France. (USAF)

A widely used technique was to place two or three vehicles under netting or tarps to mask their aspect ratio. A tank was twice as long as its width, a truck was three to five widths long. These vehicles were parked along field boundaries where their dimensions and shadows were not so evident. Along the Bocage hedgerows care was taken not to thicken their width and to cover tracks from aerial observation.

Decoys and Dummies

Decoys needed to appear real from the air and be of quick and simple construction. The Germans were masters of using dummy or decoy targets and some of their dummy objectives were attacked several times. The purpose of a decoy was to divide the enemy attack, draw attention away from the primary target, delay and confuse the enemy causing him to waste bombs and ammunition and to give time for anti-aircraft fire to come into play and then get the attacker's range. Among the decoy schemes the Germans used were irreparable and decoy trucks and tanks that were placed along roads to lure fighter-bombers into useless attacks. Setting decoy fires at the target area misled the attackers in their assessment of damage. The Germans built fighter-bomber traps consisting of dummy motor columns, depots and gun positions to attract and then bring them into the range of hidden flak positions. Dummy gun positions were set up near a target to cause the enemy avoid this potentially dangerous target or guns were set up along the lines of probable enemy approach to cause him to reroute missions. Also real guns were sometimes rotated through dummy positions once the Germans felt that Allied reconnaissance had established they were dummy positions and would route his aircraft over the area and into real AA fire. Damaged locomotives were also used in this ploy. They were set on sidings and expertly camouflaged AA guns were positioned nearby to fire on low-flying attackers. Allied air reconnaissance and experienced pilots were often able to distinguish these traps from real targets. Dummy rail operations were run on secondary rail lines to take the pressure off the major lines.

Smoke

Smoke, particles of incomplete combustion and artificial fog, clouds of atomized liquid particles, were the primary means of creating a "smoke screen." Depending on the prevailing winds smoke generators were located in irregular circular patterns around the target. The smoke generator needed to cover an area much larger than the target so as not emphasize the target. A bridge necessitated smoke to cover the river for two or three miles in each direction with additional smoke obscuring the track or road leading to the bridge. A large number of generators were needed and were labor intensive for operation and maintenance.

Barrage Balloons

The purpose of barrage balloons was to form an irregular pattern of perpendicular steel cables hanging down in the vicinity of an important target. This presented a real as well as psychological danger to fighter-bomber pilots attempting to attack under it and to force medium bombers to a higher (e.g. less accurate) altitude. The placement of barrage balloons was coordinated with AA defenses.

AA and Artillery Positions

Medium and heavy AA positions were more or less permanent while the light AA was easily moved by towed trailers. Light AA guns were relatively small and had small inconspicuous mounts and appeared on the reconnaissance photo as pinpoints and could be identified on only the largest scale photos. Often there was confusion in identifying light AA mounted on many types of military vehicles and mobile mounts because of their similarity to anti-tank and small artillery pieces.

The successful camouflage of AA positions demanded attentive planning and considerable effort. Care had to be taken not to leave the vehicle tracks and personnel paths leading to the position for the photo interpreter to discover. A framework of netting revolving with the gun needed to take an irregular shape and not the circular or triangular shape of the position and the color of the netting needed to blend in with the surrounding color. Care had to be taken to mask the shadows of the entrances to the netting. In addition to the gun position, the ammunition dumps, housing, auxiliary vehicles and trailers needed to be camouflaged. Since light AA guns consumed large amounts of ammunition, "ready" ammunition and storage dumps nearby needed to be protected and the footpaths to them needed to be camouflaged. Tracks and footpaths usually appeared lighter than the surrounding area on recon photos and were often the feature that gave the AA position away. Gun crews were encouraged to follow paths under trees but as in all armies there were individuals who would cut corners.

On easily detected long-range artillery positions the Germans hung heavily garnished netting over the barrel and around the gun site. It was a passive camouflage that did not hide the position but distracted the aim of the low-flying fighter-bomber.

AA pieces and their crews not covered by netting were protected from bomb fragments and strafing by revetments. Of course, these revetments, being round or oval were easily spotted from the air. Though differing greatly in detail these revetments could be constructed of earth, sand bags or concrete depending on the target being defended. They had common characteristics:

1) Surrounded the weapon on all sides except for a narrow entranceway.
2) Rose to a height of four to five feet either by digging out the emplacement, building the wall above ground level or a combination of both.
3) The outside face sloped while the inside face was nearly vertical.

Adapting Troop Behavior to Allied Air Superiority

By D-Day the Allies had gained air superiority. Many of the German units in Northwest Europe were occupation troops who had spent too many years in quiet, non-combat areas. Once under the strain of overwhelming Allied ground and air attacks they became demoralized and apathetic, resigning themselves to defeat, taking no or half-hearted measures to protect themselves against air attacks. But it is fair to say that under the almost daily pounding by both tactical fighter-bombers and medium bombers, even the finest troops could not endure the physical and psychological effects of these air attacks. Some German units, headed by experienced commanders, countered Allied air superiority and fighter-bomber and medium bomber attacks by:

1) Digging in and camouflaging their dispersed positions.
2) Moving, concentrating and attacking at night.
3) Avoiding built up areas, such as towns and villages that could be easily attacked and destroyed.
4) Transferring headquarters and command posts frequently.

A Wehrmacht OB West Order of 18 September 1944 ordered every soldier to keep his weapon with him at all times and to use it against low-level enemy attacks. All barracks, depots and road junctions and supply roads were to set up machine guns for use against low-level air attacks.

German Army Group B issued an order on 21 September 1944 to all newly arriving units:

"The enemy has air supremacy in the western area. The behavior of the troops must be adapted to this situation or otherwise there will be personnel and material losses that could be avoided. All movements for troop transfers and supplies are to be made at night unless, in exceptional cases, the weather prevents enemy activity. Only when the tactical situation (e.g. enemy airborne landings) urgently requires it, can movements be made during the day, also by special order. In every case, it must be considered whether it is more advisable to wait until after twilight and thus increase the probability of bringing more troops to face the enemy rather than to engage in a march by day with concomitant, inevitable higher casualties. In daily marches, there must be an air spotter assigned to each vehicle (in closed passenger cars and in trucks, he must sit on the fender). Every vehicle must carry camouflage material. Peace-type driving of closed columns is out of the question. Great intervals are to be maintained for dispersion. Through roads are to be avoided. There can be no lights showing at night. The civilian population has been instructed to aid vehicles and columns by pointing to the air when they are aware of danger. The vehicles must then stop and take cover. There are foxholes on all roads. Commander of all grades are to see to it that constant instruction is given on the proper behavior toward the enemy air force."

Wehrmacht OKH *Training Guide No. 3700/44 of 15 September 1944*, addressed movement under conditions of enemy air supremacy:

"A. Preventative Measures

1) During the day, traffic must be widely dispersed away from the main traffic routes. The armies are to pinpoint sheltered side roads which can also be traversed at night. One-way streets are to be set up. Traffic routes leading through open terrain are to be marked off by 'Low-level Aircraft', "Achtung Jabos!" warning signs also indicating the length of the open sections. Traffic is to be detoured to sheltered routes. Detour signs are required. Avoid populated areas.
2) Every driver is responsible for providing good camouflage for his vehicle.
3) Ground observers are to be spread out, also to the rear.
4) Daily weather reports provided by the Luftwaffe liaison officer are to be transmitted to the battalion staffs and particularly to the supply troops.
5) All traffic is to be diverted at night as far as possible. No headlights!
6) In clear weather, column traffic is permitted only I exceptional cases...There should be 800 meters between vehicles... Driving should be in the block system, i.e. vehicles travel alone from one cover to the next....
7) Halted vehicles are parked singly under cover.
8) Traffic must always remain fluid, even when there are distur bances from fighter-bomber attacks....There must be no piling up of vehicles.

B. Defense Against Fighter-Bombers

1) Firing with all infantry weapons (rifles, machine guns). Concentrate fire. Riders must have their weapons within reach at all times
2) When fighter-bombers appear vehicles are to take cover immediately. On nights when light signals are set, drive sharply to the right and stop. Look for available cover.
3) To deceive the fighter-bombers, dummy installations are to be set up at suitable places along the marching routes (e.g. damaged, non-functioning vehicles, dummy tanks etc.) such set ups serve purpose only when there is an AA nearby of other defensive measures.....Active combat against the enemy fighter-bombers by using fighter-bomber decoys is up to the AA division; close collaboration is required.
4) The military police are to control the execution of this order and are to handle traffic at particularly dangerous points.

C. Civilian Traffic

1) Is to be included in these measures in those areas in the immediate vicinity of the front....

10

Fighter-Bomber Scoreboard

It was the practice of AAF pilots to have their aerial victory totals stenciled or painted somewhere around their cockpit. When there were fewer Luftwaffe aircraft to shoot down and the emphasis shifted to fighter-bomber missions the pilots kept tallies of their missions in a similar fashion. Top cover missions would be denoted by a top hat symbol, escort missions by umbrellas or vertical bombs, dive-bombing missions by angled bombs and sweeps by a broom. Truck and locomotive symbols denoted motor vehicles and trains.

Record of the 405th Fighter Group

Aircraft (ground)	195-140
M/T	6,289-2,343
Armor	358-264
Locomotives	840-226
RR cars	4,410-5,220
Dumps	23-13
Oil tanks	28-8
Marshaling Yards	234
Airfields	35
Troop concentrations	82

P-47 air ace with seven victories, Capt. Edwin Fischer of the 362nd Fighter Group, is just as proud of his other accomplishments that included three V-1 victories and 25 M/T and five locomotives, 40 bombing missions, 25 dive bombing missions, and 15 sweeps. (USAF)

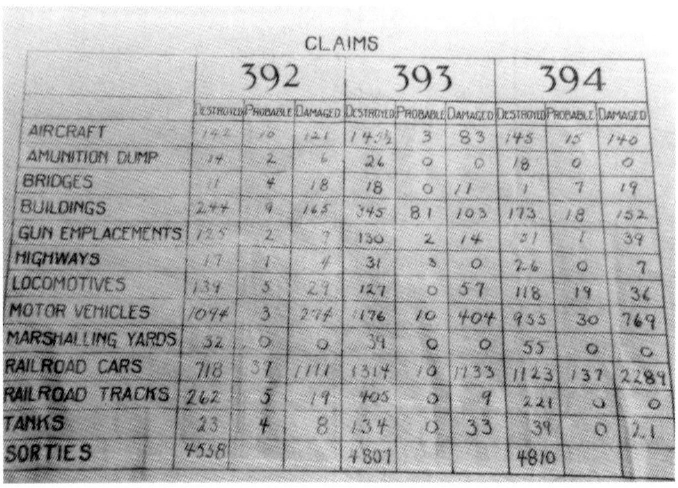

CLAIMS

	392			393			394		
	DESTROYED	PROBABLE	DAMAGED	DESTROYED	PROBABLE	DAMAGED	DESTROYED	PROBABLE	DAMAGED
AIRCRAFT	142	10	121	145½	3	83	145	15	140
AMUNITION DUMP	14	2	6	26	0	0	18	0	0
BRIDGES	11	4	18	18	0	11	1	7	19
BUILDINGS	244	9	165	345	81	103	173	18	152
GUN EMPLACEMENTS	125	2	7	130	2	14	51	1	39
HIGHWAYS	17	1	4	31	3	0	26	0	7
LOCOMOTIVES	134	5	29	127	0	57	118	19	36
MOTOR VEHICLES	1044	3	274	1176	10	404	955	30	769
MARSHALLING YARDS	32	0	0	39	0	0	55	0	0
RAILROAD CARS	718	37	1111	1314	10	1733	1123	137	2284
RAILROAD TRACKS	262	5	19	405	0	9	221	0	0
TANKS	23	4	8	134	0	33	39	0	21
SORTIES	4558			4807			4810		

The 367th Fighter Group kept a meticulous score board for its three squadrons. (USAF)

The aesthetically marked P-47D of Lt. Lawton Clark of the 78th Fighter Group. Clark was KIA in mid-September 1944 while strafing a train. (USAF)

Prolific P-47D of the 366th Fighter Group (USAF)

Combat veteran P-38F of the 1st Fighter Group/27th Fighter Squadron at Foggia in March 1944 (USAF)

Record of the 358th Fighter Group

Aircraft (ground)	201-163
M/T	4,020-2,817
Armor	212-392
Locomotives	340-595
RR cars	3,339-8,163
Dumps	79-29
Bridges	42-61
Marshaling Yards	200
Airfields	24
Troop concentrations	80
Vessels/barges	83-243
Factories/buildings	2,908-1,629
Rail cuts	661
Road cuts	165
Horse-drawn vehicles	699-315

A P-47 pilot keeps score using swastikas as markers. It appears this was quite a successful tank-buster with five. Why he reversed the swastikas on the M/T is not known. (USAF)

Lt.Col. Cy Wilson, CO of the 55th FS/20th FG, took part in 31 top cover missions (top hats), 10 escort missions (umbrellas), 9 bombing missions (bombs), and 7 sweeps (brooms). (USAF)

8th Air Force pilots felt they were fighter pilots and the only concession to ground attack was to claim victory markings for aircraft destroyed on the ground. Here *Nooky Booky IV* of 18.5 victory ace, Maj. Leonard "Kit" Carson (367th Fighter Group) shows 22 victories which includes his strafing victories. (USAF)

1Lt. Jack Ilfrey of the 20th Fighter Group was one on the few Mustang aces to include fighter-bomber accomplishments on his Mustang. (Ilfrey)

Record of the 359th Fighter Group

Aircraft (ground)	122-107
M/T	192-216
Armor	8-15
Locomotives	316-160
RR cars	278-1,087
Bridges	2-5
Factories/buildings	9-69
Vessels	6-61

Record of the 367th Fighter Group

Aircraft (air & ground)	432.5-28-344
M/T	3,225-1,488
Armor	196-66
Locomotives	382-136
RR cars	3,155-5,327
RR cuts	888-33
Bridges	30-59
Road cuts	74-15
Dumps	58-8
Marshaling Yards	126
Factories/buildings	762-528
Gun emplacements	306-65

1Lt. Paul Smith, P-61 air ace of the 422nd NFS. *Lady Gen* displays six swastikas (5 air), five locomotives and 30 missions (lightning bolts). (USAF)

These A-36s did yeoman's duty as a makeshift dive-bombers over Sicily and Italy. The Invader in the foreground has completed 117 missions. Note the two different types of marking missions on the cowlings. (USAF)

Record of the 365th Fighter Group

Aircraft (air & ground)	259-14-141
M/T	3,928-1,187
Armor	190-170
Locomotives	588-134
RR cars	3,356-1,857
Rail cuts	748
Bridges	27-35
Road cuts	141
Vessels/barges	62-43
Horse-drawn vehicles	521-52
Gun emplacements	110-59
Factories/buildings	470-258
Marshaling Yards	280

Record of the 350th Fighter Group

Aircraft (ground)	108-74
M/T	3,068-2,417
Armor	80-119
Locomotives	339-720
RR cars	1,270-7,103
Rail & road cuts	1,253
Bridges	140-156
Tunnels	33
Vessels/barges	23-266
Horse-drawn vehicles	1,842
Gun emplacements	288-352
Factories/buildings	99-628
Marshaling Yards	165
Dumps	25-326

Part Two

Fighter-Bomber Campaigns

11

North Africa

Before TORCH

The 57th Fighter Group's 72 P-40s flew off the USS *Ranger* to Accra, West Africa in July 1942 and then flew on across North Africa to Palestine at the end of the month. The Group was integrated into RAF units for training and instruction in desert air tactics. After training they operated within experienced RAF units and were dependent on them for airfields, maintenance, and intelligence. The Group, under Brig. Gen. Abby Strickland, Commanding General of the IX Fighter Command, began operations on 9 August. At the end of August Rommel began his offensive to break through to Alexandria, Egypt. In the six-day battle the P-40s of the 57th helped IX light bombers in halting the Afrika Korps offensive but their main task was bomber escort and airfield protection. AVM Sir Arthur Coningham thanked the group: "We are most grateful and full of admiration for the grand effort your pilots are making in this period of hard work and hard fighting. Well done." By the end of September, the 57th's three squadrons, the 64th (Black Scorpions), the 65th (Fighting Cocks) and 66th (Exterminators), flying with RAF units of the Desert Air Force from August, was credited with completing 46 missions, 290 sorties claiming one probable and two damaged enemy aircraft for the loss of one continuing its role as escort and interceptor. On 27 October the 57th was assigned a new role and took off in pre-dawn aided by truck headlights. The P-40s arrived at Fuka (L.G. 18) at dawn, sweeping in on the deck and completely surprising the Germans destroying a number of aircraft, motor vehicles and tents. Later that day bomb-carrying P-40s of the 65th Squadron attacked the field with the 64th Squadron flying top cover. By November the 57th was flying as many fighter-bomber sorties as escort sorties.

Operation TORCH (8-11 November 1942)

On 8 November 1942, Operation Torch was initiated with landings at Casablanca (Western Task Force-31,000 troops), Oran (Center Task Force-18,500 troops) and Algiers (Eastern Task Force-20,000 troops). Fortunately, opposition was light as the Vichy French put up a half-hearted resistance and the inexperienced American forces suffered light casualties on the ground and in the air. At Casablanca the XII Air Command assigned to Gen. George Patton's Western

P-40Fs of the 66th Fighter Squadron, the Exterminators, of the 57th Fighter Group. During 1942, the group flew the most sorties (3,608) than the other four bomber groups of the 9th Air Force combined. (USAF)

The 57th Fighter Group's 72 P-40s flew off the *USS Ranger* to Accra, West Africa in July 1942 and then flew on across North Africa to Palestine at the end of the month. The Group was integrated into experienced RAF units for training and instruction in desert air tactics. (USAF)

Classic photo of American troops, complete with Old Glory, landing at Surcouf during TORCH on 8 November 1942. (US Army)

Task Force did not get their aircraft off the aircraft carriers transporting them to the invasion until after the surrender of the city. Air cover for the invasion was to be supplied by 136 US Naval aircraft flying off four carriers, the *Ranger*, *Sangamon*, *Suwanee*, and *Sante*. The British supplied 130 fighters and 30 torpedo bombers from seven aircraft carriers. The carrier aircraft were to attack enemy airfields and provide close air support. It was essential that the French-held airfields be seized as soon as possible so that fighters based at Gibraltar could be flown in. Eisenhower wanted a combined British-American air command but had two separate commands that operated independently. The Eastern Air Command (RAF) with headquarters in Gibraltar was commanded by AM Sir William Welsh. The EAC was responsible for the assault on Algiers and covering the seas in between flying 162 fighters and 72 bombers. The Western Air Command (USAAF) with headquarters at Gibraltar was commanded by Maj.Gen. James Doolittle. The WAC was responsible for the invasions at Casablanca and Oran and the seas in between. It was to fly 240 fighters and 114 bombers to Casablanca and 320 fighters and 57 bombers to Oran. The opposing Axis-Vichy air forces totaled 1,086 aircraft (240 Axis/185 Vichy bombers, 231 Axis/218 Vichy fighters and 212 reconnaissance aircraft).

The Spitfire-equipped 31st Fighter Group under Col. John Hawkins was to take off from Gibraltar and support Patton's landing at Casablanca but the expected French Resistance never materialized nor did it at Algiers. Algiers was surrendered on the evening of D-Day and Casablanca surrendered on D-Day +2. The 52nd Fighter Group under Col. Dixon Allison was supposed to support the Oran landings where the French had based 55 Dewoitine 520 fighters and 40 obsolete bombers mainly at La Senia. Both the 31st and 52nd were based at Gibraltar and the 31st was waiting on the runway when its Casablanca mission was scrubbed. So the 31st Fighter Groups was sent to Oran where the French put up more of a fight. The 31st flew into Tafaraouri Airfield that was under attack by French artillery. Some of Hawkins' Spitfires strafed the gun positions to put them out of action until the Americans could land safely on the runway that was holed by the shelling. It was not until the 9th that the first American sorties were flown. At 0640, Lt.Col. Fred Dean and two lieutenants, Corrigan and Waltner, took off from Tafaraoui and came upon a long column of the French Foreign Legion stretching from Sidi-bel-Abbes. They strafed the column with machine guns and cannon, knocking out three trucks, a troop carrier and four tanks that were easily penetrated by the Spitfire's 20mm cannons. On returning to base, Corrigan landed too close to Dean and tore off the tail off Dean's Spitfire, totaling both aircraft to finish the first American strafing attack from North Africa. At 0800, Lt.Col. Dean and Maj. Delwin Avery attacked the French column again claiming the destruction of their three remaining tanks and causing the Legionnaires to retreat. Hawkins used his Spitfire's radio to contact the radio in an American command tank to establish communications with the task force command ship, Largs, that assigned several missions. The first mission was to attack French coastal guns that drove off the American strafers with heavy fire. The next mission was in the early afternoon to attack tanks to the west of La Macta. The airfield was being shelled as eight American pilots took off through the exploding French 75s. Soon the two flights spotted tanks and attacked them but at once they realized the tanks were

The flag was placed under the wings and on the fuselage of American aircraft in North Africa to emphasize to the vacillating French of the US presence. This P-40 belonged to the 33rd Fighter Group that had low-serviceability and sustained high losses and was replaced by the 325th Group (USAF)

American and stopped the attack. The ground forces sustained no casualties but two Spitfires were shot down. The command ship had made an error; the target was east of La Macta, not west. This was the first of many friendly fire incidents that were to plague fighter-bomber operations throughout the war and emphasized the need for coordination between ground and air forces and the establishment of a ground recognition system to alert aircraft overhead. Later that day the 31st knocked out the artillery positions that were harassing their airfield at Tafaraouri. The 31st had flown 17 missions totaling 45 sorties in it first day at war. Oran surrendered on 11 November, Armistice Day of the First World War.

After TORCH into Tunisia (12 November to mid- January 1943)
Operation TORCH was the first field test of USAAC tactical organization and doctrine. The Twelfth Air Force that had been activated on 20 August 1942 was assigned to provide air support. The XII Air Support Command formed in September 1942, was to be the tactical component but did not have any fighters as all fighters were placed under the XII Fighter Command that was to support strategic operations. There was also a major division of command between the USAAC and the RAF in the early Tunisian campaign. This division of command led to the minimal effectiveness of close support during TORCH and immediately thereafter. In response to the poor results of tactical air the Allied Air Support Command was formed on 7 February 1943 under AM Sir Arthur Coningham and his deputy, Gen. Laurence Kuter.

The next phase of the campaign was to capture Tunisia and its ports of Tunis and Bizerte that lay only 100 miles from Sicily. The 500-mile approach from Algiers through Northern Tunisia was mountainous and cut by narrow valleys supplied by a second-rate road and rail system. The railhead for the ground and air offensive was located at Souk El Arba and transport took four to six days from Algiers with a maximum capacity of nine trains per day (two for coal for the locomotives and one to supply the civilian population). The rainy season was to start in December and end at the beginning of March. Meanwhile the Germans were reinforcing North Africa from Sicily and time was of the essence. Four fighter groups, the 1st, 14th, 31st and 52nd, were based far behind the fighting in Algiers. Their ground echelons were dispersed and disorganized, airfields inadequate and even basic supplies were limited due to the lack of transportation from the docks, a problem that would trouble the American air forces during the North African campaign. The repatriated French airfields were too small to handle the large American contingent and only four had any all weather hard-surfaced runways, a factor that would affect operations that winter. The Allied advance to the east beginning in late November. was conducted with under strength armored and infantry forces moved and supplied by an inadequate motor transport system. Fortunately, the French in North Africa under Gen. George Barre, changed sides and joined the Allies and for the time were the only forces standing between the Axis and assembling American and British armies. In November and into December the Allied air forces were stretched thin. Their primary mission was flying air cover for the captured Mediterranean ports that were under constant attack from German and Italian air forces. Between C-47 escort, tactical reconnaissance, fighter sweeps and close air support missions were flown when the weather permitted. The Germans sent bombers in at night and caused significant damage to airfields that necessitated moving bombers back to Tafaraoui. By the end of November the Allies managed to advance to within 12 miles of Tunis where rains slowed, then halted Allied armor and motor transport. The German counter-attack at Teboura on 1-3 December and at Medjez El Bab on 6-10 December caused Eisenhower to break off his attack and withdraw to a more defensible position. The Allied armies had advanced beyond the effective range of their fighters. When these fighters occupied forward bases they found themselves open to debilitating enemy air attacks and poor field conditions, either plagued by dust or mud, that forced them to retreat to rear bases on the Algerian-Tunisian border. The Spitfires flown by the 31st Fighter Group had a radius of action of only 90 miles that gave them only five to ten minutes over the front. At the time the longer legged P-38s were in short supply. When the American fighters came in on fighter sweeps, the Luftwaffe had air superiority and was able to engage them. Luftwaffe bombers were able to fly from all-weather bases in Sicily and Sardinia where they were safer from Allied air attack and had short supply lines. When the rains arrived American airfields became a quagmire and aircraft, particularly bombers, were unable to fly operations. Pierced Steel Planking (PSP) was in short supply as the Tunisian rail system was inadequate and motor transport was bogged down on muddy roads. It would have taken the entire capacity of the rail system for two days to deliver the 2,000 tons of PSP needed to surface only one runway. Both the rail and road systems could barely provide sufficient supplies, ordnance and personnel to the ground forces. It was not until mid-March that the Allies were able to make an offensive move from the east. Logistics there remained a headache although airfields in Algiers and Morocco improved.

During the last month and a half of 1942, Doolittle realized he had to reorganize the command structure of the 12th Air Force to meet the requirements of the North African campaign. On 11 December he assigned the advanced echelon of the XII Fighter Command at Tebessa to the area eastward from the Algerian-Tunisian border and its rear echelon at La Senia operated from the Spanish Moroccan border to Cape Tenes and Oujada. On 12 January 1943 Doolittle moved the XII Fighter Command back to La Senia and took over command of the three Composite Air Defense Wings. The First Wing covered the Oran area, the Second covered Morocco and the Third covered Algiers from Cape Tunis to Bougie. The mission of the XII FC was 1) Patrols and sweeps; 2) fighter escort for aircraft and shipping; 3) harbor protection; 4) air raid warning; 5) homing of lost aircraft, and 6) air-sea rescue. Then on 15 February the XII FC and its defense wings became part of the North West African Coastal Air Force. Twelfth Air Force mediaum and heavy bombers attacked Bizerte, Tunis, Sousse, Sfax and Rommel's warehoused supplies. Meanwhile, Eisenhower reorganized his air command. On 5 January 1943 the Allied Air Force was activated. It consisted of all USAAF, FAF (French Air Force) and RAF units in Northwest Africa that were put under Spaatz.

American Air Forces Operating from the East

Although Eisenhower's offensive was stalled by the weather, Montgomery's British Sixth Army had moved across Tripolitania and onto northwestern Tunisia. At the beginning of 1943, the 12th Air Force listed 755 aircraft (520 operational) and the RAF 251 aircraft. Facing the Allies were 610 Luftwaffe aircraft (335 to 365 operational) and 560 Italian aircraft (half in service). Von Arnim's army was placed in the northern sector opposite the US First Army and the Italians held southern sectors. Rommel would later reinforce the southern sector with his 21st Armored Division and the central and additional Italian troops.

The second fighter group to join the 9th Air Force was the 79th, commanded by Lt.Col. Peter McGoldrick, and was composed of three squadrons, the 85th (Flying Skulls), 86th (Comanches) and 87th (Skeeters). The air echelon arrived on 2 November from Accra and five of its top officers were attached to the 57th for indoctrination in desert fighter air warfare. On 6 November, McGoldrick led six P-40s on a sweep on a German truck column near Charing Cross, Egypt. On his second pass his Curtiss fighter was hit by ground fire and he was forced to make a belly landing. McGoldrick's P-40 skidded along the desert sands and he was killed when it hit a land mine and blew up, The command of the 79th passed to Lt.Col. Earl Bates. The ground echelon of the 79th arrived on 12 November and the group went into training and was a reserve unit for several months. Some of its pilots did fly with the 57th Fighter Group to gain combat experience. In early December the British Eighth Army was preparing to launch an assault against El Agheila. El Alamein stood in the way and Coningham ordered preliminary air strikes against Axis airfields, supply dumps and troop concentrations. Airfields in the Marble Arch area were put under constant attack by RAF light bombers and 57th Fighter Group P-40s. These attacks caused the Germans to move their airfields back nearly 10 miles from the front. The El Agheilia offensive was scheduled to begin on 14 December but the Germans withdrew the day before as the 57th flew a record 17 missions dropping 38 tons of bombs on them. On 15 January 1943, Field Marshal Montgomery began his move to take Tripoli. In order to avert supply problems the port needed to be captured in ten days. The 57th flew bombing and strafing missions in support and Tripoli fell on the 2rd offering only moderate resistance. The British moved on toward the Tunisian border to attack the Mareth Line, and its strong old French fortifications located in ideal natural defensive terrain to which Rommel retreated. Through January the 57th had flown 343 missions of 3,608 sorties dropping 208 tons of bombs, claiming 64 Axis aircraft destroyed, 12 probables and 41 damaged for a loss of 26.

Tunisia (Mid- January 1943-12 May 1943)

In January 1943, US air support doctrine was based on War Department *Field Manual 31-35 (9 April 1942)* entitled Aviation Support of Ground Forces. The main premise of *FM 31-35* was the subordination of the air force to the ground force and to local circumstances. The air support commander was subordinated and functioned under the ground commander and his aircraft were subject to allocation to support these ground units. *FM 31-35* went on to grant that attacks on the enemy air forces and the acquisition of local air superiority was needed but it was to be to be secondary to attacking targets that were the most serious threat to the ground armies. The ultimate decision on target priority lay with the commander of the assigned ground unit. This doctrine opposed those so successfully developed and tested by the RAF and British Eighth Army.

An outdoor briefing of the 49th Fighter Squadron of the 14th Fighter Group a P-38 Group that was based at Youks les Bains. (USAF)

At the start of December the Germans began their aggressive defense of Tunisia. On 27 November the Germans failed in their attempt to capture the French Navy at Toulon when the French scuttled their fleet based in the port. However, the Germans were successful in disarming the French forces without resistance at the end of November. Also the Italian resolve in Africa was suspect. The Germans occupied Tunis and Bizerte to supply Rommel's retreating armies in Libya. The Tunisian coastal plain linked the Axis forces in the north and those retreating before the British Eighth Army in the west.

Tunis and Bizerte remained in Axis control until May 1943. Until then the Allies secured a line in the mountains overlooking the northern Tunisian plain from which they could launch their spring offensive. The Allies were given time to overcome their transportation problems and built up their supply and personnel strength. Forward air bases were consolidated and although useless for long periods in the rainy season would be satisfactory in good weather especially when the longer range P-38s arrived.

So at the end of January 1943, Rommel was waiting in the strong Mareth Line fortifications. The American and British were moving in from the west after TORCH, Montgomery's Eighth Army was moving up from the south after its victory at El Alamein and to the north and east was the Mediterranean and the crucial Axis supply lines from Sicily and Italy. These supply lines had not been attacked by heavy bombers due to the long distances but the supply lines were in jeopardy when the IX Bomber Command moved permanently to the Gambut area from Egypt eliminating the servicing layover.

In January 1943 Brig.Gen. Howard Craig was named the head of the XII ASC. Craig was one of the few American officers who understood air warfare in the Western Desert. His command consisted of the two under strength and low in-service P-40 squadrons of the 33rd Fighter Group; the entire poorly trained 47th Bombardment Group and P-38s from the 14th Fighter Group that were scheduled to be withdrawn. Craig asked Doolittle for reinforcements and waited to launch any significant attacks until they arrived. He received P-39s from the 91st and 92nd Squadrons and P-40s of the 94th, Lafayette Esquadrille, Squadron of the 81st Fighter Group. On 10 January, Maj. Philip Cochran, CO of the 33rd Fighter Group's 58th Squadron, led a sortie that would initiate his legendary career that would be the inspiration for Milt Caniff's comic strip character, Col. Flip Corcoran of *Terry and the Pirates* fame. Cochran dropped a 500lb. bomb directly on the *Hotel Splendida* which was the German staff headquarters at Kairouan and flattened the building. By 26 January the XII ASC had built up its operational strength but Craig had to be relieved by Col. Paul Williams when he contracted pneumonia. But problems were soon uncovered. The Lafayette Escadrille was a politically motivated unit and was poorly trained in the P-40 and its ground echelon did not follow it to Thelepte. The P-39 units found the aircraft to be an inferior fighter aircraft but would discover it to be an adequate low-level ground strafer when escorted by P-40s or P-38s. The XII ASC was fighting according as prescribed by *FM 31-35* and was stretched thin by trying to provide escort for the P-39s and A-20s, fly umbrella ground support over a large front and also to fly requested ground support missions. The Luftwaffe had increased its presence and losses were sustained. Finally the 33rd Fighter Group had to be relieved by the 325th Fighter Group and the 31st Fighter Group and two squadrons of the 52nd Fighter Groups were attached to the XII ASC. The 31st Fighter Group was left behind to wait out the weather by protecting the port of Oran and flying cover for Allied shipping convoys along the African coast. It was not until February 1943 that the group would move from the Oran area to Thelepte in Tunisia.

It was not until the Allies reorganized their air command in February 1943, that a plan was formulated to drive the Axis into northeastern Tunisia, then cut their supply lines and evacuation routes to Italy and Sicily and finally destroy the remaining trapped Axis forces in North Africa. A new air command, Northwest African Air Forces (NAAF), was activated on 18 February, commanded by Gen. Carl Spaatz and under the Mediterranean Air Command of RAF ACM Sir Arthur Tedder. The mission of the NAAF was to open the Mediterranean to the Allies and close it to the Axis then driving them from North Africa. The new command included the Northwest African Strategic Air Force (NASAF), under Maj.Gen. James Doolittle, the Northwest Tactical Air Force (NATAF) commanded by AM Sir Arthur Coningham and the Northwest African Coastal Air Force (NACAF) under AVM Hugh Lloyd. The NATAF was composed of the USAAF XII Air Support Command, the RAF 242nd Group and the Western Desert Air Force. Units of the USAAF XII Air Force and the RAF Eastern Air Command were assigned to each of these components. This new organization also resulted in a change in tactical doctrine. Previously tactical air in northwest Tunisia functioned in a defensive role providing (inadequate) air cover for ground forces and was connected closely to them for operations. When Coningham took command of the NATAF he introduced the effective tactical doctrine used in his Western Desert Campaign. At the operational field level the American ASC had learned not to allocate air units to specific ground units or to subordinate them to ground commanders. There would be no more loitering, umbrella-type operations over ground troops. They were placed under the command of the unified air and ground forces in Eisenhower's Allied Force HQ. Under this command they would be free to operate wherever they were needed, directed by the air commander in cooperation with the ground forces. However, a general pairing type of collaboration was continued between air and ground forces. The XII ASC was paired with the US II Corps and the RAF 242nd Group with the British First Army. As Coningham stated: "The Soldier commands the land forces, the Airman commands the air forces; both commands work together and operate their respective forces in accordance with a combined Army-Air plan, the whole operations being directed by the Army Commander." (W.F. Craven and J.L. Cate, *The Army Air Forces in World War II, Vol. II*, Chicago: University of Chicago Press, 1949). Coningham intended to and did use the tactical air force primarily as an offensive weapon. His TAF was principally concerned with close support of the armies but also joined in interdiction of Axis supplies, reinforcements and evacuations as well as the air battles to gain air

The early war in North Africa saw the increased use of the fighter as a fighter-bomber. Since US fighters were not prepared for the role makeshift field modifications were employed such as this duel British centerline mount on a 79th Fighter Group P-40 to carry these British bombs. (USAF)

superiority. He insisted that interdiction was not to be independent from other air force operations. Both Coningham and Spaatz maintained that the chief function of the air force was to gain and maintain air supremacy by targeting the enemy's airfields in North Africa, Sicily and Italy and destroying his aircraft in the air. Once air superiority was gained and maintained the Mediterranean became safer for Allied shipping and more dangerous for the Axis. Almost immediately Coningham directed the air support in the final phases of the Kasserine Pass battle. As spring arrived and the weather became better the airfields dried up and attacks on German road transport increased and the Axis sea and air routes across the Mediterranean were constantly harassed. The breaking of the German codes, particularly those of the Luftwaffe, and the use of ULTRA wrecked havoc on the Axis air shuttles from Sicily and Italy. The interdiction campaign in Tunisia was to support ground forces by cutting Axis supply lines from Italy, Sicily and Sardinia to North Africa. On 1 March Gen. Doolittle established target priorities for the NASAF as: 1) shipping sailing from Sicily; 2) shipping sailing from Tunisia; 3) aircraft and airfields and 4) vital communication positions in Tunisia. NATAF, under Coningham had similar priorities that overlapped those of NASAF: 1) destroy the Axis air forces; 2) disrupt Axis sea and air supply lines; 3) provide close air support and 4) prevent the evacuation of Axis troops from Tunisia. Tankers were accorded the top priority of all shipping targets.

Capt. Ralph "Doc" Watson of the 48th Fighter Squadron of the 14th Fighter Group described the early conditions faced by pilots in Tunisia (*Fighters Over Tunisia*, Christopher Shores, Hans Ring and William Hess, Neville Spearman, UK, 1975):

"The theatre of operations was peculiarly different from the standpoint of operations. We were operating off a mud field, living in pup tents and had no place to get out of the rain, even for dining; we were subject to bombing of the nuisance type every night; losses were high, replacements scarce, very little was known from an intelligence standpoint, maps were inadequate, navigation aids and homing devices were non-existent. The first forward base, on which I landed, we refueled our own airplanes from five-gallon cans lying around the field. No ammunition was available. Our field was so muddy, in order to take off or taxi an airplane, we had to load a bunch of crew chiefs on the horizontal stabilizer to lift the nose until we picked up speed, then they would jump off.... Without our aircrews we would have been lost."

The Battle of Kasserine Pass (14-22 January 1943). On 14 February, Rommel initiated an attack and by night fall had overrun two American artillery battalions, caused heavy losses to counter-attacking American armor and cut off its supporting infantry and rushed through the Pass (in background of photo). American artillery and airpower finally stopped the German advance on 22 January. (US Army)

Capt. Ralph "Doc" Watson of the 48th Fighter Squadron of the 14th Fighter Group described the early conditions faced by pilots in Tunisia, (USAF)

Kasserine Pass (14-22 February 1943)

In December 1942, the USAAF 3rd Fighter Group (12th Air Force) arrived at Thelepte flying Merlin-powered P-40Fs and was joined by the 324th (9th Air Force) and 325th (12th Air Force) Fighter Groups also flying P-40Fs in February 1943. In mid-February 1943 the Axis held its strongest position of the campaign. The Afrika Korps had retreated into Tunisia to join newly arrived German and Italian reinforcements in stopping the British Eighth Army's advance. Montgomery's Eighth Army was walled off at the Mareth Line, stymied by poor weather and waiting to build up supplies through Tripoli. This respite gave Rommel a chance to attack the ill-equipped French Army and inexperienced American II Corps. In late January and into mid-February the Axis had conducted a series of attacks and counter-attacks in Tunisia that had driven the Americans and French back. Rommel was in a commanding position to continue a more far-reaching advance to drive the Allies from Tunisia. During the period the three USAAF fighter groups and the RAF units were effective in their ground attacks on the Axis forces. On 30 January, the veteran 21st Panzer Division attacked the French forces at Faid Pass with 60 to 70 tanks and forced them to retreat to Sidi Bou Zid. XII ASC CO, Col. Paul Williams, sent out aircraft to bomb and strafe and at 1015 hours, 11 P-40s, six P-39s and six A-20s attacked the German tanks and claimed to have destroyed 12 of them. The P-39s strafed and set six trucks on fire. The Americans returned to base safely and flew another noontime mission, dropping 100lb. bombs on the German truck convoy. But air and ground attacks were not able to dislodge the Germans from Faid Pass. Rommel decided to launch his Panzers through the Kasserine Pass to capture the troublesome Allied airfields and gasoline stocks to fuel his mechanized columns. On 14 February, Rommel initiated his attack and by night fall had overrun two American artillery battalions, caused heavy losses to counter-attacking American armor and cut off its supporting infantry. The XII ASC did what it could with its fighters furnishing cover for the light bombers and strafing German trucks, tanks and gun positions. However, the German breakthrough threatened the XII ASC forward airbases and five had to be evacuated during the next week. The American II Corps were ordered to withdraw to the Kasserine Pass to hold there until the American forward airfields could be evacuated. The evacuations forced the XII ASC to retreat back to Tebessa, Le Kouif and Youks that were previous bases. The loss of Thelepte on the 17th cost the XII ASC 60,000 gallons of gasoline, 18 aircraft and a large quantity of supplies. Rommel's columns rushed through the Pass but ground to a halt after making substantial gains from 19-21 February. The Allied situation on the ground became critical as poor weather limited air attacks. Once the weather cleared sufficiently all air units focused on hitting Axis troop concentrations and advancing armor. On 22 January 1943, ten P-39s of the 81st escorted by P-40s strafed tanks, trucks and gun positions in the Ousseltia Valley of Tunisia to break up a German attack. Lt.Col. Fred Dean, CO of the 31st Fighter Group, commanded all aircraft at Youks and prepared a sunrise to sunset schedule of continuous missions against the Germans. The air attacks while not entirely successful did slow the German attack. The next day American ground forces were able to bring their 155mm howitzers to bear and sporadic air sorties (due to poor weather) stopped Rommel. During the next several days he pulled his troops and armor back to the south to face Montgomery's expected attack on the Mareth Line and was reinforced by additional Italian and German troops and armor. The attack on Kasserine Pass had inflicted a defeat on the green American troops and had disrupted the Allied timetable in North Africa. For the first time in American experience the aerial response was no longer limited to an army or corps commander in a limited area.

1Lt. Jack Ilfrey of the 1st Fighter Group. (USAF)

1Lt. Jack Ilfrey describes flying his P-38 through the Pass on the first day of Rommel's attack (*Happy Jack's Go-Buggy*, ibid.):

"On the day of the Battle of Kasserine Pass, 12 of us were assigned to ground strafe through the pass. Even one year later when I was flying over Germany with the 8th Air Force, I don't believe I saw so much flak. It seemed to come from everywhere, not only from below but also from the hills above the pass, down on us. Of the 12 pilots, only eight of us got through the pass, two of the boys managed to make our lines and crash land and six of us were able to get our P-38s back to base but we all had damage.

Our reaction to this raid was that if the Germans wanted this godforsaken place that bad let'em have it! We learned later that the concentrated air attack on Kasserine that day helped to turn the tide of battle."

In mid-February 1943, the 9th Air Force had only the 57th Fighter Group operational in the forward area. The 57th flew fighter-bomber missions from 23 February against Luftwaffe airfields near Mareth and Gabes as part of the effort to draw the Luftwaffe from supporting Rommel's Kasserine attack. Two more P-40 groups, the 79th and 324th were scheduled to become operational. The 79th ready to began operations as an independent unit on 14 March as after its CO, squadron COs, flight leaders and its intelligence and operation officers had served under the 57th. The third and last 9th Air Force fighter group in North Africa was the 324th under the command of Col. William McNown. The group was made up of the 314th Fighter Squadron (Hawks), the 315th (Crusaders) and the 316th (Hell's Belles). The ground echelon left the US in November and arrived at El Kubrit, Egypt in December and was soon joined by the air echelon. The group trained until February after which the 314th Fighter Squadron was attached to the 57th Fighter Group and the 316th Fighter Squadron to the 79th Fighter Group to gain combat experience. It would not be until May that the Group's three squadrons and HQ rejoined as a group for operations.

The Afrika Korps now numbered 100,000 men, 200 tanks and 700 guns. Rommel realized that he needed to go on the offensive soon as more men and supplies would reach the Allies the longer he waited. On 6 March he attacked Montgomery's 187,000 man veteran Eighth Army and its 473 tanks. By the next day the last great attack by the Desert Fox had been stopped and Rommel left Africa and Gen. Jurgen von Arnim took over command of the Afrika Korps. During March the Eighth Army prepared to break through the Mareth Line. On 13 March, the 79th Fighter Group moved up from reserve to Causeway Landing Ground (L.G.) just behind the Eighth Army. Causeway was nothing more than a runway built along a series of sand dunes among which their fighters were dispersed. 79th HQ was set up in an olive grove on high ground about a mile away. The 79th flew its first mission on the 14th when 12 P-40s from the 85th and 87th Squadrons escorted 11 B-25s for an attack on enemy gun positions on the Mareth Line. From 14-25 March the Group flew 590 escort sorties for Allied bombers, losing no bombers for a loss of two of their own.

Operation SUPERCHARGE (26 March 1943 and Beyond)

Montgomery went on the offensive again on 20 March trying to breach the Mareth Line and Gabes Gap along the coast and then break his Eighth Army into open country. Poor terrain, extensive minefields and a strong German counter-attack caused Montgomery to shift his attack to the western flank and pierce the Tebaga Gap which measured three miles wide and four miles long. If Montgomery's Army were to penetrate the Gap they could enter the coastal plain near the village of El Hamma and be on the road to the port of Gabes only 15 miles away. The penetration of the Gap would be difficult as the Germans had sited 88mm guns on the high ground on either side of the valley below. DAF AOC (Air Officer Commanding), AVM Harry Broadhurst planned to have his fighter-bombers concentrate a rapid attack ahead of the British infantry advancing through the Gap. This was the first time the British would attempt using fighter-bombers in close support of infantry, as that had previously been the province of the light bomber. The original attack was to take place on the 25th but the British 1st Armored Division wasn't in place and the jump off was moved ahead until the afternoon of the 26th. SUPERCHARGE was scheduled to start at 1600 hours hopefully taking advantage of the surprise of a daylight attack and also the sun would be in the Germans eyes. The air attack ironically duplicated the German Blitzkrieg tactics used so successfully in Poland, France and Russia. Pre-selected enemy strong points would be attacked immediately before the advance and then the fighter-bombers would provide continuous support for the advancing infantry. RAF G/C Jackie Darwen was stationed in an armored car close to the front and in direct contact with the assault ground commander and called down air attacks. On the 26th after an effective three-hour air attack by the Desert Air Force a New Zealand force under Gen. Bernard Freyberg flanked the Mareth Line and broke out into the open country. Tanks of the British X Corps under Gen. Brian Horrocks followed until they encountered 88mm guns sited on the hills south of El Hamma. For the advance to continue these guns needed to be destroyed or at least silenced for two and half-hours. The 57th and 79th Fighter Groups and two squadrons of the 324th Fighter Group, the 239th, the 244th and 244th RAF Wings and the 7th Wing of the SAAF participated. The 79th and the 316th Fighter Squadron of the 324th Fighter Group came in on the second wave and light flak and German infantry small arms fire were waiting. The pilots flew through the enemy fire and strafed their positions. The attack was so concentrated that the New Zealanders swarmed through the dazed German lines followed by Horrock's tanks. The air attacks, 412 sorties, were costly for the DAF with 11 pilots MIA, six from the 79th (three crash-landed and returned to the unit and three were taken prisoner). The El Hamma mission was one of several textbook examples of air-ground support in the North African campaign that were to become prototypes for later American support missions in Europe. Later that evening Montgomery radioed 79th Fighter Group CO, Col. Earl Bates:

"Please convey to all pilots the grateful thanks of myself and the entire army for their truly magnificent efforts. The results have been first class. I sincerely trust you have not suffered many losses."

Von Arnim fought an adept delaying action near El Hamma to save five Italian divisions from being captured by Montgomery's armies and to move behind the Wadi Akarit that afforded excellent defensive terrain, alleged to be the best in Tunisia.

Field Marshal Erwin Rommel was a master in desert warfare and was admired by both the Germans and Allies. It was his long lines of supply that were attacked by Allied airpower that caused the Afrika Korps' eventual defeat in North Africa. (Author/West)

Afrika Korps armor and motor transport after a strafing attack. (USAF)

The 79th flew six uneventful bomber escort missions to Sfax in the morning of 29 March and were assigned two afternoon strafing missions. Twelve P-40s of the 86th Fighter Squadron came in low and strafed a truck convoy on the coastal road south of Mahares. They had burned ten and damaged 58 trucks when four Me-109s bounced two vulnerable P-40s low on deck. Unable to maneuver the P-40s were badly shot up. One barely made it back to base but the other had its tail section shot off and crashed and burned killing the pilot. On the last mission of the day a P-40 strafing the Mahares road was hit by small arms fire and crash-landed and its pilot was captured.

By April the Allies controlled the air and had squadrons available to roam the skies looking for targets of opportunity. The flat, open African countryside offered scant cover for any unfortunate German vehicles caught by the marauding fighters. On 7 April 1943, Maj.Gen. Freiherr von Brolich, CO of the 10th Panzer Division, and his senior staff officer were to fly to Italy as the end in Tunisia was in sight and their services could be better utilized in the anticipated Allied invasion there. Following their retreating troops, the two were to travel by automobile to the airdrome. Joachim Kramarz quotes Brolich's description of the trip (*Stauffenberg*, Berlin, 1967, translated edition):

"Because of the air threat, the rule was that the divisional commander and his staff officer were not to travel in the same vehicle. So he took leave of me to go to the new command post, farther back. I said to him once again, 'Look out for aircraft. I will follow in about an hour....' When I drove back myself, accompanied only by a wireless truck and two dispatch riders, as we crossed a completely open plain, we were at once attacked by about twenty fighters. However, we managed to scramble out of our vehicles and disperse and it so happened that the machine gun bullets missed us."

As he continued his drive, Brolich came upon a car full of bullet holes with his staff officer's gravely wounded body laying a short distance away. The officer was transferred to the hospital in Carthage and then to Munich where he stayed for three months, clinging to life. He lost his left eye, right hand and two fingers of his left hand and these injuries would consign him to staff duties in Germany. The man was Claus von Stauffenberg, who placed the bomb under the table at the *Wolfsschanze* on 20 July 1944, in the failed attempt to assassinate Hitler.

Operation FLAX (5 April-12 May 1943)

The Wadi Akarit defensive line was broken on 6 April and the Eighth Army pursued the retreating Axis along the Gabes Gulf coast with Sfax falling on the 10th and Sousse on the 12th. The Eighth Army and the US II Corps met on the 16th and Enfidaville was captured on the 20th. The Axis was now cornered in northwest Tunisia and Cape Bon Peninsula. Allied air forces pounded the remaining ports of Tunis and Bizerte forcing the Axis to rely on air transport for supplies. Despite bombing attacks on their staging fields Axis air transport operations grew to over 150 flights per day. These flights picked up supplies in the Naples area and flew them to Sicily and then across the narrow strait to Cape Bon and Tunisia. The Allies tracked these air supply operations by radar and photo-reconnaissance and were ready to deal with the air transports. From December 1942 through February 1943, 187.7 tons of supplies and fuel reached Tunisia by sea from Italy with a loss of 43.2 tons (23%). During the same three-month period 42,000 German and Italian troops reached Tunisia with 3,400 (7.5%) lost in route. By March the Axis had become dependent on supply by air. In March, 3,554 aircraft had transported 8000 tons of supplies and 10,612 personnel. Ju-52 transports and Me-323 "Gigante" were sent in large numbers. The Me-323 was a huge six-engine transport with clamshell doors opening in the front and having about four times the capacity of the Ju-52.

NASAF planned a large-scale attack on the Axis air supply shuttle from Italy by a combination of fighter sweeps over the Sicilian Straits, attacks on Axis shipping and aircraft in the air and bombing and strafing attacks on Axis air bases in Sicily and Tunisia. FLAX was initiated on 5 April. At 0800 26 P-38s of the 27th Squadron of the 1st Fighter Group intercepted a flight of 31 Ju-52s north of Cape Bon, destroying 14. An additional two Me-323s and

The Me-323 *"Gigante"* were sent in large numbers to North Africa. The Me-323 was a huge six-engine transport with clamshell doors opening in the front and having about four times the capacity of the Ju-52. During Operation FLAX it was shot down in large numbers. (USAF)

two Ju-52s were destroyed while landing in Tunisia at Aouina Airdrome. The 82nd Fighter Group escorted B-25s on a sweep of German shipping. The Mitchells sunk two Siebel Ferries and an escorting destroyer while the P-38s shot down 15 German escort fighters. An attack on Palermo airport destroyed four aircraft and damaged 20 more aircraft along with a fuel dump. The Trapani airdrome was hit by B-17s that destroyed 10 aircraft, mostly Ju-52s, and damaged 65 others. After the FLAX attacks the Luftwaffe lost 25 transports in the air and ground and had 67 damaged leaving only 29 transports immediately available.

In the next several days mini-FLAX type attacks were flown. During attacks on the 6th and 7th, 14 more Axis aircraft were lost on Tunisian and Sicilian airfields. On the 10th the 1st Fighter Group led by Col. Ralph Garman went on another fighter sweep looking for Axis transport aircraft. The 71st Fighter Squadron led by Capt. John Eiland was in the low echelon and numbered most of the 20 Italian SM-75 and -82 transports and eight fighter escorts downed. By the 12th of April the Western Desert Air Force, including the 57th and 79th Fighter Groups, had its radar in position to keep vigil over the approaches to Cape Bon and on the 17th started fighter sweeps to intercept the transports but there were no intercepts on that day.

Palm Sunday Massacre (18 April 1943)

On 18 April, which was Palm Sunday, the Germans managed to successfully sneak a fleet of air transports into Tunis in the mid-afternoon (1500 hours). A mixed RAF and USAAF force patrolled the area hoping to intercept the returning German transport force. At 1700 hours the 79th Fighter Group was relieved by 34 P-40s of the 57th Fighter Group and 12 fighters of the 314th Fighter Squadron of the 324th Fighter Group flying out of their base at El Djem. Top cover was flown by 12 Spitfires of the RAF 92nd Squadron. The group patrolled uneventfully for an hour and as the sun was going down there was time for one more 15-minute sweep. The P-40s were about six miles off the coast when Capt. James Curl of the 66th Squadron saw two Me-109s coming toward him. The Messerschmitts were followed by three large V's each consisting of approximately 100 Ju-52 transports top-covered by a number of mixed German and Italian fighter types heading toward Sicily just a few feet above the Mediterranean. The RAF 92nd Squadron and the US 64th Squadron went after the enemy top cover while the 65th, 66th and 314th Squadrons pounced on the hapless transports. The transport pilots panicked and headed back toward land and were decimated. The final number of enemy aircraft destroyed could not be accurately determined, as there were a number of duplicated claims in the swirling melee. It appears that 50 to 70 Ju-52s and 16 to 18 fighters were destroyed for the cost of six P-40s and a Spitfire. Many damaged Ju-52s made forced landings in Tunisia but the "Palm Sunday Massacre" sealed the fate of the air transport supply system and with it the fate of the Axis in North Africa.

On 23 April, 16 more transports, including the last available Me-323, were shot down. So many transports were lost that Me-109s and 110s were used to transport fuel. Formation flights were discontinued and aircraft flew individually at night. The consequence of the transport losses was pointed out in the NAAF Weekly Summary of 17-23 April 1943:

"The payload of a Ju-52 flying from Sicily to Tunisia is approximately 2.5 tons, that of a Me-323 approximately 10 tons. In the early part of April, the Germans made an estimated average of 150 Ju-52 trips from Sicily to Tunis per day. Roughly eight Me323s made the same journey. This can be translated into 455 tons of war material a day or 300 tons per week....Transport activity has practically ceased since 19 April."

Despite these heavy losses, in April, the Germans averaged 78 transport flights per day (down from an early month 150 flights) carrying over 8,388 personnel and 5,040 tons of fuel, ammunition

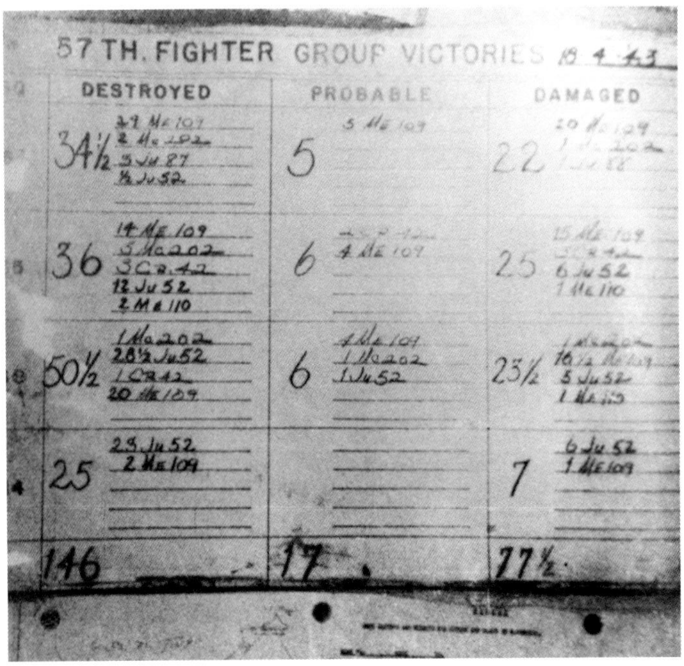

P-38s and B-25s shooting down 25 of 35 JU-52s flying at wave top level in April 1943. (USAF)

Left: 57th Fighter Group scoreboard of the Palm Sunday Massacre. (USAF)

and equipment to Tunisia. In April, 18,690 tons of supplies and 2,500 personnel disembarked by sea. However, 14 freighters, one tanker, two destroyers and 12 small craft with 15,516 tons of supplies were lost.

The Axis Ju-52s or SM-82s were a last ditch attempt by the Axis to bring in reinforcements. One can only imagine how frightened the Axis troops must have been sitting in these vulnerable transports waiting for a machine gun burst to rip through them or to go down in flames into the ocean. Many of the transport pilots lost were instructors pressed into this troop ferrying service and the fighter escort pilots lost were experienced veterans with many victories. These pilot losses would begin to tell on Luftwaffe air operations over Italy in the coming months. FLAX accounted for 116 Ju-52s and five Me-323s lost and 85 damaged.

Axis Shipping Losses (April-12 May 1943)

From early April FLAX decreased the previous average monthly naval supply tonnage of 62,500 tons to 29,233 tons in April and the loss ratio in early May climbed to 77%. Troops lost figures in March and April climbed to 12% and only 11,890 troops landed as naval troop ferry activity decreased due to the increased air attacks. The naval supply effort lost 243 ships of all types including 151 cargo ships of over 500 tons and another 242 were damaged to some degree. Allied air attacks accounted for 67% of the ships lost or damaged (8% by submarines, 7% by mines and 13% from various causes). Axis naval and air forces were limited and unable to protect their shipping lanes from Italy to Africa. A great number of transport ships were sunk both by Allied aircraft and submarines and their valuable cargoes never arrived in Tunisia. The major Tunisian ports were Tunis and Bizerte while Sousse, Sfax and Gabes were used by small transports and Siebel ferries (armed pontoon barges). The road and rail links from these ports were good and offered rapid distribution to front line depots. Railways became the primary interdiction target for NAAF bombers and were heavily damaged.

The Italian Naval High Command (Supermarina) was under pressure from the Italian Army to evacuate their troops from North Africa in this futile effort and sent several destroyers from Sicily to Tunis. Italian destroyers made 155 voyages to Tunisia evacuating 52,000 troops but 12 destroyers and 11 destroyer escorts were lost. In the mid-morning of 30 April, the 79th Fighter Group was assigned to an anti-shipping patrol and bombed Siebel ferries, barges and harbor installations in the Gulf of Tunis. In the mid-afternoon the Group sent out all four squadrons that found an Italian destroyer skulking along the Gulf of Tunis coast toward Cape Bon after evacuating troops from Tunis. The 86th and 87th Fighter Squadrons got two direct hits on the vessel's bow and scored many near misses. The smoking destroyer turned slowly back toward Tunis but soon stopped completely. Before they could finish off the crippled vessel they were bounced by 15 Me-109s and in the air battle the P-40s destroyed two, claimed a probable and damaged three others. However, two P-40s collided and the debris from the collision fell on another. All three fighters were lost but one pilot survived and was captured. The destroyer sunk later. The Group rearmed and refueled and commenced another anti-shipping patrol and came upon another Italian destroyer, escorted by ten fighters, sailing from Sicily. Twenty-four P-40s of the 87th and 316th Squadrons hit the warship hard in a concentrated and accurate attack that scored three direct hits. The ship was set on fire and began to list to port and tried to make way toward Cape Bon and safety but capsized and sunk near Sidi Daoud. The 57th Fighter Group sunk another destroyer that day and 900 Italian soldiers and the crews of three destroyers were needlessly lost.

Final Battles (May 1943)

As shipping losses mounted more and more supplies were carried by transport aircraft. The major Axis airdromes at Bizerte, Gabes, Sfax and Tunis and bases in Sicily were attacked causing such a heavy loss in transport aircraft that bombers had to be pressed into service as transports. The transport planes, largely Ju-52s, were mainly based near Palermo and Naples with some at Bari and Reggio di Calabria. Most flights originated at Naples and staged in Sicily before continuing to Tunisia. Ideally they were scheduled to arrive near midday (e.g. lunch hour) when intervention by Allied fighters was anticipated to be minimal. The transports flew at 150 feet to evade radar detection while short-legged Luftwaffe fighters provided escort only at the Sicilian and African portions of the flight. Many transport aircraft were lost in aerial combat and the attacks

After the loss of air superiority, a closely packed 21st Panzer Division supply column in North Africa was harassed during their retreat at the end of the campaign. The 21st fought in France two and a half years later and could not move in daylight and not be under constant Allied air attack. (US Army)

It was the loss of air superiority and the inability to maintain long supply lines from Italy that was the prime factor in the defeat of the Afrika Korps. Burned out Ju-52s at El Aouina Airdrome. (USAF)

on transport airfields completed the decimation of the German air transport arm so that well before the Tunisian campaign ended the aerial supply line had virtually been eliminated. Axis forces in Tunisia required 140,000 tons of supplies monthly. In February 1943, only 62,751 tons were shipped to Tunisia of which there 16,504 tons of fuel, ammunition and food (14,600 tons traveling by sea and 1,844 tons by air) and 43,966 tons (including 50 tanks, 1,293 vehicles and guns) while 2,281 tons were lost in ship sinkings.

By the end of April, the Allies had achieved total air superiority and were unconcerned by any intervention by Axis aircraft which were now based on Sicily or Pantelleria. They were able to devote the large majority of their aircraft to offensive missions and were able to fly as many as a thousand sorties a day against targets near the front lines. In mostly interdiction sorties they strafed and bombed airfields, rail and road targets and gun and troop concentrations. Fighter-bombers were particularly effective against retreating Axis motor transport on the roads or in assembly areas. The previous attention to shipping and airfield targets paid dividends, as the Axis was powerless to defend itself in the air. The Allies had expected the Axis to attempt to evacuate as many personnel as possible before the surrender but the finally won Allied air superiority in the air and over the seas prevented a mass evacuation. Von Arnim surrendered on 12 May and 275,000 prisoners were captured, of which 155,000 were Germans.

Conclusions on the North African Campaign

As the TORCH invasion began the USAAF had just begun operations over Western Europe and a large part of the 8th Air Force was transferred to the 12th Air Force when airfields in Algeria were ready. TORCH gave the USAAF a diversion from the bombing campaign over Europe for which it was not prepared. The Tunisian campaign gave the Americans their first chance to test their men and equipment in combat operations against front-line Luftwaffe units. They used four fighter (P-38, P-39, P-40 and the Spitfire) and five bomber types that created logistical difficulties of repair and replacement. For the first several months logistical support was limited with fuel, food, fresh water, bombs and ammunition, spare parts and replacement aircraft and adequate ground personnel being in short supply.

The fighting in the Tunisian campaign took place on and over a narrow strip of land and air with the Mediterranean directly to the north and the desert to the south. Initially, the Luftwaffe had superiority in men and equipment. The Me-109 and FW-190 in the hands of experienced pilots were superior to American fighters in quality and quantity. Allied intelligence and planning were lacking. Initially many squadron commanders who were promoted in the prewar Air Force were found to be incompetent as combat leaders. This process soon changed as promotions were to be based on qualifications founded in actual combat. The balance of air power in Tunisia turned with the Allied bomber force that outnumbered its Luftwaffe counterpart. The Allies did not achieve true air superiority until the end of the campaign.

During the North African campaign many of the fundamentals of tactical air power and air-ground cooperation were first elucidated and then combat-tested. Combat experience showed that air superiority was required for any ground operation to succeed. The fighting in the theater was a series of armored battles supported by infantry along the coastal strip to capture a port that would supply a further advance to another port. The terrain offered little cover and camouflage and concealment was difficult or impossible and the side that lost air superiority suffered the consequences. With the pre-requisite of air superiority, these factors made interdiction extremely successful. RAF fighter-bombers exploited the situation throughout the campaign by harassing Axis infantry, their vehicles, armor and guns that suffered heavy losses and finally the loss of their position in North Africa.

Tactical air support during the Tunisian Campaign had concentrated on the destruction of Axis airfields and aircraft, shipping, interdiction attacks on targets far behind enemy lines while close air support was rudimentary and negligible. The lack of close air support caused friction between Allied commands. The Americans claimed the inadequate close support was due to the RAF command and its new air support doctrines and not due to inadequate forces and the lack of air superiority.

Although bombers played the major role in the tactical aerial victory in Tunisia, fighter-bombers did their part by gaining air superiority, interdicting Axis supply lines in the air and on the seas, harassing Axis forces and then providing rudimentary close support. The Tunisian campaign was the first time the USAAF utilized the new tactical concepts developed by trial and error over the Western Desert by the RAF. The American tactical air force in North Africa was able to successfully coordinate with Army ground forces. However, initially this coordination was on an upper echelon basis that only took into account the broad objective of the battle but did not take into account the often-immediate needs of local ground commanders. The US fighter units were either under the control of or influenced by the RAF in North Africa. The British concept of close air support early in the campaign was to use relatively large numbers of fighters as aerial artillery in support of the infantry. Also early in the campaign there was an indefinite air command structure and operational duties. Attaining air superiority was not accomplished, as the orientation of the air forces was to support the army. The Allied bombers were mainly attacking German North African and Italian ports and some airfields in Italy and Sicily. The Luftwaffe tactical airfields in Africa were virtually untouched. It was not until the Casablanca Conference in January 1943 that the air command structure was reorganized and the North African Tactical Air Force was established. AM Sir Arthur Coningham was then able to gain air superiority and do away with "flying artillery" concept. With air superiority achieved he established the tactical principles that would become the basis of American tactical air doctrine in the form of *FM 100-20* that the AAF had been pursuing for decades. The AAF was able to establish and master the fundamentals of tactical air power at a minimal cost and in minimal time. AAF generals in Africa passed on their experience in Africa to Gen. Hap Arnold who ramrodded it through the War Department in the form of *FM 100-20* on 21 July 1943. In North Africa the true success in the air was that the tactical air force was no longer a supporting force of the Army but proved and then asserted itself as an equal and though not independent partner.

12

Pantelleria
13 May - 12 June 1943

Pantelleria is a small 18-mile by five-mile, 42 square mile, island of the Pelagain Group, situated in the Mediterranean narrows between Tunisia and Sicily. Because of its strategic location it was to be captured before the invasion of Sicily, codenamed Operation HUSKY. Mussolini proclaimed the island to be the "Italian Gibraltar," as it possessed numerous natural and man made defenses, many gun positions and fortifications and had enough supplies to hold out against a long siege. The island with its Freya radar station, airdrome capable of handling 80 fighters and submarine and E-boat bases presented a threat to the HUSKY timeable. More importantly, the Royal and US Navies were unable to provide the eight escort carriers the invasion plan stipulated. The capture of Pantelleria's Marghana airfield was required for Allied fighters and fighter-bombers to support the invasion as they would be much closer to Sicily than flying from their bases in North Africa and Malta. The weak point of the Pantelleria defense was its garrison of 11,000 untested Italian troops and an air defense that had proved mediocre in defending the island in the last days of the Tunisian campaign. Eisenhower and his planners decided that a direct invasion of the island would be too costly. Eisenhower directed Lt.Gen. Carl "Tooey" Spaatz, commander of the Northwest African Air Forces, to use Pantelleria as a "laboratory to determine the effect of concentrated heavy bombing on a defended coastline" in Operation CORKSCREW. Naval blockade and bombardment before D-Day scheduled for 11 June.

CORKSCREW was primarily a bomber action but three P-40, one Spitfire and an A-36 group were involved. Part of this fighter force was the 99th Fighter Squadron; the famed Tuskegee Airmen who were the first African-Americans to fly combat. They flew P-40s for the XII Air Support Command. On 13 May the air offensive began with nuisance raids by medium and fighter-bombers. Beginning on 18 May 50 medium and 50 fighter-bomber sorties per day were scheduled to be carried out through 5 June to isolate the port and destroy the airdrome and its aircraft. By the end of May, photo reconnaissance showed that no serviceable aircraft remained on the island and that that the airdrome facilities and supply and fuel dumps

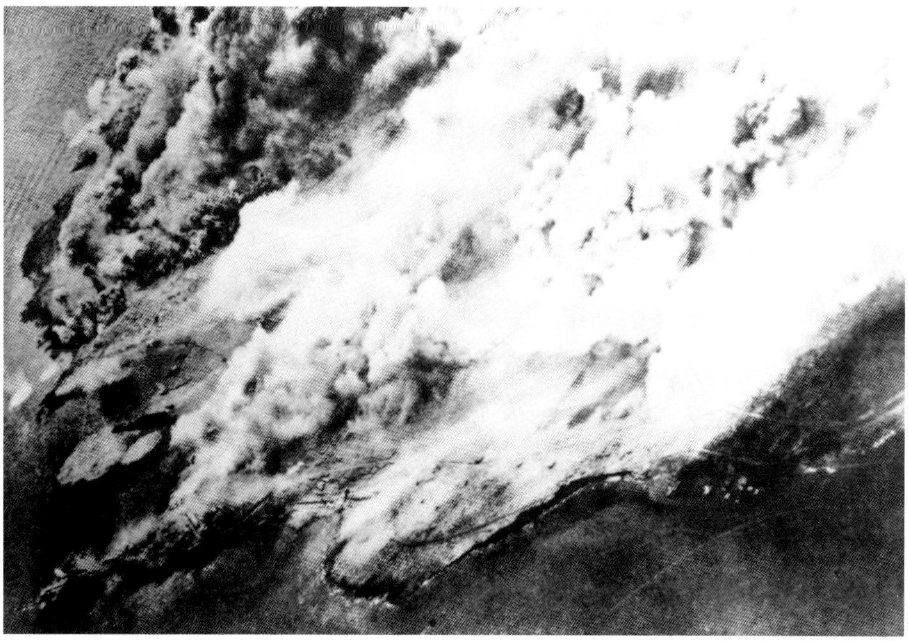

The largely Italian garrison defending the island of Pantelleria was heavily attacked by 2,294 bomber and 1,922 fighter-bombers sorties from 13 May to 12 June 1943. Mussolini's "Gibraltar" surrendered without a shot being fired during the invasion; the first time in history air power alone forced an enemy to submit. (USAF)

The Allies needed to capture Pantelleria, as planners feared that Marghana airdrome would interfere with the invasion of Sicily.The airdrome was quickly put out of action during the first air attacks and Axis aircraft posed no threat to the air offensive. Large numbers of Macchi and Fiat aircraft lay wrecked on the field. (USAF)

A large underground hanger with anti-blast doors at Marghana airfield was intact after heavy bombing attacks.The results of the Allied bombing had less to do with the capitulation of Pantelleria than did the quality of the Italian garrison.The supposed aerial reduction of the island led to the "Pantelleria Effect" on Allied air power thinking during the rest of the war. (USAF)

had been destroyed and that naval and air blockade had shattered port facilities and prevented only but a handful of small supply vessels to arrive. On 1 June B-17s joined the attack on the island after previously been occupied with isolating it by bombing airdromes in Sicily, Sardinia and southern Italy. The next attacks were scheduled to emphasize attacks on coastal batteries and gun emplacements. Over the next several days heavy, medium and fighter-bombers dropped 400 tons of bombs on these positions. On 6 June the next phase of the assault called for round the clock bombardment of increasing intensity mainly against shore batteries and gun installations until D-Day. Medium (647 sorties) and heavy bombers (598 sorties) dropped 2411 tons while fighter-bombers dropped 334 tons in 788 sorties. By 10 June the island was reduced to a ruin by the final 1,100 aircraft dropping 1,571 tons of bombs that day. Before 6 June the Axis air forces did little to prevent the air attacks but during the next several day increased their attacks, losing about 60 aircraft as compared to the 15 lost by the Allies from 18 May to 10 June. On 11 June the British 1st Infantry Division landed on the island and the demoralized garrison of 11,121 Italians and 78 Germans surrendered without firing a shot with the only casualty being a British soldier being bitten by a jackass!

Lampedusa was the largest of the Pelagian Islands and had an airstrip, 4,300 troops, radar station, two tank platoons and 33 coastal guns that made it potentially a tough target for invasion. On 13 June medium and fighter-bombers attacked the island, flying 450 sorties and dropped 270 tons of bombs heavily damaging the island's installations and knocking out about one-third of its gun batteries. Although it had received less bombardment than Pantelleria it was to be the subject of one of World War II's more implausible stories. The day before the planned invasion RAF pilot, Peter Cohen, became lost and landed on the island. He was surrounded by Italian troops and ready to surrender when the Italian commander had Cohen's plane refueled and sent him off with a letter of Italian surrender!

Operation CORKSCREW was to be a footnote of history but the ease of the victory would become a curse in the future planning of aerial operations in Italy. The aerial bombardment of Pantellaria was to become the classic air operation in the minds of some Allied strategists. But post surrender surveys revealed that Pantelleria was particularly vulnerable to air attack and even though the concentrated Allied air attacks had caused heavy damage, they did not totally destroy Mussolini's "Gibraltar." The bombardment did not undermine Italian morale, as it was already non-existent. Before the air assault, by early May, the Germans had withdrawn all but 78 of their 600 man garrison, indicating that they deemed the island as indefensible and left it to Mussolini. Italian prisoners of war stated that after the German abandonment they considered surrendering as soon as the Allies came ashore. The bombardment had killed only 200 Italians as the rest had fled to the outlying hills and did not man their posts. Only 5% (6.4% by bombers, 3.3% by medium bombers and 2.6% by fighter-bombers) of the bombs dropped fell within 100 yards of their target. Italian gun and defensive positions were poorly prepared and camouflaged and supporting troop and ammunition protection was inadequate. The survey found only ten of 80 gun positions were destroyed (only two by direct hits) and only half of the large guns had sustained damaged and could have been put into action by resolute troops. Only a few direct hits were scored on Pantelleria's heavy fortifications and underground aircraft hangers and all the bomb tonnage caused little damage. Most of the bomb damage was indirect destroying buildings, roads, communications and utilities (electricity and water). It was determined that a 500lb. bomb was more efficient than a 1,000lb. bomb as its effective radius was two-thirds that of the larger bomb. Also, they were more effective against small targets as twice as many could be dropped. A delayed action bomb was more effective than an instantaneous fuse as more damage was produced with its heavier ground shock effect. POW interrogation disclosed that fighter-bomber strafing only had a temporary effect on troops and needed to be used with bombs for a more prolonged effect on troops. General Carl Spaatz declared:

"The application of the air available to us can reduce to the point of surrender any first-class nation now in existence."

The official Air Force history stated:

"The pattern set here was probably one that would be followed in other island operations and perhaps the invasion of the Continent itself. The surrender of the Italian-held islands furnished a spectacular illustration of the intense and violent force that the Allies could bring to bear on the enemy. The reduction of the islands furnished the first proof of power of such bombardments to induce surrender."

If Pantelleria had been garrisoned by seasoned German troops it probably would only have been taken after a costly and protracted battle. The Italians were certainly not a true test of the effectiveness of air power, and the legacy of the Pantelleria success was the belief that air power could repeatedly achieve similar results. The heavy bombing of experienced German troops holed up in the town and Abbey of Cassino in February-March 1944 and of the German mountain positions near Bologna in April 1945 would be examples of this thinking that these attacks would demoralize the defenders.

USAAF Fighter-Bomber Operations Pantelleria (13 May to 12 June 1943)

	Fighter-Bombers		**Bombers***	
Target	**Sorties**	**Bomb Tons**	**Sorties**	**Bomb Tons**
Harbors & Docks	439	144.2	639	790.2
Military Installations	1,292	538.5	1,543	3,012.0
Air Bases	191	69.1	112	100.4
Total	1,922	751.8	2,294	3,902.6

(*Light/Medium/Heavy)

Although RAF units participated in the attack, USAAF units conducted 83% of the sorties and dropped 80% of the bombs.

13

Operation HUSKY: Invasion of Sicily 10 July - 17 August 1943

At Casablanca Roosevelt and Churchill agreed that a cross-Channel attack on France in 1943 was out of the question but agreed to attack Sicily, Operation HUSKY, in early July. Planning for HUSKY began in early February 1943, as a combined amphibious and airborne operation under the command of Gen. Sir Harold Alexander of the Fifteenth Army Group. D-Day was set for 10 July at 0015 hours for the airborne assault and at 0245 hours for the beach assault. Air operations on the ports and air bases on Sicily, Sardinia and Italy had begun during the Tunisian Campaign. In mid-May the tempo increased in an effort to obstruct Axis supply and communication lines and to reduce Axis air strength in order to gain the required air superiority.

After the defeat in Tunisia, the fall of Pantelleria had finally taken away any Axis offensive initiative in the Mediterranean and left them to anticipate where the Allies were going to strike next. Axis air forces were barely strong enough to meet their defensive obligations, their navies were reduced to light surface warships and submarines and their ground forces, 175,000 poorly trained Italian and 32,000 first-rate German troops, had to plan for a counter-attack to crush the inevitable invasion probably somewhere on Sicily but perhaps on the Italian boot. Axis troops in Sicily were placed in three deployments. First there were a large number of troops, mainly Italian reservists, and a few prepared positions sparsely spread a long the coast. The second was the port defense groups that protected strong points such as Messina, Palermo and Catania with flak and coastal defense guns. The third deployment were the six mobile Axis divisions that were held in a central position on the island to be ready to mount a counter-attack on the Allied forces which were being held up by the coastal forces.

After Pantelleria fell the Allied Air Forces flew missions as directed in the HUSKY air plan issued on 26 May 1943. The principal objectives were:

1) Gain air superiority by the destruction or neutralization of enemy air power within range of the invasion.
2) Protect northwest Africa and Sicily from enemy air attack.
3) Provide air cover and diversionary operations designed to disperse enemy air forces as widely as possible.
4) Carry out air operations to prepare the way and assist in its execution.
5) Air attacks on enemy shipping and naval forces.
6) Support naval operations
7) Protect the naval convoys
8) Support the assault forces.
9) Air operations to support and launch the airborne attack

There were to be three phases in the air plan with emphasis on not revealing the exact location of the invasion, although the logical choice was Sicily. The first phase was to start as soon as the Axis had been defeated in North Africa and consisted of the systematic bombing of Axis airfields and Italian industry, the bombing of Germany and Italy by RAF bombers and the bombing of the Aegean and Dodecanese Islands by bombers based in the Middle East. The second phase was to occur a week before D-Day. Strategic bombers were to attack major Axis airfields and communications on Sicily, Sardinia and southern Italy. To maintain surprise no Sicilian beachheads were attacked. The third phase was to occur in

Allied counter air attacks were so effective that by 18 July only 25 Axis aircraft were operational in Sicily. Once air superiority had been established and the beachheads consolidated the NAAF was an able attack targets without opposition. Me-109s destroyed on Agrigento Airdrome, Sicily July 1943. (USAF)

conjunction with the invasion when all local airfields were attacked. Allied leaders felt that D+1 was to be the most uncertain for Allied ships moving toward or lying off the invasion beaches as the invasion points would definitely be known to the Axis. Allied fighters would have to move from the offensive to the protection of the invasion shipping from bases in North Africa, Pantelleria and Malta until fields on Sicily could be secured. The Axis could no longer match the Allies in aircraft and their aircraft in the Mediterranean were widely dispersed with many being located in Greece and on Crete. Even with air superiority there was a lack of Allied coordination but fortunately the large Allied fleet anchored only 40 miles from major Axis airdromes suffered only minor losses because of the efficiency of the fighter control ships in directing the CAP.

Order of Battle USAAF Fighter/Fighter-Bombers

Northwest African Air Forces (NAAF)

Northwest African Tactical Air Force (NATAF)

Desert Air Force (Advanced HQ) RAF

Desert Air Force (Rear HQ) USAAF & RAF

57th Fighter Group (P-40)

79th Fighter Group (P-40)

XII Air Support Command (Advanced)

33rd Fighter Group (P-40)

111th Reconnaissance Squadron (P-51)

XII Air Support Command (Cap Bon)

31st Fighter Group (Spitfires)

86th Fighter-Bomber Group (A-36)

324th Fighter Group (P-40)

Northwest African Coastal Air Forces

52nd Fighter Group (Spitfires)

81st Fighter Group (P-39)

350th Fighter Group (P-39)

414th Night Fighter Squadron (Beaufighter)

415th Night Fighter Squadron (Beaufighter)

Fighter Aircraft Numbers

USAAF: 874 fighters/fighter-bombers

TAF: 225

XII ASC: 400

CAF: 249

RAF: 656 Fighters/fighter-bombers

Luftwaffe: 485 Fighters

Sicily and Italy (south): 260 SE Fighters/40 TE Fighters

Sardinia: 130 SE Fighters

Italy (north): 35 TE Fighters/20 Night Fighters

Italian Air Force: 530 Fighters (many obsolete or non-operational)

Sicily and Italy (south): 200 SE Fighters

Sardinia: 100 SE Fighters

Italy (north): 230 SE Fighters

The immediate emphasis was to build up the forces for the invasion and avert heavy losses to the Luftwaffe. To gain air superiority, 19 major and 12 more newly built lesser airfields on Sicily were heavily attacked along with airfields on Sardinia. These attacks forced the Axis to withdraw all bomber forces from these airfields to southern Italy but the Allies followed with attacks on the Italian mainland, especially the Foggia and Naples areas. By D-Day all but two airfields in Sicily and two in Sardinia had been destroyed or neutralized. Photo-reconnaissance attested to the efficiency of the attack by showing that over half of the enemy fighter strength fled to Italy and that over 1,000 enemy aircraft (600 Luftwaffe) had been destroyed or abandoned on Sicilian airfields and 139 shot down. The Axis air effort against the invasion on 10 July was so feeble that only 20% of the Allied air effort was against Axis airfields. The majority of the attacks on Italy and Sardinia were by bombers. The fighter-bombers contributed marginally with interdiction bombing sorties on Sicily, as escort duty was their primary function.

1Lt. J.B. Walton of the 27th Fighter Group flying out of Cape Bon, Tunisia described an attack on rail and road targets in Sicily for *YANK* newsmagazine:

"We started after a convoy of 50 or 75 trucks. The Captain (Roger Miller) went after the trucks ahead and I took those on the right. One truck started to turn back off the road and got caught in a gully and I got him just as he toppled over. Then I swung over to the side of the mountain we were passing. There were two trucks carrying about 30 men each. The men started running and I got both trucks. Then I went over the hill and got three more-all big trucks hauling men. Got them clean: I could see my tracers kicking

American landings at Gela Sicily (US Army)

Previously successful 88mm gun and German pillbox knocked out by fighter-bombers on D-Day. (USAF)

up dust around them. Then our flight ran into a locomotive and I saw it go up in steam. There was ack-ack around this and I could see men standing around the gun. I was over to the right and they didn't see me. I shot all the men on the gun and damaged the gun."

On 10 July the invasion took place and fighter-bomber activity stepped up. It was expected that Allied supporting arms, tanks and artillery could not be off loaded quickly enough to guarantee adequate support for the ground troops to hold the beachhead. Thus, the air plan called for a stepped up interdiction campaign against any enemy movement toward the beaches. Fighter-bombers were utilized to interdict the enemy's movement towards the beachheads. Two groups of P-38s were transferred on temporary duty from the Strategic to Tactical Air Forces to the eastern area to assist two groups of A-36s operating in the central and western areas. On D-Day 1,092 fighter and fighter-bomber sorties were flown covering the beachhead and escorting Allied bombers. Throughout D-Day sorties were dispatched every half hour and destroyed many enemy road and rail transport. Attacks on the eastern coastal road were very effective and also along the roads from the Enna supply concentration in central Sicily. On 12 July, nearly 1,000 12th Air Force (31st and 33rd Fighter Groups) fighter and fighter-bomber sorties were flown against enemy motor transport, blocking roads with burning trucks. The TAF flew more than 5,000 close support, interdiction and air superiority sorties and from 12-15 July the British and American beachheads moved to join. They had captured several principal airfields and were moving forward against light resistance and had captured one-third of the island. Enemy air action against infantry was inconsequential but Axis aircraft were initially able to attack the invasion fleet with little intervention, as air cover was inadequate. Fortunately, little damage was done, as the bombings were wholly inaccurate. Allied counter air attacks were so effective that by 18 July only 25 Axis aircraft were operational in Sicily. Once air superiority had been established and the beachheads consolidated the NAAF was an able attack targets without opposition. Major targets for 2,257 bomber sorties were marshaling yards. The 1,112 fighter-bomber sorties strafed and dropped 350 tons of bombs on transportation (e.g. rail and motor) targets. On 15 July the Allies pushed to capture the remaining two-thirds of Sicily and by the 17th the Germans realized the battle was lost. They decided to fight a delaying action to save their three divisions on the island. To protect the escape route over the Straits of Messina, nine additional heavy AA batteries were transferred from the mainland to bring the total to 80 batteries (excluding machine guns and 20 mm).

An A-36A in a dramatic in-flight photo over Mt. Etna, Sicily. The 27th and 86th Fighter Groups flew as part of Coningham's NATAF and the much maligned dive-bomber and did yeoman's work during HUSKY. (USAF)

Right: The Coronia Valley was a typical Sicilian terrain with a river separated by mountain ridges. Bridges were easily destroyed by fighter-bombers as the three bridges in the photo demonstrate. (USAF)

General Patton's Third Infantry Division began a rapid advance aided by NATAF close air support disrupting an armored counter-attack and nearly destroying two artillery groups. The German-Italian command was never able to form a cohesive front due to NATAF tactical air support. The Third moved 100 miles in four days and took Palermo on 22 July and the remainder of western Sicily by the 24th.

When the 27th and 86th Fighter-Bomber Groups were flying A-36 missions to Sicily they flew in 12 plane flights usually against gun emplacements shipping and strafing troop concentrations. Since they were based on the African coast only three quarters to an hour away, they were able to fly two or three missions per day. Heavy AA fire was experienced but little Luftwaffe fighter opposition. During the invasion the A-36s attacked the rail and road net while the P-40s flew cover for the amphibious landings. In the days immediately after the landings, the A-36s were based on Sicily on dirt strips near the coast with their pilots sleeping under the wings of their aircraft. Three or four sorties ranging from 15 minutes to 3.5 hours were flown per day mainly in direct ground support. The approach to the target was on deck to avoid German radar and at the target the flight would climb to 10,000 feet as quickly as possible and then dive and drop their bombs as low as possible. After the attack, depending on the AA, the aircraft would either immediately return to base or return to strafe the target area. Some low-flying A-36 pilots reported that Sicilian civilians would wave and point to camouflaged German targets The terrain took a toll on the A-36s that flew into the hills or mountains while diving or flying low-level missions or trying to evade ground fire.

On 31 July 1943, twelve A-36s of the 27th Group were thoroughly briefed with a pinpoint map on the local terrain for an attack on four heavy guns that blocked the advance of US Army infantry. Upon reaching the target area and circling three times, the pilots could not spot the guns so the flight leader decided to bomb the map pinpoint reference that was an orchard. The attack revealed no sign of the guns or their crews but on returning to base the Army congratulated the unit on destroying the four guns.

Meanwhile the British Eighth Army met stiff resistance on the Catania Plain that held them up for almost two weeks allowing the Germans time to deploy the newly arrived 29th Panzer Grenadier Division and prepare for the evacuation through Messina. Both the British and American TAFs participated in the Catania battle with systematic bombing and strafing of the routes to and from the front. From 19 July to the end of the month, 84 medium, 705 light and 1,170 fighter-bomber sorties were flown. Three German divisions; the 15th, 29th and Hermann Goering Panzer divisions, two 1st Parachute regiments and four Italian divisions remained intact. They were ordered to stabilize the front until evacuation preparations to the Italian mainland could be completed. The tactical air forces at-

The Siebel Ferry was named after its designer and was armed with 20 and 37mm AA guns and did yeoman work in the evacuation of Sicily across the Messina Straight. Called the "Axis Dunkirk" the Italians evacuated 70,000 troops and the Germans nearly 40,000 from Sicily. (US Navy)

Left: The city of Messina overlooking the narrow Straits. (USAF)

tacked ground targets located by air reconnaissance, shipping and targets of opportunity. Primary targets were towns, ports, supply dumps, roads, bridges, motor transport, ships and port facilities. During the last week of July, the busy port and seaplane base of Milazzo was heavily attacked. Between 24 and 30 July, 234 light bomber and 251 fighter-bombers attacked the town. By the end of July, the Allies had 21 Sicilian air fields back in action and 40 squadrons based on the island. The Luftwaffe mounted a successful attack on 1 August when Ju-88s and Do-217s bombed Palermo putting the main dock out of service for a short time, destroying gasoline and food supplies and blew up an ammunition train and a small ship. But this raid was the rare exception.

By the end of first week of August the Allies began their final drive on Messina to capture all the Axis forces. The Germans realized that Sicily needed to be evacuated and General Hube set up five defensive lines that would be held and abandoned on successive nights as an intended 8,000 to 10,000 personnel per night were to be evacuated over to the Straits to Italy. The Sicilian terrain, Mt. Etna and Pelorita Mountains restricted superior Allied forces to the coastal roads and relatively small Axis units were able to slow the Allied advance. The Germans placed approximately 140 88mm AA guns on both sides of the Straits of Messina and had 150 20 and 37mm AA guns either shore-based or mounted on barges. The Allied air assault by P-36s and P-40s during the first weeks of August concentrated on shipping such as freighters, barges, Siebel ferries and assorted small craft. These fighter-bombers were assigned to dive-bomb shipping but the ferries and barges that were protected by heavy onboard AA fire took a heavy toll of the fighters. On the 5th the Allies had their most successful attack on the Straits when they sunk two merchant vessels, 21 barges and a Siebel Ferry. After this loss the Germans confined their evacuation to nighttime. The port of Messina became the major target of a concerted attack by heavy and medium bombers and fighter/fighter-bombers. Despite the air attack the Germans organized a skillful evacuation that has been called the "Axis Dunkirk." Between 3 and 16 August, the Italians evacuated 70,000 men and up to 500 vehicles and 75 artillery pieces. The Germans began their evacuation on the 10th and in six days 39,569 troops, 9,605 vehicles, 47 tanks, 94 guns, 2,070 tons of ammunition and fuel and 15,700 tons of supplies crossed the Straits of Messina to safety. The B-17 attacks were curtailed on 11 August to divert them to a propaganda-inspired bombing mission on marshaling yards outside of Rome after which they were stood down for four days. The effect of the missing heavy bombers on damaging the evacuation would become evident. On the 13th the Allied advance pressured the evacuation to be continue in daylight hours and the NAAF attacked both sides of the Strait between the 13th and 17th of August with fighter-bombers flying 426 strafing sorties against docks and harbors along with attacks by the medium bombers. Despite no enemy fighter opposition the results of these attacks (three small ships sunk) were negligible due to poor intelligence and heavy AA fire which had become so intense that the medium and fighter-bombers were ordered to fly missions at higher altitudes decreasing their accuracy and results. Gen. Heinrich von Vietinghoff stated that without the troops evacuated from Sicily "it would have not been possible to offer effective resistance on the Italian mainland south of Rome" (*Campaign in Italy*, 1947). Kesselring reiterated the Allied failure to shut down the Messina evacuation: "The enemy failure to exploit the last chance of hindering the German forces crossing the Straits of Messina, by continuous and strongly coordinated attacks from the sea and the air, was almost a greater boon to the German Command than their failure immediately to push their pursuit across the Straits on 17 August" (*Kesselring: A Soldier's Record*, NY, William Morrow, 1954).

Conclusions and results

The results of the HUSKY campaign were:

1) Diverted Axis troops from the Eastern Front.
2) Secured Allied transportation lines in the Mediterranean.
3) Sardinia became indefensible.
4) Pressure on Italy intensified.
5) Forced Mussolini's resignation on 25 July 1943.
6) Led to the Italian Armistice on 3 September 1943.

Allied air interdiction during HUSKY had two major objectives; cutting off the Straits of Messina and the intensive interdiction of rail, road and coastal supply and troop traffic. Air interdiction was not particularly successful as it did not prevent the accumulation of supplies to the island before the invasion and it did not prevent the initial reinforcement and then the final evacuation from the island. Sicily's supply line was an extension of the Axis supply lines on the southern mainland. By August the Italian rail system in the south was devastated and the Axis turned to trucks and road traffic that was in turn attacked so heavily that it only operated at night. The destruction of supply ships, first during the Tunisian campaign and then in concentrated attacks on Sardinia, Corsica, the Aegean and the southern French ports, caused Kesselring to muse: "Unless our problems of new ship construction and repairs are solved at the last moment, the island can not be held against a strong enemy attack." (*Kesselring: A Soldier's Record*, ibid.) The passage across the Straits of Messina was never critically affected by air attack due to the heavy concentration of flak on both sides of the Straits. It was the lack of shipping and damage to port facilities on the mainland that reduced the amount and flow of supplies to Sicily. Then the loss of stockpiles during the retreat caused fuel and ammunition to become in such short supply that Kesselring decided that the island could not be held and ordered the evacuation.

Despite the overwhelming Allied air superiority it was amazing that the Germans could hold on to Sicily for 38 days. The Germans first reinforced then withdrew their forces across the narrow three-mile Straits of Messina; connecting Sicily to Italy. They negated Allied air superiority by placing a very heavy concentration of anti-aircraft batteries on both sides of the Strait and in between. It was the priority of the Allies to establish air superiority against the Luftwaffe that at that stage of the war was still a significant force and this required a large part of their air effort during the pre-invasion and initial part of the campaign. The tactical portion of the air campaign began only after air superiority was won. Official US Naval historian, R.Adm. Samuel Elliott Morison, criticized the lack of Allied tactical fighter support:

"Although this command (NAAF) included over 400 planes, it would give no assurance to Army or Navy as to the kind and quality of the support they could expect on D-Day or thereafter. This refusal stemmed from the reluctance of top commanders (i.e. Tedder, author) to sacrifice flexibility: 'tactical' might be wanted to support 'strategic' in action against enemy forces." (*US Naval Operations in World War II, Vol.IX*, Little Brown, MA, 1954)

Patton commented on the AAF and its initial lack of coordination with the Army. Patton, remembering the valuable support that Navy Air from escort carriers gave during TORCH, remarked to US Vice Admiral H. Kent Hewitt, commander of the American Western Naval Task Force:

"You can get your Navy planes to do anything you want but we can't get the Air Force to do a god damn thing."

The air campaign for Sicily was a bomber campaign (67% of the total sorties) with the fighter/fighter-bomber's most significant contribution being the maintenance of air superiority after the bombers had destroyed Axis airfields and aircraft on the ground on Sicily, Italy and Sardinia. This outstanding lesson of HUSKY was to be repeated in during future landings. Individual battles and the entire campaign were never jeopardized by Axis air power and air superiority significantly reduced the number of casualties and amount of damage to the Allied Army, Navy and Air Forces. Once the Luftwaffe was subdued fighter-bombers also provided another important contribution: which was the interdiction against rail, road and coastal transportation and close support sorties. Close air support during the campaign varied first with the amount of training and then the quality of the coordination and timing between the air and ground units. Air-ground cooperation was extensive and improved throughout the battle. After HUSKY the Luftwaffe strength in the MTO had diminished to 880 by 1 September due losses in the air and on the ground and withdrawals of units to the Western Front. Tactical operations to isolate the beachheads found good targets initially but as the campaign continued road and especially, rail targets were fewer. Orders were issued to discontinue rail attacks, as Allied armies would need to utilize them later during their advance. The heavy attacks on the truck concentrations and road junctions around Mt. Etna led to the collapse of the center. The road net in Sicily was sparse due to the hilly and mountainous terrain so there were few possibilities for detours and successful attacks could shut down German operational and supply movements. However, German road repair and traffic control units were extremely efficient and stymied Allied air efforts and the German withdrawal to Messina continued. In 1942, the RAF attacked a few Italian cities, intending to intimidate the Italian will to resist and to cause the Axis to move AA guns to protect these strategically unimportant targets. By the end of 1942, Milan, Genoa and Turin had the equivalent of a combined German-Italian Flak division permanently committed to their defense. The dedication of these flak units to Sicily and the southern mainland could have caused unsustainable losses to Allied air power.

The HUSKY air campaign demonstrated the need for more combined training, the need for accurate and timely information on friendly troop disposition, having the troops understand that it would require time to mount a close air support mission, targets and friendly troops needed to be identified and the need for improved ground to air liaison. During the campaign the II Corps experimented with mobile fighter control parties with VHF radio sets mounted in jeeps that later became SOP in Italy. Communications between Air HQ and Army HQ and then to their respective subordinate units was set up and refined in Sicily. Although there was a continued reluctance by American ground commanders to relinquish control to air commanders, many tactical missions were controlled by the air arm and were under a central operational control that kept air power from being used piecemeal. Kesselring commented that air-ground co-operation was extensive and improved as the campaign wore on. He considered that the Allied success in Sicily and then Italy "attributed, in the first place, to the Allied Air Forces." (*Kesselring: A Soldier's Record*, ibid.) For the first time air power in Sicily was allowed to utilize its strong points: mobility, flexibility and concentration and air superiority was achieved and maintained by the efficient and determined attacks on enemy aircraft and airfields.

Relative Contributions of the USAAF and RAF for HUSKY (May-August 1943)

	USAAF				**RAF**			
	Sorties	**%**	**Tons**	**%**	**Sorties**	**%**	**Tons**	**%**
Pantelleria	3,913	84	4,850	85	741	16	804	15
Sicily	4,986	71*	5,262	64	3,188	39**	2,926	36
Italy	3,138	76	6,476	78	1,010	24	1,659	22
Sardinia	1,351	87	1,663	82	191	13	353	18

* 71% of sorties in which bombs were dropped, 61% of all sorties
** 39% of sorties in which bombs were dropped, 29% of all sorties

USAAF Fighter/Fighter-Bomber Operations Sicily (2 July to 17 August 1943)

	Fighter/Fighter-Bombers		**Bombers***	
Targets	**Sorties**	**Bomb Tons**	**Sorties**	**Bomb Tons**
Harbors/Docks	662	67.0**	847	1,454.4
RR/RR Bridges	459	138.6	242	391.3
Marshaling Yards	60	21.0	695	1,034.4
Roads/Bridges	81	27.3	357	568.9
Military Installations	47	18.4	90	143.4
Motor Transport	767	209.2	66	24.0
Air Bases ***	149	40.5	2,162	4,061.5
Total	2,225	522.0	4,459	7,677.9

*Heavy/ Medium/Light *** 13 May to 15 July
** Mainly strafing

Allied and Axis Aircraft Losses During HUSKY

	Destroyed	**Missing**	**Damaged**	**Total**
German/Italian*	906	200	299	1,405
USAAF	157	127	691	975
RAF	52	59	87	198

*Fighters and Bombers (including 280 Me-109s, 70 FW 190s and 80 Ju88s)

14

Background: The Italian Mainland Campaign 18 August 1943 - 8 May 1945

By mid-summer 1943, the tide had turned on the German war machine with the defeat at Stalingrad, the loss of North Africa and then Sicily that caused Mussolini's abdication. Nonetheless Germany's hold on western and central Europe and the threat of a renewed German offensive in Russia caused Stalin to press for a second front. Mussolini's successor, Marshal Pietro Badoglio, immediately began secret negotiations with the Allies for Italy's surrender. The QUADRANT conference at Quebec in August 1943 made POINTBLANK, the progressive destruction of German industrial and military power, the priority as a prelude to the invasion of northwestern Europe (OVERLORD). The reduction of the German fighter force before the invasion of northwestern Europe was also a primary concern and it was agreed to accelerate the planned invasion of the Italian mainland to cope with it. From captured bases in northern Italy the two major aircraft factories in southern Germany that manufactured nearly 60% of Germany's fighter aircraft would be in bombing range as would be the oil facilities at Ploesti. To protect these resources it was thought the Germans would be forced to move half of their fighter force facing bomber attacks from the UK to the south, relieving the 8th Air Force from the heavy losses of deep penetration bombing. The British Eighth Army was to cross from Sicily to Calabria in Operation BAYTOWN on 3 September and six days later the US Fifth Army was to initiate Operation AVALANCHE, a major amphibious attack on Salerno. The Italians secretly agreed to surrender on 3 September and were to announce it on 8 September in order to confound and upset German plans during the Salerno landings.

Hitler's appointment of Field Marshal Albert Kesselring over Erwin Rommel for the defense of Italy was to be an inspired move. Kesselring had gained ground attack experience in the foot artillery in World War I and helped to reorganize the Army in the postwar Germany. He was transferred to the newly organized Luftwaffe where his administrative and organizational skills led him to become its Chief of Staff. His outstanding work during the Polish

Hitler's appointment of Field Marshal Albert Kesselring (right) over Erwin Rommel (center) for the defense of Italy was to be an inspired move. Throughout the Italian Campaign it was Kesselring's superb defensive generalship that kept Germany in the war there and took such a heavy toll on Allied personnel and resources. (Author/West)

The US Command in Italy, December 1943. (From left to right): Maj.Gen. John Cannon, Commanding General of the Northwest African TAF, Lt.Gen. Carl Spaatz, Commanding General of the Northwest African Air Forces, Lt.Gen. Mark Clark, Commanding General of the Fifth Army and Gen. Henry Arnold Commanding General of the US Army Air Forces. Note Piper L-4 in background on right. (USAF)

Campaign in 1939 with Luftflotte 1 and then Luftflotte 2 over the Low Countries led to his appointment to Field Marshal after the fall of France. In December 1941, he was made C-in-C South that gave him control over all Axis forces in the Mediterranean. In May 1943, Hitler had had vacillated between naming Rommel or Kesselring for the defense of Italy. Rommel wished to defend northern Italy where the Allies could not take advantage of their naval power to outflank the Germans by amphibious landings. With his air background Kesselring wanted to defend further south in order to keep Allied heavy bombers as far away from Germany as possible. Throughout the Italian Campaign it was Kesselring's superb defensive generalship that kept Germany in the war there and took such a heavy toll on Allied personnel and resources.

15

Operation AVALANCHE: Salerno 18 August - 20 September 1943

The invasion was planned for 9 September 1943, on the beaches just south of Salerno. Once the beachhead was established and consolidated, the invasion force was to move inland and join the British Eighth Army which landed a week earlier on Calabria (BAYTOWN) and was moving north, threatening the rear of the German forces facing the Salerno beachhead. The invasion forces were the Fifth Army, under Lt.Gen. Mark Clark, which was made up of the US VI Corps commanded by Maj.Gen. Ernest Dawley and the British X Corps under Lt.Gen. Richard McCreery. The invasion and ensuing fighting was to be supported by heavy naval gunfire. Field Marshal Albert Kesselring directed the German defense of Italy and his decisions were contingent on the political action of the Italians. If the Italians were to surrender, Hitler decided that the whole Italian Peninsula could not be defended without the aid of the Italians and he would withdraw north to Rome. However, the Italians did not surrender until 8 September, the day before the Salerno invasion and the Germans were forced to defend southern Italy as the Salerno beachhead had to be contained until the Germans could secure an orderly withdrawal of supplies and troops from southern Italy.

The air operations against the Italian mainland began before the decision to land at Salerno had been made. These air operations of January-April 1943 were bomber missions of the IX Bomber Command B-24s based in North Africa and concentrated on the port of Naples that was the main embarkation port to supply the Germans and Italians in Tunisia. In May RAF and US bombers of the NAAF hit a variety of targets along Italy's western coast in pre-HUSKY air attacks.

US Fighter/Fighter-Bomber Order of Battle
(3 September 1943)

Mediterranean Air Command
Cmdr. & Air C-in-C: ACM Sir Arthur Tedder RAF
Dep.Cmdr. & CG NAAF: Maj.Gen. Cark Spaatz USAAF
Dep. Air C-in-C: AVM H.E.P. Wigglesworth RAF
Northwest African Air Force (NAAF)
CG: Maj.Gen. C. Spaatz USAAF
Dep: AVM J.M. Robb RAF
Northwest African Strategic Air Force (NASAF)
CG: Maj.Gen. J.H. Doolittle
1st Provisional Fighter Wing *
1st Fighter Group (P-38)**
14th Fighter Group (P-38)**
82nd Fighter Group (P-38)**
Northwest African Tactical Air Force (NATAF)
AOC: AVM Sir A. Coningham RAF
Dep: Maj.Gen. J.K. Cannon USAAF
XII Air Support Command (XII ASC)
CG: Maj.Gen. E.J. House USAAF
64th Fighter Wing
27th Fighter-Bomber Group (A-36)**
86th Fighter-Bomber Group (A-36)**
33rd Fighter Group (P-40)**
325th Fighter Group**
Desert Air Force (DAF)
AOC: AVM H. Broadhurst RAF
211th Group***
57th Fighter Group (P-40)**
79th Fighter Group (P-40)**

*Temporarily detached 6 September and attached to the XII ASC to fly cover for invasion shipping and the invasion beaches.
**Flew interdiction missions supporting the Salerno invasion.
***RAF Wing which was the equivalent of a US group; while a RAF group was equivalent to a US wing.

Allied air strength in mid-August 1943 was 3,127 aircraft, 800 fewer than available for the invasion of Sicily. The total included 1,395 fighters and fighter-bombers, 461 heavy bombers, 703 medium and light day bombers, 163 medium night bombers and 406 transports. A number of heavy bombers in Africa had been withdrawn to England to take part in the strategic bomber offensive against Germany but the main reductions were in the fighter arm. On 3 September, Allied intelligence estimated that Axis air strength in Italy and Sardinia was 220 long-range bombers and torpedo bombers, 50 reconnaissance bombers and 266 fighters and fighter-bombers. The Luftwaffe serviceability rate was about 50% while the Allies was about 75%. The success of the Allied air offensive over Sicily caused its leadership to assume that a smaller Allied fighter force could have the same success against an even smaller and somewhat demoralized Luftwaffe fighter force. The Luftwaffe was unable to replace the losses of experienced pilots and aircraft due to the pressures from the Eastern Front and the defense of the Reich from the intensifying Allied strategic bombing campaign. The Germans over Sicily had too busy fighting a disorderly defensive battle to initiate the offensive to relieve the constant air attacks on the German Army and supply system. It was thought that the end of 1943 should conclude the battle for the Axis "soft under belly", but Italy tuned into a "tough old gut."

The NAAF was to support the Salerno invasion in two stages: pre-D-Day missions and missions from first light on D-Day to the establishment of a beachhead.

From 18 August through D-Day:
The NASAF was assigned to:

1) Neutralize enemy air forces in southern Italy.
2) Isolate the battlefield and obstruct the movement of troops toward the invasion area by attacking targets north of a line defined by Sapri-Trebisacca.

The NATAF was assigned to:

1) Assist the NASAF in neutralizing enemy air forces in southern Italy.
2) Force the maximum interruption of the movement of enemy troops and supplies into the invasion area (e.g. south of the NASAF operations area).
3) On D-1 provide cover for the Salerno invasion shipping.

It should be noted that before 18 August, the Luftwaffe had been driven from their southern Italian airfields and only the airfields in the Foggia were active and required attention. Nonetheless, the Luftwaffe was able to fly 90 plus bombers across the Mediterranean to attack the invasion shipping in Bizerte harbor on 17 August and a week later 40-50 bombers hit Palermo. From 18 to 31 August the majority of air missions (2,284 sorties) were conducted by heavy and medium bombers against marshaling yards first and then rail lines and bridges (442 sorties) and at a very modest third place (107 sorties), strikes against roads and road bridges. BAYTOWN, the British invasion from Sicily of the "toe" of Italy at Reggio in Calabria on 3 September, occupied NAAF activities from 28 August through the first week of September. During this period, 1-7 September, marshaling yards (446 sorties), rail lines and bridges (281 sorties: 125 by fighter-bombers) and roads and bridges/motor transport and troops (345 sorties: 55 by fighter-bombers). Although most of the air attacks were concentrated on targets in the "toe" area and AVALANCHE attacks declined, these attacks benefited both invasions. The Calabrian attacks disrupted enemy movement there and slowed the German "fighting" withdrawal towards the north to reinforce Salerno. Because of the proximity of Calabria to the captured Sicilian airfields fighter-bombers carried out a large number of sorties there. As the Salerno invasion approached, the Germans were delayed, though not prevented, from evacuating troops and supplies from southern Italy due to the extensive damage to the Italian rail network. Fuel, vehicles, tires and spare parts were in precariously short supply but food and ammunition were described as "assured." Some critically short items had to be airlifted into the area and troops marched to their destinations. During this period the Germans managed to fulfill their logistical and military operations as their ability to mount a counterattack demonstrates.

A USAAF Spitfire lies on Paestum Beach after being shot down by "friendly" fire. (USAF)

From first light on D-Day onward:
The NASAF was to continue its pre-D-Day missions.
The NATAF was to:

1) Provide air cover for the invading troops and shipping.
2) Prevent the movement of enemy troops and reserves into the battlefield.
3) Provide close support.

The XII Air Support Command of the NATAF was appointed the most difficult air assignment; to supply the air cover for the invasion and the following ground support operations. The Allied air plan called for three MASAF P-38 groups; and two A-36 squadrons, 19 Spitfire and four Beaufighter squadrons from the XII ASC to provide cover for the beachhead. The P-38s and Spitfires were to fly two sorties per day and with the A-36's and RN Seafires put an average of 58 aircraft in the air during the daylight hours. With the Allied serviceability rate of 75% they had about 670 combat aircraft available to cover the beaches and invasion shipping (322 single-engine fighters, 206 twin-engine fighters, 32 night fighters, 110 carrier-based Seafires from four escort carriers). Except for the P-38s, the other fighters and fighter-bombers were only able to reach the Salerno beachhead by using external auxiliary fuel tanks instead of carrying bombs. This limited them to providing brief patrols to prevent an enemy air attack and to strafe obvious or predetermined targets. Fortunately, on D-Day Luftwaffe attacks were minor and limited to sorties on shipping and the off-loading of troops and supplies. Because of the limited time Allied fighters were able to patrol the invasion area it was imperative that the major objective on D-Day or D+1 be the capture of Montecorvino Airfield, three miles inland and ten miles south of Salerno. Also, aviation engineers were assigned to go ashore at once to construct airstrips in the Paesrum area. From 18 August to 9 September, the MASAF bombed central and southern Italian airfields, particularly the large complex at Foggia that was the base for the majority of the Luftwaffe fighter and fighter-bomber units and limited Luftwaffe attacks to 98 sorties. It was not until D+4 that more enemy air bases were captured in fighter-bomber range of the Salerno beaches. At this time P-40s and A-36s were able to carry bombs and fly dive-bombing missions against interdiction targets. P-38s did not participate in interdiction missions until the 15th. The 33rd Fighter Group (P-40) moved to Paesum on 13 September, the 27th Fighter Group (A-36) moved to Sele on the 16th and the 86th Fighter-Bomber Group (A-36) moved to Capaccio on the 18th. The P-38s had been on TDY to the XII Air Support from the NASAF and on 17 September returned to their normal missions of escorting NAAF heavy bombers. Also, a ground-control system was established so that other ground targets were attacked upon request.

As part of the invasion of the Italian mainland a strike against Axis air power was planned for mid-August. Allied reconnaissance discovered 200-250 Axis aircraft, mostly bombers, on the ten airfields in the Foggia area. A Do-217 under attack. (USAF)

As part of the invasion of the Italian mainland a strike against Axis air power was planned for mid-August. Allied reconnaissance discovered 200-250 Axis aircraft, mostly bombers, on the ten airfields in the Foggia area. These aircraft were widely dispersed and would be difficult to destroy by conventional bombing or fragmentation bombs so it was decided to strafe them with a large low-level sweep. Several practice mission were conducted on the 2rd and 24th by the 1st and 82nd Fighter Groups. On 25 August, 140 P-38s, 65 from the 1st and 75 of the 82nd left their North African bases at 0630 and joined over the Gulf of Tunis. The 1st was led by Maj. George Rush, Group Operations officer and was assigned to attack Foggia satellite fields #1, 2 and 4 and the 82nd by Lt.Col. George MacNicol and was to attack fields #3, 7, 9 and 10. Their route had them fly at a 100 feet over the Mediterranean, skirting Sicily, crossing the Italian spine, a total of 500 miles to Foggia. The 82nd had 16 pilots abort the mission for various reasons. At just over three hours later, at the assault point, a road junction northeast of Foggia, the individual squadrons separated to attack their assigned targets. For the 82nd, the 96th and 97th headed for fields #7 and 9 at tree top level. MacNicol's 97th strafed a line of FW-190s through heavy small arms and AA fire destroying a number of fighters while the 96th hit airfield # 7, the two squadrons claiming ten destroyed and 21 damaged. The 95th Squadron led by Capt. Hugh Muse attacked airfield #3 and was the most successful claiming 11 destroyed and 22 damaged. 1Lt. Guido Lucini got three; a Ju-88, a Me-109 and a Ju-52 while 1Lt. Joseph Solko strafed a line of Ju-88s and hit nine of them in successive firing passes. The 82nd lost three pilots. The 1st was more successful as it accounted for 41 Ju-88s, a Ju-52 and a single-engine fighter and damaged 52 more. In the air, one Ju-88 was destroyed along with damage claims for ten Ju-88s and three single-engine fighters. A rail station was destroyed and a troop train at Potenza was strafed causing heavy casualties. The Group lost two P-38s and pilots although many Lightnings returned to base with AA and small arms fire damage. Both the 1st and 82nd were awarded the Distinguished Unit Citation for one of the most successful airdrome strafing missions in the MTO.

During AVALANCHE the aircraft of the XII ASC were to be directed by a fighter director control aboard the USS Ancon that was the flagship of the Western Naval Task Force. The control group consisted of Maj.Gen. Edwin House, CO of the XII ASC, and 13 officers and 42 enlisted men. The USS Hiliary was to be the secondary fighter control ship and the USS Samuel Chase was a backup. As soon as the fighters were based ashore the fighter control group would go on shore and station themselves as near as possible to the Fifth Army headquarters. Allied air superiority allowed some fighters on patrol over the beachhead to be equipped with bombs. The pilots were given their targets from shipboard controllers while in flight to the beachhead and after bombing their targets they were fly their assigned defensive patrols. The XII ASC flew a number of these sorties for the X Corps. This system gave support from ten minutes to a half hour after the request. Once American fighter-bombers were based at Salerno the air-ground cooperation actually became less efficient as the land communications lines were unreliable.

On the 11th, German Do-217 bombers directed radio-controlled Fritz-X bombs and damaged the HMS Uganda, USS Savannah and Philadelphia which caused the British to withdraw their aircraft carriers and Seafires. Several days later radio-controlled bombs seriously damaged the battleship, HMS Warspite. The increased German air activity caused the Allies to attack Luftwaffe airdromes on the 16th and 17th of September. The NASAF sent 600 bombers and 91 P-38s to bomb and strafe active fields and 300 enemy aircraft were destroyed causing the Germans to withdraw their bombers to fields in northern Italy and southern France and their fighters to Lucca and Viterbo. This withdrawal reduced German air operations from an average of 100 daily sorties to 30 and allowed the Allies to reduce their patrols from 300 to 200 per day, freeing many fighters for escort duties and fighter-bomber missions. The number of fighter-bombers was increased by the movement of a large number of aircraft based in Sicily to the Italian mainland (three 86th Fighter Group squadrons).

The Salerno Invasion was the zenith of A-36 combat operations. Flying 150 miles from San Antonio Field on Sicily, the A-36 had longer loiter time (about 30 minutes) than other Allied fighters and during the Salerno landings it was constantly flying CAP in shifts over the beachhead along with a limited number of P-38s and Royal Navy Seafires. On 13 September, A-36s of the 27th Fighter Group/522nd Squadron shot down four FW-190 fighter-bombers for a loss of one aircraft and claimed two more the next day. On 10 September, A-36s of the 86th Fighter-Bomber Group prevented three Panzer formations from reaching the battlefield. Also on the 10th the 27th Fighter-Bomber Group was awarded the DUC when it claimed 177 vehicles destroyed and 246 damaged during 12 missions totaling 102 sorties plus strafing an airfield destroying a Me-109 and damaging seven others losing one A-36 to AA. Between 9-17 September when the fate of the beachhead was in the balance, the 27th flew 98 missions with 777 sorties in support of the invasion. The German counter-attack on the Salerno beaches almost succeeded but for the heavy naval gunfire and the determined dive-bombing attacks of the A-36s of the 27th and 86th Fighter-Bomber Groups. Once the beachhead had been secured and expanded the A-36s flew right out of the beachhead from the airfield at Sele and would face AA fire on take off, over the target and then on landing. On the 17th, the 86th was ordered to attack a 12-gun 88mm battery and German troops that had been blocking the advance of the X Corps near the tobacco factory at Battipaglia. The A-36s took off at 1300 from Sele toward Salerno Bay in order to gain altitude and avoid AA fire and then flew back over their base and inland toward their target. Fifteen minutes later, with their ground personnel watching, the A-36s accurately hit the target. Later that afternoon and early the next morning, two more precision dive-bombing attacks were delivered after which the X Corps advanced unopposed. They found the pieces of the twelve guns and over a hundred dead German soldiers.

Fighter-bombers prevented the timely arrival of Panzer reinforcements until after the Allied beachhead had been consolidated. (USAF)

During B-17 and B-24 bombing missions on Naples, A-36s were assigned escort duties because they were the only US fighters with sufficient range to reach the target area. However, the superchargers on the Allison engines were not efficient at the bomber altitude and speed and maneuverability were sharply decreased. Flak and enemy fighters took their toll on both the A-36s and bombers. When returning form escort missions the A-36s were released for rhubarb type strafing of targets of opportunity.

The Germans had anticipated Salerno as a possible landing area and had deployed the 16th Panzer Division there. On the 9th, Kesselring sent the Hermann Goering Division and 15th Panzer Grenadier Divisions from north of Salerno to reinforcement the threatening the beachhead. These units had no transportation problems from the air and arrived on D+1. The LXXVI Corps was ordered from Calabria with the 29th Panzer Grenadier Division expected to arrive at Salerno late on the 9th. The division was delayed for two days because of total lack of fuel and supplies. Nine separate fuel supply columns were dispatched and all failed to arrive due to air attacks on the rail and road system transporting it. Also, the inadvertent destruction of a large fuel depot at Sapri by the Germans themselves added to the shortage. It is feasible that an earlier arrival of the 29th Panzers may have changed the result of the decisive counter-attack. The entire division did not reach the beachhead until late on the 12th, the same day the Germans mounted a powerful counter-attack against the length of the beachhead that threatened to divide Allied forces and drive to the sea. On 12 September, the XII Air Support Command HQ was assigned to Fifth Army HQ so ground and air close air support operations could be more readily coordinated. Light bombers from the NASAF and NATAF were joined by fighter-bombers to bomb and strafe the enemy counter-attack. Heavy and medium bombers continued their attacks on roads and bridges closer to the battlefront. On the 13th, fighter-bombers only flew close support sorties with the bombers continuing their road and bridge attacks even closer to the battlefront than before. On the 14th heavy and medium bombers maintained their previous attacks but the fighter-bombers roamed further a field raiding railroads, highways and their associated bridges along with motorized transport and infantry. By the 15th the German threat had been halted. 8-14 September was a week in which the beachhead had been attacked and then consolidated. The urgency of preventing enemy troops and supplies from reaching the beachhead is demonstrated by the selection of targets. During this time two-thirds of the sorties (1,933 of 3,296) and three-quarters of the bomb tonnage (3,144.7 of 4,588.3) was directed on roads and road bridges. Troops and motor transport received 794 sorties (24.1%) dropping 389.4 tons (7.8%), followed by rail line/bridges (5.9% sorties/6.1% tons) and marshaling yards (6.9% sorties/8.3%). Fighter-bombers flew 774 sorties (23.5%) and dropped 221 tons (3.9%) during the period causing a large loss of motorized transport delaying ammunition deliveries. The fighter-bombers also flew numerous close-support and strafing missions in assist ground troops. The Luftwaffe had lost 221 aircraft to the Allies 89. By the 11th all Sardinian airfields had been destroyed and by the 17th the Luftwaffe withdrew from the island. Between 16 September and 3 October the Germans performed a brilliant evacuation from Corsica, saving 30,000 troops and 600 tons of material but the Luftwaffe lost more airbases. After the Italian surrender the Germans offset some of their supply shortages by seizing large amounts of Italian supplies (fuel, vehicles, tires and ammunition) and also the supplies allocated to Italian troops were utilized by German troops.

Valiant efforts, especially by the US 46th Division, blunted the German attack. Kesselring was forced to rethink the situation especially since the British Eighth Army was moving north after BAYTOWN and posing a threat to the German rear. He decided that the defense of southern Italy would incur heavy casualties and to withdraw to the Volturno River that would provide more a defensible position especially in the oncoming fall weather. The German Panzer Lehr Division mounted an attack on the 16th to disguise the beginning of the withdrawal and the Hermann Goering Division continued these attacks until the 18th when it, too, withdrew toward Naples. During this withdrawal period, 15-20 September, the total amount of interdiction sorties decreased only two-thirds from the week before with most of the sorties being flown by medium and fighter-bombers. Their targets comprised of marshaling yards, rail lines and bridges, but the emphasis was on roads and road bridges, motor transport and troops. The last week of the campaign had 1,156 of 2,183 sorties and 1,296.4 of the 1,985 tons (65.3%) spent on roads and road bridges with remainder on troops and transport (13.3%), rail lines and bridges (13.6%) and marshaling yards (7.7%). Medium and light bombers flew 829 of the 2,183 sorties (38%) and dropped 986.6 of the 1,985 tons (50%). Fighter-bombers flew 1,107 of the 2,183 sorties (51%) and delivered 407.8 of the 1,985 tons of bombs (20.5%) but also participated in close support and strafing missions not reflected in these figures. The heavy and medium bombers were redirected to Luftwaffe airfields that had been neglected and were beginning to become more active.

Conclusion

In Tunisia and Sicily air units were no longer allocated to individual ground units but were placed under the central control of the air commander with decisions in joint operations being reached jointly at the air and army command level. During AVALANCHE fundamental air-ground practices were used to a greater extent and with use came cooperation and proficiency. There was a close connection between the Army HQ and XII ASC, the use of forward air controllers ("Rover Joes") and air and ground commanders met to select targets for the next day with the air commander having the ultimate decision. US pre-war air doctrine decreed that light and medium bombers would fly the majority of close support missions but in Italy fighters became fighter-bombers and took part in approximately two-thirds, light and medium bomber one quarter and heavy bombers one tenth of these missions.

Prior to AVALANCHE the aerial bombardment and threat of bombardment by NAAF was a key factor in Italy's surrender and then the NAAF played a major role in the success of the invasion. It had gained air superiority as it decimated the Luftwaffe on the ground and then swept it from the skies allowing 200,000 troops, 100,000 tons of supplies and 30,000 vehicles to be put safely ashore for the loss of five ships. After the beachhead was established the air force, especially their fighter-bombers in close support sorties, attacked and helped to blunt Kesselring's powerful counter-attack that threatened to divide the beachhead. After the German withdrawal the fighter-bombers followed the US Fifth and British Eighth Armies northward bombing and strafing German troops, strong points, gun positions and armor in their path. They interdicted German transport and supply to and from the battlefield. The Allied air campaign produced substantial damage and disruption to the Italian railway system, road network and motorized traffic resulting in delays in the arrival of troops and supplies. The German had a built-in duplication in their transport and supply complex that enabled them to by-pass or circumvent damage to parts. The severe shortage of fuel was not only a problem of the Italian theater but extended to all fronts and air attacks only exacerbated the situation. The damage to the transport system primarily affected troops and vehicles in the rear areas and did not significantly disrupt actual military operations. Despite causing delays, the air attacks did not prevent the Germans from consolidating the majority of their forces for the counter-attack on the beachhead. Nor did the air attacks prevent the Germans from withdrawing most of their troops and supplies from southern Italy by effectively holding the Allies inside the beachhead for a week. The Germans achieved their principal strategic goals suffering only 3,500 casualties and were able to utilize their forces more effectively than the Allies. They were proficient and well organized in confronting the damage caused by air attacks and continued to maintain high morale. The Allies won the Salerno battle by gaining air superiority that insured that the landings were successful and then being able to hold the beachhead from heavy German counter-attacks through forceful infantry fighting that was well supported by effective naval gunfire and air support.

US Fighter/Fighter-Bombers AVALANCHE (18 August to 20 September 1943)

	Fighter/Fighter-Bombers		Bombers*	
Target	**Sorties**	**Bomb Tons**	**Sorties**	**Bomb Tons**
Marshaling Yards	31	7.0	3,031	5,331.7
Railway/Bridges	544	236.1	631	986.9
Roads/Bridges	591	214.8	2,900	4,734.7
Troops/Motor Transport	1,193	369.2	341	311.0
Harbors/Docks/Ships	17	5.9	5	2.5
Misc. Military Targets	16	8.0	227	498.8
Totals	2,392	841.0	7,135	11,865.6

* Heavy, medium and light bombers

16

Volturno Campaign
21 September - 15 November 1943

USAAF Fighter/Fighter-Bomber Order of Battle
15 October 1943
Northwest African Air Force (NAAF)
Northwest African Strategic Air Force (NASAF)
Northwest African Tactical Air Force (NATAF)
XII Air Support Command (XIIASC)
64th Fighter Wing
27th Fighter-Bomber Group
86th Fighter-Bomber Group
33rd Fighter Group
324th Fighter Group
Desert Air Force (DAF)
211th Group
57th Fighter Group
79th Fighter Group

The scope of this campaign included the capture of Naples (1 October), the crossing of the Volturno River (12-14 October) and the bitter fighting from mid-October to 15 November when the US Fifth Army halted before the formidable German defensive line known as the Winter Line (the Bernhard and Gustav Lines). The situation in Italy dictated the strategic objectives that Kesselring would pursue. The Germans managed the Italian surrender competently and the Allies facilitated the German plans by invading at Salerno, south of Rome enabling the Germans to utilize the natural defenses of the hilly and mountainous terrain south of Rome. After the German Salerno counter-attacks had been beaten back, the US Fifth and British Eighth Armies met to drive the German up the Italian boot. The Germans retreated methodically north and northwest of Naples to positions along the Volturno River. The Allies exerted constant pressure against the Germans to prevent them from consolidating their Volturno positions and by mid-October fought their way across the river. During the next three weeks the Allies fought a succession of fierce battles driving a stubborn German delaying action north to an intermediate defensive position called the Bernhard Line. This defensive line crossed Italy about 50 miles north of Naples and 90 miles south of Rome and incorporated a number of hills that formed defensive anchors. Kesselring hoped to

Volturno River Valley (US Army)

After the Salerno withdrawal, Kesselring ordered elements of heavy Italian industry to be dismantled and removed along with all railway rolling stock, trucks, automobiles and buses. To fulfill this plan the Germans required adequate fuel supplies and a viable supply and transport system that came under Allied TAF attack. (USAF)

hold the Allies back until Army Group B in northern Italy under Field Marshal Rommel, could ready permanent line of fortifications in the Northern Apennines called the Gustav Line that was almost immediately north of the Bernhard Line. This line ran along the Rapido and Garigliano Rivers through Cassino and Alfadena and soon joined the Gustav Line as an in depth defensive zone. The Volturno Campaign ended in mid-November when the Allies unsuccessfully hammered the Bernhard line for two weeks.

The withdrawal of troops from Salerno to the Bernhard Line would be via the road system as dismantled heavy Italian industry would transported via the rail system. North of the Bernhard Line, the supply and transport system would deliver troops and ammunition required to fortify the line. During the Salerno withdrawal, Kesselring ordered elements of heavy Italian industry to be dismantled and removed along with all railway rolling stock, trucks, automobiles and buses. A scorched earth plan was devised to demolish railway junctions and switching points, road and rail bridges, power plants, water lines and reservoirs, transport and communication centers harbor installations, etc. To fulfill this plan the Germans required adequate fuel supplies and a viable supply and transport system. At the start of the campaign, due to German organization, resiliency and innovation, the system was satisfactory despite substantial damage suffered during the Salerno campaign. The marshaling yards were hit especially hard in the pre-Salerno invasion air attacks but German repair teams had restored the rail damage as after D-Day, Allied air activity was focused on the road system.

There was no distinct air campaign with plans or directives associated with the ground campaign. During the Volturno Campaign the NAAF continued to assist ground operations by attacking German lines of communications in two aspects: between the retreating enemy and their new defensive lines and between the German rear area and the new defensive lines. The NAAF flew 9,987 sorties and dropped 11,314 ton of bombs in interdiction missions against rail lines, roads and bridges behind enemy lines. Heavy bombers conducted sporadic attacks against rail bridges and marshaling yards in north Italy. The majority of sorties were flown against targets between the retreating Germans and the defensive positions to which they were moving: 41% of the sorties were flown against roads and road bridges were flown between the Germans and their new defensive positions, 38% against troops and military transport but only 18% were against rail lines and rail cars and only 3% against marshaling yards. These figures illustrate that the Germans were being harassed in their attempt to retreat to their new defensive positions and the movement of supplies and reinforcements from northern Italy were being limited.

During the first two weeks 21 September to 4 October the Germans were withdrawing from Salerno to the Volturno River Line. The NAAF flew 2,860 interdiction sorties and dropped 4,059 tons of bombs. At this time the fighter-bombers flew 497 sorties dropping 148.3 tons of bombs. They attacked troops and motorized military transports that were stalled by the damage created by medium bombers that had bombed the roads and bridges directly behind the front.

On 27 September, the British Eighth Army overran the German defenders of the Foggia airfields. The Foggia Plain was the only flat land south of the Po Valley and was the site of the vast Foggia air complex and nine additional satellite airfields. The capture of these fields extended Allied bomber range by 400 miles and along with missions from England gave long-range Allied bombers entrÈe to all the Greater Reich. The Luftwaffe had anticipated the loss of these fields and began to enlarge and strengthen their northern airfields using workers from the Toldt Organization. The evacuation of the Luftwaffe to these northern bases shut down German bomber activity for a month and the abandonment or capture of 832 Axis aircraft which decreased the fighter Jagdgruppen from the ten deployed in Tunisia and Sicily nine months earlier to three with 75 serviceable Me-109s. Luftflotte 2 commander, FM Wolfram von Richthofen, expertly organized his meager forces. III/JG77 was assigned to attack Allied Strategic bombers while I/JG53 and I/JG77 were to operate just behind the German Tenth Army's front to provide air support for the ground forces and top cover for II/SG4, the only FW-190 ground attack unit remaining in Italy.

In September and October the 27th an 86th attacked Luftwaffe airfields in the Rome area scoring victories on the ground and in the air. On 5 October, the 524th Fighter Squadron of the 27th Fighter-Bomber Group strafed the seaplane base at Vigna de Valle where it destroyed three Cant Z.506B floatplanes and three small trainers. On 19 October, 12 A-36s of the 524th strafed two airfields claiming 12 aircraft destroyed on the ground. But the missions took their toll

Luftflotte 2 commander, Field Marshal Wolfram von Richthofen, expertly but vainly organized his meager forces in Italy as Allied air superiority completely shut down any Luftwaffe offensive or defensive action. (Author/West)

as from 16 August to the end of the year twelve 86th Fighter-Bomber Group A-36s were lost.

The third week (5-11 October) saw the US Fifth Army reaching the Volturno and joining the British Eighth in generally bad weather. The NAAF flew 1,380 interdiction missions dropping 1,479 tons of bombs. Fighter-bombers again mopped up enemy troops and transport after bombing attacks by medium bombers by flying 786 sorties and dropping 252.5 tons of bombs.

The Germans had made Bologna into a daunting fortress defended by veteran troops and armor. To aid the Allied offensive against the city, Operation PANCAKE was planned to take place 10-23 October. As the name suggests, the aim of PANCAKE was to flatten the German defenses. On the 12th, 697 heavy bombers, 300 medium and 277 fighter-bombers dropped 1,661 tons of bombs on 74 targets around the city. The results appeared to be devastating to road traffic and supply movement, gun positions, German strong points and defenses. But when the US II Corps attacked, the determined Germans repulsed them. Poor weather limited the NAAF during the fourth week (12-18 October) as the Fifth Army crossed the river and moved north. The NAAF flew only 938 sorties/989.3 tons. Fighter-bombers (333 sorties/261.5 tons) divided their attention between the road and rail nets. The poor weather diverted many interdiction missions and increased their close-support missions.

The three weeks from 19 October to 8 November were underscored by very heavy fighting as the Germans withdrew to their second (Bernhard Line) of three defensive lines. Although bad weather continued, interdiction and close support sorties increased as the NAAF flew 4,029 sorties dropping 4,036.3 tons on rail and road targets. The NASAF operated north of Rome to the Adriatic hitting vital road and rail bridges while the NATAF operated closer to the front attacking the road net, creating roadblocks and destroying bridges in 1,661 sorties dropping 597.6 tons.

The last week (9-15 November) the Germans withdrew to their third defense line, the formidable prepared defenses of the Gustav Line. After nearly two and a half months of fighting from the Salerno beachhead, Gen. Clark decided to rest his battle weary Fifth Army.

Sunny Italy was not so sunny. During October and November 1944 the weather turned bad and allowed the Germans to retreat to the Gustav Line. (USAF)

The air effort was the lightest of the campaign due to poor weather and aircraft maintenance: 731 sorties/750.3 tons. Medium bombers and fighter-bombers hindered the movement of enemy troops to the Gustav line and motor supply to the front. Fighter-bombers flew 382 (338 vs. roads/bridges) sorties dropping 127.9 tons (106.1 vs. roads/bridges) along with close support sorties.

The total number of interdiction sorties and bomb tonnage delivered in the eight weeks of the Volturno campaign was less than then that delivered during the five weeks of the Salerno campaign. A total of 9,987 sorties were flown dropping 11,314 tons of which 4,432 sorties and 4,380.9 tons were released on roads and road bridges and 2,415 sorties and 3,237.1 on rail lines and bridges. The Germans were resolved to keep the roads open and coerced Italian men from nearby villages into road repair duty.

German troop movement was restricted by direct attacks on columns and concentrations and indirectly by attacks on roads and bridges. German motorized transport was forced to move at night and to often reroute traffic due to damage (this was especially true of the main coastal highway, the Appian Way). Despite this disruption and damage, the Germans were able to accomplish planned troop movements; withdrawing their troops to successive defensive lines i.e. holding at the Volturno and Bernhard Lines and then reaching the Gustav Line with acceptable casualties. Fuel was a problem through out the campaign and certain supplies were rationed from time to time and some critical ammunition types (especially light artillery) were in short supply and caused measured firing at times. Kesselring skillfully directed the withdrawal and the efficient German transport system and repair units were able to cope with and meet at least minimal demands.

Airmen and aircraft taking part in the Salerno campaign were exhausted and worn out and required R&R, maintenance and replacements. The Italian fall weather, notable for rain and thick, low cloud, scrubbed many missions. The poor weather and intense German resistance on the ground diverted many fighter-bomber interdiction missions to close support missions. The Luftwaffe was beaten during the Salerno battles and its bombers were withdrawn to the Po Valley and its fighters to bases north of Rome. In light of the Luftwaffe's impotence the Allies were able to allocate more sorties to the support of ground troops. To compensate the Germans added more guns and maximized their AA defenses. By mid-November, shortages of AA ammunition decreased the effectiveness of German air defenses.

US Fighter/Fighter-Bomber Volturno Campaign
(21 September-15 November 1943)

	Fighter/Fighter-Bomber		Bomber*	
Target	**Sorties**	**Bomb Tons**	**Sorties**	**Bomb Tons**
Marshaling Yards	0	0.0	997	2,350.1
Rail Lines/Bridges	798	278.4	1,618	2,959.7
Roads/Bridges	1,907	608.9	2,525	3,772.6
Troops/Transport	1,323	378.9	195	235.8
Dumps	88	36.4	117	151.4
Harbors/Docks/Ships	89	29.0	307	504.7
Misc.	12	0.7	11	9.0
Totals	4,217	1332.3	5,770	9,983.3

*Heavy, medium and light bombers

17

Winter Line Campaign 15 November - 31 December 1943

USAAF Fighter/Fighter-Bomber Order of Battle
15 December 1943
Mediterranean Allied Air Forces (MAAF)
Mediterranean Allied Tactical Air Forces (MATAF)
Twelfth Air Force
XII Air Support Command (ASC)
27th Fighter-Bomber Group (A-36)
86th Fighter-Bomber Group (A-36)
324th Fighter Group (P-40)
64th Fighter Wing
33rd Fighter Group (P-40)
57th Bombardment Wing
57th Fighter Group (P-40)
79th Fighter Group (P-40)

The Fifth Army's Volturno Offensive ground to a halt on 13 November 1943, as it had unsuccessfully assaulted the Bernhard Line that laid directly in front of the Gustav Line with which it formed a strong in depth defensive line the Allies named the "Winter Line." The Gustav Line ran ten miles deep along the rapid Garigliano River on the Mediterranean, along its narrow tributary, the Rapido River, across the backbone of the Apennine Mountains to the Adriatic north of the Sangro River. Gen. Heinrich von Vietinghoff's Tenth Army held the Mediterranean portion of the line. The area was particularly conducive to defense as the Liri valley entrance was enveloped by extensive hilly terrain that confined the roaring Rapido River and the town of Cassino. The valley was anchored by Monte Cassino that was topped by the large Benedictine Monastery.

Gen. Harold Alexander, commander of the 15th Army Group, halted his advance when his troops encountered the tough Gustav Line on 8 November. Because a standoff was evident, Alexander pressed his Eighth Army attacks from the west to the east side of the Italian Peninsula on the 19th. Once Clark's Fifth Army was rested it was to drive toward Cassino. When the two-pronged Allied thrust had pulled in German reserves, an amphibious landing was planned south of Rome in mid-January.

The German defense of the Winter Line was impeded by the severely damaged rail system and needed to keep the road net repaired and open and motor transport available to augment the rail system. The German defense used increased amounts of ammunition that already in short supply but the fuel situation was alleviated and adequate, as the Germans were no longer using fuel to withdraw. German defensive tactics and leadership were masterful and their use of ideal terrain features and the poor weather was particularly effective. The German was an eminently capable soldier and an expert in defensive fighting and maintained his high morale in extremely trying circumstances.

In late November and early December the Eighth Army advanced slowly north over the Sangro River. On 1 December the

As the Allies advanced toward the German Winter Line the fighter-bomber groups moved to the Foggia airfields and to other temporary fields. Soon after they moved there the winter rains began and the area became a bog, trucks and jeeps became stuck, clothes were caked with mud and morale ebbed to an all time low. (USAF)

restored and revitalized Fifth Army attacked the strong, fortified Monte Camino-Monte Maggiore mountain area that resisted for ten days with heavy casualties on both sides. The German's dogged resistance, constant rain or snow and appalling terrain slowed the Allied advance and by the 21st it became evident that it had been stopped. The Allies fought to the Gustav Line on the west flank but had been held seven miles from the Line in the center, opposite Cassino along the Rapido River.

On 14 November, the NAAF issued a directive outlining the priorities for the MTO:

1) Destroy the Luftwaffe in the air and on the ground.
2) Support the Italian land campaign.
3) Destroy German strategic industrial targets as part of Operation POINTBLANK.
4) Weaken the German position in the Balkans.

No explicit air interdiction directives for the Winter Line were published but the 14 November directive placed air support for ground forces second to gaining/maintaining air superiority. Air interdiction during this time would focus on obstructing transport movement from Germany to northern Italy. This was to be the responsibility of the NATAF.

During the first three weeks (16 November to 6 December) of the Winter Line Campaign the NAAF flew 1,529 sorties and dropped 1,919.8 tons of bombs. The NAAF undertaking was slowed by bad weather, a break in the fighting on the Fifth Army front and a diversion of the air effort to supporting the Eighth Army which was driving across the Sangro. Fighter-bomber interdiction action was very light: with 279 sorties/85.7 tons dropped on roads and bridges and 144 sorties/91 tons dropped on harbors and shipping. Fighter-bombers flew ground support missions.

As the Allies advanced the fighter-bomber groups moved from the Foggia airfield to other temporary fields. The 79th Fighter Group moved to Madna on 19 November. Madna was a coastal airstrip cut out of muddy lowlands just south of Termoli. Soon after they moved there the winter rains began and the area became a bog, trucks and jeeps became stuck, clothes were caked with mud and morale ebbed to an all time low. It was too cold to bathe. The food was C-rations, bread, butter and jam and the occasional Spam "treat". The field was crowded as the four 79th squadrons shared it with two RAF squadrons and a service squadron. The runway ran uphill and takeoffs were downhill and landings uphill no matter the wind direction. The PSP planking buckled into its mud base when a plane landed on it and care had to be taken in the dispersal areas that were knee-deep in mud in some areas. The 79th's P-40s remained grounded for many days in November. The weather cleared at the end of the month and the great efforts of the ground crews in rearming, gun cleaning and refueling made it possible for a record number of missions to be flown.

During this period of Allied air superiority and free-ranging interdiction it was the Luftwaffe that scored a major fighter-bomber success. On the night of 2 December there was a breakdown in Allied air defense over the east coast port of Bari. The busy Allied port had over 30 ships unloading day and night and had been carefully monitored by German reconnaissance aircraft. Aluminum strips dropped from the air initially blinded Allied radar defenses and the following Ju-88s achieved complete surprise dropping bombs and parachute mines from low level for nearly an hour. Seventeen ships were sunk with nearly 42,000 tons of cargo and six others were damaged along with fires and damage to the bulk fuel pipe system. To make matters worse, the SS *John Harvey* that was bringing 100 tons of 100lb. mustard gas bombs to the MTO presupposing Hitler introducing gas warfare was hit and exploded. Eisenhower described the Bari raid as: "the greatest single loss from air action inflicted on us during the entire period of Allied campaigns in Europe." (H. Butcher: *My Three Years With Eisenhower*, Simon & Schuster, NY, 1946) The air defense had grown complacent from a long period of air supremacy. The harbor lights were left on at night, inadequate AA defended it and night fighter forces, communications were inadequate and the radar was poorly sited or unserviceable. Ironically, that same afternoon, AM Coningham held a press conference in Bari in which he stated that the Luftwaffe was defeated: "I would regard it as a personal affront and insult if the Luftwaffe should attempt any significant action in this area." (Glenn Infield: *Disaster at Bari*, Robert Hale, 1974) Later that month Hitler ordered all six bomber groups back to Germany to prepare for large-scale attacks on England in retaliation for the Allied bombing attacks on the Reich. (Note: The Ju-88 was a jack-of-all-trades aircraft flying as a night fighter, light bomber, reconnaissance and low-level attack aircraft.)

During the two-week period, 7-20 December, air interdiction increased to 2,701 sorties and 2,907.1 tons. Pressure remained heavy on marshaling yards and rail lines/bridges there was a dramatic increase in attacks on roads/bridges near the German lines by fighter-bombers. To support the Fifth Army attacks on the Mignano Gap the MAAF flew attacks against the road net to prevent the transport of enemy supplies and reinforcements: 1,305 sorties/743,8 tons of which 1,012 sorties/448.1 tons were flown by fighter-bombers. Fighter-bombers also stepped up their attacks on harbors, docks and shipping: 289 sorties/245.3 tons dropped on the Anzio-Nuttuno, Civitvecchia and San Stefano facilities.

The Italian rail system continued to sustain damage from the persistent air attacks and even with a period of poor weather providing them with a respite, the Germans labored to keep pace with repairs. (USAF)

In the final two weeks of the campaign (21 to 31 December) the Fifth Army captured San Vittore, the last barrier before the Rapido and Cassino. Weekly interdiction sorties decreased to less than a half of the previous week, most of which were bomber sorties.

The Winter Line air campaign flew 5,687 sorties and dropped 7,063.8 tons. Fighter-bombers flew 2,378 sorties (42%)/1.038.4 tons (14.7%). The Italian rail system continued to sustain damage from the persistent air attacks and even with a period of poor weather providing them with a respite, the Germans labored to keep pace with repairs. Most rail cuts could be repaired quickly but bridge damage required laborious and protracted repair. Destruction of electric power plants made electric powered locomotives unusable and needed to be replaced by steam locomotives. The movement of locomotives made them targets for air attacks and compounded the losses. To compensate for road and rail losses the Germans depended more and more on coastal shipping that then received the attention of Allied fighter-bombers. The use of coastal shipping created delays and backlog problems in the unloading and reloading between rail and water carriers. Except for close air support, air interdiction continued to be considered part of the entire support of the Armies and not a separate entity. It is important to emphasize that the air campaign did not allow the Allies to achieve their planned objectives and did not prevent the Germans from achieving theirs.

Luftwaffe strength in the MTO, which in October had fallen 40% from the peak figure of 1,280 in July, fell to 575 aircraft in January 1944 of which only 370 were available in Italy. Luftflotte 2 was given only 35 Me-109s in November and was only able to mount an average of 75 sorties per day. Aircraft had to be conserved and used only when absolutely necessary or when the chances of success were favorable.

Fighter/Fighter-Bombers in the Winter Line Campaign

	Fighter/Fighter-Bombers		**Bombers***	
Targets	**Sorties**	**Bomb Tons**	**Sorties**	**Bomb Tons**
Marshaling Yards	118	54.8	1,580	3,403.4
Rail/Rail Bridges	315	149.1	1,101	1,889.0
Roads/Road Bridges	1,414	593.7	436	476.2
Troops/Transport	75	21.7	39	41.8
Dumps/Misc.	80	41.9	0	0.0
Harbors/Docks /Ships	376	177.2	153	214.5
Totals	2,378	1,038.4	3,309	6,024.9

* Heavy, medium and light bombers

18

Anzio (Operation SHINGLE) Cassino
1 January - 14 March 1944

Fighter/Fighter-Bomber Order of Battle 15 February 1944
Mediterranean Allied Tactical Air Force (MATAF)
Twelfth Air Force
XII Air Support Command (XII ASC)
27th Fighter-Bomber Group (A-36)
57th Fighter Group (P-47)
86th Fighter-Bomber Group (A-36)
324th Fighter Group (P-40)
79th Fighter Group (P-40)
33rd Fighter Group (P-40)

At the beginning of 1944, OVERLORD, the invasion of northern Europe and ANVIL-DRAGOON, the invasion of southern France, had taken precedence in Allied strategy. At the end of December 1943, both Eisenhower (Italian Theater commander) and Montgomery (British Eighth Army commander) departed for the forthcoming invasion of northern Europe. They were replaced by British General Sir Henry Maitland "Jumbo" Wilson and Lt.Gen. Sir Oliver Leese, respectively. Wilson was not known as an air tactician or planner but his post as Allied Theater C in C required an administrator who was able to pass directives from above to his service C-in-Cs. Gen. Harold Alexander remained as Army Group commander and Allied Army C-in-C and Lt.Gen. Mark Clark remained as Fifth Army commander. The upcoming Cross Channel and Anzio invasions drew off some seasoned divisions. The 15th Army Group received New Zealanders, French, Indian and Italian units to continue the attack on the Gustav Line. The impasse around Cassino was affecting the conduct of the Italian campaign which Allied planners wanted to resolve before OVERLORD. A landing at Anzio was planned to break the stalemate but ironically the Third Battle for Cassino and the bombing of the town and Abbey was necessary to break a stalemate at Anzio.

In the pre-OVERLORD air command restructuring, Tedder, Doolittle and Coningham left their posts in the MTO. The Mediterranean Allied Air Forces (MAAF) replaced the Mediterranean Air Command. At the beginning of 1944, Lt.Gen. Ira Eaker, who had led the 8th Air Force during the initial phases of the strategic bombing campaign, was named commander of the new Mediterranean

Sir Henry "Jumbo" Wilson (left) pins medal on Maj. Gen. John Cannon (right). In December 1943 Wilson replaced Eisenhower as Italian Theater commander. When the 12th Air Force split into the 12th and 15th Air Forces Cannon became head of the Mediterranean Allied Tactical Air Force (MATAF). (USAF)

Allied Air Force (MAAF) replacing Tedder. Eaker was a superb choice as was his deputy, AM Sir Arthur Slessor. Both leaders had made their mark earlier in the war and were highly regarded as leaders and air power sages and worked directly with Alexander. The MAAF was made up of the Mediterranean Allied Tactical Air Force (MATAF) under Maj.Gen. John Cannon and the 15th Air Force under Maj.Gen. Nathan Twining. The 15th USSAF was based in Italy for the sole purpose to join 8th Air Force and RAF Bomber Command heavy bombers in the Combined Bomber Offensive (CBO) over Germany. The 8th Air Force was losing many B-17s in its CBO deep penetration bombing of Germany and Eaker realized that soon the 15th Air Force would also be bombing the southern area of CBO. To minimize the risk, Eaker decided to draw as many Italian-based Luftwaffe fighters into the air and destroy them so they could not intercept Twining's bombers on the way to Germany and Austria or be transferred to northwestern Europe to intercept Allied bombers there.

The Northwest African Air Forces (NAAF) had to that time been almost entirely a tactical air force supporting directly or indirectly ground and sea operations by short-range tactical aircraft of the NATAF or long-range strategic bombers of the NASAF. In either case the mission of the NAAF was to support the advance of armies and navies. Only four NAAF missions were flown directly against the enemy industry. The NATAF was renamed the Mediterranean Tactical Air Force (MATAF), the NASAF became the Mediterranean Strategic Air Force (MASAF) and Coastal Air Force became the Mediterranean Coastal Air Force (MCAF). Each was a combined RAF-USAAF command. The 12th Air Force was reactivated as a fighter-bomber tactical air force. P-47s were scheduled to replace the Allison-powered P-51s and A-36s. Despite the US Chiefs of Staff's initial reluctance to become involved in an Italian campaign within months their air force was flying nearly two-thirds of all sorties, dropping 70% of the bombs and scoring two-thirds of the aerial victories.

Anzio, Operation SHINGLE, beginning on 1 January 1944 was a costly stalemate that was only broken in conjunction with the taking of Cassino by the Allies. The hills dominating the area are seen in the background and were used by the Germans in their skillful defense. (US Army)

The Fifth Army rested for two weeks and resumed its offensive on the western flank toward the Rapido, hoping to draw off German reserves from the Anzio-Nettuno invasion by the VI Corps. On 5 January, the US II Corps was in the center to exert the main offensive thrust on Rapido defenses near Cassino. The Fifth Army fought its way through stiff German resistance to the final Gustav Line along the Rapido at Cassino at the base of Monte Cassino. Alexander planned to assault Cassino in conjunction with the Anzio landings 100 miles to the north on 22 January. First the X Corps was to attack the Gustav Line at Garigliano on the 17th in an attempt to pin down German Tenth Army troops on the Line and draw off reserves that might reinforce the Anzio area. On the 20th the 36th Division crossed the Rapido south of Cassino in a poorly planed attack to exert more pressure on the Tenth Army but was driven back.

The Anzio invasion, SHINGLE, was designed to outflank the formidable Gustav Line that blocked the Allies from Rome. On 22 January the Fifth Army put two VI Corps divisions (the US rd on the north and the British 1st on the south) under Maj.Gen. John P. Lucas against light enemy opposition. The landings were virtually unopposed and only one German unit, a battalion of the 29th Panzer Grenadier Division was in the area and it was resting and being reformed after heavy losses. The road to Rome was open and the city could have been taken by a bold thrust by the Allies. Instead there was no attempt to leave the beachhead and a long period of consolidation followed. Kesselring quickly ordered all available troops to the area to deploy in the Alban Hills above the beachhead. Despite heavy Allied air attacks on the rail and road nets the Germans managed to muster two divisions by moving at night aided by their engineers who had perfected the quick repair of bridges and track cuts into an art form.

On the 30th (D+8) the US 45th Division landed and expanded the beachhead to 18 miles wide at the beach and nine miles deep with a salient at Campoleone. German 14th Army commander, Gen. Eberhard von Mackensen, masterfully regrouped and amassed 125,000 troops and counter-attacked the British 1st Division on the night of 3-4 February and by the 8th drove them back toward the beach. The Allied counter-attacks had little success. Early on the 16th the Germans initiated a major counter-attack down the Albano-Anzio road with the intention of capturing the port of Anzio. The Germans had amassed ten divisions and were opposed by less than five full Allied divisions. During the night of 15/16 February about 40-50 long-range German bombers, mainly Ju-88s from bases in southern France attacked the beachhead but sunk only one landing craft and damaged two others. At 0600, German artillery opened its barrage and knocked out the Nettuno airfield and Allied air cover had to come from Naples. Meanwhile, the Luftwaffe sent 95 carefully conserved fighter-bombers, escorted by 150 fighters to aggressively strafe Allied troops and positions. The Germans drove a gap into Allied line that was only repulsed by a powerful naval barrage and close air support. Allied intelligence predicted that the next German attack would come down the Albano Road and during the night of 16/17 February sent a number of Wellington bombers from Foggia to slow the German attack. On the 17th for once the weather was good for the entire day and A-20s, A-36s and P-40s flew powerful sorties against German artillery, troops, armor motor vehicles, dumps and positions on the battlefront. DAF and US medium bombers contributed numerous sorties against German targets. Over 800 aircraft of all types dropped over 1,000 tons of bombs on front line positions that was the greatest tonnage dropped in direct support on a single day to that time. Bad weather grounded all Allied aircraft except 127 P-40 and A-36 fighter-bombers that struck the German attack which began at dawn. A few tanks were damaged and the fighter-bomber's ground support was effective until the weather really socked in. The final German attempt to break through to the sea began at 0400 on the 19th that also was the start of the BIG WEEK (Operation ARGUMENT) Allied air offensive launched from England and Italy directed against German aircraft and aero-engine factories. During the next six days of ARGUMENT, the RAF and 8th Air Force flew 13 major strikes against 15 targets. As hoped, the Luftwaffe came up to defend and 600 German fighters were claimed top be shot down. The situation in Italy was becoming grave not only at Anzio but around Cassino as well and Eaker feared that Wilson might be forced to declare an emergency and draw away strategic bombers from ARGUMENT. However, Eaker had such a large force at hand he was able to send 105 bombers against the Germans in Italy and 126 against Regansburg. The winter weather around Anzio became so bad that almost the entire DAF was grounded and only two B-25 groups, 56 A-26s and about 160 P-40 were available. They bombed and strafed enemy troops and armor throughout the day to hamper the German attack. The Germans continued to attack until the 22nd but the US 45th and British 5th (which had replaced the British 1st) were tenacious and forced the Germans to regroup. The beachhead was placid with both sides patrolling and regrouping. On the 28th, the Germans mounted their final counter-attack at Cisterna in bad weather against the US 3rd Infantry Division. On the 29th the weather cleared and the US VI Corps and 3rd Division called for fighter and medium bombers to attack German armor and troops in close air support missions. Other fighter-bombers flew armed recon and bombed and strafed anything that moved behind German lines. Mackensen and Kesselring terminated the attack after 1 March when nearly 800 Allied aircraft operated within two and a half miles of the bombline in direct support of VI Corps. Ten groups of heavy bombers and four groups of light bombers escorted by 176 P-38s and P-47s and 360 fighter-bombers dropped 600 tons in bombs on forward German troops and artillery positions.

Between 2 January and 4 March, American SHINGLE casualties totaled 10,775, the British 10,168 and the Germans 10,306. The Germans had committed their best reserves and gained some ground and with no further reinforcements on the horizon were ultimately forced to initiate a holding action for the next two and a half months. The Allied failure should not be attributed to Lucas failure to breakout immediately after the landing. But it was the failure of the Allies in initially sending in a Corps to do an Army's job. Lucas force was vulnerable and he cautiously consolidated his position. The original 24,000 Allied troops eventually had to be increased to 110,000, losing surprise and the ever-adaptable Germans were able to reinforce and fortify their position and gain the initiative no matter how great Allied air superiority.

The MATAF was assigned air support for the Anzio invasion while continuing to support the Eighth and Fifth Army on the Gustav Line. It was assigned two responsibilities:

1) Attack Luftwaffe airfields to prevent their interfering with the invasion shipping and the landings.
2) Prevent reinforcements and supplies from moving between northern Italy and Rome and between Anzio and the Gustav Line or shifted between the two battle areas.

In three weeks before the landings (1-21 January) the MAAF flew 2,080 sorties/3,026.8 tons (fighter-bomber: 579 sorites/259.1 tons) against rail targets and 759 sorties/615.3 tons (fighter-bombers: 482 sorties/194.7 tons) against roads and road bridges. The Fifth Army offensive against the Gustav Line required large numbers of fighter and medium bombers for close air support sorties.

Luftwaffe fighter strength on 22 January 1944 was estimated at 200 Me-109s and 25-30 FW-190s. About 70 Me-109s and all the Focke-Wulfs were based around Rome to support the German Tenth Army. The remaining -109s were based in northern Italy to defend industrial and rail targets north of the Apennines and to intercept Allied bombers heading for central European targets. At the same time the MAAF had 4,658 aircraft of which 2,567 were available to support the Anzio landings. From sunrise to sunset during the landings XII ASC deployed three layers of fighter cover over invasion shipping. Four Spitfires patrolled at 20-25,000ft. while eight flew continual cover over the beaches and four over the invasion fleet at 16-18,000ft. Low cover at 8,000ft. was flown by 16 American P-40 Warhawks divided equally between the beaches and fleet. During the day 500 sorties were flown over the beaches and 135 over the fleet. The Luftwaffe sent six fighter-bomber missions and lost seven aircraft to Allied fighters who lost three. The P-40s of the 33rd, 79th, and 324th Fighter Groups were armed with two under wing bombs and six .50 caliber machine guns and utilized them to the utmost during each sortie. They dropped their bombs on their way to beach patrol, provided air cover over the beaches and then strafed targets of opportunity on their way back to base. Meanwhile, P-47 strategic fighters conducted fighter sweeps near Rome and fighter-bombers attacked rail and road targets to isolate the battlefield. The only Luftwaffe threat was from six Me-109s that slipped through beach defenses for an ineffective attack on the harbor.

In the three weeks (22 January to11 February) after the landing, the MAAF reallocated their interdiction targets from the rail to the road net flying half of the 3,338 sorties/4,149.6 bomb tons on road targets (fighter-bombers: 502 sorties/213.9 tons). At the same time the fighter-bombers were often called in for close air support missions and beachhead CAP. Between 21 and 31 January the Luftwaffe built up its bomber force with 135 bombers transferred from northwest Germany, France and Greece some of which had been bombing London. At the same time, anti-shipping units were reinforced by 50-60 Do-217s and He-177s equipped with the Hs-293 stand off guided bomb. The Luftwaffe attacked Anzio shipping and beaches 20 times. A total of 145 sorties were flown on the nights of 23/24 and 24/25 and Naples on the night of 23/24 with 50 to 60 aircraft without much success except to sink a hospital ship. On the

29th 110 enemy bombers hit the beachhead with the largest air attack since Salerno and sunk the HMS Spartan and a cargo ship. The total German tally between 23 January and 19 February was three Allied naval ships sunk and five damaged and one merchantman sunk and seven damaged.

On 30 January, 215 B-17s and B-24s of the 97th, 99th, 301st, 449th and 450th Bomb Groups escorted by P-38s of the 1st, 14th and 82nd Fighter Groups were to drop 29,000 20lb. fragmentation bombs on four Luftwaffe bomber bases in the Po Valley. German radar warned of their approach and their aircraft taxied to escape. Just as they did, P-47s of the 325th Fighter Squadron come below German radar at treetop height 15 minutes before the bombers. They shot down 36 vulnerable German aircraft for the loss of two Thunderbolts.

Despite intense Allied air interdiction of rail and road lines, the Germans moved in reinforcements and 4,000 tons of supplies to Anzio. By the end of January Kesselring moved one light and eight heavy AA battalions under Luftwaffe General Maximilian Ritter von Pohl from the Rome area to the Anzio to supplement artillery. If it were not for the extensive damage done by Allied interdiction the week before the landings the Germans would have been able to drive into the Allied beachhead.

During the final five weeks (12 February-14 March), interdiction sorties were greatly reduced by the diversion of aircraft to close support duties against the German counter-attack on the Anzio beachhead and the Cassino attacks. In the last four of eleven weeks of the campaign fighter/fighter-bombers averaged only 147 interdiction sorties/dropping 76.7 tons per week vs. 532 sorties/209.2 tons per week previously. Interdiction sorties were primarily against rail lines and bridges and then a reduced number of attacks on roads and road bridges followed by a few damaging attacks on selected fuel and ammunition dumps.

On 17 February the air battle for Anzio reached its crescendo. At 0800, 35 German Luftwaffe fighter-bombers took part in a low-level attack on Allied positions in advance of Gen. Eberhard von Mackensen's Panzer Grenadiers and their Panther and Tiger tanks. American troops fell back with heavy casualties in the face of this attack. By mid-day 48 FW-190 Jabos led another attack which drove a two-mile wide and mile deep gap in the American 45th Division's lines. Maj. General John Lucas, with his back to the wall, scrounged together his reserves and sent them into the breech. He called upon the MAAF for help and every type of aircraft flew over 800 sorties that afternoon. Over 1,000 tons of bombs were dropped on the German counterattack, most on the road between Campoleone and Carroceto. Led by L-4 Cub spotters, P-40s, Spitfires and A-36s bombed and strafed the road followed by DAF, RAF and AAF medium and heavy bombers which were redirected from their usual roles. The Allied air attacks were the heaviest in support of ground forces in one day to that time. Mackensen's grenadiers and armor were shattered and their attack ground to near stop. After regrouping Mackensen's attacks that night were ineffective and allowed the Americans to catch their breath. The 79th Falcons flew 103 of 813 of the MAAF sorties from their base at Capdichino. Of their 13 missions, 11 were in aid of the American 45th Division and all were in the face of heavy AA and small arms fire. The 79th lost one pilot KIA that day. The next day the weather turned horrendously bad and the MAAF was able to fly only 127 effective sorties of which 50 were flown by the 79th.

Throughout the Anzio campaign the Allies maintained a 10:1 aircraft superiority but were unable to shut down the Luftwaffe which flew a disruptive 100 sorties a day. It was the actual small size of Luftflotte 2 that made it a difficult target to exterminate. The Germans were experts in aircraft dispersal and the Allies placed a lower priority on German airfield attacks during this period. The seasonal poor weather canceled a great many Allied air missions and the perilous Allied ground situation caused the majority of the use of their air power for attacks on military targets of all kinds in and around Anzio and Cassino and to interdict supply targets. There was little reserve air power except for immediate targets. Allied air reconnaissance constantly monitored Luftwaffe fields for aircraft buildup that never came so they were not a priority.

During the battle of Anzio the A-36s of the 27th and 86th Fighter-Bomber Groups provided close support flying 1,385 effective sorties between 22 January and 15 February. Losses were heavy in the face of heavy AA defenses, particularly for the 86th. In January eight 86th A-36s were lost, including three on D-Day while in February eleven more were lost, four on the 15th. The 27th lost five. By spring 1944 as the battle lines became static and the German AA defenses were increased and concentrated. More than half the original A-36 fighter-bombers were lost. Since replacements were no longer available the Groups were reduced from four to three squadrons and assigned to the less dangerous general tactical duties of strafing and glide bombing which was not as accurate as dive-bombing, The A-36 groups became so depleted by January 1944, the 27th transitioned to the war weary P-40s which were left behind by the 3rd Fighter Group which left for the CBI. They transferred their remaining A-36s to the 86th. In March 1944, A-36s of the 86th Fighter-Bomber Group flying out of Naples flew 154 sorties in four days during the first battle of Cassino losing five aircraft to ground fire

The infamous and questionable bombing of the Cassino Monastery on 15 February 1944 was mainly conducted by medium bombers which demolished the target. The Germans who had honored the sanctity of the monastery to that point, moved into the rubble that afforded excellent defenses. German 88mm flak at Cassino. Note the white rings on the barrels denoting victories. (US Army)

on 13 March alone. The 86th flew the remaining 56 A-36s supporting the breakout from the Anzio beachhead in May and flew their final missions in the first eight days of July when they finally had to upgrade their A-36s to the P-47D in July in preparation to the invasion of southern France. During May, the 86th flew a great number of close support sorties during the Anzio breakout with its remaining 56 A-36s, losing 14 to AA and ground fire. On the 25th the group claimed 217 motor vehicles destroyed and 245 damaged for the loss of two aircraft and six badly damaged for which the group was awarded the Distinguished Unit Citation.

While the Germans contained the Anzio invasion at the end of January, the Allies launched the First Battle of Cassino. The town was seen as the key to breaking the Gustav Line. II Corps continued to attack the Rapido defenses near Cassino and the French Corps suffered heavy casualties attempted to encircle the town from the north. In early February the US 34th Division also launched a large attack on Cassino but the tenacious German defenders raised a strong defense and stopped the Allied attack. Alexander who ordered Clark to attack Cassino again deployed the New Zealand Corps to the Fifth Army. Monte Cassino overlooked the town from the north and it was concluded that the Germans were using the Benedictine Monastery on its summit as an observation post and a stronghold. On 15 February, Lt.Gen. Bernard Freyburg, commander of the New Zealand Corps, requested the infamous and questionable bombing of the Monastery. On the 15th, Allied air bombardment demolished the target but the Germans who had honored the sanctity of the monastery to that point, moved into the rubble that afforded excellent defenses. The New Zealanders attacked immediately after the bombing but were stopped three days later ending the Second Battle of Cassino.

On 15 March the Allies decided to mount one last attack to breakthrough at Cassino and remove the threat to the Anzio beachhead. They anticipated that the German defenders were exhausted and that after the largest close air support bombardment of the Italian Campaign would cave in. At 0830 the MAAF opened the war's largest close support attack of the war to date. 338 heavy, 176 medium and 300 fighter-bomber sorties augmented a powerful artillery attack. A total of 455 heavy and medium bombers of the USAAF and RAF dropped 992 tons of 1,000lb. bombs (2,223) on the town of Cassino in the morning with erratic results as slightly less than half of the bombs hit within one mile of the town and a number of the bombs hit friendly targets and civilian targets as far as 15 miles away. Attacks by the medium bombers were much more accurate with 90% of their bombs hitting the target. In the afternoon, despite increasing overcast, two flights of fighter-bombers took off every ten minutes over a three-hour period and the 188 aircraft effectively dropped 69 tons of bombs on German targets around Cassino. The New Zealanders again attacked but found the streets of Cassino blocked with debris stopping their tanks that were to support the advance against experienced German troops who did not crack under the intense bombardment. It began to rain and the huge bomb craters filled with water and the ground in the area became impassable. On the 16th fighter-bombers flew 325 sorties against German positions and medium bombers hit rear area reserves and supply dumps. On the 17th over 500 fighter-bomber missions were flown against German gun positions on the hills above the town After eight days the Third Battle for Cassino ended in defeat as the Germans held the line and the New Zealand Corps was so depleted that it was disbanded after the battle.

From the middle of January to the end of March the Fifth Army had suffered 52,150 casualties of which over 30,000 were against the Gustav Line. During this period fighter-bombers had flown 4,312 sorties and dropped 1,771 tons of bombs and bombers had flown 6,345 sorties and dropped 11,043 tons of bombs. The legacy of Pantelleria was evident in the tons and tons of bombs and artillery shells that fell on Cassino. It was expected that after this bombardment that the army would wipe out one strongpoint manned by dazed enemy troops after another. The bombardment did devastate the town's buildings and temporarily shock the defenders. But it also produced barriers to the quick following attack of troops and armor and allowed the defenders time to regroup. Sir John Slessor wrote to Ira Eaker (*Central Blue*, Cassell, UK, 1956):

"Another lesson which I think has been confirmed in the recent fighting in Italy is that the bomber is not a battlefield weaponÖ.

"As a general rule I am convinced that bombers of any class should be used on the battlefield as a last resort in defense. Except in those conditions, even your fighters and light bombers will contribute far more effectively to the army's battle by paralyzing the movement of enemy supply and reserves behind the battlefield than by attacking strong points, battery positions etc. on the battlefield- that is the job of artillery."

It would not be until 23 May that the 125 day Anzio beachhead stalemate would be breached by the VI Corps. During that time 478,407 tons of supplies would be off-loaded as Lucas built up his forces. The Germans had been stripped of reserves to reinforce the Cassino front.

After the Sicilian campaign the nucleus of the 12th Air Force was sent to England to form the 9th Air Force. After flying in North Africa, Pantelleria and Sicily the 324th Fighter Group was deactivated and restored and retrained as part of the 12th Air Force and

AM Arthur Slessor wrote to Lt.Gen. Ira Eaker that: "Another lesson which I think has been confirmed in the recent fighting in Italy is that the bomber is not a battlefield weapon.... As a general rule I am convinced that bombers of any class should be used on the battlefield as a last resort in defense." (USAF)

based at Cercola to support the Anzio and Cassino battles. Lt. Richard Lander of the 315th Fighter Squadron described the transition (*Aces, Pilots and Aircraft of the 9th*, 12th & 15th USAAF, David Weatherill, Kookaburra, Australia, 1978):

"Our group was the last in the European Theater to fly the P-40. We inherited the aircraft from many other groups as they were outfitted with new aircraft. This could have been the result of our successful operation with this aircraft and our excellent record of support of the ground troops in Italy. We were specifically requested by the theater commander to support the Cassino and Anzio Campaigns in close support by dive-bombing and strafing. One of our 'closest support' missions was to bomb with 1,000 pound bombs within 75 yards of our own troops, a task we carried out successfully. A unit citation was awarded to the group for this and other support missions. We had no dive brakes on these aircraft so that when we started our dive, gravity took over and our speed was uncontrolled until we pulled out. I point this out to emphasize that we took a fighter and made a fighter-bomber out of it with a fair amount of success. We were also under short rations, as preparations for the Normandy campaign were under way. As a result we were on the short end of the supplies as everything was being sent to Great Britain. In many cases we had to make do with what we had as nothing new was in the offing."

Fighter/Fighter-Bomber Interdiction Operations: Anzio/Cassino (1 January to 14 March 1944)

	Fighter/Fighter-Bombers		**Bombers***	
Targets	**Sorties**	**Bomb Tons**	**Sorties**	**Bomb Tons**
Marshaling Yards	366	158.1	2,723	5,061.7
Railroad/Bridges	1,220	552.7	1,267	2,320.1
Roads/Bridges	1,146	482.8	1,390	2,456.6
Troops/Motor Transport	408	137.6	188	145.0
Dumps	325	134.9	163	159.3
Harbors/Docks/ Shipping	679	233.6	536	792.1
Misc.	168	71.2	78	107.4
Totals	4,312	1,770.9	6,345	11,042.8

*Heavy, medium, light

19

Operation STRANGLE
15 March - 10 May 1944

USAAF Fighter/Fighter-Bomber Order of Battle
3 April 1944
Mediterranean Allied Air Forces (MAAF)
Mediterranean Allied Tactical Air Force (MATAF)
Twelfth Air Force
XII Air Support Command (ASC)
27th Fighter-Bomber Group (P-40)
86th Fighter-Bomber Group (A-36)
324th Fighter Group (P-40)
79th Fighter Group (P-40 & some P-47s)
Desert Air Force
57th Fighter Group (P-47)

Operation STRANGLE initially was not a pre-determined plan but an expansion of the continuing air battles beginning at the end of February and continuing to mid-March. It began on 15 March at the start of the Third Battle of Cassino. For the second time, Gen. Bernard Freyburg's New Zealand Corps tried to break the deadlock at Cassino. As discussed earlier, the bombardment gave the Germans useful defensive positions in the rubble and delayed the deployment of Allied armor. Continued inclement weather slowed the attack that was called off on 23 March. During the remainder of the STRANGLE campaign the Anzio and Rapido fronts were quiet.

Operation STRANGLE was to become the first full-scale, purposely planned air interdiction campaign in the MTO and led to establishing an interdiction doctrine. At this time of ground inactivity, Allied air commanders felt that air power could force the German retreat by the destruction of their supply capabilities. Wreckage of an Italian rail station during STRANGLE (USAF)

The 19 March MATAF Bombing Directive No.2. was issued by MATAF Headquarters. It was essentially similar to its directives of 18 and 25 February and defined the objective of the MATAF as "one of interdiction of enemy communications apart from whatever counter-air force and direct support activities that might be necessary." An interdiction belt in central Italy was chosen and assigned to components of the MATAF. The MASAF was continuing to participate in POINTBLANK where its responsibility was to attack rail targets in northern Italy, out of the range of medium and fighter-bombers. The Coastal Air Force (MACAF) was to attack ships, docks and harbors. To maintain the high level of interdiction against the large number of prescribed targets all the resources of the MATAF, medium, light and fighter-bombers were required to fly multiple sorties. Fighter-bombers flew more often (11,389 sorties vs. 10,299 by the heavy, medium and light bombers) as they could fly in weather that grounded the bombers and the ground stalemate released them from close support sorties. This directive was to become known as Operation STRANGLE as it was designed to concentrate air attacks on transportation and supplies in a belt about 100 miles north of the front line to strangle the movement of essential supplies to the front.

STRANGLE was to become the first full-scale, purposely planned air interdiction campaign in the MTO and led to establishing an interdiction doctrine. At this time of ground inactivity, Allied air commanders felt that air power could force the German retreat by the destruction of their supply capabilities. Mussolini's promise to the Italian people was to make the trains run on time but the Allied Air Forces were to make them run not at all. It was estimated that 96% of Italy's oil and 80% of her coal were imported by rail and it was by rail that troops and military supplies could be brought down from the north. An "interdiction belt" was set up in central Italy that was to lie between a northern line drawn from east to west from Spezia to Rimini and a southern line drawn from east to west from Cecina to Ancona. An intensive air offensive was launched against all rail lines in this belt its intention was to prevent all supplies from reaching their destination. There was a debate between the MAAF command and analysts over the most vulnerable rail targets. A group led by Sir Solly Zuckerman concluded that supplies transported over the Italian rail network could not be stopped as the system had too much capacity and only 5% was needed for military requirements. He thought that the rail system could be so disrupted that less efficient and fuel hungry road transport would have to haul supplies hundreds of miles and could be stopped and destroyed at crucial bottlenecks. Zuckerman advocated strategic attacks on the marshaling yards that were easier to locate and being larger were easier to hit. These marshaling yards were to have major repair and maintenance facilities and contain large concentrations of locomotives and rolling stock. The continual attack and disruption of major yards was to interrupt the make up and scheduling of trains causing them to be rerouted and dispersed many miles over passable portions of the system. But, unlike the French and German rail systems, the Italian system did not have many of this type of large marshaling yard. Other strategists, the "Interdiction" faction, recommended tactical attacks on bridges, defiles and rail lines were more worthwhile even though they were more difficult to strike and destroy. A MAAF directive of 19 March 1944 specified rail targets with the Florence-Rome line was given top priority. There was a wide-ranging list of targets that placated both the marshaling yard and bridge advocates in the MAAF. The German supply complex had sustained heavy damage, particularly in locomotive shortage and track cuts, during January and February. However, using locomotives and rolling stock loaded in Germany and moved into Italy would easily make up locomotive losses in Italy. By mid-March, interdiction attacks on the Italian rail system

The Italian rail system did not have many large marshaling yards to attack and disrupt the entire rail system. The "Interdiction" faction, recommended tactical attacks on bridges, defiles and rail lines were more worthwhile even though they were more difficult to strike and destroy. Note the partial German reconstruction. (USAF)

prevented trains from moving south of Rome. Supply to the fronts from the end of the rail lines was by motor transport that was attacked from the air and hindered by attacks on bridges and road junctions. Motor transport was slowed down by vehicle, fuel, tire and spare part shortages, along with a high accident rate. Coastal shipping played an insignificant role in the supply situation. Commonly used types of ammunition were in short supply and needed to be rationed.

In November 1943, the 325th Fighter Group was the first P-47 group to be assigned to the MTO joining the recently formed strategic 15th Air Force. From March to September 1943 they had compiled an exceptional record over North Africa, Pantelleria, Sicily and Sardinia flying P-40s. Their assignment to escort heavy-bombers was an entirely new concept to the group. A detachment of three 8th Air Force veterans was sent to the group to teach the tried and true tactics used over the ETO. On 19 December the "Checkertails" were assigned to cover the withdrawal of bombers from a mission to Innsbruck. On the way back, Capt. Frank Collins left the unit to strafe the airdrome at Ancona and destroyed a Ju-52 transport. Maj. Bill Chick dropped down to strafe a 200ft. boat near Rozzeto di Abrizi and barely escaped the AA fire. The group flew numerous escort missions in January and it was found that the Luftwaffe had been scrambling its fighters about a quarter of an hour before they arrived. A plan was devised to send in the Thunderbolts before the bombers to catch the Luftwaffe on the ground on the four airfields around Venice. On 30 January, Lt.Col. Robert Baseler led 60 P-47s from their base at Foggia across the Adriatic at 50ft. to escape radar detection. When the group reached the Gulf of Venice they climbed and headed toward the large airdrome at Villaorba where they caught a mixed bag of 60 aircraft: Me-109s, Macchi 202s and some FW-190s and Ju-88s scrambling to take off to intercept the bombers. A number of Ju-52s and other assorted aircraft also scrambled to escape the attack. Maj. Herschel Green described the action from his combat report:

"We arrived as scheduled, 15 minutes before the bombers were to hit. Shortly after leveling out, I spotted approximately 15 Ju-52s flying at about 1,000ft. My section of four fighters swung around to get the sun at our backs and then went into a dive toward the enemy. By the time we reached the level of the Ju-52s, they were strung out in such a manner that each fighter could fire at several aircraft as we passed through their loose and long formation. I was able to down four in this one pass. When we turned for second attack, they were all either down or in such close proximity to a couple of airfields that ground fire forced us away. Some of them apparently crash-landed off the airfields to keep from being shot down. I don't recall the number shot down by the three other fighters. We never did get back to altitude, for by this time, the remainder of the group was meeting opposition and we were kept busy taking care of the enemy aircraft that hit the deck in attempting to escape. I was able to get a Macchi 202 and a Dornier 217 for a total of six."

Air superiority was established and bombers could fly with little or no escort. The Allied strategic bombing attacks,

POINTBLANK, on German fighter aircraft manufacturing plants reduced the number of fighters and redirected many from the MTO to the defense of Germany. The capability of those remaining Luftwaffe fighters was decreased by attacks on Italian airfields. This freed the fighters to conduct interdiction missions and the fighter-bombers could fly small flights of four or eight aircraft, allowing a continuous air attack on the interdiction belt.

During the first two weeks of the STRANGLE (15-28 March), 3,927 interdiction sorties dropping 5,734.6 tons of bombs were flown by the MAAF: 1,316 sorties/2,917.4 tons on marshaling yards, 1,272 sorties/1,470.3 tons on rail lines and bridges. After these attacks, Allied intelligence determined that the attacks on marshaling yards had less effect on the movement of German supplies than did the attacks on bridges, tracks and defiles. The reason was that the Germans did not utilize Italian marshaling yards as they assembled the trains in Germany and routed them directly to the nearest available railhead to the front. From this point until the end of the campaign 2,346 sorties/4,506 tons were flown against marshaling yards and 10,075 sorties/9,560.8 tons were flown against rail lines and bridges. By 24 March, medium bombers and fighter-bombers had cut every rail line supplying the German front and kept them cut until the final day of STRANGLE. On 19 March Mt. Vesuvius made headlines as it erupted violently throwing volcanic ash 20,000ft. into the air causing the 57th Fighter Group to evacuate their P-47s from Cerola Airfield and curtail its activity for a period.

During STRANGLE, on 19 March Mt. Vesuvius made headlines as it erupted violently throwing volcanic ash 20,000ft. into the air causing the 57th Fighter Group to evacuate their P-47s from Cerola Airfield and curtail its activity for a period. (USAF)

During the next month (29 March-25 April) the MAAF flew 10,470 sorties and dropped 11,436.8 tons of bombs on interdiction targets divided among:

1) 6,303 sorties (4,405 by fighter-bombers)/5,886 tons against rail lines and bridges,
2) 915 sorties (478 by fighter-bombers)/591.1 tons against dumps
3) 852 sorties (173 by fighter-bombers)/1,334.1 tons on harbors docks and shipping.

At the end of the period it became evident that the air offensive alone could not force the Germans to retreat. On 28 April the MAAF issued a new directive that "defined the object of the air operations as being as to make it impossible for the enemy to maintain his forces on their present line in Italy in the face of a combined Allied offensive." The "combined Allied offensive" mentioned in the directive meant that it would be necessary for Allied ground forces to put pressure on the Germans through brutal ground combat. On 15 April the 79th Fighter Group, the Comanches, used a full bomb load on their P-47s for the first time hanging a 1,000lb. bomb on each wing and a 500lb. bomb under the fuselage.

During the final two weeks (26 April-10 May) the MAAF flew 7,291 sorties (3,861 by fighter-bombers) and dropped 8,203.4 tons mainly against rail lines and bridges: 3,772 sorties (2,537 by fighter-bombers)/3,674.8 tons. The severe damage to the rail system forced the Germans to rely on other transport nets:

Motorized transport drew the attention of 1,077 sorties (963 by fighter-bombers)/774.2 tons;
Harbors, docks and shipping: 452 sorties (203 by fighter-bombers)
Dumps: 528 sorties (309 by fighter-bombers)/299.1 tons.

The Reichsbahn made up divisional supply trains in Austria, north of the Alpine passes and unloaded them onto road transport north of Rome and later north of Florence and at times north of the Apennine passes. Therefore, the bombing of marshaling yards was not necessary as loaded trains by-passed them. After the battles of February and early March had depleted German ammunition supplies, the German Quartermasters could not replenish them and they remained perilously low through April and into the May DIADEM battles. The German 14th Army's attack against the US VI Corps at Anzio was discontinued because of ammunition shortage, as was Von Senger's withdrawal from the Gustav Line. During the DIADEM battles the Allies also suffered from an ammunition shortage and evidence suggests that overall, German troops had sufficient ammunition to meet these attacks as they dropped back to existing ammunition depots. STRANGLE had destroyed fuel and material and labor was expended to repair the damage. But the effort could have been better expended on stopping the movement of troops rather than material, especially in January and February, when the movement of troops occurred between the Gustav Line and Lombardy Plain to reinforce Anzio. Interdiction was found to be effective in conjunction with ground operations but that did not happen from mid-March until the opening of DIADEM in May.

STRANGLE did not achieve its goal of a denying adequate supplies to the Wehrmacht, because the inactive ground situation did not force the Germans to use supplies at a level to cause critical shortages. The Germans employed every means to bring up necessary supplies. Pictured: 57th Fighter Group P-47s attacked this retreating German horse-drawn artillery column. (USAF)

During both STRANGLE and DIADEM fighter-bombers and medium bombers flew almost equal numbers of sorties. The bombers concentrated on marshaling yards while the fighter-bombers took on the rail and road networks. B-25s of the 310th Bomb Group attacking Po River bridges. (USAF)

STRANGLE did not achieve its goal of a denying adequate supplies to the Wehrmacht, because the inactive ground situation did not force the Germans to use stores at a level to cause critical shortages. On 7 April Eaker wrote Arnold: "What we need more than anything is some Army support....What we ask the Army to do is put enough pressure on the enemy to force him to discharge some ammunition and further reduce his reserves of fuel and ammunition." The most significant effects of STRANGLE was that it severely handicapped the German supply effort and tactical mobility which would become evident in the next phase of Allied operations, the intensive ground fighting of DIADEM. It did cause a gradual loss of German tactical mobility as motor transport was diverted from tactical to logistical service. During STRANGLE Field Marshal Kesselring and the Germans again demonstrated that they were masters of supply and defense.

Fighter/Fighter-Bomber Interdiction Operations
STRANGLE (15 March-10 May 1944)

	Fighter/Fighter-Bombers		Bombers*	
Targets	**Sorties**	**Bomb Tons**	**Sorties**	**Bomb Tons**
Marshaling Yards	463	229.8	3,199	7,193.5
Rail Lines/Bridges	7,414	3,840.4	3,933	7,190.7
Roads/Bridges	1,229	711.2	295	473.6
Troops/Transport	741	339.1	198	191.1
Dumps	1,076	486.3	716	638.7
Misc.	68	34.0	—	—
Harbors, Docks, Shipping	398	212.8	1,958	3,832.9
Totals	11,389	5,853.6	10,299	19,520.5

* Heavy, Medium and Light

Celebrated Hollywood film director, William Wyler (*Little Foxes*, 1941, *Best Years of Our Lives*, 1946 and *Ben Hur*, 1959), chronicled the fighter-bomber activity of this period for the Air Force in his outstanding documentary, "*Thunderbolt*." In 1944, Wyler had directed the documentary, Memphis Belle, and was awarded the DSC and promoted to Lt. Colonel for his efforts. He and another future director, Capt. John Sturgis (*The Great Escape*, 1963), also served as cinematographers. The movie was introduced by actor Jimmy Stewart and narrated by Lloyd Bridges and starred the pilots and ground crews of the 57th Fighter Group, specifically the 65th Fighter Squadron under Lt.Col. Gilbert Wymond, when it was based at Alto, Corsica. Col. Archie Knight was the technical advisor. The film followed the Fighter Squadron as it participated for two months during Operation STRANGLE for which it was awarded the Presidential Unit Citation. Much of the film was taken from innovative remote 16mm cameras mounted under the wings, on the tails and in the cockpit of the Squadron's P-47s. Start and stop toggles in the cockpit allowed the pilots to operate the cameras anytime during a ground attack sortie. A B-25 camera plane took additional footage of the P-47s in the air. The 43-minute Technicolor movie was completed in October 1945 but was not released to the general public until 1947.

Lt.Col. Gilbert Wymond of the 65th Fighter Squadron of the 57th Fighter Group, being filmed for the William Wyler documentary "*Thunderbolt*" filmed in 1944 when the unit was based at Alto, Corsica. Capt. John Sturgis who would direct the *Great Escape* (1963) is on the far right. (USAF)

20

Operation DIADEM
11 May - 22 June 1944

Fighter/Fighter-Bomber Order of Battle 11 May 1944
Mediterranean Allied Air Force (MAAF)
Mediterranean Tactical Air Force (MATAF)
XII Tactical Air Command*
27th Fighter-Bomber Group (P-40 & some P-47s)
86th Fighter-Bomber Group (A-36)
324th Fighter Group (P-40)
79th Fighter Group (P-47)
Desert Air Force (DAF)
No USAAF units
87th Wing
57th Fighter Group (P-47)**
*Changed 15 April 1944; was XII Air Support Command
** Administratively part of the Desert Air Force

As an air interdiction campaign, DIADEM was a continuation of STRANGLE with two differences. The zone of interdiction was deepened to all rail lines crossing the Apennines. This would put 140 miles (STRANGLE had 100 miles) between German railheads and the front that was to further burden the motor transport system. The second was to increase night interdiction by light bombers to put around the clock pressure on the German supply lines. In the previously mentioned directive of 28 April, The Outline Plan for Air Participation in Operation DIADEM, the MAAF, in effect amended STRANGLE "to make it impossible for the enemy to maintain his forces on his present line in Italy in the face of combined Allied offensive." The directive specified three air assignments:

1) Maintain air superiority
2) Maintain the obstruction of German supply movement in the Rome area so as to decrease the supplies available to front line troops to such a low level that they would be unable to offer any sustained opposition to the impending Allied ground offensive
3) Assist the ground offensive with ground support sorties.

Locomotives and rolling stock were the primary targets in DIADEM's main objective of maintaining the obstruction of German supply movement in the Rome area. Here a locomotive boiler was damaged by a direct hit by a 100lb. bomb. (USAF)

The directive divided the plan into three phases: a preparatory phase from 15 March to D-Day, an assault phase during the first few days of the offensive and a sustained offensive phase afterwards. The primary objective of DIADEM was to eliminate the German military as a viable force in Italy along with the propaganda benefits of capturing Rome and to prevent the Germans from siphoning troops to France. In March 1944, the Germans had invested 23 divisions in Italy and an Allied ground offensive was needed to coordinate with air offensive. The Allies were importing 32,180 tons of supplies daily while the Germans opposing the Allied Fifth and Eighth Armies were subsisting on 4,000 tons per day in a static defensive posture which was 1,000-1,500 tons less than needed once the Allied offensive got underway.

The DIADEM close air plan divided air support obligation for ground forces. The Desert Air Forces would operate in the west with the XII TAC (the renamed XII ASC) and the newly formed

Fifth Army Commander, Lt.Gen. Mark Clark made his controversial decision on 1 June 1944 to alter his attack plans and move toward Rome. Kesselring had no plan to defend Rome but continued fighting as long as possible so that the Fourteenth Army could retreat across the Tiber. However, Clark's decision to take Rome allowed the battered German armies to escape to the north in a frantic but masterful retreat that continued until the 20th when they arrived at a newly prepared Trasimene defensive line. (US Army)

XII TAC was to operate with the Fifth and Eighth Armies until the direction of the ground battles permitted the reestablishment of the previous Fifth Army/XII TAC and Eighth Army/DAF alliances. For interdiction missions, the XII TAC was deployed to the indefinite area south of Rome, the central area north of Rome to Lake Trasemene, and the Tyrrhenian coast as far north as Lake Bolsena. The US 8th Fighter Wing based on Corsica was assigned the west coast area north from Lake Bolsena and bounded in the east by a line through Lake Trasemene, Arezzo and Florence. DAF was assigned to the eastern area from a line east of Rome to the Adriatic and then north to the east of Lake Trasemene and Arezzo. Tactical reconnaissance was to be covered by three squadrons with the Eighth Army and two with the Fifth and were interchangeable.

On 28 April, a directive was issued calling for the intensification of air interdiction attacks and the reduction of Luftwaffe air power by attacking airfields to D-Day. The Tactical Air Forces were to operate south of the Pisa-Rimini line and the Strategic Air Forces to the north of that. The Coastal Air Force was to unite with the Tactical and Strategic Air Forces in hammering Italian west coast ports and shipping. Both fighter-bombers and medium bombers were to cut all rail lines south of Pisa-Rimini causing German rail traffic to concentrate in northern Italian marshaling yards where it would be attacked by heavy bombers. Besides attacks on the air and transportation targets, other vital targets of the preparatory phase were to destroy enemy supply dumps (in order): gasoline, oil and ammunition,. The assault phase added close air support of the D-Day attacks by the Tactical Air Force and an attack on German corps and army headquarters by the Strategic Air Forces. The sustained offensive phase ordered the Tactical and Coastal Air Forces to continue undiminished attacks supporting the ground offensive with the Strategic Air Forces returning to its usual strategic capacity. On 15 May, MAAF HQ amended the air plan in Operations Order No. 35, BIGOT-DIADEM. It ordered a maximum effort by all available aircraft to support D-Day and slated specific targets for attention on D-Day plus1.

Ground forces opened Operation DIADEM on 11 May 1944, with three fundamental objectives: 1) to crack the Gustav Line, 2) to overwhelm the Hitler Line which was being prepared to defend the Liri Valley behind the Cassino front, 3) to break the Anzio stalemate and link up with the Allied Armies moving up from the south to cut off the German Tenth Army.

On 11 May, the British Eighth Army was assigned to mount the primary attack, a powerful offensive to overrun major defensive positions on Gustav Line near Cassino. The US Fifth Army on the west was to launch a secondary attack simultaneously to aid the British attack. The opening British attack on Cassino was again driven back by the Germans but the Americans succeeded in breaking through on their front. The II Corps and French Expeditionary Corps (FEC) of the Fifth Army attacked through the mountainous terrain and advanced toward Anzio. The VI Corps attacked from inside the Anzio beachhead eleven days after D-Day and two days later met the II Corps. The united forces then drove toward the Tiber Valley, intending to split the German Tenth and Fourteenth Armies, cutting off the retreat of the Tenth and pushing the broken Fourteenth westward toward Rome and the Mediterranean. It was

Alexander's intention to cut off the German Tenth Army at Valmontone and under the circumstances there should have been no problems. Besides the German Army's supply problems and the constant air attacks, its leadership was in disarray. Army Group Chief of Staff, Gen. Siegfried Westphal and 10th Army CO, Heinrich von Vietinghoff both became ill and Mackensen was relieved of command of the Fourteenth Army on 2 June. At this time (1 June), Fifth Army Commander, Lt.Gen. Mark Clark made his controversial decision to alter his attack plans and move toward Rome. Kesselring had no plan to defend Rome and on 2 June asked permission to evacuate the city. He was told to continue fighting as long as possible so that the Fourteenth Army could retreat across the Tiber. However, Clark's decision to take Rome allowed the battered German armies to escape to the north in a frantic but masterful retreat that continued until the 20th when they arrived at a newly prepared Trasimene defensive line. In their retreat the Germans were forced to travel along roads surrounded by steep Ravines and mountains, making German transport sitting ducks for fighter-bomber attacks. Between 1-6 June 1,100 vehicles were destroyed and another 1,100 damaged but these attacks did not stop the resourceful Germans from escaping. The "Pantelleria Effect" led the Allies to forget the lesson the Germans learned at Dunkirk; that it took an army to prevent an army from moving. The Trasimene Line was a quickly built line was intended to delay the now determined Allied pursuit until Kesselring could complete the fortified Gothic Line then being prepared across the northern Apennine mountains which lie just south of the Po Valley. On 22 June, the Germans again stopped the Allied advance bringing DIADEM to a close.

The initial devastating D-Day, 11 May air attack came as a complete surprise to the German commanders especially as their command posts and control centers were targeted by 276 sorties that seriously restricted command and combat for the next 24 hours. The catalyst for the Allied ground offensive thrust through the Gustav Line during the first week was close support and air interdiction sorties by all types of aircraft against all types of targets. Heavy bombers hit marshaling yards and harbors, docks and shipping. Medium bombers also hit harbors and shipping but the rail and road net was their primary target (917 sorties/1,824 tons). Fighter-bombers cut rail lines and bridges with 1,407 sorties and 873 tons, hit the road net with 815 sorties and 401.1 tons and flew an additional 123 sorties/85.1 tons on command posts to prevent their restoration to normal from the first attacks.

The bad weather in the second week (18-24 May) grounded heavy and medium bombers for several days and total sorties dropped over one-third to 4,244 of which fighter-bombers flew 2,267. The fighter-bombers actually increased their efforts against the road net with 1,053 sorties but flew only 677 sorties against the rail system. They also flew a great number of close support missions as the Fifth Army broke through the Gustav Line and the US II Corps advanced along the coast and the VI Corps broke out of the Anzio beachhead to meet up with the II Corps.

On 24 May the 79th Fighter Group had flown its 20,000th combat sortie and on that day had set a single day record for a fighter group by dropping 153 tons of bombs. Falcon ground crews worked unceasingly from their base at Pomigliano to rearm and refuel their P-47s that flew two or three missions that day. The 86th Squadron, the Comanches, particularly distinguished itself during this period. On the 26th it flew a mission south of Rome, attacking a supply train getting 16 direct hits. The 20-car train was totally destroyed when the last hit exploded an ammunition car sending bits and pieces of locomotive and rolling stock high into the air. The 86th then hit a large truck convoy in two attacks and it too exploded into a violent end. On 4 June the Comanches outdid themselves when they set a single day record for a single squadron when they destroyed 114 trucks and armored vehicles on a road north of Rome. The entire 79th was credited with 121 motor transport and 154 destroyed.

During the third week (25-31 May) the MAAF flew 5,119 interdiction sorties dropping 6,443.3 tons of bombs divided almost equally between the rail and road nets. Fighter-bombers flew 930 and 1,189 of their total 2,356 weekly sorties against rail and road targets respectively. During this week the fighter-bombers flew close support attacks in the Velletri-Valmontone area where Kesselring was attempting to contain the VI and II Corps from driving a wedge between his Tenth and Fourteenth Armies. When the Anzio and Cassino fronts met and the Germans were in full retreat there were fewer supply dumps, fixed positions and strong points and command posts to hit and Armed Reconnaissance became the main fighter-bomber mission seeking out targets of opportunity particularly transport and troop concentrations. In his war diary, Gen. Heinrich von Vietinghoff bemoaned the potency of the fighter-bomber: "The effectiveness of the fighter-bomber lay in that their presence alone over the battlefield paralyzed every movement." From 11 May to 15 June, the Allies counted 290 Axis aircraft abandoned on 14 captured airfields. On 29 May 19 FW-190 fighters were lost during an Allied air attack on their field at Piacenza and all FW-190 fighters in Italy were withdrawn from operations. Two days later, after suffering crippling losses FW-190 fighter-bomber unit SG4 was withdrawn from Italy to rest and refit and then to be sent to the Eastern Front. At the end of May, the Luftwaffe High Command in Germany ordered that all Gruppen based outside the Reich had to transfer a Staffel to Reich homeland defense. The Luftwaffe relegated ground support to a secondary role and strategic and air defense of the Reich became its primary function. Flak guns and radar were moved to northern Italy to defend against strategic Allied bombers flying to bomb targets in Germany, Austria and Hungary. The ever-resourceful Germans also used AA guns in an anti-tank and anti-aircraft role to hamper the Allied advance while retreating to the north. The Germans lost over 200 AA guns between Rome and the Apennines; 90 to enemy action and air attacks and the remainder were destroyed by their crews for want of transportation to move them.

The greatest number of weekly interdiction sorties of the air campaign were flown between 1-7 June with 5,185 of the 6,599 sorties being directed almost equally at the road and rail net. Fighter-bombers flew 1,060 (of 2,286) and 1,377 (of 2,899) sorties against the rail and road nets, respectively and 304 (of 399, the most for the campaign) sorties against troops and military transport. They supported the Allied breakthrough the Gustav Line at Valmontone which drove through the Hitler Line 75 miles to the north and northwest and was not stopped until it arrived at the Trasimeno Line two weeks

Both Operations STRANGLE and DIADEM targeted the Italian transportation system. Here spans of the road and rail bridges over the Piave River in northeastern Italy have been destroyed. (USAF)

later. The interdiction campaign harassed the retreating Wehrmacht by causing roadblocks at bridges and road junctions with fighter-bombers attacking by day and light bombers at night.

During the final two weeks (8-22 June), the MAAF interdiction attacks subsided due to poor weather: 7,646 sorties/8,632.7 tons. Again road and rail systems were primarily hit with 1,188 against rail and 2,316 sorties against road targets of 3,996 total sorties. As targets became more and more scarce the Germans protected those remaining with mobile flak batteries and fighter-bomber casualties became higher. On 9 June the DAF discontinued strafing sorties due to the lack of targets and heavy losses.

The Luftwaffe averaged about 50 sorties per day and at no time exceeded 200. The largest Luftwaffe attack occurred on the night of 12/13 May on US B-25 bases on Corsica. During the first week of the attack there were two missions against US infantry in the Minturno area and a few smaller attacks on Allied shipping and supply bases in the Naples area.

Results of DIADEM

During the DIADEM air interdiction campaign (11 May through 22 June 1944) the MAAF flew 30,079 sorties (13,747 by fighter-bombers) dropping 39,821.9 tons (7,445.1 by fighter-bombers) of bombs. The rail (excluding marshaling yards) and road nets received the brunt of the attacks with 21,970 sorties (12,012 by fighter-bombers)/26,395.6 tons (6,785.5 by fighter-bombers) divided about equally between the two targets. The marshaling yards in the north congested by rail traffic unable to proceed any further south received 3,525 sorties flown mainly by heavy bombers. Harbors, docks and shipping received 1,863 sorties/3,580.7 tons (295 sorties/136.5 tons by fighter-bombers) followed by attacks on troops and military transport, 1,317 sorties and 914.5 tons mainly by fighter-bombers (736 sorties/221.2 tons). It was found that before a bombing mission a preliminary attack by formations of fighter-bombers quieted German AA opposition and accuracy and the following bombers achieved more damaging results and fewer losses.

During DIADEM the Germans lost 25,000 men, 2,000 machine guns, 500 heavy machine guns, 429 anti-tank guns, 148 tanks and 295 artillery pieces. Because of their air superiority, between 12 May and 22 June the MAAF claimed only 176 Luftwaffe destroyed, 44 probables and 93 damaged. The MAAF lost 438 aircraft the great majority to flak as the Germans concentrated their AA guns at all principal points along their road and rail net.

The German supply system was only satisfactory at the onset of DIADEM due excellent logistical management and the inactive combat situation. But there was no regular rail traffic to Rome and regular traffic was stopped at Florence where it was off loaded and transferred to motor transport. Due to attrition from air attacks and wear and tear the Army Groups in the interdiction zone could only supply two-thirds of the motor transport needed to move these supplies to the front and their Armies in the combat zone had to supply the remaining one-third from tactical transport. The Tenth Army Quartermaster's report of 15 May described this predicament: "Because of the great distances to the army support bases and the necessary troop movements, the corps and divisions are unable to take care of their own supplies. The army is therefore compelled to use its transport capacity to support the troops and their tactical movements." The renewed Allied ground offensive had a "Catch-22" effect on the German armies. They needed their motor transport returned for tactical duties (e.g. movement of troops and local supply) but the increased supply requirement; especially fuel and ammunition, due to combat could not be met.

The cutting of one rail line in Central Italy caused an increase in traffic on other lines that resulted in the congregation of rolling stock, which in turn, became easier targets, particularly for strafing attacks. The line cuts could cause delays of supplies as far back as Germany where trains were already loaded and waiting. Priority supplies had to be unloaded and reloaded to arrive at the front. Trains carrying ammunition and fuel and then those carrying weapons, and armored vehicles were given priority. The concentrated attacks on the important Brenner Pass line led the Germans to concentrate heavier AA defenses there which reduced the protection at other points and made them more vulnerable to air attack. The only repairs attempted on the rail system south of Florence was to repair some bridges temporarily to allow valuable locomotives and rolling stock to escape north of the interdiction lines. There was an increase in rail cutting activity that demanded immediate attention to maintain the flow of supplies. The widespread and recurring damage to the rail and road systems necessitated more and more repair personnel. The core of the repair organization were engineers but it became increasingly necessary to employ civilians and troops and materials that could have been better used to support combat activities. The management of the German rail system in Italy was tenacious, skillful and flexible in the shuttling and transloading supplies. But as the air attacks continued the remaining rail system was cut into smaller and smaller portions and it began to deteriorate.

The incessant air attacks rendered the rail net less able to operate inside the interdiction zone forcing Kesselring to rely on the road net to move supplies from the northern edge of the interdiction zone to the combat zone. It was critical that the roads remain open. The German Tenth Army Quartermaster ordered, "every officer in the supply troops must become involved in repairing road destruction and disentangling traffic jams without regard to his own person." A Tenth Army Quartermaster's report of 28 May stated: " The systematic enemy air operations against supply routes and traffic junctions are threatening, despite the most stringent traffic control measuresÖto hamper traffic to such an extent that grave supply disruptions are expected." Two days later his report went on to state: "Because of the increasing air strikes against the remaining roads in the combat area, there are constant road disruptions and severe losses of troop and supply vehicles. Even though all available officers are being committed to get the supply columns through, the times required for round trips are increasing so that it is no longer possible to calculate the amount of time needed for these trips. Hence unloading and transport performance is declining steadily." While the daily amount of supplies delivered was adequate to meet the demands of an inactive battlefield on 11 May once DIADEM was launched the daily expenditure of ammunition and fuel in combat increased as the supply capability decreased through increased motor vehicle losses and traffic delays. As noted previously, the front line vehicles were needed for tactical duties once the Allied attack began. The gravity of the situation is described in the report of Army Group C Wehrmacht Patrol Service for June 1944:

"As a consequence of direct combat and especially of strafing, many troop vehicles broke down, so that even guns had to be transported by hitchhiking. Since no more transport could be rounded up at the front, units sent commandos to the rear, as far as northern Italy, with orders to requisition vehicles, bicycles, and horses at any price."

Even Wehrmacht vehicles, parked briefly without guard (contrary to Army orders) were not safe from these wild commandos. The commanding general issued a sharp order on 23 June against this program and assigned patrols to stop it.

On the day Rome fell, the German Fourteenth Army War Diary for 5 June portrayed the chaotic transport situation:

"The roads leading north on 4 June, despite traffic controls, were so filled with burning motor vehicles and ammunition, and there were so many bomb craters and air attacks, that no north-south traffic was possible. Hence the troops currently have only small amounts of ammunition and fuel. The corps has no convoy capacity to bring up ammunition and fuel tonight....The attempt to move fuel and ammunition by day has proved to be futile because of air attack and it led to great losses of vehicles."

The limitations put on the goods carrying capacity of the supply system by air attacks caused the exclusion of the transport of food from Germany that could be purchased from Italian agriculture and processing complex. This resulted in rising price levels and inflation. Ammunition and fuel were the two most essential items required by the army to stop the Allied offensive. Ammunition supplies to the front line depots and troops were sufficient to continually supply the low daily requirements of an inactive front line but adequate only to meet the first few days requirement once the Allied offensive began. Fuel was vital to both combat and supply vehicles but supply vehicles were unable to deliver adequate amounts to the combat vehicles once the offensive began. So while fuel and ammunition stocks in depots could be at adequate levels the vehicles to distribute it to the front in adequate amounts were not available. The major reason that the German withdrawal did not become a total rout was that the army was falling back on its supply depots. The German Quartermaster corps instituted a well-organized and systematic plan to resupply the retreating troops and to evacuate as many supplies as possible to the rear. Despite the continuous proficient and resourceful German effort to curtail its effects, the DIADEM air interdiction campaign was a notable success. Through unceasing and effective attacks on the rail and road systems in both the combat zone and interdiction zone; supply, transportation and command problems gradually became so monumental and forbidding that even the combat capability of an well-organized, well-disciplined German army could not endure.

Luftwaffe General Erich Ritter von Pohl, head of Axis AA defenses in Italy stated in a post war interrogation (US Army, Europe, Historical Division, *Ms. No. D-191*, 1947):

"Then the Allies began to conduct systematic harassing attacks (i.e. STRANGLE and DIADEM) against our routes of communication in Central Italy in connection with their operations in southern Italy and the landings at Nettuno (i.e. Anzio), combined with occasional heavier attacks against communications centers in upper Italy. The vulnerability of the Italian railroad net suddenly became apparent with terrifying clarity.... In this precarious situation it was fortunate for the German command that Allied air activity against the German rear area at this time was conducted only when ground operations at the front freed the air force and diminished to a minimum as soon as the Allied armies launched a decisive offensive at one place or another....I personally feel that if the Allied air force had concentrated its attacks on the German lines of communication as early as the beginning of 1944, Army Group South would have been forced to withdraw to the Apennines."

It was the fighter-bomber campaign that disrupted German operations and leadership at all levels and prevented the Germans from massing reserves and supplies or to coordinate counter-attacks. After DIADEM and the retreat from Anzio and Cassino German troop movement could be made only at the expense of supply and supply movement. Once forced out onto the roads and no longer entrenched on static defense lines the Germans became increasingly vulnerable to air attack. Faced with the prospect of diminishing reinforcements and with their supply lines and transportation inadequate and under siege, the Germans from that point on were no longer concerned with Rome or mounting counter-attacks but only with sheer survival. Except for all-weather and nighttime capabilities the American fighter-bomber in mid-1944 was able to operate over the entire air power gamut. But despite this impressive display of airpower during STRANGLE, the main objective; to make it impossible for Kesselring to maintain his armies south of Rome, was not realized until Allied ground armies forced the Germans into battle. DIADEM and the concurrent ground attack was more effective than STRANGLE as it consumed German resources more rapidly and finally flushed the Germans into the open from their defensive positions to be exposed to attack from the air and ground. DIADEM also bolstered the concept that tactical air operations were more effective when land and air forces are equal partners working together toward destroying the enemy.

Fighter/Fighter-Bomber Interdiction Operations DIADEM (11 May-22 June 1944)

	Fighter/Fighter-Bomber		Bombers*	
Targets	**Sorties**	**Bomb Tons**	**Sorties**	**Bomb Tons**
Marshaling Yards	232	123.1	3,293	7,478.5
Rail Lines/Bridges	5,262	3,044.3	5,664	11,463.4
Roads/Bridges	6,750	3,741.3	4,294	8,146.6
Troops/Transport	736	221.2	581	693.3
Dumps	222	97.0	592	599.3
Harbors/Docks/Ships	295	136.5	1,568	3,444.2
Command/HQ	230	79.2	340	550.8
Misc.	20	2.6	—	—
Total	13,747	7,445.2	16,332	32,376.1

*Heavy, medium and light

Attack on Ploesti (10 June 1944)

The eleven vital oil refineries located near Ploesti Rumania were a priority target for the 15th Air Force as they supplied the Reich with one third of its oil. Ploesti was the third most heavily defended target in Europe as the Germans and their Rumanian allies had based fighter squadrons there to intercept any Allied air attack and more importantly had positioned the heaviest concentration of anti-aircraft batteries in the world. The USAAC first attacked Ploesti on 11 June 1942 doing little damage and caused the Germans to further strengthen its defenses. It was over a year later that the USAAF launched its famous Ploesti raids of 1 August 1943. The raid did do substantial damage but it came at a high cost, as 54 B-24s were lost with 532 crew. Eight months later on 5 April 1944, the 15th Air Force reinstated the bombing campaign against the refineries and their rail yards. Again the results of eight bomber missions were mediocre as the targets were too dispersed and Axis defenses took a heavy toll. Advance warning alerted the AA and fighters of the approaching 15th Air Force B-17s and B-24s and smoke generators were utilized to obscure the targets. It was decided that the P-38s of the 82nd Fighter Group would be assigned to hit specific targets in low-level surprise attacks escorted by P-38s of the 1st Fighter Group. The 10 June mission would be the longest dive-bombing mission in the MTO at 1,300 miles round trip to attack the former Standard Oil plant, the Romana Americana refinery.

At 0530, 46 P-38s took off from their Italian base at Vincenzo led by Group CO, Col. William Litton, rendezvousing with the 1st Fighter Group escorts ten minutes later. The two groups crossed the Adriatic and Yugoslavian mountains at low altitude and entered the Danube Valley heading toward Bucharest. The 82nd was attacked by enemy aircraft but were ordered not to engage in order to retain their drop tanks and bombs. The 1st was hit by a large group of enemy fighters and engaged them; downing 26 but suffered 14 losses. When the 82nd was only four miles south of the target the group began to climb to bombing altitude at 6,000 feet. Smoke pots had been lit and smoke covered the main boiler house target that had been assigned to the 96th Fighter Squadron. The boiler plant could still be distinguished by its two tall smoke stacks but most of the Lightnings had to rely on instruments on the pull out from their dives. Hits had been scored but pinpoint targeting was not possible. The 95th Squadron dove on the main distillation plant that, too, was covered by smoke and results could not be observed. The 97th Squadron bombed last and attacked the main cracking plant that was not as covered with smoke and reported bomb hits. The AA barrage was heavy and seven P-38s returned to base with damage and four were lost to AA fire. A 1.5 million-gallon storage tank was hit and set on fire. On their return to base the 82nd strafed targets of opportunity, claiming 11 locomotives and four aircraft on the ground losing eight pilots MIA and ten aircraft lost. The Group was awarded the DUC and did achieve heavy damage to the Romana American refinery's output. However, 11 more missions were flown by 15th Air Force heavy bombers which finally reduced Ploesti output to 20% by the time the Russians over ran the area in late August 1944. The cost again was high with 245 bombers being lost in the 11 missions

Friendly Fire

The 82nd Fighter Group was to have a strange encounter on 7 November 1944. The 95th and 97th Fighter Squadrons of the 82nd Fighter Group/15th Air Force out of Foggia under Group CO, Col. Clarence "Curly" Edwinson, were to attack transport and German troops retreating from Greece. The 95th Fighter Squadron strafed and destroyed a locomotive and then flew on to attack a truck convoy. After inflicting considerable damage to the convoy the pilots discovered that they were over the wrong road and had attacked Russian trucks and troops. As they were pulling up from the deck, their top cover (97th Fighter Squadron) cautioned them that "bogeys" were taking off from a field in front of them. The Russians had scrambled Yak fighters under Capt. A.I. Koldunov to protect the convoy. The P-38s and Yaks both climbed for altitude but a Yak pulled up its nose and fired on the last P-38 piloted by Lt. Philip Brewer whose Lightning crashed and exploded. Lt. Kenneth Katschke flying top cover at 7,00 feet dove on the "enemy" and shot it down at about 4,000 feet. Katschke only saw the red stars, as the fighter was about to crash. A bogey crossed in front of Lt. Thomas Urton who was leading the 95th Fighter Squadron flying medium cover. Urton broke toward him. and four P-38s and six Yaks engaged in a dogfight. Urton finally identified the fighters as Soviet Yaks and called the information to his flight. Just as he did, he was warned to break and he looked back to see a Yak on his tail shooting at close range. Lt. John Blumer closed in and flamed the Soviet to rescue Urton. The other Yaks continued to press the attack and a second was hit by Urton and was seen to spiral, smoking towards the ground (probable). Urton chased and hit a third Yak that was on the tail of another P-38 and chased it off, damaging it..

2Lt. Eldon Coulson's P-38 was hit and seen to crash and burn. The fighters finally separated and when Urton waggled his wings the Yaks did likewise and allowed the P-38s to withdraw.

In the mean time, a Yak attacked Edwinson's flight head on and the P-38s broke and after two or three passes Lt. William Blurock got on its tail and got a few hits causing it to smoke heavily and partially drop its wheels (claimed as a probable). The Russian waggled his wings and Edwinson replied and the unfortunate battle ended with two P-38s and two Yaks destroyed and two Yak probables and one damaged.

The air battle ended but the incident caused diplomatic repercussions, as one of the dead in the strafing attack was a Soviet Lieutenant General along with two officers and three enlisted men and 20 vehicles. The Russians demanded an immediate investigation from Gen. Ira Eaker and the Joint Chiefs of Staff and the discipline of those responsible. Gun camera film concluded that the Russians were in deed strafed and the target road was 55 miles (10 minutes) away. On 25 November 1944, a seven-page report was sent to the War Department and Joint Chiefs of Staff. The JCS sent a message to the Red Army General Staff saying that the P-38s had made a navigational error and attacked a Red Army column by mistake. It went on to state that the P-38s were "justifiably attacked by Soviet fighters defending their column" and "the Soviet flight Leader courageously closed into formation with the US Flight Leader and mutual identification was confirmed". The message concluded: "Please accept my heartfelt regrets and be assured that every precaution has been taken to prevent such errors in the future". Edwinson was relieved of his command on 20 November and awarded the DFC the next day and on the 22nd was on his way to the States to explain the "incident".

21

Operation ANVIL-DRAGOON
The Invasion of Southern France
15 July - 28 August 1944

From late 1943, it was evident to the Germans that an Allied invasion threatened the French Riviera. The German war machine was in retreat on the Eastern Front after its defeat at Kursk and then struggled to contain the Allies on the Normandy coast at the same time as the Allies broke out in Italy and captured Rome. A large fraction of the allotted German resources to Italy were transferred to these fronts. By August 1944 only ten divisions were found south of the Liore River and only seven of these were deployed on the French Mediterranean coast. The Luftwaffe in the area had been battered for more than a year by Allied strategic bombing and possessed only about 200 operational aircraft of which 130 were anti-shipping bombers. An additional 50 bombers and 80 fighters could be deployed from Italy and northern France. The Allies could muster over 5,000 aircraft and five aircraft carriers. The Germans also deployed 450 heavy AA and 1,200 light AA guns mostly along the coast. Three problems faced the Allies in this build up:

1) The Allies had no chance of tactical surprise as German reconnaissance aircraft had long discovered the build-up in Corsica,
2) The redeployment of forces could not interfere with the US Fifth and British Eighth Armies in Italy
3) The build up of Corsica into an effective base of operations.

Planning

Planning for the invasion of southern France began in December 1943 and had been thrashed out long and often by Roosevelt, Churchill and the Combined Chiefs of Staffs. Finally, in early July, Gen/ Sir Henry Wilson, Supreme Allied Commander, MTO, was directed to proceed with the invasion on 15 August. The Mediterranean Allied Air Force (MAAF) released the initial air plan on 12 July. The Tactical Air Force (MATAF) was responsible for overall planning. The XII TAC under Brig.Gen. Gordon P. Saville was to provide air support for the battle with help from the Desert Air Force based in north central Italy, MATAF medium bombers based on Corsica and Sardinia, MASAF at Foggia and the Coastal Air Force which was based at various sites.

Lt.Gen, Ira Eaker, Maj.Gen. John Cannon, Lt.Gen. Jacob Devers and Maj.Gen. Thomas Larkin meet to discuss US strategy during DRAGOON. (USAF)

It had been the intention of the High Command in the MTO to drive up the Italian Peninsula and move into the Hungarian Plain. However, the Pisa-Rimini defense line stalled the Allied advance from Rome and in northern France the Allies were moving behind schedule from the beachheads. ANVIL-DRAGOON was scheduled to be launched on 15 August. Worried that there was a possible security compromise of the code name ANVIL, the operation was renamed DRAGOON on 1 August. Churchill suggested the name as he felt he was dragooned into going along with it. During that week Churchill had unsuccessfully tried to cajole Roosevelt to use the ten divisions earmarked for DRAGOON to reinforce OVERLORD for the capture of the Brittany Peninsula and the Channel ports. The purpose of ANVIL-DRAGOON was:

1) Assist the Normandy operation by engaging German units that could be sent to reinforce the battle in northern France.
2) Capture a major port through which sizable reinforcements and supplies could be moved.
3) Liberate southern France.
4) Link up with forces driving from Normandy and engage the German Army in a decisive battle in central Europe.

Each of the three major components of the MAAF was to draw up a plan for its part in the invasion. The Coastal and Strategic Air Forces were to continue their normal activities. The Tactical Air Force was confronted with the problem of planning the assault, to reorganize itself and build new bases on Corsica without impairing the operations in Italy. To continue the support of operations in Italy the MATAF had to split its command. It left the Desert Air Force the responsibility of air support in Italy and moved the XII TAC to Corsica to prepare for the invasion.

The build up on Corsica was difficult as there were only two ports on the island. Ajaccio, the main port, could handle only one Liberty ship a day and Bastia could only accommodate small vessels. Every road and rail bridge and tunnel had been destroyed during the Allied air interdiction campaign. Under German occupation there were only two small airfields but by 10 August the Allies built 14 all-weather and semi-weather operational fields that could accommodate 18 tactical groups.

Air operations began at the end of April and by 10 August the MAAF had flown 6,000 sorties dropping 12,500 tons of bombs on southern France. A quarter of the effort was in support of the invasion while the majority was normal anti-sub and anti-air sorties, interdiction of supply lines into Italy and attacks on French marshaling yards in cooperation with the Normandy front. The MAAF plan called for the following:

1) Gain air superiority by neutralizing the Luftwaffe.
2) Afford air cover for the invasion convoys, the invasion troops and ensuing air operations.
3) Prevent or impede the movement of German forces into the battlefield.
4) Support the invasion and subsequent operations of the ground forces.
5) Transport and drop airborne troops and provide air support.
6) Support operations of the French Underground (Marquis) by air action and air supply.

On 28 July, the 12th Air Force issued its tactical plan:

1) To neutralize the Luftwaffe on the ground and in the air.
2) Disrupt enemy communications and prevent the movement of his reserves into the battle area.
3) Attack specified enemy defensive installations in the invasion area.
4) Destroy submarine pens and block ships in Toulon Harbor.
5) Provide air cover over the invasion beaches and to shipping 40 miles out.
6) Provide close air support.

The air operation was divided into three phases:

1) D minus 30 to D minus 1: airfields and communication lines in southern France were to be primary targets. (It was not until 2 August, D minus 13, before these attacks began)
2) D minus 1: isolate the invasion area.
3) D-Day forward: Provide close support to ground troops

This plan was later structured into two pre-invasion operations: NUTMEG and YOKUM. NUTMEG (D minus 5 to 0350 hours on D-Day) was to support the invasion area directly by attacks on defending troops, coastal batteries and radar installations. YOKUM (0550 to 0730 on D-Day) was to be a concentrated attack to prepare the beaches by destroying coastal and beach defenses. All aircraft were assigned definite approach lanes to the assault area. Bomb loadings were to be instantaneously fused fragmentation and demolition bombs not exceeding 260lbs.

Air operations following the landings were coded, DUCROT which was to:

1) Destroy remaining enemy beach and coastal defenses.
2) Isolate the battlefield by destroying rail and road bridges across the Rhone-Isere-Durance rivers and by blocking roads and rails in the passes and valleys through the Alps from the Isere River south.
3) Attack troop movements in the XII TAC area.
4) Neutralize Luftwaffe airfields within range of the beachhead.

USAAF Fighter/Fighter-Bomber Forces (15 August 1944)

Mediterranean Allied Air Forces (MAAF)

Mediterranean Tactical Air Force (MATAF)

12th Air Force

XII Tactical Air Command

87th Fighter Wing

86th Fighter Group (P-47s)

79th Fighter Group (P-47s)

57th Fighter Group (P-47s)

64th Fighter Wing

27th Fighter Group ((P-47s)

324th Fighter Group (P-47s)

14th Fighter Group (P-38s)

The German defense of Southern France was charged to Army Group G under General Johannes Blaskowitz (center). (Author/West)

The forces were 816 USAAF fighters vs. 25 Luftwaffe fighters that were reinforced by one fighter unit after D-Day. All Germans air activity ceased after 21 August when the Germans withdrew their remaining fighters to Metz.

The German defense of southern France was charged to Army Group G under Gen. Johannes Blaskowitz. The 19th Army, commanded by General of the Infantry Friedrich Wiese, deployed seven infantry divisions along the coast and held eight in reserve at Grenoble. In areas of potential invasion the Germans built numerous defensive coastal batteries and pillboxes, spotted machine guns and light artillery and mined the beaches and installed underwater obstacles. Because the Germans were unable to guess the specific invasion area the defenses were thin and unevenly distributed along the coast.

When the pre-invasion air attacks on southern France began in July 1944, the Germans possessed sufficient stores of supplies to fulfill the requirements for their defensive plans. Their supply dumps had been widely dispersed and were well camouflaged. Army Groups had stockpiled additional supplies in anticipation of an attack. The transport network in the area was adequate before the air attacks but rail shipments from northern France had been infrequent due to the Allied air attacks there. The key rail link to the area ran along the Rhone Valley and thus became a primary Allied air target. In the months before the invasion, air attacks on transportation and communication targets had been made intermittently with some success by 15th Air Force heavy bombers and medium bombers of the MAAF. Because the MAAF was also responsible for air operations in Italy and southern France they had neither the time nor resources to strike pre-invasion targets until two weeks before the landings.

Pre-invasion attacks of Operation NUTMEG destroyed or damaged many transportation targets before D-Day; particularly railroad bridges over the Rhone River south of Lyon. Of the six bridges only one had been repaired to carry a single track. Three of the four bridges between Italy and the Riviera were cut and the Germans found it was almost impossible to move reinforcements into the area. Because of the increased heavy air attacks in southern France and the inactivity in the air over northern Italy, the Germans correctly interpreted that an invasion would soon take place somewhere along the southern French coast. They had great difficulty in moving the 11th Panzer Division from Toulouse in southwestern France to join the 19th Army. The vast majority of the bomb tonnage dropped was by medium bombers of the XII TAC and heavy bombers of the 15th Air Force. No determined air attacks were made to destroy supply, ammunition and fuel dumps, as they were well dispersed and camouflaged and thus represented only 3.2% of the sorties and 2% of the tonnage of the air campaign. Sabotage by the well-organized French Resistance, the Maquis, also contributed a large proportion of the damage to the transportation system.

The concentrated air attacks of YOKUM on the morning of D-Day, 15 August, were mainly close support missions by medium and fighter-bombers to destroy gun positions and to soften up the beach defenses. Transportation targets also received sizable effort outside the battle area to prevent the movement of troops and equipment into the area of the invasion that was now revealed. Fighter-bombers flew 87 sorties dropping 52.5 tons of bombs on rail equip-

A First TAF P-47 strafes a mountain road in Southern France. US fighter-bombers were very effective in harassing the German retreat that became a rout. (USAF)

ment and bridges and 214 sorties dropping 170.4 tons of bombs on road and highway bridges. After the air attacks, naval guns bombarded the beaches for the half hour before the landings. The 3rd, 36th, and 45th Divisions of VI Corps under Gen. Lucian Truscott made the landings between St. Tropez and St. Raphael on the French Riviera against light or no opposition. They secured the landing area by nightfall and were ahead of their timetables. The Luftwaffe flew very few sorties in the area and was quickly and easily driven off. Enemy reinforcements never arrived and no large-scale counterattacks were launched. Because of the quick success of the landings, Truscott had a difficult option: either consolidate the beachhead or to immediately attack the demoralized and retreating Germans. An attack would be without adequate supplies that were in the process of being off loaded on the beaches. Truscott's VI Corps attacked and rapidly advanced over the mountains of Provence and up the Rhone Valley. Soon the attack was outrunning its supplies. The capture of a port was necessary as soon as possible as supplies were to delivered via the beaches until D plus 20. The Germans made an orderly retreat but left the 242nd and 244th Divisions to hold the ports of Toulon and Marseilles as long as possible. In their withdrawal the Germans were ordered to destroy military installations, railways, airdromes, ports, ships at anchor, power plants etc. Weapons, food and ammunition were to be transferred to the garrisons at Toulon and Marseilles that were to be defended to the last man.

Allied air supremacy was so effective that on D-Day the Luftwaffe flew only 60 missions over southern France and 70 the next day. German fighters were powerless to counter the invasion or protect their troops, supply lines and airfields. Only 30 Me-109s were available as reinforcements but soon returned to their bases in northern Italy. The German bomber force had to be pulled back to Lyon. There were a few ineffective dusk bombing sorties by a small number of Ju-88s on the 15th through 19th.

During the first week of DURCROT, medium and fighter-bombers bombed and strafed roads, tracks and yards at Marseille and Avignon, destroying 42 locomotives, 633 rail cars and 843 trucks. On the ground the Allies had driven a wedge and were moving rapidly after the retreating Germans. Over 100 road and rail bridges were attacked. The MATAF decided to cease the air attacks, as the further destruction of these targets would hamper Allied ground movement chasing the retreating Germans. Less intense air attacks intended to obstruct the German retreat continued but left selected routes open for the advancing Allies. After securing the beachhead on the first day, by the end of the first week the Seventh Army had surged forward surrounding Toulon and Marseille and then reached the Rhone River and were headed toward Lyon. On 21 August, Lt. Gen. Jacob Devers, Deputy Commander of AFHQ wrote to Lt. Gen. Ira Eaker, Air C-in-C: "...I wish to tell you what a grand job you, Cannon, Twining and Saville did and are continuing to do in our present effort in southern France. Your aerial preparation and later support made possible our great gains."

After the first week of the invasion the 15th Air Force no longer took part in air operations except for a few fighter-bomber sorties. The MASAF was withdrawn completely and the Coastal Air Force flew only a few sorties. During the second week the Germans lost 1,402 motor vehicles. Substantial losses, of weapons, ammunition, fuel and food did not appear to be a problem for the Germans either at the beaches or during the withdrawal, as they moved back to established dumps and depots.

As the Allied advance drove away from the beachhead the fighter-bombers based on Corsica had problems keeping up. The Allied engineers quickly repaired captured airfields and built new landing strips often gouged from vineyards so that by week's end six were available to three P-47 groups.

Utter devastation of a retreating German motorized column outside of Montelimar in southern France during the last week of August 1945. The destroyed motor and horse-drawn vehicles had been bulldozed aside so that advancing American vehicles could pass. (USAF)

Left: Demolished German tracked vehicles and a staff car lay in a ditch after a XII TAC fighter-bomber attack in the Montelimar road bottleneck. Despite the heavy loss in men and material much of the German Nineteenth Army managed to escape. (USAAF)

Montelimar (24-31 August 1944)

The eight day battle for Montelimar took place in an area bounded by the Rhone River and Highway 7 on the west and the Drome River (Livron) on the north and the Roubion River (Montelimar) in the South. The rail and road center of Montelimar was the southwest pivot lying on Highway 7 (the main Marsailles-Lyon road) and a parallel rail line running through the deep Rhone River Gorge, the only northern escape route. The American infantry divisions of VI Corps, the 3rd, 36th and 45th, moved forward to cut off Gen. Frederich Weise's Nineteenth Army.

On the 26th American TacR fighters came upon a column of retreating German vehicles stretching several miles along Highway 7. They dove to strafe the front and rear of the column to cause a road block in the narrow valley. They called XII controllers at St. Tropez who dispatched all available fighter-bombers in the air to the area. After the attack more than 500 German vehicles were left burning. For the next three days VI Corps tanks and artillery and XII TAC fighter-bombers blasted the fleeing Germans. The 27th Fighter Group distinguished itself in its attacks at Montelimar and Salon and was awarded the DUC. On the 29th the 79th Fighter Group out of St. Raphael harassed the Germans throughout the day. In the early morning the 86th Squadron blocked Highway with 30 trucks destroyed and 50 more damaged. The 85th Squadron attacked rail targets on the tracks parallel to the highway, setting a long line of cars on fire, and then moved along the Rhone and sank two river barges. The 87th Squadron had the best target of the day when they took off on a late afternoon mission to investigate the highway north of the advancing American infantry. They came across over 500 vehicles moving north on the highway 15 miles south of Lyon. At first Capt. Bill Colgan, Lt. Philip Bagian and F/O Russell Jennings thought it was an American column moving below them but soon found that the solid mass below was the enemy. Colgan and his "Red Flight" dropped down to strafe the front of the column and Lt. John Boone led his "White Flight" down on the rear of the column and together they blocked off the road with burning vehicles at each end. The Squadron repeatedly attacked until it ran out of ammunition leaving 47 vehicles destroyed and another 64 damaged. The Germans fired on their attackers with small arms and automatic weapon fire. Begian and Jennings were hit and crashed and three of the five other fighter-bombers were badly holed. Colgan reports (*Fighter-Bomber Pilot*, ibid) that he had over a 100 holes in his aircraft when he quit counting. Bagian made a dead stick crash landing while German soldiers fired into the landing area. He soon was rescued by the French Resistance and was back with the squadron within a week. Jennings was KIA when his Thunderbolt crashed into a hill near the highway. The 79th went on to attack the retreating Germans for the next four days and in the six-day air battle accounted for 143 destroyed and 216 damaged vehicles and numerous horse-drawn vehicles and claims against river and rail traffic. Seven ammunition trains were attacked and destroyed in spectacular fashion.

Moving up the Highway at the end of the battle the American Seventh Army counted over 2,000 contorted bullet-riddled and blackened vehicles and the rotting and bloated corpses of over 1,000 horses and numerous German soldiers lying along the highway in almost unbearable stench. The *War Diary of the 79th Fighter Group* describes the carnage as they moved up Highway 7 to their new base at Valence:

"As we moved up the Rhone Valley the destructive powers of the fighter-bombers became apparent with a grim clarity which none of us had ever fully realized. For a distance of roughly 30 miles, centered on the little town of Montelimar, was a shambles that may well have had no counterpart in this war. Here had been created a bottleneck of traffic, lined bumper-to-bumper, that had been ceaselessly attacked for days on end. Vehicles of every description were blocking each other until all became victims of Allied air power. There were great diesel buses such as once were used on the streets of Berlin, there were tanks and horse-drawn carts, there was in actuality everything that could move on wheels, and all were now abandoned in flight. Only the odor of decaying bodies, both animal and human, remained to connect the spectacle with the part it had once played for the Wehrmacht. The debris had been cleared from the road to the ditches alongside by a bulldozer which was still occupied as we hurried on northward."

Despite a shortage of supplies, the VII Corps carried out a spectacular drive across the mountains but it arrived too late to cut off and trap the majority of the Germans in southwestern France. Most of the 19th Panzer Division and 198th Reserve Division escaped. Fighter-bombers had easy targets as the roads were congested with bumper-to-bumper columns of troops, armor, motorized vehicles and horse-drawn guns and equipment. An estimated 4,000 vehicles, tanks and guns were destroyed and 15,000 prisoners were taken. The French Army B and the US 45th Division laid siege on Toulon and Marseilles supported by artillery and naval barrages and fighter-bombers that flew close support missions. The cities fell on 28 August, only 13 days after D-Day and provided the Allies with their ports and by the end of the war over 900,000 troops and four million tons of supplies would be off-loaded. By the 28th the battle for southern France was virtually over. The US Seventh Army had *almost* closed off the Rhone Valley but the Americans faced shortages of fuel and ammunition and the Germans, as usual, were able to mount tactical counter-attacks and skillful defensive stands to allow the withdrawal their troops. Some 57,000 Germans had been captured and an estimated 50,000 killed and masses of material had been lost but over half of the Germans escaped the incomplete trap. The Americans lost 2,700 and the French 4,000 men (mostly in the reduction and capture of the ports). The Allied advance continued and Lyon was captured on 3 September and Dijon on the 10th. The three US Divisions advanced northeast in an attempt cut off the retreating Germans at the Belford Gap that was 40 miles west of Basel and the German-Swiss border. The Germans under Col.Gen. Johannes Blaskowitz counter-attacked and held long enough for the bulk of the German Nineteenth Army to again escape to the Rhine River Afterward the VII Corps slowed down and conducted a mopping up campaign. Meanwhile the XII TAC was moving units to France from Corsica as fast as advanced airfields were prepared. On 10 September Field Marshal James Wilson called for the return of the XII TAC to Italy and all its units stationed in southern France.

This move would leave the Allied troops in southern France without air cover. A concerned Eisenhower sent his representative, Gen. Toohey Spaatz, to meet with Wilson's representative, Gen. Ira Eaker, and it was agreed that XII TAC would remain in France under the control of the USSTAF. But also it was agreed that AAF units "on loan" to the XII TAC and the XII AFSC would be returned to the 12th Air Force and MTO. On 15 September operational control of the XII TAC was no longer under the MATAF and the 12th Air Force, but transferred to the USSTAF and 9th Air Force. The 324th Fighter Group (64th Fighter Wing) and the 415th Night fighter Squadron would remain in France with the XII TAC. The 12th Air Force's 27th, 57th and 79th Fighter Groups were to be sent back to the MTO.

On the 13th of September, the US Seventh from DRAGOON and Third Army from Normandy met near Dijon. All DRAGOON forces were consolidated into the Allied Sixth Army Group and the front in Northwest Europe was continuous and poised to advance into Germany.

Results and Conclusions on DRAGOON

After a yearlong debate and despite Churchill's opposition, DRAGOON was launched and was an archetypal tactical military success. In a month the US Seventh Army's experienced troops led by enterprising leaders had liberated the southern two-thirds of France and captured two critical ports, Toulon and Marsailles and inflicted devastating losses of men and materiel on Gen. Frederich Weise's Nineteenth Army. They joined Eisenhower's troops advancing east from Normandy two months earlier than anticipated to form a united battle front extending from Schwitzerland to the North Sea. Eisenhower wrote (*Crusade in Europe*, ibid.):

"There was no development which added more decisively to our advantages, or aided us more in accomplishing the final and complete defeat of the German forces, than the attack up the Rhone Valley". Distinguished naval historian, Samuel Eliot Morison, added (*History of United States Naval Operations in World War II, Vol. XI*, ibid.): Dragoon "was an almost perfect amphibious operation from the point of view of training, timing, Army-Navy-Air Force cooperation, performance and results." Craven and Cate, the official USAAF historians (*The Army Air Forces in World War II, Vol. III*, ibid.), wrote:

"....its success predicated on planning, preparation and execution. So it was that DRAGOON was easy, not only because the enemy was weak but because the Allies had added to their superiority in men and material the lessons learned from earlier invasions."

Some historians, political figures and military strategists argued that DRAGOON was of little strategic military importance and ultimately allowed the Russians to occupy and control the Balkans. Five years after the war, Gen. Mark Clark, still a principal military figure at the time, wrote (*Calculated Risk*, Harper & Bros., NY, 1950); "The weakening of the campaign in Italy in order to invade southern France, instead of pushing into the Balkans, was one of the outstanding political mistakes of the war." Churchill was always opposed to DRAGOON but not for the same reason as Clark in his hindsight assessment. Despite his suspicions about Soviet post war designs on Eastern Europe, in mid-1944 he wanted to strengthen the British position in Italy. British and Empire troops had fought there in large numbers and suffered heavy casualties in what Churchill originally described as the "Soft underbelly of Europe" and which subsequently became a "tough old gut." The American leaders were naïve about the political realities regarding Stalin's post war objectives in the Balkans but an Allied drive through north Italy and then turning the Adriatic corner into Yugoslavia would have been costly and logistically problematical. The Americans and British were no longer equal partners and Marshall and Eisenhower got their way. DRAGOON had weakened the Italian Campaign irreparably and committed the Allies to a Western Europe strategy for the remainder of the war.

Fifteenth Air Force Fighter-Bomber Interdiction Operations: ANVIL-DRAGOON (15 July-14 September1944)

	Fighter/Fighter-Bombers		Bombers*	
Targets	**Sorties**	**Bomb Tons**	**Sorties**	**Bomb Tons**
Rail Lines/Bridges		—	526	1,323.5
Marshaling Yards	—	—	407	1,185.0
Roads/Bridges	50	19.7	—	—
Military Installations	58	23.5	362	868.5
Motor Transport/Troops	21.3	—	—	
Totals	110	44.5	1295	3377.0

*Heavy, Medium and Light

XII TAC Fighter/Fighter-Bomber Interdiction Operations: ANVIL-DRAGOON (15 July-14 September 1944)

	Fighter/Fighter-Bombers		Bombers*	
Targets	**Sorties**	**Bomb Tons**	**Sorties**	**Bomb Tons**
Rail Lines/Bridges	1575	16.8	1,690	2,970.6
Marshaling Yards	157	66.5	16	33.0
Roads/Bridges	1,315	790.7	1,464	2,658.1
Military Installations	66	23.5	310	374.7
Motor Transport	264	123.8	219	194.6
Harbors/Docks, Shipping	86	44.5	100	200.2
Totals	2,945	1,565.8	3,799	6,431.2

*Heavy, Medium and Light

Note: 1,113.104 rounds of .50 caliber ammunition were also fired during 1,124 sorties.

22

Arno-Gothic Line
23 June - 31 December 1944

Fighter/Fighter-Bomber Order of Battle 31 August 1944
Mediterranean Allied Air Force (MAAF)
Mediterranean Tactical Air Force (MATAF)
XII Fighter Command
XII Tactical Air Command
87th Fighter Wing
57th Fighter Group (P-47)
27th Fighter Group (P-47)
86th Fighter Group (P-47)
324th Fighter Group (P-47)
Desert Air Force
79th Fighter Group (P-47)

MATAF Interdiction operations subsequent to DIADEM continued to follow Operational Directive No. 11 of 22 June 1944: which were to continue "the destruction and disruption of the enemy's lines of communications." An analysis of the rail system in the Po Valley determined that its complexity negated attacks on lines on specific routes as had been done on the southern routes in the DIADEM interdiction zone. There were 22 bridges crossing the Po between Turin and the Adriatic: half were permanent bridges and half recently built pontoon military bridges. The destruction of six of these and two over the Trebbia River at Piacenza and the viaduct east of Genoa would effectively stop all rail traffic coming from Germany, France, Austria and the Balkans. The road bridges were to be untouched as it was expected that the rapidly advancing Allied armies would need to have these bridges intact to continue their advance. But the Allied armies advance slowed to a crawl and on 11 July, medium bombers were ordered to destroy the Po bridges.

In early June, Gen. Harold Alexander's plans to exploit the DIADEM success needed to be revised when the Combined Chiefs of Staff decided to launch Operation ANVIL to which they committed Alexander's VI Corps, the 36th and 45th division and a French division. A month later, the Chiefs of Staff ordered another two French divisions, several supply units and 70% of Alexander's air power to ANVIL. This move relegated Italy to a secondary theater status behind Northwest Europe and the Pacific and severely affected morale there. In the meantime, Kesselring had again proved

Field Marshal Albert Kesselring had proved to be the master of defensive warfare during the withdrawal up the Italian boot. On 1 June 1944, the Gothic Line was no more than a 200-mile line drawn across a map of the Italian Peninsula. Plans were drafted and orders cut for the construction and by August the Germans had stopped the Allies at the newly constructed defensive line. (Author/West)

to be the master of defensive warfare. On 1 June 1944, the Gothic Line was no more than a 200-mile line drawn across a map of the Italian Peninsula. Plans were drafted and orders cut for the construction. The equivalent of three German divisions had been annihilated in the retreat from Anzio and Cassino. Hitler sent four new divisions to Kesselring and promised four additional divisions complemented by Czech and Italian divisions for guard and coastal duties freeing additional German troops. Kesselring needed time to build and man the Gothic Line. The Allies were of no little help, first aided by Mark Clark's decision to go for the capture of Rome, allowing the escape of a large number of German troops and then by drawing off troops chasing the Germans for ANVIL. In early July, German forces took up positions in the Arezzo Line and stopped the Allied advance for ten days. Kesselring withdrew; blowing bridges behind him and an able rear guard action slowed the Allied advance. On 5 August the Germans stopped at the Arno Line that ran from the north bank of the Arno from Pisa to Florence across the Apennines to the Metauro River.

By the end of August 1944, Eisenhower had 103 air groups under his command in France while there were 46 in Italy. But during the summer the transfer of the Twelfth Air Force and Fifth Army to France was being contemplated instead of allowing them to stagnant in the inert command structure of Italy. As German naval and air threats diminished in Italy the Mediterranean Allied Coastal Air Force became superfluous and its strength fell from 56 squadrons in January 1944 to 33 by September. The MAAF decided to compensate for its loss of the XII TAC to ANVIL by withdrawing XII Fighter Command from the MACAF and designating it a tactical air command responsible for close support operations for the Fifth Army. XII Fighter Command was ready for its new role on 20 September with only six squadrons of the 57th and 350th Fighter-Bomber Groups and a night fighter squadron available. It was to be augmented when necessary by the DAF. Two P-47 fighter groups from the XII TAC remaining in Corsica after ANVIL were transferred to the XII FC. The unexpected rapid advance of the Seventh Army up the Rhone River put it beyond the range of the Twelfth Air Force and on 16 September the Chiefs of Staff divided the Twelfth between Italy and south France. On 19 October, the command was established in Italy with 25 squadrons and was officially designated as the XXII TAC and was to support the US Fifth Army.

When the battle for the Gothic Line began Kesselring had 26 German and six Italian divisions that were opposed by 21 Allied divisions which was about five and a half fewer than it had after the fall of Rome. The Germans confronted their shortage of reinforcements, equipment and supplies and the daunting Allied air attacks with excellent leadership, continued high morale and superb fighting skill. Even though their air forces roamed the skies unopposed, the Allies did not have sufficient ground forces to take advantage of their air superiority and to exploit German weaknesses or breaks in the Gothic Line. The Allies also suffered from reinforcement and supply deficiencies but due to different reasons. Italy was a secondary theater receiving only adequate personnel, equipment and supplies that were being held up by an early winter and poor roads. These factors and the continued stubborn German resistance gnawed away at Allied morale. From the fall of Rome to 15 August the Fifth Army had lost nearly 18,000 killed, wounded or missing while from July to September the British Eighth Army suffered nearly 20,000 casualties during its offensive.

The stubborn German defense caused the Allies to change their strategy. The British Eighth Army was to transfer its forces east and move along the Adriatic coast, attacking the Gothic Line over the low hills of eastern Italy and then break through to the Lombardy Plains. The US Fifth Army was to move east and attack the mountainous center of the line after the Germans had shifted troops east to oppose the new Eighth Army attack. The Allies hoped that when the Fifth attacked on 10 September the Germans would again have to transfer troops back to oppose their attack, allowing the Eighth to then advance in force in the east. Kesselring quickly concluded that the British attack was the major offensive and ordered a general withdrawal to the Gothic Line and ordered the newly arriving divisions there. The Fifth Army was then able to cross the Arno against light opposition to attack toward the Gothic Line and force its way northward. But bad weather, a stiff German resistance and the arrival of reinforcements Kesselring had sent from the Eighth Army's front slowed the advance on Bologna on 18 October. The transfer of these German reinforcements allowed the Eighth to advance 20 miles and by early December it had reached beyond Revenna. Soon the expert German defense of rugged terrain and the oncoming Italian winter stopped both the Fifth and Eighth Armies again. During the first 12 days following the fall of Rome the Allies advanced 87 miles then between 16-23 June it slowed to 20 miles and then only another 20 miles in the next three weeks. Kesselring accumulated 19 under strength divisions with six in reserve, three of which were building the Gothic Line. The Allies moved slowly and cautiously giving Kesselring time to prepare his

Operation MALLORY MAJOR began on 12 July with medium bombers ordered to destroy the 22 Po River bridges. Fighter-bombers were to attack in the following days to prevent repairs and also to destroy the pontoon bridges. After two days, of the 11 permanent steel and concrete bridges, one was totally destroyed, three were half destroyed and seven were impassable. At the end of four days of the 21 bridges; 12 were considered totally destroyed, eight were closed to traffic and only one was open but a destroyed bridge to the south blocked the line leading to it. The Borgoforte Po River Bridge was destroyed during Operation MALLORY MAJOR during mid-July 1944. (USAF)

defenses and while they continued their vigorous air interdiction campaign, they would have been better served by attacking the hapless targets retreating from the battlefield. However, Kesselring always considered that the Allies might again try another flanking amphibious operation to the north that at that time had a high probability of success. But after the Anzio fiasco the Allies were more than reluctant to try another.

During the first six weeks (23 June-3 August) Allied infantry advanced from the Trasimeno Line through the Arezzo Line to the Arno River Line. The MAAF flew 18,480 sorties and dropped 19,423.3 tons of bombs; half against rail lines and bridges (8,803/9,346 tons), a quarter against roads and bridges (4,860 sorties/3,760.7 tons) and dumps received 1,822 sorties/2,484.4 tons. During this period Operation MALLORY MAJOR began on 12 July with medium bombers ordered to destroy the 22 Po River bridges. Fighter-bombers were to attack in the days following to prevent repairs and also to destroy the pontoon bridges. After two days, of the 11 permanent steel and concrete bridges, one was totally destroyed, three were half destroyed and seven were impassable. At the end of four days of the 21 bridges; 12 were considered totally destroyed, eight were closed to traffic and only one was open but a destroyed bridge to the south blocked the line leading to it. From Piacenza southward, all north-south rail traffic was stopped. MAJOR MALLORY concluded, but the MAAF continued its attacks on Italian bridges and by 20 July 90% of the bridges in northern Italy were cut. By 4 August Genoa was isolated, all lines from Milan to the south and east were cut and only one along the Apennines was usable. Fighter-bombers operating out of Corsica while waiting ANVIL assignments carried out numerous sorties. Medium bombers were more effective against the permanent bridges so the fighter-bombers hit the pontoon and smaller bridges on the lines leading to the main bridges north and south of the Po. They also harassed bridge repair crews and took a heavy toll on roads, road bridges and the motor transport on them. At the end of the period the Allied armies had reached the Arno and the air forces were diverted to the ANVIL pre-invasion preparation. To protect the Po bridges the Germans transferred AA guns from Italian factories and other areas. In 1944 a total of 1,482 bridges were destroyed mainly by air attacks but several due to partisan sabotage. In the six month period May through September 864 were destroyed with 226 in July.

Luftwaffe General der Flakartillerie Wolfgang Pickert (German Air Force Monograph Project No. 184: *The Impact of Allied Air Attacks on German Division and Other Army Forces in Zones of Combat*, Karlsruhe, Germany USAF, 1958) commented on the loss of the Po River bridges:

"This situation (the effect on front line German units) changed in the late summer of 1944 when air attacks, the precise date of which cannot be established, suddenly destroyed all Po River bridges. Only one of the railway bridges was capable of only temporary repair and from then on all rail traffic across the Po River, in both north-south and south-north directions ceased. All rolling stock south of the river was thus cut off from normal traffic. All supply and personnel traffic had to be adjusted to motor vehicle transportation, which meant that large quantities of motor fuel had to be made available for the purpose at the expense of units in combat at the front.

In spite of continuously repeated air attacks, very efficient night-time ferry services were maintained at various points along the Po Valley by German engineer units, which also were thus lacking at the front, where they were sorely needed.

Mention must be made here of the exceptionally serious delays in the movement of personnel on furlough and of replacement personnel; and of the way in which such personnel, as well as shirkers, were held up at certain congested points, with the well known results which were exploited by enemy propaganda:

'....the attacks against the Po River bridges belong in the same category as the air attacks against supply movements in the German rear in North Africa, or the attacks against the rail and road systems and Seine River bridges prior to and during the battles in Normandy or during the Battle of the Bulge.'"

The retreating Germans had sabotaged their Corsican airfields through demolition, mine laying and plowing up tarmacs and the damage was so great that it was easier to build new fields. American engineers were able to build a field in five days. XII TAC strips were 6,000 feet and DAF fields were 3,600 feet. The engineers were so efficient that one survey team forged ahead of the infantry and was captured by advancing Fifth Army infantry!

During the next three weeks (4-24 August) there was little ground action as the Allies were repositioning their forces for their new plan of attack on 25 August. The MAAF concentrated on ANVIL that was to take place on 15 August and only 6,542 sorties and 5,967.6 tons were flown; again against rail lines and roads and their associated bridges. Fighter-bombers flew the majority of these missions (3,948 sorties/1,987.7 tons). Despite all the hardship and destruction from the ground and the air, German armies south of the Po were never routed. Their skill and resourcefulness again saved the day. The German Rail Repair Organization was expert at expediting repairs using conscripted Italian labor units and pre-posi-

A 57th Fighter Group dive-bombs a bridge over Po River in 1944. Arrows point to two P-47s leaving the target and two diving toward it. (USAF)

After Allied interdiction had destroyed the rail and road net in northern Italy, Armaments Minister Albert Speer, extended and reorganized the northern Italian inland waterway system. So-called "Speer barges" of the Transportflotte carried essential materials and armaments. This photo shows the destruction of a Speer barge and its landing dock on the Po River. (USAF)

tioning repair materials along important lines. Pontoon bridges were assembled at night and dismantled before dawn. Ferries were used at more than 50 crossings along the Po. Cable cars were installed across the Po to carry troops and supplies. The expanse of the rail and road system in northern Italy prevented the Allies from cutting all lines and roads simultaneously. The diversion of Allied air units to ANVIL took a considerable portion of MAAF activity as the 4,249 sorties flown on the first day of that invasion demonstrate. Ground strategy, not air execution limited the overall effect of Allied air power in Italy and deferred final victory. The land strategy was too cautious and instead of battering Kesselring's divisions while they were in full retreat south of the Po it attacked in small thrusts that allowed the Germans to take up prepared defensive positions.

The 325th Fighter Group Attacks German Airfields in Hungary (21 August 1944)

In August and September, the 325th Fighter Group, operating out of Tarquina A/D, accounted for numerous Luftwaffe aircraft on the ground. As the Germans retreated from the Russians on the Eastern Front the Luftwaffe and Hungarian Air Force withdrew their aircraft into Hungary and into operational range of American fighters and bombers operating from Italy. The 325th Fighter Group was to conduct a low-altitude fighter sweep on the Hajdu Boszormeny

Unable to cross the Po River because there were no bridges intact, the retreating German forces were sitting ducks for fighter-bomber attacks as was this motorized column trapped along its banks. (USAF)

Left: Camouflaged portion of a German pontoon bridge used to cross the Po River, (USAF)

Airdrome while heavy bombers dropped fragmentation bombs. The fighters arrived at the field first looking to shoot down any enemy opposition. As the fighters were orbiting the bombers came over and dropped their loads which were off their mark so much so that the fighters found themselves inside the bomb pattern and had to break away from the danger of falling bombs. As the bombers left, the orbiting fighters saw that the bombers had missed the target. Maj. Hershel Green was leading the mission and had been instructed not to do any strafing. But seeing the unscathed aircraft sitting on the field defended by only light AA defenses, Green decided to attack the field and led his squadron on a destructive strafing pass. With limited ground fire, Green then broke the cardinal rule of ground strafing; never make a second pass. In fact he led his pilots on six passes and the Group was given credit for 37 destroyed, 13 probably destroyed, and 17 damaged. Green personally destroyed eight Me-410s and two Me-109s, claimed six Me-410s as probably damaged, and damaged three more Me-410s. 1Lt. Robert Bass got

Maj. Herschel Green, 18 victory air ace of the 325th Fighter Group, claimed ten aircraft destroyed on the ground while strafing a German airdrome in Hungry on 21 August 1944. (USAF)

four destroyed, one probable, and four damaged. The raid was so devastating that the Hungarian unit there was deactivated and the airdrome closed. Green was given a mandatory, but mild, reprimand by his CO, Col. Chet Sluder, and then was awarded the DSC for his action that day.

On the 1st of September the 325th was assigned a rhubarb mission on Bedrecen, Yugoslavia. Top cover was provided for 11 P-51s and the other fighters attacked in three sections, one strafing, West to East, the second from North to South and the last from East to West. The Luftwaffe lost 59 aircraft on the ground and three in the air. 1Lt. Arne Arneson made five passes over this field and then moved on to another field 15 miles to the south. Here he made eight passes on the nine bombers parked there, expending most of his ammunition to destroy three. Two Checkertails were shot down by flak. On 8 September, Ecka A/D in Yugoslavia was attacked by the 325th whose pilots made between five and eight passes each. Their totals were 22 Ju-52s, 19 Ju-88s, 7 FW-190s, five Fi-156s and five assorted aircraft. On their way back to base the Group came upon an airfield at Petrovrad and added three Ju-52s and a pair of Fi-156s. After the mission the Group was commended by XV Fighter Command, GC Brig.Gen. Dean Strother who stated: "This is the most thoroughly effective strafing attack I have ever known in terms of completeness of the destruction accomplished."

During the next two months (25 August-12 October) the Allied armies had broken the Gothic Line, moving toward Bologna in the center and past Rimini in the east. The MAAF flew 17,882 interdiction sorties dropping 22,689.9 tons: 6,941 sorties/9,794.3 tons against rail lines and bridges, 5,139 sorties/4,566.1 tons against roads and bridges. Fighter-bombers flew the majority of these sorties.

In mid-November Allied medium bomber strength was reduced. 42nd Wing HQ and two of its B-26 Groups were moved to France and in December the 319th Bomb group and its new B-25s were sent to the Pacific. The decrease in medium bomber strength increased the importance of fighter-bombers. From 26 November to 2 December, 148 sorties were flown against the Brenner Line. During one attack a train and 900 feet of track were destroyed near Sant' Ambrogio. On 28 November 46 P-47s put ten large gaps in 40 miles of track on the lower Brenner isolating rolling stock to be picked off later. During December a daily average of 20 P-47s attacked up and down the Brenner Line cutting 149 tracks. By 15 January, the Germans abandoned the rail electric grid south of Trento.

The Luftwaffe was a non-entity as in mid-September its fighter strength was estimated as 30 Me-109s. US medium bombers could be sent on missions unescorted freeing the fighters for fighter-bomber duty. In the middle of October 2d Gruppo of the Fascist Republic Air Force that had been trained and equipped in Germany arrived in northern Italy to defend transport lines in the Brenner Pass area. On 19 October, the Gruppo attacked 30 B-26s of the 319th, who had not experienced an enemy air attack in eight months and shot down three Marauders. By mid-November, Luftwaffe fighters also became very contentious attacking bombers in formations of up to fifty. On 5 November, they attacked a formation of B-26s, shooting down three and damaging six. In early November, German fighters based in northern Italy intercepted MASAF heavy bombers attacking nearby targets. The Luftwaffe had reinforced its bases at Aviano, Udine and Villafranca with over 100 fighters. Escorted heavy bombers were attacked in the Udine area by 30 to 40 fighters and lost 14 bombers for a loss of eight destroyed, two probables and two damaged to the P-51 escorts. This new Luftwaffe activity and the notable success of 2d Gruppo, caused the MATAF to cancel its no escort policy for medium escort on 14 November. To counter the Luftwaffe opposition, MASAF bombers, escorted by Mustangs, bombed their bases on 17 and 18 November.

On 26 December, newly arrived Italian units, trained in Germany combined with German units and five battalions assaulted the left flank of the Fifth Army in the Serchio Valley and by midday had punched a large hole in Allied lines. After the German Ardennes Offensive the Allies feared that the Axis assault could threaten the Allied port of Leghorn. The US 92nd Division was in disarray and the XXII TAC dispatched several small P-47 missions

Gen. Heinrich von Vietinghoff was the skillful commander of the Tenth Army who took over for Kesselring for three months in late 1944 and early 1945. On 23 October, the popular Kesselring visited his front line troops when an artillery piece, paying more attention to the sky than to the road, pulled out of a side road without stopping and collided with Kesselring's staff causing him a serious concussion. (Author)

which failed to knock out their assigned road and rail bridges. The 19th Indian Brigade was put into the line and the next day "Rover Joe" directed 145 sorties of the 350th Fighter Group, the 86th Fighter Group and the 1st Brazilian Squadron restored the situation. In three days the Germans and Italians were in retreat and harassed by THII Thunderbolts.

By mid-1944, Kesselring and the German Army in northern Italy, through organization and experience, had become masters of withdrawal and defense. They systematically moved supply dumps far behind the front lines, sent only necessary supplies to the front and upon withdrawal supplied retreating troops with remaining supplies instead of abandoning or destroying them. The German repair system was exceptional in its organization and efficiency and became expert at repairing damage to roads and rail lines and repairing or replacing damaged bridges. The transportation administrators became adept at transferring supplies from rail to road transport, re-routing supplies when rail lines and roads were cut and bridges destroyed. Movement could be only made at night and open river crossings were only known at the end of the day's attacks. Convoys and individual trucks had to drive along the banks of the Po until a crossing point was reached. Also, the load capacity of repaired and pontoon bridges were limited. Both factors led to a large backup of waiting vehicles. German ground operations and methodical withdrawals were coordinated with the supply situation. The morale, determination and combat capability of the German soldier remained high as he learned to cope with and overcome these obstacles and again was able to stop the Allied advance.

Kesselring usually visited the front at three days a week. At 0500 on 23 October, the popular Field Marshal left his HQ by staff car to visit his front line troops that had stopped the Allies at the Apennines. Despite being harassed by fighter-bombers throughout the day he continued his visit late into the afternoon. Fighter-bomber paranoia was everywhere on the roads. An artillery piece, paying more attention to the sky than to the road, pulled out of a side road without stopping and collided with Kesselring's staff car. Kesselring suffered a severe concussion that put him in a German hospital, putting von Vietlinghoff in command for almost three months. Kesselring's troops were told that the field Marshal was doing well but the gun had to be scrapped (Ken Macksey, *Kesselring*, Greenhill, 1996)!

Operation BINGO and the Attacks on the Brenner Line

In the summer of 1944, the Italian rail network was supplied by four systems: the French, Swiss, Yugoslavian and German. By November the French system had been eliminated. The "neutral" Swiss continued to allow raw materials to move through their country; iron and chrome to Germany and coal for the Italian munitions industry from Germany. The Swiss contribution was a minor one and could be eliminated by bombing several of their important tunnels into Italy. Three German and four Yugoslavian lines remained which were interconnected and grouped into three lines: the Brenner, the Venetian Plain and the northeastern frontier. The Brenner Line was the most important carrying two-thirds of all supplies. Of the minimum daily 5,500 to 6,000 tons of supplies, 3,600 to 4,000 were shipped over the Brenner Line. It was a 168-mile standard gauge electric and steam line from Innsbruck to Verona. When the attacks on the line began in early November there were 366 AA guns concentrated around four main areas along the line: Verona, Trento, Bolzano and Innsbruck. Flak units were transferred from the front including key areas in the Po Valley and eventually one-third of all heavy flak in Italy was placed along the Brenner Line. In 1944 the Allies had lost 713 aircraft to Axis flak. By the beginning of April 1945 there were 1,012 heavy and 2,194 medium and light flak guns in Italy. On the southern end from Verona north to Trento there were 33 bridges. The longest was 135 feet and heavily defended by AA and ten others were strongly built, attack resistant, masonry types crossing small streams. The middle section of the Brenner line north of Trento ran through a wide valley to Bolzano. The most vulnerable site was the 3,000-foot long viaduct of 35 spans at Lavis. There were two 350-foot bridges crossing the Adige north of Trento

When the attacks on the Brenner Line began in early November there were 366 AA guns concentrated around four main areas along the line: Verona, Trento, Bolzano and Innsbruck. Flak units were transferred from the front including key areas in the Po Valley and eventually one-third of all heavy flak in Italy was placed along the Brenner Line. In 1944 the Allies had lost 713 aircraft to Axis flak. Luftwaffe General Erich Ritter von Pohl (right), head of Axis AA defenses in Italy seen here with Luftflotte 2 commander Field Marshal Wolfram von Richtofen (left) (Author/West)

but the Germans realized their vulnerability and completed a diversion by early December. The northernmost section from Balzano to Innsbruck ran through 7,000 to 10,000ft. Alps cut by deep, narrow valleys that clouded over with winds that could reach 70mph making attacks difficult. The targets were small and difficult to detect and attacks were usually along one narrow axis with little time for accurate bomb aiming. The Germans increased their AA defenses along the entire Verona to Innsbruck section to nearly 1,000 guns with over half comprised of heavy 88 and 105mm pieces. Of 16 replacement pilots assigned to the 57th in November 1944, nine had been lost to accidents or combat in Brenner Line attacks by early February 1945. In mountainous terrain with long steep gradients, electric power was more efficient than steam power for locomotives. To supply the electricity large transformer stations were placed about 20 miles apart to feed the electric lines between Verona and the Brenner Pass. As the gradients became steeper these stations were placed about ten miles apart. If two adjacent stations were shut down limited service could continue but shutting three stations down stopped the system. Operation BINGO was authorized on 27 October to destroy the Brenner electrical grid. It was not until 6 November that the weather was good enough to launch the attack. Four transformers between Verona and Trento were assigned to DAF and XXII TAC fighter-bombers while 57th Wing B-25s. B-26s were to bomb three other stations along the same line. The MASAF heavy bombers attacked three stations north of Trento. The heavies did poorly missing all their targets but the fighter-bombers did very well. The rocket-firing P-47s of the 86th and 87th Squadrons of the 79th Fighter Group along with RAF 239 Wing P-40s scored 18 direct hits on main buildings and 23 on the transformer southwest of Verona. By 12 November only steam locomotives were in operation and long lines of motor transport were moving supplies on roads parallel to inoperative rail lines. The German repair organization became mobile and efficient. Material dumps were skillfully camouflaged and dispersed near areas exposed to air attack. As the weather worsened and air attacks subsided these crews opened more lines. The Ala Bridge that had been destroyed seven times in 24 attacks was put back online again. Luftwaffe General of Flak in Italy, Erich Ritter Von Pohl, stated in a post war interrogation (US Army, Europe, Historical Division, ibid.): "…. It seemed that German commanders in the defense could predict almost to the day when new large-scale (air) attacks would begin. These attacks began invariably when, after the hard and unceasing repair work of thousands of engineers and workers, the restoration of destroyed railway facilities and thus the entire line or important sections of the line seemed just about complete. The only question which could never be answered was: "Where will the next attack occur?" The everyday BINGO attacks were interrupted by recurrent poor weather in December and January but by then the electrical network supplying the railways was beyond repair south of Trento and the Germans repair system focused on other areas. BINGO was not designed to completely stop all traffic on the north Brenner Line but it achieved its objective of reduced volume which with recurrent bombing could keep the German supply requirements to a point below the basic minimum amounts.

The Brenner Line, a 168-mile standard gauge electric and steam line from Innsbruck to Verona, was the most important rail line in Italy carrying two-thirds of all supplies. A German troop train and the bridge at Arezzo were destroyed in one attack by MAAF fighter-bombers. (USAF)

The direct effect of the attacks on the Brenner Line did not include the effect of fighter-bomber attacks on trains that moved safely over the Brenner Pass towards the front lines. These trains often did not reach their destination to deliver their supplies. The Germans often tried to by-pass the Brenner. Oil from Ploesti was routed from Vienna to Genoa by moving it via Linz, Regansburg, Nuremburg, Karlsruhe, Lyons and Ventimiglia. The total distance was 1280 miles or twice the distance via the Brenner.

The intensive flak defenses under von Pohl was responsible for the passage of supplies along the Brenner Line until the end of the war. But the Allied interdiction campaign moved the forward railheads back to Verona and then to Balzano as the AA defenses of these forward railheads were removed to protect the Brenner and left them vulnerable. As much AA as practicable was taken, the defense of large cities, coastal defenses, the defense of dams and industrial areas, from forward road and bridge defenses across the Po River and particularly from frontline units. At first only half a battery or small AA units were transferred to individual Allied targets. In mid-March 1944, Kesselring ordered that one-third of all flak in Italy be transferred to protect the railway network. The vital rail centers at Verona, Bovereto, Balzano, Sterzing and Innsbruck were reinforced with this AA and allowed at least the minimum necessary movement of rail traffic to be maintained until the very end. In a post-war interrogation (US Army, Europe, Historical Division, ibid.): von Pohl stated: "Thus, there can be no doubt that the functioning of the Brenner railway until the last days of the war, next to the unceasing and heroic work of the railway engineers, was primarily due to the efficiency of the Flak, whose accomplishments in this instance can be compared with those at the Straits of Messina."

The concentrated flak along the rail lines was effective and the Allies extended the scope of their interdiction campaign to increase their attacks on motor transport system at the end of 1944. Important road bridges in northern Italy were systematically attacked and caused great disruption, continually causing long detours, wasting time and precious fuel. Fighter-bombers able to put a stop to daytime road travel as enemy AA defenses had been stripped for railway protection.

Operation BLOCKADE

After the German surprise Ardennes Offensive in mid-December 1944, the Allied Command worried that the Germans would abandon Italy or gradually withdraw their troops back into Germany. Spaatz appealed to Generals Twining and Cannon in Italy to paralyze the Brenner and Tarviso routes into Italy to prevent German troops there from being withdrawn into northern Europe. This was to be the MAAF's most important contribution to the Allied effort in northern Europe.

Operation BLOCKADE. After the German surprise Ardennes Offensive in mid-December 1944, the Allied Command worried that the Germans would abandon Italy or gradually withdraw their troops back into Germany. Spaatz appealed to Generals Twining and Cannon in Italy to paralyze the Brenner and Tarviso routes into Italy to prevent German troops and equipment there from being withdrawn into northern Europe. This was to be the MAAF's most important contribution to the Allied effort in northern Europe. (USAF)

The slow, costly movement of the British Eighth Army up the eastern Italian coast and the failure of the US Fifth Army to take Bologna at the end of October called for continued interdiction missions to stem the flow of supplies to the resolute defenders and to prevent their withdrawal to northern battlefields in France and Germany. The Allies had blasted Italian bridges month after month but the Germans continued to move just enough men and supplies whenever and wherever they wanted. Once troops and supplies were unloaded at the front the Germans then loaded the empty trains with Italian food, industrial equipment and raw materials for shipment back to the Reich. In September as many as 33 trains per day were moving through the Brenner Pass and in October the average was 28 per day. To stop this movement the Allied air strategists decided that to be effective the air offensive during the winter needed to be continuous and be directed at isolating Italy from Germany. On 11 November the MASAF was designated to only attack targets in Germany and on the 16th attacks on all Italian targets were to be approved by or requested by Brig.Gen. John Cannon, CO of the TAF.

Operation BLOCKADE initiated in early November 1944, took on new significance and a reassessment stated: "While losing none of its significance as a strangle operation, was increasingly motivated by the further desire to hamper the transfer of German manpower reserves from this to other theaters." In early November, the MATAF also initiated the BLOCKADE campaign that was designed to isolate "international routes" (e.g. Germany to Italy) but the weather hampered its full implementation. P-47s flew missions during BLOCKADE but poor weather and heavy AA fire made the missions difficult and dangerous.

At the start of 1945, the Allied Air Forces numbered 280 squadrons and were the most powerful weapon in the Allied arsenal. Their mission in Italy was amended. The northeast interdiction zone was extended to include the border routes into Italy north of the Venetian Plain. DAF medium bomber squadron operations were shifted from south of the Po to blockading the border routes. As soon as they were able to detach from supporting the armies that weren't expecting to be committed to much activity during the winter; fighter-bombers were committed to a concerted offensive against vital areas on the routes connecting Italy and Germany The purpose was to deny the Germans the supplies to resist and prevent any withdrawal from Italy. The MAAF Operational Directive No. 23 of 9 January 1945 stated the aim of air interdiction in Italy was: "to maintain the isolation of northern Italy and to disrupt the enemy supply organization, in order that his fighting capabilities may be reduced by the time our ground offensive is resumed." Previously about 75% of rail track cuts were made in open areas and stations and only 25% at bridges. No longer would air attacks punch easily repaired holes in tracks but would concentrate on bridges which would reduce rail traffic and force an increasing amount of traffic to the roads where the Germans had a shortage of vehicles and gasoline.

Fortunately for the Germans winter had brought about a stop to Allied ground operations and the German daily supply requirement were much less. The Allies hoped that their air interdiction program on the German supply system during the winter would with not allow them to build any reserve supply capacity to resist when the spring 1945 fighting began as happened after STRANGLE and DIADEM in May 1944.

Assessment

Figures from Luftwaffe General Karl Kollar, the Chief of Air Staff, stated that in 1944, the Luftwaffe in Italy flew 28,664 sorties and lost 966 aircraft or one in every 31 sorties. Allied figures for 1 January to 22 December 1944 were quite different: In air combat the Luftwaffe lost 3,753 destroyed, 899 probable and 1,262 damaged and 1,818 destroyed and 1,143 damaged on the ground. German flak defenses claimed 713 MATAF aircraft in 1944.

From 13 October until the end of the year, poor weather hampered the MAAF campaign. During the three-week period, 13 October to 2 November, poor weather virtually stopped MAAF interdiction sorties (1,894, mostly by fighter-bombers-72.5%). The weather between 24 November and 22 December halved the average number of sorties (3,939) and tonnage (3,165.8). These sorties were again flown mostly by fighter-bombers (73%) that could drop below the weather to attack targets.

From 23 June-31 December 1944, the MAAF flew 61,101 interdiction sorties dropping 65,714.7 tons of bombs with fighter-bombers contributing the majority of the sorties, 33,585/16,095.3 tons. Rail lines and bridges were hit by 29,618 sorties/33,631.8 tons (16,768 sorties/8,125.7 tons by fighter-bombers), roads and bridges by 14,783 sorties/11,632.4 tons (10,744 sorties/5009 tons by fighter-bombers) and dumps by 6,019 sorties/6,526.2 tons (2,375 sorties/ 1,112.2 tons by fighter-bombers).

Fighter/Fighter-Bomber Interdiction Operations
25 June-31 December 1944

	Fighter/Fighter-Bombers		**Bombers***	
Targets	**Sorties**	**Bomb Tons**	**Sorties**	**Bomb Tons**
Marshaling Yards	1,294	700.0	3,562	7,463.0
Rail Lines/Bridges	16,768	8,125.7	12,850	25,507.3
Roads/Bridges	10,744	5008.0	4,039	6,624.4
Troops/Transport	863	344.1	1,905	2,051.7
Dumps	2,375	1,112.2	3,644	5,414.1
Harbors/Docks/ Shipping	1,001	536.4	1,294	2,204.4
Misc.	540	268.9	244	354.7
Totals	33,585	16,095.3	27,538	49,619.8

* Heavy, medium, light

23

Po Valley
1 January - 2 May 1945

US Fighter/Fighter-Bomber Order of Battle (1 January 1945)
Mediterranean Allied Air Force (MAAF)
XXII Tactical Air Command*
62nd Fighter Wing
350th Fighter Group
27th Fighter Group
57th Fighter Group
86th Fighter Group
Desert Air Force
79th Fighter Group
* Was XII Fighter Command until November 1944

On 27 November 1944, Sir Harold Alexander was promoted to Field Marshal, retroactive to June when his troops entered Rome. There were no problems when the popular Alexander was named to replace Sir Henry Wilson as Supreme Allied Commander Mediterranean on 12 December. Lt.Gen. Mark Clark assumed command of Allied armies in Italy while Lt.Gen. Lucian Truscott returned to Italy to assume command of the Fifth Army. Lt.Gen. Sir Richard McCreery had taken over command of the British Eighth Army in October.

Allied high command in Italy. In mid-December 1944, Sir Harold Alexander (left) replaced Henry Wilson as Supreme Allied Commander Mediterranean. Lt.Gen. Mark Clark (center) assumed command of Allied armies in Italy while Lt.Gen. Lucian Truscott returned to Italy to assume command of the Fifth Army. Lt.Gen. Sir Richard McCreery (right) had taken over command of the British Eighth Army in October. (US Army)

At the year's end Truscott had moved three of the Fifth Army's divisions to the endangered left flank and called off its attack on Bologna as heavy winter snows and stiff German resistance stopped their advance. Alexander issued orders to his Armies to go to on the defensive. At the start of 1945 the Germans, the terrain and the weather had stopped the Allied armies. The front went into static, holding disposition. Both sides regarded Italy as a secondary action to the larger battles taking place in northern France. The Allies were short on manpower and ammunition and would be unable to mount an offensive until April. By mid-January Kesselring returned from his convalescence to find the situation much the same when he left in late October. The Allies transferred two Canadian divisions from the Eighth Army but the personnel losses were made good with Polish, Jewish and Italian units. The Fifth Army was strengthened by the US 10th Mountain and 1st Brazilian Divisions but lost two 12th Air Force fighter groups to the ETO. The Allies reorganized and trained troops for their planned spring offensive while the Germans lost three divisions to the defense of Hungary and Czechoslovakia but used the lull to strengthen their defenses, especially around Bologna which was be the Allied spring objective. The German predicament on the Russian Front and the impending Allied advance into Germany caused the German High Command to divert supplies intended for the Italian front. The shipment of supplies to Italy was only sufficient to maintain an inactive front and no stockpiles could be accumulated to stop the future Allied offensive. As a result when the offensive began, ammunition became in critically short supply and was strictly rationed. Kesselring realized that his forces could not stop the Allies and accordingly readied plans for a serial withdrawal to the north bank of the Adige River located in the foothills of the Alps.

Air interdiction did prevent the Germans from withdrawing troops from Italy to France and Germany. They withdrew the 356th Division from the front and transferred them through Verona and three weeks later they had not gotten out of Italy. The normal time of the trip of 330 miles should have been 12 hours from Bologna and the Austrian border. There were long waits for tunnels and bridges to be repaired or long detours around damaged areas, trucks ran out of gas and living off the land then became the order of the day. There are stories of German units buying gasoline on the black market to fuel their trucks.

In February 1945, the TAFs in Italy became the first air force to fly half a million sorties. By 8 February they created four critical blocks of the Brenner Line and by the end of the month there were ten. The Germans withdrew their besieged railheads back from Ora/Trento to north of Bolzano that meant motor transport was needed to transship the stalled supplies. Since the fighter-bombers of the DAF had a shorter range they were assigned close support for both the Eighth and Fifth Armies, freeing the longer-legged P-47s for interdiction sorties further north which in turn allowed medium bombers to attack even further north than previously, even into Germany. All this air activity still did not shut down the German system.

The Casarsa Bridge had been a difficult and frustrating target for the Allies during the winter of 1944-45. It was constructed over a dry riverbed and was readily repaired. Time after time it was thought to have been destroyed and soon air reconnaissance brought back photos of traffic moving over it. The Germans had placed heavy AA defenses around it and on three successive missions the Desert Air Force had lost five aircraft. On 23 February 1945, the 79th Fighter Group was assigned to destroy the bridge. The Group sent three flights ahead of the main force armed with rockets and 20lb. fragmentation bomb clusters. The frags were designed for bomb bay use but 79th armorers devised a method to mount them on underwing racks. The three flights attacked the German AA batteries with the frags and rockets and the three Thunderbolt flights that followed were able to drop their 500lb. bombs accurately on the bridge without interference.

The air effort in the fall and winter of 1944 was neutralized by bad weather, short winter days and the highly efficient German repair organization. The earlier STRANGLE and DIADEM operations had demanded all of the Allies air power but in January 1945,

During 1945 the shorter ranged fighter-bombers of the DAF were assigned close support for both the Eighth and Fifth Armies, freeing the longer-legged P-47s for interdiction sorties further north which in turn allowed medium bombers to attack even further north than previously, even into Germany. All this air activity still did not shut down the German system. Pictured: 27th Fighter Group P-47s of the XXII TAC armed with two 500lb. bombs and carrying belly drop tanks fly over the Apennines. (USAF)

Ponte di Piave rail and road bridges destroyed in February 1945. (USAF)

Main rail line on the Brenner Line between Padua and Vicenza after a dive-bombing attack on 17 February 1945. (USAF)

with somewhat less strength, more sorties were flown than before with more accuracy, destroying or damaging more locomotives, rolling stock and motor vehicles along with more bridges and cut tracks. The reason for the increased aerial success was that the Axis was pushed further north and constricted in a smaller area of northern Italy. This smaller area was commensurate with their decreased air strength and ability to restrict German movement and access to their source of supply. In February the German rail system south of Verona and the repair organization was overwhelmed and less efficient due to the lack of repair supplies and ability to move quickly to areas of damage. The vital rail and road bridges over the di Piave River were destroyed and could not be repaired. February was a good flying weather month and demonstrated that even with good weather and complete air superiority, it required many thousands of continuous sorties to destroy the transport and supply lines of a resourceful enemy and then to maintain the level of destruction. The increased activity caused the Allies to lose 323 aircraft. By the end of March, Allied air power had disabled German transport and deprived them of fuel to meet the upcoming Allied spring offensive but still Axis transport and supply was never completely halted and met minimal short term requirements.

Operation HERBSTNABEL

The Tenth and Fourteenth German Armies included some more experienced divisions that were now up to strength, rested and had carefully conserved supplies and ammunition. Kesselring realized, after DIADEM, that he could not hold the front against a major Allied offensive supported by an air force benefiting from complete air superiority in good spring weather. "HERBSTNEBEL" was Kesselring's plan for a patient, controlled retreat to and then across the Po. His troops in western Italy were to fall slowly back to Ticino to hold the industrial area in the northwest as long as possible. After Salerno and Anzio, Kesselring always was aware of the possibility of another Allied amphibious landing. Luftwaffe aerial reconnaissance was non-existent and unable to discover this threat or even the when and where of the upcoming Allied ground offensive. When the offensive did come, Kesselring had been recalled to replace von Rundstedt as C-in-C West and von Vietinghoff had again assumed command.

In February the Allied Chiefs of Staff had decided that the Italian campaign had served its purpose and was to become a holding operation with offensive thrusts to strike German weak points and withdrawals. The Allied armies and armored units were rested and resupplied after the winter hiatus. The arrival of the 10th Mountain and 1st Brazilian Divisions provided the manpower for the Allies to put pressure on the Germans by mounting an attack in mid-February in the rugged high mountains southwest of Bologna in order to gain a better jumping-off point for the spring offensive.

Operation WOWSER

On 15 March, AM Sir Guy Garrod relieved AM Slessor as Deputy Air C-in-C and on 22 March, Maj.Gen. John Cannon was promoted to assume Eaker's position as commander of the MAAF (Eaker was appointed as the new USAAF Chief of Staff in Washington). Gen. Chidlaw succeeded Cannon as commander of the MATAF and the 12th Air Force. Except for Garrod who had been in command in Southeast Asia, the others were experienced MTO commanders. The Allies had achieved air superiority and their air-ground teams worked in near perfection. On 7 April the MATAF issued a short, five paragraph directive that conceived Operation WOWSER that was to commit a maximum air effort to support the Allied ground offensive. In support of this forthcoming offensive the MATAF flew massive attacks on the areas of the intended attack. After supporting the initial attacks the MATAF was to continue its isolation of northern Italy aided later by MASAF whose bombing of Germany would be concluded by mid-April and would be available to attack Italian targets. Fighter/fighter-bombers flew thousands of close support missions during the period aiding greatly by the Rover Joes. The Luftwaffe offered no resistance and bombers could fly without escort, freeing fighters for support sorties. Small fighter-bomber formations flew continuous missions against the harried Germans.

In February the Allied Chiefs of Staff had decided that the Italian campaign had served its purpose and was to become a holding operation with offensive thrusts to strike German weak points and withdrawals. Close support "Rover Joe" became a staple in war in northern Italy. (USAF)

Rover Joe in action near Bolongna, Italy. German artillery had been harassing American troops on the static front. Joe radioed in MAAF fighter-bombers to take them out. (USAF)

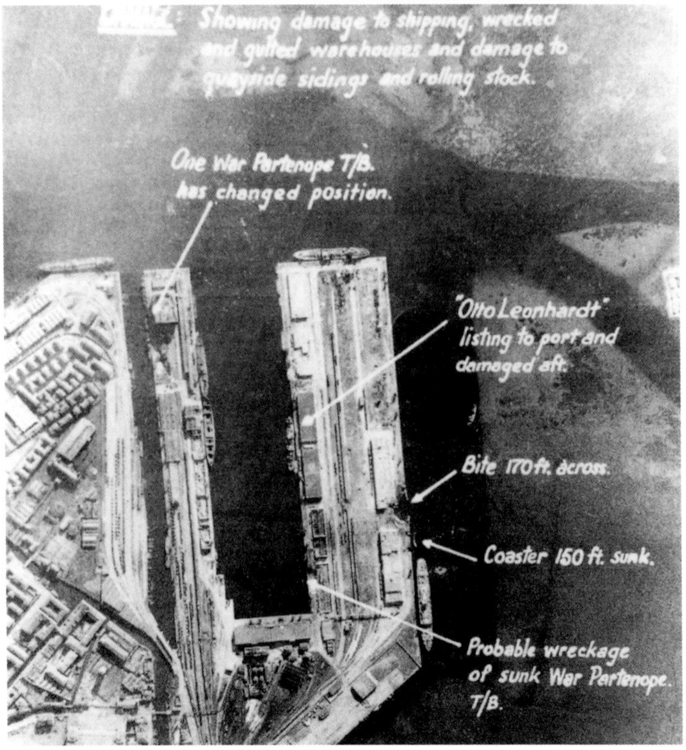

Damage assessment photo, Operation BOWLER mission over Venice in March 1945. The damaged transport *Otto Leonhardt* is pointed out. The 79th Fighter Group struck the transport with two quick direct hits and it caught fire and settled to the bottom. (USAF)

In mid-March, reconnaissance discovered numerous enemy aircraft on Campoformido Air Drome, near Udine, one of the largest in northern Italy. There were about 120 enemy aircraft in Northern Italy but the lack of fuel had limited their effectiveness. As the British 8th Army drove toward Udine it was decided that the A/D needed to be neutralized. On 18 March, the 79th Fighter Group sent 50 P-47s over the A/D in four individual rocket and strafing attacks. The missions did negligible damage as only two Ju-88s were on the field but did disrupt the AA defenses. Four P-47s returned full of holes and one pilot was lost. On 20 March, recon photos showed numerous aircraft on the field and the 79th attacked again. Known AA positions were attacked first with machine gun fire, rockets, frags and phosphorous. After the gun positions were neutralized the Group repeatedly attacked the field, flying a group record number of daily sorties: 260 in 24 missions. Many of the pilots flew three missions that day as Campoformido's buildings, revetments and runways were shattered and 21 aircraft were destroyed on the ground.

Operation BOWLER

By mid-March the German supply lines in northern Italy and the Balkans had been so badly damaged that the Germans needed to ship supplies via the water in the Adriatic. The short distance between the ports of Trieste and Venice allowed a crossing that could be made entirely in darkness. The DAF devised Operation BOWLER to cope with the problem. Venice had become the center of this supply activity and on 21 March the 3,200-ton transport, *Otto Leonhardt*, had docked there along with two 1,000-ton coastal tankers, two torpedo boats and many barges. At the time Venice had been declared an open city to spare its numerous treasures and DAF commander, W/C G. H. Westlake made it very apparent that any officer whose units hit the city would be "bowler-hatted" (fired). To further emphasize his point he stationed orbiting recon aircraft over the dock area to take strike photos. The 79th Fighter Group, joined by RAF 239 Wing Mustangs, participated in the mission with 20 P-47s led by Capt. Benjamin Cassiday on the mid-afternoon of 21 March. The two groups hit 43 AA positions with machine gun rounds, rockets and frags. After the AA suppression, the precision main attack on the harbor took place under the gaze of Venetian citizens watching from their rooftops. The first 79th flight struck the *Otto Leonhardt* with two quick direct hits. The transport caught fire and settled to the bottom. The next three flights destroyed three barges and set another on fire. Docks and quays were shattered and warehouses bombed. One ammunition warehouse exploded so violently that a British recon Spitfire flying overhead was flipped on its back. One of the tankers was set aflame, a torpedo boat sunk and a destroyer damaged. One RAF pilot was downed but quickly rescued, maximum damage was done and Venice's nearby cultural treasures were spared.

WOWSER did not include any continuous pre-jump off aerial softening up sorties as throughout March intense Allied air attacks had destroyed the German transportation net cutting supplies and preventing withdrawal. By the time of the Allied offensive on 9 April all principal rail line north of the Po had been severed and Army Group C was trapped.

Operation BUCKLAND

Within WOWSER, Operation BUCKLAND was the combined heavy, medium and fighter-bomber plan to support the Eighth Army on D-Day and D plus 1. At 1350 heavy bombers dropped carpets of GP and large fragmentation bombs across British V Corps and Polish II Corps lines. At 1400, fighter-bombers were to attack German HQ and communications targets and flew armed recce of all roads leading to the front. Medium bombers were scheduled to attack German artillery at 1450 to 1520 and 1535 to 1550. Air and artillery attacks were coordinated with the latest time, 1920 (one hour before dark), the fighter-bombers could attack the forward German positions without jeopardizing Allied positions. For the two days after D-Day, 1,673 heavy and 624 medium bombers bombed German targets directly behind the battlefront in closely coordinated attacks. Immediately after these attacks, 740 fighter-bombers struck command posts, HQs, gun positions, armor, troop concentrations and targets of opportunity.

Fifth Army's D-Day was scheduled for 12 April but poor flying weather postponed the attacks for two days. Previous to D-Day XXII TAC attacked German communications directly forward of the front. On the 14th, H-Hour had been set for 0600 but fog covered Allied airfields but by 0800 the fog began to lift and H-Hour was moved to 0900. From 0900 throughout the morning 459 P-47 and RAF Spitfire and Kittyhawk strafing sorties were flown first against German artillery and then against pre-arranged and "Rover Joe" directed targets that greatly aided the infantry advance.

Congressional Medal of Honor recipient, 1Lt. Raymond Knight of the 350th Fighter Group/346th Fighter Squadron, poses with flak damage sustained on an earlier mission. Knight is the only fighter-bomber pilot to receive the CMH. (USAF)

Medal of Honor Strafing Ace
Pilot: 1Lt. Raymond L. Knight
Unit: 346FS/350FG/12AF
Time: 24-25 April 1945
Place: Northern Po Valley
A/C: P-47 *"Oh Johnnie"*
Action: Texan, 1Lt. Raymond Knight joined the 346th Fighter Squadron, "Checkerboard", of the 350th Fighter Group on 7 December 1944. The Group's three top aerial scorers only had three victories each and during its entire tour the Group had 50 aerial and 108 ground victories. Knight had flown 82 missions without having an aerial claim. At the time the American Fifth and the British Eighth Armies had cracked the stubborn German defenses that had held up the Allied advance for several months. On the morning of 24 April 1945, Knight volunteered to lead two P-47's to the heavily defended Luftwaffe airdrome at Ghedi. Once over the target he risked heavy AA fire to recon the field, discovering eight camouflaged aircraft. Pulling back up, he radioed the location to the waiting P-47s and led a strafing run in which he claimed five aircraft and his wingman two. After returning to base, Knight again volunteered to lead a flight to the airfield at Bergamo that was in the same area as Ghedi. He ordered his flight to stay at 5,000 feet while he dropped down to contain the AA. Approaching the target, heavy 88mm flak damaged his left wing root but he pressed on and discovered camouflaged enemy aircraft. He called to his flight and led them into battle. He made ten passes and was hit twice more. He was credited with destroying six fully loaded twin-engine bombers and two fighters while his flight got four other TE bombers and a fighter. Knight was able to bring his damaged fighter back to base. The next morning Knight led another flight to Bergamo. He destroyed three more TE bombers but his aircraft was badly damaged. He choose not to divert to British-held Brinisi or bail out but climbed with his wingman to try to cross the Apennines to Pisa. His Medal of Honor citation reads: "Realizing the critical need for aircraft in his unit, he declined to parachute to safety over friendly territory and unhesitating attempt to return his shattered plane to his home field. With great skill and strength, he flew homeward until caught by treacherous air conditions in the Apennines Mountains, where he crashed and was killed". These missions helped the Allies maintain a bridgehead across the Po River at a critical time during which German air interdiction may have made a difference. Knight's wife accepted his posthumous award.

Bologna (8-21 April 1945)
In the beginning of April, Von Vietinghoff had 349,000 German and 45,000 Italian troops, 261 tanks, 450 self-propelled guns and 400 medium anti-tank guns and 1,436 artillery pieces. Bologna was the center of Axis resistance in northern Italy and was heavily fortified and reinforced by the Germans. Back in mid-October the Allied Air Forces initiated Operation PANCAKE that as its name implies was to flatten the city but it continued to hold out. There were 23 German and four Italian divisions against Alexander's 17. The Allied spring offensive was to surround the German armies south of the Po River with a coordinated attack by components of the British Eighth Army on 9 April and the US Fifth Army on 14 April. Both attacks were preceded by heavy artillery and air bombardment. On 5 April, "Bomber" Harris and the RAF had no targets left in Germany and discontinued area bombing. On 16 April General Spaatz sent Generals Doolittle and Twining a directive declaring the Combined Bomber Offensive to be at an end and that Strategic Air Forces in Europe be for the "direct assistance to the land campaign." On the 15th, the MAAF concentrated its resources to the Fifth Army advance, mounting the greatest heavy bomber close-support missions ever in the MTO. From 15-18 April the MASAF sent 4,829 bombers and fighters against targets between Bologna and Highway 9, along the Eighth Army's line of advance and on Highways 64 and 65, the Fifth Army's line of advance. XXII TAC flew over 1,200 sorties in support of the Fifth Army. The British and US units moved into the Po Valley and by the 20th advanced along the entire front facing varied resistance. Von Vietinghoff was forced to throw in his last reserves but was unable to hold off the US VI Corps. Von Vietinghoff held his position until his forces were about to be surrounded when he instituted Kesselring's HERBSNEBEL and ordered a withdrawal from Bologna to the foothills of the Alps. But the Germans stubbornly hung on and it was not until 21 April 1945 that the US 24th finally took Bologna which the Germans abandoned. The weather cleared and the roads were dry and the Allied advance raced past the temporary delaying defensive lines. The Germans moved in large rag-tag convoys north towards the Po. They were hunted from the sky, ammunition and fuel in short supply, communications spotty or lost. In April the MAAF supported the ground offensive and the entire air campaign focused on the circumscribed German front. The MAAF flew 65,959 sorties, 2,200 per day. In four days, 21-24 April, the Germans lost 5,876 vehicles with 2,347 being lost on 23 April. When they finally reached the river they found that the DAF and XXII TAC had destroyed the permanent bridges, the pontoon bridges that were under construction and ferries. The Germans had their backs to the river waiting for something to take them across, but Hitler demanded

that they defend the Po. The German troops defended fiercely in hope of reprieve but as they waited under round-the-clock air assault more Allied artillery was put in place to bombard them. Fighter-bombers ceaselessly hit German signal communications so that frontline commanders were out of contact with their forward units and reserves. Any daylight movement on any level was impossible without sustaining heavy losses. Von Vietinghoff requested permission to withdraw but Hitler refused threatening him with death in absentia. Nonetheless, in face of the multiple Allied breakthroughs von Vietinghoff succeeded in withdrawing a large number of his troops across the Po but thousands of troops and most of his army's equipment were left behind. Many units had no alternative but to swim across the Po but 54,000 preferred to surrender. The river crossing barely slowed the pursuing Allies who chased the collapsing Wehrmacht into north Italy. On 29 April von Vietinghoff approved an unconditional surrender that was to take effect at noon on 2 May.

During this final phase of the war in Italy (1 January-2 May) the MAAF flew 59,563 sorties and dropped 62,611 tons of bombs on interdiction targets the majority by fighter-bombers with 33,543 sorties and 16,176.9 tons. Rail targets; marshaling yards, rail lines and rail bridges, were pounded by 35,604 sorties dropping 43,464.4 tons of bombs of which fighter-bombers flew 18,527 sorties dropping 9,687.5 tons. Roads and road bridges were attacked with 10,377 sorties and 9,504.2 tons (5,436 sorties/2,444.5 tons by fighter-bombers), dumps by received 5,354 sorties and 3,703.4 tons (3,988 sorties/1,718.4 tons by fighter-bombers and troops and military transport by 3,909 sorties and 3,132.7 tons (2,169 sorties/1,718.4 tons by fighter-bombers).

During this final phase of the war in Italy (1 January-2 May) the MAAF flew 59,563 sorties and dropped 62,611 tons of bombs on interdiction targets the majority by fighter-bombers with 33,543 sorties and 16,176.9 tons. After DRAGOON the 57th Fighter Group 1945 was transferred from Corsica to Grosseto, Italy to attack the Brenner Pass and Po River Bridges until the end of the war. (USAF)

By the end of March 1945, German flak strength in Italy had grown to 1,012 heavy and 2,194 medium and light AA guns that caused Allied aircraft to fly higher and more carefully and reduced their accuracy. At the same time the Allies 4,393 front line aircraft on hand versus 130 serviceable Luftwaffe aircraft. Luftwaffe CG Italy Max von Pohl estimated on an average day in late in early 1945, the Allies were able to put up 1,000 fighter-bombers, 250 medium bombers, 70 non-escort fighters, 80 tactical reconnaissance aircraft, 20 night fighters and 20 intruders along with the 700 strategic bombers which over flew Italy on their way to targets in Germany and Austria. Not only did the Luftwaffe have insufficient aircraft to combat the Allied air armada, significantly it didn't have enough for basic reconnaissance to keep track of the onrushing Allied armies once their offensive began. Aircraft, ammunition and air supplies earmarked for Italy were often waylaid in Germany for the defense of the Homeland. Furthermore, many essential non-flying Luftwaffe personnel were being conscripted as soldiers. By March the 130 Luftwaffe aircraft remaining in Italy faced 30:1 odds and their fuel was restricted to nine tons per day versus 407 tons for the Eastern front and 403 tons for the Western Front and defense of the Reich.

On 2 May, Maj. Edward Gabor's (345th Fighter Squadron/350th Fighter Group) P-47 was hit by light flak while strafing near Udine and became the last air casualty in the MTO and one of 402 lost from the beginning of April. The same day, von Vietlinghoff surrendered unconditionally to Alexander without Hitler's consent.

Fighter/Fighter-Bomber Interdiction Sorties
(1 January-2 May 1945)

	Fighter/Fighter-Bombers		**Bombers***	
Targets	**Sorties**	**Bomb Tons**	**Sorties**	**Bomb Tons**
Marshaling Yards	1,538	807.4	5,416	11,667.0
Rail Lines/Bridges	16,989	8,890.1	12,661	22,100.1
Roads/Bridges	5,436	2,444.5	4,941	7,059.7
Troops/Military Transport	2,169	918.4	1,740	2,214.3
Dumps	3,988	1,718.4	1,366	1,985.0
Harbors/Docks/ Shipping	2,377	1001.7	826	1,298.2
Misc.	1,046	396.4	70	110.1.
Totals	33,543	16,176.9	27,020	46,434.4

* Heavy, medium, light

24

Results and Conclusions Italian Tactical Air Campaign

The topography and geography of the Italian Peninsula made it an obvious target for air operations designed to cut an army's supply lines. The mountains that separate the top of the Italian boot from the rest of the European Continent and the chains of mountains and hills that course its length tend to constrict the territory in which roads and rail lines were able to operate in high capacity. Italian rivers tend to run east and west across the peninsula requiring many vulnerable bridges and viaducts to cross them. While the many thousand missions flown in the air campaigns in North Africa and Sicily validated the concept of air interdiction its potential was unappreciated and tactics were not validated until Italy. Before a large-scale interdiction air campaign could be initiated, air superiority needed to be established by destroying the Luftwaffe in the air and on the ground. It was not until before the Anzio campaign that total air superiority was achieved. Early in the battle for Italy there were not sufficient aircraft available to carry out the task and all the air objectives and attacks on transport lines needed to be prioritized. The success of these early attacks prompted the initiation in March of a concentrated air interdiction campaign, STRANGLE, which was "to reduce the enemy's flow of supplies to a level which will make it impossible for him to maintain and operate his forces in central Italy." The objective of STRANGLE was to prove presumptuous and was modified in DIADEM to "make it impossible for the enemy to maintain his forces on his present line in Italy in the face of a combined Allied air offensive." The impressive success of the Italian interdiction campaign proved in theory and in fact the importance of interdiction as an integral part of air operations and later was used in Northwest Europe.

Air Superiority: Undoubtedly, Allied air superiority assured the success of interdiction and close air support missions. But despite having almost complete air superiority the Allies lost 8,011 aircraft and Italy demonstrated that the expert use of anti-aircraft could help negate the aircraft numbers game. Air superiority gained just before the Anzio landings negated the Luftwaffe both in preventing attacks on the transportation system but also in army close support that the Germans virtually invented and perfected. In the steep terrain and often-static battlefields of Italy, Allied artillery was most damaging to the Germans and was not neutralized by the Luftwaffe. German troops were irked when enemy artillery-spotting observation aircraft lingered unmolested overhead for hours directing accurate artillery fire.

Close Air Support: A general tenant of air power is that whoever controls the air also controls the ground. In Italy this was true but it did not bring about a quick and expeditious victory. Without it the invasion of Italy would have been very costly, if not impossible and with it, victory was inevitable but long and costly. Air power could never be a substitute for hard- fought land battles but Armies alone could not defeat a well-led and disciplined enemy in terrain suited for defense without suffering onerous losses.

Interdiction: The definition of interdiction is to: "destroy, obstruct, nullify or delay the enemy's fighting potential before it can be brought to bear." But interdiction alone could not force the Germans to withdraw only ground battles did so. Interdiction isolated the battlefield by destroying transportation networks thus cutting off supplies, paralyzing battlefield mobility and cutting communications and thus turned orderly withdrawals into shattering retreats. During the slog up the Italian boot air interdiction played a continuing vital role of damaging the enemy frontline potential by cutting off a large quantity of his supplies and reinforcements.

Air power unquestionably was used as a psychological weapon during the Italian campaign. The hardened veteran German soldiers on the Italian front expected and were prepared for heavy air attacks. Thus they suffered fewer casualties, less loss of morale and fighting capacity. The psychological effect of air power was negated by the quality of the individual German soldier and his leaders.

General Field Marshal Albert Kesselring (*Kesselring: A Soldier's Record*, ibid.):

"The supply situation, which is always of decisive importance for the success or failure of an operation, was satisfactory toward the beginning of 1944. The opinion that the supply situation was bound to improve the further northward the Army group withdrew was one of the worst delusions of my subordinate commanders. The longer the approach routes were, the less was the enemy able to carry out concentrated attacks on the supply lines; the more numerous the existing means of communications (railways, roads, inland waterways, sea and air transportation), the greater was the probability that one of the other means of communication would remain intact owing to the enemy's inability to concentrate his air attacks on all of them. As an airman I personally had no doubt that the difficulties would increase from the moment when we moved into the Apennines position, and that the entire supply service would collapse when the Alps were reached. This opinion was later borne out by facts."

During the 20 months of the Italian Campaign, the Allies lost 313,495 casualties while the Germans lost 336,650. Why was it so costly and why did it take the Allies so long to move up the Italian Peninsula? Three factors dominated land operations in Italy: topography, weather and the remarkable talent of the German commanders, especially Kesselring, in utilizing terrain and weather, in the face of overwhelming Allied air superiority, to mount a superb defensive war. The Allies were always cautious and moved forward too slowly so that the Germans were able to move up reinforcements and regroup. The Allied soldier relied on air power to do the dirty work for them. Tedder stated: "All land battles are confusion and muddle and the job of airmen is to accentuate that confusion and muddle to a point where it gets beyond an enemy's capacity to control." It was the Pantelleria mentality that plagued Allied thinking throughout the Italian Campaign. Concentrated airpower alone could not demoralize and defeat the well-disciplined and veteran German infantryman. The masterful defensive stalemates created by the Germans expended fewer supplies that could be brought to the front despite the massive destruction of rail and road targets and the supplies carried by them. From March 1944 onwards, the Luftwaffe transferred most of its units from Italy and focused on northern Europe and the remaining few units were shunted around to meet each new emergency. The air offensive in Italy was one of cooperation with Allied armies and also between Allied air forces and then between the strategic and tactical air forces and their aircraft.

Fighter/Fighter-Bomber Interdiction Operations in the Italian Campaign (18 August 1943-2 May 1945)

	Fighter/Fighter-Bombers			Bombers*		
Targets	**Sorties**	**%**	**Bomb Tons**	**Sorties**	**%**	**Bomb Tons**
Marshaling Yards	4,042	4.1	2,080.1	23,801	23.2	49,950.0
Rail Lines/Bridges	49,310	49.7	25,116.7	38,725	37.7	74,416.2
Roads/Bridges	29,217	27.3	13,804.1	20,820	20.3	33,773.9
Troops/Military Transport	7,508	5.4	2,730.9	5,187	5.0	5,884.7
Dumps	8,155	7.2	3,631.1	6,598	6.4	8,948.9
Harbors/Docks/Shipping	5,232	4.6	2,333.0	6,647	6.5	12,293.8
Misc.	2,099	1.7	857.0	948	0.9	1,630.8
Totals	105,563	100.0	50,552.9	102,726	100.0	186,898.3

*Heavy, medium, light

25

Northwest European Campaign: Background and Command

Churchill and Roosevelt named General Dwight Eisenhower as overall Supreme Commander of all land, sea and ground forces for Operation OVERLORD, the invasion of France. Field Marshal Bernard Montgomery was named commander of ground forces and Air Chief Marshal Trafford Leigh-Mallory as commander of the Allied Expeditionary Air Forces (AEAF). A major consideration in the planning for OVERLORD was the decisive role of the Allied Air Forces. Experience in the MTO showed that in decisive land battles air cooperation with the armies could not be a specialized function of part of the air forces but one of the entire air force. OVERLORD planners realized that the array of responsibilities facing the Allied air forces required the involvement of every RAF command: bomber, fighter, coastal and transport and the US 8th (Strategic) and 9th (Tactical) Air Forces. The Allied Expeditionary Air Force (AEAF) was formed with purpose to support the Allied Armies across Northwest Europe. At the time of his appointment, ACM Leigh-Mallory was the AOC (Air Officer Commanding) of the fighter command and he was thought to be a wise choice, as the success of the invasion would depend on air superiority over the beaches. Maj.Gen. Ira Eaker commanded the Eighth Air Force and Maj.Gen. Lewis Brereton commanded the newly reformed Ninth Air Force. There was a distinction in planning and executing the Normandy Invasion air war. Leigh-Mallory was the chief of the AEAF and he and his joint British-American staff, headquartered near London at Stanmore, planned the air campaign that was known as the "Transportation Plan." Eisenhower's deputy for air operations was RAF ACM Sir Arthur Tedder who was based with Eisenhower's operational staff at Bushy Park, London, just a few miles from Stanmore.

Ninth Air Force Resurrected (25 August 1943)

General H.H. Arnold decided not to expand the Eighth Air Force to support the invasion, as it would become too large and unmanageable. Arnold resurrected the 9th Air Force on 25 August 1943 as the tactical arm and the VIII Fighter Command was to escort 8th Air Bombers during Operation POINTBLANK. On 16 October 1943 the 9th Air Force was officially launched in the UK at Sunninghill when Maj.Gen. Lewis H. Brereton was assigned command.

New Allied leadership February 1943. (Bottom row, left to right): Gen. Dwight Eisenhower, ACM Arthur Tedder, Gen. Harold Alexander, and Adm. Andrew Cunningham; (Top row, left to right): Harold Macmillan (British minister, AFHQ), Maj.Gen. Walter Bedell Smith, Commordore Royer Dick and AVM H.E.P. Wigglesworth. (USAF)

British leadership. ACM Trafford Leigh-Mallory (overall commander of the Allied Expeditionary Air Force, AEAF), ACM Arthur Tedder (Deputy Supreme Commander of Allied Forces) and FM Bernard Montgomery. (Author/West)

Gen. Henry "Hap" Arnold (General of the Air Force), Lt.Gen. Carl "Tooey" Spaatz (CG of the US Strategic Air Forces, USSTAF) and Maj.Gen. Hoyt Vandenberg was the Deputy Commander of the AEAF under Leigh-Mallory) (USAF)

Brig.Gen. Victor Strahm continued as his Chief of Staff as he had for a long time in the MTO. Brereton and a small cadre of 9th Air Force staff officers moved to England from the Egypt to provide close air support for OVERLORD. Eaker pledged some 8th Air Force units to the 9th but the majority of the 230,000 men and 4,000 aircraft coming from America through the spring of 1944 were deployed to the Ninth. Brereton seemed to be an excellent choice for the command of the Ninth being one of America's senior aviators. In World War I he commanded the 12th Aero Squadron in France and received successive promotions during the war to Lt. Colonel. Between the wars he attended and instructed at various tactical and training schools. He was the commander of the Far East Air Force in the Philippines at Pearl Harbor and then was named C-in-C of the Allied Air Forces in Java. In March 1942, he organized and commanded the 10th Air Force in India and in June 1942 became commander of the Middle East Air Force (MEAF) which would become the Ninth Air Force in October 1943, when he was appointed its CG. In late May 1943, Eaker wrote Arnold that, "You could not have selected a better man for the Ninth Air Force." The commander of Brereton's IX Fighter Command and its two tactical air commands, the IX and XIX, was Lt.Gen. Elwood "Pete" Quesada. He had commanded the 12th Fighter Command in North Africa and also was the Deputy CG of the Northwest African Coastal Air Force and had participated in many operational missions over Tunisia, Pantelleria, Sicily, Corsica and Italy. Tactical air power theory and practice at the time was in flux and the inexperienced Quesada would have to employ known air support practices recently learned in Africa and Italy and then revise them along the way. Quesada was an impatient, temperamental, perfectionist who endured neither incompetence nor excuses and had problems in assembling a staff that would ultimately be the backbone of the world's best tactical air force.

It was intended to equip the IX Fighter Command beginning in November with P-51s but Gen. Doolittle, CG of the 8th Air Force quickly ended that notion and the IX FC received P-38s and P-47s. The first P-47 group was the 362nd. Through January the 354th Fighter Group was the only operational IX fighter group but its P-51Bs were assigned bomber escort duties. The new but not yet operational 357th Fighter Group that flew P-51s was traded from the IX FC to the VIII FC for the operational P-47 equipped 358th Fighter Group. The planned growth for the IX FC by D-Day was projected at 35,000 men and 1,600 aircraft of five fighter wings, 19 fighter groups, one tactical reconnaissance group, three night fighter squadrons and all the support units.

The successful landings in Normandy on 6 June 1944, were the product of almost five years of war to which the fighter-bomber only began to contribute as part of the pre-invasion process. It was the during the breakout from the beaches, the race across Western Europe to the West Wall, liberating France Holland and Belgium and then repelling the German Ardennes Offensive and the final drive across the Rhine into the heart of Germany that the soundness of the fighter-bomber concept was proven.

Commanding General of the 9th Air Force, Maj.Gen. Lewis Brereton (left) CG of the newly reformed Ninth Air Force meets with Lt.Gen. Carl Spaatz, CG of the USSTAF (center) and Gen. Dwight Eisenhower, Supreme Commander in April 1944. (USAF)

Maj. Gen. Ira Eaker (left) commanded the Eighth Air Force, and ACM Arthur Portal was Eisenhower's deputy for air operations. (USAF)

26

D-Day/Normandy Pre-Invasion

Fighter Groups Assigned to the VIII Fighter Command (1 February 1943)

Order #	Fighter *Group	Date Assigned	Fighter Type
1	4FG	09/12/42	P-47C/D
2	78FG	11/29/42	P-47C/D
3	56FG	01/12/43	P-47C/D
4	353FG	06/07/43	P-47D
5	352FG	07/06/43	P-47D
6	355FG	07/05/43	P-47D
7	356FG	08/25/43	P-47D
8	20FG	08/25/23	P-38H/J
9	55FG	09/16/43	P-38H/J
10	359FG	10/19/43	P-47D
11**	358FG	10/20/43	P-47D
12	361FG	11/30/43	P-47D
13***	357FG	01/31/44	P-51B
	(364FG	02/10/44	P-38J)
	(479FG	05/14/44	P-38J)

* In order of assignment
** To the 9AF
*** From the 9AF

TAC Order of Battle

9th AF TACs:

IX/Quesada: First Army/Hodges (6 June 1944)
- 70 FW
- 71 FW
- 84 FW
  - 48 FG (P-47)
  - 50 FG (P-47)
  - 365 FG (P-47)
  - 366 FG (P-47)
  - 367 FG (P-38)
  - 368 FG (P-47)
  - 370 FG (P-38)
  - 371 FG (P-47)
  - 404 FG (P-47)
  - 405 FG (P-47)
  - 474 FG (P-38)
  - 67 TRG (P-38)
  - 422 Squadron (P-61)

XIX/Weyland: Third Army/Patton (6 June 1944)
- 100 FW
- 303 FW
  - 354 FG (P-51)
  - 358 FG (P-47)
  - 362 FG (P-47)
  - 363 FG (P-51)
  - 36 FG (P-47)
  - 373 FG (P-47)
  - 406 FG (P-47)
  - 10 PRG (P-38)
  - 425 Squadron (P-61)

XXIX/Nugent: Ninth Army/Simpson

9th AF Organization

HQ/Vandenberg
IX Service/Wood
IX Engineer/Newman
IX Air Division/Anderson
IX Air Defense Command/Richardson

Note: Seventh Army/Patch worked with the British 1TAC

Allied Air Command Structure

Combined Chiefs of Staff (CCS)
RAF
- 8th Air Force
  - VIII Fighter Command (13 fighter Groups)

Supreme HQ Allied Expeditionary Force (SHAEF)
- **Allied Expeditionary Air Force (AEAF)**
  - 9th Air Force
    - IX Fighter Command (8 fighter groups)
    - IX Tactical Air Command
    - XIX Tactical Air Command *

* Under the operational control of IX TAC until the US Third Army became operational on 1 August 1944. At that time it became co-equal with the IX YAC under command of the IX Fighter Command

On 1 March 1944, the 9th AF had 1602 fighter-bombers available and the 8th AF 1400.

Pre-Invasion Fighter/Fighter-Bomber Objectives

1) Gaining and maintaining air superiority over the invasion area by the progressive destruction of the Luftwaffe in France. Bombers were assigned to continuously and systemically bomb Luftwaffe airfields within a 130-mile radius of Caen in order to force the Luftwaffe to operate as far from the invasion area as possible.
2) Destroy rail facilities such as major marshaling yards, railway centers, repair, maintenance and storage depots, switching centers, roundhouses etc. The object was to isolate the battlefield.
3) Disrupt rail traffic and rail equipment by attacking all moving trains in France and Belgium.
4) Destroy selected rail and road bridges over the Seine, Liore, Meuse and other rivers to isolate the battlefield.
5) Destroy coastal batteries, fortifications and communications along the Atlantic Wall.

Note: Not heeding the Pantelleria lesson, the destruction of the Atlantic Wall batteries was assigned to the 8th Air Force heavy bombers, RAF Bomber Command and 9th Air Force medium bombers. The 9th began its attacks in early May as a second priority and continued through the month without significant results and with a great drain on its resources. The 8th Air Force and Bomber Command dropped a massive amount of bombs in the two weeks prior to the landings. Post-invasion surveys showed that very few enemy batteries had been destroyed.

Invasion Responsibilities of the IX TAC

On 15 April the AEAF issued a massive and comprehensive air plan calling for maximum effort by the RAF Bomber and Fighter Commands, the RAF Coastal Command, the Air Defense of Great Britain, two US and one British airborne division, the VIII Bomber and Fighter Commands, IX Bomber Command, and the IX and XIX Tactical Air Commands. The responsibilities of the IX TAC were:

D minus 30 to D minus 1

1) Be employed in the training and preparation for the invasion.
2) Provide fighter escort for bomber attacks of the USSAF and IX BC
3) Provide fighter-bombers for offensive operations as directed by the 9th AF
4) Provide tactical recon supplemented by photo recon as directed by the 9th AF
5) Provide necessary units and personnel to implement fighter control of fighter units of the Command
6) Establish liaison with the US First Army and execute the necessary details incidental to future joint operations.
7) Coordinate with the Commanding General, XIX TAC, in training and preparation of those units of his command that will be attached to IX TAC in future operations.

During assault, build-up and subsequent phases

1) Provide five groups of P-47 aircraft as high cover over the assault beach area.
2) Provide one group of P-38 aircraft in convoy cover and coordinate the participation of four groups of P-38 aircraft of the VIII FC in convoy cover.
3) Provide two groups of P-38 aircraft and four groups of P-47 aircraft for the direct air support of the ground forces.
4) Coordinate the employment of six groups of P-47 and three groups of P-51 aircraft of the VIII FC in the provision of bomber escort for the IX BC.
5) Maintain four groups of P-47 aircraft and two groups of P-51 aircraft in reserve for use as directed by the Commanding General, 9th AF. It is probable that the major part of these groups will be used as fighter-bombers for attacking coast defense batteries and other strong points in the enemies defense system.
6) Be prepared to operate all fighter and fighter-bomber groups on a scale of four group sorties a day.
7) Be prepared to furnish escort for troop carrier operations on D-Day and D+1.
8) Provide one group of tactical recon aircraft to execute tactical recon missions in direct support of the ground forces, on a scale of three group sorties a day.

On 15 April 1944 the AEAF issued a seven-point directive for the responsibilities of the IX TAC for D minus 30 to D minus 1. (USAF)

Before D-Day the 2nd TAF flew reconnaissance and contributed to the Transportation Plan, with its rocket-firing Typhoons destroying locomotives and rolling stock and its medium bombers destroying communication centers. A 2nd TAF Typhoon if the 122 wing on a French airfield. (USAF)

9) Be responsible for night fighter control through the 85th Group until relieved by the IX Air Defense Command.
10) Be responsible for aircraft warning and day fighter control activities in the American sector.
11) As soon as R&R (refueling and rearming) strips are available, coordinate their use by fighter groups of the command for the execution of such missions as may be ordered by the Commanding General, 9th AF.
12) As advance landing grounds and airfields become available, occupy them with fighter groups and execute fighter and fighter-bomber missions in support of the US First Army and other missions as may be ordered by the Commanding General, 9th AF.
13) Provide the necessary headquarters personnel and operational agencies to conduct operational control and command of all 9th AF units located on the far shore, until such time as the Commanding General, 9th AF, establishes his operating headquarters on the far shore and announces his assumption of command.

RAF 2nd Tactical Air Force

The 2nd Tactical Air Force was created on 1 June 1943 for OVERLORD under AM Arthur Coningham. It was fashioned after the Desert Air Force and the Anglo-American Tactical Air Force in Tunisia. Since OVERLORD was to be fighter and fighter-bomber inclined, the 2nd TAF was to have them on strength. Along with the US 9th Air Force, Britain's 2nd TAF was part of the Allied Expeditionary Air Force (AEAF). Four RAF groups made up the 2nd TAF: No. 2 (Bomber) Group No. 83 (Composite) Group, No. 84 (Composite) Group and No. 85 (Base) Group which was under the temporary operational command of No. 11 Group attached to RAF home defense command. The joint command organization of the 2nd TAF was:

Supreme Commander (Eisenhower)
AEAF (Leigh-Mallory)

21st Army Group<———>	**2TAF**
(Montgomery)	(Coningham)
2nd British Army<———>	83 Group
(Dempsey)	(Broadhurst)
1st Canadian Army<———>	84 Group
(Crerar)	(Brown)

The joint command system paired headquarters at each level of command. The 2nd TAF supported Montgomery's 21st Army Group under which was Dempsey's 2nd Army and Crerar's 1st Canadian Army headquarters which were supported by Broadhurst's 8rd Group and Brown's 84th Group respectively. Under this system both the British Army and RAF were independent and at no level could an Army commander order air support; a system which would rankle the Army. 83 Group consisted of one Mustang III Wing, five Spitfire IX Wings and four Typhoon IA Wings {plus reconnaissance (Mustang I and Spitfire IX and artillery spotting (Auster V) units}. 84 Group consisted of one Mustang III, six Spitfire IX and three Typhoon IA Wings (plus recon and spotting units). The objectives of the 2nd TAF were:

1) Achieve air superiority to allow fighter-bombers, bombers and reconnaissance aircraft to operate without interference.
2) Provide air support for the Army through indirect and direct air support.

Indirect support was "attacks on objectives which do not have an immediate effect on the land battle." Indirect support targets included transportation, rail, road and shipping targets and lines of communication.

Direct support was "attacks on enemy force actually engaged in the land battle." Targets were tanks, artillery, defensive positions and infantry.

By D-Day the 2nd TAF was comprised of 14 bomber squadrons, 65 fighter squadrons (HQ-2, 83 Group-25, 84 Group-26 and 85 Group-12), seven recon, seven spotting (A.O. P.) and one met squadron. During the air battle over the ETO the 2nd TAF fighter-bomber groups were engaged in: 60% armed reconnaissance, 25% planned missions and 15% target requested missions.

Before D-Day the 2nd TAF flew reconnaissance and contributed to the Transportation Plan, with its rocket-firing Typhoons destroying locomotives and rolling stock and its medium bombers destroying communication centers. Radar stations and Luftwaffe airdromes were also frequent targets. On D-Day the 2nd TAF were to provide an "air umbrella stretching from England to the landing beaches.

Allied Air Strategy

By late March 1944, after nearly two and a half years of war, the Allies had not yet formulated even a broad plan for the engaging its air forces or what the air organization was to be for the invasion which was only two months away. The bomber escort and ground support factions of the senior Allied leadership were at odds at a personal level. The reserved, stuffy, Leigh-Mallory was held in low regard by everyone, fellow Brits and Americans alike. Brereton also came under personal scrutiny. Both Lt.Gen. Omar Bradley, First Army Commander, and Eisenhower had qualms about Brereton and the 9th Air Force feeling he was more interested in the Ninth's medium bombers and didn't grasp the potential of ground support and made half-hearted efforts to solve air-ground problems. Quesada and his command basically drafted the American tactical air support plan for OVERLORD and ground generals referred to the 9th Air Force as "Quesada's Air Force." The Allied command arrangement for OVERLORD included Gen. Carl Spaatz, commander of the US Strategic Air Forces in Europe (USSAFE) and ACM Arthur Harris, AOC of the RAF Bomber Command neither of whom was disposed to take orders from Leigh-Mallory. By mid-March, Eisenhower could no longer tolerate the situation in his air command and he brought in some of his reliable North African air cronies. Hoping to placate the anti-Leigh-Mallory camp, he named Sir Arthur Tedder, his chief air assistant in the desert, as Deputy Supreme Commander under Leigh-Mallory. Carl Spaatz was appointed to head all American air forces in England. Jimmy Doolittle became 8th Air Force commander, replacing Ira Eaker who went to Italy to replace Spaatz. But Eisenhower's moves only increased the personality issues among his top echelon of officers. Leigh-Mallory, Brereton and Coningham viewed Ike's new appointees as intruders. Montgomery then undermined Coningham by naming the highly respected AVM Harry Broadhurst as Coningham's fighter commander. Eisenhower as Supreme Allied Commander in effect directed all air components of OVERLORD and implemented his position through Tedder, his newly appointed deputy and Tedder then was the actual air commander-in-chief, though not in name.

Personalities aside, the underlying problem for the discord was doctrinal questions. There remained unanswered questions of what was the role of air power in the invasion scheme. Harris, Spaatz and Doolittle were proponents of the strategic use of bombers in the invasion while Leigh-Mallory advocated a more tactical use of bombers. Leigh-Mallory's resolute stand for tactical air power led Eisenhower to reconcile the two camps and finally the fighter forces were freed to train with ground forces and the bombers were to begin to interdict invasion targets. In April and May, 8th Air Force bombers hit tactical targets with twice the sorties and two and a half times the bomb tonnage as strategic targets.

ACM Trafford Leigh-Mallory was the C-in-C of the AEAF (Allied Expeditionary Air Force) which gave him command of the Allied tactical air forces but did not decide his authority over the strategic air forces. Problems with Tedder and strategic bomber advocates, Arthur Harris and Carl Spaatz who had agendas for their strategic bombers arose and Leigh-Mallory gradual lost control of OVERLORD air strategy. (Author/West)

German Air Strategy 1944

By early 1944, the Allied air offensive had placed the Luftwaffe in a compromised strategic position. Allied bombers had severely damaged the German aircraft industry. In February the 8th Air Force launched a concentrated attack, BIG WEEK, which destroyed the root of the German aircraft industry, its factories and power plants. While the bombers were shattering the German air industry their escorts had destroyed many defending Luftwaffe fighters. The P-51 Mustang was able to escort the bombers to the target and was superior to the defending Luftwaffe aircraft and pilots. The Luftwaffe had initiated retaliatory attacks on England and suffered heavy losses (329 of 550 bombers) without offsetting results. Then in May the 8th Air Force began attacks on the German synthetic oil industry and by D-Day the German war machine and Luftwaffe was feeling the results. The Luftwaffe had achieved success against RAF night bombing raids on Germany but Bomber Command switched to attacking the transportation system and was successful in isolating the invasion beaches. The Luftwaffe had hoped that the groundbreaking Me-262 jet fighter/fighter-bomber would be available in numbers to have a significant effect on the invasion. The production schedule was delayed due to the problems with the Jumo turbo-jet engine compressors and the Me-262 did not fly over the invasion beaches. The Germans had developed the V-1, Flying Bomb, the first cruise missile, and had built the ski launch sites along the Channel coast. The German V-1 threat was designed to terrorize the British civilian population and hopefully force the stop of Allied bombing of the Reich. Secondly it was to disrupt the invasion by destroying supplies and troop concentrations. But Allied air reconnaissance discovered the sites and Operation CROSSBOW destroyed the sites and delayed the V-1 launch schedule until after D-Day. With the losses in fighters and bombers the Luftwaffe decided that it had to continue defend Germany until the invasion came and then it would move fighter units west to France to counter the Allies on the beaches. When the invasion did come the Luftwaffe bases in France had been destroyed and reattacked after they were repaired. The Luftwaffe fighter-bomber force was in Russia waiting for the spring offensive there. Luftwaffe pilots in the west were trained in air-to-air combat and were found to be ineffective and vulnerable as fighter-bomber pilots.

The von Rundstedt-Rommel Controversy on the Potential Impact of Allied Air Power

Hitler had placed his best generals in charge of defending against the invasion. The German senior commanders of OB West, Field Marshals Erwin Rommel and Gerd von Rundstedt, opposed each other over the location of German operational reserves ready to repulse the Allied invasion of France. Von Rundstedt felt that the landings could not be prevented and wanted to drive the Allies back into the sea by a mobile counter-attack by a large reserve force located in a central position in the rear for more flexibility to attack once the exact location of the invasion had been established. Rommel felt that the Allies almost complete air superiority would prevent the movement of von Rundstedt's reserves and opted to crush the invasion by deploying all his reserves near the beach to immediately drive the enemy into the sea.

Other than Rommel, the Germans had not learned the lessons at Salerno and Anzio when the Allies succeeded in landing a large force under air-sea superiority and established a beachhead. Panzer reserves were stationed too far to the rear and could not be brought into action soon enough due Allied air superiority. It is now obvious that Rommel's plan to deploy Army Group B and its reserve panzer divisions was the correct one. Based on his experience in North Africa and Italy Rommel knew due to Allied air superiority and effective air interdiction that reserves needed to be close to the beaches in order to commit them as soon as possible before they could be cut apart by Allied medium and fighter-bombers. Von Rundstedt backed by other German generals, mostly from the Russian front (von Kluge and Model), who never experienced Allied air interdiction thought Rommel's plan contradicted the tried and true strategic and tactical concept of defense in depth and to make use of the German superiority in armored mobile warfare such as von Rundstedt practiced in Russia. This concept could have succeeded if the Luftwaffe and Kriegsmarine had been equal in strength to the Allies air-sea power. Rommel knew that strategically defense in depth would be impossible against Allied air superiority. The coast defense line was thin and would be battered by the overpowering pre-invasion air-sea bombardment and would then be vulnerable to the establishment of beachheads. The only prospect of defeating the Allied invasion was to quickly concentrate a large force in a counter-attack on the landing beaches before they could become organized and consolidated. A minimum of five or six panzer divisions would be required to stop the Allies the first two days on the beaches. Rommel position was: "If we cannot get at the enemy immediately after he lands, we will never be able to make another move, because of his vastly superior air forces. If we are not able to repulse the enemy at sea or throw him off the mainland in the first 48 hours, then the invasion will have succeeded and the war will be lost for the lack of a strategic reserve and the complete absence of the Luftwaffe." (Hans Spiedel, *Invasion 1944*, Regenery, Chicago, 1950)

Hitler had placed his best generals in charge of defending against the invasion. The German senior commanders of OB West, Field Marshals Erwin Rommel and Gerd von Rundstedt (pictured), opposed each other over the location of German operational reserves ready to repulse the Allied invasion of France. (Author/West)

Unfortunately Rommel and von Rundstedt disagreed on strategy and Hitler sanctioned neither plan and a provisional arrangement resulted. Influenced by FORTITUDE, the decoy invasion at Calais by Patton's bogus 1st Army Group, Hitler took charge of the anti-invasion plans and his plan was a compromise. The Fuehrer demanded that the defense would be at the Atlantic Wall and the disposition of the one available combat ready panzer corps and five panzer divisions in formation were to be stationed miles behind the beaches with an emphasis on repelling the invasion at Calais.

Air Superiority

In North Africa and Italy air-to-air combat and attacks on German airfields and AA positions primarily gained air superiority. Bombers attacking the Reich and its aircraft and oil industry gained early air superiority over Europe. The attacks were designed to draw up the defending Luftwaffe in order to have aerial gunners and the escorting fighters destroy them. Air superiority was looked upon as a by-product of the strategic bombing campaign but as D-Day approached the tactical strategy changed. Tactical missions by medium bombers and fighter-bombers were to attack and neutralize Luftwaffe airfields within 130 miles of the landing beaches and interdict German transportation and supply systems in France.

The air planning for the invasion was the responsibility of Leigh-Mallory, overall commander of the Allied Expeditionary Air Forceproved to be a poor choice for this position. Leigh-Mallory controlled over 3,000 heavy bombers of the 8th, 12th, 15th US Air Forces, the medium bombers of the 9th Tactical Air Force and approximately 3,000 fighters. He was generally held in low regard not only by American counterparts such as Gen. Carl Spaatz and

Maj.Gen. Elwood Quesada but also by his fellow Brits: Eisenhower's Deputy Supreme Commander of Allied Forces, AM Sir Alfred Tedder and subordinate, AM Sir Arthur Coningham. The Tedder, Coningham, Leigh-Mallory triangle played like a bad soap opera with all the requisite back-stabbing, name-calling and infidelities. When discussing what was required to achieve air superiority, Coningham said that Leigh-Mallory "didn't have a clue!"

At the time of his appointment as C-in-C of the AEAF Leigh-Mallory, Operation POINTBLANK, the intended destruction of vital German industry especially synthetic and natural oil facilities, ball bearing factories and aircraft assembly factories, was underway, directed by Spaatz. As part of POINTBLANK was the supposition that the Luftwaffe would have to defend these vital targets and thus expend itself in attacking the daily stream of fighter escorted Allied bombers thus leaving fewer planes and pilots to fly over the invasion beaches. On 8 February 1944 Gen. H.H. "Hap" Arnold issued Field Order No. 237, the "Down to Earth" edict, directing the American air effort in the ETO "to destroy the Luftwaffe in the air and on the ground." No. 237 stated:

"If bombers are not being attacked, [fighter] groups will detach one or two squadrons to range out searching for enemy aircraft. Upon withdrawal, if the endurance permits, groups will search for and destroy enemy aircraft in the air and on the ground."

To make the prospect of dangerous ground strafing more appealing the 8th Air Force decided to allow ground victory claims toward total victory credits and ace status. This enabled P-38, P-47 and P-51 escort pilots to make surprise attacks on Luftwaffe units massing to attack the bomber stream. These fighter attacks, if rapidly deployed, would disrupt the Luftwaffe response, enabling many bomber groups to fly through areas without being attacked. VIII Fighter Command CO, Gen. William Kepner, encouraged ground strafing as he knew this change in tactics would cause the Luftwaffe to lose more aircraft, disrupt organized response, destroy valuable fuel supplies, wreck facilities and demoralize ground crew.

In POINTBLANK, Spaatz had planned to turn the poor weather over Europe that had grounded countless bombing missions into an

The confident Quesada guaranteed Churchill that the German Air Force would not appear over Normandy and on 6 June he was good to his word. (USAF)

Left: The Tedder, Coningham, Leigh-Mallory triangle played like a bad soap opera with all the requisite back-stabbing, name-calling, and infidelities. When discussing what was required to achieve air superiority, Coningham said that Leigh-Mallory "didn't have a clue!" Coningham is pictured with Harry Broadhurst (left), his brilliant field leader of the 2nd TAF 83 Group. (Author/West)

ally by using radar-directed blind bombing from above the clouds. Spaatz' plan never materialized as the radar bombing sets were in short supply and those sent were inaccurate. Long-range escorts were also in short supply and those that did arrive were initially sent to the 9th Air Force tactical groups. The poor weather of the winter of 1943-44, time, vested interests, personalities all conspired to defeat Spaatz' air plan to simultaneously destroy German oil and air power. His plan to attack German oil was put on hold and his bombers were to be used in pre-invasion close support tactical missions under the control of Leigh-Mallory. Spaatz went to Eisenhower and insisted that American aircraft should not be put under the control British control and particularly under the control of Leigh-Mallory but to no avail. Instead, Ira Eaker, a Spaatz friend and advocate, was sent to the Mediterranean to head the 12th Air Force and was replaced by Jimmy Doolittle. The decision had little to do with who was right or wrong but the American High Command was playing the age-old military blame game. After Leigh-Mallory had secured Spaatz' heavy bombers he told Eisenhower he would also require the RAF bombers under Sir Arthur Harris to insure that all road and rail targets behind the beaches were demolished. Spaatz argued that this demand would totally sabotage POINTBLANK and that tactical missions squandered heavy bomber resources that could better be used and that these tactical attacks on rail and road targets would never force the Luftwaffe to come out to protect them like attacks on oil would. Spaatz notes in his Command Diary on 3 January 1944:

"Am not sure whether L-M (Leigh-Mallory) has proper conception of air role. Apparently accepts possibility of not establishing air supremacy until landing starts."

Pete Quesada had a similar experience with Leigh-Mallory when he asked him how he intended to achieve air superiority over the beaches. Leigh-Mallory replied:

"What is air superiority? When the Germans come up to contest our invasion, we will win the battle for air control at that time."

Arthur "Bomber" Harris called Leigh-Mallory "an imbecile" for diverting his bombers from their nightly raids to attack "secondary targets" and bypassed Eisenhower by going directly to Churchill with vigorous objections. He told Churchill that Leigh-Mallory's plan to use RAF bombers against tactical targets had no chance of success and went to say that after this failure, the Army would look for a scapegoat and blame it on the RAF. Harris was so bold as to offer to put his prediction in writing! Churchill consulted his Air Force Chief, AM Sir Charles Portal, who had three years previously rendered a similar oil plan that could not be implemented at the time as the British did not have the resources. Portal agreed with Harris and Spaatz but Churchill mindful of the heavy losses suffered on the disastrous Dieppe "D-Day rehearsal" raid of August 1942 he had to accede to Leigh-Mallory's and the US Army's demand to use both USAAF and RAF heavy bombers in a tactical pre-invasion role. Churchill did agree to keep these bombers out of Leigh-Mallory's direct control. A major OVERLORD briefing was held on 15 May 1944, attended by all the principal Allied leaders: Churchill, Eisenhower, Montgomery, Smuts, Tedder, Ramsey, Leigh-Mallory and the American and British Corps and Division commanders and King George. Leigh-Mallory described the air plan in detail to the group. After 1 June he was to gain temporary control of all strategic air power in Europe in addition to the USAAF 9th Air Force and the British 2nd Tactical Air Force. During the early phases of D-Day 1,900 American and British bombers would drop nearly 11,000 tons of bombs on the beaches and then return to refuel and rearm. Back in the air they would concentrate their attacks on bridges and towns. When it was Lt.Gen. Lewis Brereton turn to speak he deferred the 9th Air Force briefing to Quesada who had just turned forty and been made a Major General. When VII Corps commander, Maj.Gen. J. Lawton Collins asked how Quesada was going to keep the Luftwaffe from interfering with the landings, he told him that there wasn't going to be any German Air Force there. Churchill interrupted asking him how he could be so sure. The confident Quesada guaranteed that the German Air Force would not appear over Normandy as the fighters and fighter-bombers of the US 8th and 9th and RAF 2nd Tactical Air Forces would destroy the Luftwaffe as far inland as Brussels and Paris and on 6 June he was good to his word.

The Mustang and Thunderbolt Change Roles

When the P-51B was re-engined with the Packard-licensed Rolls Royce Merlin the fighter was able to fly to Berlin. But it was sent to England as a ground support fighter-bomber for the newly formed 9th Air Force. The P-38 and P-47 were eminently unsuccessful in flying escort for the VIII Bomber Command and when the 354th Fighter Group, "Pioneer Mustang Group," arrived in the UK in early November 1944, it was transferred to the VIII Fighter Command for escort duties. This transfer was the first of the AAF's change in policy. The 357th Fighter Group flying the Mustang was next when it was exchanged for the 358th P-47 group. From that point on the 9th Air Force would receive the P-47 groups for tactical missions and the 8th Air force would receive the P-51s for escort missions. It was ironic that the P-47 designed as a high altitude escort and the P-51 designed as a tactical fighter-bomber as the Mustang I for the RAF would trade roles for which each would become outstanding. The only P-51 Group retained by the 9th was the 36rd Fighter Group that later would become an effective tactical reconnaissance unit.

355th Fighter Group Harasses Luftwaffe Airdromes (March-April 1944)

In March 1944, the 355th Fighter Group earned their nickname the "Steeple Morden Strafers" as part of "Ramrod" bomber escort missions. Lt. Clarence Barger described a hair-raising attack on a German airdrome in an encounter report (*Steeple Morden Strafers*, Ken Wells, Egon Publishers, UK, 1994):

Lt. Clarence Barger of the 355th Fighter Group vividly describes a harrowing Ramrod mission on 8 March 1944. (USAF)

"Attack Made on Enemy Airdrome in the Vicinity of Hosepe on 8 March 1944

Pilot: Clarence R. Barger, 354th Fighter Squadron

Time of Attack: 1530 First attack

A/C Encountered: Five Ju-88s and one Me-109 on the ground

Claims: Three Ju-88s destroyed on the ground

I was flying Haywood Black No.2 on Captain Johnston's wing. At 15,000 feet near the rendezvous point in the vicinity of Dummer Lake, Lt. Brown called to say he had spotted an aerodrome with two aircraft on it. Captain Johnston called and said we would look it over. We dived and as we got lower the flak got heavier with the light flak coming up to 10,000 feet. We altered course and intended to make a pass from a distance of five miles from the aerodrome, down sun. Captain Johnston and I missed the field and looking behind I saw Lt. Sweat and Lt. Brown about a half mile behind us and also on the treetops. Lt. Sweat made a sharp turn into the field so I did a steep left turn, which brought Captain Johnston out as my wingman. We came out in this order for our pass on the field-Lt. Sweat leading, then myself, followed by Captain Johnston and Lt. Brown.

I saw a line of four Ju-88s with others strung out around the perimeter. Lt. Sweat opened fire at the first Ju-88 from 200 yards and practically zero feet. I saw it burst into flames and black smoke starting pouring out. (Note: Sweat was shot down and killed after this pass) I opened fire on the next Ju-88 from zero altitude and at a range of about 250 yards. I saw strikes on the ground before the aircraft, and the same pattern finally engulf it, hitting the fuselage and wings, it then began to burn. I pulled up and in doing so my tail hit the top of the fuselage of a parked plane bending a base of the vertical fin. I was too close to the fire on the third aircraft so I held my fire until I got the fourth Ju-88 in my sights. Still at zero altitude, I fired at this enemy aircraft and saw strikes on the fuselage and wings. I passed over it too quickly to see it catch fire. During this pass over the field the machine gun fire was quite heavy and concentrated but all of us flew through it okay.

The third aircraft had not been hit and as I did not see any fire break out in the last aircraft I decided we might as well finish them all off. By this time I was in the lead and thought Captain Johnston and Lt. Brown were still behind me. I did a steep left turn and made another run down the line of enemy aircraft. This time I "essed" until I got into position to fire on the last two enemy aircraft-I fired and saw strikes on both these aircraft.

. I whipped around to the left again and made a third pass. I didn't even dare fire, as the machine gun fire from the ground by that time showed tracers on all sides of me. Since I was the only one making this pass, all the guns seemed to be concentrated on me.

By this time I was all above it and at a distance of two to three miles from the aerodrome I started to climb because I didn't have enough gas to come home on deck. My fuel gauge indicated that I had about 105 gallons.

At about 3,000 feet I saw one of our fighters about a half mile ahead of me and 2,000 feet above me. Flak was bursting around the plane all this time. When I reached the plane it turned out to be Lt. Brown. We climbed to about 7,000 feet, flying in a westerly direction, when Lt. Brown suddenly started a steep dive. I didn't know where he was going but I followed. At the time I thought perhaps hr didn't have enough gas to get home or was injured and had decided to a last big "do" before he got it. We were only five or ten miles from the first aerodrome. When we dropped at about 3,000 feet I saw that he was heading for another aerodrome on which I spotted a Me-110.

Lt. Brown opened fire at the enemy aircraft and I saw many strikes and smoke coming out of it by the time I got within firing range. I opened fire at some of the aircraft at about 350 yards but I think I overshot the target and missed. Machine gun fire was very heavy. We continued on the deck for almost a half a mile and then began to climb. Flak was bursting on all sides of us and machine gun fire was still heavy.

An explosive shell burst at my tail and shook the plane terrifically. I called Lt. Brown and asked him to throttle back as my plane had been hit. No sooner had I finished talking than the damn stuff came tearing through the right side of my cockpit through the rear panel. Some hit the armor plate so close to the edge of it that it chipped off and the shrapnel from this hit me in the back of my head, stunning me for a few seconds.

I called Lt. Brown again and I guess I sounded quite excited by now. Anyhow, I said I was hit in the head and that my ship was in a very critical condition. I looked at the gas gauge again and I saw I only had sixty gallons, noticing at the same time that my air speed indicator was reading zero; the glass of my suction pump gauge had been broken. Half of the glass of my gunfight was also shattered. The control wires of my left aileron had been shot off and it was flapping up and down in the wind. My flaps, likewise, were useless and flapping since my hydraulic system had been shot out. There was also a hole about a foot in diameter through the trailing edge of my left wing root; smoke came out of it all the way back to England.

By this time Captain Johnston heard our radio chatter and joined our formation. I didn't know how badly my tail assembly had been shot up so I asked him to fly close and have a look since my plane was vibrating so that it almost shook my shoes off. Captain Johnston said my tail looked okay but after we had landed he told me he had thought it would shake off but hadn't wanted to tell me because I might had got excited.

Captain Johnston and Lt. Brown kept 'essing' around me to protect me from any enemy aircraft which could have come up on my tail. I came out across the enemy coast at 7,000 feet with 1,500 rpm. My fuel warning light came on while I was still over the Channel. I weighed the two possibilities; either bailing out as soon as we hit England or trying to crash land the aircraft. There was a layer of clouds 2,000 feet thick with a base of 1,000 feet and Captain Johnston wanted me to fly on his wing but I didn't want to try it as I feared that the wires of my right aileron would give way, flicking my aircraft into his. Coming out of the clouds I saw a large aerodrome on my right. I made one complete right hand circuit (right hand because of the dead aileron) to land into the wind. I released my undercarriage about 100 feet above the ground and rocked the wings as much as I dared so the wheels would lock. By this time my gas gauge read empty.

At about ten feet off he ground Lt. Brown was screaming over his R/T, 'Pull up, your wheels, only one of them is down!' Without any hydraulic system they had to stay down, fortunately they locked just before I touched the ground. A shell had blown my left tyre and the plane was swinging off to the right towards a group of B-26s. I quickly turned off all switches, unlocked the tail wheel and ground-looped violently to the left. The plane went half way around and stopped. The hole in my left wing was blazing so I jumped out of the aircraft and ordered the fast assembling ground crew to get a fire extinguisher and put the fire out.

An ambulance took me to the hospital and the medical officer sterilized the five holes at the back of my scalp. The next day a piece of shrapnel was dug out of my scalp by my own flight surgeon."

On 28 March, Lt.Col. Gerald Dix led the 355th Fighter Group in their newly arrived Mustangs (late February to early March) and made rendezvous with the B-17s over Chateau Thierry. For the second time that week the 354th Fighter Squadron was bounced by two flights of P-38s without any damage being done but increasing the animosity toward the Lightning pilots. After the escort Maj. Edward "Jonesy" Szaniawski's 357th Fighter Squadron strafed the Dijon Airdrome. The "Jone's Boys" established an ETO record by destroying 19 German aircraft on the ground and adding one probably destroyed and damaging 31 others. Szaniawski was credited with four and Ben Johnston with three to become ground aces with a total of six and five, respectively. The 354th Squadron claimed four total ground victories and the 358th one, when William Hovde hit a He-111 near Compeigne. The 355th suffered no losses for a total of 24 ground victories. Szaniawski would be shot down by flak strafing German airfields on 19 May. He would become a POW, and attempted two escapes. He was recaptured after the first but was successful in April 1945.

On 5 April 1944, the 4th and 355th Fighter Groups flew bomber escort missions to Munich through poor weather. As part of the escort they attacked 11 airfields around Munich and destroyed 96 Luftwaffe aircraft. The 4th would lose four pilots, including 17.33 victory ace, Capt. Duane Beeson. While sharing one-third victory over a Ju-88 Beeson's P-51 was hit by flak near Brandenburg but he survived to become a POW. Col. William Cummings led a 355th Fighter Group sweep on six airfields southwest of Munich for which the group was awarded the Distinguished Unit Citation. After making landfall at Ostend, Cummings dropped through the undercast and "by a remarkable feat of navigation, arrived in the vicinity of the target after flying on instruments for a hour and a half. Only one other group of the original force was able to locate the primary

Right: Col. William Cummings led a 355th Fighter Group sweep on six airfields southwest of Munich for which the group was awarded the Distinguished Unit Citation. (USAF)

objective. The formation (the group split into three squadron attacks-ed.) descended through a break in the clouds approximately four miles from the target, and despite a furious snow squall which made even normal flying difficult, launched a bold attack. In the face of withering fire from ground defenses which increased in intensity with each successive sweep over the airdromes, the 355th Fighter Group tenaciously pressed the attack, wreaking destruction upon parked aircraft and enemy planes attempting to frustrate the attack. Oblivious of personal danger, the pilots of the groups continued the assault for 40 minutes, strafing not only the primary objective but also adjoining airfields which were in the traffic pattern."(from the DUC). They claimed 51 destroyed, two probably destroyed and 81 damaged, a record that would stand for five months before being broken by the 479th Fighter Group:

"This daring assault, carried out in exceptionally adverse weather and against strong opposition, materially contributed to the weakening of the enemy's airborne defenses against heavy bombers." (DUC)

The 358th Fighter Squadron claimed an ETO record 24-1-41 for an individual squadron. Forty-two 355th pilots destroyed or damaged German aircraft for the day. Maj. Claiborne Kinnard of the 354th Squadron had one air victory and four ground victories, Byron Houston and Lee Mendenhall of the 354th Fighter Squadron and Lawrence Dissette and Raymond Myers for the 358th Fighter Squadron all scored triple ground victories. Two Mustangs were shot down by flak. On 11 April the 355th got nine in the air and 14 on the ground but lost two pilots to flak. On the 13th the Group claimed six in the air and 22 on the ground sweeping the Oberpfaffenhofen and Grailsheim Airdromes. The 354th Fighter Squadron took top honors with 19 strafing victories on Oberpfaffenhofen with Kinnard getting four. On the 15th, the Group got 13 more ground victories but lost three to flak (all became POWs) and would conclude its pre-invasion airdrome attacks. For the war the Steeple Morden Strafers would rank fifth in the 8th Air Force in total aerial victories with 352 but ranked first in ground victories with 510.5.

On 8 April, improved weather conditions gave the AAF escorts to down a record 88 Luftwaffe in the air and 49 on the ground. On 15 April the 8th and 9th Air Forces conducted mass strafing attacks on airdromes in Germany. The cost was high as bad weather was the major factor in the loss of 33 aircraft and 30 pilots MIA. Aces, Raymond Care of the 4th Fighter Group (6 victories) was hit by flak and made a POW and LeRoy Schreiber, CO of the 62nd Fighter Squadron (12 victories) was KIA when his fighter was hit by flak over the Flensburg Airdrome. On 20 April the 339th Fighter Group made it first combat appearance when it coupled with the 353rd's P-47s in dive-bombing the Romorantin/Prunieres airdrome in an attempt to draw away German fighters from the heavy bomber formations and damage to the airdrome facilities and aircraft. The 339th led by second leading ETO strafing ace, Col. Joseph Thury with 25.5 victories would become the first group to score 100 ground victories and was the only group to score 100 ground victories in a day twice.

The bombing of German industry especially on the German aircraft industry, notably BIG WEEK, 22 to 27 February, when 8th Air Force groups from England joined 15th Air Force groups operating from Italy took their toll on the Luftwaffe. The freelance fighter sweeps and the heavy and medium bomber missions over France in preparation for D-Day also served to decimate the Luftwaffe. Leigh-Mallory had forecast and ordered the preparation for a significant air battle over the Normandy beaches that never occurred. The first priority of the pre-invasion air campaign was the attainment of air superiority. During the year and a half before D-Day AAF heavy bombers had attacked German industry and forced the Luftwaffe into combat and the bomber fighter escorts destroyed a major portion of the Luftwaffe. Between January and May 1944 the German fighter arm lost almost 100% of its average personnel strength of 2,283 as 2,262 were killed or severely wounded. The Jagdwaffe lost 1,432 fighters (and 18% of the pilots available at the start of the month) in February, 2,012 (22% of the pilot strength) in March, 2,540 (20% of the pilot strength) in April and 2,461 (25% of the pilot strength) in May. By June Pete Quesada could even more confidently assure Churchill that the Luftwaffe would not appear over the landing beaches.

Interdiction Missions

By the end of February 1944, the IX Fighter Group had only escorted heavy bombers and had not prepared for their tactical duties. Joint air-ground practice exercises on the English coast had to tolerate the diversion of the fighter force to escort 8th Air Force heavy bombers. During Operation DUCK at the end of December 1943, the 29th Infantry Division was supposed to practice close support procedures with fighters but no fighters appeared as the landing craft approached the shore on the first day. During the four-day exercise only a handful of fighters participated as also happened during Operation KNOCKOUT in January. Operation FOX, a large-scale amphibious exercise in March at Slapton Sands, comprised 18,000 troops, 1,700 vehicles and hopefully 740 aircraft that were scheduled to work with air force ground liaison parties on the beach. Again, escort duties along with poor weather, limited the air part of the exercise to only one squadron. Operation BEAVER, held on 30-31 March, was the first ground-air exercise held after Eisenhower released fighters for tactical operations. BEAVER was to approximate combat conditions with most naval and air support and some ground fire being live. The exercise was a disaster, plagued by bad weather and with the reoccurring ground-air communications problems. It took three hours for ground requests to reach AEAF Uxbridge HQ and that turned out to be a blessing in disguise as the ground troops had inaccurately marked their "front line" and would have sustained real casualties if the air support arrived in time to drop live ordnance. So with only three months to D-Day, the Americans had not tested their ground-air capabilities.

Meanwhile, Quesada was gathering an accomplished staff. Able administrator, Brig.Gen. Alvin Kincaid replaced Col. John Whitley as chief of staff and relieved Quesada of bureaucratic routine. Col. Lorry Tindal was the new IX FC operations officer and developed American ground-air methods after studying Luftwaffe tactical procedures. Col. Raymond Stecker who was with the desert IX Air Force and a All-American back at West Point in 1932 was named Quesada's delegate at AEAF Combined Operations at Uxbridge. Quesada's was blessed with capable Wing and Group commanders. The most able of the lot was Brig.Gen. O.P. Weyland who arrived on 29 January 1944, with his 84th Fighter Wing and so impressed Quesada that on 4 February he urged the appointment of Weyland as commander of the XIX TAC. The leaders of IX TAC groups were Colonels Gilbert Meyer and Dyke Meyer (not related), James Ferguson and James Howard. All were consummate fighter pilots and leaders. Howard had experience with the Flying Tigers in the CBI where he became an ace and then became an ace and was awarded the Congressional Medal of Honor in the ETO. All these men reflected Quesada and his fighter-bomber tactical philosophy, knowing the strengths and limitations of the fighter-bomber and had a first-hand knowledge and concern for their pilots. Quesada initially considered brash, impatient and a relatively inexperienced political appointee, also earned the respect of not only his men but also recognition from his superiors as on 28 April, George C. Marshall approved his promotion to Major General.

Initially OVERLORD planners considered a short interdiction campaign designed to isolate the Cotentin Peninsula by destroying bridges there. But in early 1944, British Professor, Sir Solly Zuckerman, pushed his "Transportation Plan" which would produce a "railway desert" in France. The Transportation Plan will be discussed later in the Plan to Attack the Rail System.

Quesada's IX Fighter Command initiated its first major interdiction missions on 8 April when over 100 P-47s attacked rail repair shops in Belgium followed by 56 P-51s on the 10th on the same target. On the 9th, the P-47s disrupted freight and troop train movement in northern France and damaged several road junctions. In the last two weeks of April, the IX FC attacked 22 targets and for the first time tactical missions outnumbered escort missions. But the results were unsatisfactory as Allied intelligence investigation found that the German rail and road networks in France had not experienced the damage that was claimed. The Germans used forced French laborers to repair damage to marshaling yards and track cuts within days and even hours of their damage. At the end of the April interdiction missions Allied intelligence estimated that the Germans still had three times the rail capacity needed for their military requirements, four times the required rolling stock, eight times the number of locomotives and ten times the requisite servicing facilities.

The conventional view of the fighter was that it was considered to be either a high altitude escort or air-to-air interceptor. But the proposed tactical, dive-bombing/strafing role would necessitate the fighter to utilize new equipment and tactics from their traditional function. Shortsighted pre-war American planners had failed to design a pure ground support aircraft and all three fighters in the USAAF inventory in 1944, the P-51, P-47 and P-38, had deficiencies which would make them wanting in the ground attack role and would require equipment modifications. Also, IX FC pilots required attitude modification as in training they prepped for aerial combat and escort functions with a minor in ground support. Quesada solicited Maj.Gen. John Cannon of the MAAF for help on ground support as Cannon's fighter-bombers had learned valuable lessons in Italy. In April and May 1944, 227 IX officers were sent to Italy and Cannon sent his pilots to England to teach in air support schools there. Over 200 hundred IX FC pilots attended these schools and in turn taught pilots in their command what they had learned. At the end of April, the 365th and 405th P-47 groups were sent to the gunnery range at Southampton to develop new and better use of dive-bombing techniques and ordnance. Basic lessons were learned, none revolutionary, and most were changed later. But it was a start and in early May, Quesada ordered his now, fighter-bombers, to attack German locomotives that were considered the weak link in the French transport system.

On 20 May, Leigh-Mallory authorized other AEAF commands to conduct wide-scale fighter sweeps against moving rail traffic, coded Operation CHATTANOOGA CHOO CHOO. The fighter-bomber attacks were aimed at locomotives and rolling stock north of the Loire River to supplement attacks on marshaling yards and bridges. In the next two weeks over 500 locomotives were destroyed

In February 1944, Sir Solly Zuckerman developed the "Transportation Plan," to attack the French and Belgian rail marshaling yards to isolate the battlefield. Zuckerman maintained that the destruction of 101 rail centers and maintenance facilities over a three-month period with 45,000 tons of bombs would paralyze the French rail system. (Author/West))

or damaged and tracks cut at 150 sites. On the 21st, 11 group missions (two were weather aborts) of 561 9th AF fighter-bombers attacked trains in France north of the Loire River. The ground claims were 46 locomotives destroyed, 11 probably destroyed and 21 damaged for the loss of nine aircraft and many damaged by ground fire. The 8th Air Force also sent out 500 fighters and attacked trains in Germany.

The Plan to Attack the Rail System: The Transportation Plan
The rail system in northwest France SNCF (French National Railways) and Belgium SNCB (Belgium National Railway) was large and interconnected. From mid-1942 the Reich Transportation Ministry coordinated this system with the complex and well-developed Deutsch Reichsbahn (German National Railway) in the Rhineland and Saar industrial areas of western Germany. The French and Belgium systems were operated by resident manpower but supervised by the Reichsbahn. In 1943 a large volume of military and industrial traffic moved between Germany and occupied Western Europe as the Germans pillaged the economies of France, Belgium and Holland. By January 1944 85% of all French rail traffic was operated for the Reich, 33% for the German Army. As the invasion neared the Reichsbahn established a reserve of 484 trains with about 20,000 cars in eastern France and western Germany. When the invasion came these trains loaded with supplies and troops were to be sent to the front under the control of German Reichsbahn personnel. The Wehrmacht often interfered with train schedules and French and Belgium railway personnel were purposefully inefficient, absent from work and even sabotaged schedules and trains. To add to the Reichsbahn woes, the Maquis, French Resistance, began a large-scale campaign to destroy bridges, tunnels, to cut track, derail trains and ambush German railway personnel. From March 1944, the Allies began their attacks on the rail system in northwestern Europe that was the most dense in the world.

Air Chief Marshal Arthur "Bomber" Harris was the commander-in-chief of the RAF bomber command and protested vigorously when his Bomber Command and the USSTAF were placed under Eisenhower's SHAEF command as he felt that a continued strategic air offensive against Germany cities and industry would eventually bring the Reich to surrender. He was overruled and reluctantly supported his role in the Transportation Plan. (Author/West)

Air Chief Marshal Arthur Tedder joined Eisenhower in believing that OVERLORD would be successful only if Allied air superiority was complete. Tedder was behind the Transportation Plan and used his influence to convince Eisenhower of its worth and ramroded it through opposition, especially that of Leigh-Mallory. (Author/West)

Northwest Europe Rail System

Country	RR Miles/100sq.mi.	% Double Track
Belgium	27.5	58.3
Germany	20.8	35.3
Holland	15.3	50.8
France	12.6	47.2
US	8.3	11.9

The objective of the Allied air interdiction campaign before D-Day was to prevent the movement of German troops, equipment and supplies along the rail and road net. Professor Sir Solly Zuckerman who worked with Tedder in the Mediterranean had been named by him to help the AEAF plan and evaluate the Allied air operations. While in Sicily Zuckerman saw that the bombing of six rail centers there had immobilized the rail system. In February 1944, Zuckerman developed the "Transportation Plan," to bomb the French rail centers to isolate the battlefield. He maintained that the destruction of 101 rail centers and maintenance facilities over a three-month period with 45,000 tons of bombs would paralyze the French rail system. Some 41% of the total pre-invasion bomb tonnage were to be devoted to the Transportation Plan and only 11% to POINTBLANK. The 8th Air Force was to contribute 45% of the pre-invasion tonnage and Bomber Command 35%. The USAAF endorsed an "Interdiction Plan" to block German military movements close to the battlefield by destroying critical transportation targets, such as bridges roads and railways and the transport on them. Both Eisenhower and Tedder preferred the Transportation Plan as it would bring the Strategic Air Force under SHAEF control and the Interdiction Plan was not suited to heavy bombers. Leigh-Mallory ramroded the Transportation Plan although many Allied bombing advocates did not believe it could accomplish its objectives. Jimmy Doolittle, head of the 8th Air Force, did not believe his B-17s could hit what he considered pinpoint targets that needed to be attacked in good weather. Of course, "Bomber" Harris objected to the Transportation Plan, as it would divert his heavy RAF bombers from destroying German cities. Leigh-Mallory argued that the Luftwaffe would oppose the destruction of the rail system but Spaatz did not agree. He wanted to have the authority to attack any target necessary to make the Luftwaffe come out to fight and opposed Leigh-Mallory's assignment of targets. Harris and Leigh-Mallory also had a similar disagreement over Bomber Command's role. Finally Tedder had to intervene and proposed a joint planning committee to resolve the matter. This committee was directed by Eisenhower who demanded that everyone in his command accept his "Air Preparation Plan" (e.g. Transportation Plan) as doctrine.

Lt.Gen. Carl "Tooey" Spaatz was the commanding general of the US Strategic Air Forces (USSTAF). Spaatz supported the Oil Plan to bring the Luftwaffe and Wehrmacht to their knees but was overruled by the Transportation Plan espoused by Eisenhower and Leigh-Mallory. Nonetheless, Spaatz accomplished the difficult task of maintaining the AAF strategic bombing campaign and aiding OVERLORD. (USAF)

Soon the Interdiction camp gained more advocates. AAF Bombing expert, Gen. Fred Anderson, USSTAF's director of operations, felt the French rail system was too large, had too much equipment and was too efficient and thus could not be disabled by bombing its marshaling yards. Even though bombing would do heavy damage to the system, the Germans would reduce civilian traffic in favor of military traffic and be able to reroute traffic around the damaged marshaling yards until they could be repaired. Since marshaling yards were located in towns and cities, bombing them would cause heavy French and Belgian civilian casualties and deprive them of fuel and food. The British Air Ministry favored the Interdiction Plan and endorsed a concerted interdiction offensive to begin shortly before D-Day. The influential EOU (Enemy Objectives Unit of the Economic Warfare Division) that was affiliated with the OSS came out for Interdiction. By destroying key selected rail targets, especially bridges, tunnels, viaducts, selected marshaling yards and then cutting tracks at 500 foot intervals over 30 to 40 miles. Rail interdiction could interrupt the movement of German troops and supplies would utterly inundate repair crews. Great numbers fighter-bombers were able to continually attack trains and road and water traffic down to single boxcars, staff cars, motorcycles and horse-drawn vehicles. To isolate the battlefield interdiction targets were chosen in "rings" extending back from enemy frontline. Pressure could be increased or decreased in each ring as dictated by the battlefield situation and the amount of traffic coming to it. A short powerful interdiction campaign just before the Invasion would prevent the Germans from making any extensive repairs and prevent troops and supplies from entering the battle.

So it was, the powerful trio: Leigh-Mallory, Tedder and Zuckerman, backed by Eisenhower vigorously endorsed the Transportation Plan against an ever-increasing number of Interdiction advocates who had collected more and more evidence to back their position. To refute Zuckerman's claims that attacks on Italian bridges were ineffective and uneconomical, the EOU sent OSS agents to Italy to investigate. Zuckerman's report that included only two ineffective attacks on Italian bridges and did not include the 18 of 30 bridges knocked out by air attacks. The OSS report went on to compare the 200 tons of bombs dropped to block a bridge as compared to the 1280 tons of bombs dropped on the Messina marshaling yards. Gen. Ira Eaker, who was commander of the 8th Air Force, was transferred to Italy and was replaced by Doolittle and his deputy, ACM John Slessor. Eaker had came out against the AEAF plan and cited his experience that attacks on marshaling yards did not stop traffic for more than a few hours. Slessor also was against the AEAF plan and in his book, *The Central Blue* (London, Cassell, London 1956) stated:

"One of the remarkable developments in the past three months to my mind has been the emergence of the bridge as a worthwhile bombing objective. At the present time, of 25 clean cuts in the Italian railways, 16 are bridges."

Air Chief Marshal Charles Portal was instrumental in passing the control he had on the Combined Chiefs of Staff over Allied strategic air power to Eisenhower before and during the Invasion and backed the Transportation Plan. (Author/West)

To settle the dispute, Marshal of the RAF, Sir Charles Portal, called a meeting but there was a new card in the deck. By early 1944 the Germans had been driven from natural oil sources and faced a fuel shortage. Before the war they had built hydrogenation plants to convert plentiful coal to oil and Spaatz planned an attack on these installations. Spaatz' proposal called the "Oil Plan" would attack 27 plants producing 80% of German synthetic oil and 13 refineries generating 60% of the refined from crude. Spaatz was to pitch his Oil Plan to Portal but Tedder got Portal to restrict the meeting to the question of utilizing the strategic air force for the Oil Plan or the Transportation Plan. By concentrating on the use of the strategic air force he circumvented the Interdiction Plan that was conducted by tactical air forces. Tedder was confident he could discredit the Oil Plan by pointing out that RAF Bomber Command and the AEAF would not be effective in carrying out the oil attacks. The USSTAF defended its assertion that it could put the synthetic oil plants and refineries out operation for many months and cause the defeat of the Luftwaffe. The USSTAF contended that the Luftwaffe would defend German oil to the death but would not do so for French rail targets. The loss of oil would affect the German armies and air forces on all fronts and thus aid the Normandy Invasion. By this time Eisenhower was tired of the arguing among his air commanders and felt they were jeopardizing the Invasion and undermining his command.

A conference was called on 25 March at Norfolk House in London at which Eisenhower and Portal would meet with senior air commanders. Tedder, Spaatz, Leigh-Mallory, Harris, Anderson and others were present. The articulate Tedder eloquently explained the Transportation Plan and gave assurance that the Luftwaffe would remain the first priority objective and that rail centers would remain as second priority. The Transportation Plan would obliterate 76 rail centers in France and Belgium and paralyze the rail network leading to the Invasion beaches. Eisenhower vigorously and immediately broached his primary concern that when the invasion got ashore and stayed there that it be given all possible support. Eisenhower said that the AEAF Transportation Plan gave the strategic air forces the opportunity to make a significant contribution to the success of OVERLORD. Spaatz gave a plain and unimpressive presentation of the Oil Plan. After he finished his proposal, it was refuted by the Ministry of Economic Warfare, an organization that previously supported the Oil Plan, stated that it would not have any effect for four or five months. Portal rejected the Oil Plan as it was demonstrated that it would not help OVERLORD in the first several critical weeks. He did concede that the Oil Plan was attractive and should be reconsidered after the first critical weeks of the Invasion. The crafty Tedder had somehow had preserved his Transportation Plan. Portal did not want the Transportation Plan to be raised as an issue again and directed the unenthusiastic Harris and Spaatz to work with the AEAF on planning attacks on the rail centers. In April, RAF Bomber Command began an intensive bombing attack against the rail centers and killed thousands of civilians and was branded as air terrorists by German propaganda. When Tedder ended the campaign on 25 May after 48,795 tons of bombs had been dropped severely damaging 42 of the 73 marshaling yards, destroying 4,000 locomotives and killing 4,615 French and Belgium civilians. SHAEF intelligence analysis stated that the rail center attacks did not significantly decrease the enemy's capacity to transport essential daily supply requirements to the front. The Germans had three times the number of rail lines required, four times the number of rolling stock and eight times the number of locomotives and more than adequate servicing facilities for normal operation. On 15 April, Eisenhower issued an order that the USSTAF and RAF Bomber Command would be under SHAEF command and Tedder would oversee OVERLORD air operations.

The Reichsbahn reacted to the Allied rail attacks by increasing AA protection for trains and placing more of its personnel in vital operating posts in the SNCF and SNCB. More locomotives and rolling stock were sent to France and Belgium to make up the losses. Specialized repair crews for locomotives were sent from Germany, 10,000 Todt Organization foreign workers were transferred from military projects to repair the rail system along with nearly 16,000 German troops. As the damage increased French and Belgium civilians were conscripted for rail repair. The Wehrmacht cut all non-essential civilian traffic and gave priority to military traffic. As a consequence the French economy suffered from a coal shortage that shut down industry and decreased utility service. Despite these measures, at the beginning of May more than 1,700 trains were stalled in bombed areas and from mid-May trains could not operate with any schedule west of a line from Orleans-Paris-Brussels. The Allied rail attacks caused problems into Germany as loaded trains waiting in the Saar backed up, as they could not be sent into France where rail centers were damaged and impassable. There were thousands of damaged locomotives and rail cars in France in need of repair along with miles of cut tracks. By late May the required 100 daily military supply trains moving from Germany to France were cut to only 32. By mid-May only 40% of the French railway's locomotives were in service due to repair organization problems and only 50% of its rolling stock was in service as compared to early March. By late May the SNCF transported 45% less freight than in

Capt. Gerald Johnson, a 16.5 air ace with the 56th Fighter Group, was hit by flak during a strafing run on a train and crash-landed. (USAF)

January 1944 and as the invasion occurred it was operating at 10% normal capacity.

The rail interdiction campaign did not come without a cost. On March 27 the 56th Fighter Group was scheduled for a 1,000 hour escort mission that was scrubbed at 1230 due to poor weather. Capt. Gerald Johnson, a 16.5 victory ace, took off his flight clothes and rested in his room when the combat mission alarm sounded. Thinking that any mission now would only be a milk run, Johnson dressed in slacks and street shoes and hurried for take off. The squadron R/V'd with the bombers and continued on an uneventful mission. On the way home, Johnson and his wingman descended to 8,000 feet looking for something to shoot at. They spotted a long freight train winding its way through a shallow canyon carrying supplies into France for the expected Allied invasion. Johnson dropped down first and strafed the train getting hits causing small explosions indicating the train was carrying ammunition. The following fighters caused more explosions and fires and by the time Johnson turned to start his second pass, the train was badly damaged. But Johnson and the 8th Air Force were inexperienced in strafing and he violated two cardinal strafing rules; don't make a second pass on a target and if you do, come in fast, hit the target and get out fast. His run was low and slow but he scored more hits on the train. Now over-confident, he again came in low and slow for a third pass and made him vulnerable to ground fire that was now ready for him. Johnson describes the pass in his biography (*Called to Command*, Turner, KY, 1996):

"I was overconfident. It seems by the time I started my third pass, the anti-aircraft defenses on the train were prepared for action. The barrage of fire I ran into sounded something like the sound of large hail hitting a car. Almost immediately the windscreen was bathed in oil and I heard horrible noises from the engine. It shook the entire airplane as it struggled to keep turning but it could not make it. I was about 200 feet in the air with low air speed and a dead engine. Instinctively I pulled back on the stick and reached for the canopy handle. The airplane was too slow to climb.

Now I was trapped—I was too low to bail out and had only heavily wooded and rugged terrain to crash into. I had no options. This airplane was going to crash in seconds. I could only help it crash as safely as possible. In this situation the aileron was ineffective because of my low speed, I could maintain the wings level only by use of the rudder, known as "walking the rudder pedals." This I did and the airplane came down and just slapped the tops of these big trees when suddenly to my utter amazement I saw a small open and cultivated field right ahead. The airplane mushed through the tops of the trees and dropped to the ground at the edge of the field. It could not have skidded 200 feet. My head hit the gunsight and my left arm hit something else, but I felt no pain, There has never been any doubt in my mind that this was one of several times in my life when God was with me.

I opened the canopy, got out of my parachute and pulled the ripcord. The parachute billowed out in the cockpit. I pushed it down under the fuel primer pump, pulled out the pump, kicked it until fuel leaked onto the parachute, and with my Zippo lighter started a fire. I did this to keep the Germans from getting the airplane."

Col. Lance Call, CO of the 365th Fighter Group, the *Hell Hawks* (USAF)

As Johnson was torching his P-47 he noticed one of the Thunderbolts from his flight with its wheels down. After the war Johnson learned that his wingman attempted he to land and rescue him but hit some trees causing serious damage to his aircraft and left the area. The wingman later called in a "Mayday" but never was heard from again. Johnson tried to escape through a woods but as he tried to cross a road he was fired on and surrendered and spent the remainder of the war as a POW in Stalag Luft I. That same day the 56th lost another ace when Capt. Walker "Bud" Mahurin, 19.75 victories, was either hit by flak or fire from the rear guns of a Do-217 bomber he had attacked at low level. He bailed out and with the help of the French Resistance evaded back to England on 7 May.

Attacks on the Seine, Meuse, and Loire Bridges: Bombers or Fighter-Bombers?

In spite of the decision to attack marshaling yards airpower advocates pressed Leigh-Mallory for bridge interdiction. On 7 May the 9th Air Force Advanced HQ recommended to Leigh-Mallory a plan to attack rail bridges over the Meuse and Seine. Fighter-bombers were to focus on two bridges over each river and medium bombers on one over each. With no Seine bridges to be attacked until 24 May, the Meuse bridges were attacked first. Leigh-Mallory at AEAF HQ also authorized the experimental bombing of the Seine bridges. Quesada wanted his IX FC to participate to demonstrate their capabilities. It was thought that 1,200 tons of bombs would be required to destroy each steel and concrete bridge and since fighter-bombers could carry only two tons each Quesada had to almost resort to begging to get a chance for his fighter-bombers to show their stuff. On 7 May, the 365th Fighter Group, led by Col. Lance Call, attacked two concrete rail bridges at Mantes-Gassicourt and a steel rail span Vernon in the late morning. Twelve P-47s approached the Vernon Bridge at 10,000 feet and dove through the overcast as they neared the bridge. The aircraft were armed with two 1,000lb. GP bombs, fused at 8-11 second delay. Col. Call flew at high speed low along the river, below the level of the span and drove his bombs at point blank range into the north bridge abutment and climbed away. Call climbed and circled to direct further attacks. After the smoke began to clear Call saw that the north end of the bridge had collapsed into the Seine. The last flights were ordered to focus on the center span and the entire north span fell into the water. Two IX fighters were lost to flak. The concrete Mantes-Gassicourt bridge was tougher and suffered light damage. The concrete abutments were hit repeatedly but the bombs bounced off into the water. On the 9th and 10th of May the 365th Thunderbolts returned to Mantes and again it was hit by bombs without effect.

On 10 May, Leigh-Mallory suspended the Seine bridge attacks that were drawing attention towards Normandy and the Invasion. In the meantime the Operational Research Section (ORS) studied bridge attack methodology and determined that aircraft employed (fighter-bombers or bombers), bombs, fusing, and tactics should be selected according to the bridge's characteristics. The ORS emphasized that each bridge was different and careful attention to bomb size and fusing would be required. The Vernon mission on 7 May had been an unqualified success and influenced Leigh-Mallory who authorized the attacks on the Seine bridges to resume on 24 May. B-26s of the IX Bomber Command and fighters of the IX Fighter Command were joined by the RAF 2nd TAF and the 8th Air Force to attack bridges. Fighter-bombers utilized three bridge busting techniques:

1) zero altitude on the deck drive bombing
2) a steep glide from about 4,000 feet, releasing bombs at 2,000 feet and
3) dive-bombing from 8,000 feet, releasing bombs at between 4,000 to 6,000 feet.

Appropriate bombs and fuse settings were selected so that bombs would damage vulnerable parts of the bridge and not bounce off the concrete or steel portions and explode harmlessly in the water or air. B-26s armed with 2000lb. bombs of the IX Bomber Command, augmented by fighter-bombers (primarily by USAAF P-47s armed with 500 lb. bombs and secondly, rocket-firing RAF Typhoons), led the bridge attacks and a large amount of ordnance was expended but the bombing campaign achieved results.

On the 24th, seven rail and four road bridges over the Seine between Paris and Rouen were targeted. On the 26th, ten Seine bridges were given top priority. As the Germans tried to repair the bridges, the repair crews were strafed around the clock by fighter-bombers. On 31 May of the rail bridges crossing the Seine from Le Havre, the mouth of the river, to Paris, 22 had been destroyed; five damaged and only two remained usable. The attacks on the road bridges were also highly successful that by D-Day only one road-bridge, at St. Pierre du Vauvray, remained standing between Conflans and Rouen. From 27 May to D-Day IX TAC fighter-bombers flew 1,181 sorties against 13 bridges, destroying 12 with 854 tons of ordnance. The results of the air campaign by the 9th Air Force and the RAF 2nd TAF to destroy these bridges became evident once the invasion began. Wehrmacht divisions were forced to detrain often from 50 to 150 miles from the front. Tank regiments of the 9th and 10th Panzer Divisions were forced to detrain at Fontainebleau and travel eight days to Caen, the same amount of time it took to travel from Russia to Paris.

Seine-Meuse-Loire-Orleans Road and Rail Interdiction

In preparing for the invasion Allied planners realized that the railway and road system in Northern France needed to be destroyed or badly damaged to prevent the Germans from bringing up replacements and supplies to confront the Allied invasion beaches. If the transport system was not interdicted the Germans could conceivably bring in troops and supplies at a rate to exceed that of the Allies and drive them from the beaches. Air attacks on rail facilities throughout Northern France began as early as February 1944. By May, the Seine-Loire interdiction program on rail and road bridges began. To conceal the location of the invasion beaches the preliminary attacks were wide-ranging. As D-Day approached attacks concentrated on the Seine and Meuse River bridges, marshalling yards and rolling stock. For security reasons it was not until D-Day that attacks on the Loire River bridges were initiated. By that time only one of the Seine rail bridges was standing and only five road bridges from Paris to the Channel was intact.

4 June Attacks on Rail Bridges

On 4 June three fighter groups left their bases in England to attack the few remaining bridges on the Continent. Col. Harold Holt led 48 P-47s of the 366th Fighter Group from Thruxton to attack the bridge at Le Fitte Bridge. The 365th Hell Hawks under Col. Lance Call leading 48 P-47s out of Beaulieu targeted the resistant Vernon Bridge over the Seine. Forty-eight Thunderbolts of the 368th Fighter Group left Chilbolton under Col. Gilbert Meyers to attack the bridge at Gent Belgium.

The Vernon and Le Fitte bridges were important, as they were main rail spans running from Nancy across France and terminating in Brest. The line passed through the marshaling yards at Dijon where they could be routed to Normandy. The 365th and 366th were escorted by 32 P-38s of the 370th Fighter Group as the Luftwaffe had fighters stationed in Holland and Belgium out of the way of the persistent pre-invasion attacks. The P-38s rendezvoused with the two fighter groups midway over the English Channel with the 402nd Squadron under Maj. Seth McKee protecting the 366th and the 470th under Capt. John Howell trailing the 365th. The American fighters crossed over the French coast north of Dieppe and at Argentan the two groups separated to attack their individual targets simultaneously. Meanwhile Luftflotte 3 tracked the formations and sent JG 54, the famous Green Hearts under ace, Col. Erich Rudorffer, to intercept the P-47s. Rudorffer led 18 FW-190s of JG 54/III toward the 365th and Maj. Franz Eisenach JG54/I took another 18 Focke Wulfs against the 366th. The escorting P-38s were alerted by radar

64th Wing P-47s strafe and set fire to a German train in France. (USAF)

Left: The Seine River rail bridge at Conflans, the first of seven bridges north of Paris. By 12 June 1944 all seven rail bridges and the 13 road bridges from Paris to the Channel were destroyed. (USAF)

to the incoming Germans and flew above them hid by the overcast. The Lightnings bounced Eisenach's fighters and quickly shot down four and damaged five others. Holt's fighter-bombers were free to attack the Le Fitte Bridge. The P-47s paired off and attacked in 30-second intervals at deck level. At about 75 to a 100 feet each fighter dropped its 500lb. delayed fused bombs. Holt and his wingman put three of four bombs against the right pier near the riverbank. After three attacks by the squadron Capt. Zell Smith and his wingman finished off the span that collapsed into the river. The next squadron came down and the first pair put three of four bombs into the center span and succeeding pairs put this span into the river. The final attacks put one end of the third span into the water. The attack was not losses as AA fire shot down three P-47s.

Meanwhile Call's 365th and Howell's 470th headed toward the beautiful old ornate Vernon Bridge. Rudorffer raced in to intercept the P-47s but was surprised by the P-38s. Experten Rudorffer claimed the final two of his 222 victories while his pilots downed another four and damaged two others. Despite the heavy losses Howell's P-38s evened the score by shooting down six FWs including two by Howell but more importantly prevented the Germans from interfering with the attack on the bridge. As Call came to the bridge he saw that a locomotive and its cars were crossing it. Call and his wingman attacked first and they put three bombs on the trestle and one hit the locomotive stopping the train. By the time Call's 386th Squadron finished it had collapsed one span taking 28 rail cars with it. The 387th hit the middle span with 13 bombs collapsing it and putting the locomotive and ten cars in the river. The 388th weakened the third span but could not collapse it. German anti-aircraft fire shot down two Thunderbolts.

The 368th Fighter Group left the other two groups at the English coastline and headed across the North Sea to the bridge at Gent, Belgium. Rail traffic on the main route though Belgium into northwest France was carried over this four-span bridge over the Meuse River. The line also led to Lille, whose bridge was also targeted that day, and then headed southwest to Le Havre. The destruction of these two bridges would effectively stop rail traffic from reaching the Normandy coast from the northeast. Col. Gilbert Meyers led his group at 3,000 feet through heavy cloud and light rain and shortly after leaving the English coast was joined by P-38s of the 370th Fighter Group. German radar at Zeebrugge, Belgium picked up the American formations and alerted the small airdrome at Obier that sent 15 Me-109s to intercept them. Soon a raging dogfight took place as Col. Howard Nichols sent his 401st Squadron P-38s into the fray. For a quarter hour the fighters battled in and out of the low overcast. When the battle was over five Messerschmitts were destroyed and four damaged while the Americans suffered four destroyed and three damaged. But despite their losses Nichols men succeeded in their mission of keeping the Luftwaffe away from the bridge busters. Meyers led his squadron in pairs at river level against the Gent Bridge. As he approached two 88mm AA shells exploded his wingman's aircraft. Meyers pressed his attack and at point blank range dropped his two 500lb. bombs blowing away part of the second span and loosened the steel trestle. Capt. Robert Johnson and Capt. Walter Mahurin (back in combat, returning from his March 27 shoot down) attacked through the thick AA fire and three of their four bombs hit the weakened second span and it dropped into the Meuse. Over the next quarter hour the remaining 44 P-47s scored at least 26 more hits dropping two more spans into the river and severely damaging the supporting piers and trestles making repair more difficult.

The destruction of the Saumur Bridge over the Loire River. The Loire bridges were attacked just after the invasion to prevent the movement of German reinforcements and supplies to the beaches. (USAF)

The Loire bridges needed to be taken out shortly after D-Day. The distance to the bridges from UK bases made it difficult for medium bombers or fighter-bombers to attack them. The width of the river and the flying distance made these bridges suitable targets for the heavies. Bad weather hampered bombing from the 7th to 11th and many bombers returned with their bombs or bombed alternate targets. But by the 16th the heavy bomber's persistence claimed that seven Loire bridges had been destroyed. Mediums of the IX Bomber Command took up the attacks on the remaining Loire bridges in July and by the end of he month blocked 19 of 35 aided by track-cutting fighter-bombers with 23 rail cuts, 13 locomotives and 51 rail cars destroyed on 6 July alone.

Of all the Allied air interdiction objectives the pre-invasion air plan to disrupt the French rail network was eminently successful, particularly against bridges. The Germans efficiently rebuilt roads, marshaling yards and airfields but replacing bridges was more difficult. A trestle near Rouen was rebuilt seven times and by D-Day not a single bridge remained intact over the Seine. By drastically reducing the number of locomotives and rolling stock, repair facilities and depots the Allied air attack caused the calamitous failure of the rail system in a very short period. The system was diminished from exceeding the German's economic and military requirements in northern France to one, at D-Day, that could not supply its occupation troops. As Allied troops hit the Normandy beaches, the rail system was powerless to move in reinforcements and had to resort to road transport which itself was uncertain due precarious fuel supplies and motor transport numbers. Motor transport and the few trains operating slowly through the wrecked railway system were easy targets for the marauding fighter-bombers flying armed reconnaissance sorties in increasing numbers after the landings. The fighter-bombers added to the mayhem by attacking bridges and the remaining few uncut tracks.

Once the invasion had taken place, secrecy was no longer an issue and the TACs initiated increased air interdiction on German transport directly on and behind enemy lines at the beachheads. The final repaired and undamaged bridges in the Seine-Loire area were attacked. Attacks on the rail and road bridges, marshalling yards, rolling stock and rail cutting in the Paris-Orleans area were begun. The German rail movement inside the Seine-Loire area was limited to the movement of supplies. Troops had to be detrained outside the area causing considerable delays in movement to the front. Half of the troops detrained had to march six to twelve days in company or platoon units along roads to the front suffering repeated fighter-bomber attacks. The continued attacks by patrolling fighter-bombers finally relegated all supply and personnel movement to be made at night causing more delays and confusion.

By D-Day the Allies had dropped 71,000 tons of bombs on 80 rail centers and the late May fighter-bomber attacks on bridges had cut over all French rail traffic by 40% and to a greater extent closer to the Normandy beachheads.

9th AF Fighter/Fighter-Bomber Sorties Pre-Invasion 1944

March	4,627
April	7,369
May	19,479 (7743 escort/3660 interdiction/2561 sweeps)
Total	31,475 (Bombers flew 16,795)

Sweeps were attacks on railroads, roads and airdromes in northern France. Upon completing their escort and bombing sorties, fighter-bombers were free to strafe targets of opportunity.

9th Air Force Fighter/Fighter-Bomber Interdiction Operations: Pre-Invasion (1 March-6 June 1944)

	Fighter/Fighter-Bombers		Bombers*	
Targets	**Sorties**	**Bomb Tons**	**Sorties**	**Bomb Tons**
Rail Lines/Bridges	2,742	1,204.4	1,977	3,219.8
Marshaling Yards	4,151	2,093.0	4,068	6,385.0
Roads/Bridges	720	557.1	1,136	1,881.0
Military Installations	252	143.0	555	897.2
Motor Transport	42	22.8	—	—
Harbors/Docks	—	—	101	186.0
Totals	7,907	4,020.3	7,837	12,569.0

*Medium and light

9th AF Strafing Targets	Rounds	%
Railroads and Railway Bridges	461,113	69
Marshaling Yards1	32,893	20
Military Installations	41,40	6
Highways and Bridges	23,351	4
Harbors and Docks	8,280	1
Miscellaneous	720	-
Total	667,758	100

8th Air Force Fighter/Fighter-Bomber Interdiction Operations: Pre-Invasion (1 March–6 June 1944)

	Fighter/Fighter-Bombers		Bombers*	
Targets	**Sorties**	**Bomb Tons**	**Sorties**	**Bomb Tons**
Rail Lines/Bridges	292	227.4	132	333.3
Marshaling Yards	70	52.4	3,699	10,082.4
Roads/Bridges	288	87.6	92	270.0
Military Installations	—	—	52	124.8
Motor Transport	6 3.0	—	—	
Totals	656	370.4	3,975	10,810.5

* Heavy

Note: 705,678 rounds of .50 caliber ammunition were fired.

27

Normandy Landings/D-Day
5 - 6 June 1944

Command and Organization

USAAF Fighter/Fighter-Bomber Units (6 June –25 July 1944)

8th Air Force
- VIII Fighter Command
  - 65th Fighter Wing
  - 66th Fighter Wing
  - 67th Fighter Wing

Allied Expeditionary Air Force (AEAF)
- IX Tactical Fighter Command
  - IX Tactical Air Command
    - 70th Fighter Wing
    - 71st Fighter Wing
    - 84th Fighter Wing
  - XIX Tactical Air Command
    - 100th Fighter Wing
    - 30rd Fighter Wing

OVERLORD air objectives

1) Protect the cross-Channel movement from air attack.
2) Neutralize coast and beach defenses
3) Protect the landing beached from air attack
4) Reduce German ability to launch counter-attacks
5) Provide air-ground cooperation in the advance of the ground forces from the beachhead

The Allied Expeditionary Air Force (AEAF), the US 9th Air Force and British 2nd Tactical Air Force and the US 8th Air Force had the primary duty of fighter-bomber operations during the landings and afterward. Bombing was to be the basic means of attack but strafing would inflict significant damage. Targets of opportunity for strafing were to be selected visually by pilots returning from bombing attacks, unsuccessful armed reconnaissance sorties or after bomber escort missions.

The VIII Fighter Command was assigned three missions on D-Day: bomber and troop carrier escort, protect Allied shipping and

A March 1944, pre-D-Day inspection of 9th Air Force airfields in England. Quesada is on the far left with AEAF commander, Trafford Leigh-Mallory, on his right. Eisenhower is partially obscured to the right of the pilot in the foreground while Maj.Gen. Lewis Brereton, 9th Air Force commander, is in the trench coat on the right. (USAF)

Eisenhower with his field commanders: (left to right) Bradley (First Army), Gerow (V Corps) and Collins (VII Corps). (US Army)

Aerial view of Normandy Beachhead looking south onto the hedgerow country that would hold up the Allied advance. (USAF)

to attack any air or ground movement toward or over the beaches. P-38s flew high altitude cover for the invasion fleet. P-51s and P-47s conducted an early morning sweep called Operation FULL HOUSE and then formed an umbrella east of the invasion fleet and beaches in a 50 mile semi-circle and maintained the patrol until relieved at noon. The afternoon missions for the VIII FC consisted of interdiction missions against rail, road and barge traffic in operations codenamed STUD and ROYAL FLUSH. These missions provided included specific assigned targets and armed reconnaissance concentrated in the Seine-Loire-Paris-Orleans area. On D-Day the VIII FC flew 1,800 sorties, characterized by a diversity of targets. They destroyed 17 bridges, ten marshaling yards, 85 trains along with a variety of other targets: motor convoys, barges, tugboats, barracks, troop concentrations, warehouses, and military buildings. They prevented any Luftwaffe aircraft from reaching the D-Day armada and destroyed 28 enemy aircraft and damaged 14 in the air for a loss of 25 to all causes.

On D-Day, five P-47 IX Fighter Command fighter groups were assigned to high beach cover, two P-38 groups to convoy cover, five in reserve and six P-47 and P-38 groups for direct support of the crossing and landing operations, with specific targets in the beachhead area. They were to halt German movement behind the beaches by attacking six bridges and a rail embankment southwest of the Ste. Mare Eglise and near Ste. Sauvuer le Vicomte. A failure of the OVERLORD air plan was that inadequate provision, only 47 group sorties, was made for unforeseen emergency calls from the ground forces as it was thought that planned missions would encompass close support needs. When emergency requests were made they had to go through the same unwieldy process that was unsuccessful during the pre-invasion exercises. Infantry requests were sent to assault battalions that forwarded them to fighter direction control ships offshore then on to AEAF HQ at Uxbridge that then directed their orders to air force units in the task force. It took an hour and a half to three hours for fighters to respond and about two hours for light bombers. The lessons from pre-invasion exercises FOX, KNOCKOUT, and BEAVER were not learned. On D-day the IX TAC only had 10,129 of a planned 63,100 bombs on inventory and 9,000 of 20,000 drop tanks.

On D-Day a total of 2,185 fighter and fighter-bomber sorties were flown as every 8th and 9th Air Force unit flew at least one mission to sustain a continuous air umbrella over the landing beaches. Of the 2,185 aircraft, 1,719 were escort or patrol while 466 were fighter-bomber sorties. The American fighter units lost 24 pilots and 25 aircraft. The 4th Fighter Group was bounced while strafing and lost seven pilots (six KIA and one evader) including two aces, Capt. Bernard McGratten (8.5 victories) to enemy aircraft and F/O Evan McMinn (five victories) to flak.

Allied fighter-bombers were to provide air cover and interdict the Luftwaffe and provide close support for the invasion. Their first mission never developed as only a handful of enemy fighters appeared over the invasion beaches. In the previous four months Allied medium and fighter-bombers had destroyed the Luftwaffe in the air and on the ground and utterly devastated German airfields, radar and communications. However, close support for the invading troops was a failure. Naval gunfire was given the task of suppressing German beach defenses. The Atlantic Wall was made up of reinforced concrete fortifications and pillboxes expertly sited and heavily gunned. Allied strategists for OVERLORD, particularly Leigh-Mallory, had failed to profit from the lessons learned by the US Navy in the Pacific when heavy naval bombardment had failed to destroy Japanese beach fortifications and dislodge their defenders. Veteran Navy dive-bomber and close air support pilots were then called in to suppress the Japanese. Leigh-Mallory had left the neutralization of beach fortifications to naval gunfire alone. When the Allied infantry waded ashore they were cut down by fire from the nearly intact German defenses which naval bombardment had failed to knock out. The few Allied fighter-bombers that were called in also failed to knock them out. Despite the previous extensive attacks on bridges, rail and road targets the Allied tactical air forces were untrained and unprepared to attack the Atlantic Wall targets they encountered on the beaches. Ground-to-air and air-to-ground communication between the troops trapped on the beaches was absent as was the communication between infantry on the beach and the fire support ships waiting offshore. Active radio frequencies were few and undependable or did not work. More importantly there were only a very few experienced and proficient Forward Air Controllers flying in light aircraft over the beaches. They could have received messages from infantry on the beaches concerning enemy strong points and verified them and relayed their coordinates to tactical aircraft and fire support ships. After the landings, until the beachhead was secure, fighters ranged over the battle area and in hundreds of strafing attacks along roads leading to the beach, harassed and destroyed German infantry and equipment laboring to reach the battlefield.

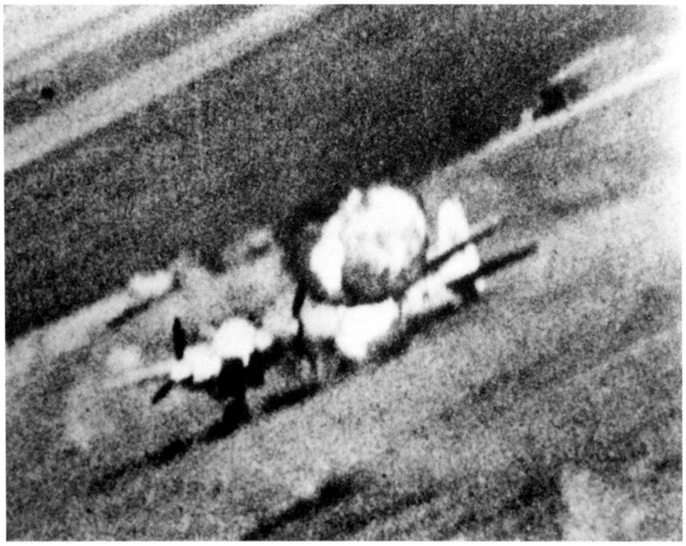

A Ju-88 is cut down on the ground by a comprehensive plan which effectively eliminated the Luftwaffe at D-Day. The complete Allied air superiority over Normandy provoked the following comment from German infantry: "If it's silver (aircraft), it's American; if it's dark, it's British and if it can't be seen it's German." (USAF)

Where is the Luftwaffe?

The complete Allied air superiority over Normandy provoked the following comment from German infantry: "If it's silver (aircraft), it's American; if it's dark, it's British and if it can't be seen it's German." Conversely, Lt.Gen. J. Lawton Collins, VII Corps Commander, complained to Gen. Omar Bradley that one of his regiments had been heavily attacked by German fighter-bombers. Bradley checked with Quesada who looked into the matter and found that the regiment had been "heavily" attacked by two Me-109s! The definition of heavy differed on the north side and south side of the front. It meant relative ease of movement. It meant that the Allies could stockpile mounds of supplies on the beaches. It meant that Allied soldiers only needed to look forward as up only contained friendly aircraft.

While escorting 8th Air Force heavy bombers the VIII Fighter Command helped establish Allied air superiority when they defended the bombers against Luftwaffe fighter attacks. But it was 9th Air Force fighters and fighter-bombers along with medium bombers that were assigned to attack the Luftwaffe at their airfields in northern France, Holland and Belgium intending to neutralize all airfields within 130 miles of the landing beaches. The 9th stepped up these attacks in April and more so in May 1944 until D-Day. Between 1 May and 5 June, they attacked 36 airfields, nine in particular, located from the Brittany coast to Holland and Belgium. These nine included Abbeville/Drucat, Achiet, Beaumont Le Roger, Beaumont sur Oise, Beauvais/Tilly, Chartres, Cormeilles en Vexin, Denain/Prouvy and Evreux/Fauville. The increase in attacks as the invasion date approached damaged runways, taxiways and hangers and associated buildings and gave the Germans less and less time to repair them. By D-Day the airfields closest to the beaches had been hit by 6,717 tons of bombs. The 9th Air Force dropped 3,197 tons, the 8th Air Force dropped 2,638 and the RAF dropped 882.

As mentioned previously, Leigh-Mallory had predicted and prepared for a large Luftwaffe presence over the beaches. As Quesada predicted, this never took place and the massive air umbrella was soon folded and its aircraft was put to other uses. Gen. Arnold was in England at D-Day and was upset at the extravagant waste of airpower that could be better used in other theaters. He thought the English had purposely overestimated Luftwaffe strength despite the intelligence advantage they possessed in Ultra. On 25 May, the British Joint Intelligence Committee assessed Luftwaffe strength at 2,350 aircraft when German figures put the Luftwaffe strength (Luftflotte 3) at just over 200 aircraft of all types. Arnold felt that the RAF Fighter Command had done virtually nothing after the Battle of Britain especially as they did not increase the range of any of their fighters. This was the reason the British wished to have as many longer range US fighters on hand as possible to fly and fight across the Channel..

Order of Battle/Third Air Fleet
6 June 1944

Third Air Fleet
FM Hugo Sperrle
X Air Corps
Lt.Gen. Alexander Holle
Anti-shipping & Missile-carrying Bombers
(136 Do-217 & FW-200, 136 Ju-88)
IX Air Corps
Maj.Gen. Dietrich Peltz
Conventional Bombers
(261 Ju-88, Ju-188 & Do-217)
II Fighter Corps
Maj.Gen. Werner Junck
Single-engine Day Fighters
(350 Me-109 & FW-190)
II Air Corps
Lt.Gen. Alfred Buelowius
Tac Recon & Close-Air Support Aircraft
(67 FW-190, 42 Recon, 52 Ju-88)

On D-Day the Luftwaffe was divided into seven regional air forces (Luftflotten) each controlling the combat units in a defined area. The Third Air Force (Luftflotte 3) under FM Hugo Sperrle controlled France, Belgium and Holland and was assigned to attack the Allied invasion. By June 1944, only the 115 FW-190s and Me-109s of JG2 and JG26 were available to face the 8,560 (3,440 Strategic heavy bombers, 930 medium and light tactical bombers and 4,190 day and night fighters and tactical fighter-bombers). In the year and a half before D-Day, the 8th Air Force had sent its heavy bombers had attacked German industry and the Luftwaffe was forced to defend and suffered huge losses, not so much in aircraft but in experienced pilots.

Before D-Day the Allies attacked German airfields in northern France. To protect their aircraft the Luftwaffe withdrew the aircraft to safer areas to southern France and to the east toward the German border to be moved up when the invasion was imminent. German plans also called for the rapid transfer of Home Defense fighter units from Germany to France soon after the first Allied troops landed. But when the Allied troops finally hit the Normandy beaches, the Luftwaffe plan went astray. Oberkommando West delayed the transfer, as it believed that the Normandy landings were a feint and that the real landings were to be made at the Pas de Calais. Luftflotte 3 could only launch 100 sorties on D-Day. Key Luftwaffe ground personnel were flown in by Ju-52s transports many of which were shot down and the other personnel transported by the rail system were delayed in arriving up to a week late disrupting the command and communications system. The Germans stocked these vacant airfields in France with fuel, ammunition and ordnance but the Allies had systematically attacked these fields. Once the Allies landed, Luftwaffe pilots found their assigned fields destroyed and had to fly from inferior, ill-equipped, secondary fields east of Paris. These fields put them out of the range of Allied fighter-bombers but also caused them to use more fuel flying to and from the beaches decreasing their time over the target. When the Germans fighters approached the beachhead they had to do so from the flank that was easier for the Allies to patrol so most of the Luftwaffe was intercepted away from the beaches. These pilots had previously flown interceptor sorties against Allied bombers and their fighter escorts and were inexperienced in low-level fighter-bomber operations. Operating as fighter-bombers they were attacked and decimated by large numbers of Allied fighters and were forced to defend themselves and to jettison their bombs long before they neared the beachhead. In the first two days of the Invasion an additional 200 fighters were moved from Germany to France and 100 more followed on the 10th. By the end of the first week the Luftwaffe abandoned the use of their fighters as fighter-bombers and directed them to resume their role in aerial combat to hopefully lessen the numbers of Allied aircraft attacking the German frontlines. Also the transfer of these fighters to France meant fewer fighters to defend Reich industry, especially the synthetic oil plants which were under increasing attacks. Even as late as the end of June, Luftflotte 3 build up was only 233 fighters and 419 pilots as it lost almost half of its aircraft reinforcements. For every sortie launched by the Luftwaffe the Allies countered with a dozen. The Luftwaffe on the Western Front not only was inferior in numbers but its inexperienced pilots flew too many missions in now inferior aircraft using inflexible and unsuitable tactics. The airfields were vulnerable, the ground facilities inadequate, communications poor and maintenance and spare parts lacking. In the first two weeks of the invasion the Germans lost 594 aircraft. The bottom line was the lament of the German soldier, "Where is the Luftwaffe?" Eighth Air Force Fighter Command CO, Gen. Bill Kepner, visited the frontline and commented on the value of air superiority in Normandy:

"The relatively unmolested landing of 200,000 vehicles and a million men and the construction of a dozen airstrips practically within sight of the front created advantages beyond the fondest dreams of the Army."

The beachheads and the supply ports in England were to remain a He-111 bombardier's fantasy.

The II Jagdkorps controlled the single-seat day fighter units of the Third Air Fleet in northern France. On D-Day it consisted of six Gruppen of 168 Me-109s and FW-190s and was reinforced by 200 more fighters from Home Defense units by the end of D+2 and another 100 by D+4. On these French airfields the Luftwaffe fighters were at a disadvantage as they had been used to working out of well-equipped permanent fields with radar ground control that would direct their operations. II Korps fighters conducted escort for FW-190 fighter-bombers of the II Air Corps under Maj.Gen. Alfred Beulowius that was armed with only 67 FW-190 fighter-bombers. The II Jagdkorps itself was then pressed into fighter-bomber duties when they were equipped with 250lb. bombs on D+3 and D+4 in futile attacks against Allied shipping and beach positions. Sorties were flown to protect German troops that resulted in decimating dogfights with numerous patrolling Allied fighters. German airfields were either bombed by medium bombers or bombed and strafed by

German trucks in Normandy are trapped at a crossroads without cover and easy prey for the oncoming fighter-bomber attack. (USAF)

A P-38 with Invasion stripes on its wings strafes a locomotive bringing up supplies toward Normandy. (USAF)

the ever-present Allied fighter-bombers. The Luftwaffe lost replaceable aircraft but experienced pilots were either killed or captured. Replacement pilots were poorly trained and quickly perished and the II Korps was steadily worn down by attrition.

Luftwaffe Sorties D-Day to D+4

Date	**Fighter Sorties**	**Sorties> Ground Attacks**
D-Day	70	?
D+1	300	60-70
D+2	525-550	75-100
D+3	500	110-120
D+4	260-270	60-70

Confusion and destruction in Normandy

The following was written by Goetz von Berlichingen, a staff officer with the 17th SS Panzer Division (Intelligence Summary No. 299S, 6 January 1945):

"On 7 June 1944 the 17th SS Panzer Grenadier Division received orders to leave the marshaling area in Thouars and to move to the invasion front in Normandy. Everyone was in a good mood and eager to see action again, happy that the pre-invasion spell of uncertainty and waiting had stopped at last. In some minds....that perhaps this was only a repetition of the Dieppe incident in which the Allies would withdraw after a German show of force. Perhaps Goetz von Berlichingen would even be too late to get into the scrap.

Our motorized columns were coiling along the towards the invasion beaches. Amidst this rumbling of motors and grinding of vehicle tracks the Panzer Grenadier was in his element again. Then something happened that left us in a daze. Spurts of fire flickered along the columns and splashes of dust staccatoed the road. Everyone was piling out of the vehicles and scuttling for the neighboring fields. Several vehicles were already in flames. This attack ceased as suddenly as it had crashed upon us fifteen minutes before. The men started drifting back to the column again, pale and shaky and wondering that they had survived this fiery rain of bullets. Had that been a sign of things to come? This had been our first experience with the "Jabo." The march column had now been completely disrupted and every man was on his own, to pull out of this blazing column as best he could, And it was none too soon because a hour later the whole thing started all over again, only much worse this time. When this attack was over, the length the road was strewn with splintered AT guns (the pride of our division), flaming motor vehicles and charred implements of war.

It dawned on us that this opponent that had come to the beaches of Normandy was of a somewhat different format. The march was called off and all the vehicles that were to be left hidden in the dense bushes and barns. No one dared show himself out in the open anymore. Now the men started looking at each other. The first words were passed. This was different from what we thought it would be like. If things like this happened here, what would things be like up there at the front? No, this did not look like a feint attack upon our continent. It had been our first experience with our new foe-the American.

During the next few days we found out how seriously he (Americans) was going about his business. Although we only traveled at night and along secondary roads rimmed with hedges and bushes, we encountered innumerable wrecks giving unmistakable testimony that some motorist had not benefited from the bitter experiences we had had earlier. After about five days we moved into our assigned sector east of Periors. The Division staff, to which I belonged, crawled into a small village, obviously intent to have as many trees, sunken roads and as much other cover as possible. But now the 'Jabo' plague became even more serious. No hour passed during the daytime without the nerve-frazzling thunder of strafing fighters overhead. And wherever we cared to look we could see smoke billowing from some vehicle, fuel depot or ammunition dump and mushrooming into the sky.

The common soldier began to think. What would all this lead to and what was being done about it? Where was the Luftwaffe and why had it not been committed during the past few days? If he asked his superiors about it, they shrugged their shoulders and remarked that German planes would make their appearance at the opportune moment. But that moment never came. Instead, bad tidings reached from the front as all around us ambulances were carting away victims of strafing. And when the soldiers became more insistent in their queries they were finally told that the Luftwaffe was operating in adjoining sectors where the situation was even more serious than ours. This excuse calmed them for a while until contact had been made with those adjoining sectors and the soldiers found out that the absence of air power there was just as conspicuous. And in those sectors the soldiers had been told that the German planes were operating in our sector.

...Complaints became more frequent that artillery ammunition stores were running low, that weapons needed replacement that communications were out due to air attack. The hope of driving the Americans back into the Channel had already given way to a hope of being able to hold our own against the invaders. And then came the great American breakthrough in the direction of Coutances. The way of the cross for the German soldier had begun."

TACs aid the D-Day airborne troops

The Normandy airborne operations of the 82nd and 101st Airborne Divisions were assisted by the TACs achieving Priority One, air superiority and flying pre-jump counter flak sorties and attacks on communication centers. Once the paratroopers were on the ground, most of TAC missions flown were pre-arranged sorties against bridges on the Cherbourg Peninsula, on lines of communications opposite the paratroopers or armed recce missions behind enemy lines. The most notable armed recce missions were against the 17th Panzer Division as it moved toward its assembly area. A number of tanks were damaged or destroyed. Close air request missions were infrequent and those flown were appropriated from armed recce missions by TALOs who "talked" the fighter-bomber pilots to the target, a method that would soon become an accepted routine. Losses of the airborne TALOs and/or their equipment in the drops also limited the effectiveness of any anticipated air support. It was fortunate that in these early days of close support that the paratroops were able to quickly link up with the beachhead on 8 June, as both fighter-bomber support and aerial reconnaissance information were inadequate to assist these lightly armed troops. The losses sustained by the paratroops due to the lack of close air support were too large when considering the large numbers of fighter-bombers available over the invasion beaches.

TACs over Normandy: D-Day to D+10

Between 0352 and 2340, on D-Day, 18 groups of 9th Air Force fighters flew approximately 2,000 sorties comprising air cover, armed reconnaissance, bomber and troop transport escort and a number of close support strikes. Priority One: Air Supremacy sorties were particularly effective as only a handful of German fighters appeared over the beaches during daylight hours of 6 June. VII Corps commander, Maj.Gen. Troy Middleton, on Utah Beach stated: "the air forces provided the greatest assistance in these operations by protecting our troops from enemy aerial attack and by disrupting his communications and limiting the movements of enemy reserves". However, large-scale Priority Three: Close air support sorties were limited and relatively unproductive as direct air-to-ground communications had not been established. The 0635 landings on Omaha Beach did not clear enemy resistance and move inland until late afternoon. First Infantry Division commander, Maj.Gen. Clarence Huebner, credits fighter-bombers with meaningfully aiding the Omaha Beach assault: "The Air Force (fighter-bombers) gave assistance by area cover which was superb, fighter sweeps and dive-bombing and strafing which proved effective, preliminary communication interruption and continuous interruption of enemy troop movements. Sorely needed was a softening up by medium and heavy bombers. This (the bombing) would have to be accurate and of sufficient strength to insure the elimination of certain strong points immediately prior to the assault. The lack of this success was keenly felt during the Normandy assault." These fighter-bomber sorties were attacks on targets of opportunity by aircraft on station over Omaha Beach. These fighter-bombers were unable to communicate directly with ground forces and were thus unable to aid them directly. The ground units had to call a Headquarters ship, which then relayed the ground request to central control at Uxbridge in the UK. There a decision was made and relayed to the appropriate

The Normandy hedgerow, the infamous Bocage. The light swatch in the upper of the photo is ALG, A-9, under construction. (USAF)

Left: First Infantry Division commander, Maj.Gen. Clarence Huebner, credits fighter-bombers with meaningfully aiding the Omaha Beach assault. (US Army)

air unit. This procedure took a very long time to implement and so there were only six close air support requests made by V Corps to Uxbridge on the critical morning of D-Day and only 13 were made all day.

On Omaha Beach the American VIII Corps under Maj.Gen, J. Lawton Collins ran into strong German resistance, poor beach conditions and weather that only remarkable courage by ground troops and quick and effective air support saved the day. Aided by 13 close support missions assault battalions worked their way inland. Quesada directed three fighter-bomber groups from Bradley's headquarters on the beachhead. The P-47s attacked mortar and artillery positions threatening the beaches. Lt.Gen. Lewis Brereton considered this air support to be responsible for the establishment of the beachhead, "History may show that they saved the day" (*The Brereton Diaries*, NY, William Morrow, 1946). Vandenberg blamed some of the troubles on American landing beaches, particularly Omaha, on AEAF fighter control neglect. On D-Day he found that AEAF battle HQ had all British beach front lines marked but the two American beaches were neglected. As the Deputy Commander of the AEAF he forcefully protested and got more much needed air support for US troops.

After the landing constructing airstrips from the dense Bocage hedgerows of Normandy under German fire was found to be almost impossible. By the evening of D-Day only one of the two planned temporary 2,000-foot landing strips had been completed behind Utah Beach and it would not be until D+3 that one of two refueling and rearming strips had been completed. The invasion was held up and the proposed four airstrips to be completed by

IX TAC P-47s share a Normandy airfield with the British and cattle. (USAF)

D+4 and eight by D+8 fell far behind schedule. Germans ignored the initial airfield construction and waited until heavy equipment was moved in and then shelled the fields.

Two hundred and twenty command personnel of the 70th Wing were to come ashore late on D-Day but delays keep them aboard their landing craft until 1600 D+1 when they waded through the human and material wreckage of the invasion beaches. As they proceeded toward their base at Cricqueville by truck German snipers fired at them. They were forced to bivouac for two days as Cricqueville was still in enemy hands. Finally by 10 June Col. Blair Garland, head of IX Signals, had established a landline to

ALG 9th Air Force Fighter Group headquarters on one of the first Advanced Landing Grounds in France after D-Day. Included in this photo is the mobile control tower (center under netting). (USAF)

Left: Throughout the centuries the roads sunk deeper and deeper into the hedge rows making it an idea area for defensive fighting and hiding from American fighter-bombers. (US Army)

Eisenhower in England, to the First Army and to two corps at the front. Only two of five forward directing posts were ashore and most of his support personnel were caught up in the traffic jams behind the beachheads. There were 1,600 engineers making their way toward the areas where airstrips were to be constructed and soon the first two operable strips would be ready but in the meantime the IX would have to fly out of Middle Wallop in the UK.

On 7 June P-47s of the 365th, 366th and 368th Groups began operations at 0600 to attack chokepoints caused by interdiction missions and were on call for close support by American infantry divisions. During the day 467 aircraft from these three tactical groups flew 35 squadron strength request missions. Other 9th Air Force groups flew invasion shipping patrol and other missions. The 8th Air Force flew 820 patrol and escort sorties and 653 strafing sorties and lost 14 aircraft and 12 pilots.

By 8 June Allied invasion plans had fallen far behind schedule and it was imperative that Omaha and Utah Beaches be linked together so that the Germans could not put reinforcements into the area. The 101st Airborne Division was chosen to attack bringing the beaches together in a battle near Carentan. Being an airborne division meant that they were lightly armed and without artillery and faced well-equipped portions of the German Sixth Parachute Regiment and the 17th Panzer Grenadier Division closing in on the area. To aid the lightly armed 101st the IX TAC was to provide air support. At dawn on 9 June the first requests for air support arrived over the IX radio net but bad weather prevented any sorties from being flown. By 0900 the weather improved and offshore air controllers sent out a mission against four concrete gun emplacements holding up the 101st advance. American lines were marked with colored panels and the P 47s dropped their 500lb. bombs to take out the guns.

P-51s flew armed recce sorties 30-50 miles behind the battlefront and discovered 10-12 trains carrying a two-division strong battle group, Kampfgruppe *Heinz*, which was to lead the German counterattack on the beaches. The Mustangs destroyed one train before running low on fuel and ammunition and radioed the *Heinz* position to HQ. More P-51s were dispatched and destroyed another train and assisted by medium bombers cut tracks on both sides of the area. On the 10th the weather was clear and Allied fighter-bombers were able to answer all calls for ground support. In the early morning three waves of 70 aircraft supported the advance to the outskirts of Carentan. Then on the 11th low ceiling prevented dive-bombing and all requests for support, including five from Lt. Gen. Lawton Collins personally. There was no fog or rain over him, but Collins and his infantry did not understand that low ceiling was a weather condition that could prevent air attacks on the first units of *Heinz* arriving in the area. The next day the weather cleared somewhat and over 200 aircraft smashed the trucks, horses and men of a German infantry company. Lt. Wilford Crutchfield of 362nd Fighter Group dropped below the low cloud and discovered a train and road convoy headed toward Carentan. He radioed its position and dove destroying seven troop trucks. Soon after other fighters added 41 trucks, seven locomotives and 15 flatcars carrying vehicles. Capt. Bob Stephens of the 354th Fighter Group attacked near Le Mans and destroyed 50 railway cars, a radio station and several flak towers. *Heinz* continued to move toward Carentan despite the incessant four day aerial pounding it received. Its troops were hungry, tired and in total disarray and their attack toward Carentan was abandoned in the afternoon of the 12th. Allied air planners believed that air interdiction would be the bulk of early air operations over Normandy. Close air support sorties would occur only after the Allies had established a secure beachhead 30+ miles deep and the battle fronts had stabilized so that air support would not jeopardize friendly troops. US ground units requested 184 ground sorties in the first week of the invasion while British troops, stopped by strong German defenses requested even more support sorties. It wasn't long before Allied ground commanders, lacking strong artillery support, began to rely on air support as a quick and efficient means of hitting the enemy. Starting at 0530 on the 8th Eighth Air Force fighter groups flew 1,353 escort, sweeps, patrols and ground attacks sorties losing 22 aircraft and 21 pilots including eight victory ace, Lt. Robert Booth of the 359th Fighter Group to German flak who was to become a POW.

On 9 June, very bad weather grounded the entire Allied air campaign. The weather improved the next day and although bomber operations were curtailed the American fighters were able to fly 1,491 sorties claiming 30 Luftwaffe aircraft in the air for the large loss of 24 pilots. Despite sustaining their largest casualty rate of the war, over the next several days Allied pilots were able to claim nearly twice as many German aircraft in the air as they lost. At this point in the war, American pilots were better trained and equipped and had a numerical superiority of three to one. The new attacks on fuel supplies and German aircraft on the ground further added to the German woes. The only factor in the German's favor at the time was the overcast over German targets. Control of all tactical missions in France was taken over by the IX TAC in advanced headquarters on the Continent. On the 16th the first American fighters operated from a primitive airstrip, called A-2, cut into the Normandy countryside near the front at Criqueville by the IX Engineer Command. These advanced fields saved time as the pilots could operate from sunrise to sunset from France without returning to England to be refueled and re-armed. Several days later, the 48th Fighter Group

German Panzer units shipped to the front via train but often had to off-load many miles from their destination. Here the 78th Fighter Group strafes a train carrying an armored division on its way to the Normandy front. (USAF)

was operating out of at A-4 at Dreux, France. On the 19th, the Ninth, announced that the 368th Fighter Group would be stationed at a "permanent" base in France, A-3 at Cardonville. Another notable innovation also began on the 16th when the VIII Fighter Command conducted the first organized fuel tank raid. It had been found in the absence of napalm bombs in the ETO that 8th Air Force pilots could hit large targets with their long-range fuel tanks and then could increase the destruction by strafing the blazing target. On the 16th over 500 8th Air Force fighters dropped their auxiliary tanks on rail targets in France destroying over 400 rail cars.

In the weeks after the landing, primary targets for the fighter-bombers continued to be railroad equipment and rail and road bridges. Although most of the bridges on the Seine and Meuse had been destroyed the Germans were masters of improvisation and repair. Constant surveillance by reconnaissance aircraft revealed when bridge repairs were about to be completed and the bridge was attacked again as it neared completed repair. The result was that only one train crossed the Seine between D-Day and the arrival of Allied troops at the river. Both carefully planned missions and armed recce missions were deployed to stop German troop and supply movements and to isolate the battlefield. German transport, rail and road, were forced to move only at night or on bad weather days when Allied fighters were grounded. To deny German access to the front from the south, fighter-bombers aided in the destruction of bridges over the Loire River between Orleans and the sea and cut track in specified areas. Between 7 and 19 June, rail targets, especially marshalling yards, continued to receive major interest from medium bombers (1,579 sorties/2,422 tons of bombs) and fighter-bombers (2,898 sorties/1,246 tons). These attacks limited German use of the well-developed rail system west of the Seine and north of the Loire. As part of the von Rundstedt/Hitler plan to withhold reserves until after the invasion began, the Germans had prepared plans for the French rail system to bring up troops to the front as quickly as possible for a decisive counter-attack. But this plan was critically disrupted when the main sections of the rail system were so badly damaged it caused the Germans to re-route troop and supply trains to single-track lines moving north. The reserves had to detrain miles from their intended jump off point and move slowly by motor transport and by foot. So instead of a concentrated counter-attack the reserves were fed piecemeal into the battle to strengthen the deteriorating front. The situation had gotten so bad that locomotive personnel left their trains when Allied aircraft only flew over. Orders were given that they could only stop and leave their trains when actually under air attack. No consideration was given to returning the empty trains and they accumulated and blocked these few remaining open lines. German road movement met long delays forced by long detours that, in turn, caused the use of gasoline that was in critically short supply, increased wear and tear that led to increased maintenance problems for motor vehicles and armor which were lacking spare parts. Rail and road traffic accumulated behind destroyed bridges. Many tracked armored vehicles broke down on the long detours as a tank motor required overhaul after 400 miles. All of which provided splendid targets for fighter-bombers.

Maj.Gen. Fritz Bayerlein, the Commander of the Panzer Lehr Division, was a seasoned veteran of North Africa and Russia. His division was reinforced specifically to repel the invasion and stationed in central France to be moved immediately after the invasion location was determined. (Author/West)

Panzer Lehr Division trucks strafed and burning on their way to stop the Allies at the Normandy Beachhead. (US Army)

Maj.Gen. Fritz Bayerlein, the Commander of the Panzer Lehr Division, was a seasoned veteran of North Africa and Russia. His division was reinforced specifically to repel the invasion and stationed in central France to be moved immediately after the invasion location was determined. It was supplied with more armor and motor transport than the average German division and two-thirds of its troops were veterans. Bayerlein received the alert that the invasion was to be on the way at 0200 on 6 June and he was ordered to assemble and move north at 1700. Air attacks were heavy and Bayerlein requested a delay until twilight to escape the Jabos but was refused. The division moved as ordered and was immediately attacked by fighter-bombers and lost 20-30 vehicles by nightfall. The next day Bayerlein was ordered to continue moving toward the beaches at daylight and the first fighters appeared at 0530 near Falaise. They continued a sustained attack not only on the division but also on road junctions and bridges in its path. By the end of the day the losses were shattering: 130 trucks (40 carrying precious fuel), 84 half-tracks, prime movers and self-propelled guns and five tanks. Bayerlein personally had to take refuge twice from fighter-bomber attacks.

From the onset of the invasion both sides raced to build up their forces realizing the winner of the battle would be the side with the better logistics. In the month following D-Day the Germans had planned to transfer 23 divisions to Normandy to increase their total to 30, a figure that the Allies could not immediately match. Thus air interdiction would remain a critical factor in Allied strategy. Except for RAF Bomber Command, all Allied air forces were diverted to interdicting German transport. The 8th Air Force flew only two strategic missions from 2 to 17 June. On 15 June alone over a thousand B-17s destroyed seven Loire bridges. In eight days, its strategic bombers flew 5,900 tactical sorties, dropping 14,000 tons of bombs in direct support of ground operations. They were credited with attacking 38 bridges, 22 trains, nine motor transport convoys and 58 marshaling yards. Medium bombers of the IX Bomber Command and RAF 2nd Tactical Air Force added to the harassment of marshaling yards and bridges.

Field Marshal Erwin Rommel had planned to commit German troops into the invasion area in the first days of the attack but all were delayed by Allied air attacks and as he stated in *The Rommel Papers* (Harcourt Brace, NY, 1953): "far too late to smash the enemy landing by counter-attacks." Rommel comments on the complete Allied air superiority in a report to Generalfeldmarschall Wilhelm Keitel, Chief of the Armed Forces High Command on 11 June 1944:

"Especially by day, the Luftwaffe and German navy are in no position to prevent the enemy to an essential degree from increasing his forces on land. The extremely strong enemy air superiority kept us from moving up the I SS Panzer Corps...The Army Group intends to launch its main operation in the Carentan-Montebourg area in order to destroy the enemy there and avert the danger to Cherbourg. This operation can have no more support from our fighter formations since we have no more airports near the front.

As my officers and I have repeatedly ascertained ourselves, and as the troop commanders, especially Sepp Dietrich (a Hitler favorite-ed.), report the enemy completely dominates the air space over the battle terrain to about 100 kilometers behind the front. Every day, with strong fighter-bomber and bomber formations, he halts nearly all traffic on the roads and paths and on open terrain. Movements of our troops onto the battlefield by day have been made almost impossible, while the enemy can operate freely. In the rear, all tight spots are subjected to constant attack. It is very difficult to bring up necessary supplies of ammunition and fuel to the troops. Even the movement of smaller organizations on the battlefield, the emplacement of artillery, the preparation of tanks, etc., is immediately bombarded up to a point of annihilation. Troops and staff must hide in covered terrain by day in order to escape the constant form the air.

In the battlefield of the I SS Corps, the condition was such on June 9 that many enemy fighter-bomber squadrons circled above the battlefield without pause and heavy bomber formations intensely bombarded troops, towns, bridges and traffic intersections without any regard for the civilian populace. Neither our own anti-aircraft not the Luftwaffe seem able to hinder the crippling and destructive effect of the enemy air forces."

A typical example of the problems faced by the Germans in moving troops and equipment occurred on 7 June. The 275th Infantry Division based in Brittany was ordered to move about a 100 miles by rail from Rennes to the Lison-Bayeux area of Normandy. At 1300 five trains were in route and three more were being loaded. An hour later it was reported that the first train had been held up at Avranches and that the other trains had been attacked. At 1600, the lines between Rennes and Dol were cut. Detours were being scheduled but three more cuts on these new routes were reported at 1800. A detour was finally worked out but in the next two hours it too was disrupted no less than 19 times! Another detour was arranged. While waiting, the first train was attacked about ten miles north of Avranches with the loss of the train and all the division's equipment and heavy casualties to the troops. The second train could proceed no further and was unloaded 12 miles southwest of Avranches. Also unable to proceed, the other trains were unloaded near Rennes on the 9th and it was until the late on the 11th that units arrived piecemeal near Bayeaux. The 12th SS Panzer Hitler Jugend was forced to march 75 miles northwest of Caen during which time they were continually attacked by fighter-bombers and sustained such heavy losses that upon their arrival they could not mount an attack. The 3rd Parachute Division required six days to move 135 miles from Brittany to St. Lo too late to make its scheduled counter-attack on Bayeaux.

The Germans attempted to move the outstanding 271st, 272nd, 276th and 277th motorized divisions into the breech but their movement was thwarted but fighter-bomber attacks at every road junction, town, clearing and destroyed bridge. They also had to contend with effective sabotage by the French Resistance. Units of the 272nd tried to move by train four different times before finding the 180-mile night time march preferable and safer than facing constant fighter-bomber attacks.

Troops ordered to the reinforce the Normandy front from the southwest of France were able to move from 120-150 miles per day until they reached the broken bridges over the Loire River. Troops arriving from the west (e.g. Germany, Holland, Rumania or Russia) were stopped at the Seine and had to detrain near Paris. Ferries, small boats and temporary pontoon bridges got the troops across the rivers but their armor and artillery was often left behind. If only one permanent bridge been open the movement could have been accomplished much more quickly. Because of the threat of air attacks, movement to the front was made on a less vulnerable company or platoon level. The result of this type of movement was confusion and disorder upon arrival and disrupted command organization that led these troops to be fed into battle in a piecemeal fashion. Depending on the motor transport available, the movement to the front, which was about 150 miles away, could take from two days to two weeks. A march to the front by foot and any available transport such as bicycles, and horse-drawn vehicles was made in night marches of six or seven days on secondary roads. Major towns and cities were avoided as because the bomb damage to the roads within these areas slowed travel and exposed the movement to further attack. The summer nights were shorter allowing more daylight for air attacks. Night movement was inherently slow but interrogations of German officer POWs indicated that the lack of large-scale and regular nighttime interdiction by Allied night fighters and the subsequent ability of the Germans to move at night was the major reason that their forces remained operational.

Cherbourg (17-26 June)

As soon as Utah Beach was secured the Americans turned their attention to Cherbourg, 16 miles to the northwest. The German LXXXIV Corps was left on its to protect the west flank by Rommel who needed to check Montgomery at Caen and Bradley at St. Lo before they broke out of the hedgerows and roared into the flat terrain to the south. Lt.Gen. Lawton Collins' VII Corps and the 90th Infantry Division and 82nd Airborne attacked on the 11th trying to drive to Cotentin and cut the LXXXIV Corps in two. On the 12th, Gen. Erich Marcks, commander of the LXXXIV Corps was attacked by a fighter-bomber on a road west of St. Lo and hit in the right leg by a bullet and bled to death before help arrived. A temporary replacement was named further hindering the direction of the defense. On the 15th, the 82nd Airborne led the breakout and Collins exploited the situation and drove to cut off the Cherbourg Peninsula. The 709th Infantry Division under Lt.Gen. Wilhelm von Schlieben was able to pull together a ragtag force from retreating remnants. Group von Schlieben and the newly arrived 77th Division pulled back toward Cherbourg. The retreat was hampered when Lt.Gen. Heinz Hellmich of the 234th Infantry Division was killed by another fighter-bomber. Lt.Gen. Rudolf Stegmann, commander of the 77th, decided to defy Hitler's orders and tried to break through the American lines to connect with German forces to the east. The 77th's horse-drawn columns were attacked by fighter-bombers near the village of Bricquebec and Stegmann was too was killed by a fighter-bomber. Col. Rudolf Bacherer assumed command and was successful in leading his troops to safety the next day.

The battle for Cherbourg was a strategic failure because the port had been destroyed and would not be in use in full capacity for months. Cherbourg was the first major use of tactical air power in direct support of ground objective in Northwestern Europe. The role of air power in the victory is debatable. The TAF flew 1,822 sorties; dropping almost 500 tons of bombs on heavily fortified positions manned by determined, well-led troops. As it had been throughout military history, it required the foot soldier, at great risk and high cost, to dislodge the enemy and force their surrender. (USAF)

On 17 June the Allies launched their final attack to isolate Cherbourg from the rest of France. Von Schlieben withdrew into Cherbourg. At 0830 the 36rd Fighter Group attacked German troop concentrations outside the coastal town of Carteret at the far end of the Cotentin Peninsula. Later that morning, 48 P-38s again attacked Carteret but three other strikes were canceled because of inaccurate identification panels laid out by ground controllers. The panel problem was corrected and over 200 fighter-bombers carried out five more afternoon missions allowing the US army to nearly cut the Cotentin Peninsula in two cutting off Cherbourg.

On 18 June, the weather cleared and eight fighter-bomber groups flew 384 aircraft from their bases in southern England. The 367th sent 45 P-38s toward La Rouche and attacked a power station and bridge there and turned the town into a shambles. On the way back to base they strafed targets of opportunity strafing anything that moved: M/T, rolling stock and even a vegetable cart. The 392nd Squadron Operations Officers was killed when ground fire hit his cockpit. The 366th under Harold Holt attacked a truck convoy hiding in the trees near Periers. Also 405th hit armored column. 370th cut 38 rail lines and 45 freight, ammo and gasoline railcars. 371st in a fighter sweep near Valognes knocked out 98 trucks and killed 800-1,000 men to finish the isolation of Cherbourg.

For all the planning, the weather was the one intangible. On the morning of the 20th, a great storm and heavy gales hit the Normandy coast and Bradley's army attacked without air support but made headway nonetheless. The storm continued into the next day and wrecked the artificial harbors built along the invasion beaches. The Allied supply situation already overstretched became critical and the capture of Cherbourg's harbor and dock facilities became an overriding objective in Allied plans. The siege of the city began and Hitler issued another one of his fight to the death edicts

On the 21st, Bradley enlisted Quesada's support in a massive air operation but the IX did not have sufficient resources to do the job alone. Bradley's plans had divided the area in front of the city into grids that were to be attacked by saturation bombing. To fulfill the plan over 2,000 aircraft would be needed in an effort not seen since the Cassino attack earlier that spring. Quesada and Collins met near Ste. Mere Eglise to discuss what Collins described as "air pulverization" across twenty miles of the front. The bomb lines were to be marked with yellow and white smoke and since the less-accurate heavy bombers were scrubbed, Collins wanted the front marked as close as possible so his troops would be able to quickly attack any breaks in the German lines. Quesada and Col. Harry Holt, CO of the 366th Fighter Group, agreed but insisted that a buffer zone of several hundred yards be established to minimize the jeopardy to American troops from short and inaccurate bombing. Quesada quickly flew to England and presented the plan to the Allied Air Commanders at Hillingdon House. Quesada flew back to Europe late the same day to meet with Bradley and VII Corps commander, J. Lawton Collins to prepare the operational orders for the next day. Through his experience at Guadalcanal, Collins was a firm believer in cooperation between combined forces: army artillery, engineers, air and when possible, navy.

Brereton took the plan back to England where the air staffs of many commands worked feverishly on the details of the final order that included 1,500 aircraft. Long gone were the days in North Africa and Sicily when TAC air was in its infancy and such a large effort on such short notice would have been impossible. Several hours before sunrise on 22 June, the final order was drafted and flown to France by Brig.Gen. Richard Nugent. The plan included ten Spitfire squadrons and twelve IX fighter squadrons to strafe German positions at the front an hour before the attack. As the infantry moved forward from only 300 yards from the bomb line, eleven groups of medium bombers would attack pinpoint targets in a rolling carpet of bomb. The weather on the 22nd was ideal as Quesada, Collins and Nugent watched the air show from a point only a half-mile from German lines. American mortars fired WP (white phosphorous) shells on German strongpoints to mark them for the fighter-bombers and infantry pulled back 1,000 yards along the front as a precaution. Over 100 RAF Spitfires and Typhoons swept the front strafing and bombing German positions at 1240 hours. A flight of Typhoons swept along the front close to the watching American Brass and opened fire. The three generals hit the ground as 20mm cannon shells whizzed around them. As they got up they saw angry soldiers nearby throw yellow smoke grenades intended to mark American lines. Next 557 IX TAC fighters crossed the Channel and reached Cherbourg at 1300 hours. The 2nd TAF attack had alerted the German AA defenders and also covered the area with smoke and dust. The Americans were assigned to attack six defended areas over the 25-mile front but the AA and smoke and dust forced them to attack targets of opportunity. The yellow smoke grenade markers thrown earlier around the CP did mark the American lines but newly arrived P-47s mistook their intent and again strafed Quesada and his guests who again took cover. Wave after wave of fighter-bombers hit the German positions to great effect but not without loss as two dozen were lost. At 1400 hours the infantry moved across the fighter-bomber bomb line through the stunned German lines. The 400 medium bombers flew in as clouds from the sea rolled in to cover the battle. The medium bomber pilots were inexperienced in close support and blind bombed the area. The mediums hit the 9th Division twice and the 79th Division put itself in jeopardy by over running the bomb line but fortunately the overcast prevented the mediums from finding the area. The medium bombers failed to hit any of their assigned targets and their performance only caused contempt for them by the infantry. Collins' forces made small gains against the well dug in and determined German defenses but did not penetrate them.

On the 2rd poor weather returned and limited air support to only three minor missions but Collins tough troops aided by skillful artillery and assertive and capable leadership on regiment and battalion levels moved well into the city and were within two miles of the harbor in certain areas.

On the 24th good weather returned and P-47s attacked targets along the main harbor road and the American infantry drove into the city detouring around several strong points in order to keep their momentum. One of these bypassed points was La Mere a Canard, a fortified hill with entrenched artillery that began to fire and caused the infantry to stop their advance and take cover. An artillery duel ensued but the Germans held fast. At 1615 hours Bradley asked Quesada to mount an air strike to take out the artillery. Quesada radioed Col. Gilbert Meyers whose 368th Group had recently moved to France and had not expected to see combat for several more days. At 2027 hours Meyer's deputy commander, Lt. Colonel Frank Perago, took off with 24 P-47s and headed toward Cherbourg. After the P-47s finished dropping their 1,000lb. bombs the German artillery had been silenced and American infantry was again advancing. The German defenders throughout the city crowded together in underground fortifications and tunnels waiting for the American artillery and air attacks to stop and American infantry attack to continue. On the 25th only pockets of determined resistance remained which had to be mopped up in bitter fighting. Fort du Roule was the last German strongpoint located on the coast. It was surrounded on three sides by steep cliffs and approachable only by a narrow ridge protected by mine fields, barbed wire and an anti-tank ditch. Pillboxes and trenches bristling with mortars and

Cherbourg's port facilities were made usable for months by Allied bombing and German demolition. (USAF)

On 26 September 1944 after a resolute defense, German commander, Lt.Gen. Wilhelm von Schlieben, surrendered Cherbourg and was publicly denounced by Hitler. The city was finally cleared on the 29th but not before the Germans had completely destroyed the port. (US Army)

automatic weapons covered the approach from the roof of the Fort. A flight of P-47s armed with 500lb. bombs opened the attack but most of the 24 bombs missed the small target. After an artillery and mortar barrage the fort had to be taken the old-fashioned way by costly infantry attack. On the 26th, German commander, General von Schlieben surrendered and was publicly denounced by Hitler. The city was finally cleared on the 29th but not before the Germans had completely destroyed the port.

The battle for Cherbourg was a strategic failure because the port had been destroyed and would not be in use in full capacity for months. The battle cost Collins' VII Corps 22,119 casualties (2,811 killed) and the Germans 47,000 killed, wounded or captured. Cherbourg was the first major use of tactical air power in direct support of ground objective in Northwestern Europe. The role of air power in the victory is debatable. The TAF flew 1,822 sorties; dropping almost 500 tons of bombs on heavily fortified positions manned by determined, well-led troops. As it had been throughout military history, it required the foot soldier, at great risk and high cost, to dislodge the enemy and force their surrender.

Results and Lessons Learned in June 1944

In three weeks of combat twenty-five years of tactical air power theory were found to be flawed and had to be improvised and revised over the battlefield. A new tactical air power prototype plan was developed, still flawed and sometimes ineffective, but one that was operable in the present and adaptable to changes in the future.

By the end of June, IX fighter-bombers flew over 25,000 sorties in 800 missions destroying 24 bridges and 14 tunnels, 17 ammunition and supply dumps and 53 marshaling yards, 1,300 motor transport, 506 locomotive and rolling stock and cutting 170 tracks. There were five advanced landing fields in operation by mid-June each enabling three fighter groups to rearm and refuel between missions without returning to their bases in England. These fields delivered over 30,000 gallons of gasoline, hundreds of thousands of rounds of ammunition and many tons of bombs.

German generals were unanimous about the disastrous effects of Allied air superiority, particularly those generals who had served on the Russian front before being assigned to the West. An anecdote demonstrates Allied confidence in their air superiority. On 4 July 1944, Eisenhower was touring the front with Omar Bradley. Late in the afternoon they were at an advanced field where they met Pete Quesada, who had a personal two-seat Mustang. On a whim Ike asked Quesada to take him up for a bird's eye tour of the front. Bradley was worried about the situation and asked Ike not to go. Eisenhower replied, "Brad, I'm not going to Berlin!" For the next 45 minutes Quesada and his passenger proceeded to fly over the front and even into German territory.

Field Marshal Gerd von Rundstedt:

"After the first few days I had no hope of defeating the invasion. The Allied Air Forces paralyzed all movement by day and made it very difficult even at night. They smashed the bridges over the Liore as well as over the Seine, shutting off the whole area. These factors greatly delayed the concentration of reserves there-they took three or four times longer to reach the front than we had reckoned." (Basil Liddel Hart, *German Generals Talk*, Morrow, NY, 1948)

Field Marshal Guenther von Kluge:

"The enemy's command of the air restricts all movement in terms of both space and time and renders calculation of time impossible. For armored or motorized troops in divisional strength upwards, it limits the possibilities of command and maneuver to night or bad weather operations, which cannot as a rule develop into anything more than operations with limited objective." (*Rommel Papers*, ibid.)

Confidence in Allied air superiority. On the 4th of July 1944, less than a month after D-Day, Pete Quesada took Ike up in his personal two-seat P-51 for a tour of the battlefield. Bystander, Omar Bradley, disapproved of the flight but Ike replied, "Brad, I'm not going to Berlin" and the Ninth Air Force commander flew the Supreme Allied Commander over and behind the front for the next 45 minutes. (USAF)

Field Marshal Walther Model (via Lt.Gen. Bodo Zimmerman):

"Field Marshal Model, who had hitherto seen action only on the Eastern Front did not immediately grasp the full gravity of the situation in France and hoped that he might restore it. But he was soon to realize the unimaginable effects of the enemy's air supremacy, the massive destruction in the rear areas, the impossibility of traveling along any major road in daylight without great peril, in fact the full significance of the invasion." (Seymour Freiden and William Richardson, *The Fatal Decisions*, Sloane, NY, 1956)

Finally Rommel:

"Support by our air force was not forthcoming on the scale originally foreseen. The enemy had command of the air over the battleground up to a point some 60 miles behind the front. In sorties of immense strength he smashed the defense installations in the coastal zones and effectively the approach march of our reserves and the supply of our troops, principally by damage to the railway system." (*Rommel Papers*, ibid.)

Rommel went on to comment:

"The enemy air superiority limits all movements in time and space and rules out the possibility of any time calculations. It limits the command and operational potentials of the tank and motorized divisions, from the division organization upward, to night operations or to combat during bad weather. The enemy air superiority makes it necessary for mobile reserves to be kept as close to the coast as possible....When distances are too great, the tank organizations lose some of their tanks to breakdown en route....The enemy has systematically attacked all traffic intersections, roads and railroads and destroyed all bridges. There were bombing and strafing attacks on columns and individual vehicles. With enemy air superiority, it is difficult to supply the tank organizations and so no more should be in operation than can be supplied." (*Army Group B Situation Reports*, 25 June 1944)

Requests for planned air support missions were tendered by armies to Main HQ 21 Army Group G (Air) Section at Uxbridge (UK) that then forwarded them to the Air Force for implementation. Requests from advanced ground units for direct air support were radioed directly by Air Support Party Officers stationed with the ground units to Uxbridge. Theoretically, air officers on HQ ships in the assault area controlled fighter-bombers flying over the area and were to vector the aircraft to vital targets. The excessive delay and ineffectiveness in this type of system was soon obvious. The Air Support Party Officers (later called Tactical Air Liaison Officers-TALOs), immediately realized the deficiency and improvised to obtain fighter-bomber support by making direct radio contact with squadron leaders in the air. This procedure was not in practice at the time but pleading by the Air Liaison Officer could divert a sympathetic squadron leader to attack an urgent target. The result of this deficiency was to lead to the initiation of armored column cover.

During the month after D-Day, IX TAC airman Quesada and First Army ground commander Bradley established a bond that benefited close air support aviation. The two set up command posts in neighboring mobile vans and had a common distrust of Brereton's disinterest in ground-air operations and worked closely together to remedy the situation. Every night at 2000 hours their two staffs met to plan the following day's operations. Col. Robert McClenahan, IX Intelligence Officer, began the meeting with a short summary and synopsis of the battle. The First Army weatherman gave the forecast and its ground officers presented operations and intelligence reports. In light of this information the First made its requests for air support. Col. Lorry Tindal, IX TAC Operations Officer, assigned fighter groups for each request while holding back reserves for bomber escort duty. Both, Bradley and Quesada had to sign off approval that was essentially a rubber stamp as both commanding officers had confidence in their junior officers. The operational orders were cut and sent to the selected units and the AEAF at Uxbridge. Leigh-Mallory seldom interfered with plans, as to his credit; he realized the benefits of decentralized command in conducting the air war. Both Quesada and his RAF opposite number, Sir Harry Broadhurst, were permitted unusual freedom in their employment of air power. The plan was usually in place a little after midnight.

Despite the outstanding ground-air cooperation at this level Montgomery thought the Leigh-Mallory/Tedder/Coningham rift added to lack of Allied success on the ground by not taking advantage of their great air power superiority. Montgomery stated in his personal diary that he suspected that RAF 2nd TAF chief, Arthur Coningham and Eisenhower's Air Deputy, ACM Sir Arthur Tedder were in collusion to deny his armies of the support in the field it required. Tedder thought Montgomery was too cautious and by not advancing had given the Germans time to build up their forces in Normandy and restore the transportation system the Allied air forces had destroyed at great cost before D-Day. Montgomery's failure to advance prevented the RAF from establishing airfields on the Continent and its short-ranged fighters had to operate from UK bases.

Tactical air power was particularly effective in interdicting the battlefield but was not effective against fortified positions and towns. The rudiments of diverting aircraft in the air to requests for immediate air support and to turn away friendly fire were being laid.

9th Air Force Fighter/Fighter-Bomber Interdiction Operations: OVERLORD (6 June-24 July 1944)

	Fighter/Fighter-Bombers		Bombers*	
Targets	**Sorties**	**Bomb Tons**	**Sorties**	**Bomb Tons**
Rail Lines/Bridges	7,284	3,663.9	3,090	4,843.4
Marshaling Yards	1,848	797.6	743	1,238.6
Roads/Bridges	2,533	1,130.4	2,115	3,349.7
Military Installations	1,229	555.0	2,511	3,931.5
Motor Transport/Troops	1,382	623.7	143	240.0
Totals	14,276	6,770.6	8,602	13,603.2

*Medium and light

8th Air Force Fighter/Fighter-Bomber Interdiction Operations: OVERLORD (6 June-24 July 1944)

	Fighter/Fighter-Bombers		Bombers*	
Targets	**Sorties**	**Bomb Tons**	**Sorties**	**Bomb Tons**
Rail Lines/Bridges	2,928	918.0	3,031	7,587.9
Marshaling Yards	1,520	415.4	2,229	6,089.4
Roads/Bridges	687	261.3	575	1,399.0
Military Installations	420	142.0	572	1,591.9
Motor Transport/Troops	271	81.8	93	1.0
Shipping	79	17.5	35	86.5
Totals	5905	1,836.0	6,451	16,785.5

8th and 9th Air Force .50 Caliber Ammunition Expended Interdiction Operations: OVERLORD (6 June-24 July 1944)

	8th Air Force		9th Air Force	
Targets	**Sorties**	**Rounds**	**Sorties**	**Rounds**
Railways/Bridges	2,829	611,502*	2,414	1,000,336**
Marshaling Yards	1,585	583,562***	778	240,630
Roads/Bridges	421	156,403	790	362,148
Military Installations	269	76,435	484	185,167
Motor Transport	870	186,449	1,128	509,684
Totals	5,174	1,614,351	5,594+	2,297,965++

* Includes 2,536 rounds of 20mm ammunition

** Includes 4,267 rounds of 20mm ammunition

*** Includes 18,098 rounds of 20mm ammunition

+ Includes 102 Medium bomber missions

++ Includes 17,594 rounds of .50 caliber ammunition fired by medium bombers

28

Breakout from the Normandy Beaches 7 July - 13 August 1944

Elle River to St. Lo-Bayeux Road (7-18 July)

On 3 July J. Lawton Collins' VII Corps, Troy Middleton's VIII Corps and Peter Corlett's XIX Corps began an attack south toward Coutances and St. Lo in hopes of capturing St. Lo in a week. But soon the advance stalled from Middleton's VIII Corps in the west to Gerow's V Corps on the English flank. The Germans quickly learned to diminish the effects of Allied air attacks by disciplined moves at night off the main roads. After weeks of great effort a large number of German troops had arrived at the front, drained and disorganized, but ready to go into battle aided by favorable defensive terrain and poor weather. Once in the hedgerows, the German soldier used foxholes and slit trenches expertly and changed front line positions frequently at night.

After the port of Cherbourg fell, the First Army regrouped to attack south along the Cotentin Peninsula to reach the road net that would allow them to mass their forces and attack along a line from Coutances on the west to St. Lo on the east (the west boundary of the British sector). Their objective was to break out of the beachhead. In early July, Corlett's XIX Corps was assigned to attack and take the strategic communications center of St. Lo. The 29th and 30th Infantry Divisions attacked the front side by side with the 29th designated to take the town. The surrounding terrain was referred to as "Bocage"—low, rolling countryside divided into small fields by hedgerows and many narrow, sunken roads. The Bocage complex was earthen embankments of various shapes and sizes about four feet high, covered with intertwined hedges, shrubs and small trees that French farmers used for a 1,000-years to reduce topsoil erosion. The Germans dug machine gun nests and gun emplacements, foxholes and interconnecting trenches into the Bocage and each field became a miniature battle that had to be taken individually in costly small unit actions. It was not until 18 July that the 29th took St. Lo. The Germans utilized these terrain features to conceal infantry, armor and self-propelled guns. US progress was slow as the determined Germans defended their well-concealed positions and made frequent counter-attacks to regain or hold important defenses. With the destruction of the artificial harbors by the storm of the 19th and German sabotage of Cherbourg's port the Allies encountered supply problems. The constant combat during the past

General Bernard Montgomery was the commander of the British 21st Army Group in France. Most American and many British commanders disliked the controversial and abrasive Montgomery who was contemptuous of the "amateur" Americans and stridently insisted he alone knew how to win the war. His lack of aggressive action and failure to capture Caen and airfield sites in the area led to the failure to trap and destroy the German army in France and end the war more quickly. (Author/West)

month and high casualty rates had mentally and physically exhausted American troops. As on the Russian and Italian fronts the Germans again showed themselves to be the superlative defensive soldier and the Bocage hedgerows afforded them the ideal terrain.

In the meantime on 18 July, three British armored divisions, under Lt.Gen. Richard O'Connor began an offensive codenamed GOODWOOD to take Caen. A massive air attack by heavy and medium bombers of the RAF and USAAF again failed to dislodge or dishearten the well dug-in German defenders under Gen. Heinrich Eberbach. Although Caen was finally taken, it was at an exorbitant cost and the final objective, the breakout onto the Falaise plains was not achieved.

The XIX Corps attack was aided by tactical air support from the IX Tactical Air Command/First Army Combined Operations Center. On request fighter-bombers attacked specific targets and armed air reconnaissance sorties were flown to deny the Germans use of the roads. Close support missions were flown against strong points, field fortifications, emplaced and self-propelled guns and troop concentrations. The presence of fighter-bombers alone weakened German resolve and attacks on defended towns and villages, enemy field fortifications and strong points were facilitated when the Jabos were overhead.

During the initial stages of the US offensive in early July, the elite Panzer Lehr Division was to counter-attack along the Vire River and contain and then drive a wedge into the US sector. Panzer Lehr commander, Maj.Gen. Fritz Bayerlein wanted to move his armor into position and attack at night to escape the fighter-bombers. Wehrmacht HQ directed him to move and attack in daylight. At 0830 Panzer Lehr attacked and made initial gains but later in the day, fighter-bombers of the IX TAC broke up the attack and forced Bayerlein to retreat to defensive positions. The next day, the Germans brought up a unit of 1,500 poorly trained paratroops who were immediately strafed and bombed by ten P-47s. Besides suffering 200 casualties, the attack so unnerved the unit that they could no longer be counted upon as a viable fighting force.

The Armed Recce sorties were so successful that FM Gerd von Rundstedt commented, "(fighter-bomber) aircraft were dominating the main combat area and main supply approaches to depth of 150-200 km......the closer the area is to the combat zone, the more frequently appear the fighter and fighter-bombers in road hunting......the main effort of enemy air attacks now is directed in a zone of about 20km. Behind the main line of resistance, against any kind of movement, be it secondary road or cross country....Whenever, assembly areas are detected an attack by fighter-bombers is launched without delay."

Bad weather seriously curtailed air operations during the first three weeks of July. When not on their primary assignment of close support, the fighter-bombers of the IX TAC on armed recce and those of the IX Fighter Command inflicted massive damage to rolling stock (615) and locomotives (33) in July and were especially successful in cutting rail lines (168). On a mission on 13 July an ammunition train exploded on a siding, destroying 25 tanks. They destroyed six bridges that were vital to the Germans. They flew 2.958 sorties against rail equipment and bridges dropping 1,283 tons of bombs and 856 sorties dropping 332.6 tons of bombs on marshalling yards.

On 15 July Rommel commented on the transport system: "Destruction of the rail network and the great threat from the air to the roads and rails up to 150 kilometers behind the front, have made supply movement so difficult that only the most vital needs can be brought forward and there must be a very sparing use of artillery and mortar ammunition in particular. These conditions will not improve. The transport tonnage keeps sinking more and more as a result of air strikes and the enemy air forces will become more effective as they take over airports in their beachhead. No noteworthy forces can be brought up to the front. The Seventh Army alone urgently needs two fresh divisions. On the enemy side, new forces and material stream in every day." (*Army Group B Situation Reports*, 15 July 1944) Two days later Rommel would personally suffer the effects of Allied air superiority.

On 17 July Field Marshal Erwin Rommel was touring the Normandy front in his staff car. This tour was described in a report written by Captain Helmut Lang in Desmond Young's classic biography *Rommel: The Desert Fox*:

"About 4PM Marshal Rommel started on the return journey from General Dietrich's headquarters. He was anxious to get back to Army Group B headquarters as quickly as possible because the enemy had broken through on another part of the front.

All along the roads we could see transport in flames; from time to time the enemy aircraft forced us to take second class roads. About 6PM, the Marshal's car was in the neighborhood of Liverot. Transport which had been just attacked was piled up along the road and strong groups of enemy dive-bombers were still at work close by. That is why we turned off along a sheltered road to join the main road again two and a half miles from Vimoutiers.

When we reached it we saw above Liverot about eight enemy dive-bombers. We learnt later that they had been interfering with traffic on the road to Liverot for the past two hours. Since we thought that they had not seen us we continued along the main road to Liverot to Vimoutiers. Suddenly Sergeant Holke, our spotter, warned us that two aircraft were flying along the road in our direction. The driver, Daniel, was told to put on speed and to turn off onto a little side road to the right, about 100 yards ahead of us, which would give us some shelter.

Before we could reach it, the enemy aircraft, flying at great speed only a few feet above the road, came up to within 500 yards of us and the first one opened fire. Marshal Rommel was looking back at this moment. The left hand side of the car was hit by the first burst. A cannon shell shattered Daniel's left shoulder and left arm. Marshal Rommel was wounded in the face by broken glass and received a blow to the left temple and cheekbone which caused a triple fracture of the skull and caused him to lose consciousness immediately. Major Neuhaus was struck in the holster of his revolver and the force of the blow broke his pelvis.

As a result of his serious wounds Daniel, the driver, lost control of the car. It struck the stump of a tree, skidded to the left of the road and turned over in a ditch on the right. Captain Lang and Sergeant Holke jumped out of the car and took shelter on the right of the road. Marshal Rommel, who at the start of the attack, had hold of the handle of the door, was thrown out, unconscious, when the car turned over and lay stretched out on the road about twenty yards behind it. A second aircraft flew over and tried to drop bombs on those who were lying on the ground.

Immediately afterwards, Marshal Rommel was carried into a shelter by Captain Lang and Sergeant Holke. He lay on the ground unconscious and covered with blood which flowed from the many wounds on his face, particularly his left eye and mouth. It appeared that he had been struck on the left temple. Even when we carried him to safety he had not recovered consciousness.

In order to get medical help for the wounded, Captain Lang tried to find a car. It took him about three-quarters of an hour to do so. Marshal Rommel had his wounds dressed by a French doctor in a religious hospital. They were very severe and the doctor said that there was little hope of saving his life. Later he was taken, still unconscious, with Daniel to an air force hospital about 25 miles away. The doctors there diagnosed severe injuries to the skull-a fracture at the base, two fractures to the temple and the cheekbone destroyed, a wound to the left eye and wounds from glass and concussion. Daniel died during the night in spite of a blood transfusion.

A few days later Marshal Rommel was taken to the hospital of Professor Esch at Visinet, near St. Germaine."

On 20 July, while he was at St. Germaine, anti-Hitler conspirators attempted to assassinate the Führer at the "Wolf's Liar" in Rastenberg. Count von Stauffenberg had placed a briefcase filled with explosives under the map table near Hitler, but a thick table leg absorbed most of the explosion. Hitler recovered more rapidly than Rommel who returned to his home at Herrlingen to recuperate to the German press announcement that he had been injured in an automobile "accident." Before arch-conspirator, von Stulpnagel, died after attempting to shoot himself, he uttered the name, "Rommel." The Field Marshal's fate was sealed but he was left to convalesce. But by mid-October, he was given the choice of taking poison or facing a humiliating public trial in Berlin. Rommel ingested the poison and on 17 October, he was given a lavish state

The IX Fighter Command sent out eight groups of 350 fighter-bombers flying in three-minute intervals of fighter-bombers and between H minus 85 minutes to H minus 64 minutes (0938 and 0957) they bombed and strafed an area just south of the St. Lo-Periers road measuring 7,000 yards long by 250 yards wide. Panther tanks destroyed near le Desert, France. (US Army)

funeral. Hitler told the German nation that Rommel had died of the severe injuries he had received in a motorcar accident in the course of a journey at the front.

Although the Allies had not gained as much ground as they projected in their planning by the end of June 1944, Allied armies were firmly established in northern France. A few days after D-Day, the US First Army under Gen. Omar Bradley and the British Second Army under Maj.Gen. Sir Miles Dempsey had broken through German beach defenses and joined their two beachheads. Maj.Gen. Leonard Gerow's V Corps had taken Caumont and advanced toward St. Lo before being stopped because the supplies to the V Corps were diverted to the VII Corps of Maj.Gen. Lawton Collins to clear the Cotentin Peninsula and Cherbourg. Montgomery's 21st Corps made good initial advances until gritty German opposition near Caen stopped it. After capturing the critical port of Cherbourg, on 3 July the First Army launched an offensive south from the Cotentin Peninsula and after an intense battle captured St. Lo on 16 July. The British-Canadian stalemate at Caen was broken at great cost in Operation GOODWOOD with the support of a massive air attack and Montgomery moved south across the Orne River toward Falaise before being stopped again. Meanwhile the US First Army was engaged in a succession of slow, bitter battles in the hedgerows beyond the Normandy beaches. To relieve the First Army, Bradley launched Operation COBRA.

Operation COBRA/Falaise-St. Lo (25 July 1944)

By mid July, ground forces had become more dependent on air support and looked at it as a substitute for hard and costly ground fighting. In the face of artillery shell shortages these requests grew even more frequent. Eisenhower encouraged his generals to make maximum use of air support. The upshot was overwhelming and arbitrary requests for air support and Brereton was forced to set up more stringent guidelines for calling in air support. Air support officers canceled missions they thought unnecessary and inevitably ground commanders became upset that their judgment was being questioned. The Germans had skillfully deployed their forces in Normandy and air targets were fewer and more difficult to find. As GOODWOOD had shown, massive bombardment by heavy bombers of enemy positions was found not to have the desired effect as the German defenders put up an unexpected stubborn and costly defense. Nonetheless, Eisenhower and Bradley were determined to use air power as the keystone in Operation COBRA. Again the Pantelleria effect entered Allied planning.

After Cherbourg had been captured, the First Army conducted limited objective attacks across its entire front in preparation to breaking out of the beachhead. By the third week in July preparations for Operation COBRA were completed. VIII Corps units extended from the west coast of the peninsula east along the Periers-St. Lo highway to the vicinity of le Mesnil Vignot; VII Corps units from this point east to the Vire River and near St. Lo; XIX Corps units from St. Lo proper to a point near La Barre de Semilly; and V Corps units from there east to the inter-army boundary.

Before COBRA the German Army was severely affected by the disruption of the rail and road system. Besides the acute lack of fuel and ammunition; for each division per month the following were required: two replacement battalions, one or two mortar brigades, more heavy artillery, guns and machine guns. The deliveries of fuel and ammunition needed increased protection, especially at the bridges by anti-aircraft and fighters. The German soldier was demoralized by the absence of the Luftwaffe to deal with the Allied fighter-bombers and the bothersome artillery spotting aircraft.

The general objective of COBRA was to penetrate the enemy line with a powerful thrust along a narrow front. VII Corps in the center was assigned the main thrust while the V, VIII and XIX Corps were to exert continuous pressure against the enemy, harassing any attempted retreat and to prevent him from disengaging. Bradley hoped that COBRA could help the Allied command problem when he mused on the day before the operation (*General's Life*, Omar Bradley with Clay Blair, NY, Simon Schuster, 1983):

"Cobra thus assumed vast importance in my mind. If it succeeded, I was certain it would give everybody a much-needed shot in the arm. It would help eliminate the backstabbing. It would put such momentum in the war that the very speed of it would heal the seams of our rupturing alliance. Conversely, if it failed, it could develop into much more than just another military set back. It could bring on dangerous open warfare in the alliance that might lead to Monty's relief and perhaps Ike's and my own."

COBRA was a three-phase plan that included:

Phase One: Intensive aerial bombardment by heavy, medium and fighter-bombers, coordinated with heavy artillery fire, was to be followed by a breakthrough of the enemy positions by three infantry divisions. These divisions were to open up a hole and secure the flanks of the breakthrough area.

Phase Two: Two armored divisions and one motorized infantry division would exploit the breakout by moving through the hole and advancing along the two main routes beyond.

Phase Three: Consolidation and pressing the attack on the retreating Germans on the ground and in the air.

The forward boundary of the target area was the straight St. Lo-Periers highway. Front line troops were withdrawn 1,200 yards to the north of this road and this new front line was marked with fluorescent panels. The enemy's forward positions were marked with red smoke by artillery shells and a strip 300 yards wide on the forward edge of the target area was to be bombed by fighter-bombers only. Plans also included the marking of tanks and armored vehicles with cerise panels, the repainting of the Allied white star marking on all breakthrough vehicles and the installation of two-way ground–air radio sets in tanks and armored vehicles leading the command columns of the 2nd and 3rd Armored Divisions. Experienced fighter-bomber pilots were assigned to travel forward in these vehicles, communicating with close support air units by means of the radio, designating targets for attack by air. Ground liaison officers at the airfields of the TACs assisted in the briefing of pilots on air cooperation missions, familiarizing them with the ground situation and in interrogating pilots upon the completion of the mission. These methods of air-to-ground identification were found to be suitable for fighter-bombers and small formations of medium bombers but not for high altitude heavy bombers. Planners did not foresee that the first bombing attacks and prevailing winds would result in smoke and dust obscuring the marking panels. Centralized VHF radio control of bomber formations would have prevented the short bombing

COBRA began on 25 July and realistically did not end until it literally ran out of gas at the Siegfried Line on the German frontier. It was the most effective sustained close air support battle of the war and the first and only time saturation bombing of enemy ground positions by heavy and medium bombers on a large scale was attempted in the ETO. H-Hour, the infantry ground attack launch time, was set for 1100 and the saturation bombing of an area approximately 3,000 by 7,000 yards south of the St. Lo-Periers highway by 1,500 heavy bombers, 400 medium bombers and 550 fighter-bombers (both 9th and 8th Air Force) continued for a period of two and a half hours. The IX Fighter Command sent out eight groups of 350 fighter-bombers flying in three-minute intervals and between H minus 85 minutes to H minus 64 minutes (0938 and 0957) they bombed and strafed an area just south of the St. Lo-Periers road measuring 7,000 yards long by 250 yards wide. The fighters flew in a column of groups, with squadrons in a column of flights, to an initial point over ALG A-10 Carentan. At three-minute intervals each group would check in with the air controller at A-10 and then proceed to its target. The first group attacked the eastern area, the second the western, etc. alternating until all areas were attacked. Their targets were defined by exploding artillery shells, red smoke pots and panels to define the troop line. There were so many fighter-bombers, that to avoid air traffic, pilots had to fly alternate bomb runs between the eastern and western sectors. The combined 8th and 9th Air Force fighter-bomber missions dropped 143.2 tons of GP bombs and 68.7 tons of fragmentation bombs. Of the 15 groups in the attack, nine groups were armed with 500lb. GP bombs, three groups carried 260lb. frags, two carried a combination of GP and

US Infantry dig out after COBRA short bombing. Short bombing was a bugaboo throughout the war especially by heavy and medium bombers. (US Army)

frags and a P-38 groups carried two belly tanks filled with napalm. They dropped 500lb., incendiary and fragmentation bombs on defined positions causing Ninth Division commander to radio Bradley of the "perfect support" he had received. Immediately after the fighter-bomber attacks, between 1132 and 1223, 341 medium and light 9th Air Force bomber sorties dropped 677 tons of bombs. Light bombers carrying 500lb. GP bombs and medium bombers carrying 260lb. fragmentation bombs attacked strong points close behind the lines but out of artillery range. After a brief lull B-17s and B-24s of the 8th Air Force 1,508 attacked at right angles to the front between 1003-1055 dropping 3,429 tons of bombs. The bombers saturated an area one mile long and five miles deep lying just behind (south) the area just attacked by the fighter-bombers. Unfortunately, the third and final wave of bombers hit friendly troops waiting to attack. The VII Corps that was the nucleus of the attack bore the brunt of the short bombing. An entire battalion command of the 9th Division was destroyed, every assault company of the 4th Division was hit and the 30th Division recorded more casualties than in any previous day of the war. To make matters worse Lt.Gen. Leslie McNair became the highest-ranking officer to be killed in combat in the ETO during the war. Never again would heavy bombers be allowed to take part in close support missions in the ETO.

On schedule, at 1100 hours, the US First Army attacked aided by IX TAC fighter-bombers. Between 1135 and 2104 hours, IX TAC flew 13 armed reconnaissance missions of squadron strength or less against selected targets such as troop concentrations, armor, communications centers, HQs and observation posts. That evening the fighter-bombers dropped delayed action bombs on the crossroads near Coutances. Fused to explode one to twelve hours later they would disrupt German vehicle movement. The awesome aerial bombardment did substantial physical and psychological damage but the surviving Germans denied the Allies, discouraged by the short bombings, their initial objectives that were thought to be necessary to begin an armored offensive. But the Germans were beginning to crack and Collins wisely pressed the attack committing his armor. On the 26th the 2nd Armored Division moved out to continue the momentum of the attack and was joined the next day by the rd Armored division.

On the second day of *COBRA*, 26 July, the IX TAC began to fly a new type of mission, armed column cover. American armor broke through the German front and moved in three columns to drive toward Coutances, Granville and Villedieu. The retreating Germans put up an improvised defense of strong points, anti-tank positions and occasional armor. Constant air cover was supplied by fighter-bomber flights of four aircraft armed with bombs or rockets that would fly in 30-minute relays over their assigned armored column. Air-ground communications between flight leaders and tank commanders was by VHF radio while the IX Air Service Command equipped air force SCR-522 sets in the tanks. When the armored column ran into difficulties, it called for air support that was only minutes away and then designated what action should be taken. Ideally, pilots were attached to the armored command to consult about the feasibility of the fighter-bombers to attack the desired target and how best to direct the flights to the target. The flight leader was able to initiate attacks on targets he discovered from his aerial vantage point. On the 26th more than 70 flights flew column cover and the next day over the IX TAC flew a 100.

The American armor advanced to within two miles of Coutances where they met determined German opposition charged with holding open an escape route for the Seventh Army that was retreating from the VIII Corps. In *Column Cover* Col. Harold Holt, 366th Fighter Group commander, described an armored column cover for Brig.Gen. Maurice Rose's 2nd Armored Division Shermans. Holt sent out his P-47s so that there would always be flights of four over the lead tanks. As Holt called the command tank he asked if there were any targets? The Germans had blocked the road to St. Gilles with a 88mm gun and Holt was directed to its position. With the accurate directions Holt took out the gun and the tanks continued on to the next German roadblock. On the same day, Maj. Randall Hendricks, CO of the 368th Fighter Group, discovered three German armored vehicles moving toward American lines. Hendricks dove and the Germans evacuated their vehicles and scurried toward a ditch, waving a white flag. Hendricks radioed the American command tank and circled the area until the Shermans arrived. In *Thunder Monsters Over Europe* (Reginald Nolte, Sunflower, KS, 1986) Capt. Joseph McLaughlin was described as seeing a column of Shermans stopped, stretching far to the rear. His flight followed the column forward and found two German Tiger tanks blocking the way. The P-47s dove, one after the other, and put the Panzers out of commission. The day was a turning point for armed column cover and tactical air power. Collins tactical resourcefulness and Quesada's armored column cover had finally broken the Normandy deadlock. After weeks of virtual standstill American troops were about to rout the German forces. On the 27th the good weather continued and Bradley, hoping for a breakthrough, ordered the VIII and XIX Corps to attack the breech in the German lines and the remaining Germans found their position indefensible and retreated. On the 28th, Coutances fell and the orderly German withdrawal disintegrated into a chaotic retreat as American columns moved five to eight miles ahead. And by the end of the month the advance was encountering only scattered resistance.

405th GC, Colonel Robert Delashaw was commended by Quesada for the superlative work done by his group. (USAF)

IX TAC also flew armed-reconnaissance missions during the last week of July. On the 26th, 16 eight-plane missions were flown; on the 27th, 11 squadron strength and seven eight-plane missions were flown. On the 28th, the 405th Fighter Group flew ten such missions between 1510 and 2140 hours. The Group's War Diary describes their actions for that afternoon. Poor weather grounded the Group until mid-afternoon when eight P-47s of the 515th Squadron led by Maj. William Coleman took off from their ALG at Picauville (A-8). They headed for Villedieu and after finding no worthwhile targets they patrolled roads toward Gavray where they discovered a large German motor convoy. The two flights carried no bombs but strafed, destroying 67 trucks and five horse-drawn vehicles. The 510th Squadron took off at 1715 hours under their new CO, Capt. Ralph Jenkins. Avenging the loss of their CO, Lt. Colonel Bruce Parcel, the previous day they destroyed 76 trucks, four half-tracks, three armored cars and 16 horse-drawn vehicles in the same area. Twelve P-47s of the 509th Squadron led by Maj. Frederick Kinne, left Picauville at 1809 hours and destroyed 40 vehicles and an ammunition dump. During the remainder of the day the 405th continued its attacks flying over a 100 sorties destroying 318 trucks, 11 tanks, eight half-tracks, 15 staff cars and 23 horse-drawn vehicles. This day the 510th was particularly effective, claiming 150 trucks destroyed (24 damaged), 12 tanks destroyed (five damaged) and ten staff cars destroyed. At a press conference the next day at 9th Air Force HQ, the 405th Fighter Group was cited as the outstanding group on the 28th. The following days saw no abatement of the group's activity in attacking the retreating Germans. It flew 114 sorties on the 29th, 110 on the 30th and 182 on the last day of the month. In these four days they had four pilots MIA and one seriously injured. While visiting Picauville, Pete Quesada told 405th GC Colonel Robert Delashaw:

"I'm so grateful for what your Group has been doing in this fight and for your leadership. This work on the Peninsula may well be the greatest victory an American Army has had in any war."

During the remaining daylight hours of the 25th and then on the 26th and 27th, armed recce flights were flown to the west, south and east of the breakthrough area to prevent the movement of enemy reserves and destroy units which were trying to retreat. From 26 July to 1 August over 400 armed column support missions were flown by fighter-bombers over the armored spearheads and were credited with destruction of large numbers of enemy armored vehicles and tanks, motor transport and personnel.

On 28 July, fighter-bomber claims were over 1,000 vehicles damaged or destroyed. An additional 300 fighter-bomber attacks called in by ground and air units on specific targets. Night movements of enemy troops and supplies were hindered by the use of delayed action bombs dropped on key road junctions and timed to explode at night when the Germans were forced to move because of the intensive daylight attacks.

Infantry wasn't the only personnel to suffer from friendly fire. On 24 July, the bombardier of an 8th Air Force bomber accidentally hit his bomb toggle when a bundle of anti-radar chaff hit his B-17. The bombs hit the 404th Fighter Group at Chipelle, killing four, wounding 14 and destroying two Thunderbolts.

Results and Conclusions of the COBRA Air Operations

The results of the heavy and medium bomber attacks prior to the breakout once more did not achieve maximum results. Enemy communications in the area were disrupted but casualties were not severe. The shock effect was shattering as reported by POWs but the lag time before the ground attack gave the German infantry some time to recover and resist. Due to inadequate communications and the difficulties in visual identification of the target areas there was the regrettable short bombing by heavy bombers of friendly troops waiting to attack. Armed Column Cover was initiated and was vital in the relatively narrow gap through which the break out by armor and infantry was made. This column cover intended to protect ground troops and armor from enemy air attack, discovered and broke up enemy troop concentrations, possible counter-attacking forces and gun positions and strong points in their path. Armed reconnaissance out ahead of American columns gave timely information of the enemy and frequently gave the earliest report of our own front line locations. Armed recce often broke up enemy reserves, supply and troop transport moving to the front and otherwise harassed the enemy. Air-ground coordination in COBRA was conducted by the existing liaison process. Coordination with the 9th Air Force and its tactical air commands was effective due to air-ground combined operations centers that had come online soon after D-Day and already had enjoyed the advantages of joint planning. This did not take place in the 8th Air Force whose liaison was distant or non-existent.

In the seven weeks after the Allies came ashore at Normandy, fighter-bombers contributed significantly to the success of COBRA and the air campaign over northern France. Their contribution went beyond the measurable effects such as troops killed, tanks and guns put out of action, locomotives, rolling stock and motor vehicles destroyed, bridges made impassable, Luftwaffe aircraft destroyed in the air and on the ground. The intangible effectiveness of the fighter-bomber campaign was:

1) The reduction of the number of German troops reaching the front.
2) German battle plans were disrupted and ineffective as the arrival of troops, equipment and supplies could not be relied upon.
3) Reduction of the amount of ammunition and the resultant reduction in the firepower available to the Germans.
4) Tactical vehicles were taken from the battlefield and used for transport as the railways were inoperative and other motor transport in short supply.
5) Required the use of limited stocks of gasoline for non-tactical transport and concurrently limiting fuel stocks by damaging fuel dumps and fuel transport.
6) Fighter-bomber missions were able to operate at maximum capacity and minimum costs by its reduction of the supply of AA ammunition and the attainment and maintenance of air superiority.

Before COBRA, first at Pantelleria, the Allies tried to gain the upper hand on the ground by utilizing its air power as a sledgehammer in its support of ground troops. But after the failure of the initial massive air bombardment, COBRA did demonstrate that the air-tank team could accomplish a breakout. But COBRA to this day is remembered for the massive air bombardment of 25 July and not the hundreds of individual fighter-bomber sorties that truly paved the way for the breakout. After the battle Pete Quesada commented:

"Had tactical air been given those kinds of resources, (e.g. that allotted to the heavy bombers) we would not only have made a breakthrough but we could have hammered the enemy all the way to Paris."

On 31 July Gen. Walter Warlimont met in Paris with C-in-C West, FM von Kluge, and reported the following: "Commander-in-Chief West describes the seriousness of the situation with impressive eloquence. Whether the enemy can be stopped at this point is questionable. The enemy air superiority is terrific and smothers almost every one of our movements. Every movement of the enemy, however, is prepared and protected by its air force. Losses in men and equipment are extraordinary. The morale of the troops has suffered very heavily under constant murderous enemy fire." (Milton Shulman, *Defeat in the West*, Dutton, NY, 1948) Note: For this meeting Warlimont was supposed to fly to Paris but could only fly to Strasbourg due Allied air superiority and had to drive to Paris at night for the meeting.

IX TAC Operations 25-31 July 1944

Date	Fighter Sorties	Bomb Tons	E/A Claims	IX TAC Ftr Losses Air	Total	Dam.	Recce Sorties
25	1,546	451.5	7-0-7	1	4	24	79
26	1,561	507.0	17-1-6	2	16	43	122
27	1.451	344.0	11-0-5	0	17	43	104
28	1,250	157.6	12-3-1	2	10	18	96
29	1,038	285.8	0-0-0	0	8	17	29
30	1,320	294.0	15-7-6	2	14	67	84
31	1,019	241.2	5-0-2	3	9	6	141
Totals	9,185	2,281.1	67-11-27	10	78	218	655

IX TAC Ground Claims 25-31 July 1944

Tanks	384
Artillery	71
Motor Transport	2,287
Horse-drawn Vehicles	125
RR and Road Bridges	33
Road Junctions damaged	85
RR Lines Cut	46
Locomotives	14
Rolling Stock	194
Troop concentrations	38
Gun Emplacements	71
Dumps	12
Military Buildings	45

American Command Changes, August 1944

On 1 August, Bradley's army controlled a large number of corps and divisions over a wide, rapidly expanding front and was an administrative nightmare. The Third Army was activated in France and put under control of the Twelfth Army Group along with the First Army. Lt.Gen. George Patton was given command of the Third and Lt.Gen. Courtney Hodges took command of the First from Bradley who moved up to the command of the Twelfth Army Group. When the First Army was the only American army in France, Quesada's IX TAC had operated close air support operations. O.P. Weyland's XIX TAC remained in England and his fighter-bomber groups came under Quesada's operational control as they moved to France. When the Third Army was activated, Weyland moved his HQ to Normandy and regained command over some of his fighter-bomber groups and began to provide close air for Patton. When Bradley moved up, Quesada lost the productive daily association with him and faced establishing a similar rapport with Hodges. Hodges was an old line West Pointer who was highly regarded by both Eisenhower and Bradley but was the antithesis of Quesada, being mild-mannered without temper and emotion. Hodges was unimaginative and a pure military tactician, preferring to forge ahead rather than maneuver. The two did form a good working relationship but never the strong bond and friendship of the Bradley-Quesada partnership. The 9th Air Force also was assigned a new commander as Brereton was reassigned, supposedly kicked upstairs, to the Allied Airborne that was not to become active for months. Brereton never had the confidence of American ground leaders and totally alienated them during a 27 July press conference when he blamed the COBRA short bombing on the infantry. Brereton was a careless leader; living in a luxuriant French chateau, while subordiantes, Quesada and Maj.Gen. Samuel Anderson of the IX Bomber Command, were allowed almost total control of the Ninth's fighters and medium bombers. Quesada had hoped to replace Brereton as he was the senior subordinate and had shown his colors as the best tactical leader in the AAF during the previous months. But Eisenhower and Arnold relied on the recommendation of Gen. Carl Spaatz who nominated Maj.Gen. Hoyt Vandenberg. The personable and handsome Vandenberg was a 1923 West Pointer who had graduated in the bottom 10% of his class but was an adept self-

In October 1944, Ninth Air Force CO, Pete Quesada, dines with the three ground generals to whom his air force provided ground support. From left: Quesada, Lt.Gen. J. Lawton Collins (VII Corps), Lt. Gen. Courtney Hodges (First Army) and Lt.Gen. Omar Bradley (XII Army Group). (USAF)

promoter. He was an first rate pilot who, after Pearl Harbor, had risen from major, serving as Eisenhower's air advisor in 1942 and then became Doolittle's chief of staff in Africa. He was the nephew of influential Michigan senator, Arthur Vandenberg, and used his social skills to smooze his superiors. He attended the Quebec, Cairo and Teheran Conferences as Hap Arnold's aide. Immediately before his appointment he had been Leigh-Mallory's AEAF Deputy commander were he spent more time in AEAF politics and nurturing a relationship with Spaatz than spending any time in France learning air power precepts. So it was that a desk general who had never flown or led in combat would become 9th Air Force commander. To his credit Vandenberg realized his shortcomings and gave the disappointed Quesada broad autonomy in his command. Bradley's promotion gave him greater control over Allied operations. Quesada used his friendship with Bradley to gain what he needed and to influence tactics when more American armies were activated in Europe and there were more competing tactical commanders at Quesada's level.

In his memoir, *A Soldier's Story* (ibid.), Bradley remembers Quesada's contribution to tactical air support:

"As a result of our inability to get together in England, we went into France almost totally untrained in ground-air cooperation. But we also went with an offsetting advantage in a breezy young major general named Elwood P. Quesada....

He succeeded brilliantly in a task where many airmen before him failed, partly because he was willing to dare anything once. Unlike most airmen who viewed ground support as a bothersome diversion war in the sky, Quesada approached it as a vast new frontier waiting to be explored."

Maj.Gen. Hoyt Vandenberg was the Deputy Commander of the AEAF which placed him between the difficult and disliked Leigh-Mallory and the senior US airman, Lt.Gen. Carl Spaatz. The consummate politician Vandenberg was successful in placating both and was named CO of the 9th Air Force in August 1944. (USAF)

Maj.Gen. Otto P. Weyland was the commander of the XIX TAC preferred to be called "Opie". Weyland's XIX TAC protected Patton's Third Army flank from German interference from the south while they roared west into central France. (USAF)

XIX TAC/Third Army

XIX TAC

The XIX TAC, commanded by Brig.Gen. Otto P. Weyland, originally operated from England as part of the IX Fighter Command as the XIX Air Support Command. Weyland was assigned command of two wings and seven fighter-bomber groups on 4 February 1944 at Aldermastok Court, near Reading Berkshire. The IX FC was assigned the task of in-theater training of new fighter groups for six weeks and on 18 April the XIX Air Support Command was redesignated the XIX TAC. The XIX was assigned veteran groups from the IX TAC. The units of the XIX TAC were:

100th Wing: 354th, 358th, 362nd, and 363rd Groups
303rd Wing: 36th, 373rd, and 406th Groups
(The 354th and 363rd were P-51 groups and the remainder were P-47 groups.)

When the XIX TAC began operations it divided its headquarters into advanced and rear echelons. The advanced echelon was made up of operations, intelligence and communications personnel and a small detachment of administrative officers with Weyland actively planning and directing operations. This advanced echelon moved often and usually was only two days behind the Third Army command. The "X-ray" unit of the XIX TAC chief of staff and several of his assistants were assigned directly to the Third Army command at all times to maintain a close, personal liaison. The rear administrative echelon moved less frequently and was stationed close to the attached air units where it could administer to their logistical, personnel and administrative requirements.

The 354th Fighter Group was the first operational P-51 group in the ETO and was referred to as the "Pioneer Mustang Group." All four of the 100th Wing's fighter groups had previously flown numerous escort missions from East Anglican bases for the heavy bombers of the 8th Air Force during the winter and early spring of 1943-44. The 30rd Wing arrived on 8 March and all seven groups of the XIX began operations from the advanced bases in Kent. Their initial task was to take part in the pre-invasion air attacks and to support the D-Day landings and the ensuing breakout into Normandy. During this time the First Army was the only American Army in France and the XIX TAC groups flying from Normandy were under the operational command of the IX TAC that was supporting the First Army. When the IX TAC relocated to France with the First Army, Gen. Weyland took over command of the IX Fighter Command in England and with it operational control of all fighter-bomber groups of the IX and XIX TACs stationed in the U.K. These groups were transferred to the Continent as soon as airfields became available. When Weyland arrived in France in early July the IX Fighter Command was disbanded.

Rover Joe, Air Liaison Officer (ALO), with radio headset on jeep carrying communication equipment. The M-4 Sherman tank in the background indicates that this ALO was directing Armored Column Cover operations. (USAF)

The XIX's advanced HQ initially arrived in France on 2 July stationed near Cricqueville. After a brief stay there moved to the Nehou area which was in the near vicinity of Patton's HQ. The Army and Air Commands had operated together in England during the training and planning phases and were consequently ready to serve as a closely integrated unit.

The Third US Army under Lt.Gen. George S. Patton Jr. finally became operational on 1 August. It had been stationed in southeastern England and used as a decoy to have the German think the D-Day invasion was going to cross at Calais. The Third joined Lt.Gen. Courtney H. Hodges' First Army in Lt.Gen. Omar N. Bradley's 12th Army Group that became operational on 1 August. To support the Third Army, the XIX TAC under Brig.Gen. O. P. Weyland also became operational that day. When the XIX TAC became operational it had only three fighter groups available but by the 5th it had five and by the 7th it had its full complement of seven.

Armored Column Cover and Armed Recce in Brittany (1-5 August 1944)

Patton's Third Army armored columns advanced so quickly through Brittany they often outran their communications with the bomb line changing by the hour as it moved west toward the end of the Peninsula. Since this was the case the XIX TAC fighter-bombers were allowed to find targets of opportunity rather than being given planned targets. The XIX TAC conducted its own version of the German Blitz. During the first five days of August, XIX TAC fighter-bombers flew 1,088 sorties and destroyed 250 motor vehicles, 12 tanks, 9 horse-drawn vehicles, four locomotives and nine rail cars, bombed and strafed 21 troop concentrations, seven fuel and supply dumps, a gasoline storage dump and a headquarters. The Germans in Brittany were widely dispersed and their gun positions and armor were difficult to locate and attack. The XIX TAC destroyed 17 gun posts with the 365th Fighter Group's 500lb. bombs knocking out three 88mm self-propelled guns that were standing in the infantry's line of advance. The 358th Fighter Group destroyed guns that were concealed in hay wagons. In the morning of 2 August, a flight of 405th Fighter Group P-47s flying armed recce along the northern coast of Brittany discovered a Panzer assembly area and destroyed seven Tiger tanks that were trying to hide themselves under a smoke screen. On 4 August, the 4th Armored Division radioed an urgent request for an immediate attack on an enemy armored column hidden in a wooden area. A squadron of the 358th Fighter Group dropped 16 bombs obtaining a good bomb concentration on 15 German tanks.

One daylight air attack in the first five days comprised the only Luftwaffe resistance so armor column cover air units were allowed to range up to 30 miles ahead of the advancing tank columns searching for targets that might obstruct the advance. These sweeps yielded a large number of motor and horse-drawn transport. By 6 August, Rennes, the capitol of Brittany had fallen without a fight and its airfields were in American hands. The remaining Germans were withdrawing to strong points at Brest, St. Malo, Lorient and the Painpol Peninsula.

"Model" Attack on Luftwaffe Airdromes (4 August 1944)
Col. Hubert Zemke, CO of the 56th Fighter Group describes a "model" strafing attack (*The Hub, Fighter Leader*, ibid.):

"The next day....we got together with our good neighbors, the 363rd Group at Raydon. This was another result of co-operation their respective intelligence officers, our Dave Robinson and their Hank Bjorkman. The 353rd had for some weeks scouted and plotted developments at airfield Plantlunne, east of Nordhorn, and earlier that day had seen it stocked with aircraft. We were invited to participate in giving this place a working over. Setting out in the late afternoon with a combined force of 69 P-47s, most lugging two-250lb. bombs, the Luftwaffe was caught off guard. Leading the show, the 353rd did some excellent strafing of the defenses, allowing the 56th to follow up with some dive-bombing. We then strafed every aircraft and military installation to be seen. The known flak positions were silenced on the first pass and, as others were found, individual pilots would silence them. When we were finished there were between 25 and 30 aircraft burning on the field and the whole place was covered with a pall of smoke. It was the finest exhibition of saturation strafing I ever witnessed and a model for how such an attack should be carried out. My greatest difficulty in this race track to strafe was to stay out of the way of other P-47s and their fire."

Mortain (29 July-14 August 1944)
From the start of its advance the Third Army was threatened from the rear. North of Avranches, the First Army held the Cotentin Peninsula; to the south, the Third Army was expanding in all directions. These two large areas into which the American armies had penetrated were connected only a narrow corridor that was intersected by roads and bridges along which reinforcements were speeding southward.

After the breakout at St. Lo, the First Army attacked the German's uncertain defenses south and west of Vire and Patton's Third Army moved south through Avranches to pivot into the Brittany Peninsula or east toward Mayenne. The Germans realized that their position was exposed and their forces were in danger of being encircled. Patton's Third Army raced through the lightly defended Brittany Peninsula and Hodge's First Army was in the center and stopped to protect Patton's flank and to regroup. Von Kluge also used this time to regroup and bring in additional armor and troop reinforcements that he positioned opposite the juncture of the US First and Third armies near Mortain. Von Kluge intended to use these forces to allow an orderly withdrawal from Normandy. However, Hitler saw this accumulation of armor as an opportunity to drive a wedge between the two American armies, break through to the Golfe de St. Malo at Avranches dividing the First and Third Armies. The thrust would cut the narrow corridor through which the Third Army was receiving it supplies and reinforcements and cut off Patton's twelve divisions. The Fuehrer also promised von Kluge he would provide large-scale Luftwaffe support

The German counter-attack at Mortain failed in part due to fighter-bomber attacks that took a toll on German motor transport and armor. (US Army)

Bradley realized that Collins' VII Corps was exhausted and vulnerable and decided to replace it with the rested 30th Division but just as the divisions were in the process of relief the Germans attacked. On 7 August the Germans opened a heavy counter-attack against the VII Corps with five Panzer Divisions The Panzer Tiger tanks smashed through the disorganized Americans and by midnight had overrun Mortain and were headed for main objectives near Avranches. By dawn scattered American units regrouped and threatened the German exposed German flanks on the salient they had driven. Lt.Gen. J. Lawton Collins moved the Second Armored Division into position to attack the German flanks aided by IX fighter-bombers. Capt. Joseph McLachan of the 368th Fighter Group led his P-47 flight and tuned into their close support radio channel waiting for instructions upon their arrival over the Second Armored Division which was moving toward the flank of the German salient. McLachan was surprised to hear the voice of 1Lt. Joseph "Noodles" Nolan who had left two days earlier to assume his role as a forward air controller. Nolan directed the P-47s toward two self-propelled 88mm guns. After a reconnaissance run the flight attacked and destroyed these guns. The IX TAC knocked out 20% of the German strength heading toward Avranches: 28 tanks, ten half-tracks, and several more 88mm guns. The promised Luftwaffe support was intercepted in the air or on their airfields and only a handful of the 300 German aircraft reached the battlefront. The Luftwaffe only sent single aircraft or small formations against the key bridge at Avranches and day and night attacks against US troops and the Germans lost the initiative

During the battle TAC units convincingly confirmed their value. It was apparent that the Germans planned to force a wedge between the First and Third Armies. The infantry and armor of the elements of the VII Corps in their path were out manned and out gunned by the concentrated German armor. The First Army requested that IX TAC give priority to assist them in the battle and on 7 August all fighter-bombers not assigned to beach air cover or escort were committed to the battle. The teamwork between the ground and air was outstanding with fighter-bombers answering most calls for close air strikes, the armed recce attacking targets of opportunity and breaking up troop and armored concentrations and other squadrons providing armored column cover for armored divisions. On 8 and 9 August IX TAC flew 998 sorties over Mortain and destroyed 76 tanks and almost a 1,000 motor vehicles. Ground forces called in the majority of these sorties.

As the battle continued there were more targets than aircraft to attack them and fighter-bombers from the XIX TAC and a RAF rocket-firing Typhoon squadron were called in as reinforcements. The weight of Allied fighter-bomber attacks in close air support was instrumental in decisively overcoming this counter-attack by damaging or destroying the enemy's armor and troop concentrations and disrupting his attacks by bombing and strafing. The ability of the TAC organization to transfer and mass fighter-bomber units to meet specific requirements of the battle was a major factor in the victory. From that point the Germans were persuaded that it was imprudent to launch a major counter offensive in daytime against a tenacious, well armed and well supplied enemy who had the benefit of formidable air strength.

Gen. J. Lawton Collins rated the battle for Mortain as:

"...one of the outstanding small-unit actions of World War II and said the "fighter-bombers, as usual, were highly effective. It should be rated as one of the best single close air support fighter-bomber operations of the war."

The German Seventh Army Chief of Staff, Maj.Gen. Rudolf-Christopher Freiherr von Gersdorff, credited American fighter-bomber operations as the reason for their defeat. Eisenhower stated: "The chief credit in smashing the enemy's spearhead, however, must go to the rocket-firing Typhoon planes of the 2nd Tactical Air Force. They dived upon the armored columns and with their rocket projectiles, on the first day of the battle destroyed 83, probably destroyed 29 and damaged 24 tanks in addition to quantities of 'soft-skinned' MT. The result of this strafing was that the enemy attack was effectively brought to a halt and a threat was turned into a great victory."

General J. Lawton Collins rated the battle for Mortain as "one of the outstanding small-unit actions of World War II and said the "fighter-bombers, as usual, were highly effective." Burned out trucks of the German Seventh Army clustered around a Normandy farmhouse during the breakout. (USAF)

By 10 August the German threat at Mortain was contained but Hitler ordered the attack to be continued and allowed his irreplaceable armor and troops to be squandered. In the intense fighting of the next several days the Mortain area changed hands several times in hand-to-hand combat and armored clashes. But by the 14th the enemy attack had been beaten off and he began a general withdrawal. The continued German attack gave the Allies the opportunity to trap thousands of Germans.

9th Air Force Fighter/Fighter-Bomber Interdiction Operations: COBRA (25 July-13 August 1944)

	Fighter/Fighter-Bombers		Bombers*	
Targets	**Sorties**	**Bomb Tons**	**Sorties**	**Bomb Tons**
Railway/Bridges	2,082	818.6	2,741	4,836.4
Marshaling Yards	455	219.1	134	173.7
Roads/Bridges	689	319.3	402	550.3
Military Transport	851	393.8	830	1,104.2
Motor Transport/Troops	1,125	427.1	—	—
Harbors Docks/Shipping	34	11.0	98	169.0
Totals	5,236	2,188.9	4,205	6,833.6

* Medium and light

8th Air Force Fighter/Fighter-Bomber Interdiction Operations: COBRA (25 July-13 August 1944)

	Fighter/Fighter-Bombers		Bombers*	
Targets	**Sorties**	**Bomb Tons**	**Sorties**	**Bomb Tons**
Railways/Bridges	1,493	530.1	599	1,900.6
Marshaling Yards	893	281.0	843	2,128.9
Roads/Bridges	248	92.8	1,261	2,853.5
Military Installations	88	49.5	911	2,484.7
Motor Transport/Troops	230	67.4	—	—
Totals	2,952	1,020.8	3,614	9,367.7

* Heavy

8th and 9th Air Force .50 Caliber Ammunition Expended Interdiction Operations: COBRA (25 July-13 August 1944)

	8th Air Force		9th Air Force	
Targets	**Sorties**	**Rounds**	**Sorties**	**Rounds**
Railways/Bridges	2,677	1,289,903*	303	197,212+
Marshaling Yards	848	553,598	107	96,099
Roads/Bridges	243	93,799**	—	—
Military Installations	58	48,618	78	92,986
Transport/Troops	303	210,424	423	302,150
Totals	4,129	2,196,342	911	688,447

* Includes 5,948 rounds of 20mm ammunition
** Includes 1,682 rounds of 20mm ammunition
\+ Includes 7,229 rounds of 20mm ammunition

29

Falaise
14 August - 21 August 1944

Prelude to Closing the Trap (August 6 to 12)
Between 6-12 August the trap began to close around the German Seventh Army. Rennes had fallen and all Brittany was in American hands except the ports. The Third Army began its encircling movement to strike the rear of the German armies facing the First Army and the British near Mortain and Vire. Soon the Third Army had captured Laval and Mayenne and was advancing south and east from Le Mans and the trap was set to surround the Germans in the Mortain-Falaise pocket. During this period the weather was generally good and the XIX TAC flew over 3,500 sorties. Pilots flew as army as five sorties a day. The XIX TAC was assigned to:

1) Protect Patton's Loire flank
2) Neutralize the Luftwaffe
3) Fly armed reconnaissance
4) Provide close support
5) Fly missions against the surrounded ports; Brest, St. Malo and Lorient

Air-Ground Cooperation. Third Army CO, Gen. George Patton (left) and Brig.Gen. O. P. Weyland (right), CO of the XIX TAC like the Bradley/Quesada team developed their air-ground cooperation to WW-2 state of the art. (USAF)

In early August, Patton had limited forces available to protect his southern flank along the Loire River. He had driven eastward, seizing the major cities on the north bank of the Loire, leaving only small garrison in each. The Germans had sufficient troops available south of the river to cause problems if they were able to concentrate and cross the river. Patton asked Weyland to protect this flank by preventing troop concentrations and movements through armed and tactical reconnaissance. This was the first time in air warfare history that a ground commander would have an air commander defend his flank. The XIX TAC concentrated its armed recce missions southward to the Loire to keep roads and railways under constant observation. The fighter-bombers attacked any German movement discouraging them from crossing the river.

Patton in his autobiography, *War as I Knew It* (Houghton Mifflin, Boston, 1947) discussed his decision to entrust Weyland and the XIX TAC to protect his flank:

"If I had worried about flanks, I could have never fought the war. Also I was convinced that our air service could locate any groups of enemy large enough to be a serious threat and then I could always pull something out of the hat to drive them back while the Air Force in the meantime delayed their advance."

Weyland described the autonomy Patton gave in guarding his flank:

"I had full control of the air. The decisions were mine as to how I would allocate the air effort. He ran the ground and I ran the air whether it would be close air support, interdiction, something to do with air superiority or perhaps helping out somebody else or doing something General Eisenhower directed as a joint effort of all air power." (Post war interview, USAFHRA)

Between the 7th and 10th August the Luftwaffe was defeated both on the ground and in the air. On the 7th the Luftwaffe went on the offensive to prevent the encirclement of von Kluge's armies south of the Seine. The same morning Luftwaffe bombers damaged an American supply column southwest of Mortain. The XIX TAC spent the day against the Luftwaffe and ended the day destroying 14 in the air and 19 on the ground. Twelve P-51s of the 36th Fighter Group were flying armored column cover for the IV Corps and were radioed to attack the airdrome at Chartres. Only eight bombs were dropped but they destroyed six aircraft and damaged three more. On a well-camouflaged field six miles east of Chartres, three flights of the Pioneer Mustang Group, the 354th, destroyed a dozen Me-109s and a Ju-88 but at a cost of three aircraft. On the next day the Luftwaffe sent up 20 to 40 aircraft at a time and attacked only when they had local superiority. They were beaten off and by the end of the day had to go on the defensive to protect their bases around Paris. On the 9th the 354th Fighter Group flew a far-ranging armed recce to the Reims-Champagne airdrome. They had to dive from 6,000 feet to the deck to attack through heavy enemy AA to strafe and destroy six Ju-88s and damage two others along with destroying two light AA guns and a flak tower. The next day the XIX destroyed 13 German aircraft in the air and then claimed another four the next day. On the 11th no Luftwaffe aircraft appeared over the area.

The XIX armed reconnaissance campaign was focused on the rail system north, south and east of Paris, attempting to isolate the eastern battlefield and paralyze all rail lines and rail traffic leading to Paris. For the period the XIX TAC claimed 75+ locomotives, nearly 1,000 rail cars, almost 1,000 motor vehicles and over 125 horse-drawn vehicles. On 8 August, the 362nd Fighter Group deployed 40 P-47s on an armed reconnaissance sweep north and east of Paris. Their total for this mission was:

"Four 500lb. bombs dropped on enemy guns-guns silenced; dropped two fragmentation clusters on a enemy gun position with the same results. Eight fragmentation clusters and two 500lb. bombs dropped on 40 box cars; destroyed 40 box cars and a locomotive by dropping four frag clusters and two 500 pounders on a marshaling yard. Damaged eight RR cars by dropping eight 250-pound frags on a second marshaling yard. Damaged 25 more freight cars at another point. Dropped two frags on an airdrome. Destroyed seven MT. Strafed 15 freight cars loaded with 155mm guns."

Later that day the 362nd flew their third group mission of the day. They dropped 26 bombs on seven Tiger tanks, claiming three. They moved on to drop 16 bombs on a marshaling yard, destroying a workshop. After dropping their bombs they went on to strafe road targets claiming two armored cars, two ammunition trucks, a gasoline tanker, and a dozen miscellaneous vehicles. The cost to the 362nd for the day was four aircraft lost.

Close support was to provide an important means of closing the trap as the fighter-bombers covering the XV Corps tank columns between Laval and Mayenne attacked German Panzers around Mortain and Vire. From 6-12 August, the XIX TAC knocked out over 150 tanks and 30 gun and flak positions. On 8 August, eight P-51s of the 36rd Fighter Group strafed over 100 horse-drawn carts, killing many horses and troops. Another 36rd Mustang squadron destroyed 50 motor transport and damaged 80 and destroyed 25 horse-drawn vehicles, killing over 200 soldiers. The fighter-bomber attacks became so feared by the Germans that a motorized and horse-drawn column finally raised a white flag until American troops closed in to capture them.

Hitler's continuance of the Mortain offensive threatened his entire position in France and Montgomery and Bradley ordered their forces to close on Falaise and Argentan, far behind the German armor and troops at Mortain. Patton's Third Army was ordered to abandon its assault into Brittany and turn 180 degrees and drive through Mayenne and Alencon and on to Argentan to meet the Canadian First Army that was moving south toward Falaise. To support the Canadians, Montgomery ordered a massive air attack code-named TOTALIZE which was similar to COBRA. The lessons of COBRA went unheeded and TOTALIZE killed even more friendly troops than COBRA and had the same questionable effects on German troops. After the Eighth Air Force B-17s short bombed Canadian troops they fired back and actually cheered when a Flying Fortress was hit.

Closing the trap (12 to 14 August 1944)

On 12 August Vandenberg summoned his first general staff meeting at 9th Air Force HQ to coordinate tactical air operations in the American zone. Quesada's IX TAC fighter-bombers in conjunction with British 2nd TAF were ordered to attack German forces inside

A common sight in the Wehrmacht of 1944 as a spotter scans the skies for Allied Jabos which seemed to be everywhere. (USAF)

the developing pocket. The primary mission of the Allied air plan was to cover XV Corps in its advance north from Alencon and by strong-armed recce between Le Mans and Paris cut off the battlefield and clear the way to Paris. The protection of the Loire flank and reduction of the ports was to continue. The Third Army drove northward while the Canadian First Army drove south to try to close the trap near Argentan. The name Falaise translates as "cliff" and the area out side the city consisted of gorges and deep valleys that the retreating Germans were forced to use. Vehicles and troops concentrated there are became easy targets for the Allied fighter bombers. The 21st Panzer Division had been transferred from the Eastern Front to Normandy and many of its Grenadiers felt overwhelmed by the Allied material strength in the air and on the ground. Against the Russians the battles were man against man and tank against tank and the Luftwaffe had at least parity in the air to keep the Soviet Sturmovik fighter-bombers at bay.

After being stopped on 9 August the First Canadian Army, recommenced its offensive at 1200 on 14 August and advanced to within three miles of Falaise. On the 16th the Canadians captured the city and advanced towards Trun and Chambois. On the north the British Second and the US First Armies were pressing attacks against the sides and end of the salient, attempting to dislodge the tenacious German units that were trying to hold open the mouth of the salient to allow the escape of the nearly trapped Seventh and Fifth Panzer Armies. The US 80th and 90th Divisions, transferred from the V Corps of the First Army, attacked toward Trun and Chambois from the south on 18 August but were unable to make much progress as they met stiff resistance from the German Eberbach Group which was holding open the escape to the east. On 19 August the 90th Division reached Chambois but the 80th that had been trying to capture Argentan was stopped. South of Trun, US V Corps and Canadian armored units finally linked up and closed the gap through which the Germans were hurrying through to escape. A small number of German units continued to break out through in areas where Allied units were stretched thin but 50,000 were trapped. The beaten troops that did escape headed east, leaving behind most of their equipment as they tried to cross the Seine. Until 21 August, when heavy rain halted air operations, movement by day was impossible as the retreating Germans were constantly harassed from the air.

Missions were flown as quickly as possible. Briefings were short, as they were always the same. Every day a list of roads was noted which could be assumed to have German vehicles and could be attacked immediately without further identification. The IX played havoc with the Germans tying to escape the pocket. On 13 August, a forward air controller Col. Charles Young's 367th Fighter Group to a large armored column. The fighter-bombers attacked for two hours destroying 45 tanks. That same day IX TAC also destroyed 106 armored vehicles and 570 motor transports for the loss of eleven aircraft that was the largest single day loss for the IX TAC. That day, the entire Ninth Air Force, XIX TAC, IX TAC and IX BC claimed 958 vehicles of all types. The Germans called the escape corridor "Jabo Rennstrecke," or "fighter-bomber race course."

On the 14th, Patton and Montgomery were closing the trap and the desperate Germans exposed themselves in daylight to try to escape. The forward controllers led P-47s to numerous rich German targets. On the 14th the 511th Squadron of the 405th Fighter Group circled a group of 300 to 400 German soldiers about five miles northeast of Argentan. The soldiers waved a white flag and fighter control was radioed their position to the nearest American infantry so they could pick up the prisoners. Late that day the Luftwaffe made a rare appearance. North of Flers, 16 Me-109s and FW-190s bounced a squadron of 405th Fighter Group P-47s. The 405th pilots were not used to aerial combat in the cumbersome Thunderbolt and quickly lost four aircraft and three pilots. The outnumbered Americans turned into the German attack and evened the score, downing four Luftwaffe aircraft. On the day, the Luftwaffe lost 27 aircraft and the IX TAC seven. The aerial combats of the day were just part of destruction. At day's end fighter and medium bombers had a two-day total of 63 tanks, 75 armored vehicles, ten half-tracks, 1,081 motor transports, 33 trucks, 29 artillery guns, 16 flak guns, seven staff cars, eight horse-drawn vehicles, nine rail cars and eight ammunition dumps. The IX lost 24 aircraft and 17 pilots. The British 2nd TAF also scored high claims and 13-14 August became two of the best days in the tactical air war in Europe.

The Luftwaffe had been noticeably absent and ineffective since D-Day and needed to make excuses to German ground troops who had been under constant Allied air attack. A document circulated by the German military governor in France to German infantry and Panzers stated: "The ground soldier in action on the invasion front feels himself depressed most of all by enemy air superiority. In spite of the numerical inferiority of our air force, there have been successes accomplished, however, which the single soldier, tied down to his own narrow section of the front, cannot appreciate. The following air force information should be known to the troops so that they may know what great support the fighting forces are receiving from their own air force." This was followed by figures on Luftwaffe supposed successes against invasion shipping.

The Trap is almost closed (15-21 August 1944)

Field Marshal Hans von Kluge, commander of Army Group B, had begged Hitler to allow the withdrawal of 300,000 troops over the Seine before they were surrounded but the Fuehrer again issued one of his infamous "stand and fight" edicts. In the morning of the 15th he drove to visit Sepp Dietrich's headquarters and his motor convoy was attacked by Allied fighter-bombers after which he disappeared for the entire day. Von Kluge reappeared at his headquarters in the late evening saying he was out of contact as his radio van had been destroyed in the strafing attack. Hitler suspected that von Kluge was trying to negotiate surrender with the Allies (there is circumstantial evidence of this and in his agreement to support the conspirators when Hitler was assassinated). On the 16th FM Walther Model, who Hitler considered "the savior of the Russian front" and was fanatically devoted to Hitler, was called upon by the Fuehrer to take over from the deceitful von Kluge who had secretly began to withdraw troops and vehicles from the Gap. Model met von Kluge at his headquarters at St. Germain outside Paris delivering Hitler's letter relieving von Kluge. Model had no idea of the dire situation and called a meeting at Fontaine l'Abbe chateau with his generals Heinz Eberhard, Paul Hausser and Sepp Dietrich. It had taken Eberhard eight hours to drive the 27 miles from the center of the pocket to the conference due to roads blocked by traffic jams and wrecked vehicles and incessant fighter-bomber attacks. Eberhard recited his dismal report to Model who reluctantly agreed to begin a retreat through the Gap.

The advance became so rapid that Bradley did not know were Patton's Third Army was located and became worried that the impetuous Patton would accidentally engage Montgomery's army. Patton reported to Bradley that he had forward troops in Argentan and asked, tongue in cheek, "Shall we continue and drive the British into the sea?" Bradley stopped Patton's advance without consulting Montgomery. J. Lawton Collins VII Corps was also halted. Both Patton and Collins begged Bradley to allow them to close the pocket but the cautious Bradley persisted. His controversial decision allowed the 15-mile Falaise Gap to remain open and nearly 100,000 German soldiers of the Fifth and Seventh Armies and numerous officers to escape across the Seine. The Allies finally closed the pocket on 20 August.

On 15 August, the 404th Fighter Group squadrons attacked on the Gap in relays. Col. Leo Moon leading two flights of 506th Squadron P-47s attacked troops and motorized vehicles for an hour before they were relieved by Maj. Harry Shook's 506th. On his withdrawal, Moon detected 20 German tanks but couldn't pinpoint their exact location to Shook over the radio. Moon quickly dropped down to mark the target by strafing. Shooks' squadron attacked claiming 15 Panzers destroyed. That afternoon the 404th flew another series of missions against the Gap. The 507th Squadron spotted a long line of German vehicles hiding along a tree-lined road suppressed the AA fire with fragmentation bombs and bombed and strafed the column. Still later, the 404th flew an improvised mission to the same area and destroyed five more armored vehicles, two trucks, a flak gun and strafed dug-in German infantry.

On the 17th the Germans began a concerted withdrawal in the daylight and as the early morning mist lifted to clear skies Allied reconnaissance pilots reported the gigantic number of German vehicles crowded bumper-to-bumper in the 13-mile wide gap. Literally thousands of USAAF Thunderbolts, Mustangs and Lightnings and RAF Typhoons and Spitfires took off on multiple sorties from their fields in France and England to storm the hapless Germans

Field Marshal Hans von Kluge replaced Rommel at Army Group B. He had begged Hitler to allow the withdrawal of 400,000 troops over the Seine before they were surrounded but the Fuehrer again issued one of his infamous "stand and fight" edicts which led to the loss of these troops. (Author/West)

Right: On 15 August Hitler replaced von Kluge who committed suicide with Field Marshal Walther Model who in turn was replaced by Gerd von Rundstedt on 5 September. (Author)

American soldiers watch their artillery and air force pound German Seventh Army positions near Falaise. (US Army)

trapped in the "Jabo Rennstrecke". The fighter-bomber attack was so concentrated that the fighter-bombers had to line up to attack. Southwest of Lisieux, 100+ tanks and 200+ motor vehicles had been discovered. When two flights of 37th P-47s came into attack, the column had already been strafed by four P-51s and eight Typhoons that had started 50 or more fires. When the P-47s made their attack, dropping two 500lb. bombs and 24 frags they were unable to see the results. Near Falaise the 36th Fighter Group discovered over 1,000 vehicles moving north almost bumper to bumper. When the 36th radioed their find back to base they were told not to attack as the area was under the control of the RAF 2nd TAF. The British fighter-bombers went on to destroy over 3,000 vehicles in a series of attacks that day. The stalled German columns extended for miles and the fighter-bombers came in relays, once out of ammunition and bombs, the depleted aircraft would give way to newly arrived units eager to continue the pounding. The German troops were caught in the open, too tired or unable to dig foxholes for protection from the bombs, rockets and machine gun bullets from the sky. Under the intense air attacks, the drivers of troop-filled trucks, often on fire, ran off the road or into other vehicles. Soldiers and horses intermingled with the blazing vehicles, writhing and shrieking multitudes. Soldiers were blown to bits or lay trembling in the slaughter while horses by the hundreds stampeded in terror dragging their carriages down roads and over cowering troops.

The RAF 2nd TAF played a large part in the air operations at Falaise. During the retreat towards the Seine, 15 to 21 August, Typhoons, Mustang IIIs and Spitfires flew an average of 1,200 sorties per day. Several Typhoons would initiate the attack on the densely packed motor columns on the roads, knocking out the lead vehicle to stop the column. Then their squadronmates would swoop down in a high-speed dive to shoot up the rest of the column with their rockets and 20mm cannon. After they were finished the Spitfires or Mustangs would come in to strafe the survivors. On 18 August the 2nd TAF destroyed 1,159 vehicles and damaged 1,700 more while German tanks suffered 124 lost and 100 damaged. The 2nd TAF averaged 2,100 missions a day between 6 June and 1 September suffering 1,701 losses which was 80% of the number of fighters available on 6 June or 44.5% of all fighters flown. The Typhoons sustained the heaviest losses at 56% followed by the Mustang III at near 50% and the Spitfire at 41%.

Allied Fighter-Bomber Sorties and Claims
Falaise Pocket-August 1944

Sorties/Claims	2nd TAF	IX TAC	Total
Sorties	9,896	2,291	12,787
MT destroyed	3,340	2,520	5,860
Armor destroyed	257	134	391
Total claims	3,597	2,654	6,251
Claims per sortie	0.36	0.91	0.49

By the afternoon the pocket was packed with two army and four corps headquarters, remnants of six infantry, five panzer and one parachute division. Many of the roads through the area were sunken and prevented the Germans from taking cover in adjacent fields and would become mass graves. After the Allies swept eastward, they found movement along these roads was impossible as hundreds of dead German soldiers lay among bloated horses, wrecked trucks, automobiles, motorcycles and armor trapped by embankments, fallen walls and scorched shrubs and trees. Among the destruction there were undamaged tanks and guns that were abandoned by their crews in an almost hysterical effort to escape the carnage. There were concentrated areas of destruction where the fighter-bombers had done their work. Burned out vehicles with the burned bodies of their occupants spilled out next to them stretched for hundreds of yards. The last weeks of August were particularly hot and human bodies and animal carcasses quickly decomposed and the fetid odor covered the areas for miles around. Between Moissey and Chambois the dead German bodies were stacked four high for over a kilometer. The road was bulldozed clear and the bodies buried in a mass grave.

The 2,000 to 3,000 daily Allied air sorties in the close quarters of the pocket did produce friendly fire accidents as the pocket became so constricted that Allied ground forces were operating so closely to each other. On 18 August Leigh-Mallory abolished the bomb line around the battle zone making the pocket off-limits to the fighter-bombers so as not to incur more friendly fire accidents. However, there were few worthwhile targets remaining inside the pocket to attack and most of the Germans had already escaped. The fighter-bombers then flew sorties against targets of opportunity outside the pocket. American artillery south of the Gap and Canadian artillery to the north opened a massive barrage to continue the carnage. But the trap could not be closed by fighter-bombers and artillery and as always in warfare the infantry, American, British, Canadian and Polish, aided by armor had to do the dirty work of facing the enemy man-to-man. Nevertheless the desperate Germans managed to keep the Gap open. On the 18th, the disheartened von Kluge headed back to Germany and on the way stopped along the road. He strolled off into a wood and bit into a cyanide pill and was dead in seconds. That morning the pocket had shrunk to an area of six miles by six miles as the Germans savagely fought for their lives.

When Patton's tanks reached the Seine at Mantes Gassicourt and Vernon, the XV Corps immediately swung east along the riverbank, closing a large new trap around the remnants that had escaped from Falaise. On the 19th, the Germans desperately tried to get to the Seine and cross it by any means including swimming. The XIX and IX TACs flew relentless sorties over the river to devastate the harassed Germans. The approaches to Chambois were being held by the Germans to keep elements of the US 80th Division from linking up with the Canadians and Poles only two miles to the north. Allied artillery and airpower were called in to attack the small pocket that was packed with German troops and vehicles. SS Gen. Paul Hausser was meeting with his Chief of Staff, Maj.Gen. Rudolf von Gersdorff and Brig.Gen. Kurt Meyer when the area was attacked by fighter-bombers. A nearby ammunition truck was hit and exploded and von Gersdorff was badly wounded. Late in the afternoon the Poles moved into Chambois driving through streets littered with destroyed vehicles and armor. Among the hundreds of dead enemy soldiers there were many wounded moaning for help. So many horses were wounded, bellowing and laying writhing in pain or moving, dragging their intestines that the orders were given to the Allied troops put them out of their misery.

Results and Conclusions

In the opinion of many senior officers interviewed by 12th Army Group Historian, Col. Ralph Ingersoll "the failure to close the Argentan-Falaise gap was the loss of the greatest single opportunity of the war." The explanation for this tactical blunder can be found in the personalities, egos and jealousies among the Allied command structure. Eisenhower had allowed Bradley and Montgomery to pursue their own objectives at critical times and never took firm control of operations. Also, at the time the Allied leaders, Eisenhower, Bradley and Montgomery, were buoyed by the great success of OVERLORD and expected the war to be over by Christmas. They had ignored the basic doctrine of warfare: believing that the capture of territory was more important than the destruction of enemy forces. While heavy fighting was going on Argentan-Falaise these leaders were more concerned with getting to the Rhine and over running Germany rather than closing the pocket. To this day

An Opel Blitz truck and Sd Kfpz 251 half-track are destroyed on narrow road out of Falaise. (USAF)

Devastation of a retreating German motor column at Falaise by the 368th Fighter Group. In four days, 24-28 August the 368th Fighter Group under Colonel Gilbert Meyers destroyed 426 vehicles and damaged 125 others. (USAF)

When Patton's tanks reached the Seine at Mantes Gassicourt and Vernon, the XV Corps immediately swung east along the riverbank, closing a large new trap around the Germans who had escaped from Falaise. On the 19th, the Germans desperately tried to get to the Seine and cross it by any means including swimming. A US M-10 tank of the 79th Infantry Division crossed the Seine over a newly constructed pontoon bridge as all permanent bridges had been destroyed by Allied air power. (US Army)

German POWs who didn't escape the Falaise pocket. An estimated 10,000 Germans were killed and 50,000 captured but about that number escaped. Also 260,000 German troops crossed the Seine. (US Army)

historians argue these points. Although the battle to close the Falaise Gap was a failure it was not a complete loss. Only a small portion of German equipment was not destroyed. None of the 27th Panzer Division's 127 tanks and 40 assault guns survived the battle. From seven Panzer divisions in the pocket, only 24 tanks and 60 artillery pieces escaped through the Gap while 200 tanks, 1,000 guns, 5,000 vehicles and 2,000 wagons and 1,800 horses were lost. These divisions lost 10,000 dead, 50,000 captured. The end result was that although the battle of the Argentan-Falaise pocket did not result in the complete annihilation of the German forces in Normandy, after that time the German army was no longer an effective force and France could not be defended. General Omar Bradley reported that 70,000 Germans were killed or captured and that 19 German divisions had been destroyed in the pocket. Various historians put the number of escaping Germans at 20,000 to 50,000 but those who did escape did so without their equipment, armored vehicles, M/T or field guns. However, the great resurrection of the German Army in the fall of 1944 and their ability to counter-attack in the Ardennes was due in some respect to the Allies inability to annihilate the Germans at Falaise.

In his book, *Crusade in Europe*, (Doubleday, NY, 1948) Eisenhower described the battle:

"The battlefield at Falaise was unquestionably one of the greatest 'killing grounds' of the war. I encountered scenes that could be only described by Dante. It was literally possible to walk for hundreds of yards at a time without stepping on nothing but dead and decaying flesh."

On 21 August, Leigh-Mallory flew to France to meet with Montgomery. The two assumed that the Seine bridges had been destroyed even though the Germans had moved large numbers of troops across the river since D-Day. Leigh-Mallory had ordered attacks on the bridges be discontinued and the fighter-bombers were to concentrate their attacks to the east and north to prevent the Germans from establishing new defensive lines at the Somme and Marne Rivers. Bad weather and no aerial reconnaissance of the area prevented the discovery of the crossings. Thus, the ever-resourceful Germans were able to repair some of the bridges and build three pontoon bridges. The bulk of their forces crossed the Seine via 60 ferry and boat crossing sites along with a multitude of small boats and rafts. The number of German troops in the pocket and on the roads to the Seine numbered 270,000 with an additional 50,000 coming from elsewhere west of the river. About 80,000 troops of this 320,000 were lost between the 19th and 31st of August. During that same period, 240,000 troops and 28,000 vehicles and several tanks crossed the Seine.

After Falaise the Allies pushed into northern France and the first American troops crossed the Seine on 19 August and Charles DeGaulle's Free French forces entered Paris six days later. On 15 August, the Allies invaded southern France in Operation ANVIL-DRAGOON and were driving the few Germans left to defend that area back toward Germany. Hitler replaced von Kluge with Model. During the last week in August the Allies began a head long motorized rush along the main roads through France, into Belgium, Luxembourg and toward Germany. No one walked; everyone rode until the advance literally ran out of gas stalling further progress that then was stopped completely by an early winter and stiffening German resistance which stretched from the North Sea to Switzerland. The Allies had not eliminated the German armies at Normandy but only dislodged them.

30

Reduction of the French Ports August - September 1944

Brest (25 August-18 September 1944)
Hitler instructed Gen. Hermann Ramcke, who was commander of the defense of the Brittany ports to hold for at least 90 days. On 23 July Hitler sent an order to all fortress-port commanders:

"Strong garrisons commanded by officers of proven courage and resourcefulness must be sacrificed to defend the main French ports and deprive the enemy of their use."

During the first week of August 1944, the US Third Army advanced swiftly up the Brittany Peninsula towards its objective, the strategic deep-water port of Brest that was intended to supply the Allied advance to the east. The deep-water port was south of the city and was virtually land-locked by the curving Crozon Peninsula. By the 18th the peninsular city was surrounded and cut off far from retreating German troops in north central France. The German intention was to deny the use of the port and its facilities and tie up as many Allied troops for as long as possible. The Brest defenses formed a large circle around the city proper with 75 heavily defended strongpoints. The outer defenses were comprised of a series of modernized old French forts supported by German built field works. The inner defenses were a complex of large, interconnected pillboxes and blockhouses and a favorable defensible geography that was incorporated with the cities ancient moat and immense wall. Previously the city was an important U-boat base and was well protected by numerous large caliber coastal artillery and AA guns that were positioned to protect the city from land, sea and air attack. There also was an extensive system of underground air raid shelters. Most importantly, Lt.Gen. Hermann Ramcke, a hard-nosed veteran who had served in North Africa and Russia, commanded three divisions totaling 20,000 resolute troops and 23,000 auxiliaries.

A joint ground-air attack was initiated against the formidable German defenses. The land assault plan was to be a persistent attack by the 2nd, 8th and 29th Infantry Divisions from the north, surrounding the city and then drive into it. The VIII Corps was to drive down the peninsula that protruded into the bay south of the city. The infantry was supported by attacks by heavy and medium bombers on the city defenses and by fighter-bomber attacks supporting each division. The XIX TAC left behind two fighter groups, the 358th and 362nd, to fly missions from nearby bases. Because of the rapid advance and the distance from the American armies advancing to the east, communications was marginal between Corps and higher ground HQ and Corps and air HQ. Fighter-bombers were assigned standard air-ground cooperation to give continuous cover. Initially, inefficient ground-air coordination involving essential information on bomb lines, troop positions, target details made both heavy and medium bomber and fighter-bomber attacks less effective. White smoke shells were used to indicate enemy targets but the Germans came to fire white smoke shells on American positions to cause confusion. The use of colored shells came into use. When air-ground support was unable to furnish targets the fighter-bomber unit was given predetermined targets at takeoff. Soon, fighter-bomber effectiveness was greatly improved by placing them on an air alert status while the heavy and medium bombers continued to struggle on. Poor weather over fighter-bomber airfields or over Brest often reduced the weight or continuity of the attack. The daily progress of the ground attack was grudgingly slow, measured in thousands of feet as the Germans defended zealously, surrendering ground only when overwhelmed.

In the three weeks of the assault fighter-bombers flew 15 days, averaging six missions and 82 sorties per day. On a typical mission on Brest bomb loads were pre-determined by target type. The heavily fortified targets warranted the full P-47 load of two 1,000lb. bombs but most sorties utilized two 500lb. or two 250lb. bombs. Three flights, twelve P-47s, were readied; eight armed with two 500lb. bombs and four were to fly top cover. The Thunderbolts flew in a wide "V" with the top cover at 12,000ft. and the fighter-bombers at 10,000ft. As the fighter-bombers approached the port they dropped to 7,000ft. and turned out to the sea for several minutes while each pilot was radioed his instructions to attack definite targets. The pilots paired up and dived on the target at the recommended 60-degree angle using the gunsight. The bombs were released when the huge nose of the P-47 covered the target, usually at 2,000ft. and indicated air speed of 350mph. At the end of the dive each pilot would pull up in a tight turn to observe the outcome of his attack before rejoining top cover to return to base.

On 25 August, the 362nd Fighter Group attacked naval and merchant vessels in Brest harbor deploying squadrons at two-hour intervals on four missions. It was feared that the Germans were going to evacuate troops from Brest to Crozon. Twelve P-47s of the 378th Squadron dive-bombed through intense AA fire from ships in the harbor. Lt.Col. Joseph Laughlin got two hits on the stern of a light cruiser. Later, Laughlin led the 377th Squadron back to finish off shipping in the harbor and as he dove on the light cruiser hit earlier it blew up violently and sunk. Two hits were gotten on an auxiliary cruiser and four large ships and a dozen smaller ships were damaged. The 362nd was awarded the DUC for these actions. On 27 August, 12 P-47s coordinated with heavy artillery fire to neutralize the bunkers and emplacements of Battery Domaine.

After days of ground attack the German defenses retreated to a more confined area so that further bombing by heavy and medium bombers jeopardized friendly troops. Fighter-bombers capably worked directly with ground troops, attacking strong points, fortifications and defended buildings, armor, artillery and AA positions immediately over the frontlines. Fighter-bombers supporting the 2nd Infantry Division flew 97 missions (705 aircraft), 65% of which were called by front line battalions or forward observers. The 29th Infantry Division, in its attack on the Fort of Pte. Du Grand Ninou, called for bombing strikes by two flights of P-47s. Two direct hits were observed and many near misses and shortly the fort was surrendered.

With more forts and vicious street fighting in the future, on 13 September Maj.Gen. Troy Middleton sent Ramcke a surrender proposal that was turned down. Fort Keranroux and Montbarey were in the line of the advance and Middleton ordered a concentrated attack supplemented by artillery, bombers and fighter-bombers. Fort Karenroux was first to fall. Its hundred shell shocked survivors crawled out of the fort whose outline was obliterated and pock marked. Montbarey was more difficult as it had walls 25 feet thick, a 50 foot dry moat and extensive mine fields and gun emplacements. Initial assault units took heavy casualties and the attack was suspended. It was decided to bombard this fort by land and air before further action. The three-day bombardment was so intense that the dazed defenders surrendered with half of their garrison dead.

In the Brest operation maintaining air superiority and the interdiction of enemy reinforcements and supplies was not necessary. This, along with generally good weather during the period, allowed the full brunt of fighter-bomber attack to be concentrated to the small area the Germans were confined. This was the most concerted American fighter-bomber close air support operation to that time. Infantry called 331 missions involving nearly 3,700 sorties by fighter-bombers on air alert status. Air alert over the city allowed maximum flexibility and minimum delay from request to attack. Planned attacks required two to six hours compared to ten to twenty minutes for air alert calls (pre-planned bomber attacks required two days). Almost half a million rounds of artillery, heavy and medium bomber raids and constant fighter-bomber strafing and bombing missions reduced Brest to rubble and its defenders will to resist. The port had been demolished in the assault and then by German demolition and was useless. The Americans suffered 9,831 casualties. The port of Antwerp was captured in the beginning of September and plans to salvage the port of Brest were abandoned as were plans to capture the French ports of Lorient (15,000 garrison), St. Nazaire (12,000 garrison), Quiberon Bay and Nantes.

The Brest Forts, Karenroux and Montbarey, stood in the way of the advance. They were reduced to rubble by initial artillery and air bombardment that caused the shell shocked survivors to surrender. (13-16 September 1944) (USAF)

Lt. Gen. Hermann Ramcke, hard-nosed defender of Brest at his surrender on 19 September 1944. (USAF)

The fall of Brest marked it as a memorial to the extravagant use of air power. Huge numbers of aircraft, unopposed in the air, had been used to bombard a surrounded city while American armies in the east were driving into France and were without their support. This advance toward Germany ran out of momentum by mid-September. SHAEF had hoped that Patton's Third Army could advance long enough to allow the flanking of the Siegfried Line in the north and then to cross the Rhine River to Holland. If Patton were given the total assistance of the IX TAC could he have had advanced further than he did before the Third Army needed to regroup and resupply?

Fighter-Bomber Air Operations Against Brest (25 August-18 September 1944)

Date	Missions	Sorties	Date	Missions	Sorties
25 Aug*	17	157	7 Sept	18	205
26 Aug	9	143	8 Sept	49	574
27 Aug	7	144	9 Sept	24	189
28 Aug	3	45	10 Sept	11	172
29 Aug	0	weather	11 Sept	21	168
30 Aug	0	weather	12 Sept	12	99
1 Sept*	11	108	13 Sept	2	16
2 Sept	22	4	14 Sept*	6	48
3 Sept*	20	313	15 Sept	0	weather
4 Sept	11	2	16 Sept	12	69
5 Sept*	42	544	17 Sept	9	56
6 Sept*	39	463	18 Sept	5	32
19 Sept	5	27			
			Totals	331	3,698

*Days 9AF Medium and light bombers attacked (2,059 dispatched and 1,573 attacking)

St. Malo (7-18 August 1944)

The port of St. Malo lies 40 miles west of Avranches on the River Rance with the small resort towns of Dinant and Dinan on the estuary. The small, heavily fortified Isle of Cezembre commanded the channel to St. Malo. The area contained 13-14,000 defenders, mostly Russian prisoner-soldiers, under the fanatical command of Col. Andreas von Aulock who vowed to his Fuehrer that he would defend the port to the last man. Von Aulock had about 1,000 diehard paratroops and another 1,000 experienced Grenadiers of the 17th SS Panzer Division along with troops evacuated from Guernsey. Patton sent Maj.Gen. R.W. Gerow's 6th Armored Division to St. Malo which they reached on 7 August. The Americans surrounded the port and von Aulock ordered the demolition of the port facilities. The garrison put up stiff resistance even in the face of shelling by the battleships, HMS *Warspite* and *Malaya*. The Allies had refrained from bombing St. Malo, Dinant and Dinan to reduce casualties to the civilian population but when their own casualty figures mounted the two resort towns were bombed and taken with heavy casualties, Dinant on the 13th and Dinard on the next day. St. Malo's old town had to be cleared street by street, house by house. Artillery fire and bombing reduced the town to rubble but von Aulock held up four US regiments before he surrendered. On 17 August

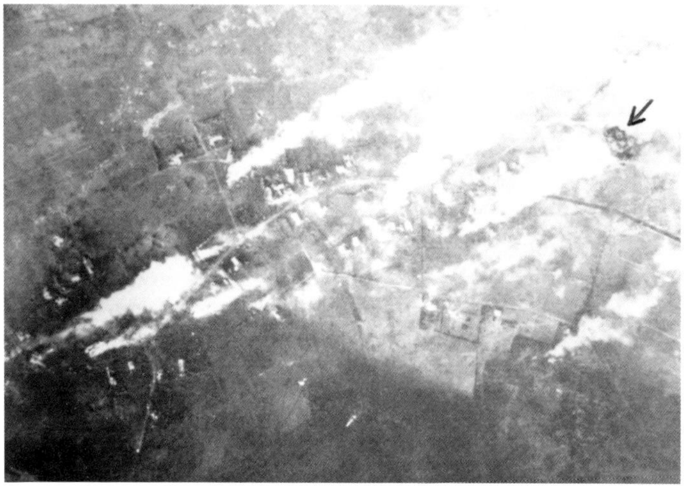

Droopsnoot P-38s dropping napalm bombs (exploding at arrow) on Isle de Cezembre, off St. Malo. (USAF)

Capture of the Citadel at St. Malo which was destroyed by combined attack by bombers, fighter-bombers and battleships. (US Army)

P-38s drop napalm "fire bombs" on the Isle of Cezembre on 31 August 1944. A TacR P-51 can be seen in the photo flying between the two smoke plumes (arrow). A newly dropped napalm bomb is exploding on the upper left side of the isle. (USAF)

the Third Army had surrounded the citadel at St. Malo and issued an ultimatum that was ignored by von Aulock. The 9th Air Force sent in 36 P-38s carrying two 165-gallon napalm tanks. The first flights dropped their napalm and the inferno induced von Aulock to surrender to the 8rd Infantry Division. The fall of St. Malo netted 11,600 prisoners mostly Russian and the Americans found the port too damaged to repair quickly.

But the fighting was not over as the small Isle of Cezembre, about two miles off shore, blocked the entrance to St. Malo and its batteries shelled the captured port. Another fanatical German officer, Lt. Richard Zeiss, commanded the isle garrison that was well protected by fortifications from the absolute decimation of everything above ground by artillery, naval shelling and aerial bombing. The P-38s that did not drop their napalm on the St. Malo citadel on the 17th flew to Cezembre and unloaded. Still Zeiss and his 300 troops held out and by the end of August some 20,000 shells and bombs had landed on the quarter-mile by half-mile isle. On 31 August 56 P-38s dropped 112 napalm tanks on the fortifications and the next day the garrison surrendered in the face of continued attacks, the loss of their water supply and an impending amphibious invasion. Interrogation of the survivors revealed that the napalm had seeped into some shelters and forced the occupants to evacuate. An AAF report on the napalm attack stated: "It is felt that the Fire Bomb accomplished a certain definite portion of damage to personnel, equipment and morale that was not accomplished by the use of HE. It is not to be construed, however, that this indicates the Fire Bomb would have accomplished this alone. Experience indicates that the Fire Bomb has a definite place when used in conjunction with HE or on rubble and damage that was not the result of HE bombing."

9th Air Force Fighter/Fighter-Bomber Interdiction Operations: Pursuit to the West Wall (14 August-14 September 1944)

	Fighter/Fighter-Bombers		Bombers*	
Targets	**Sorties**	**Bomb Tons**	**Sorties**	**Bomb Tons**
Railways/Bridges	962	264.7	444	789.5
Marshaling Yards	368	103.8	52	65.0
Roads/Bridges	329	104.8	564	972.3
Military Installations	476	213.2	1,317	1,765.9
Motor Transport/Troops	4,578	1,389.7	522	944.3
Horse-Drawn Vehicles	67	13.0	—	—
Shipping	384	158.1	—	—
Totals	7,164	2,247.3	2,899	4,536.0

* Medium and light

8th Air Force Fighter/Fighter-Bomber Interdiction Operations: Pursuit to the West Wall (14 August-14 September 1944)

	Fighter/Fighter-Bombers		Bombers*	
Targets	**Sorties**	**Bomb Tons**	**Sorties**	**Bomb Tons**
Railways/Bridges	794	352.8	1,014	2,965.3
Marshaling Yards	473	207.2	1,986	5,293.6
Roads/Bridges	801	334.4	97	239.5
Military Installations	—	—	610	1,502.8
Motor Transport/Troops	56	19.2	68	161.0
Shipping	31	12.6	2	4.0
Miscellaneous	108	33.4	216	434.7
Totals	2,263	959.6	3,393	10,600.9

* Heavy

9th Air Force Operational Strength 1 March-12 September 1944

Date	B-26	A-20	Total Bombers	P-38	P-47	P-51	Total Fighters
1 March 1944	265	0	265	109	244	89	442
6 June 1944	542	174	716	185	853	126	1,164
24 July 1944	541	206	747	147	644	116	907
14 August 1944	457	171	628	160	685	119	964
12 September 1944	512	207	719	144	741	77	962

31

The German Retreat Across Northeast France 21 August - 15 September 1944

The Retreat

The Allied pursuit of the Germans from Normandy across northern France began on 14 August when the Allied pincers closed on the German Seventh and Fifth Panzer Armies at Falaise and Argentan. This portion of the pursuit lasted for a month as the retreating German Panzer Armies escaped eastward in confusion until they reached the West Wall (Siegfried Line). There were no new plans for a co-ordinated interdiction program for this period and interdiction operations were basically an extension of what happened before COBRA. The IX and XIX TACs continued three missions as spelled out by *FM 100-20*:

1) Gain and maintain air superiority
2) Interdict the movement of enemy troops and supplies into and within the battleground
3) Provide close air support

The 9th Air Force Summary of Operations stated: "Just which phase was most important at any one time was determined by the progress of the war. When the army was advancing, Phase 3 operations required a large part of the TACs effort. When the front was relatively static, Phase 2 operations were by far the most numerous. On those rare occasions when the GAF got off the ground in considerable force the maintenance of local air superiority was of paramount importance."

Air interdiction during this period changed as instead of trying to stop movement toward the battlefield fighter-bombers tried to prevent the Germans from withdrawing from the battlefield. The targets remained the same but the reason in attacking them changed. As the Allies advanced rapidly east they realized that they would need a more or less intact rail system to continue their advance. On 17 August the AEAF ordered that bridge attacks needed to be authorized and on the 27th rolling stock without locomotives or stranded

As the Allied armies advanced across France new ALGs had to be built to accommodate fighter groups trying to keep up with the advance. The 37rd Fighter Group on a large Continental ALG. The 411th (foreground) and 412th (background) Fighter Squadrons still flew some Razorback P-47s (left foreground). (USAF)

Tents on ALG B-48 at Amiens, France. While these tents were adequate in the summer months they were totally insufficient for winter use with their thin canvas walls. Note the ubiquitous GI transport parked in the front of the tent. (USAF)

In the rapid advance across France in the summer of 1944, the IX TAC took over Luftwaffe airfields just days after they were abandoned. Here is a P-38J, probably of the 485th Fighter Squadron of the 370th Fighter Group is being serviced in front of a burned out German aircraft. (USAF)

by rail cuts not be attacked unless they carried military supplies. During this period systematic attacks were conducted against transportation targets east of the West Wall into Germany. In mid-September the IX and XIX TACs were assigned missions to attack rail lines east and west of the Rhine.

The Germans had planned to set up a defensive line at the Touques River but the Allies advanced so quickly the Germans had race to reach and cross the Seine. The Allies had intended to stop at the Seine to regroup and augment their dwindling supplies. But their rapid advance and Patton's Third Army already having crossed the Seine to the north and moving east, it was decided to take advantage of the situation and not allow the Germans to reorganize. To cut off the retreating Germans elements of the US First and Third Armies moved north up the west bank of the Seine near Paris. The British and Canadian armies moved east and south while the remainder of the Third Army moved to the east. For the time being Paris was to be by-passed to off set any political problems with DeGaulle and the French and to prevent any damage to the city. On 22 August Eisenhower decided to concentrate Allied forces on the recapture of Belgium. Montgomery's 21st Army Group was to evict the Germans from the Pas de Calais and move east to capture the Channel ports. The US First Army was to cross the Seine south of Paris and take Lille while the Third Army would continue its move east toward Strasbourg and Metz.

The Third Army was outrunning its fuel supplies and needed to revise their objectives along the Seine to conserve fuel supplies. The First Army was mopping up the area between the Third Army and the British and then moved toward the Seine. By the 22nd Eisenhower decided to move on Paris and delegated the 2nd French Armored Division to do so by the night of the 24th. The US 4th Infantry moved on the French capitol from the south and the German commander, Gen. Dietrich von Choltitz, surrendered the city on the 25th.

The desperate Germans fought ferociously to hold off the Allies before the Seine so the retreat over the river could be carried out on the only two bridges that remained intact over the Seine, the damaged road bridge at Rouen and a pontoon bridge at Le Bas de Poses. Although most of the retreat was over these two bridges, ferries, barges and assorted boats carried retreating forces at night. Bad weather grounded the Allied air forces for several days but on the 27th it cleared and the fighter-bombers were again harassing the Germans on the Seine.

The XII Corps of the Third Army continued to advance to the east. On 29 August elements crossed the Marne while others moved on to Chalons-sur-Marne. By 2 September two divisions crossed the Meuse River and the XX Corps captures Reims on 29 August and Verdun on 1 September. On 2 September the Third Army was stopped by lack of fuel.

After the German debacle at Falaise the US First Army in the north drove easily across France toward the German homeland. On 31 August they drove past the Soissons, drove across the Belgian border on the 2nd, captured Sedan on 7 September, Liege on the 9th liberated Luxembourg the next day. They then entered Germany on the 11th and three days later approached the Siegfried Line near Aachen. Patton's Third army breached the Somme-Marne defensive Line before the Germans could man it, crossed the Meuse on the last day of August and was in Metz on 10 September. On 11 September the Third Army joined with the Allied armies driving north from the DRAGOON beaches in southern France and on the 15th were in Nancy.

All along the front the German commander, FM Model tried to set up lines of defense only to have them over run. The German Fifteenth Army on the coast was under heavy attack from the British who were trying to stop it from withdrawing into Germany. The German Fifth and Seventh Armies fought delaying actions and tried to hold a line at Marne-Somme, then at the Meuse River and at the canal at Maastricht all fell of which fell the armies were forced to flee to the east. The German First Army did manage a holding action at Verdun. The four divisions of the Fifteenth Army were that were attempting to break through Allied lines while the Fifth Panzer Army had only three to four panzer divisions and about two infantry divisions remaining. Antwerp fell and on 5 September Hitler replaced Model with the retired FM Gerd von Rundstedt as com-

During the race across France throughout August the IX and XIX TACs registered a spectacular performance. A German half-track is a sitting duck while stopped along a French road that affords no cover. (USAF)

mander of Army Group B. Von Rundstedt was saddled with a disorganized defense as his troops had lost their heavy weapons and armor and decided the only viable solution was the withdrawal to the West Wall.

At the end of August, four large Allied armies were rapidly advancing north and northeastward on a front stretching from the mouth of the Seine to the Meuse River at Verdun and stood only 60 miles from the German border. On 2 September Eisenhower decided that Patton's Third Army should have the bulk of the reserve gasoline to drive through the West Wall, cross the Rhine, and capture the Ruhr and Saar. Hodge's First Army was also to advance as far as it could toward Cologne and Koblenz. Despite the awesome fuel and supply problems the Allies moved quickly toward the Rhine and German border liberating large areas of France, most of Belgium and Luxembourg and portions of Holland. By 10 September the US First Army approached the West Wall at Aachen and the Third Army crossed the Moselle River. The V Corps crossed the Luxembourg border and moved into Germany on the 11th while the VII Corps advanced slowly on Aachen through difficult terrain and fortified German positions. As the Allies moved into Germany they met with and were slowed by the prepared West Wall defenses. By the 14th the Allied advance was slowed or halted along the entire front due to the lack of fuel giving the defeated Germans the opportunity to reorganize and strengthen their defense of the Fatherland.

The Fighter-Bombers

Throughout August fighter-bombers registered a spectacular performance. In four days, 24-28 August the 368th Fighter Group under Col. Gilbert Meyers destroyed 426 vehicles and damaged 125 others. For the month the IX TAC flew 12,305 sorties/378 missions claiming 98.5-18-35 in the air and 63-2-19 on the ground for a loss of 123. The XIX TAC flew 12,292 sorties claimed 163-16-34 in the air and 66-4-28 on the ground for the loss of 114 aircraft. The XIX TAC's August totals were:

4,058	motor transport
598	horse-drawn vehicles
466	tanks and armored vehicles
222	gun positions
11	ammunition dumps
13	fuel and supply dumps
44	troop concentrations
58	enemy barracks and buildings
246	locomotives
2,956	railway cars
122	railway cuts
39	marshaling yards
155	barges and river vessels
18	merchant vessels
8	naval vessels
17	airfields
68	enemy aircraft destroyed and 28 damaged on the ground

On 25 August the Luftwaffe in France collapsed. Fighter-bombers of the 8th and 9th Air Force destroyed 178 Luftwaffe aircraft, probably destroyed 13 and damaged 63 others. The XIX had totals of 31-1-8 in the air, 18-4-0 on the ground. The 354th Fighter Group conducted a number of squadron-sized sweeps over Luftwaffe airfields north and northeast of Paris. Late in the day P-51 flights encountered 45 Me-109s and FW-190s destroying 13 while losing four. Another 354th squadron destroyed 13 Luftwaffe fighters on airfields near Reims and Beauvais. At sundown the Luftwaffe evacuated their remaining aircraft eastwards as their bases around Paris were captured by Patton's Third Army Several days later their Marne bases were captured and the Luftwaffe retreated to bases behind the Siegfried Line. By the end of August no Luftwaffe aircraft were in the air and the few remaining on French fields were sought out and destroyed. The air war against the Germans on the ground continued. Also, on 25 August 632 sorties were flown and 266 motor vehicles were destroyed, four tanks, 44 locomotives and 164 rail cars.

The weather was generally good during this period (only three down days) and the IX and XIX TACs continued their destruction. On 1 September the 405th Fighter Group flew six squadron strength missions to Arlon, Thionville, Metz, Nancy and Toul. The Group's total for the attack was 200 trucks, 28 horse-drawn vehicles five tanks and four horse-drawn artillery. Meanwhile, the 36th Fighter Group attacked German units retreating from Poitiers-Chateauroux, south of Loire. Four two-flight missions were sent out at 0645. The

Col. Raymond Stecker CO of the 365th Fighter Group was an All-American back at West Point in 1932 and was one of Quesada's many talented Group commanders. (USAF)

flights came upon a long German column and dropped low and attacked through intense AA fire. After destroying a large number of vehicles it was relieved by a second mission that finished off the column. The third mission also discovered a column in the same area and demolished it. The fourth and last mission of the day found yet another column and smashed it. For the day the 36th destroyed over 500 German vehicles and was awarded the DUC. On 3 September, Capt. Raymond Stecker of the 365th Fighter Group came upon a large conglomeration of German trucks, half-tracks, staff cars and wagons near Mons. His pilots destroyed 294 trucks and after two other groups came in and continued the destruction. On 3 September the US First Army took Mons, Belgium and trapped German troops in a pocket south of the city. The IX TAC attacked the pocket and got its largest single day's claims of the war: 919 trucks, 58 armored vehicles and 757 horse-drawn-vehicles. The 368th Fighter Group was outstanding that day winning the DUC. It flew seven missions of 83 sorties bombing and strafing German targets that were heavily defended by AA and small arms fire. They destroyed 262 trucks and damaged 30, destroyed 230 horse-drawn vehicles and a large number of personnel. During two-day period fighter-bombers flew 1,053 sorties destroying almost 1,200 vehicles. On the 7th, 36 P-47s of the 406th Fighter Group left Le Mans (A-35) at 1505 to search for large concentrations German troops attempting to escape the Chateauroux area to the east and then to continue their escape through the Belfort Gap. They found the road between Chateauroux and Issoudon choked with trucks, horse-drawn vehicles, armored vehicles, artillery and troops. The Thunderbolts dove through heavy small arms fire and hit the strung out column with bombs, rockets and strafing. The road was blocked for 15 miles with over 300 smoking vehicles. The Group returned to base and quickly refueled and rearmed and hit the same column again destroying an additional 187 vehicles harassing the column well into dusk causing them to make a hazardous night landing, After they left the French Forces of the Interior (FFI) mopped up the dazed German column taking many prisoners. The 406th was awarded the DUC for the action.

On 18 August Mustangs of the 354th Fighter Squadron of the 355th Fighter Group were making a low-level sweep searching for targets of opportunity. Squadron Commander, Capt. Bert Marshall spotted a marshaling yard northwest of Paris, near the German border. Marshall left his squadron to orbit overhead out of the range of the German light flak while he dove to test the strength of the defenses. Marshall's P-51 was immediately hit by flak and caught on fire. Marshall radioed 1Lt. Royce Priest to take command of the squadron and return to base. Marshall was able to control his wounded fighter into a crash landing in a wheat field. While Marshall was making his landing, Priest radioed Marshall that he was going to attempt to rescue him by landing in a nearby field. Marshall ordered Priest to go home but the Lieutenant ignored the order and landed. Priest taxied as near as possible to his CO and Marshall ran up and again ordered Priest to return to base. Priest replied by throwing out his parachute/dingy pack and getting out of the cockpit. Marshall had no choice and climbed in followed by Priest who sat on his lap. To close the canopy the six-foot tall Priest had to put his head on the front windshield. Marshall successfully maneuvered the fighter to take off over some haystacks and pursuing German soldiers firing at them. On their return to Steeple Morden, Priest dropped the wheels and Marshall lowered the flaps to make a textbook landing. For his unauthorized rescue, Priest was awarded the DSC.

As discussed previously the outstanding use of the fighter-bomber in the ETO was Weyland's use of his XIX TAC to protect Patton's Third Army's exposed flank by holding and then pursuing German forces south of the Loire. This action culminated on 16

Maj. Bert Marshall, CO of the 355th Fighter Group, was hit by flak on a fighter sweep and crash-landed his wounded P-51 near the German border. 1Lt. Royce Priest landed and rescued his CO who flew the P-51 back to base while Priest sat on his lap. (USAF)

Quesada's IX TAC was only half the size it was in July but in August it flew more sorties (8,712), dropped more bombs (21,237 tons), destroyed more German tanks (634) and Luftwaffe aircraft (26) than any other month in its history. Ninth Air Force P-47 pilots examine the German tank they destroyed. It appears that the rear engine compartment has been blown off. (USAF)

September when Lt.Gen. William Simpson, commander of the newly formed Ninth Army, and Weyland were present at the surrender of German Marche Gruppe commander, Maj.Gen. Eric Elster, and 20,000 troops at Beaugency Bridge. Elster and his men had been effectively prevented from moving from the south of France by Weyland's fighter-bombers. On 10 September, negotiations with Elster were underway and the German General signaled his intent on surrender if air attacks were discontinued. The mere threat of American Jabos kept him to his word until the capitulation.

Quesada's IX was only half the size it was in July but in August it flew more sorties (8,712), dropped more bombs (21,237 tons), destroyed more German tanks (634) and Luftwaffe aircraft (26) than any other month in its history. The major problem for the TACs was to keep up with the rapidly advancing Allied ground offensive. IX Engineer Command built over 60 new airfields in August and September. During the six weeks, mid-July through August, a fighter-bomber group moved to a new base three times on average, each move being about a 100 miles or less. Optimism ran rampant from the Allied High Command down to the infantry soldier. But soon the fantastic advance slowed as supply could not keep pace with distance and demand. By September there were serious shortages of food, gasoline and ammunition at the Allied front.

Lt.Col. David Schilling led a late afternoon mission of 29 P-47s to Gelnhausen Airdrome. (USAF)

56th Fighter Group Drops Down to Strafe Luftwaffe Airdromes (5 September 1944)

On 5 September, the VIII Bomber Command sent out 882 B-17s and B-24s to bomb synthetic oil and aircraft factories in southeast Germany. The 56th Fighter Group was to fly in advance of the bombers to catch the Luftwaffe on the ground before they could take off to intercept the bombers.

Maj. Lucien Dade led 36 P-47s of the 61st, 62nd, and 63rd Fighter Squadrons at 0938 and arrived near Koblenz an hour and a half-later and attacked Mershausen Airdrome. The 61st (8) and 62nd (7) destroyed 15 aircraft as they strafed the field. Dade was the top scorer with three. The 62nd under Capt. Mike Quirk moved on to the Limburg Airdrome where 30-40 aircraft were parked and destroyed six, three by Capt. Michael Jackson. Capt. Harold Comstock led the 6rd from its top cover position to strafe the Autobahn northeast of Koblenz. They were bounced by ten or more Me-109s and in a dogfight and shot down seven and damaged one. After subduing the Messerschmitts they returned to strafing and claimed six trucks, an automobile and a locomotive. One pilot was lost flak (POW). The 61st attacked a train near Siegberg and lost another pilot to flak (KIA) from a nearby airdrome. Two other P-47s were hit by flak but both managed to limp to friendly territory making successful belly landings in France. The 62nd moved to Wetzlar and Grozenlinden Airdromes where they claimed six destroyed and three damaged. Capt. Herman King destroyed three and half aircraft.

Lt.Col. David Schilling led a late afternoon mission of 29 P-47s to Gelnhausen Airdrome and was supplemented by eight P-47s of the 61st to provide top cover. When they reached Gelnhausen there were about 50 parked, mostly single engine aircraft. Schilling reported the following in his combat report:

"I was leading the 63rd Squadron and when we reached Gelnhausen, Germany, airdrome, I told my Red and Blue Flights to orbit the field while I took my flight across the field to draw out any flak that might be around. On our first pass we came across the field from east to west along the south side of the airdrome. My number two man (2Lt. Charles Rotzler-ed.) and I were the only ones to fire on this pass, silencing flak positions on the west side of the field on the way in. I also fired at two FW-190s located near the southeast corner of the field and raked my fire through a blister hanger near the center of the south side. Lt. Rotzler, my wingman, also strafed the entire length of the field, damaging some FW-190s which were lined up just in front of the hanger on the west side of the airdrome. The flight then dropped to the deck and pulled up about two miles from the field.

The flight's second pass was made in the same direction over the southern hanger line. Lt. Rotzler destroyed a FW-190 camouflaged under a tree, and Lt. Albright (Edward-ed.) blew up a Ju-52 in flames in the southeast corner.

The third and fourth passes were made the same as the second. This time I destroyed an FW-190 east of the large hanger near the southwest side. Lt. Rotzler destroyed an FW-190 and Lt. Daniel (Robert-ed.) destroyed an FW-190 in the same area.

I then called in that the flights should change their direction attack due to the smoke and the availability of the target and come

Gelnhausen Airdrome near Frankfurt was attacked on 5 September 1944 by the 56th Fighter Group and the 62nd and 63rd Fighter Squadrons claimed 47 destroyed/16 damaged on the ground. (USAF)

in from the south to the north on the west side of the field. Three passes were made in this direction by my flight.

On my sixth pass I saw two planes in a hanger near the southwest corner of the south side of the field and concentrated on them. Lt. Albright spotted another one inside the hanger and destroyed it. The hanger burst into flames from my attack and burned to the ground, destroying everything in it. Lt. Rotzler destroyed a FW-190 in the southwest corner on his fifth pass. On his sixth pass he suspected flak firing from the hanger on the west side of the field. Raking his fire down the entire length of the building, he scored many hits on the planes inside. On his seventh pass Lt. Rotzler destroyed what he believed to be a Me-109 on the north side of the field."

As the 63rd left Gelnhausen Schilling spotted a FW-190 flying along the Rhine and called for one of his pilots to make an attack as he was out of ammo. Lt. Eugene Timothy hit the 190 and forced the enemy pilot to bail out. For the mission the squadron claimed 16 destroyed and four damaged. Both Rotzler and Schilling were credited with five destroyed and two damaged for the mission.

The 62nd Squadron attacked Gelnhausen and had even better results destroying 29 and damaging 16. Top-scorers for the 62nd were Capt. Robert Keen with six FW-190s, Capt. Michael Quirk and Lt. Darrell McMahan with four FW-190s each. The 61st Squadron came down and damaged five more of the aircraft that were left on the field. There were four 56th Fighter Group aircraft hit and downed but all four pilots returned to the group within days.

The 8th Air Force scored well that day claiming 119-82 on the ground and 27-1-2 in the air. The 55th Fighter Group claimed 13 destroyed and 19 damaged during attacks on Boblingen and Echterdingn airdromes in the Stuggart area. The 479th claimed 45 destroyed and 20 damaged primarily during attacks on Bad Nauheim and Ettinghausen. The 434th Squadron had a good day at Ettinghausen with Capt. J.M. Hollingsworth claiming six ground victories (four Me-410s and two Do-217s) and Lt. T.C. Olson with five (four Do-217s and a Me-110). The 8th lost seven KIAs, four POWs and one MIA for the day (nine by flak).

Right: The object of the USAAF fighter-bomber campaign from 15 September to 15 December 1944 was to cut German supply and transport lines supplying the West Wall defenses and German frontier. Despite the abundance of targets the German rail system offered the Allies did not embark on a concerted interdiction agenda such as had been so successful in northern France. A twisted troop train demolished by 8th Air Force P-47 at Gisors, France. (USAF)

USAAF Fighter-Bomber Campaign Against the German Transport System (15 September-15 December 1944)

The object of the USAAF fighter-bomber campaign from 15 September to 15 December 1944 was to cut German supply and transport lines supplying the West Wall defenses and German frontier by attacking railway marshaling yards and stations, tracks and bridges. It was to provide close support to ground forces. Despite the abundance of targets the German rail system offered the Allies did not embark on a concerted interdiction agenda such as had been so successful in northern France. The British Air Ministry and Deputy Supreme Allied Commander, ACM Sir Arthur Tedder, urged a concentrated air campaign on the Reichsbahn in western Germany. But US Strategic Air Force commander, Lt.Gen. Carl Spaatz, was adamant that his bombers should pursue the "Oil Plan." Spaatz was backed by 8th Air Force HQ, SHAEF Intelligence and, most importantly, by Gen. Hap Arnold and AAF HQ in Washington. They believed the attacks against the smaller rail system in northern France had sidetracked the strategic air forces from the "Oil Plan." Tedder "complained that current air attacks on Germany constituted a rather patchwork effort and argued that the one factor common to the entire German war effort was the country's rail and water communications system. If the Allies directed the entire weight of their air power against this target in the western Reich, they would have a good chance to produce the collapse of the Nazis within a matter of weeks." (Craven & Cater, *Army Air Forces in World War II*, Vol.III, ibid.)

The decision was made by SHAEF at the end of October to pursue oil as the primary objective for the strategic air forces followed by transportation attacks. The Combined Strategic Targets Committee established nine transportation zones with marshaling yards designated as the principal target and repair installations and power centers as secondary targets. Medium bombers and fighter-bombers were to assist the heavy bombers in these attacks. On 5 December this plan was amended and the Transportation Plan was moved to third priority after the oil attacks and saturation bombing of the German front lines. As their part in the transportation attacks, during the first week in September the 9th Air Force developed a plan of attacks to cut rail lines. A month later the Rhine bridges were added to their target list as the Allies had expected to cross these bridges soon but were halted at the West Wall and needed to interdict German supplies.

The German rail system was the most complex and efficient in Europe. It included 119 major marshaling yards (43 large yards in the Ruhr area) and hundreds of medium yards capable of handling 2,000 or more railway cars and more hundreds of smaller yards. There was adequate rolling stock available as the Germans had earlier removed cars and locomotives from the rail systems of occupied countries. The German railway system was essential to sustain military operations and also to the continued function of German industry. It was understood that if rail services could not provide traffic for both, the military would get priority.

Having experienced the devastating effects of the Allied air campaign against the railway system in northern France, German commanders understood and feared the significant effects of a similar air campaign against the German rail system. The shortage of gasoline greatly curtailed movement by motor transport so the Germans were dependent upon the continued operation of the railroads. The Germans were conscious of the potential of the Allies to severely restrict German military operations and industrial output by destroying the rail system. They took precautions to counteract the potential damage to the rail system east of the Siegfried Line and Rhine which had largely been untouched. Repair units were reinforced, re-equipped and given the means to reach and repair damaged lines and facilities quickly and efficiently. In anticipation of attacks on the Rhine bridges the Germans reinforced their structure, added tracks to highway bridges and planked rail bridges for joint motorized and rail use, added ferries and pontoon bridges and pipelines to the river crossing system. Potent anti-aircraft defenses were placed at strategic crossings. The system was made more efficient by planning alternative routing around damaged areas and trans-loading of shipments. To a lesser extent than had been necessary in France, the Germans were able to substitute motor transport for trains as at this time there was sufficient fuel available. German strategists anticipated these delays in the planning of their military actions. These and other measures were sufficient to meet the Allied effort expended in damaging the system. The Allies decided not to make the German transportation system the top priority air target which, along with poor weather and a rapid, efficient repair program allowed the continual flow of German supplies and troops to the front and prevented Allied aircraft from repeatedly returning to take out rail targets and keep them out of action.

In Germany it was not possible to limit rail transport to military requirements, as it had been in France as the supply of raw materials and transport of finished products from the Saar and Ruhr industrial areas had to be considered. The military was given priority and deliveries to the battle area were sufficient to maintain optimal supply levels. Despite shortages, particularly of artillery ammunition and fuel, the Wehrmacht was able to sustain its defensive effort at a level that prevented the Allies from making continued rapid advances after it had overran its supply lines in its race across France in the previous summer and needed to stop and regroup. The American logistical problem allowed the Germans also to regroup and strengthen the West Wall defenses. The ability of the Germans to move the volume of infantry, equipment and supplies in preparation for their Ardennes counter-offensive demonstrates that the tactical air offensive against the German transport system was only minimally effective. German records of carloads of supplies shipped to the Panzer Armies assembling for the counter-offensive between 1 September and the end of December show that of 9,649 carloads totaling 144,735 tons only 62 carloads were destroyed by air attack. The air attacks on rail targets both on the strategic and tactical level was generally periodic and without systematic planning. Had the effort been more coordinated and concentrated and reconnaissance more effective and accurate the build up for the Ardennes counter-offensive could have been reduced and the attack itself prevented and the Allied drive into Germany would have begun much sooner.

Both the 422nd and 425th NFS were flew some night intruder missions but were not effective due the lack of air/ground radar. French civilians repair the asphalt on a 425th Night Fighter Squadron Coulommiers in France in September 1944. (USAF)

Role of USAAF Nightfighters in the Interdiction Role

The 422nd Night Fighter Squadron had arrived at Charmy Down, England in early March 1944 with trained pilots but without any aircraft. Their P-61 Black Widows would not begin to arrive until 23 May and the lack of an operational strength of 12 and additional training prevented the 422nd from participating in the D-Day landings. During this period a belated controversy arose comparing the Black Widow's performance to that of the Mosquito, further delaying its entry into combat. In a fly off between the two aircraft on 5 July, the P-61 demonstrated that it was superior in speed, turn and rate of climb. On 16 July the P-61 entered combat in "Anti-diver" sorties against the V-1 Buzz Bomb. The 425th NFS arrived at Charmy Down on 26 May and received its first P-61 on 15 June and would not have enough aircraft to become operational until the end of July.

The European Black Widows were equipped with four 20mm M-2 cannons located in the belly (fed by a type AN-M1 Chatellerault power feeds that were charged on the ground). The cannons could be provided with 800 rounds but 600 rounds was the normal load. The cannons fired forward through a horizontal range of 1/4 degree from dead ahead and a vertical range of +1/4 degree and a –1 degree from the horizontal that made both a converging and diverging line of fire. The standard factory dorsal turret, containing four .50 caliber machine guns was removed in the ETO.

The Luftwaffe was sending Ju-87s, 88s and 188s night intruders to harass American troops and important material concentrations and two night fighter squadrons were sent to France. The 422nd was posted to Maupertus (A-15) in France on 25 July to coordinate with First Army and the 425th to Vannes, France (A-33) on 18 August to aid the Third Army that was attempting to clear the Brittany Peninsula. Their missions from these Continental bases were primarily against these Luftwaffe aircraft and the 422nd's 1Lt. Raymond Anderson and his radar operator (R/O) John Morris were finally credited with the first ETO aerial victory, a Ju-88, on the night of 7/8 August.

The 425th was stationed on the Brittany Peninsula between the ports of St. Nazaire and Lorient that the Third Army had surrounded, trapping several German divisions in each. Just as they arrived, the Germans broke out of the two ports and attempted to link up and drive east. HQ urgently requested the 425th to provide air support but had not established radio communications so Capt. Leon Lewis, CO of the squadron declined. After some urging, Lewis sent up his P-61s in a maximum daylight ground support mission. They attacked an armored column and broke it up with each aircraft flying two passes. The squadron lost its first aircraft and pilot. When Lewis finally set up radio communications he found that he had been relieved of his command for his refusal to fly the requested mission! He was reinstated the next day after discussing the circumstances of his refusal to fly the mission.

As the Allied Armies advanced the NFS were reassigned to support various armies. The 422nd was initially assigned to the IX TAC on 12 March 1944, then to the 71st Fighter Wing on 4 May 1944 and back to the IX TAC, 70th Fighter Wing on 7 October for the remainder of the war. The 425th was shuffled around, starting with the 9th Air Force on 23 May 1944, then to the IX Air Defense Command on 10 June, to the 71st Fighter Wing on 20 June, then back to the IX Air Defense Command on 6 August and then to the XIX TAC, 100th Fighter Wing on 7 October for the duration. The 425th conducted a much larger number of interdiction missions compared to the 422nd.

The 425th War Diary reports a nighttime train-busting mission near Berlin by Capt. Earl Bierer and his R/O, 2Lt. James Lathrop. In the moonlight Lathrop saw a train and dove on it strafing it with their belly-mounted four cannon. The locomotive was hit and dragged the cars it was pulling off the tracks into a burning pile. They continued their patrol and soon spotted two trains coming towards each other on parallel tracks. Bierer tried to judge where the trains would meet so he could get both on one run. Flying through flak he hit the firing switch and hit the engine of one and derailed the other.

The two NFS were always short on aircraft. The 422nd received only one replacement aircraft in its first five months of operations. During late 1944, the lack of spare parts for its SCR-720 radar and the poor weather grounded the P-61s. The 422nd only had an average of four aircraft available for daily operations. November 1944 had 28 of 30 days of bad weather and it continued into December. This period of time was particularly vital as the Germans were building up their forces for their Ardennes attack to start in mid-December. When the German offensive began, low clouds characterized the winter days but the nights were clear. The Germans sent out nighttime intruders that had to be intercepted by the diminished P-61 squadrons and their interdiction of the advancing enemy ground forces took a backseat and the Germans were able to move at night virtually unimpeded. A few German columns were detected and attacked by the A-20s and P-61s of the 422nd and 425th squadrons. The Germans were so desperate to get supplies through that they often used their headlights at night to gain speed. The Germans gambled between being seen by the rare Allied nightfighter and their need for getting the critical supplies through. From 16-27

December the 425th claimed five enemy aircraft shot down in combat, three locomotives, 16 railway cars and 598 trucks destroyed. For December, the 422nd claimed 16 aircraft destroyed, one probably destroyed and two damaged in the air, three locomotives destroyed/one damaged, 57 railway cars damaged, seven motor transports damaged and six factories damaged. The 422nd was awarded the Presidential Unit Citation for its efforts in destroying five enemy aircraft on the nights of the 16/17 and 27/28 December. The Citation went on:

"In addition to their normal role of intercepting and destroying enemy aircraft the 422nd NFS attacked marshaling yards, road and rail networks, motor transport and locomotives on intruder missions thereby effectively continuing the air effort to isolate the battlefield to cover a full 24 hours each day."

The 422nd was operating with as few as four serviceable aircraft per night and some aircraft went out on two, three or even four sorties. The 422nd lost five aircraft (three P-61s and two A-20s) during the Ardennes Campaign due to bad weather. These missions could been more productive and losses could have probably could have been prevented if the aircraft would have been fitted with auxiliary fuel tanks to give the lost aircraft additional range to find the enemy and then their way back to base.

After the Battle of the Bulge was won, Allied forces prepared to move into Germany in February. The 425th's P-61s and A-20s took part in the air missions to knock out the German transportation system. Of 117 sorties, 51 were intruder missions using 500lb. GP bombs (22 tons), 5-inch HVAR rockets (84) and 165-gallon napalm tanks (48). Because of the darkness the total results were unknown but the squadron claimed 30 locomotives and over 100 rail cars either destroyed or damaged and a similar total against motor transport.

As the Allied troops were moving rapidly into Germany and their exact positions were not known, the nightfighter squadron saw little activity and were restricted from flying into "forbidden zones."

The wartime totals for the 422nd NSF were:

Sorties flown:	1,576
Bombs dropped (tons)	147
Aircraft claimed (air):	43-5-5
V-1s destroyed	5
Locomotives destroyed/damaged:	14-36
Railcars destroyed/damaged:	41-435
Motor Transport destroyed/damaged:	14-434
Factories destroyed/damaged:	11-29

Note: It appears that the damage totals were high as the sorties were carried out at night preventing accurate claims that would be credited as damaged.

Moselle River (7-12 September 1944)

The Third Army advanced rapidly across eastern France in August 1944, capturing Verdun on 1 September. It was ordered to attack east to acquire a bridgehead over the Moselle River and then capture the city of Metz. The attack began at 0800 on 7 September against light resistance. The next day the bridgehead was forced and secured. Air support helped neutralize German small arms, machine gun and mortar fire which jeopardized the crossing. A heavy German counter-attack was repulsed inflicting heavy casualties. Expansion of the bridgehead was met with heavy resistance and frequent local German counter-attacks intended to push the American troops back over the Moselle. During this time the XIX TAC flew armed recce and provided column cover along the front. Fighter-bombers on column cover operated directly with ground control and repeatedly attacked German Panzers, gun positions, and troops. Armed recce sorties, operated ahead of and to the flanks of the bridgehead, destroying the reinforcements, reserves, armor and supplies used in the German counter-attacks.

By 12 September, the bridgehead maintenance and consolidation was in its final stages. Fighter-bombers bombed gun positions and strafed infantry and tanks moving between towns and to the

P-61s of the 422nd and 414th NFS during the Battle of the Bulge taxiing from their base at Florennes (A-78) Belgium. (USAF)

front. Following the bombing attacks the strafing of German gun positions, artillery observation posts and fortifications obtained good results. A 5th Infantry Division report stated:

"Air (fighter-bombers) played an important part in enabling the division to hold the bridgehead and attack and expand it. During the first few days after the crossing by the 10th Infantry, the air provided ample cover and scattered enemy personnel and equipment when the enemy was forming up to counter-attack. The cooperation was excellent and in one case support was as close as 200 yards from our front lines. Close support of ground troops was provided without pilots being briefed prior to takeoff, targets being indicated by coordinates or colored smoke, using the communications of the air support party."

Nancy (9-15 September 1944)

The XII Corps was moving east to take the city of Nancy but the Foret de Haye, a densely wooded and heavily fortified area to the west blocked its capture. The Foret was in an easily defensible hilly area comprised of well-organized strong points supported by armor and recently reinforced troops. A network of strongly defended roads and extensive belts of minefields connected these strong points.

During the period of the attack, 9-15 September fighter-bombers close support sorties and planned missions were unable to destroy or neutralize individual enemy positions due to the density of the woods. The need for IX Bomber Command heavy and medium bombers became clear with many aircraft participating in the dropping of 100lb. and 500lb.GP bombs and 100lb. fragmentation bombs that reduced fortified positions and destroyed troop concentrations through the total weight of the attack. But XIX TAC fighter-bombers provided Armed Column Cover and Armed Recce missions. Fighter-bombers did play an important role maintaining air superiority and were persistent in their attacks on tanks and armored vehicles, motor and rail transport and prevented troop reinforcement to make good heavy losses. In a notable attack XIX fighter-bombers strafing 15 tanks, stopping their advance and destroying or damaging all.

On 14 September, the Germans withdrew from their positions in the forest and at noon on the next day, the lead elements of the XII Corps entered the city. The victory was credited to the smooth functioning of ground forces, medium and heavy bombers and fighter-bombers.

Activation of the XXIX TAC (14 September 1944)

In September the US Ninth Army moved to the front from the Brittany Peninsula and to support this army its own tactical air command, the XXIX TAC was activated on 14 September at Vermand, France with Brig.Gen. Richard Nugent as its commander. The HQ and HQ Squadrons were derived from the 84th and 30rd Fighter Wings that were originally attached to the IX TAC for organization, training and operations. The XXIX TAC was assigned the 36th, 366th and 37rd Fighter Groups when it opened its operational HQ at Arlon on 1 October and was joined by the US Ninth Army HQ at Arlon on

First TAF commander Maj.Gen. Ralph Royce (left) meets with his superiors, commander of the USSTAF (center), Maj.Gen. Hugh Knerr, commander of the USSTAF Engineering Command and Ninth Air Force head Lt.Gen. Hoyt Vandenberg (standing). (USAF)

Left: In September the US Ninth Army moved to the front from the Brittany Peninsula and to support this army its own tactical air command, the XXIX TAC was activated on 14 September at Vermand, France with Brig.Gen. Richard Nugent as its commander. Quesada is pictured with Nugent. (USAF)

6 October. On 22 October the XXIX TAC and Ninth Army were moved to the extreme north flank of the US front at Maastricht, Holland. On that day the 366th Fighter Group was returned to the IX TAC and the 48th and 404th Fighter Groups were assigned to the XXIX TAC.

Formation of the First TAF (P) (September-November1944)

The US Seventh Army was positioned at the southern end of the American flank and began to receive direct support from the XII TAC that had accompanied it from the Mediterranean. At the end of September, the 9th Air Force assumed direct operational control and in October administrative control of XII TAC units. On 20 October, only 13 days after it had been proposed, General Order 81 established the First TACAF (P) that was the newest and last ETO TAC. The Seventh Army and the French First Army that was operating with it were given their own TAC made up of XII TAC, French First Air Force and some Ninth Air Force units. This force was designated the First Tactical Air Force (Provisional) and became operational in November as a separate command under the USSTAF and Spaatz. The 50th and 371st Fighter Groups were assigned from the XII TAC on 1 November and the 358th Fighter Group on 15 November. Maj.Gen. Ralph Royce, former Deputy Commander of the AEAF, was named the first CG. The 1st TAF(P) flew its first mission on 1 November 1944 when its P-47s bombed and strafed the Breisach railroad bridge and Neustadt marshaling yards.

Tactical Air Force Assignments:

TAC and 1st TAF UNIT ASSIGNMENTS

XI TAC			
70FW	XIX TAC	XXIX TAC	1st TACAF
100FW	100 FW	84 & 303FW	
365FG	354FG	36FG	50FG
366FG	358FG*	48FG	324FG@
367FG	362FG	373FG	371FG
368FG	405FG	404FG	415NFS@
370FG	406FG		
474FG	425NFS		
422NFS			
67TRG	10PRG	363TRG	PRG
107TRS	12TRS	160TRS	111TRS@
109TRS	15TRS	161TRS	162TRS
30PRS	31PRS	33PRS	34PRS
	155PSN		

* to 1st TAF(P) on 15 Nov 1944

@ units from 12AF

Note: 1945 9AF composition was: 1945 1st TACAF composition was:

43% fighter/fighter bombers 50% fighter/fighter bombers

43% light/medium bombers 29% light/medium bombers

2% night fighters 4% night fighters

12% recon a/c 17% recon a/c

32

West Wall Operations
15 September - 15 December 1944

USAAF Tactical Air Commands 16 September 1944
AEAF (Allied Expeditionary Air Force)
US 8 Air Force
US 9 Air Force
IX TAC
XIX TAC
XXIX TAC
US XII TAC

American tactical air forces had 1,819 fighters and 48 night fighters operational and the RAF 723 fighters and 180 night fighters against approximately 300 German fighters and no night fighters that had been concentrated against the British night bombing campaign.

Comparative Air Strengths
(15 September 1944)

Aircraft	**USAAF**		**RAF**		**GAF**	
	Assigned	**Operational**	**Assigned**	**Operational**	**Assigned**	**Operational**
Bombers*	3,674	2,873	2,038	1,657	161	106
Fighters	2,679	1,819	903	723	392	295
Night Fighters	48	482	28	180	—	—
Recce	526	516	238	157	73	44

* Includes heavy, medium and light bombers

West Wall (Siegfried Line) concrete and steel fortifications, minefields, interconnecting pillboxes, trenches and tank traps and the ubiquitous Dragons Teeth. (US Army)

In September 1944 both American ground and air forces felt the shortage of gasoline. The shortage became so critical that the 302nd Air Transport Wing, created in July 1944 carried emergency 9th Air Force fuel supplies by C-47 in Jerry cans. (USAF)

Siegfried Line (September-October 1944)

After the COBRA breakthrough the First Army raced across Northern France and Belgium until it reached the Siegfried Line, the vaunted West Wall, in the Aachen area and the Third Army was halted at the Moselle River. Here these Armies were forced to stop to regroup and resupply as they had outrun its supply capabilities. This break in the rapid advance gave the Germans time to occupy, supply and further reinforce their West Wall defenses. In July only parts of three German armies were stationed in this very strong defensive position but by fall there were six armies of a size matching the four Anglo-American armies. FM Gerd von Rundstedt had replaced FM Walter Model as head of the German Army Groups B and G on 5 September. Many of the units were understrength and there were 10,000 Volksgrenadier personnel comprised of hospital returnees, teenagers, converted Luftwaffe, Kriegsmarine and industrial personnel.

The same supply shortages hampered the American air forces. In September, the nine fighter-bomber groups reported that they had inadequate fuel and ordnance supplies. Five groups had shortages that caused them to be unable to operate on eleven different days. The 365th Fighter Group had no aviation fuel available on four days in September. Once resupplied the American armies captured the cities of Aachen and Metz and attacked and reduced the Siegfried Line and Hurtgen Forest. These bloody battles placed the First and Ninth Armies in position to drive to the Rhine River where they again were halted by German defenses.

The Germans mounted a stiff resistance along the West Wall and the progress of the First Army was slow and costly. IX TAC close air support was a modification of the system used in the Normandy Beachhead area, with fighter-bombers attacking specific vital enemy positions very close to the front and making the use of colored smoke for marking necessary identification. At one-hour intervals, fighter-bomber squadrons were to contact either Corps TALO or Division TALO for assignment of specific close support targets along the front before continuing on an armed recce mission behind the lines. The fighter-bombers hit their targets with sufficient accuracy often neutralizing or destroying German defensive positions hindering the offensive. However, the effect of the blaze bombs (napalm) did not have the expected effects on the pillboxes and fortifications. The area between the West Wall and the Rhine was effectively isolated by the destruction and interdiction of German rail, road, supply and communications lines. The major effect of the fighter-bomber force in the Siegfried attack was its maintenance of air superiority and the armed recce missions behind the lines. They were often hampered in their objective by the shortened daylight hours of late fall and bad weather.

The 4th Armored Division attacked east from Nancy on 24 September and was counterattacked in the early morning northwest of Chateau Salins. At 0918 two Squadrons of the 405th Fighter Group at St. Dizier (A-64) was called in despite rain and low ceiling. Immediately after takeoff the P-47s had to go on instruments and were vectored to the target by MEW controllers. Twelve P-47s of the 509th Squadron under Capt. Thomas Collins and another 12 Thunderbolts of the 510th under 1Lt. Edward Ziegewald arrived at the target. It was socked in at 8/10th's cloud down to 1,800 feet with poor visibility in the overcast at 800 feet. Eight of the fighter-bombers carried two 500lb. bombs and four were designated to fly escort. The 509th dove through intense flak and found Patton's Shermans, low on fuel and ammunition, under attack by a superior force of German Panzers. The Thunderbolt's timely arrival broke the brunt of the German attack. Meanwhile, the 510th could not locate the tank battle but came upon a motorized column of over 100 trucks and armored vehicles that they bombed and strafed with devastating effect. After the attack the pilots needed to return safely back to base through the overcast. At their briefing they had been instructed to fly west and bail out over friendly territory if they could not find their base. After flying until their fuel was almost expended a sharp-eyed pilot saw a field through a break in the clouds and the two squadrons landed at Rouvres, France (A-82). Later that day in the continued bad weather, Maj. T.A. Bohr led the 511th Squadron against a fortified position blocking Patton's advance. Through intense light AA fire the fort and adjacent buildings were put out of action. The 405th, "Thunder Monsters," were awarded the DUC for the action.

Commanding General Georg Keppler of the I SS Panzer Corps reported the following on his Corp's retreat from Falaise to Aachen, from mid-August to mid–October 1944: "Owing to the absolute superiority of the enemy with regard to material and our own lack of anti-aircraft weapons and support from our own air force, the effect of air raids of the Allies was immense. As all movement (during the day) was almost impossible the combat activity was considerably impeded by the air force of the Allies; the bringing up of reserves, supply, etc., was very delayed, particularly as the roads were overcrowded during the night. The losses in personnel and material caused by the air activity of the Allies were heavy. The attacks of the Allies on the ground were not much feared since, generally, they were carried out very cautiously, hesitantly and without vigor. It often occurred that an Allied attack stopped when a few of their tanks had been knocked out and it was not continued until considerable reserves and renewed air support had been procured." (Gen, Georg Keppler, *I SS Panzer Corps: Falaise to the*

Vicinity of Aachen, US Army, Europe, Historical Division Foreign Military Studies, Karlsruhe, no date.)

Bill Colgan of the 79th Fighter Group described his reaction on flying into Germany for the first time (*Fighter-Bomber Pilot*, ibid.):

"I had a definite feeling as we crossed the border flying into Germany itself. Now we were hitting the enemy in his homeland instead of battling him in countries he had occupied. I guess I was quite anxious for a first look at Germany. I'm not sure what I expected to see-perhaps some sort of tremendous fortress of a country or countryside. What I did see-in addition to targets-was some picturesque towns and villages, and very pretty green countryside on the fringes of the Black Forest."

During the month of September the IX TAC flew 307 missions of 9,708 sorties dropping 1,993 tons of bombs, claiming 70-11-33 Luftwaffe aircraft in the air and 24-10 on the ground. The XIX TAC flew 7,791 sorties dropping 2,015 tons of bombs and claiming 32-0-5 Luftwaffe aircraft in the air and 34-30 on the ground. They also registered the destruction of 2,122 trucks, 196 armored vehicles, 276 locomotives and 892 railway cars.

Aachen (12 September-21 October 1944)

The Germans had planned to use Aachen as an essential part of the Siegfried Line defense as a breech there would give the Allies access to the Rhine Plain to the east. With a population of 165,700 the city was the first major obstacle on the German border. The city defenses consisted of inner and outer rings of mostly concrete construction manned by experienced troops. The options were to encircle and by-pass the city or attack and capture it as part of the combined effort to penetrate the German West Wall. The decision was to attack. The VII Corps was to surround the city from the west, south and east while XIX Corps was to push down from the northwest to cut off any reinforcing German troops. Once these US troops were in place, an ultimatum to surrender was to be issued threatening to destroy the city.

The victory at Aachen was due to the American superiority on the ground in men and materials applying established attack doctrine. The most beneficial effects of TAC air power in the battle were the interdiction and armed recce missions to isolate the battlefield. No air strike was directly responsible for an infantry advance and only infrequently did a fighter-bomber knock out a bunker or pillbox. These air factors allowed the ground forces to achieve victory only in somewhat less time with only a minimal reduction in casualties and loss of material. (USAF)

The combined ground-air attack began during the second week of September. For the first week Lawton Collins' forces hammered the fortresses around Aachen, advancing only three to five miles and suffering heavy casualties. The IX TAC had been escorting medium bombers against Rhine River bridges for ten days when Hodges asked Vandenberg and Quesada for close air support. IX TAC was to cooperate with the First Army to conduct an agenda of armed reconnaissance to isolate the battlefield. Squadrons were to verify with 1st Infantry (VII Corps) and 30th Infantry (XIX Corps) TALOs before flying into the designated-armed recce areas and then attack targets specified by TALOs. Fighter-bombers provided close support attacking centers of resistance, and key targets such as gun emplacements, small-fortified positions and road junctions. Five fighter-bomber groups were assigned. The 366th and 368th were assigned to armor column cover and the 48th, 50th and 367th were to fly close support against targets requested by the infantry. On the 22nd, Col. Harold Holt of the 366th Fighter Group, assigned to the Third Armored Division, flew rotating flights of six P-47s over the tank columns. But unlike COBRA in July, strong German defenses on each flank slowed the advance of the tanks. The pillboxes and gun emplacements withstood the 500lb. bombs but as in the past no new air strategy was planned and these targets were continually and mostly ineffectually battered. From 25 September to 7 October the German Seventh Army had six divisions totaling 50,000 troops defending the city to the death.

Hodges ordered the XIX Corps to encircle Aachen from the north and west and the VII Corps to close the ring from the east and south. Two additional fighter-bomber groups were assigned and on 7 October the 1st and 30th Infantry Divisions attacked, hoping to join, surrounding the city. Two air plans were considered, one threatening an 'all-out" air attack to destroy the city by heavy, medium and fighter-bombers. However, the this plan was not viable as the air forces required for an attack were unavailable for a saturation attack on such widely spaced defenses. The attack would have had a minimal effect and possibly could have created another "Stalingrad rubble defense." Instead, a plan threatening a combined artillery-air attack, coordinated with armor and infantry attack was formed and presented to the Germans as an ultimatum. The Germans rejected the ultimatum and the battle escalated until the inner defenses were penetrated and vicious street fighting took place. Close air support missions were called by attacking ground units on the city's many pillboxes and fortified buildings. From the 2nd to 21st October 13 of the 20 days saw at least half of the IX TAC daily missions comprised of ground support. On the 12th and on the 15th the air-ground support ratios were 30 of 38 and 18 of 24 respectively. These missions were usually flown at squadron strength (12 fighter-bombers) although entire groups flew on occasion. From 8-18 October, 525 fighter-bombers flew over 5,000 sorties dropping

2,000 tons of GP and fragmentation bombs. If there were no targets immediately available or unused bombs on hand, squadrons and groups on armed recce were ordered to fly over the city and bomb designated areas. On 15 October, the 48th Fighter Group flew nine squadron strength missions against the town's gun positions and entrenched infantry. While on its way back to base the 492nd Squadron was called by the XIX Corps to halt a German counter-attack led by 30 Panzers. The squadron was low on fuel but made two effective low altitude strafing attacks through heavy ground fire. The German attack was beaten back and the squadron was awarded the DUC. On three different days, the strategic air forces also joined in by dropping 1,800 tons of bombs on the city's center. While this produced little in tactical results, it did add to the destruction and had a demoralizing effect on the defenders. The American infantry advance was slow and costly averaging under two thirds of a mile a day. Despite Quesada's request to reduce close air support for fear of accidental attacks on friendly troops, Vandenberg ordered the continued attacks. On the 16th, IX fighter-bombers strafed troops of the 120th Regiment causing 50 wounded and eight deaths. The incident did not receive the usual bad PR as that day the two American spearheads joined to surround the city, trapping 13,000 Germans.

On 21 October, the first major German city was surrendered, three-quarters destroyed and the majority of its defenders killed, wounded or captured. The victory that was estimated at its start to take 15 days and one US Corps and three divisions took 39 days, two corps and five divisions and marked an end to the slapdash German retreat across France. The TACs lost 79 aircraft and 58 pilots flying over 10,000 sorties and dropping 8,616 tons of bombs that were in short supply and could have been better used elsewhere. Fighter-bombers were taken from bomber escort duty and consequently the IX medium bomber losses to the Luftwaffe were twice the normal in October. The victory was due to the American superiority on the ground in men and materials applying established infantry attack doctrine. The most beneficial effects of TAC air power in the battle were the interdiction and armed recce missions to isolate the battlefield. No air strike was directly responsible for an infantry advance and only infrequently did a fighter-bomber knock out a bunker or pillbox. Neither, Armor Column Cover or the tanks below reproduced the results of July and early August, Medium bombers and fighter-bombers continued persistent and effective second and third priority missions while fighters maintained air superiority. These air factors allowed the ground forces to achieve victory only in somewhat less time with only a minimal reduction in casualties and loss of material.

Hurtgen Forest (September-December 1944)

The VII Corps attacked the Siegfried Line in the Hurtgen Forest, south of Aachen. Some of the most bloody and vicious battles of the European Theater took place in this heavily wooded area. The forest was dense with few open areas that severely limited close air support missions. Fighter-bomber interdiction and armed recce missions against troops and supplies coming into the area did have a perceptible, if indirect effect on the battle. On 2 December, the 370th Fighter Group was ordered to attack a heavily fortified strongpoint at Bergstein in conjunction with an attack by the Third Army. The P-47s flew through poor weather and heavy AA and small arms fire to set the village ablaze with a concentrated napalm bombing. The dazed Germans put up minimal resistance and the Third Army was able to clear that section of the forest with minimal losses. The 370th was awarded the DUC for its action that day.

After the breakout from the Forest the American VII Corps were forced to clear the villages to the east that the Germans vigorous defended. Fighter-bombers were called in and devastated one village after another, burning out each with incendiary attacks. But each time the Americans penetrated the German defense it was soon met with a stiff counter-attack.

Metz/Operation MADISON (17 September-20 November 1944)

The French city of Metz is situated on the east bank of the Moselle River and blocked the Allies from sweeping into the Saar Valley. A chain of hills and ridges is located on the western bank and domi-

A P-47 of the XIX TAC attacks Fort Driant, Metz. On 26 September, a combined ground-air attack was initiated against Fort Driant. Three missions of 35 sorties were flown dropping napalm tank and 1,000lb.GP bombs. After the air attack strong infantry patrols ran into heavy mortar and machine gun fire. The large-scale attack was called off, as it became evident that despite the power and accuracy of the fighter-bomber attack, its effect on a permanent concrete and steel fortification was ineffective. Note P-47 upper left at arrow. (USAF)

nates its western approaches and provides a geographical barrier to attacks from the southwest, west and northwest. The available approach corridors, the north and south, were under observation from the high ridges running along the east bank. The city had been a fortress from Roman times and the French had improved the defenses in modern times. The Germans had integrated an inner and outer band of permanent forts with field fortifications sited on high ground and arranged to be mutually and individually supporting. Covering fire protected the approaches and the recently reinforced Fortress was considered to be impregnable to direct attack. The troops defending the Fortress were zealous SS and officer candidate personnel. The Germans in their training programs and exercises used the region and thus they were thoroughly familiar with the terrain and the problems of defending the area. The road and rail system in the area was satisfactory and heavily used to supply the garrisons of the city.

On 17 September 1944, the XX Corps attacked the city in force, with its 5th Infantry Division attacking from the south, the 90th Infantry Division from the west and the 7th Armored Division attacking the heights to the northwest. Two days later the attack had made little progress in the face of heavy mortar and artillery fire. It was decided to reduce the Fortress through a series of coordinated ground-air attacks on a series of limited objectives. Medium and heavy bombers supported the fighter-bombers but their attacks were only partially productive. On 26 September, a combined ground-air attack was initiated against Fort Driant. Three missions of 35 sorties were flown. The first squadron of 12 P-47s, eight armed with a napalm tank and four with two 1,000lb.GP bombs. Six bombs and six napalm tanks hit inside the fort and then it was strafed. Five minutes later the second squadron, armed with the same ordnance loading, put six GP bombs and all eight napalm tanks inside the fort causing reported direct hits and many fires. The third squadron dropped seven 1,000 pounders and seven napalm tanks. After the air attack, the 5th Infantry sent out strong patrols that ran into heavy mortar and machine gun fire. The large-scale attack was called off as it became evident that despite the power and accuracy of the fighter-bomber attack, its effect on a permanent concrete and steel fortification was ineffective. The 90th Infantry Division attacked Fort Jeanne D'Arc in conjunction with fighter-bomber attack. A forward ground controller reported that 21 1,000lb. bombs and 24 napalm tanks had hit the fort. But as the attackers approached the fort they were hit with heavy mortar and machine gun fire and forced to retreat.

Most of the missions flown were coordinated with a ground controller but pre-briefed targets were attacked. The Germans had placed a 231-ton 280mm railroad gun with a range of 31 miles in the railroad tunnel at Teterchen that was located about 20 miles northeast of Metz. The Germans would roll the gun out of the tun-

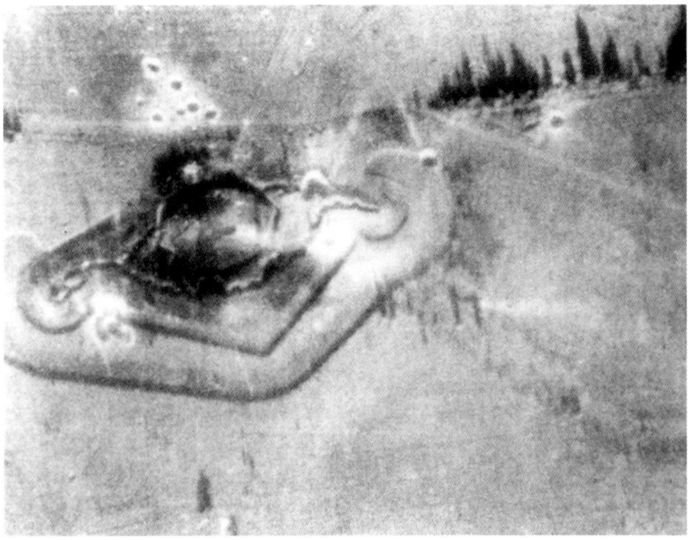

A strike photograph (left) of napalm bombs dropped on the Metz forts by 9th Air Force P-47s on 26 September 1944 and a post strike photo (above) of the damage. The Thunderbolts carried a mixed load of napalm and 1,000lb. bombs. (USAF)

nel at night and fire rounds at the Metz-Nancy area. One shell broke the windows of Patton's HQ in Nancy. The 359th Fighter Group was assigned to knock out the tunnel. Lt. Rae Preston led 11 Thunderbolts, which encountered bad weather and heavy flak on the way. The pilots had to take evasive action through the haze and there was an air collision that severed the tail of one P-47 that resulted in a KIA and had the other fighter barely able to return to base with a badly damaged prop. The squadron was vectored to the target by the ground controller and five fighters dropped ten bombs on the west-end of the tunnel one scoring a direct hit on the entrance. The bomb had skipped into the mouth of the tunnel and burst near the rear of the gun damaging its carriage and killing 12 men. The next night the Germans evacuated the gun to the east.

The German garrison skillfully defended Metz with a line of fortified villages and strong points stretching from Thionville ten miles north of Metz and to the Moselle River to the south. Very wet October weather all but stopped the American advance. By mid-October, XX Corps abandoned its direct assault on the forts and decided to encircle them. The XIX TAC Control Center was moved forward so bad weather operations could be conducted. The XIX fighter-bomber groups were based within 50 miles of the front but even with this new forward control could operate only operate one day out of two. The fighter-bombers no longer attacked the forts but bombed and strafed supply points, command posts, and the communication system around Metz. This shift in targets produced the best results as they decreased the amount of ammunition and supplies to the forts. The fighter-bombers also neutralized German troop concentrations that were forming for counter-attack and destroyed gun emplacements supporting the forts. It was the medium and heavy bombers that had the most destructive effect on the forts. However, the infantry did not follow up soon enough after their bombing to take advantage of the shock effect and reduced return fire to minimize their casualties. A salient continued to protrude west around Metz and a ground offensive, Operation MADISON, was scheduled for 8 November to strike the southern and northern flanks of the salient and surround the city and move on to the Rhine.

In the early days of November, the weather limited air operations. In preparation for the ground offensive from the 1st to the 7th about a 1,000 sorties were successfully flown against ordnance and supply dumps and Luftwaffe airfields destroying 31 aircraft on the ground. On the 2nd, 6th, and 7th the weather prevented all fighter-bombers operations. The XIX TAC was assigned to support the US Third Army in its attack against Metz forts and to open an advance northeast to the Rhine.

On 8 November fighter-bombers flew 471 sorties in support of the opening of MADISON. The XIX TAC flew 389 sorties destroying four enemy command posts, 34 buildings, nine trucks, 22 locomotives/12 railcars and one bridge. The 405th Fighter Group flew 80 sorties and destroyed the CP of the 17th SS Panzer Division. The attack killed several high-ranking officers, and 17th SS Panzer that was the German mobile reserve was unable to function at this critical juncture. During the bad weather the Germans built increased the number of AA batteries. The 405th Fighter Group lost 12 aircraft and 11 pilots in November and had 79 aircraft damaged by flak.

The next day medium and heavy bombers of the XIX TAC (162 medium bomber sorties), 8th Air Force (1,223 heavy bomber sorties) and the 9th Bomb Division (111 effective sorties of 514 dispatched due to bad weather) attacked targets in support of the attack. The bombers attacked primary and secondary targets in the Metz and Thionville areas by visual and radar. XIX TAC fighter-bombers were assigned planned low-altitude missions against nine enemy HQ and command posts and armed recce missions within the area of the ground attack. Eighth Air Force fighters were assigned to bomb and strafe airfields east of the Rhine. The bombing results were more disruptive than destructive. The bombing results were low as the forts did not sustain much damage but dazed the defenders with their intensity. The 312 fighter-bomber sorties in cooperation with the ground attack were more directly effective. They strafed and bombed German troops, armor, gun and AA positions with 61 tons of GP and fragmentation bombs and 34 napalm tanks. The XX Corps led by the 90th Infantry crossed the Seille River in three places and captured eight villages. The next day the Moselle River was crossed and eight more villages were captured. The final encircling attack calculated to reduce and trap the Metz garrison was underway. Despite very bad weather that curtailed air support the Metz forts were taken one by one. Five small forts to the east and south were captured on the 13th, and the Fifth Division took Fort Verdun on the 18th. The next day the 90th and 5th Infantry met, encircling the city and the remaining forts were reduced individually. The next day, the garrison, minus a few SS fanatics, surrendered the city. During the first weeks of December, the Third Army advanced against heavy opposition and by the middle of the month had captured almost all of the Saar region and most of its major cities.

From 10 November to 15 December the weather limited fighter-bomber operations. Twelve days were non-operational and 16 were only partially operational. On only eight days did sorties exceed 200 daily and for three days, 17 to 19 November, could 300 or more sorties be flown. On these three days attacks were concentrated on German road and rail systems. The fighter-bombers were very successful claiming 162 locomotives, 1,096 rail cars, 842 motor transport, 62 armored vehicles and 113 gun positions. The Patton-Weyland affiliation during the start of MADISON, then the continued interdiction of the transportation system when weather permitted and the continued air supremacy contributed to the Third Army's success at Metz. But again it was the foot soldier that had to take the Metz forts one after another and struggle without air support which was grounded by the weather day after day.

Lindre Dam (20 October 1944)

The Lindre Dam, located near the town of Dieuze in eastern France, held back the waters of the Etang de Lindre and the US Third Army's 35th Division needed to cross the Seille River in the area. The 1,200 foot long earth and masonry dam was to be breached beforehand so that the Germans could not blow the dam and flood the Americas as they were crossing the River and thus cutting off their lines of supplies and communications. Elaborate plans were made for the attack as 378th Fighter Squadron 362nd Fighter Group CO, Lt.Col. Joseph Laughlin, obtained photos, diagrams and specs on the dam.

It was felt that the main dam was too massive to breach and that the small sluice at the south end was vulnerable and hits on it would allow the water to drain. In the morning of 20 October, Laughlin led 378th and 379th Squadron P-47s armed with 1,000lb. bombs to the dam. They dove through heavy flak and scored nine hits and three near misses on it. As they left they observe a small flow of water running over the dam near the sluice. The 379th Fighter Squadron returned that afternoon and got a few more 1,000lb. bomb hits on the dam and near misses on the sluice. Although the damage did not appear to be significant the water was undercutting the dam's structure and would drain the lake in several days and not cause the massive flooding that would be brought about by a German demolition.

Night Fighter Operations (October-November 1944)

During October the 422nd (IX TAC) and 425th (XIX TAC) Night Fighter Squadron operated intruder missions along with their air defense missions. The two squadrons were, as they had been throughout the fall, acutely under strength as the average operational roster of each was about ten P-61s and a few war-weary A-20s. The 425th had meager success with 16 of its first 20 sorties making no claims. The other four sorties claimed only five locomotives, three motor vehicles, two factories, one railway station and a signal tower. The 422nd claimed two locomotives destroyed and eight damaged with 26 rail cars destroyed and 140 damaged for October.

355th Fighter Group Freelance (2 November 1944)

Maj. John Elder led 56 Mustangs of the 355th Fighter Group on a freelance support mission to the First and Second Air Division attacking Merseburg. The Group took off at 1012 and R/V'd west of Merseburg at 1216 and provided area support north of Merseburg and to the main bomber track. Just before reaching the target, the 354th and 357th Fighter Squadrons intercepted several Me-262s flying in from Berlin. Simultaneously the 358th Fighter Squadron came upon six Me-109s attacking a B-17 box at Lille near Merseburg destroying one Messerschmitt and damaging another. Two 354th Fighter Squadron pilots shot down a Me-109 apiece as 25 of them were forming up to attack a B-17 formation near Naumburg. The 357th lost the Luftwaffe jets as they broke for the deck but ran into a number of Me-109s and FW-190s and shot down five that were landing at an airdrome near Werngerode. Dropping to the deck they destroyed 25 more German aircraft in the air and on the ground. 1Lt. William Cullerton had shot down a FW-190 and Me-109 in the

The Lindre Dam near Dieuze was attacked by P-47s of the 362nd Fighter Group on 20 October 1944. The Thunderbolts attacked the vulnerable sluiceways of the dam with 1,000lb. bombs. The rushing white water can been seen on the upper edge of the dam. (USAF)

air and got six more on the ground while Elder got one on the air and five on the ground. Cullerton was the first 8th Air Force pilot to destroy eight aircraft in a day and scored the highest number of combined air and ground victories in a day. For a total of 33 enemy aircraft destroyed two pilots were lost in the attack, one bellied in and the other bailed out, both to become prisoners of war.

Operation QUEEN (16-29 November 1944)

After the battle for Aachen a meeting was called by 12th Army Group air-operations liaison officer, Colonel Sheffield Edwards to discuss tactical air power at Aachen. The air-liaison officers of corps, divisions and HQ questioned company and regimental officers along with TAC officers to identify successes and failures and incorporate them into a new system for the TACs. The conclusions were that the thick forests and fortifications restricted TAC efficiency and that TAC was only effective against a retreating enemy. Its effectiveness against dug in and fortified defenders was to remain an open question. At the TAC level, a number of changes were suggested. Group commanders wanted orders to be issued the night before assigned operations instead of at 0400 so that there would be more time for adequate briefings and squadron coordination. The airfields were thought to be too far from the front lines and new construction had not kept up with the rapid advance due to the time factor and the logistical shortage in base-building materials. Communications were always a problem and required constant adjustment and modification. On a command level, for ease of control wings were eliminated as the three IX TAC had only a few fighter groups as compared to the 18 under the IX TAC in July.

IX Fighter Command (1 November 1944):

IX TAC:
- 70th Fighter Wing: 365th, 366th, 367th. 368th, 370th, and 474th Fighter Groups
- plus 67th TRG and 422nd NFS

XIX TAC:
- 100th Fighter Wing: 354th, 358th, 362nd 405th and 406th Fighter Groups
- plus 10th PRG and 425th NFS

XXIX TAC:
- 84th Fighter Wing: 36th and 48th Fighter Groups
- 303rd Fighter Wing: 373rd and 404th Fighter Groups
- plus 363rd TRG

1st TAF:
- 50th and 371st Fighter Groups

Previously new airfield construction had taken a back seat to the supply of the ground armies that were short on food, fuel and ammunition. The advantage of new airfields nearer the front was offset by delays and shortages of supplies reaching them. Despite, these adjustments, air response time only decreased slightly from 74 minutes in September to 71 in October and 70 in November. Ground leaders were coming to realize that TAC was limited by the enemy defenses and terrain factors and could not be counted on for much more. Meanwhile the TAC airmen continued to make modifications while investigating new tactics and procedures. But, in retrospect and unrecognized by command and pilots, October 1944 saw the most efficient use of tactical air power thus far in the war for both the IX and XIX TACs. But in November ground and air officers returned to COBRA tactics to smash the Siegfried Line.

To prevent short bombings that had plagued COBRA and GOODWOOD an intricate marking plan was developed. Infantry units were to lay large, football field-size, red panels at one-mile intervals 1,500 feet behind the front lines while artillery batteries were to fire red burst shells to detonate at 5,000, 10,000 and 15,000 feet, creating a bomb line in the sky. Ninth Air Force Signals Section instituted special homing frequencies to aid heavy bomber approach and was granted temporary control over all ETO navigational aids.

The First Army/IX TAC and Ninth Army/XXIX TAC were to launch a coordinated attack toward Julich-Duren, cross the Roer River and break into the west German plains in the Cologne-Bonn area. To augment this plan, Operation QUEEN was framed as a cooperative effort of the strategic and tactical air forces and was to be the largest air-ground effort undertaken by the Allies to date. A thorough examination was made of the targets in the area of Eschweiler, Julich, Linnich and Duren. Like COBRA, QUEEN was devised to aid a ground offensive to penetrate a resolute German defense but unlike COBRA, there was to be no saturation bombing of the area. The large target area was divided into smaller, specific areas where photo recon and intelligence reports had identified the heaviest concentrations of enemy defenses. Single targets or target areas at Einsweiler and Linnich were then assigned to heavy, medium and fighter-bomber units of the 8th and 9th Air Forces (the RAF was assigned Julich and Duren). The initial date was to be the first day of good weather to support such a large operation but was to be no later than 16 November when the ground armies were to attack with or without air support.

Operation QUEEN commenced on 16 November, at 1115 hours, with approximately 1,200 8AF heavy bombers, 250 9th Air Force medium bombers and 300 9th Air Force fighter-bombers and 1,000 RAF bombers covered by 8th Air Force fighters (300 heavy bombers and 350 medium bombers subsequently aborted the mission due to poor weather). The air attack was a complete surprise and persisted during the shortened late autumn daylight hours dropping 10,000 tons of bombs before the infantry and armor jumped off. After the heavy and medium bombers finished their attacks (1113 to 1248 hours) the fighter-bombers of the IX and XXIX TAC continued to support the attack by covering the advance of the infantry divisions. At 1305 hours, fog and low ceilings allowed only 350 fighter-bomber sorties along the front. The First Army had three fighter groups provide cover and armed reconnaissance to the front of three infantry divisions. Three other fighter-bomber groups were assigned to special targets in front of the attack and after these attacks were to continue armed recce to the front and flanks of VII Corps. It was found that the strafing attacks were ineffective as they were not concentrated along the German front but were too far ranging behind the front line. Only ten of 2,809 aircraft were lost to combat and only one Luftwaffe fighter appeared to defend. The bombing results, both by the bombers and fighter-bombers was less accurate than expected due to smoke and haze but there was only one incident of short bombing. Although 10,000 tons of bombs dropped on a small area devastated towns like Julich, Enschweiler and Duren German casualties from air attack were very light with the heavily attacked German 47th Division sustaining only 3% casualties. The average German air casualty rate was 2%, as the Germans had built a large number of bomb shelters along the front. The withdrawal of American troops to protect them from short bombing had the effect in places of delaying their advance until after the psychological effects of bombings on the enemy were lost. The US infantry gained an average of three-fifths of a mile and the greatest gain was about a mile. The V and VIII Corps did not even attempt to move that first day.

On the 17th, the weather prevented any effective air support. The XXIX TAC flew 78 sorties and the IX TAC flew 129. The weather cleared on the 18th and 19th and 1,737 fighter-bomber sorties were flown by the two TACs in a continuous series of air-ground cooperation sorties against enemy troop concentrations, fortified villages and gun positions. From the 18th to 2rd, the IX TAC flew 1,215 sorties for the First Army that was still unable to gain substantial ground. Ground operations were restricted to limited attacks and the consolidation of objectives and beating off counter-attacks. It became apparent that QUEEN was another failure, as despite the extensive ground and air preparation, the ground attack, unlike COBRA, did not achieve a break out. The infantry met with determined and costly resistance that slowed its attack, giving the Germans time to regroup. The advances were less than three miles after a week of fierce battle and fell far short of the Rhine and had not even reached the Roer River. The pattern bombing of selected smaller areas within a larger area by heavy and medium bombers was too far forward to be exploited quickly by the attacking troops. It did not cause large numbers of enemy casualties and had minimal effect in reducing enemy resistance. It required two to three days to penetrate the German lines. The fighter-bombers were outstanding in their Armored Column Cover and close support roles after the first day. On the 18th the 48th Fighter Groups flew 24 four plane armored column cover relays and 25 more the next day. There were instances of successful interdiction missions. On the 18th the XIX TAC claimed 74 locomotives and 456 railcars. On the 19th the 405th and 367th Fighter Groups destroyed 25 locomotives in group strength missions. On the 20th, the XXIX TAC sent the 48th and 404th Fighter Groups on three major attacks on German tanks resulting in the breaking up of two strong German counter-attacks in the Bourheim area. On the last day of November, a squadron each from the 366th and 368th Fighter Groups was flying air-ground cooperation near Euskirchen. A train hauling German armor was spotted by 67th TAC R and reported to ground control. The 366th's Squadron destroyed eight tanks and a fuel car while the 368th's Squadron claimed ten to 12 tanks destroyed and many more damaged. No US aircraft were lost to combat, Luftwaffe opposition was non-existent and most importantly, there were no friendly fire accidents. However the IX TAC lost 45 aircraft and 39 pilots mostly to AA fire.

Von Rundstedt summarizes the effect of fighter-bomber interdiction during the period: "In the early static phase of the battle, the defense of the Siegfried Line from the end of September to mid-December, fighter-bomber efforts were decidedly unpleasant." (Bradley, *Effect of Air Power on Military Operations*, ibid.)

During November the TACs were credited with:

Target	**IX TAC**	**XIX TAC**	**XXIX TAC**
Aircraft in air	37-6-14	23-0-6	1-0-1
Aircraft on ground	1-0-2	50-1-18	0-0-0
Motor transport	131	95	31
Armored vehicles	57	79	19
Horse-drawn vehicles	47	145	?
Locomotives	43	275	25
Railway cars	136	957	197

QUEEN ended on 30 November with the two TACs and the 9th Bomb Division having flown 16,200 sorties and dropped 11,000 tons of GP and fragmentation bombs and hundreds of napalm tanks. But QUEEN was a failure with only a few villages captured and the front lines moved four to ten miles to the east. The Allies had anticipated the destruction of the German armies west of the Rhine but failed to do so in spite of the great outlay of men and materiel. First Army commander, Courtney Hodges, blamed the weather for reducing the scheduled number of fighter-bomber attacks and Quesada blamed the failure of the infantry to follow the air attack immediately with a determined large-scale attack. But both were wrong in their assessment. The aerial portion of QUEEN was generally successful in most aspects. To date no other close air operation had ever utilized so many aircraft or used so much ordnance that was so accurately aimed. Against similar defensive targets, more ordnance was expended in the first hour of QUEEN than was employed in the entire Meuse-Argonne offensive in World War I. Also, the Third Armored Division and the 104th Infantry Division reached the forward enemy lines much quicker than armor or infantry in COBRA. Fighter-bomber operations were again successful. Their close support attacks augmented artillery and armor against German strong points and armor and broke up the numerous counter-attacks launched by the Germans. Armed recce attacks delayed the movement of enemy reinforcements and supplies to the battlefront. Air superiority was again nearly complete as only 107 Luftwaffe aircraft were lost in November and ten for the first half of December. The American air forces lost 106 aircraft almost all to AA fire. Again the ground generals asked the air generals to dislodge a well-entrenched and determined enemy, now with his back to his border. QUEEN was another large-scale air attack failure due to its high-level leaders persistent dedication to strategic air power the USAAF. They continued not adhere to a clearly defined tactical air power doctrine and again this failure led to the improvised nature of the QUEEN air and ground plan and its subsequent failure. So, after QUEEN in late 1944, American air leaders began to realize that tactical air support had its limits and needed to be utilized with these limitations in mind.

Roer River (16-29 November 1944)

Because the US First and Ninth Armies failed to breakthrough into the Cologne area in Operation QUEEN, the goal of the attack was narrowed to reach the Roer River. The German defense in the heavily

As the cold weather arrived in late 1944 living and field conditions for pilots, ground crews and aircraft deteriorated. P-47Ds of the 354th Fighter Group sit in crude bulldozed earthen revetments on an ALG in France. (USAF)

populated area west of the river was a prepared perimeter of closely spaced, mutually supporting village strong points that protected a larger town. The defending German soldier was ordered to hold the villages and towns at all costs. The US ground offensive was hindered by long periods of rainy weather that limited TAC air support and thus became one of attrition, with infantry attacks supported by artillery reducing each village and then town.

After QUEEN, when the weather cleared, fighter-bombers played an important role and reverted to their previous agenda of attacking the road and rail systems, bridges and missions in support of infantry attacks that added to the weight of fire of the ground attack on strong points and reduced casualties. Unlike the Bocage hedgerows and the natural camouflage of the Saar-Moselle Triangle, the targets on the Roer were very apparent from the air: defended villages and towns and enemy reinforcements and counter attacks moving from rear areas. The fighter-bombers also attacked rail and road traffic in rear areas during daylight, decreasing the enemy's ability to get ammunition and other vital supplies to the defended villages and towns. The majority of fighter-bomber ground support attacks were against the numerous defended towns and villages in the way of the infantry advance. On 23 November, 19 missions totaling 209 sorties were flown by seven fighter-bomber groups of the IX TAC. The 365th Fighter Group flew four requested missions for the 104th Infantry Division, attacking three villages. Fires were started in the first village and heavily defended buildings were destroyed in the other two and in the third, armor was attacked. On the fifth mission, it jettisoned its bombs to chase 40 FW-190s. The fighter-bombers were joined by medium bombers in the support of the air-ground support missions. This concentration of air resources to the Roer River advance came at the time the Germans were building up their resources for the upcoming Ardennes Offensive to the south.

Life on the ALGs in the winter of 1944 was uncomfortable at best living in canvas tents with wooden floors and walkways. Note piled cord firewood and chimneys poking through apex of tent roof. (USAF)

First TAF personnel mop mud off the Hessian runway on a French airstrip. The tarpaper on a Hessian surfaced field was supposed to keep moisture from seeping through to the surface but once on the surface it only collected into large mud pools. (USAF)

Hundreds of Jerry cans being hand-emptied into a fuel bowser on a 362nd Fighter Group ALG in France. The cans were trucked in by IX TAC trucks from Normandy and emptied into the ALG bowser to make fueling there quicker. (USAF)

Sixth Army Group at the Rhine-Lost Opportunity? (Late November 1944)

On 24 November Eisenhower and Bradley visited the Allied southern front where they first visited Patton's Third Army that had come to a halt near Nancy. Later Lt.Gen Jacob Devers, CG of the Southern Group of Armies and Lt.Gen. Alexander Patch, CG of the Seventh Army, joined Eisenhower and Bradley. Patch's Seventh Army's VI Corps under Maj.Gen. Edward Brooks and XV Corps under Maj.Gen. Wade Haislip were about to move east and attack and seize bridgeheads over the Rhine and move into Germany. In the previous six weeks the Seventh Army had heavy fighting through the Vosges Mountains and across the Alsatian Plain to the banks of the Rhine. The XII TAC's fighter-bombers had focused on the area between Karlsruhe and Landau, the speyer-Mannheim-Darmstadt area, Strasbourg and the Muhlhouse-Colmar Pocket. By mid-December Patch's held a front of 165 miles along the Rhine across from the Saar Industrial Basin and Strasbourg. Eisenhower ordered Patch to abandon his proposed attack across the Rhine and to move north to assist Patton. Both men left the meeting extremely angry at each other's plans but, of course, Ike prevailed. Perhaps, if Eisenhower would not have played it safe and allowed Patch to cross the Rhine, this unexpected crossing could have moved north and enveloped the Ardennes area and eliminated the German Offensive there.

33

Ardennes/Bulge Operations
15 December 1944 - 7 February 1945

The German Build-up (Mid-November to Mid-December 1944)
Despite the complete surprise of the German attack, code-named WACHT am RHEIN, against the US First Army that was recuperating in the inactive Ardennes region from its dash across France there were indications that the Germans were rushing a build-up in the area. In late November to mid-December both air reconnaissance and ground intelligence had discovered subtle and not so subtle evidence of a build-up. Although weather was often dreadful in the first half of December, the recon missions that were flown disclosed increased road and rail activity west and west of the Rhine especially toward mid-month. The Germans had selected their assembly areas far to the north or south of the proposed breakthrough to disguise the point of attack.

When the Germans were ready to launch the attack there was a shortage of fuel, motor transport and ammunition for an operation of this magnitude. The shortages were due to several factors:

1) Destruction of supplies by air attacks inside Germany
2) Destruction of the Rhine bridges
3) Destruction of the rail lines east of the Rhine
4) Air attacks on the rail system that obligated the Germans to use M/T west of the Rhine
5) Restricting German transport to nighttime

From 1 to16 December the IX TAC and the medium bombers of the 9th Bombardment Division attacked the numerous towns and villages on the First Army's Front. The fighter-bombers bombed and strafed, mostly in squadron and group strength, the troops billeted in these towns and the ordnance and supplies stored there. Some towns like Zulpich (ten times), Euskirchen (nine) and Bergstein (six) were hit numerous times. During the time The XXIX TAC attacked the towns and villages in the Ninth Army's area. But despite the apparent intensity, this activity was no more than the normal reaction to the enemy by a superior number of aircraft in short periods of good weather.

For the Ardennes Offensive the Luftwaffe transferred 47 heavy and 51 medium and light flak batteries. Lt.Gen. Wolfgang Pickert commanded the heavy batteries that included 120 pieces of 88mm or more. Pickert who spent the war on the Russian front was to provide AA defense, anti-tank and artillery capability. Although Goering had promised Hitler 3,000 fighters to support the offensive, more responsible members of the Luftwaffe estimated that the actual air strength to be 1,700 with only about half operational. The Luftwaffe had assigned 23 Gruppen from Reich defense and three FW-190 Gruppen from Russia leaving only two fighter groups to defend the Reich. These Gruppen were dispersed over a 250-mile front extending from Rheine-Main to Oldenberg, making the coordination of operations difficult. So WACHT am RHEIN could not depend on the Luftwaffe to gain any fleeting control of the air. It would need surprise, poor weather and to be able to run over the initial weak opposition and then to move quickly to exploit the expected breakout.

US Air-Ground Command/Fall 1944. (Left to right): Lt.Generals Carl Spaatz, George Patton, and James Doolittle, Maj.Gen. Hoyt Vandenberg, Brig,Gen, O. P. Weyland. (US Army)

USAAF Tactical Air Commands: 16 December 1944

SHAEF

US 9th Air Force (Lt.Gen. Hoyt Vandenberg)
IX Tactical Air Command (Brig.Gen. Elwood Quesada)
XIX Tactical Air Command (Maj. Otto Weyland)
XXIX Tactical Air Command (Brig.Gen. Richard Nugent)
US First Tactical Air Force (Maj.Gen. Ralph Royce)

On 16 December 1944, the USAAF had 2,452 fighter aircraft (8 AF: 1,102; 9 AF: 988; 1 TAF: 362) and the RAF 1,582 available against an estimated 850 Luftwaffe fighters

Luftwaffe West: December 1944

Luftwaffenkommando West (Lt.Gen. Josef Schmidt)
II Jagdkorps (Maj.Gen. Dietrich Peltz)
III Jagddivision (Maj.Gen. Walter Grabmann)
(7 Geschwader/20 Gruppen)
Jagdabshnitt Mittelrhein (Oberst. Hannes Trubenbach)
(6 Geschwader/16 Gruppen)
III Flieger Division

Only 18 hours before the German attack, on 15 December, Eisenhower's G-3 briefed the air commanders and wrote off the Ardenne's area as having "nothing to report." The abject failure of American intelligence to decipher information on a German buildup and its shift by mid-December to the Ardennes area was a grand malfunction of many parties that were responsible for data interpretation. Basically there was no interface between air and ground intelligence to pass down and then interpret the air reconnaissance data.

The Attack (16 December 1944)

The German counter-offensive through the rugged Ardennes Forest began in the early morning of 16 December 1944 and came as a complete surprise to the Allies who were slow to react. Under the cover of darkness and bad weather the Germans deployed troops and materiel of the Fifth and Sixth Panzer Armies and the reconstituted Seventh Army to assembly areas near the jump off points. The Germans planned a rapid penetration along a sixty-mile front through the weakly held line of Hodge's First Army from Echternach in the south and Aachen in the north. The attack was to drive west in the Monchau-St. Vith/Bastogne area, then north to cut off American armies east of Leige, Brussels and Antwerp. Diversionary attacks were scheduled along the entire American front from Monchau to Luxembourg City. For the first time in the war the German High Command launched a major attack without having air superiority. To compensate for this lack of air superiority, the counter offensive was planned to take place during a period of predicted bad weather that would hinder both aerial reconnaissance on interference by USAAF tactical air forces.

The Germans had early success and over ran several US units as the attack moved west with American units retreating to the Dinant area. The German penetrations in the Monchau-Malmedy and south Luxembourg areas were contained, Bastogne was vigorously defended and held and St. Vith was held until a southerly defensive line was formed in the Malmedy-Stavelot-La Roche area in the north. This line along with defense and ensuing buildup at Bastogne forced the German attacks along the east-west road net.

American Air Reaction

The German offensive plans were correct in depending on poor weather as from 16 to 23 December as almost all medium bomber air operations were canceled. Fighter-bombers flew 2,818 sorties of all types during the period, a major proportion of which were counter-air missions as the Luftwaffe appeared in large numbers for the first time to support the offensive and distracted the Americans from their primary close support missions. On the 16th, the Luftwaffe flew 150 sorties and on the 17th, they flew 600-700 sorties and 450-500 on the 18th. Thereafter, the number fell to half due to weather and due to the loss of 200 aircraft that had been destroyed by US fighters and AA fire.

On the 17th and 18th, the IX TAC achieved some local successes by flying dangerous very low-level missions in poor visibility. As the Germans drove southwest from Moschau through the Lorshiem Gap the threat to Stavelot became grave. On the 17th Maj. John Motzenbecker of the 365th Fighter Group's 387th Squadron led 16 P-47s from Chievres at 1041 toward the Roer River south of

Maj. John Motzenbecker of the 365th Fighter Group (USAF)

Duren. Leaving his flight as top cover, Motzenbecker dropped below the clouds south of Monschau and discovered a large column of German tanks, half-tracks and transport on the main road heading toward the American lines. The column stretched for four and a half miles and many more vehicles crammed the side roads. While crossing the column Motzenbecker's P-47 was hit in the wing by flak. He returned to top cover and sent four flights of four aircraft to the deck against the enemy that began to quickly disperse off the roads into the trees. The fighter-bomber's .50 caliber machine guns ravaged the column on the main road and then went after the vehicles on the side roads with their 500lb. bombs. There were burning vehicles everywhere and when Motzenbecker's squadron was finished the 388th Squadron under Capt. Robert Fry was diverted to the area by the MEW controller. Six to eight more tanks were attacked with 500lb. bombs and 40 additional armored vehicles and assorted horse-drawn transport were attacked. The 365th 'Hell Hawks" weren't finished as 12 P-47s of the 386th Squadron led by Maj. George Brooking left at 1259 and arrived south of Roetgen. Brookings soon found 150 armored and horse-drawn vehicles on a secondary road between Monschau and Simmerath. The Germans were concentrated in bunches of 20 to 30 which were bombed and strafed several times despite intense and accurate flak and automatic small arms fire. The attack destroyed over 60 vehicles, probably destroyed 15 more and damaged 20 others. Continuing their reconnaissance they found a column of 15 guns, including at least three 88mms. The column was attacked but the measure of the damage could not be assessed. It had been a banner day for the 365th as they claimed 107 German vehicles destroyed, 20 probably destroyed and 45 damaged. Fifteen 88mm guns were also destroyed. Near Bullingen the 366th Fighter Group attacked the First SS Panzer Division which was heading toward Stavelot and Malmedy. The Panzers had already by-passed American positions on the front and were about to surround the US Second and 99th Divisions. The air

A Mark V Panther tank of *Kamfgruppe Peiper* was knocked out by fighter-bombers of Col. Ray Stecker's 365th Fighter Group on 18 December 1944. (USAF)

attack and a courageous attack by the Seventh Armored Division drove the Panzers to the southwest and prevented the encirclement. Before the 366th could inflict further damage 150 Luftwaffe aircraft come on the scene and the P-47s gave chase, claiming seven for a loss of three.

On the 18th the Germans threatened the crucial supply base at Liege and Hodges was forced to commit the 82nd and 101st Airborne Divisions. Until these divisions could be deployed only a few troops and air power were available to slow the onrushing German *Kampfgruppe Peiper*. As the predicament on the ground became more precarious fog kept the IX TAC fighter-bombers grounded. IX TAC CO Pete Quesada needed to make a difficult decision; to send up his fighter-bombers in the dangerous weather or wait for it to clear. For the first and only time in his career, Quesada

A captured German photo of a P-47 attacking the armor of *Kampfgruppe Peiper* near Bullingen on 17 December 1944 during the first days of the Battle of the Bulge. (USAF)

Left: Col. Ray Stecker. On 18 December the onrushing German *Kampfgruppe Peiper* threatened to break through thin American lines held by service troops, cooks and clerks.. Fog kept fighter-bombers grounded and IX TAC CO Pete Quesada needed to make a difficult decision, to send up his fighter-bombers in the dangerous weather or wait for it to clear. For the first and only time in his career, Quesada chose to fly combat over the preservation of the lives of his pilots. Stecker's 365th Fighter Group volunteered and routed Peiper's Panzers. (USAF)

chose to fly combat over the preservation of the lives of his pilots. He asked Col. George Peck, CO of the 67th TRG, for volunteers to search for Peiper's Panzers. At 1200 hours, Capt. Richard Cassidy and 2Lt. Abraham Jaffe took off in their F-6 photorecon Mustangs into heavy 10/10 overcast and were guided through the fog shrouded Ambleve Valley often just above tree level toward Stavelot by MEW radar and then by SCR-584 radar. The F-6 pilots were flying toward the target area when they were told to drop through the 200-foot overcast where they located 60 tanks and armored vehicles. They called in the target and made three attacks before retiring. Quesada's Chief of Operations, Col. Gil Meyers, sent Col. Raymond Stecker's 365th Fighter Group against the column that was about to break through thin American lines held by service troops, cooks and clerks. Stecker sent four plane flights at 20 to 30 minute intervals from their fogged-in airfield to find the Germans through the overcast. The first flight led by Capt. Robert Fry left at 0912 but had to turn back due to 10/10 cloud at 500 feet and on their return several P-47s had close calls upon landing through dense fog. It looked as though there would be no more flying for the day but the situation was critical and the Germans were driving toward Liege after breaking through at Stavelot. Meyers asked Stecker to try to send one flight out. Stecker asked for volunteers and Maj. George Brooking who had been in the area the day before took off at 1305 hours with Capt. James Wells, 1Lt. Robert Thoman and 2Lt. Roy Price. Other flights were to follow at 20-minute intervals with each Thunderbolt carrying two 500lb. delayed action bombs. Brookings circled for a half-hour for the fog to lift or for a break in the clouds but had no choice but to send the two newly arrived squadrons back to Chievres. Brookings knew of the dangers of the Belgian hills and ridges in the thick fog and clouds below but bravely dove blindly into fog-shrouded valleys looking for the Germans. After finding a valley empty he pulled up and continued his harrowing search to the next valley. Finally, Brookings found Peiper's columns and called in his three companions. The T-Bolts descended cautiously in single file to only a few feet above the ground and just below the overcast. Capt. Wells dropped his two 500lb. bombs in the midst of eight tanks spaced no more than a few feet apart on a road at the top of a hill. Two of the tanks were wrecked and six others rolled over on their sides off the road and down the hill. The road was blocked and the other P-47s did extensive damage with their bombs and then their strafing runs. 2Lt. Price's Thunderbolt was hit but he managed to parachute into friendly territory. 1Lt. Wells was also hit and Brookings directed Capt. Wells back to base. Brookings continued to orbit the area in order to direct the 368th Fighter Group that was on the way. While waiting Brookings searched two nearby valleys and found more Panzer columns in them. He strafed the led vehicle of each column effectively halting the entire column that could not maneuver around the burning lead vehicles in the narrow valleys. Flights of fighter-bombers began to arrive and Brookings very low on fuel was forced to leave after directing the 368th Fighter Group to the abundant targets. The 368th was followed by the 67th Fighter Group and then the 366th and 404th Groups were called in. The 365th flew a total of ten missions that day taking off and landing in thick fog. Several of the missions were turned back for fear of mid-air collisions, as there were so many attacking aircraft in the area. The sixth mission, a four plane flight of the 387th Squadron led by Maj. Arlo Henry arrived at Stavelot at 1500 and found a hole in the clouds and dive-bombed and then strafed a widely spread column of vehicles. Despite the distance between the vehicles they destroyed 40, probably destroyed 15 and damaged ten. The column was equipped with flak guns and two of the American aircraft were severely damaged but managed to return to base safely. The seventh mission, four planes of the 387th led by Capt. Neal Worley arrived at Stavelot at 1530 and dove on the same column destroying 40 trucks and damaging several tanks. Two more fighter-bombers were hit by flak but also landed safely in the heavy fog. At 1540 four more fighter-bombers of the 387th led by Capt. Robert Robinson found another group of German tanks and vehicles that were dive-bombed and strafed. Three tanks were destroyed and two damaged and five half-tracks were destroyed and three damaged in the initial dive-bombing pass. Robinson then led the flight on a strafing attack that netted four tanks destroyed and one damaged. One of the P-47s was hit by AA but returned to base belly-landing safely. On the ninth attack Capt. Samuel Saunders also of the 387th led another flight of four to Stavelot and again pounced on a convoy of tanks and trucks. The convoy was dive-bombed and strafed and the flight left destroying four tanks and five trucks. Flak damaged one P-47 that barely limped back to base. Finally, GC, Col. Raymond Stecker took off with 17 aircraft of the 388th Squadron but was unable to relocate the German columns. For the day the "Hell Hawks" were credited with 126-6-34 motor and armored vehicles for a cost of one P-47 lost over enemy territory, one bellied in and seven severely damaged. Peiper's Panzers were routed and turned away and although still a threat to Stavelot, Liege and the Allied fuel stores the Germans desperately needed were now out of danger.

From the 19th to 2rd December the weather was so bad over the Continent that the three TACs were only able to fly a few close support and strafing sorties. There was rain and snow over the battlefields and fog and low ceilings socked in the ALGs. The three 9th Air Force TACs did not fly more than 250 sorties on any of these days. The Germans used the poor weather to press attacks against vital road junctions at Bastogne and St. Vith. US infantry commanders called for air strikes that never took off and on the 22nd St. Vith was abandoned. The Germans had driven a "Bulge" into the Allied lines which severed Bradley's Twelfth Army line, placing Patton's Third Army on the south of the Bulge and Hodges' First Army and Simpson's Ninth Army on the north. Eisenhower decided that in order to counter-attack he would have to transfer Bradley's northern, First and Ninth, Armies to Montgomery's Twenty First Army Group. Bradley then could stop the German advance and then attack the south edge of the Bulge while Montgomery's new combined force would attack the north. Bradley was outraged with Eisenhower's move and, if not for his personal friendship with the Supreme Commander, would have resigned. The changes on the ground led to changes in the TACs. Quesada's IX and Nugent's XXIX were moved from supporting Hodges and Simpson to Coningham's British Second Tactical Air Force. But, unlike the changes in command on the ground, there were no such changes in the air. In fact, on the 21st, Coningham met with Quesada and Nugent and put all his fighter-bombers under Quesada's control as he was the nearest commander to the battle and most able to plan and control the coming air battles once the weather cleared. For once the Allied high air command made the right decision that was to soon pay dividends. Vandenberg transferred three fighter-bomber groups to Weyland's XIX to support Patton's offensive to relieve the surrounded Americans at Bastogne. On the 27th, three of the IX TACs groups, the 365th, 367th and 368th were temporarily transferred to the XIX TAC to balance the air power to ground forces. The move left Quesada with only three groups but he had Coningham's aircraft and was given temporary control two 8th Air Force fighter groups stationed in France.

On 23 December the weather broke and the IX and XXIX attacked the middle and north sections of the Bulge. The 370th supported the 82nd Airborne in its attempt to recapture St. Vith while other groups aided the Third and Seventh Armored Divisions that were trying to hold the Germans in the north. On this day 669 fighter sorties were flown knocking out 320 German motor transport and armored vehicles. The IX Bomber Command and 8th Air Force sent over 1,000 medium and heavy bombers to rail targets, marshaling yards and bridges behind the front. The air effort greatly heartened the infantry at the front. The next day armed reconnaissance missions were flown in the St. Vith-Stavelot area and *Kampfgruppe Peiper* was again attacked and further decimated, losing the majority of their motor transport and tanks. Over 1,400 heavy and medium bombers attacked 11 Luftwaffe airfields east of the Rhine to ease the persistent air attacks while medium bombers hit supply lines to the front. By Christmas the Allies had stopped the German attack and were about to regain the initiative. The fighter-bombers continually hit German supply lines and Panzers that soon would have no reserves and would run out of fuel. On Christmas Day, Collins VII Corps engaged the Second Panzer Division near Celles on the Meuse River. The German tanks were low on gasoline and unable to maneuver. Collins requested an air attack and the next morning Quesada sent in three groups and in a coordinated attack smashed literally hundreds of tanks and armored vehicles. Coningham's Second Tactical Air Force flew 370 fighters along with P-38s of the 370th Fighter Group into the breach between the First and Third Army. The fighter-bomber Christmas present to the Germans was over 500 armored and motor vehicles and 50 gun positions destroyed.

Not since their devastating attacks on the Argentan-Falaise pocket did the tactical air forces (on 4,281 armed recce sorties) ravage the German road net and the motor transport and armor traveling on it. The destruction could have been greater if a large number of fighter-bombers were not diverted to fighter sweeps and bomber escort missions to counter a rejuvenated Luftwaffe that flew 800 fighter sorties. During this time, fighter-bombers were effectively diverted from armed recce missions to close support missions on specific targets requested by ground troops. These strafing and bombing sorties on German troops inflicted both great physical and psychological damage. The German bid to regain at least local air superiority, albeit temporary, but was denied and served only as an annoyance to American air. Strategic bombers also operated successfully in a tactical role flying both interdiction and close support missions inside and outside the battle area. As a result of the courageous ground and air operations from 23-27 December the German attack in the Ardennes was completely checked.

Maj.Gen. Ludwig Heilmann led the 5th Parachute Division that was one of the last elite, battle-hardened units remaining but had not yet experienced the withering fighter-bomber attacks encountered on the western front. Heilmann writes the following about the utter disregard his officers and troops had for possible fighter-bomber attacks:

"The Allied air forces did not make any appearance at all during the first week of the offensive, because the skies in the combat areas were covered by low-hanging clouds.....The morning of 25 December brought the first blue skies and the Allied fighter-bombers commenced searching the roads but without attacking; they first had to identify the units spearheading the attack. By afternoon already, however, numerous vehicles standing unconcealed on a road were in flames and in this way one panzer division lost its fuel supply trucks... In the night an uninterrupted trail of burning vehicles extending like torchlight procession from Bastogne to as far back as the West Wall.

In my opinion the Ardennes Offensive was irretrievably lost when the Allies sent their air forces into action on 25 December, a fact that even the simplest soldier realized. It was terrible to see how helpless the members of the elite divisions were when opposed by air forces. Not one of the responsible commanding officers paid any attention to camouflage and concealment. Instructions given by me to my military police units to prevent concentrations of personnel were considered as assign of cowardice by an SS division and disregarded. This naturally cost casualties. Innumerable vehicles were left parked at quarters and premises within localities although wooded sections were to be found an all sides for the purpose.

From these personal observations I came to the realization that the Ardennes Offensive would fail because of the effects of the Allied air attacks no matter what happened." (Maj.Gen. Ludwig Heilmann, 5th *Parachute Division*, US Army, Europe, Historical Division, Ms. No. B-023, n.d.)

Work of 9th Air Force fighter-bombers at Bastogne. (USAF)

Bastogne (18-31 December 1944)

The German counter-attack in the Ardennes struck the Americans in the St. Vith-Bastogne area in force. On 18 December, The 101st Airborne Division at Neufchateau was moved to Bastogne to block the German advance from taking this vital communications center. The Germans continued the attack and by the 21st had surrounded the town. The next day the German commander offered a divisional surrender or face annihilation to Brig.Gen. Anthony McAuliffe who replied with his now famous rejection: "Nuts." The Germans continued heavy artillery, infantry and armor attacks without interference from the American air forces that were grounded by bad weather.

On the 2rd the weather cleared and fighter-bombers attacked targets near the town that could not be engaged by artillery due to the shortage of ammunition. Panzer columns northwest of the town were also attacked. On the 2rd and 24th the IX and XIX TACs continued effective close air support and maintained air cover for 241 C-47 transports that re-supplied the town by a parachute drop on the 2rd and for 42 gliders on the 26th and 27th. Night fighters flew cover against German night intruders that harassed the defenders. Due to the fluidity of the battlefield situation the night fighters were restricted to intruder missions, patrolling the area against enemy night fighters. However, German night intruders were not intercepted and caused some serious damage. The fighter-bombers continued to effectively fly close support, armed recce and sweeps. Bombing and strafing sorties near the front were very effective against infantry, armor, artillery and reinforcements.

The 26th was a key day in the battle for Bastogne as early that morning American armor tried to relieve the surrounded city from the southeast. After an early rapid advance the Shermans met stubborn resistance near the village of Remichampagne. Air support was called in by the tankers and 20 minutes later two P-47 squadrons arrived, dropping their bombs on the German position that was soon abandoned and moved to the main German fortified defensive line at Clochimont and Assenois, southeast of Bastogne. Assenois was a small town of about 49 buildings that controlled the road to Bastogne. P-47s and P-38s of Weyland's XIX were armed with napalm and 11 flights of four aircraft descended to 1,000 feet at 1400 hours. The firebombs destroyed buildings and the heat drove the defenders out into the waiting fire of American infantry. At 1650 hours, coordinated ground-air support opened a corridor to Bastogne for the 4th Armored Division and normal supply and reinforcement were resumed. Napalm had been particularly effective, as it had been in the entire Battle of the Bulge. Earlier it had been no more effective on armor, buildings and fortified positions than bombing or strafing. In the Bulge the Germans often hid from view but did not have access to bunkers or pillboxes and napalm forced them into the open. Even though the German siege of Bastogne had been broken, the American position was in doubt for several more days as the Germans continued their attacks until the 31st. The Luftwaffe continued night bombing and strafing attacks before breaking off. The Germans were hampered in their retreat by the damage to the rail system behind their lines.

The 406th Fighter Group provided conspicuous air support over Bastogne for which it was awarded the DUC. On the 23 December the weather cleared and the group's P-47s took off from Mouemelon-le-Grand (A-80) early in the morning on the first of 81 missions and 529 sorties which attacked targets within a 10 mile radius of the surrounded town. The P-47s of the 512th, 513th and 514th Squadrons bombed, strafed and launched rockets on German tanks, motorized vehicles, buildings and gun positions which were heavily defended by AA fire. On three successive mornings the P-47s arrived just as the Germans were about to launch attacks to overrun the surrounded Americans. Aggressive air attacks blunted the German resolve. During the 23-27 December period the Group knocked out 194 tanks and armored vehicles, 610 motor transport, 43 horse-drawn vehicles, 226 gun positions, 59 defended buildings, 13 ammunition or fuel dumps, 12 bridges and destroyed or damaged 13 Luftwaffe aircraft. The 405th Fighter Group was honored for its actions during the Battle of the Bulge in a letter from Patton (*1 January 1945 General Order Number 1*):

"From the bloody corridor at Avranches, to Brest, thence across France to the Saar, over Saar into Germany, and now Bastogne, your record has been one of continuous victory. Not only have you invariably defeated a cunning and ruthless enemy, but also you have overcome by your indomitable fortitude every aspect of terrain or weather. Neither heat nor dust nor floods nor snow have stayed your progress. The speed and brilliancy of your achievements is unsurpassed in military history."

Friendly fire continued to be problem as on the 26th P-47s were responsible for killing 37 Allied personnel and a number of civilians in three different attacks. But friendly fire was also endured by the fighter-bombers as American anti-aircraft crews fired on them on four different instances during the last week of December. On Christmas Day, George Preddy, top 8th Air Force ace at the time with 27 victories, was leading the 328th Fighter Squadron of the 352nd Fighter Group. He was returning to his ALG base in Belgium after being separated from the rest of his squadron and was joined by two other lost 474th Fighter Group P-51s. Flying low over the Hurtgen Forest, the Mustangs were heading for the 12th AA Group

Smashed German tank destroyer during the Battle of the Bulge. It was estimated that Allied fighter-bombers knocked out 751 German tanks and armored vehicles during the battle. (USAF)

that had been warned of approaching Me-109s. Not waiting to identify the low-flying aircraft the quad .50 caliber machine guns briefly opened fire before the 109s were identified as P-51s. Preddy's aircraft bellied into a nearby field, its occupant fatally wounded by two .50 bullets. The German use of Allied equipment and uniforms in Battle of the Bulge prompted the rumor that the Luftwaffe was using American aircraft that made the gunners even more trigger-happy. Patton and Hodges then ordered that their batteries were not to fire on any aircraft unless attacked first.

As December ended the German High Command realized that their ground armies and air forces had been stopped by Allied air power. It was the joint effort and effectiveness of the fighter-bomber, tactical reconnaissance aircraft and heavy and medium bombers that greatly aided the American defense of Bastogne. But the ground battle was frequently on a platoon or company level and the timely and effective appearance of fighter-bombers was often the deciding factor in the battle.

9th Air Force Fighter/Fighter-Bomber Interdiction Operations: West Wall (15 September-15 December 1944)

	Fighter/Fighter-Bombers		Bombers*	
Targets	**Sorties**	**Bomb Tons**	**Sorties**	**Bomb Tons**
Railways/Bridges	7,543	3,509.0	1,263	2,152.3
Marshaling Yards	2,170	961.3	828	1,411.9
Roads/Bridges	1,324	700.0	168	308.3
Motor Transport/Troops	1,446	585.9	202	411.0
Military Installations	1,044	533.2	1,167	2,040.8
Shipping	393	168.2	—	—
Unidentified	673	333.2	6	6.0
Totals	14,593	6,790.8	3,634	6,330.3

* Medium and light

First TAF Fighter-Bomber Interdiction Operations: West Wall (15 September-15 December 1944)

	Fighter/Fighter-Bombers		Bombers*	
Targets	**Sorties**	**Bomb Tons**	**Sorties**	**Bomb Tons**
Railways/Bridges	331	149.7	28	54.5
Marshaling Yards	386	169.7	—	—
Roads/Bridges	164	77.8	—	—
Motor Transport/Troops	88	45.4	—	—
Military Installations	100	56.4	—	—
Shipping	8	3.3	—	—
Totals	1,077	502.2	28	54.5

*Medium

8th Air Force Fighter/Fighter-Bomber Interdiction Operations: West Wall (15 September-15 December 1944)

No fighter-bomber operations
Bombers flew 22,721 sorties dropping 61,113.1 tons of bombs.
Marshaling Yards: 19,500 sorties/52,365.9 tons
Railways and Bridges: 1,257 sorties/3,333.0 tons

Breaking the Bulge (28 December 1944-31 January 1945)

Patton's Third Army moved north and Montgomery got his American and English forces organized and moved south. The Germans were now in danger of becoming surrounded themselves and von Rundstedt wanted to retreat across the Rhine and establish a strong defense there. Hitler adamantly refused to allow any retreat and consigned 21 hastily rebuilt or poorly trained divisions to the battle. The movement of these troops and their weapons gave the Allied air forces new and numerous targets. IX BC and 8th Air Force heavy and medium bombers hit rail and road traffic and bridges, supply depots and communication centers in late December. The weather after the 27th reduced fighter-bomber operations of Quesada's IX TAC and Nugent's XXIX TAC on the north of the rapidly withering Bulge and Weyland's XIX TAC on the south.

Operation BODENPLATTE was the Luftwaffe's New Year's Day 1945 surprise attack on Allied air bases on the Continent. Here all that is left of a 365th Fighter Group P-47 based at Metz/Frescaty airfield is its starboard wing. (USAF)

The German High Command knew that if their offensive was to continue and Germany was to be saved from being totally overrun, Allied fighter and medium/light bombers based near the front needed to be destroyed. In a shocking surprise attack, code-named Operation BODENPLATTE, on New Year's Day morning, the Luftwaffe sent over 900 planes, under the command of Maj.Gen. Dietrich Peltz, to bomb 16 crowded Allied air fields in France, Belgium and Holland. The Germans hoped that they could regain air superiority and reduce the constant Allied harassment of their retreating troops. The Allies had become indifferent to air defense over months of Luftwaffe inactivity. The lack of sufficient airfields, the poor weather and need for aircraft to meet the Ardennes Offensive added to the concentration of aircraft on the Allied airfields. Quick action at the ALG base at Asch, Belgium (Y-29) thwarted the Luftwaffe attack there. Lt.Col. John Meyer led the 487th Squadron of the 352nd Fighter Group that shot down 23 Germans without a loss. Meyer was awarded the DSC and the 487th the DUC. Claims on both sides are contradictory. Danny Parker (*To Win a Winter Sky*, Combined Books, PA, 1994) has estimated Allied losses as high as 300 aircraft on the ground and another 70 in aerial combat. The RAF recorded losses at 144 destroyed and another 84 badly damaged. The USAAF only admitted 134 losses, 62 damaged beyond repair. Neither the RAF nor the USAAF included the 70 lost in aerial combat. Norman Franks credits the Germans with 159 British aircraft destroyed or damaged and 55 American aircraft lost on the ground. It seems that AA gunners on both sides were guilty of nerves. While returning to base 85 Luftwaffe aircraft were shot down by their own nervous AA batteries that were unaccustomed to seeing their aircraft in the air. While visiting front line bases that day, Generals Carl Spaatz and Jimmy Doolittle almost became the victims of friendly fire when Patton's AA gunners fired upon their twin-engine aircraft. Fortunately their aim was bad and the Generals escaped unscathed. The Luftwaffe loss estimates also varied from 200 to 300 replaceable planes. More importantly the Luftwaffe lost over 214 irreplaceable pilots and crew including 20 experienced commanders: eleven *Staffel*, six *Gruppe* and three *Geshwader*. In addition to the largest single day loss during the war of men and aircraft the Luftwaffe had squandered its carefully stockpiled fuel supplies.

Operation BODENPLATTE sounded the death knell the Luftwaffe fighter arm and Reich Air Marshal Hermann Goering needed a scapegoat and he sacked General of the Fighters, Adolf Galland, and replaced him with Oberst Gordon Gollob. The Luftwaffe after the Ardennes Offensive lost 125 aircrew in the last two weeks of January as the average pilot life expectancy was only three missions! The Luftwaffe was spread thin as only four fighter wings were left to defend the Homeland and the attrition rate there was an unsustainable 30%. Meanwhile the Allies were dropping 2,000 to 4,000 tons of bombs per day on the Reich at a very economical loss of 0.2% of sorties flown.

After the Luftwaffe morning attack, that afternoon, on a day when the Allied air forces should have been destroyed, they went out and claimed 22-28 (destroyed-damaged) tanks, 37-13 armored vehicles, 320-187 motor transport, 37-22 locomotives, 336-504 rail cars and 73 rail cuts. Also that day the 8th Air Force, based safely in England, flew 800 bombers, escorted by 700 fighters against marshaling yards at Limburg and Kassel and the oil industry at Magdeburg.

On New Year's Day Eisenhower ordered four US Corps, the VII, VIII, XII and XVIII Airborne, to attack the northern and southern flanks of the Bulge and the British Thirtieth Corps to attack its spearhead. Fighter-bombers flew repeated armed reconnaissance sorties and heavy and medium bombers increased their efforts against German transportation hubs. The relentless air attacks chipped away at morale and German soldiers refused to move from their foxholes and many deserted. The renewed Soviet offensive on the Eastern Front allowed the Allies to advance rapidly toward southern Germany. On the 16th, elements of Patton's and Hodge's armies met at Houffalize. On January 22nd and 2rd, fighter-bombers were everywhere and the tactical air commands destroyed 2,000 motor vehicles. On the 2rd, the US Seventh Armored Division recaptured St. Vith. The five Corps converged and moved east and by the end of January completely reduced the Bulge, ending the last German threat of the war in the West.

Fighter-Bomber Air Contributions

The heavy and medium bombers of the 8th and 9th Air Forces were widely credited with helping to blunt and turn back the German attack by cutting off German supplies and reinforcements. Close air support and armed reconnaissance missions also played a major part in the air. The Germans had anticipated Allied air attacks on main supply roads and had detours and alternate routes were planned

The 370th Fighter Group was based at A-78, Florennes/Juzaine, Belgium. Its P-38s carrying 500lb.bombs are seen here taxiing for take off to blunt the German Ardennes Offensive which was closing in, only 15 miles away. (USAF)

in advance. However, the continuous fighter-bomber attacks on these routes were so effective that the German transport system became paralyzed. It was not only the loss of so many motor vehicles that was critical but also the loss of the supplies they carried, particularly the fuel. The shortage of fuel denied the Germans mobility. Losses of supplies while in transit were greater than those losses in the bombing of dumps, parks and depots that were dispersed and camouflaged. Over the front, sudden and unexpected low-flying strafing attacks on the enemy supply system had a great destructive effect on materiel and morale as it caused heavy casualties and deprived frontline troops of those supplies just destroyed and future supplies as the M/T to carry them was destroyed. Level-bombing of rear areas was more effective than fighter-bombers as it was more accurate and concentrated but caused fewer casualties. There were fewer aircraft losses as the Germans received sufficient warning of the impending attack, but the bombers were safer from flak at their higher altitudes. Corps and division commanders had high regard for the fighter-bombers that attacked and slowed advancing Panzer columns, made any troop or transport movement along the Belgium roads impossible and flushed dug in Germans from their fortified positions. Fighter-bombers knocked out 751 tanks and armored vehicles, 299 gun positions, 6,000 motor vehicles, 1,200 buildings, numerous locomotives and rolling stock and the morale of the entire German army on the Western Front.

In his book, *The First and the Last* (Henry Holt, NY, 1954) Luftwaffe Fighter Commander, Adolf Galland, stated:

"The Third Reich received its death blow in the Ardennes Offensive. In unfamiliar conditions and with insufficient training and combat experience, our numerical strength had no effect. It was decimated while in transfer and devastated while in action and the Jabos were especially proficient at intercepting much needed reinforcements at critical times. The American Jabos destroyed us."

Von Rundstedt (Bradley, *Effect of air Power on Military Operations, Western Europe*, ibid.) stated that "the loss of supplies through fighter-bomber attacks on supply trucks and rear dumps at the divisional and corps levels had been a greater factor of loss than level bombing attacks on army dumps farther to the rear." He felt that the German advance had been "devastated" by fighter-bomber attacks that drove back the forward railheads supporting the offensive and caused the breakdown of the German transportation system slowing and then halting the offensive.

By the fall of 1944 IX TAC communications system between ground and air extended with great efficiency from forward director posts to radar centers to radar centers to fighter control stations to a combat command post and finally to a fighter-bomber group. MEW directed aircraft to and from targets, united bombers with their fighter escorts and detected the few aircraft the Luftwaffe sent out. J. Lawton Collins of the VII Corps wrote to Quesada to thank him for the "part played by the Air Force, particularly the fighter-bombers, in support of the VII Corps. We would not possibly have gotten as far as we did, as fast as we did and with as few casualties, without the wonderful air support that we consistently had." The old infighting over air power policy and air support had been forgotten. The daily close contact and cooperation between all levels of command of the ground armies and air forces in the tactical air war led to this new era of Army-Air Force goodwill, at least for the time being. Quesada was convinced that the success of the fighter-bomber in the Battle of the Bulge had finally given it a place in air power along with the aerial dog fighter and bomber escort.

Roer River Line (19 December 1944- 23 January 1945)

In early December 1944, the Ninth Army failed to capture the Roer River dams' preventing the continuation of attacks east of the river forcing the First into a defensive posture on the west bank. Then on 16 December, the Germans unleashed their Ardennes counter-offensive to the south and troops from the Ninth were withdrawn to reinforce the "Bulge." Only five divisions were available to hold a 45-mile front but the area was well suited for defense with the Roer River presenting a formidable physical barrier along most of the front. Intelligence feared another large scale German offensive against the weakened Roer front. Probably for the first time in ground defense planning, a comprehensive air plan, coded Operation BOBCAT, was devised mutually by air and ground staffs. The XXIX TAC that had been assigned to the Ninth (e.g. Roer front) was diverted to support the First Army in the Ardennes. A few close support missions were flown over the Roer Front to assist limited Ninth Army ground attacks, which were mainly aggressive patrols and to attack German troop concentrations and disrupt enemy attacks. The majority of the missions flown were armed recce with priority given to attacking rail and motor traffic towards the Ardennes. No medium or heavy close support bombardment was used in this static defense.

By the end of December, the German Ardennes Offensive had been stopped and, so too, the potential threat of a major attack on the Roer Front. During the last week of January and early February the XXIX TAC concentrated on destroying the rail system east of the Roer and west of the Rhine in order to aid the Ninth's attack across the Roer in February 1945.

From 15 September to 15 December the USAAF contributed the following:

Heavy Bombers	48,323 sorties	129,521 tons
Medium & Light Bombers	9,150 sorties	15,595 tons
Fighters & Fighter-Bombers	106, 822 sorties	15,495 tons

9th Air Force 1945	**# Squadrons**	**%**
Fighter/Fighter-Bomber	45	42.8
Light/Medium Bombers	45	42.8
Reconnaissance	13	12.3
Night Fighters	2	1.9

First TAF 1945	**# Squadrons**	**%**
Fighter/Fighter-Bomber	24	50.0
Light/Medium Bombers	14	29.1
Reconnaissance	8	16.6
Night Fighters	2	4.1

9th Air Force Fighter Groups to TACs 1945

16 January			1 February			8 February		
IX	**XIX**	**XXIX**	**IX**	**XIX**	**XXIX**	**IX**	**XIX**	**XXIX**
48FG	354FG	36FG	36FG	354FG	366FG	36FG	354FG	366FG
366FG	362FG	373FG	48FG	362FG	370FG	48FG	362FG	370FG
370FG	365FG		365FG	367FG		365FG	367FG	373FG
404FG	367FG		373FG	368FG		404FG	368FG	404FG
474FG	368FG		404FG	405FG		474FG	371FG*	406FG
	405FG		474FG	406FG	*From 16 Feb.			
	406FG							

Retreat From the Bulge: Another Falaise-Type Rout (22-26 January 1945)

The Allied air forces interdiction campaign had sealed off the Ardennes in December and in January had left the retreating Germans only a few roads and rail lines open. The German engineers aided by days of poor weather managed to keep a number of these lines open to allow the withdrawal during the first three weeks of January. In the early morning of 22 January Capt. Wilfred Crutchfield leading the 378th Squadron of the 362nd Fighter Group spotted over 1,500 vehicles of the Sixth Panzer Army heading east in the Prum area in preparation to move to the Russian front. Quesada called out all available 9th Air Force resources to attack all retreating German forces. Both IX and XIX TAC Groups were dispatched. The 362nd Fighter Group claimed 312-106 (destroyed-damaged) motor transport, 11-1 tanks, 6-1 armored vehicles, 15-0 horse-drawn vehicles and 44-10 gun positions. The 406th Fighter Group claimed 119-111 motor transport and 10-0 horse-drawn vehicles while the 405th claimed 179-71 M/T there. A liaison pilot flying an artillery mission on main and secondary roads spotted another huge concentration of over 1,500 German vehicles moving bumper to bumper west along the Our River which formed the border between Luxembourg and Germany. The Dasburg Bridge, 16 miles south of St. Vith, was destroyed by B-26s of the 387th and 394th Bomb Groups creating a bottleneck trapping German traffic. Two XIX TAC groups were dispatched to the Our River concentration and half of the 1,500 German vehicles were destroyed or damaged. The 368th Fighter Group claimed 422-117 motor transport at Dasburg. The 367th Fighter Group operating both at Prum and Dasburg claimed 98-30 motor transport. The XIX TAC flew 550 sorties netting 1,162-531 motor transport, 20-4 tanks, 10-1 armored vehicles, 41-18 horse-drawn vehicles and 49-13 gun positions. The IX TAC flew 350 sorties that recorded 409-625 motor transport, 8-19 tanks, 20-23 armored vehicles, 8-0 horse-drawn vehicles and 13-14 gun positions. The XXIX TAC flew 163 sorties by two groups concentrating on rail traffic in the Duren area; The 36th Fighter Group claimed 7-0 locomotives, 282-125 rail cars, 17-2 buildings and three aircraft on the ground. The 37rd Fighter Group got 8-1 locomotives, 346-126 rail cars and 40-27 buildings. Seven XIX TAC aircraft were lost: five from the 362nd and one each from the 367th and 368th. Six IX TAC aircraft were lost: two each from the 404th and 370th and one each from the 48th and 366th. The XITH TAC losses were: the 36th Fighter Group lost two aircraft and had eight damaged while the 37rd suffered four damaged fighters. Weyland was elated over the results he noted in his diary: "....worse than the Falaise Pocket, Biggest day in the history of TAC destructions..."

On the 2rd the three TACs flew 750 sorties, 313 less than the day before. The XIX was able to put up only four groups due to the weather. It flew 183 sorties, mainly to the Dasburg area, and declared 317-168 motor transport, 6-0 tanks, 3-0 armored vehicles, 11-0 horse-drawn vehicles, 12-4 gun positions and 26-8 defended buildings. The 362nd Fighter Group flew 52 sorties yielding 194-121 M/T, 3-0 armored vehicles, 12-4 gun positions and nine buildings destroyed. The 368th Fighter Group flew 32 sorties with 102-41 M/T, 6-0 tanks, 9-0 horse-drawn vehicles and 10-0 defended buildings. The 354th got 1-0 locomotives, 22-38 rail cars, 3-0 M/T, 2-0 horse-drawn transport, 7-8 defended buildings and nine rail cuts in 56 sorties. The 365th Fighter Group flew 43 sorties for 18-6 motor transport. The IX TAC sent out 408 sorties and again took a large toll of German vehicles: 661-737 M/T, 3-13 tanks, 17-24 armored vehicles, 5-8 horse-drawn vehicles and 5-3 gun positions. The 48th, 370th and 404th Fighter Groups operated in the Blankenheim to Ahrdorf area and the 366th and 474th Fighter Groups operating in the Dasburg, Prum and Blankenheim area. The IX TAC lost five aircraft. The 36th and 37rd Fighter Groups of the XXIX flew 159 sorties to Duren area and got 15-24 M/T, 1-0 armored vehicles, 2-0 horse-drawn vehicles, 6-1 locomotives, 150-89 rail cars, 65-15 defended buildings, 46 rail and three road cuts. Gen. Fritz Bayerlein's once proud Panzer Lehr Division was fighting to keep the Gemund bridgehead over the Our River open at Hoscheid. The fuel shortage had become so critical that 53 operable tanks had to be left behind. In the late evening Bayerlein drove to his Command Post at Eisenbach and found the road backed up with heavy traffic. At sunrise the American Jabos attacked and Bayerlein's driver was forced to weave in and out of burned wreckage of trucks, armored vehicles and wounded horses bellowing in pain. The next day his grenadiers would retreat from the frantic street fighting in Horsheid across to the West Wall and the German border. The Panzer Lehr Division had lost 80% of its strength and only 400 men and 18 tanks crossed the Our. The ever-present Allied Jabos had made the Panzer Lehr's seven and a half month retreat from the D-Day beaches to the West Wall a living Hell.

On the 24th during armed recon missions in support of the ground troops the fighter-bombers took a further toll of the German motor column. Total claims, mostly by the IX TAC were 359-298 M/T (the 366th Fighter Group claiming 159-199), 12-27 tanks, 30-8 armored vehicles, 4-0 horse drawn vehicles and 47-1 gun positions. Losses for the 24th were: XIX TAC lost none, the IX lost five and had 19 damaged (two beyond repair), the XXIX TAC lost one and 11 damaged. On the 25th 463 sorties by the IX and XIX TACs (the XXIX TAC was operating to the north) claimed 623-566 M/T, 9-25 tanks, 40-30 armored vehicles, 8-4 horse-drawn vehicles and 22-3 gun positions. IX TAC lost two fighters and had 25 damaged while the XIX lost one.

The four-day totals were astounding as the three 9th Air Force TACs destroyed or damaged 6,618 motor transport, 159 tanks, 237 armored vehicles, 188 gun positions, 47 locomotives and 2,227 rail cars. The almost complete destruction of the rail system west of the Rhine and the shortage of motor vehicles made it necessary to carry a large proportion of supplies by horse-drawn vehicles. Although these losses were enormous they did not bring about a disordered rout but with the aid of deteriorating weather the German continued their disciplined withdrawal. For the remainder of the month and into February the weather closed down air operations for both sides.

The Ardennes Offensive cost the Germans 507 locomotives, 6,266 rail cars, 974 rail cuts, 11,378 M/T, 1,161 tanks and armored vehicles, 472 gun positions, 421 road cuts and 36 bridges. These resources could have been better expended on establishing a strong defense of Germany's eastern and western borders. The Russians began their winter offensive on 12 January and by the end of the month the tattered remnants of the Panzer armies retreating from the Bulge were being transferred to the cauldron in the east.

Operation NORDWIND (1-26 January 1945)
The Second Battle of the Bulge

Hitler had ordered FM Walter Model to retake of the French Provinces of Alsace and Lorraine against Patch's depleted Seventh Army in a pincers movement north of Strasbourg. Unlike the Ardennes Offensive Devers and Patch were not surprised as ULTRA intelligence intercepts gave them the time, place and order of battle for the attack.

On New Year's Eve the Germans launched their attack and that night and into New Year's morning the outnumbered Americans held fast, gave ground and in places were over run. The Luftwaffe launched BODENPLATTE that morning but no damage was done to First TAF fields or aircraft by the surprise air attack. Four XII TAC P-47 Groups took off to aid the beleaguered Seventh Army flying armed recce against fuel and ammunition depots and engaged in some of the largest air battles of the war along the southern front. On the 2nd Eisenhower ordered Devers' exposed VI Corps to retreat back to the Vosges Mountains and hold the vital passes there. During the withdrawal the P-47s bombed and strafed the attacking Germans but were intercepted by the revitalized Luftwaffe. On the 3rd, the Germans continued their attack in cold, fog and deep snow. The dogged Americans, without close air support due to the continuing bad weather, held fast and mounted counter-attacks to regain lost ground and the initiative. Devers withdrawal left Strasbourg abandoned to potential German reoccupation. General DeGaulle vehemently protested the loss of this historic city for political and morale reasons to Eisenhower. Churchill took the side of the French and Eisenhower backed down and Gen. De Lattre's First French Army to defend the city.

After the 324th Fighter Group moved to Luneville (Y-2) all four 64th Wing fighter groups were based on fields within much shorter range to the battlefront but the weather did not cooperate. On the 5th, under overcast weather, Hitler ordered a change in the attack and directed it toward the Wissembourg Gap, north of Strasbourg and drove the green US infantrymen back. The German 19th Army drove nine divisions toward the French defending Strasbourg. By the 8th, the Germans had driven to seven miles north of Strasbourg before being stopped by American reinforcements while the German 19th Army's move out of the Colmar Pocket reached 13 miles south of Strasbourg before the French stopped them. On the 9th the weather cleared and the XII TACs flew mission after mission to stop the German attacks on the Seventh Army. Fighter-bombers flew close support missions on the front lines and interdiction missions against armor, trucks and trains behind the lines. Also on the 9th the Germans reinforced their attack with elite SS units but after initial losses US artillery, armor and the individual soldier repelled and stopped the attack.

On the 12th the Russians began their gigantic offensive that would put them to within 50 miles of Berlin in the next month. In response, Hitler was forced to scale down NORDWIND and transfer three divisions to the east. After 13 of 14 days of poor weather that grounded the medium bombers, good flying weather on the 14th allowed the fighter-bombers, especially the 324th Fighter Group with 12 missions of 131 sorties, to give the withdrawing German divisions a rousing send off. Over the next several days the B-26s and P-47s attacked the flow of reinforcements and supplies into Colmar but the Germans nonetheless received enough of each by night and during bad weather. On the 17th fighter-bombers were able to block both ends of the Kaiserslaautern-Neustadt tunnel. Two days later XII P-47s flew 16 missions of 190 sorties and destroyed 27 German Panzers and beat off a determined Panzer attack. The Germans attempted one last desperation attack in bitter cold and driving snow on the 24th. The Germans advanced to cross the Moder River and breakthrough American lines at Huguenot supported by more than 20 FW-190s and Ju-88s. The American Seventh Army and the French stopped the Germans and the German called off the offensive that had gained them only a small area of the Alsace Plain and 25,000 casualties (vs. 15,600 US casualties). NORDWIND had delayed the American move toward Germany for six weeks and when it was over the American Sixth Army Group moved to eliminate the Colmar Pocket and the remaining enemy forces west of the Rhine.

Operation CHEERFUL: Eliminating the Colmar Pocket (20 January-12 March 1945)

Held by 50,000 German troops, the Colmar Pocket was a 30 mile deep by 50 mile wide bridgehead running west of the Rhine to the Vosges Mountains and from south of Strasbourg in the north to Mulhouse on the southern end. In December the First French Army under Gen. Jean de Lattre was assigned to reduce the Pocket but failed due to poor weather, stout enemy resistance and unfavorable terrain. The failure of NORDWIND and the Ardennes Offensive and the onrushing Russian offensive in January led to Operation CHEERFUL that was to eliminate the Colmar Pocket. US and French troops were to attack the north, center and south sides of the Pocket and converge on Breisach, a German city on the eastern bank of the Rhine. Eisenhower reinforced the NORDWIND-depleted US Seventh Army with three additional divisions. The First TAF was to carry out a three priorities within CHEERFUL. The first priority was to maintain air superiority by conducting sweeps and escorting medium and fighter-bombers and artillery liaison aircraft. The second priority was fighter-bomber close support requests. The third was for medium and fighter-bombers to interdict the movement of supplies and reinforcements on the Black Forest rail and road system, east bank of the Rhine defensive positions and to attack the retreat of the Germans from the Vosges area. To accomplish this the First TACAF had four P-47 groups and two B-26 groups and operational control of four 9th Air Force fighter-bomber groups.

Four divisions of the French I Corps initiated CHEERFUL on 20 January but were halted by the next day by a blizzard and strong German defenses, suffering severe losses. On the 22nd, four French Divisions and the 3rd and 28th American Divisions attacked to take the Breisach bridge but the blizzard also soon stopped their advance. Only on the 2rd were units of First TACAF able to take off. P-47s hit road and rail facilities, transport, bridges and supply routes in and to the pocket. Armor and troop concentrations were heavily attacked. Fighter-bombers flew mission after mission, sortie after sortie in support of the French attack south of Strasbourg in the continued good weather the next day. Maj.Gen. Frank Milburn XXI Corps attacked the Pocket from the center and on the 25th made advances and with French forces succeeded on encircling the Germans at the south end off the Pocket. The next day German counterattacks stopped the 3rd Infantry Division at Holtzwhir and Wickerswhir until 50th Group P-47s appeared and smashed the Panzers. The XXI Corps moved forward trying to cut off escape routes from the Pocket while XII TAC and French First Air Force Thunderbolts flew close support missions against German armor, gun positions and troop concentrations and interdiction missions against motor and rail transport, bridges, marshaling yards and rail lines. First TAF medium bombers had been grounded for ten days by bad weather and heavy snow and flew interdiction missions to prevent supplies from coming into the Pocket.

On the 29th Brig.Gen. Gordon Seville took over the First TACAF from Ralph Royce and Col. Nelson Jackson became CO of the 64th Fighter Wing. Intelligence reports found that the Germans had adequate supplies on hand in the Pocket and were continuing to bring in more despite Allied air interdiction. On the 30th the First TAF began its second phase of the Colmar air campaign and extended its interdiction well east of the Pocket. The accelerating Russian offensive caused Hitler to strip elite units from the Pocket and send them east. By 1 February, the XXI Corps and the French moved into the weakened German front and reduced the to 25 miles and to within five miles of the Breisach Bridge. On the 2nd French and American P-47s flew sorties all day against anything moving on the roads and rails. The Breisach Bridge was a key Rhine crossing and was a priority for destruction. The bridge defenses were the

A mobile, jury-rigged control tower fabricated from the Plexiglas nose of a B-17 by the 370th Fighter Group in late January 1945 at Ophoven, Belgium (Y-32). (USAF)

Right: The winter weather was some of the worst experienced in years in northwestern Europe. Here ground crew try to keep warm and brew coffee as their charges taxi for take off. (USAF)

PSP was used to "winterize" ALGs but supplies were limited. A 371st Fighter Group (404th Squadron) P-47D taxiing off a PSP hardstand in France. (USAF)

Keeping 'em flying was a problem during the winter of '44. Here a 474th Fighter Group ground crew struggles to get a P-38 ready for a mission an engine heater sits under the port wing. (USAF)

strongest of any on the southern front. There were over 160 guns defending the bridge and another 100 plus defending the Neuenberg Bridge to the south. In addition to the heavy flak concentration, the continued poor weather and the terrain around the bridge made attacks difficult for both medium and fighter-bombers. Low-level missions were confined by the terrain and flak chewed up any fighter-bomber attack. Finally, heavy B-26 Marauder attacks on the 3rd and 4th blocked the bridge and the Germans blew it up. Colmar fell on the 5th and the German 19th Army was surrounded. Von Rundstedt asked Hitler for permission to withdraw but was refused. On the 8th the First TAF flew 136 Marauder and 253 Thunderbolt missions against the reeling German transport and troop concentrations. They destroyed five bridges, including the Neuenberg Bridge. The Pocket was eradicated on 9 February with only about 4,000 of 15,000 to 18,000 remaining troops escaping. The eight divisions of the 19th Army had suffered 30,000 casualties (American and French lost 18,000). Despite atrocious weather initially the fighter-bomber undertaking increased in quantity and quality as the weather improved as the campaign progressed. The First TAF flew 1,980 sorties during the three weeks of CHEERFUL and both Brig.Gen. Frank Milburn of the XXI Corps and Gen. Jean de Lattre of the French First Army praised the First its efforts.

Warm oil is being poured into the engine of a P-47 waiting for pre-flight in the snow. (USAF)

P-38 pilots of the 367th Fighter Group are transported to their aircraft by improvised sleds pulled by a jeep. (USAF)

9th Air Force Fighter/Fighter-Bomber Interdiction Operations: Battle of the Bulge (16 December 1944-7 February 1945)

	Fighter/Fighter-Bombers		Bombers*	
Targets	**Sorties**	**Bomb Tons**	**Sorties**	**Bomb Tons**
Railways/Bridges	1,783	982.6	2,515	4,463.3
Marshaling Yards	2,084	1,126.7	187	289.1
Roads/Bridges	1,323	1,001.3	650	1,556.5
Motor Transport/Troops	4,281	2,422.3	275	444.5
Military Installations	343	183.4	589	1,003.8
Shipping	56	27.3	11	21.0
Totals	9,870	5,743.6	4,227	7,778.2

* Medium and light

8th Air Force Fighter/Fighter Bomber Interdiction Operations: Battle of the Bulge (16 December-7 February 1944)

No fighter-bomber sorties

All heavy bomber: 21,543 sorties dropping 58,368.3 bomb tons

First TAC Fighter-Bomber Interdiction Operations: Battle of the Bulge (16 December 1944-7 February 1944)

	Fighter/Fighter-Bombers		Bombers*	
Targets	**Sorties**	**Bomb Tons**	**Sorties**	**Bomb Tons**
Railways/Bridges	2,081	1,161.8	181	386.5
Marshaling Yards	1,006	535.6	25	48.6
Roads/Bridges	311	173.6	—	—
Motor Transport/Troops	464	234.9	99	197.0
Military Installations	658	366.6	167	350.3
Shipping	22	12.1	—	—
Totals	4,542	2,484.6	472	982.4

* Medium

Note: The 9th Air Force had 845 fighters and fighter-bombers operational and 1,241 attached and the total AAF had 3,821 fighters and fighter-bombers operational and 4,245 attached in February 1945.

34

Attack on Germany
8 February - 8 May 1945

The Continuing Assault on German Railway System

From mid-September to mid-December 1944, the first priority of the tactical air forces was the destruction of the German transport system and in particular the German railway system. It was to cut German supply and transport feeding the Wehrmacht in its battles to slow the rapid Allied advance towards the German homeland. German reports show that the damage from air attacks on the transport system did not significantly interfere with the movement of troops and supplies and that the German transport system instead of being crippled was mostly inconvenienced by the attacks. The Germans were able to reroute trains and make efficient, rapid repairs. It had a large amount of rolling stock and locomotives and made a practice of liberating rail stock from occupied countries. Also, during this period there were a large number of operational days curtailed due to shorter daylight hours and to poor weather. When the weather permitted the fighter-bombers were called to fly many close support missions first and then attack the transportation system. Transportation targets took second priority after oil targets for the heavy and medium bomber offensive. At the turn of the year, Allied intelligence determined that the transportation attacks had about reached a point in mid-December that the system, if the attacks were now increased, could no longer be sustained.

In mid-February Reich Armaments and War Production Minister, Albert Speer was placed in control of the German transport system. After taking over he found:

"The traffic emergency requires most extreme measures and also makes it necessary to have a uniform distribution of those traffic capacities that are still available. In recent months, traffic has no longer been able to fill the demands which have been placed on it. It is true that this is not the fault of those who are responsible for the traffic but that the air war situation and the course of the Russian offensive in the east have created this heavy traffic crisis. Our entire economic life is endangered by this heavy traffic crisis.

The armaments industry is getting only limited amounts of raw steel for processing. Only an increase in this volume of traffic can determine whether the industries and economic capacities we still have left and the feeding of our people can be assured. Everything needed to maintain the power of the German people has, of course, first priority. Food and supplies for the populace must be assured to the greatest possible extent.

Over and beyond this, however, transport space can be made available only for direct armament requirements and the most basic industries necessary for this. It is a matter of course that troop transports, above all, have priority and will be carried out unconditionally. It is, however, also a matter of course that the other Wehrmacht freight can be only transported to the extent permitted for the rest of the economy." (Speer Memorandum, 19 February 1945)

In mid-February Reich Armaments and War Production Minister Albert Speer was placed in control of the German transport system. Hitler and Speer inspect a new truck off the production line. (Author/West)

In early March rail transport priorities were:

1) Army transport for operations and supply
2) Coal
3) Food
4) Emergency program of the Reich Ministry for Armaments and War Production
5) Refugees

Armaments Minister, Albert Speer, in a memorandum on 18 February:

"In recent months, (rail) traffic had no longer been able to fill the demands which have been placed on it. It is true that this is not the fault of those who are responsible for the traffic but that the air war situation and the Russian offensive in the east have created this heavy traffic crisis. Our entire economic life is endangered by this weakening of the traffic system."

By mid-February the loss of locomotives and rolling stock had become a major problem.

By mid-February the rail situation neared crisis proportions. The loss of rolling stock was reduced to 28,000 rail cars when 36,000 were deemed to be essential. A minimum of 13,000 carloads of coal was required to maintain the economy. On 14 February 10,000 carloads were delivered, 8,000 on the 21st and by 9 March only 700 carloads were delivered. In January Army Group B received a daily average of 9.5 trains carrying supplies. By mid-April it received 6 trains and by the first of March only 4.3 daily trains. At the end of February the Wehrmacht Seventh Army was scheduled to receive just over 52,000 replacements but received fewer than 13,000.

Attack on the Bullay Bridge (10 February 1945)

Ninth Air Force medium bombers had tried to knock out the Bullay Railway Bridge on several occasions without success, only causing minor damage. On 10 February P-47s of the 368th Fighter Group had succeeded in putting the center span into the river. When Maj.Gen. O.P. Weyland saw the post strike photos he wrote Maj. General Samuel Anderson, CO of the IX Bombardment Division:

"Dear Sam:

Here's the newest picture of that Bullay Bridge you were interested in for some time. Any time find some little job that's too tough for your mediums, just call on us for a few of our P-47 heavy bombers.

Insultingly yours,
O.P. Weyland
Major General, USA"

Anderson replied:

"Dear Opie:

"Congratulations on the Bullay Bridge job! In view of the fact that it had been severely weakened by medium attacks on 14 and 16 January (photographs inclosed), I am not surprised that your pea shooters were able to collapse the span.

Also in view of the fact that O.R.S. tells me that your claims as to bridges destroyed and railroad cuts are about 70% greater than actual damage, I can appreciate your elation over having one picture to prove one claim.

Equally insultingly yours,
Samuel E. Anderson
Major General, USA"

Operation CLARION (22-23 February 1945)

On 17 December 1944, a *General Plan for Maximum Effort Attack Against Transportation Objectives* was issued under the code name CLARION. It was to be a "wholesale and widespread" attack on rail and water transportation facilities with the object to overwhelm the German repair service and seriously disrupt the ability to supply the battlefield. It was hoped that the Germans would be forced to make use of motor transport for supply and be thus deplete their

CLARION, the *General Plan for Maximum Effort Attack Against Transportation Objectives* was to be a "wholesale and widespread" attack on rail and water transportation facilities. A 358th Fighter Group Thunderbolt dives to the attack. (USAF)

The 358th Fighter Group fighter-bombers strafe and bomb the rail facilities in the town of Gudingen, Germany. (USAF)

precious fuel and oil reserves. Another objective of the continued heavy attacks on the transportation system was to cause a crisis among German transportation workers and result in mass defections. Also, 7,000 bombers and fighter-bombers were to carry out widespread attacks on lightly defended transportation targets over all of Germany to emphasize to the German people the effects of war. The German Ardennes Offensive had put CLARION on hold until late February.

After the great success of the air power, particularly fighter-bombers, in the Battle of the Bulge there was a renewal of the undercurrent for a post war independent Air Force. Although tactical air had gained its place in air warfare, senior American air leaders were "bomber boys" and the role of strategic bombing would be the keystone of the post war independent Air Force. Ninth Air Force commander, Hoyt Vandenberg, was the consummate military politician and realized that his position as the leader of America's largest tactical air force could jeopardize his future in the post war Air Force. An article in the 15 January issue of *Time* magazine lauded Vandenberg and the 9th Air Force for their tactical support of the ground forces. The article was generally flattering but one paragraph implied that Vandenberg was under the control of the generals on the ground and that he had a ground support mentality. The insecure and self-serving Vandenberg needed to rectify this perception. From that point, to distance himself from tactical air he referred all air support requests from Bradley's Twelfth Army Group for approval by the tactical air command involved. However, his self-serving decision also had the effect of slowing the request process for air support that cost time and infantry lives. Vandenberg asked his head of intelligence, Col. Richard Hughes, to formulate some plan to prove that he had a strategic air mentality. The Allies were about to surround the Ruhr, trapping thousands of German troops and Hughes made a list of cities, roads and bridges along the periphery of the Ruhr Valley to be attacked to prevent the Germans from escaping. Hughes and Vandenberg flew personally to pitch the plan to Eisenhower in Paris. The use of tactical air forces in a strategic role intrigued Eisenhower's staff and the plan was approved as part of CLARION. Ira Eaker opposed the plan in that it was intended to break down German morale by inflicting most of its casualties on the German population and that it would have no long-term effect on the massive and redundant German rail system. However, the plan gained the support of Marshall and Spaatz and the attacks were scheduled for the next clear day. Vandenberg's strategy paid off in the future as he was named the Chief of Staff to lead the new independent Air Force in 1948, replacing Spaatz.

358th Fighter Group pilots personally inspect the damage they inflicted on a bridge they had bombed. Later bridges were spared as their destruction impeded the swift Allied advance. (USAF)

CLARION was aided by some of the best flying weather since the previous summer. While the operation was planned to be a one-day affair the good weather, the large amount of bombs dropped from lower altitudes and relatively small losses led to a similar operation the next day. On the 22nd and 2rd of February Bomber Command, 8th and 15th Air Force strategic bombers attacked eastern, southern and north-central Germany. The US IX and British 2nd TAF hit targets nearer to the front in western and northwestern Germany. The 2,125 bombers dropped over 6,000 tons of bombs on 80 targets and the TACs dropped another 2,500 tons on 37 targets. The three 9th Air Force TACs flew 1,082 effective sorties comprising armed recon, air-ground cooperation missions and escort missions after which they conducted bombing and strafing sorties on assigned targets and targets of opportunity. The results were impressive: 117 destroyed and 78 damaged motor transport, 87-33 locomotives, 631-962 rail cars, 6-10 tanks, 10-18 rail and 182 road cuts, 0-22 bridges for a loss of 13 fighter-bombers. Four missions flying 48 P-47s of the 404th Fighter Group under GCO, Col. Leo Moon were assigned anti-flak support for 9th Air Force medium bombers. As the flak was light, the Group was free to bomb and strafe. The 404th returned to base with 25-6 locomotives, 124-68 rail cars, 12 buildings and three factories destroyed and 24 rail cuts for a loss of four planes damaged by flak.

The demonstration of bomber and fighter-bomber air power was imposing as it almost totally disrupted the enemy transport system across Germany in an arc from west of the Rhine to north and south of Berlin. But the expectation of CLARION to have lasting effects on German industry, transport and morale again proved wrong. After CLARION it was not possible to accurately access the damage inflicted on the German rail system as the reconnaissance and photographic methods of the time were not proficient enough. But after CLARION there was no evidence of a large-scale breakdown of the Reichsbahn's ability to transport supplies, or of a large-scale disruption of its repair organization, or of mass defections of railway workers nor did CLARION have any lasting effect on German civilian population that had already had suffered extensive air attacks. The Joint Intelligence Committee investigation showed that CLARION had only temporary and local effects on the rail system and that military traffic continued to go through. It concluded that it had no effect on the over all capacity of Germany to go on with the war. Sir Charles Portal agreed with the JIC conclusion and recommended against further CLARION-type operations. To defend their fundamental thinking on air power Tedder, Spaatz and Doolittle were obligated to disagree with the JIC but dispatched no further large-scale CLARION-type operations during the war. There would be no ultimate display of Allied air power that would finally bring Germany to its knees.

Operation GRENADE (23 February 1945)

Immediately following CLARION, in the early morning of 23 February, the US First Army began its drive to the Rhine and the US Ninth Army to the south drove across the Roer River toward Cologne and the Rhine River. The Ninth had some problems with accurate German artillery during its crossing of the Roer but it was put out of commission by air operations during the day. The XIX TAC supported the US Third Army as it approached the Pruem River. These attacks were christened GRENADE.

CLARION had taken the place of the heavy pre-assault missions originally planned for the XXIX TAC as their fighter-bombers ranged throughout the area. The hastily retreating Germans had loaded tanks on railroad flatcars and tried to hide in tunnels to escape. Near Ehrany a train tried to hide in a tunnel only to find that cars protruded from both ends of the tunnel and the 371st Fighter Groups was able to destroy the train by blocking both ends of the tunnel. The 368th Fighter Group flew 28 missions into the Pruem-Bitburg Pocket and destroyed 262-69 M/T, 56-54 tanks, 58-47 armored vehicles, 30-9 buildings and 7-5 gun positions. For the day, flying 71 missions of 527 sorties from 0850 to 1910, the XIX TAC claimed 336-134 M/T, 64-58 tanks, 58-48 armored vehicles, 16-12 locomotives 460-817 rail cars, 81-34 buildings. A total of 194 tons of GP and RDX, 14.1 tons of fragmentation bombs, 12 tons of incendiaries, 12 tons of white phosphorus and 28 leaflet bombs were dropped. They claimed 4-1-1 in aerial combat but lost seven fighter-bombers. XXIX TAC in the north claimed 260-338 M/T, 6-9 tanks, 11-3 armored vehicles, 50-13 locomotives and 751-429 railcars and 201-158 buildings for the loss of three aircraft. It had flown 613 sorties for the day, a new record for the command.

Due to the air support, the Third Army penetrated the Siegfried Line and advanced all along the front and established a bridgehead across the Saar River southwest of Trier. Once the strong fixed defenses of the Siegfried Line had been breached, German resistance became disorganized especially after the important communications center at Bitburg and the pivotal defensive position at Trier had been reduced. The VIII, XII and XX Corps joined to begin their own blitzkrieg attack toward the heart of Germany.

Continuing Attacks on the German Rail System (until the war's end)

Except for interruptions by poor weather and the Ardennes Offensive, the role of the American tactical air effort from late summer 1944 to the end of the war was to attack the well-developed rail network inside Germany upon which its military was dependent. Initially the objective of the attacks on marshaling yards, rail lines and railway bridges was to decrease the German's ability to move troop, equipment and supplies without interference to the battlefront. However, because of the size and complexity of the rail system in western Germany the Allies did not have the same carefully planned and coordinated interdiction strategy that had just been so successful in northern France. The destruction of the Reichsbahn remained the immediate objective of the tactical air force.

As the Allies advanced to the German border, a number of Allied strategic air power advocates determinedly pressed for a concentrated effort of the strategic air forces to destroy the railway system in western Germany. Although the strategic air campaign had had success in France an analysis of the complex German rail network concluded that a similar undertaking would be too great to be effective. As a result the 8th Air Force was ordered to continue its campaign against the German oil industry as its first priority and the German rail network as its second. However, rail marshaling yards were the specific target which were most attacked by the 8th Air Force from December 1944 until the end of the war.

As the Allies approached the Rhine, the weakened German Wehrmacht had only four armored divisions and ten to twelve infantry divisions available to defend the Homeland. However, they only had to defend 350 miles of front from the Scheldt to Switzerland and supplies for this force involved its movement over shorter distances on a better road and rail system than France and Belgium. It was hoped that the Rhine bridges could be preserved for Allied use rather than be destroyed. A SHAEF G-2 Memorandum of 11 September 1944 suggested that a long term, large-scale program of

14th Fighter Group P-38s attack Weiheim marshaling yards in Germany on 19 April 1945. At this time nothing of value could move or stand still in Germany without the attention of Allied fighter-bombers. Note a P-38 flying over the yard (arrow). (USAF)

interdiction was not suitable but strafing and bombing strikes should vigorously attack profitable targets of opportunity or those revealed by intelligence or reconnaissance. Attacks on the dense rail network in western Germany, particularly rail centers and rail line cutting (especially on either side of the Rhine bridges) were to be vigorously pursued but limited to those which were directly connected to the ground battle.

While the strategic bombers were bombing marshaling yards and other rail targets well behind the battlefield, the tactical air forces were attacking rail targets related directly to the front. The intention of the tactical air forces was to reduce or eliminate the movement of German infantry and supplies to the front or away from it. Ammunition, fuel and supply dumps received little interest because the rail targets were deemed more important and also because dumps were well dispersed and camouflaged so as to be difficult to identify and destroy. Highways and motor transport, except as close support targets, were of less importance because of the acute shortage of gasoline limited the use of motor vehicles to a minimum. As the Russians advanced from the east and the British and Americans from the west, strategic targets became of minor importance. The need for close support also lessened as German resistance weakened. Interdiction attacks continued at a declining rate as the Germans lost more and more territory and much of their rail system and locomotives and rolling stock.

In late 1944, when the battlefront was stabilizing at the German frontier, rail-cutting operations were resumed to isolate the battlefield. According to *Operational Assessment of Rail Interdiction by Fighter-Bombers Attacking Open Rail Lines* (IX TAC Re port No. 67, Operational Research Section) systematic air attacks were required to destroy all the rail lines supplying a specific battle area in order to isolate it. (The report used attacks on the eight rail lines carrying east-west traffic west of the Rhine for its analysis.) The plan was to send out two group missions to attack rail lines selected to prevent rail traffic from moving east and west. Rail lines west of the Rhine were designated the GREEN systems and the ones east of the Rhine were known as the RED or BLUE systems. The lines of the GREEN system were changed often as the battlefronts changed. Approximately 70% of the sorties flown against the rail lines were by fighter-bombers. Report No. 67 showed the following results. A network of eight rail lines leading to a battle area could carry five to ten times the required military traffic. Cutting one track only inconvenienced the enemy and meant that there was one less track to cut to make isolation total. One track left uncut continued to allowed traffic to carry the necessary supplies to the front. It was found that three sorties were required to cut one line. A force of four flights was necessary to give 90% probability to cut *one* rail line. To cut eight rail lines leading to the front, at 90% probability, 260 fighter-bombers were required. With perfect pre-attack reconnaissance the 90% probability of cutting all eight lines required 100 fighter-bomber sorties. Rail-cutting was made using a dive-bombing attack with the 500 lb. GP bomb armed with an 8-15 second delay fuse. The object of the 500 lb. bomb was to create as large a crater as possible. No reliance was given to pilot's post-mission assessment that their particular assigned rail line had been cut as dive-bombing bomb bursts were not observed by the pilot at close range. It was reported that it took only five to eight hours to repair even a direct hit on a line by non-essential labor (e.g."slave" or POW from occupied countries). With these seemingly mediocre results, rail cutting was used as a stopgap to other, more effective long-term isolation operations such as against bridges. IX TAC Report No. 67, found:

"With the present number of fighter-bomber aircraft available, the bombing accuracy, weapon effectiveness and nature of the German rail network (unlike Italy ed.) it is impossible to achieve isolation or paralyzation over a period of time by the sole use of F/B attacks against open rail lines....The results of these attacks then were of a harassing nature, for isolation was probably never attained."

Report No. 67 seems to contradict findings after the occupation of the areas involved in France and Belgium rail cuting missions. At this time the TACs had so many fighter-bombers on hand for all missions that rail-cutting was a profitable under taking as it further stretched the rail system capacity for movement and repair.

As a result of attacks on the German rail system, ammunition supply became critically low at the beginning of February as the ammunition on hand was fired and only small amounts arrived at the front. In a memo from von Rundstedt to Model (OB west), 13 February 1945, it was predicted that the Army would out of heavy and light howitzer shells in seven days. The situation was exacerbated on 5 March when three ammunition trains were attacked, destroying 450 tons of light howitzer ammunition, 450 tons of 150mm rocket launcher rockets and 225 tons of 240mm gun ammunition. Hitler made up the deficit to OB West by releasing howitzer and rocket launcher ammunition from the Fuehrer reserve.

Tank maintenance also suffered. As air attacks destroyed large tank maintenance and repair areas small repair teams were organized and sent to the front. It was increasingly impossible to transport damaged tanks back from the front for repairs, as special cars were required to carry them back. These special cars were destroyed one-by-one and could not be replaced.

Motor transport was not to be a replacement for rail. The heavy bomber campaign against the German oil industry so reduced the gasoline supply that it had to be rationed carefully. On 30 March 1945, Hitler directed:

"....the fuel situation requires continued extremely minimal fuel allocations to the Wehrmacht.... Exclusive use of these slight amounts for combat purposes must be assured. I therefore order that liquid fuel be used only for vehicles directly involved in combat (tanks, assault guns, etc.). For command and supply vehicles, when the trip cannot be made by wood-gas vehicles or by using horses, liquid fuel can be used only in exceptional cases."

On 22 January 1945, as the Russians moved toward Berlin, Hitler ordered the Sixth Panzer Army to transfer from the western front to help protect the German capitol. Despite, having rail and fuel priority, the unit never left the front due to fighter-bomber attacks, lack of fuel to move its tanks, the transporting trains non-arrival due the fighter-bomber attacks and the disruption of communications that made it impossible to locate the trains that had been delayed. By the end of January German fuel supplies had become so critical that von Rundstedt asked Jodl to restrict Luftwaffe operations, except for reconnaissance, and release their fuel to the Army. In February, von Rundstedt requested 52,215 men for his Seventh Army but only received 12,902. Until mid-March the German repair organization was able to keep rail tracks open and bridges repaired. The continuous attack and destruction of the Weser River bridges stopped trains there. Troops and supplies there had to be off-loaded onto vehicles to be transported to the front. There were not enough trucks or fuel available to complete the trip.

As mentioned the Allied command did not pursue the same well planned, concentrated interdiction plan against the Reichsbahn in western Germany as it did in France and Belgium earlier. There should have been a firm rail interdiction plan in place as the rail system in Germany was more extensive, more heavily defended by AA, had more substantial and better-defended bridges, a more capable repair organization and probably most important, flying weather that was worse than that over France. With a plan the Allies' great excess of fighter and medium bombers could have overcome these obstacles and produced even better results. The escorts of the 8th Air Force had no Luftwaffe opposition and were released for fighter-bomber duty and there were more IX TACS and fighter-bombers than ever before. The German ground armies had mostly been reduced to a fleeing mass with diminished defensive capabilities not requiring the attention of fighter-bombers except in less frequently requested close support sorties and major attacks and breakouts. The problem with the rail interdiction program was that it was spread throughout Germany and should have been concentrated initially in the area between the West Wall and Rhine. If this area had been saturated the attacks could have broken the German ability to deliver supplies and its repair ability. As the front moved east, a defined interdiction area behind the front such as was established in Italy would again stress German rail capabilities and so on until there was no further capability. As it was the effectiveness of this anti-rail air campaign was reduced by the German's decision to assign first priority on the increasingly diminished rail system to its military requirements. But the Catch-22 of their decision was that German industry experienced a reduction in the transport of raw materials and of finished products causing the entire German economy to degenerate at an accelerating rate.

Clearing the Saar-Moselle Triangle (19-23 February 1945)

The Saar-Moselle Triangle was bounded by the Saar River on the east, the Moselle River on the west and the Siegfried Line to the south. The 130 square mile area blocked the XX Corps path in its attack to capture the city of Trier. Plans were to capture the high ground west of Saarburg that ran parallel to the Saar River and then to advance to the east and northeast to positions south and southeast of Trier to prevent a German retreat from the city. The rough, hilly and often densely wooded terrain made armored attack difficult and was suited for enemy defense. The XIX TAC was assigned to provide air support.

The 94th Infantry and Tenth Armored Divisions began the offensive on 19 February. Poor morning weather grounded fighter-bombers but after noon they flew air cooperation missions for the XX Corps. Despite low clouds and poor visibility seven armed vehicles and tanks, 19 motor transport, 35 railway cars, four gun positions, 24 defended building were either destroyed or damaged.

The next day the 94th advanced five miles under heavy artillery fire and a tenacious defense while the 10th armored Division advanced through heavy mine fields but against light resistance. Poor weather hindered fighter-bombers air cooperation but again they achieved admirable results: 14 armored vehicles and tanks, 39 motor transport, six locomotives, 28 railway cars and 22 defended buildings were destroyed or damaged and the towns of Eschied, Taben and Trassen were set ablaze.

On the 21st, the weather cleared and the XIX TAC fighter-bombers flew 32 four fighter-bomber cooperation missions for the XX Corps providing almost continuous cover throughout the day. The results were outstanding and greatly aided the advance: seven armored vehicles and tanks, 140 motor transport, four locomotives, 188 railway cars, one gun position and 53 defended buildings were destroyed or damaged and many towns within and near the German perimeter were bombed and strafed at the call of ground control.

On the 22nd, the 94th and Tenth continued their advance and the Saar River was crossed and a bridgehead established. The XIX TAC was assigned to provide medium bomber escort as because of their previous success the Triangle had been cleared of virtually of all worthwhile enemy targets. However, they flew two missions of 23 sorties outside the Triangle in an armed recce/isolation mode. The claims were: three tanks, 20 motor vehicles, and 140 railway cars. Night fighters flew nine patrol and four intruder sorties along the front targeting motor convoys, trains and towns.

On the 24th, the last pockets of German resistance in the Triangle were mopped up and XX Corps forces reinforced the bridgehead. Fighter-bombers again flew missions unrelated to the fighting in the Triangle. Twenty-three four-plane flights were flown as XX Corps forces reinforced the bridgehead. Fighter-bombers again flew missions against rail marshaling yards and rail traffic with many flat cars carrying tanks or motor transport being destroyed or damaged in violent ammunition explosions.

During the initial stages of the battle for the Triangle the fighter-bomber force successfully engaged in close support missions but did not determine the final outcome. They contributed to the relatively easy ground victory by adding to the destruction and attrition of military hardware and the logistics system. As the ground forces thrust into the Triangle the number of close air targets diminished and the fighter-bombers were released by the XX Corps and conducted armed recce/interdiction missions outside of the Triangle in areas that would be the next objectives of the XX Corps.

Roer River (23 February 1945)

After the German Ardennes Offensive was defeated, the plans for the crossing of the Roer River and an advance toward the Rhine, north of the Ruhr, were prepared. Along with these plans a detailed air study was prepared pertaining to the most effective use of air power in the operation.

After an long and intensive artillery barrage, the assault crossing by the Ninth Army began at 0330 on 23 February 1945, and was accomplished that day without significant German resistance and only moderate losses. The Ninth exploited the easy crossing and moved rapidly to the west bank of the Rhine by 11 March. The XXIX TAC came to full strength in late February when the two former wings consisted of five fighter groups and one TAC recce unit were added. On the 2rd Brig.Gen. Richard Nugent's XXIX TAC attacked the extensive rail and road net to the east, with 602 aircraft destroying 64 locomotives and 1,182 freight cars and 175 M/T. P-38s of the Lt.Col. Morgan Griffin's 370th Fighter Group hit the Honig area. Squadrons led by Maj. John Crouch and Capt. James Buskley destroyed 35 locomotives, 344 flatcars, 14 passenger cars, cut 26 rail lines and blew up two bridges. After five days of good weather, the XXIX had seen the biggest days in its history when it flew 2,469 fighter-bomber sorties bagging 192 locomotives, 2,693 rail cars destroyed or damaged, 377 rail cuts, six rail bridges destroyed and 1,064 buildings destroyed or damaged. Lt.Gen. Hoyt Vandenberg, CG of the 9th Air Force congratulated Gen. Nugent: "The results obtained in your close cooperation with attacking ground units and the destructive blows dealt the enemy movements in the rear areas reflect great credit on the training, technique of operations and superior leadership throughout your command."

The success of the operation was attributed to the cooperation of the tactical air forces. Medium bombers were outstanding in their attacks on vital communication centers and marshaling yards. Fighter-bombers of the XXIX TAC provided excellent close support to the infantry by attacking defended towns and villages, motor transport, tanks and gun positions. They flew armed recce missions to interdict enemy lines of communication and provided air cover for pre-crossing troop and equipment concentrations and for engineer bridges by day. A major failure was that the Luftwaffe destroyed two newly completed engineer bridges during the night of 23-24 February, which delayed the movement of essential equipment and supplies. A stronger night fighter presence could have prevented this loss.

Strafing the Luftwaffe on the Ground (February-March 1945)

The 8th Air Force fighters engaged in air-to-air action against a reluctant Luftwaffe in February but if the Luftwaffe wasn't in the air then they had to be on the ground. On the 3rd the 8th Air Force claimed 21-1-7 in the air and 21-11 on the ground. The 84th Squadron of the 78th Fighter Group accounted for 16-6 of the ground victories and Lt. K.R. McGinnis of the 55th Fighter Group was high ground scorer with four Fi-156 destroyed. Nine pilots were lost, six POWs.

On 9 February the 8th claimed 22-5-8 in the air and 43-44 on the ground. The 77th Fighter Squadron of the 20th Fighter Group had a steller day with 39-5 on the ground and 2-1-0 in the air. Maj. Merle Gilbertson led the squadron down to a grass field at Esperstedt that was covered with 60+ single and twin-engined aircraft. The squadron attacked for 20 minutes until most P-51s ran out of ammunition. On their return home they were attacked by 15 Me-109s that were taken on by the pilots who had some ammo remaining. Two Germans were shot down and one probably destroyed with no losses to themselves. Top ground scorers for the day were Capt. Lowell Einhaus (6 FW-190s), Capt. Charles Cole (6 FW-190 destroyed and 1 damaged) and Lt. R.D. Jones (4 FW190s and one Me-109). The 20th suffered three aircraft with flak damage but lost none of the six pilots were lost that day (5 KIA).

On the 20th the claims were 16-1-1 in the air and 46-32 on the ground. Again the 20th Fighter Group led the way with 6-1-0 in the air and 26-23 on the ground. The only ground ace for the day was Capt. F.A. Morgan of the 356th Fighter Group who destroyed five on the ground. The 20th also claimed 15-5 locomotives and 25-115 rail cars. The 55th Fighter Group claimed 89-10 locos and 24-64 rail cars. Thirteen pilots were lost (6 KIA-1 MIA-1 ASR-5 POW).

On the 25th the claims were 22-1-3 air and 23-17 ground. The 55th Fighter Group was 6 air and 8-3 ground. The 4th Fighter Group had 11-8 ground and 2-1-0 air. Ten pilots were lost (4 KIA-2 MIA-4 POW)

On 9 February 1945 20th Fighter Group (8th Air Force) P-51s hit Eperstedt Airdrome near Gotha. There are 21 burning hulks on this field. For the day they destroyed 43 aircraft. (USAF)

A Do-17 has just been forced to crash land on a snow-covered field (note skid marks of tail wheel) and is being strafed. There is a prone body laying at the rear of plane. (USAF)

The 27th was a big day for the 353rd and 4th Fighter Groups. For the day the 8th Air Force claimed 2 air and 83-28 ground. After being released from bomber escort duty to Leipzieg the 350th Squadron of the 353rd Fighter Group searched for targets of opportunity in the Botha area. Squadron commander, Maj. Walker Boone spotted over 50 aircraft on the Rohrensee Airdrome. Boone dropped down and made a quick pass to check the AA defenses and when he wasn't fired on, he led the squadron on a "ring-around-the-airdrome" strafing attack. When they finished there were 37 burning enemy fighters (10 FW-190s, 10 Me-410s, 5 Ju-88s, 4 Me-110s, 2 He-219s, 1 Me-109, 1 Ar-240, and 4 unidentified aircraft) and 16 more damaged. Boone accounted for 7 destroyed and 4 damaged (2 Fw-190s, 2 He-219s, a Me-110, the Ar-240 and a unidentified twin-engined aircraft). Capt. Herbert Kolb got 5-3 destroying 3 FW-190s, 1.5 Me-410s and 0.5 unidentified twin-engine aircraft. 2Lt. Roland Lanoue also was a strafing ace in a day with 5 including 3 Focke Wulfs and 2 Me-410s. Col. Everett Stewart led "B" Group of the 4th Fighter Group on a bomber support mission to Halle and after the mission was completed, the 335th Squadron remained with the bombers and the 334th strafed targets of opportunity and Weimar Airdrome. All fighters made four to six passes on the airdrome and destroyed 43 German aircraft with 1Lt Donald Malmsten getting seven. The squadron lost two MIA (subsequently POWs).

On 2 March the onslaught continued as the 8th claimed 67-7-23 air and 34-26 ground. The 364th Fighter Squadron of the 357th Fighter Group did the most damage on the ground with 15 destroyed and 15 damaged. Lt. Dale Karger claimed 4 destroyed and 4 damaged on the ground and .5 in the air while Lt. D.R. Williams destroyed 2 on the ground and damaged 9 more plus .5 in the air. Fifteen pilots were lost (5 KIA and 10 KIA)

The TAC Situation in March 1945

In March the TACs were almost able to supply continuous daily air support as the weather in the month was generally good and missions were canceled only on three days. The TACs were able to fly more often and in greater numbers than ever before causing increasing damage to German rail and road communications lines and to their supply depots. From D-Day the German ground forces were more or less numerically equal to the Allied ground forces. In addition, the German soldier had demonstrated skill, courage and tenacity that made him arguably the best soldier of World War II. But the TACs, in conjunction with the bombers, had complete air superiority. Allied fighter-bombers were able to dictate the enemy's ability to maneuver its forces and supplies by the destruction of its rail and road lines of communication. But from this point it was realized that with final victory was close at hand and it would be the grunt on the ground who would have to destroy the enemy and drive him east to eventual surrender. While the TACs could not be credited with winning any ground battle they helped make each victory possible and with fewer casualties.

Kyll River to the Rhine (1-12 March 1945)

At the end of February 1945, the XII Corps was in a position to force a crossing of the Kyll River, giving the Fourth Armored Division the opportunity to make a run to the Rhine. The XIX TAC was assigned to support the operation beginning 1 March (no medium or heavy bombers were utilized during this period). On 2 and 3 March, XIX fighter-bombers maintained air superiority, provided "superior and accurate" close cooperation and were especially effective against enemy movements and provided superlative armored column cover. On 3 March, with this assistance from the XIX TAC, the Fifth Army was able to establish a bridgehead was across the Kyll. On 4 March, a second bridgehead was established and was consolidated. The 4th Armored Division crossed into the bridgehead and began a spectacular dash to the Rhine, covering 52 miles in 58 hours. By 8 March, the 4th had by-passed Mayen and Koblenz held positions along the Rhine and was patrolling across the river. The 5th Infantry Division followed, mopping up the by-passed enemy pockets. However, during this breakout rain and fog grounded all aircraft.

From 9-12 March the Third Army consolidated the break through clearing enemy pockets left by the 4th Armored Division and advanced toward the Rhine. During this period the weather cleared and the fighter-bombers flew very effective Armored Column Cover and armed recce attacks and were instrumental in reducing enemy pockets. Enemy aircraft that counter-attacked were quickly destroyed or dispersed.

Rhine Bridges and the Remagen Bridgehead (9-27 March 1945)

The success of the Allied attacks on the bridges over the Seine and Loire in France had so restricted the movement of German forces that it was only natural to direct similar efforts against the Rhine bridges. These bridges were larger and more strongly constructed and more heavily defended than the French bridges. The AA defenses made the heavy and medium bombers attack from higher altitudes, which were less accurate. The construction of the bridges made them unsuitable for fighter-bomber attack. These bridges were repeatedly attacked in the fall and winter and the minimal damage

The Ludendorff Bridge at Remagen in mid-March 1945 was the scene of frantic German operations to destroy it after their demolition charges failed to explode. Note the pontoon bridge down river. (USAF)

was quickly repaired and the Germans continued to use them until they demolished them after they withdrew over them in February and March. There were 63 bridges (29 railway, 22 road and 12 pontoon road) over the Rhine between Rotterdam and Basle along with 100 ferry crossings. Some of the bridges were among the largest in Europe ranging from 700 to 7,000 feet in length.

As early as mid-September 1944 the Germans began provisions for the destruction of the Rhine bridges. Work began on the construction of ferries and plans were made for three over water and three underwater pipelines to cross the river. However, the shortage of fuel and the ability of the railroads to carry adequate fuel to the front led to the abandonment of the pipeline plan. By mid-October the Allies stepped up their air attacks on the bridges but any damage was quickly repaired and none became impassable. By mid-December 17 bridges were damaged by bombing but only four were total losses. The Germans placed demolitions and destroyed threatened and expendable bridges and floods on the northern Rhine made several more bridges impassable.

The 9th Armored Division of the First Army moved towards the Rhine and surprisingly found the Ludendorf Railroad Bridge at Remagen intact. To exploit this stroke of luck and to permit as many troops to cross safely into the bridgehead on the eastern bank was to provide protection of the bridge from Luftwaffe air attacks. AA units were given priority of movement and within two days after the capture of the bridge, a bristling AA defense was in place. First Army and IX TAC brass agreed that IX TAC would assist in the defense of the area by its usual means of armed recce in front of the bridgehead to prevent the movement of enemy reserves and supplies into the area and to break up any potential counterattacks. But in addition to this function, they were to fly continuous patrols over the area to intercept Luftwaffe aircraft. These patrols were to be flown at high altitudes, as the AA batteries were to control close air defense.

On 13 March the IX TAC had its best day in its air defense of the Bridge when it scored 9-5-6 Luftwaffe aircraft. At 1100 on the 14th, the 36th Fighter Group flew a mission to Lippe A/D and discovered over 50 aircraft, mostly Ju-87 Stukas, armed and ready to takeoff to attack Remagen. The P-47s attacked for 40 minutes dropping 500lb. bombs, launching rockets and then strafed leaving 23 Stukas and one Me-109 destroyed and damaging 29 others. The 404th Fighter Group followed the 36th Fighter Group and destroyed 21, mostly Ju-87s and damaging 19 more. However, two of their P-47s collided in mid-air, killing both pilots. That afternoon the 2rd Squadron of the 36th returned to destroy eight Ju-87, (damaged six) and three Me-109s. The 22nd Squadron followed destroying two FW-190s and damaging a Me-109. The total for the day was 37-27 that would remain on the ground not to attack the bridge. Between 7-14 March 372 Luftwaffe aircraft had attacked the bridge and 80 were shot down by AA fire.

An assessment of the effectiveness of the air defenses confirmed that the AA batteries were more effective than the fighters in combating enemy air attacks. Poor weather conditions reduced the effectiveness of the US fighter high cover. Individual enemy fighters were able to slip through the overcast, under the fighter high cover patrols, to make quick attacks on the bridge and surrounding area. However, the fighter-bombers carried out a program of armed recce against the movement of supplies and reinforcements to the area and interdiction missions against key communications centers that prevented the Germans from attacking the vulnerable bridgehead.

Third Army Attacks Toward the Rhine (13-22 March 1945)

Early on 13 March three divisions of the XX Corps began attacks through the Schwartzwald forest that was an obstacle lying before the rich industrial Saar basin. The first day of the offensive was helped by good weather and 52 missions totaling 430 sorties were flown of various types; close support, armed recce and bomber escort. Aerial claims were 8-0-4, 140 M/T, 21 armored vehicles and tanks, nine locomotives and 300 rail cars and 92 buildings were damaged or destroyed. The next day the Moselle River was crossed aided by 70 missions of 492 sorties which claimed 245 M/T, 17 locomotives and 315 rail cars, 26 gun positions and 135 buildings. The good weather continued and on the 15th, a record number of missions were flown by the XIX TAC in cooperation with the Third Army that was clearing out German opposition north of the Moselle. The XIX TAC flew 101 missions flying 643 sorties were launched, many of which were four-plane close cooperation missions. The 367th Fighter Group hit a motor transport depot at Gelnhausen, a repair shop at Friedburg and the Wiesbaden marshaling yard. Ground claims included 219 M/T, 38 tanks and armored vehicles, 15 locomotives and 393 rail cars, 13 gun positions, 65 horse-drawn vehicles and 161 buildings. Patton's Third Army, led by the Fourth Armored Division, advanced out of the Moselle bridgehead against scattered and disorganized resistance as the Germans were attempting a mass withdrawal. Close cooperation missions continued to take its toll on motor and rail transport. As the VIII Corps attacked Koblenz and moved toward the Rhine the XIX TAC had a field day against motor transport. The retreating Germans crowded the roads and the fighter-bombers recorded 1,033 M/T in 76 missions of 714 sorties. Along with the M/T; 106 tanks and armored vehicles, 49 locomotives and 488 rail cars, 18 gun positions, 416 horse-drawn vehicles and 13 horse-drawn guns and 72 buildings were damaged or destroyed. With the support of what Patton described "superb air cooperation" his 4th Armored Division captured the important Rhine river city of Worms on the 20th. Patton's tanks and infantry burst into the German rear between the Rhine and Saar to begin one of the foremost routs in armored warfare. His tank columns, followed closely by infantry, took a page out of German Blitzkrieg doctrine and drove deeply into the Rhine-Moselle-Saar Triangle. Supply dumps were over run and large numbers of prisoners were taken. On the 19th 8,355 POWs were taken and on the 20th over 15,000 were captured. XIX TAC fighter-bombers were active in preventing the Germans from crossing the Rhine. They flew 67 missions of 655 sorties flying close air support for the XII and XX Corps, armed recce along and beyond the banks of the Rhine, attacked airfields, M/T and rail targets. Claims included 859 M/T, 38 locomotives and 173 rail cars, 283 horse-drawn vehicles and 22 horse-drawn guns, ten armored vehicles and tanks, 30 gun positions and 104 buildings. The Third Army having breached the Siegfried Line and cleared the Saar basin continued its drive to the Rhine at Worms,

Mainz and Ludwigshafen. It joined with the Seventh Army that had driven northward through the Siegfried Line. On the 22nd heavy fighting was encountered by the XII Corps around Mainz while the remainder of the Third Army rolled up to the west bank of the Rhine. The weather remained excellent as the XIX TAC flew 68 missions of 661 sorties in cooperation with the XII and XX Corps, armed recce east of the Rhine and a continuation of the road and rail interdiction campaigns. By the end of the day the Third Army had occupied the west bank of the Rhine from Koblenz and Ludwigshafen. The Third Army now occupied more German territory than all the other Allied armies combined having taken 4,600 miles since 13 March and was poised to conquer more.

The success of the Third Army prompted Patton to write XIX CG, Maj. O.P. Weyland the following letter on 21 March:

"The XIX Tactical Air Command and the Third Army have again between committing treason in reverse as we did so happily in August and September.

By this I mean instead of giving aid and comfort to the enemy, we have been giving him pain and discomfort and doing it in a big way.

Let's keep it up!"

Weyland added the following to the letter forwarded it to his command:

"1) With apologies to Patrick Henry I say, if this be treason, let us make the most of it.

2) XIX TAC-Third Army again is showing the world what a perfectly coordinated fighting air-ground team can do. I knew that you would be with me to a man when I assured General Patton that we could 'keep it up' with the Third Army."

"Spy Fry." On 16 March 1945, two flights of 50th Fighter Group P-47s flew a mission using napalm and 500lb. bombs, attacking a German espionage school. The photo shows the direct hit of a napalm bomb exploding on the building. (USAF)

Attack on the Nazi Espionage School (16 March 1944)

In early March the Seventh Army captured a German spy who was turned over to G-2 counter-espionage for interrogation. To save his life, the prisoner who could be executed for spying, readily provided the necessary information about his "alma mater" such as location, construction and class schedules. The 50th Fighter Group was briefed on the school and a mission plan was devised. It was decided that the attack should take place between 0900 and 1130 hours when the "students" would be in class. Since the building was of heavy brick construction an attack plan was formulated using a mixture of bombs and napalm. The first squadron would fly ten P-47s carrying two 500lb. TNT bombs fused at eight to 11 second delay and two P-47s carrying two 75-gallon napalm tanks. The second squadron would dispatch eight napalm-carrying Thunderbolts and four aircraft with two instantaneously fused 500lb. RDX bombs. The RDX was used as it was more powerful than TNT against deep fortifications or cellars in this case.

On 16 March, Col. Harvey Case, 50th Group CO, led the first squadron down to the deck and circled to identify the target and then attacked the school in two ship elements from the southeast at tree-top level. The two napalm fighter-bombers attacked first to keep the students from leaving the school. The TNT bombs followed and tore off the roof and a portion of the top floor. Maj. David McDonald, Deputy Group Commander, led the napalm squadron low from the northeast and enveloped the school in orange fireballs followed by thick black smoke that rose up to 2,000 feet. Lt. George Stucky finished the mission by leading three Thunderbolts in a dive-bombing attack to drive their instantaneously fused RDX bombs into the basement to kill any personnel taking refuge there. The successful mission became known as the "Great Spy Fry" among members of the 50th.

Attack on the German C-in-C, West at Ziegenberg (19 March 1945)

At 0100 on 19 March the 367th Fighter Group was assigned to attack the HQ installations of the German C-in-C West at Ziegenberg, Germany. That morning 367th pilots found it unusual that a maximum effort mission had been scheduled at a time when even squadron level missions were not flown. Only experienced pilots were assigned to the mission which was specially briefed by teams from Weyland's HQ. It had been found by Allied Intelligence in England that the FM von Rundstedt and his staff had occupied the castle at Ziegenberg about 30 miles north of Frankfurt. Most of staff worked in bunkers and tunnels cut in the mountainside but they took their lunch hour at 1330-1430 above ground in the castle. After listening to the briefing, Col. Edward Chickering and his squadron commanders and Ops officers formulated a plan of attack. The first squadron was to dive-bomb at minimum altitude to gain surprise followed by a second squadron that would also dive-bomb. The third squadron would come in and drop napalm into the broken wreckage, burning and suffocating personnel in their underground shelters. West Point graduate and 90 combat mission veteran, Maj. Charles Matheson was chosen to lead the 394th Squadron in the first wave. Each of Matheson's P-47s was armed with two 1,000lb. demolition bombs with 8-11 second delayed action fuses. The 392nd Squadron also

On 19 March the 367th Fighter Group was assigned to attack the HQ installations of Gen. Gerd von Rundstedt, the German C-in-C West at Ziegenberg, Germany. Unknown to the Americas was that von Rundstedt had been replaced by Albert Kesselring and an unexpected visitor that day was Armaments Minister, Albert Speer. This photo recon post strike photo shows the damage to the entire complex. (USAF)

armed with two 1,000lb. bombs was to be the second wave. 392nd CO, Maj. Elmer McTaggart chose 1Lt. Allen Diefendorf to led the squadron. The Lieutenant was outstanding at identifying targets and was an accurate dive-bomber. Maj. Chester Slingerland was to lead the 393rd Squadron in the napalm attack. Col. Chickering flew with Slingerland to act as air commander and observe the mission and direct any changes during the mission. The 48-plane mission was to fly an indirect route to Ziegenberg so as not to alert the Germans. There were no low-level recon photos available, as recon flights would have warned the Germans of an impending attack. The castle was sited on a mountain slope in rugged territory and the amount and position of flak guns was not known. The 367th had only transitioned to the P-47 from the P-38 at the end of February and wasn't totally convinced of the Thunderbolt's superiority as a fighter-bomber.

The 367th's mission began as Matheson and the 394th Squadron took off from the short runway of their new base at Jarney at 1220 followed by Diefendorf's 392nd at 1234 and the napalm-carrying 393rd at 1240. Unknown to the Allies, earlier in the month von Rundstedt had been replaced by FM Albert Kesselring who had so brilliantly conducted German operations in Italy. Also unknown was that German Armaments Minister, Albert Speer, was visiting the castle that day for a noon conference with Kesselring. Their conference had just concluded when the 367th neared Frankfurt at 7,000 feet, high enough to remain out of the range of light automatic AA fire and low enough to evade radar detection. The Group was flying a widely spread formation with the 394th Squadron to the north, the 392nd in the center and the 393rd to the south. As they flew between Frankfurt and Hanau 88mm guns blasted the formation causing the 393rd to pass beyond its scheduled turn. The 394th was only minutes away from Ziegenburg and began its descent at minimum altitude. There was haze up to 4,000 feet that limited Matheson's vision to only a few miles. Diefendorf saw that Matheson turn up the wrong valley and when he looked back he couldn't see the 39rd . Diefendorf broke radio silence to inform Chickering of Matheson's error. Diefendorf spotted Ziegenburg and told Chickering that in several seconds he would be in perfect position for an attack. Chickering needed to make a quick decision, either to allow Diefendorf to attack from a higher altitude and compromise surprise or to recall the Group and return to attack the next day with the German now perhaps alerted. Chickering decided to go for it and Diefendorf and his wingman, Capt. John Adams, dove on the

An immediate post strike photo of the chateau taken by an attacking pilot. Delayed fused 1,000lb. demolition bombs and then a napalm was used in the attack. The 367th was awarded the DUC for the mission. (USAF)

Photos of the chateau after the Allies occupied the area. Despite the apparent heavy damage both Kesselring and Speer escaped harm by retreating to the building's cellar. (USAF)

target at 1335. As the Americans dove, Kesselring was toasting Speer's 40th birthday. Diefendorf picked the front castle door as his aiming point, strafing on the way down. He dropped his bombs at 500 feet followed closely by Adams. Kesselring and Speer rushed through smoke and dust from the explosions into the bunkers. As the 392nd attacked Matheson led the errant 394th back into position and went into drop their bombs and as they left 11 hits from the 60 bombs dropped were counted on the castle. The 393rd arrived at 1355 as the other two squadrons turned back to base. The smoke made it almost impossible for the squadron to find an aiming point for its napalm. Seven containers did hit the castle and two landed nearby.

Post-strike reconnaissance photos showed the complete destruction of the castle's east wing and the remainder to be heavily damaged. Interrogation of German prisoners several days later revealed that 30 soldiers had been killed by the first bombs but most of the officers and Speer and Kesselring had escaped safely down to the bunkers. Kesselring was slightly wounded on the head by a falling chandelier and although the attack did not kill the German commander it did disrupt his communications to his troops, as the Americans were about to cross the Rhine. Kesselring moved his HQ to Thuringia on the 27th and would not be able to duplicate the brilliance he had shown in Italy with the now totally demoralized troops he commanded. As Speer drove from Ziegenburg he passed thousands of retreating German soldiers who cursed him. The 367th was awarded the DUC for its attack on Ziegenburg.

Rhine River/Third Army (23 March 1945)

It was expected that the Rhine River would be a daunting obstacle and crossing it would necessitate significant delays and substantial casualties. However, the Third Army easily crossed with an entire division crossing in 14 hours. Despite repeated counter-attacks, the Third advanced rapidly east, before the west bank had been secured.

No detailed air plan was developed. XIX TAC flew fighter sweeps and ground controlled close cooperation missions over the crossing. The next day it increased its efforts under perfect weather conditions to keep in step with the rapid advance of the ground forces. Area cover and direct cooperation missions were for the advance and armed recce in the Mainz-Frankfurt area. XII Corps

The Bad Durkheim-Kaiserlautern Road after the XIX TAC attacked on 24 March 1945 as part of Operation UNDERTONE. (USAF)

An American jeep weaves through fighter-bomber destruction of a retreating German column on the Kaiserlautern-Neustadt road on 19-20 March 1945 during Operation UNDERTONE. (USAF)

evaluated XIX TAC's efforts as being "excellent." For the day 21 close support missions of 147 sorties were flown against rail facilities, motor transport and gun positions. Twenty-three area cover missions (180 sorties) were flown during which 19 fighters were destroyed and four damaged as Luftwaffe activity was temporarily revived. Five armed recce missions (178 sorties) were flown resulting in the destruction of motor and rail transport and aircraft on the ground. Night fighter patrols flew seven sorties resulting in the unsuccessful pursuit of enemy aircraft and the strafing of convoys. By the 24th, the advance drove eastward, aided by XIX TAC fighter-bombers. Fourteen air cover missions (112 sorties) were flown with claims against motor and rail transport. Close cooperation with ground units accounted for seventeen missions (125 sorties) destroyed or damaged motor transport, rail cars and locomotives, tanks and armored vehicles, and gun positions. Armed recce accounted for five missions (73 sorties) on rail equipment. XII Corps assessment of XIX TAC stated:

"XIX TAC continued its excellent support of the attack of the divisions. Fighter cover was continuous from first light to dusk. Fighter-bombers effectively attacked gun positions, vehicles and command installations."

For the day 84 missions for a five group record 775 sorties were flown.

On the 24th the Third Army, again led by the Fourth Armored Division, continued its Blitzkrieg east of the Rhine, breaking out of the Offenheim bridgehead advancing toward Darmstadt. By the 25th, the Third Army took Darmstadt and its thrust again developed into a rout as the retreating German could offer only weak resistance and their demoralized troops surrendered in record numbers, 18,818 POWs.

Night fighters were initially limited due to the lack of targets. After the crossing, Luftwaffe activity increased and they maintained air superiority and carried out small-scale harassment of enemy troops.

Rhine River/Seventh Army/UNDERTONE (15-24 March 1945)

On 14 March the US Seventh and Third Armies began a combined offensive to crack the Siegfried Line defenses in the Saar-Palatine Triangle under the codename Operation UNDERTONE. Opposing the American armies were some of the strongest West Wall concrete and steel fortifications, minefields, interconnecting pillboxes, trenches and tank traps and the ubiquitous Dragons Teeth. Gen. Paul Hausser's Army Group G consisting of the German Seventh Army defended the 75-mile northern end of the Wall and the First Army the 80-mile southern end. Patton's Third Army VII Corps spearheads quickly broke through the German Seventh Army on the lower Moselle River and drove behind the Germans facing the US Seventh Army. The move caught Hausser by surprise as he thought Patton would cross the Rhine at Remagen. The US Seventh Army jumped off on the 15th and advanced despite meeting heavy resistance.

The fighter-bomber groups of the 64th Fighter Wing flew maximum effort during the ten days of UNDERTONE. The First TAF flew an extraordinary 12,392 sorties during the operation. The pilots and ground crews worked from dawn to dusk flying two, three and sometimes four missions a day mostly without rest or food. During the first two days of the offensive the fighter-bombers flew mostly close support missions hitting strongpoints, defended towns and villages and troop concentrations along the front. A 64th Wing record total of 943 fighter-bomber sorties, 300 more than the previous record, were flown on the first day, 96% were on close support missions. The 358th Fighter Group set a one day record for bomb tonnage with 145 and the 50th Fighter Group set a record for most buildings destroyed with 220. French and American B-26 Marauder medium bomber groups also were out in force and contributed heavily to the damage with precision saturation bombing of West Wall fortifications, totally demoralizing their defenders. On the 16th the First TAF fighter-bombers were again in the air from sunrise to sunset totaling 947 sorties to set another 64th Wing record. The 358th Fighter Group set a one-day record by destroying 12 tanks. Again American and French B-26s hit the increasingly disorganized Germans. Weather on the 17th grounded most air action but it cleared on the 18th and every fighter and medium bomber hammered the now retreating Germans. There were only two escape routes, the main east-west highway through the Pfaelzer Forest or the secondary road that ran close behind the West Wall. Soon the roads became crowded and then clogged when the P-47s shot up everything moving on them. The 27th Fighter Group set a daily 64th Wing record when it caused 15 roadblocks. By the 19th the US Seventh Army was making large gains on the south flank and Patton's Third Army was attacking the West Wall from the rear and racing through the center of the Palatine, only ten miles from Mainz. P-47s flew close support missions for the Seventh Army's armored spearheads. The constant fighter-bomber attacks totally disorganized and demoralized the German retreat that became a rout. The Germans were withdrawing east of Kaiserlautern, the geographical center of the Rhine-Moselle triangle, along roads twisting through steep forested hills that led to the plains bordering the Rhine. Large columns of German armor moved on secondary roads that wound through steep hills that made bombing and strafing very difficult. The 358th Fighter Group had spent the preceding five days supporting the Seventh Army in breaching the Siegfried Line and suffered heavy losses in aircraft and personnel. On the 19th, the Group flew through haze and discovered the long German columns and over the next two days virtually annihilated the Germans destroying 790 M/T and damaged 622 more. The 324th Fighter Group established two daily 64th Wing records when it flew 264 sorties for average of almost four (3.94) sorties per aircraft available that day (this also thought to be an ETO sortie/aircraft record). Maj.Gen. Frank Milburn, THI Corps commander, wrote to Brig.Gen. Glenn Barcus, CO of the XII TAC: "In one case, after a group of woods had been bombed and strafed, 130 Germans emerged and surrendered rather than be subjected to further air action. Close support missions have been successful to the point that front line infantry consider fighter-bomber pilots fellow members of their offensive team." On the 20th the First TAF fighter-bombers reset their daily sortie record with 1,005 that would be their wartime record. The 358th destroyed the record daily number of motor transport with 457, the 50th Fighter

Group the most horse-drawn vehicles with 74 and the 324th Fighter Group destroyed the most barges in a day with five. The German withdrawal was so confused and rapid that a close cooperation bomb line could not be set. On the 21st the 6rd Infantry Division broke through at Oberwurzbach and the Germans left the West Wall defense in droves despite Hitler's "stand and die" order. Lack of usable rail lines due to fighter-bomber interdiction forced the Germans to mob the few main roads that funneled into Gerersheim on the Rhine. The traffic jam provided the P-47s with numerous targets that they preceded to bomb and strafe mercilessly. On the Kaiserlautern-Neustadt road 12 Thunderbolts would attack, line abreast, perpendicular to the retreating columns and climb to make another pass. Often they had to wait their turn to attack, as there were so many fighter-bombers in the air. Thousands of vehicles were destroyed and damaged along the route. The same fate waited the retreating Germans on the Landau-Bad Durkheim-Frankenstein highway. Over 500 vehicles were lost on a narrow mountain pass west of Bad Durkheim. By the evening of the 24th a few thousand German rearguard troops remained west of the Rhine as the German Seventh and First Armies were virtually destroyed. They had lost 38,000 KIA and another 100,000 were taken prisoner. The American Sixth Army Group had broken the Siegfried Line and captured the Rhineland and stood along the Rhine ready to move into the Reich. First TAF fighter-bombers claimed 51 tanks, 46 guns, 2,542 motor vehicles, 284 horse-drawn vehicles, 40 locomotives, 1,091 railroad cars, 1,281 buildings, and two bridges. The 358th and 50th Fighter Groups received the DUC for their action in UNDERTONE. In eight days the 50th had flown 1,304 sorties (163 average per day) while on 19-21 March the 358th had flown 40 missions of 352 sorties destroying almost 800 vehicles and damaging another 600. The 358th was awarded a cluster to its DUC. Seventh Army CG, Lt.Gen. Alexander Patch congratulated XII Commander, Brig.Gen. Glenn Barcus:

A German StuG III tank destroyer with its track off and expended shell casings lies along the side of the road with the carcass of a dead horse on the lower right after the strafing of a road near Bourheim, Germany. (USAF)

"I have just returned from a visit to the front line units and every member of my command is grateful for the all-out effort you have put forth. I wouldn't trade the 358th for any fighter group in any theater."

Rhine River/Ninth Army (24 March 1944)

By the middle of March the Ninth Army's advance from the Roer River to the Rhine had been completed. The Ninth was directed (Operation FLASHPOINT) to attack across the Rhine north of the Ruhr industrial basin, establish and secure a bridgehead from which it was to isolate the Ruhr and then thrust into the heart of the Reich.

An interdiction line was set east of the Rhine to prevent enemy movement between the Ruhr and the battle area by destroying the transportation system to the east of the Rhine. Heavy and medium bombers were to take out the rail centers and waterways. The extensive road system in the battle area was unfeasible to attack so fighter-bombers of the XXIX TAC were to cut rail lines and bridges on the Ems River and Dortmund-Ems Canal, rolling stock, rail junctions and railheads. Secondary targets such as ammunition and fuel dumps, storage areas, military transport parks etc. were also to be attacked.

On 20 March, the 373rd Fighter Group of the XXIX TAC flew six missions to aid in the preparation for the Rhine crossings. The P-47s attacked both enemy supply lines and airfields. They destroyed or damaged 119 aircraft and facilities on three airfields that the Luftwaffe had intended to use to repulse the crossings. The other missions attacked rail and road transport cutting off supplies to the area from the east. The 373rd received a DUC for its actions that day. The 371st Fighter Group of the XIX TAC also was awarded the DUC for its actions from 15-21 March as it attacked German forces retreating across the Rhine. In that week, the 371st flew 1,035 effective sorties and destroyed 18 tanks and damaged 47 others, destroyed 16 gun positions and damaged 14 others, destroyed 1,237 trucks and damaged 1,061 others, destroyed 366 horse-drawn vehicles and damaged 280 and destroyed 158 buildings and damaged 80 more. Only three aircraft were lost.

On D-Day, 24 March, XXIX TAC provided cover for each attacking division. Other fighter-bombers attacked communication centers close to the front of the attack and armed recce were conducted. Heavy and fighter-bombers attacked airfields to prevent intrusion by the Luftwaffe. A bridgehead was quickly established

Men of the Fifth Armored Division look over a P-47 of the 366th Fighter Group that crash-landed near their position in Germany. It appears that the fighter suffered a hit in the engine as there is oil spattered on the tail plane. (USAF)

As the final total decimation of the Reich neared a 57th Fighter Group P-47 could fly unmolested over Hitler's "Eagles Nest" retreat at Bershtesgaden. The ravages of previous air attacks are evident. (USAF)

and reinforced with minimal losses. Steady progress was made on the 25th but German resistance increased significantly until the end of the month when XIX Corps broke out and dashed 35 miles to the east.

Fighter-bombers supported the lead assault units by attacking tanks and armored vehicle, defended buildings, gun positions and infantry. Fighter-bombers on armed recce and division cover prevented movement of enemy troops into the battle. A XVI Corps report stated: "A large movement of enemy tanks was observed and attacked on 25 March. A POW of the 116th PZ Division stated that his unit was attacked while forming up for a counter-attack. He stated that the counter-attack was canceled because of the losses and confusion resulting from air attack."

In this operation, fighter-bombers provided protection for the concentrated troops and materiel from the Luftwaffe and Wehrmacht. They accomplished this by gaining air superiority, providing close support on resisting enemy positions, isolating the bridgehead area either by immobilizing enemy movement near the front or by armed recce behind the front.

Breakout from the Rhine Bridgehead: The Ruhr Pocket (29 March-11 April 1945)

The Ninth Army built up and expanded its bridgehead east of the Rhine in late March 1945 and was poised for dash into Germany. On 30-31 March and 1 April, the Ninth Army made spectacular gains to the east. Meanwhile, the First Army located south of the Ruhr and the Ninth, moved northeast and met on 1 April, trapping 350,000 German soldiers in the Ruhr Pocket. Leaving units to reduce the pocket, the two armies then continued to the east, making large gains daily, covering 200 miles in two weeks until on 11 April the Ninth reached the Elbe River.

As the Allies moved into Germany more and more ex-Luftwaffe airfields were captured and put to use. P-47s of the 404th Fighter Group being serviced in a former Luftwaffe hanger. The hanger seems to have survived Allied air attention. (USAF)

354th Fighter Group P-51D maintenance at Y-64, Ober Olm, Germany in mid-April 1945. (USAF)

During the first days of the break through bad weather curtailed fighter-bomber attacks. No close support missions were flown on 1-2 April and on the 3rd, only 38 close support and 30 second priority missions were flown. During the remainder of the break through the weather was clear except for one non-operational day. Armed Column Cover sorties were the most numerous and effective missions flown. Column cover allowed the attacking echelons to reduce roadblocks and overcome strong point, armored vehicles and tanks, defended and occupied buildings, troop concentrations and field fortifications.

On 5 April the 406th Fighter Group was flying air support for the Fifth Armored Division which was crossing the Weser River. The Group flew seven missions between 0745 and 1430 sending 58 Thunderbolts against a number of targets ranging from 100 trucks and troops hiding in a woods, the Hamelin marshaling yards in which trains loaded with aircraft parts and called-in German strong points. Utilizing a variety of weapons, 500lb. GP and RDX bombs, 75 gallon napalm, rockets and strafing they claimed 26 M/T, a locomotive and 21 rail cars, three horse-drawn vehicles three tanks, two armored vehicles and nine gun positions.

The role of armed recce in this operation was to provide aerial protection to attacking armor which was very vulnerable to air attack and to prevent the rapid and orderly retreat of enemy troops to reinforce defensive positions in weakly defended areas which were the targets of an armored attack. After the initial penetration, armed recce and armored column cover produced excellent supporting results.

After relieving von Kluge at Falaise and failing to hold France and then failing to drive the Allies into the sea during the Ardennes campaign, FM Walther Model, the savior of the Russian front, found himself surrounded in the Ruhr pocket. Rather than be taken prisoner along with 375,000 troops and 30 generals and failing his beloved Fuehrer he committed suicide by shooting himself in the head with his pistol.

35

Decimation of the Luftwaffe on the Ground 9 - 17 April 1945

With the Russians advancing rapidly from the east and the Allies racing from the west, the German transportation complex and their remaining operational airfields were being compressed into a smaller area filled with lush targets. As the Allied advance moved into Germany the Luftwaffe was faced with a lack of fuel, few skilled pilots and the loss of airdrome after airdrome. This meant that the Luftwaffe had fewer and fewer fields to accommodate their aircraft and crowded them into southern and western Germany, northern Czechoslovakia and Austria.

9 April

The 55th Fighter Group was assigned an escort mission to the Munich area. As the bombers reached Munich, Lt.Col. Elwyn Righetti leading three squadrons had them leave the bombers southeast of the city to avoid AA fire. The three squadrons orbited waiting for the bombers to complete their bomb run. Maj. Edward Giller spotted a Me-262 and chased it back towards its base. He fired, getting several hits on its wings and fuselage and the jet crash-landed trying to land at the base. Righetti sent a flight in after the jet to strafe its base. A Me-410 was strafed and burned but the AA was too heavy to continue and the 55th's squadrons chose to orbit until more bombers came over and reduced the flak. While circling Capt. Robert Welch saw a He-111 being towed along the autobahn south of Munich. As Welch dropped to investigate he saw more camouflaged aircraft parked just off the autobahn and in the surrounding woods. Welch's flight went down to strafe and when its ammunition was expended, Righetti led 35 P-51s down against light flak for eight to ten passes each. There were over 100 aircraft packed almost wing tip to wing tip in the area and the Group left 49 destroyed and 22 damaged. Many of the aircraft were noted in the after combat reports as difficult or slow to burn.

10 April

The week of 10-17 April 1945 saw the utter decimation of the Luftwaffe on the ground. On 10 April, roving 8th Air Force fighters claimed only two victories in the air but claimed an astounding 309 ground victories and 235 more damaged. That day the 8th Air Force sent out 1,300 bombers and the VIII Fighter Command 900 fighters.

As the Allies advanced into Germany more Luftwaffe bases were captured and flight times to targets was short so several missions could be flown daily. A 354th Fighter Group P-51 rests on a newly captured ex-Luftwaffe airdrome at Ober Olm Germany in early April 1945. (USAF)

The Germans effectively hid their jet aircraft along the autobahn in the latter stages of the war. The MK-108 cannon on a captured Me-262 being inspected by an American intelligence officer. (USAF)

On his 30th birthday, Lt.Col. Righetti led his 55th Fighter Group to strafe the Reiss/Canitz A/D where there were a large number of FW-190s parked on the runway and in the hanger area. Righetti's P-51 was hit by flak as he destroyed nine German aircraft on the Ground. He crash-landed and post war investigation showed he was possibly killed by either by his civilian or military captors. (USAF)

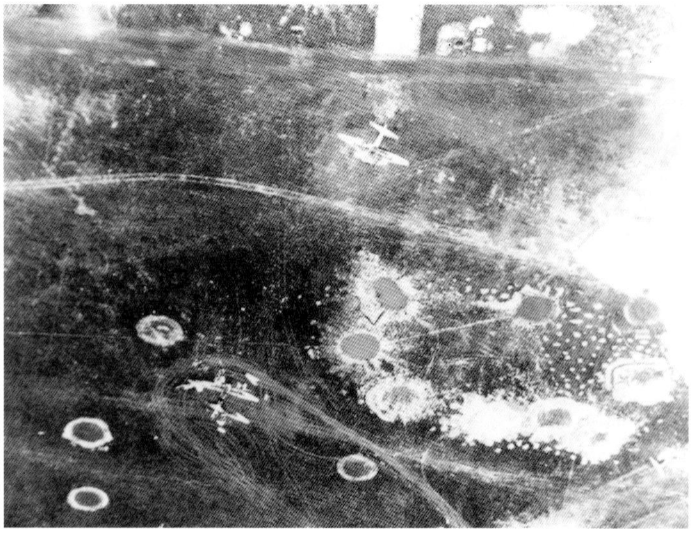

Burg Airdrome after 10 April 1945 attack by the 55th Fighter Group. Enemy aircraft were dispersed along the edges of the field and in the surrounding forest. Many of the aircraft were the Ju-88/FW-190 Mistel piggyback combinations and Me-262 jets. The 55th left 27 aircraft destroyed for the loss of one. (USAF)

The 56th Fighter Group led by Maj. James Carter dispatched 62 Thunderbolts on a sweep ahead of the bombers to Lubeck. Arriving at Lubeck at 1415 they found no productive targets and moved on to Muritz Lake at 1435. Capt. William Wilkerson took a part of the 62nd Squadron down to strafe. He destroyed a twin-engine aircraft and his wingman, F/O Clinton Albright, got one destroyed and one damaged. The other part of the squadron flew to Neuruppin Airdrome and claimed 13 aircraft including a Ju-88/Me-109 Mistel piggyback combination. The 63rd Squadron separated into an "A" group, led by Capt. John Fahringer, and a "B" group led by Capt. George Bostwick. As the group was a quarter of a hour ahead of the bombers which were heading to Brandenburg, Bostwick had time to attack the Briest Airdrome. While heading there he saw P-51s attacking Werder Airdrome and since there was no flak and many sitting targets there he led his group down to "assist" the Mustang pilots who were not happy over this intrusion. In the mean time, Fehringer led "A" squadron to Stendal. The claims for these two targets were 17 destroyed and 13 damaged. Maj. Carter led the 61st squadron to Muritz Lake and Rechlin Airdromes. In the face of light flak the squadron claimed 14 destroyed (seven flying boats on Muritz Lake) and 28 damaged. The destroyed total would have been higher if the damaged aircraft would have been fueled and thus easier to set on fire. Three P-47s were lost but two managed to crash land in Allied held territory and 13 were damaged by flak. Leading strafers for the day were Captains Walter Flagg and George Bostwick with four apiece. The 44 aircraft claimed destroyed that day put the 56th's total to 907.5 or 912.5, with depending on the source, destroyed for the war.

Capt. George Bostwick led the 63rd Fighter Squadron P-47 Thunderbolts on a rodeo mission to Berlin and then attacked the Werder Airdrome (1450 to 1510 hours) and recorded the attack in his combat report of the action. Bostwick destroyed four enemy aircraft and damaged two more on the ground and two on the air escort. (Bostwick)

Capt. George Bostwick led 63rd Fighter Squadron P-47 Thunderbolts on a rodeo mission to Berlin and then attacked the Werder Airdrome (1450 to 1510 hours) and recorded the attack in his combat report of the action. Bostwick destroyed four enemy aircraft and damaged two more on the ground and two on the air escort. The Squadron claimed 15-0-9 for the mission. Bostwick described his part in the mission:

"I was leading 56th 'B' Group on a sweep and escort mission to in the Berlin area. We reached the city approximately 15 minutes early, so I flew down to the vicinity of Briest Airdrome with the intent on making a few strafing passes before leaving to make rendezvous with our bombers. I spotted an airdrome (later identified as Werder) which had five or six oil fires on it and which was being strafed by about 12 P-51s. They seemed to be getting practically no flak and there were 75/100 enemy aircraft of all types on the field, so I decided to join their pattern.

I had 12 aircraft with me at the time, so left one flight up as top cover and took eight aircraft down to strafe, each of us making three passes on the airdrome. The P-51s changed their pattern a few times but we did not have too much difficulty conforming to it. All three passes were made generally from northwest to southeast.

On our first pass I destroyed a Ju-88; Lt. Naylor an unidentified single-engine E/A; Lt. T.W. Smith a Ju-88; Capt. Flagg a Do-217; Lt. Hoffman an unidentified twin-engined E/A; and Lt. V.A. Smith a Ju-88. In addition to these Lt. T.W. Smith damaged a Ju-88 and Lt. Hennessey damaged a Do-217.

Our second pass was made almost north to south. I damaged an unidentified twin-engined E/A on the north edge of the field and then continued on across the field firing into the open end of a hanger. I scored strikes on one unidentified twin-engined E/A which burst into flames. As I pulled up the whole hanger burst into flames. I saw one other E/A in the hanger and there may have been more.

Our third pass was made from the northwest again. I concentrated my fire on a Ju-88 and a Me-109 which were parked close together. The Ju-88 burned as I pulled up. Lt. Naylor destroyed a Me-109 and Capt. Flagg an unidentified single-engine E/A. Lt. Naylor also damaged a Do-217; Capt. Flagg a Me-109; Lt. Hennessey a Do-217 and Lt. V.A. Smith an unidentified E/A.

Upon pulling up from each pass I took pictures with my K-25 camera. All aircraft seemed to have plenty of gasoline in them and most of them burst into flames after having been hit two or three times. The 78th Group P-51s which were strafing with us estimated in their mission summary that we had started 20-25 fires and we were claiming 15 as destroyed. The P-51s started 10-12 fires on the field proper while we were there and were working over a dispersal area to the west of the field as we left. After out third pass we re-formed and escorted out bombers out to Dummer Lake."

For his combat tour of 92 missions Bostwick scored eight victories and one damaged in the air and seven destroyed and two damaged on the ground.

The 56th Fighter Group's fierce competitor in the ETO victory race was the 4th Fighter Group that had been neck and neck with the Wolf Pack. Lt.Col. Sidney Woods led 61 P-51s on a support mission to Rechlin-Lars Airdrome and claimed only four ground and one air victory for the to give it 893 in the race to reach 1,000 for the war.

The 339th Fighter Group was assigned bomber support duty to Neuruppin. The 50rd Squadron was to remain with the bombers but while Lt.Col. Dale Shafer was photographing the bombing he came upon Neuruppin A/D that was loaded with over 100 dispersed aircraft. Shafer called in the 504th and 505th Squadrons and while they were waiting, he and his wingman, 1Lt. Robert Frisch made seven strafing runs on the field. Shafer destroyed two and damaged four while Frisch got four destroyed and two damaged. The 504th under Maj. William Julian arrived to join Schafer and Frisch. Although 20 and 37mm flak heavily defended the airdrome, the attackers were able to strafe the dispersed aircraft while mostly staying out of danger (several P-51s were hit but were able to return to base with minor damage). The 504th spent 35 minutes over Neuruppin with

Maj. Joseph Thury followed as the second most prolific ETO strafer with 25 1/2 ground (2 1/2 air) victories as CO of the 505th Fighter Squadron/339th Fighter Group. (USAF)

Right: On the 10th, Lt.Col. John Landers led the 82nd Squadron of the 78th Fighter Group to a rendezvous with the Third Air Task Force. John Landers probably had one of the most varied scoring records of any pilot in the war: six Japanese in the Pacific, 8.5 ETO air victories and 20 ground victories in the ETO. Here Landers' P-51 shows 31 total ETO victories 2.5 more than published totals. (USAF)

each man averaging ten passes. The squadron claimed 36 destroyed and 39 damaged. The strafed aircraft did not explode or burn as they were not fueled but once started engine oil burned satisfactorily and the smoke soon made locating targets difficult. Eight 504th pilots destroyed three aircraft each. The second leading ground ace in the 8th Air Force was Maj. Joseph Thury, CO of the 505th Fighter Squadron/339th Fighter Group, with 25.5. Thury's best days also came in mid-April 1945. The 505th dropped off escort just before the bombers began their bombing run. Thury responded to Shafer's call to Neuruppin and split his squadron taking 11 Mustangs and leaving eight with Maj. Archie Tower. The squadron discovered a large dispersal area that ran north from Neuruppin for almost two miles. The P-51s stayed out of range of the German AA and the German airdrome personnel with small arms who were still in hiding from the bombing. Each pilot made 10 to 15 passes and left only when their ammunition ran low. Thury counted 35 large and 20 smaller fires. Thury attributed the effectiveness of the raid to the installation of incendiary bullets in two of their guns. Thury's 505th component claimed 26 destroyed and 14 damaged with Thury getting four destroyed and two damaged. Tower's part of the squadron attacked 30 aircraft parked in a wooded area and another 30 or so parked wing tip to wing tip near hangers. Towers' pilots made 12 to 15 passes and claimed 37 destroyed and 19 damaged with five Mustangs suffering damage from light flak. Tower destroyed eight and damaged three; 1Lt. Jerome Murphy was credited with five destroyed and three damaged while 1Lt. Harold Burch got five destroyed and two damaged. The 339th was the first fighter group to score 100 ground victories in a day.

On the 10th, Lt.Col. John Landers led the 82nd Squadron of the 78th Fighter Group to a rendezvous with the Third Air Task Force. John Landers probably had one of the most varied scoring records of any pilot in the war. He was an ace in the Pacific with six victories in the P-40 with the 49th Fighter Group/5th Air Force and then became an ace in the ETO with five victories. He had four victories in the P-38 with the 55th Fighter Group and one in the P-51 with the 357th Fighter Group. He had scored 3.5 victories in his P-51, *"Big Beautiful Doll"*, with the 78th since becoming its CO in late February 1945. The bombers bombed the Luftwaffe jet fields near Brandenburg and after the escort the 8rd went down after the jet dromes. Their first target, Briest A/D, was aborted after a few cautious passes, as the flak was too intense. Landers led the squadron to Burg A/D near Magdeburg which was still recovering from the very recent bombing but after one solo pass on that field he moved on to Werder A/D which was under attack by P-47s that had already burned ten to fifteen aircraft there. Landers put out a call on his R/T for the other to join in, as there were about 70 Luftwaffe closely parked aircraft on the edge of the runway and in the nearby trees. Twelve passes were made against light to moderate AA fire and although the undamaged aircraft were difficult to spot through the smoke of burning hangers and aircraft the group was credited with 52 destroyed and 43 damaged. The 82nd destroyed 33, the 8rd got 11 and the 84th claimed 8 while Landers was credited with eight and four pilots claimed four each. Three pilots were listed MIA.

The 55th Fighter Group was to escort the Third Air Division to attack Burg A/D. On their way to the target the 55th had to beat off persistent attacks by Me-262 jets. One squadron of P-51s checked out the field prior to the bombing and then orbited while the B-17s boxes bombed the large field and between bombing boxes they continued to check the number of aircraft, AA opposition and wind. After the last bomb run the escort P-51s jettisoned their drop tanks swooped through the smoke and dust. The Germans had placed flak guns on either side of the large field that could concentrate on strafing aircraft. Aircraft were dispersed along the edges of the field and in the surrounding forest. Many of the aircraft were the Ju-88/FW-190 Mistel piggyback combinations and Me-262 jets. The 55th left 27 aircraft destroyed for the loss of one.

The USAAF daily total of 309 surpassed the high of 177 scored on 5 September 1944. There were eight losses for the day: seven to flak and one to mechanical failure (due to flak damage?) There were three POWs, two KIAs and two MIAs.

11 April

On 11 April, a field order was issued banning strafing as Patton's Armies were advancing rapidly and might be endangered by the eager strafers. The fighters of the 8th Air Force were on escort duty to various marshaling yards around Germany.

Ninth Air Force fighters roamed the skies looking for Luftwaffe fighters in the sky and on the ground. The 354th Fighter Group destroyed 20 and damaged six more Luftwaffe fighters in the air and then went on to claim 2-3 enemy on the ground. The 373rd Fighter Group was bounced by three flights of 20 FW-190s while attacking an airfield and shot down 17 with 2-4 probable-damaged. The air claims for the 9th Air Force were 39-2-10. The ground claims were 70 destroyed and 61 damaged with the 474FG/9AF claiming 27-35, the 368th with 14-2 and the 373rd with 10-6.

12 April

36th Fighter Group destroyed the largest number of enemy aircraft on the ground in one day for the 9th Air Force. A 11-plane P-47 mission left its base at 0745 to strafe airdromes in the Kothen area. At Schkeuditz the Group descended to destroy 14 He-111s, three Do-217s and a hanger. They moved onto Leipzig/Mochau where there were over 300 parked aircraft. They destroyed 16 Ju-88s, ten training aircraft, nine FW-190s, seven Me-109s, six He-111s, five Me-410s, a Me-262, a Stuka and a captured P-47. The total for the two attacks was 73-23 plus four damaged gliders. All Thunderbolts returned to base, four with flak damage. The Group was awarded the DUC for the action.

13 April

On 13 April, the ban was lifted and the day would be unlucky for the Luftwaffe as 285 aircraft were destroyed and 220 damaged on the ground. It was becoming more difficult for a fighter pilot to gain a ground victory as the parked aircraft had no fuel in their tanks and couldn't be seen burning on the gun camera films. The 56th was assigned to a fighter sweep led by Col. Lucian Dade on Eggebeck A/D near Kiel in north Germany. The day was the second anniversary of the 56th's first of 458 missions in the ETO. Arriving over Eggebeck at 1510 after flying for one and three quarter hours, its 51 Mustangs found 175 to 200 parked aircraft. The squadrons took their briefed positions. The 62nd Squadron was to fly top cover at 15,000 feet; the 61st was to orbit at 10,000 feet. The Yellow and Blue Sections of the 63rd were to orbit their P-47s at 5,000 to spot any flak opening up on the White and Red Sections which were to go in and strafe line abreast at 400 to 450 mph. No flak was met on the first pass so Dade called down the Yellow and Blue Squadrons. During the second pass three flak positions opened fire causing the only casualty of the day. Lt. William Hoffman's P-47 was hit and he tied to gain enough altitude to bail out but his parachute failed open soon enough and he was killed. The three flak positions were put out of action and Dade called in the squadrons. The 63rd Squadron made eight or nine passes and expended its ammunition in destroying 45 aircraft and damaged 36. The 61st Squadron came down and claimed 26 destroyed and 24 damaged in 94 individual passes. The 62nd that had been flying top cover finished up the mission by destroying 25 and damaging 33 others in 105 passes. The daily total for the group was 339 individual firing passes that expended 78,073 rounds of .50 caliber ammunition destroying 96 aircraft and damaging 93. After two years in battle these victories made the Wolf Pack the first to destroy over 1,000 aircraft much to the chagrin of the 4th Fighter Group, which could only claim a few moored seaplanes off the coast of Denmark that day. 1Lt. Randal Murphy of the 63rd Fighter Squadron set a record by destroying ten aircraft on the ground in one location: five He-111s, three FW- 190s, one FW-200 and one He-177. He also damaged a Me-109 and four unidentified aircraft. Murphy was an outstanding marksman and after this success was sent back to the States to teach new pilots on strafing techniques. Other strafing aces in a day were Lt. Russell Kyler (61st) four Ju-88s and a Me-210 and Lt. Philip Kuhn (63rd) with five. Lt. Vernon Smith (63rd) destroyed four and damaged four and Lt. Ernest Treff (61st) destroyed three Ju-88s and damaged five others, Lt. Lloyd Geren (62nd) destroyed four He-111s and damaged three others. The 63rd was using the newly developed T-48 .50 caliber ammunition that had a higher muzzle velocity and incendiary quotient. The 96 claimed destroyed put the 56th at either 1002.5 or 1007.5 victories to put it over the coveted 1,000 destroyed mark for the war.

Randal Murphy (63rd FS/56th FG) set a record by destroying ten aircraft on the ground in one location on 12 April (he also damaged five others).

The 355th Fighter Group, the famous "Steeple Morden Strafers," that had set airdrome strafing records in March and April 1944, flew a ramrod to Hagenow Airdrome, led by Lt.Col. Claiborne Kinnard. As landfall was made near Hasum, Capt. Bert Marshall discovered over 50 German aircraft on the airdrome there. After escort release, Kinnard led the 354th Squadron back to Hasam. The flak positions were silenced on the first pass and the squadron made seven attacks on the field. The squadron claimed 37-0-17 for the highest squadron total in the 355th in the war. Capt. Joseph Mellen and 1Lt. Duran Vickery became strafing aces-in-a-day with five victories each followed by Marshall with four. The 357th and 358th Fighter Squadrons strafed Flensburg, Leck and Schleswig airdromes to score 32-0-14 that included a dozen newly delivered He-111s parked wing tip to wing tip at Leck Airdrome. The Heinkel bombers probably weren't refueled and didn't burn so the 357th went to Schleswig to help the 358th. There the two squadrons scored 29-0-1 with John Tullock getting four. On its way home the 358th attacked Flensburg and got four more aircraft to give the Group 69 aircraft destroyed and 31 damaged for the day. This was a new group record that gave it back the ground victory lead from the 339th Fighter Group that it would hold until the end of the war.

The 8th Air Force lost nine pilots, three known lost to flak but the rest crashed for unknown reasons, probably flak damage. Four were POWs, two KIAs and three MIAs.

14-15 April

No ground claims were made as fighters were on escort duty.

16 April

On the 16th, John Landers' 78th Fighter Group was assigned to support 760 B-17s of the First and Second Air Divisions to the Regensburg area and then go on to strafe airdromes in the Prague-Pilsen area of Czechoslovakia. While the 84th Squadron led by Landers was on escort duty, the 82nd Squadron free-lanced into individual flights and attacked airdromes. White flight led by Capt. Croy attacked Straubing A/D and destroyed a FW-190 before he was hit by flak and bailed out but he was too low for his chute to open. 1Lts. James Parker and Eugene Peel destroyed three aircraft but Peel too, was hit by flak and forced to crashland. Red flight led by Capt. Robert Holmes attacked Straubing and destroyed five aircraft which didn't burn as they were not fueled. They went on to other airdromes and scored more victories but Holmes was hit by flak and KIA. Yellow flight attacked Marienbad A/D and took four passes to set one Do-217 on fire. 2Lt. Fred Swauger was hit by small arms fire and crash-landed and was captured. He was freed by advancing US troops a few days later. The rest of the Group completed its escort with its drop tanks in place that allowed them to fly into Czechoslovakia and attack the airdromes around Prague where hundreds of German aircraft were concentrated trying to escape the advancing Allied Armies. At 1530 hours Landers saw over 80 aircraft parked in scattered groups of two to five on Cakowice Airdrome. First the Group dropped to 3,000 feet and flew over the field to look into the flak situation. Landers then ordered the remaining 82nd Squadron Blue flight to fly top cover while he led the 83rd and 84th Squadrons south out of sight past the airdrome and then turned back on deck. On his first pass Landers burned four He-177 bombers, burned two more on his second pass, another two on his third pass and on his last five passes flamed three more. The first two flights across the field burned 13 enemy aircraft and after five passes over 50 aircraft were on fire. The 78th Mustangs came in time after time to ravish the damaged aircraft smoldering on the field. By the time the attack was finished every German aircraft had been destroyed and the Group moved over to nearby Letnany A/D that had over 50 aircraft. The AA batteries were knocked out after the first few passes and then textbook gunnery passes were executed for the next 25 minutes. Ten to 12 passes were made and many enemy aircraft were hit but again refused to burn. Finally the smoke and dust became so thick that individual firing runs were initiated for safety. 1Lt. Clyde Taylor destroyed four Ju-52s, three Me-109s and a FW-190. During these attacks on Prague no 78th aircraft were lost and one pilot was wounded by small arms fire. When the Group returned to Duxford, intelligence sorted out the gun camera film and determined that the group had destroyed a record 135 destroyed and 89 damaged. The 82nd had destroyed 19 and damaged 28, the 83rd 58-28 and the 84th 58-31. Of the 11 aircraft Landers flamed he would be officially credited with nine. Taylor was credited with eight; Capt. Edward Kulik had seven, Lt.Col. Olin Gilbert and 1Lt. Anthony Colletti had six strafing victories and six pilots were ground aces in a day with five victories: 1Lt. Gene Doss, Capt. Donald DeVilliers, 1Lt. Danford Josey, Capt. Dorian Ledington, Capt. Duncan McDuffie and 1Lt. Dale Sweat. Lander's 20 total ground victories made him the fourth highest ETO strafing ace.

Capt. Robert Ammon of the 339th Fighter Group destroyed 11: four Me-109s, three Ju-88s, two FW-190s, and two He-111s breaking Randal Murphy's record of 10 set three days earlier with the 56th Fighter Group. (USAF)

On the 16th, the 339th Fighter Group flew 62 aircraft on a sweep, area patrol and strafing mission also to the Regensburg area. Each squadron split off to attack separate targets. The 50rd found and attacked five airfields but three were passed up as heavy flak was encountered. The remaining two were vigorously strafed including one that was being attacked by the 78th Fighter Group. The 50rd made eight or nine passes but the pickings were slim and they claimed four destroyed and ten damaged. Capt. Robert Ammon led a single four-plane flight to Praha/Kbely airdrome. Ammon passed over the periphery of the field to draw flak and shot up a He-111 on the way. Two batteries opened fire and were silenced on the second run. The flight started 24 fires before P-51s of the 78th Fighter Groups interfered in an undisciplined attack. Ammon's debriefing report clearly showed his anger with the "Duxford Squadron":

"They came in shooting up everything in sight. They did not ask to join us in our pattern but came in from all directions. They forced me to break off two passes and endangered my whole flight."

Ammon was hit by AA that filled his cockpit with smoke and forced him to head back to base. His flight had scored 27 destroyed and nine damaged with Ammon getting 11 destroyed: four Me-109s, three Ju-88s, two FW-190s, and two He-111s breaking Randal Murphy's record of 10 set three days earlier with the 56th Fighter Group. Ammon also damaged four aircraft, 1Lt. Steven Chetneky got six destroyed and three damaged while 1Lt. John Byers got five destroyed and one damaged. Lt.Col. William Clark led the 504th to Klatovy A/D and set up strafing runs on the 25 aircraft parked there and left several flights to take care of these Germans. He proceeded to Bedejovice where he discovered at least 500 aircraft crowded on the field. Clark set up an exploratory pass to flush out the flak. His flight came in low from the south with the sun at their backs and was fired upon by intense flak. Clark's flight hit four aircraft that burned very readily after only a few rounds had been fired. A FW-190 exploded under his fighter and a large piece hit his port wing. Due to the heavy flak Clark cut the attack short and moved to another field near Platting that also had a large number of dispersed aircraft. Flak was also heavy here and the attack was canceled after a few passes that destroyed a number of Me-109s and FW-190s.

Again Clark moved on to another airdrome south of Platting and attacked several times before again being driven off by flak. Clark's Squadron made one pass on Straubing A/D and returned to base with 48 destroyed and 13 damaged. Clark claimed eight (five FW-190s, two Me-109 and a Ju-52) destroyed and one damaged. Thury split up the 505th Squadron to cover more area in its patrol. He took nine P-51s and descended to 10,000 feet looking for targets of opportunity between Lake Chiem and Munich. One of the pilots spotted movement on the autobahn and Thury descended to investigate and saw an aircraft being towed along the road. Dropping even lower he discovered more aircraft well hidden in the adjacent trees and confirmed that the Luftwaffe was using the autobahn as an airfield. The squadron descended to 1,000 feet and the flights divided and widened out to make firing runs. Thury strafed a Me-109 but met no flak. The Major and three P-51s of his flight turned to make a second pass. The German flak often waited until the second pass to fire and fired on the incoming flight. Thury instructed his pilots to concentrate on the gun positions that were identified and put out of action. Four Mustangs sustained minor flak damage but pressed their attack and swooped on the airfield. Thury added a Me-262 jet and his squadron claimed 20 aircraft destroyed on the day 1Lt. Vernon Carr led two 505th Fighter Squadron flights to an airfield near Wallersdorf but found only a few aircraft there and moved on across the Isar river where he found a small grass field with 40 aircraft. They made one pass through heavy AA getting two destroyed, moved on to Passan, made another pass through heavy flak and destroyed four and left for home with six destroyed and two damaged for the day. Capt. Philip Loveless led five other Mustangs to check other fields but shied away as all bristled with flak. They came upon an A/D under attack by the 353rd Fighter Group and joined in and shot up 13 and damaged five more. The 339th scored 143-45 for the day without a loss and became the only fighter group to be credited with over a 100 ground in a day twice.

Lt.Col. Righetti led 58 P-51s on escort for Second Air Division B-24s to Salzburg. The energetic and personable CO had made the 55th Fighter Group a leading 8th Air Force group taking the headlines away from the 4th and 56th Fighter Groups in early 1945. After the escort, Righetti led the group checking airdromes along the Danube Valley from Linz to Landshut strafing airdromes along the way. The 38th Fighter Squadron found over 50 aircraft on the autobahn near Brunnthal and went on to Neubiberg. The 338th Fighter Squadron attacked 40 aircraft at Landshut destroying 12 and then flew on to Erding and Linz and destroyed 13 more. The 343rd Fighter Squadron went to Brunnthal that had just been strafed by the 38th Fighter Squadron and found undamaged aircraft to attack. They flew through heavy flak and destroyed ten and then went on to Lake Chiem and sunk two BV-138 flying boats in a dry dock at the west end of the lake. The daily tally for the day for the 55th was 52 destroyed and 26 damaged for the loss to AA fire of three pilots KIA and one POW.

Reicherberg Airdrome. Strike photo of the 353rd Fighter Group mission led by Col. Ben Rimmerman that destroyed 61 aircraft on the ground on 16 April 1945. (USAF)

Left: Col. Ben Rimmerman took over the 353rd Fighter Group from Glenn Duncan who was shot down by flak and led his group on numerous successful fighter-bomber missions. (USAF)

The 352nd Fighter Group, "The Bluenosed Bastards of Bodney", had just moved back to Bodney four days earlier after being based at ALGs at Asch and Chievres, Belgium. The Group flew escort for the First Air Division and released half of the escort, six flights, to patrol and search for Luftwaffe airdromes. The 486th and 487th Squadrons under Lt. Col. Willie O. Jackson pounced on Ganacker A/D that was loaded with parked aircraft. Jackson sent in three sections, one to fly top cover, one to lure the flak batteries into firing and the last to suppress the flak. Jackson led his section across the field without firing and 15 to 20 flak guns opened fire. After four or five passes the guns were silenced and a gunnery pattern was set up. The Bluenosers then beat up the field for 30 minutes and was credited with 40 destroyed and 27 damaged. Jackson claimed four destroyed (two FW-190s and two Me-109s) and one damaged. Top-scorers for the day were Capt. Edwin Heller (486th Fighter Squadron) with seven destroyed and 1Lt. Charles "Buck" Pattillo (486th) and 1Lt. Henry Sykes with five destroyed and two damaged. It is interesting to note that "Buck" Pattillo's twin brother Cuthbert "Bill" was credited with two destroyed and three damaged for the day while flying for the 487th. On the mission Bill's fighter was hit by ground fire and he crash landed in a field and was captured by the Germans and made a POW. Buck did not know Bill's fate until he returned to the Group on 17 May after being liberated by advancing American infantry. The twins remained in the post war Air Force and were members of the "Skyblazers" USAFE Aerial Demonstration Team and later organized the "Thunderbird" aerobatic team. Bill retired as a Major General in 1980 and Buck as a Lt. General in 1981. The 328th Fighter Squadron attacked Landau and destroyed five and damaged nine there. The Group claimed 43 destroyed and 33 damaged for the loss of one KIA and one POW.

The 353rd Fighter Group led by Col. Ben Rimmerman flew 64 Mustangs to the Munich area where they were to attack Luftwaffe airdromes and then escort the B-24s back to England. At 1455 the 351st Fighter Squadron attacked Reicherberg A/D and attacked the packed field for a half-hour before withdrawing to escort B-24s from Stuttgart. The Squadron scored 61-22 with 20 pilots scoring ground victories. The aces in a day were 1Lt. Gerald Miller with nine victories (six FW-190s, two Me-109s and a Do-217) and Capt. Gordon Crompton who claimed five (three Ju-188s and two Ju-88s) and four pilots had four aircraft destroyed. Col. Ben Rimmerman who had taken over the 353rd from Glenn Duncan who was shot down by flak on 7 July 1944 destroyed six (three FW-190s, a Me-109, a Me-108 and a Ju-87) while leading the 351st Squadron. From 1530 to 1600 hours the 350th Fighter Squadron under Capt. W.J. Lane attacked Pocking A/D and its satellite fields that were also packed with parked aircraft. The Squadron ended its day with 55-18 with Capt. Herbert Kolb leading the scoring with 9.5 victories (five FW-190s, two Me-109s, 1.5 Fi-156s, 0.5 Fi-156 and 0.5 Hs-126 along with two Ju-87s damaged). 1Lt. Bruce McMahan destroyed four FW-190s and shared two Fi-156s and a Hs-129 with Kolb to give him 6.5 victories. Other strafing aces in a day for the 350th were 1Lt. James McClure with six and Capt. Melville Hightshoe, F/O Richard Gutske and 1Lt. Joseph McMullen all with five. The 352nd Squadron claimed 15-13 in its attacks on Pocking and Bad Aibling. The total for the day was 137-53 for the loss of three KIA by flak.

The 56th Fighter Group sent out on a Ramrod escort mission for three B-24 combat wings to Rosenheim. Maj. James Carter with 31 P-47s led "A" group and Maj. Felix Williamson with 20 Thunderbolts led "B" group. Williamson's group went hunting over several Luftwaffe airdromes several of which were being strafed by P-51s. Only two enemy aircraft were destroyed and five damaged by the 56th for a loss of one KIA and five flak damaged P-47s. Williamson's crash landed his fighter in flames from a ruptured fuel line at the ALG at St. Trond. These were the last two victories of the war for the 56th.

The 4th Fighter Group got 61 destroyed claims free-lancing over Prague and 44 more strafing Gablingen A/D after it was released from escort to put the group over 1,000 victories. The 4th sent out two groups, "A" group led by Lt.Col. Sidney Woods and "B" Group by Maj. Louis "Red" Norley. "A" group, Cobweb Squadron (334th Fighter Squadron) was to strafe the Gablingen Airdrome near Augsburg. There was some light flak that damaged five P-51s and caused one MIA pilot. The mission's total was 44 aircraft destroyed and 22 damaged. Two pilots, 2Lt. William Antonides 1Lt. Kenneth Helfrecht, each was credited with five aircraft destroyed. "B" group was assigned to a support mission to Rosenheim and Prague to be followed by a strafing mission to the Karlsbad-Salzburg and Prague areas. "B" (335th Fighter Squadron) split into two squadrons, "Becky" led by Woods and "Caboose" Squadron by Maj. Pierce McKennon. Becky came into Praha/Kbely Airdrome on the deck and Caboose flew top cover, looking for flak positions to attack. There was light flak but heavy small arms and machine gun fire was encountered. Becky claimed 28 destroyed and 14 damaged while Caboose got 33 and 22. The total for the day was 105 destroyed but the cost was high. Eight aircraft and pilots (two KIA and six MIA) were lost to flak including Woods who was a POW. McKennon was had a 20mm shell burst in his cockpit wounding him above the eye. He had to land at an ALG in France to be treated before returning back to England. 1Lt. Douglas Pedersen got eight Ju-52 victories. He strafed Praha/Kbely were he made 15 passes destroying four Ju-52s. After three Mustangs of his flights were MIA after being hit by flak Pedersen moved onto Praha/Letnany and Praha/Cakovice Airdromes. He made six more passes, expending his ammunition destroying four more Ju-52s. F/O Donald Baugh also became a strafing ace in a day by claiming five Ju-88s for Becky Squadron. The 105 victory credits put the 4th Fighter Group at exactly 1,000 aircraft destroyed in the war but it continued to trail the 56th.

The 355th Fighter Group finished its illustrious ground strafing career when Lt.Col. John Elder led a Ramrod mission to Traunstein, initially to escort Second Air Division B-24s and then to strafe the target after the bombing. The Liberators were R/V'd over Trier at 1405 and the 355th's 62 P-51s escorted the bombers to the target and back to Gunsbert at 1555. Ten Me-262s were reported in the area but could not be found and Elder took his charges to the Regansburg area to strafe. Elder's 357th Fighter Squadron strafed three fields around Linz for claims of 29-0-36 for a loss of two pilots. Elder and Capt. Henry Bille claimed four each. Lt. Joseph Lake suffered a fatal direct hit by flak, exploded and spun in. Lt. Thurman Long's Mustang was hit by flak near Linz and crashed just short of Russian lines and he was taken POW. Capt. Lawrence Dissette led the 358th Fighter Squadron to Straubing for claims of 18-0-6 with 2Lt. Halbert Marsh getting five and Lts. Francis McCollom and Grant Seeley claiming four each. It was an expensive day for the 358th as it lost four pilots and five fighters to accurate flak over Straubing. Lt. William Lynch was hit by flak and was captured and later escaped, Lt. John Rogers was hit by flak and bellied in his Mustang and evaded capture, Lt. McCollom was hit by flak but flew his Mustang to Rosenburg before bellying in and Capt. Dissette bailed out ten miles after being hit and evaded capture. Lt. Donathan was severely wounded in the leg but managed to crash-land his P-51 inside friendly lines to have his wounds treated.

The daily totals for all 8th Air Force fighter groups were astounding: 743 e/a were destroyed and 406 were damaged on the ground for a loss of 31 P-51s and one P-47 for the day. A total of 32 pilots were lost, all by flak: 14 POWs, nine KIAs and nine MIAs.

The 9th Air Force also scored its biggest day for the destruction of enemy aircraft on the ground with 215 destroyed and 190 damaged. The IX TAC claimed 54-69 with the 365th Fighter Group being the leading Group with 43-50. The 365th was assigned close cooperation with the 3rd Armored Division and 104th Infantry division. When no targets could be found they flew armed recce hitting transportation targets and Luftwaffe airfields. The fourth mission, 14 aircraft of the 387th Squadron under Capt. Andrew Smoak attacked the airfield at Pretzsch where 45 aircraft had been dispersed. In the ensuing attack 19 were destroyed and 23 damaged with 1Lt. Herbert Prevost getting two DO-217s, three Me-109s and one Me-110. On the sixth mission, Capt. William Rodgers took 14 fighters of the 386th Squadron to Wahrenbruck where 15+ aircraft with several dummy aircraft dispersed in between were discovered on the airdrome there. Nine planes were destroyed and four damaged. The seventh mission took off at 1434 with Capt. Neal Worley leading 14 aircraft of the 387th Squadron. The 3rd Armored Division was stopped outside the town of Bernberg where a controller requested the Squadron to buzz the town. After the buzzing the Squadron circled the town for 20 minutes and then came down to strafe the Saale River that ran through the center of town. They strafing was so intimidating that the German civilians surrendered the town! The eighth mission 14 fighters of the 388th Squadron under Capt. Herbert Rogers were directed by a controller to attack the airdrome at Oschatz where there were over 45 aircraft dispersed. Their strafing attack claimed 15 destroyed and 25 damaged.

On 16 April 1945 the 405th Fighter Group claimed 67 destroyed and 40 damaged in 70 sorties supporting the XIX Corps. Capt. William Myers, leading the 511th Squadron, claimed 11-0 and 1Lt. Charles Riedel claimed 7-2. (USAF)

The XIX TAC accounted for 84-74 German aircraft on the ground with the 367th Fighter Group getting 60-39. At one airdrome it destroyed 43-21 including 25-18 Me-109s and 2-1 Me-262s. Two other missions of 23 P-47s strafed Marienberg and Michelsberg for 17-18.

The XXIX TAC claimed 77-47 with the 405th Fighter Group garnering 67-40 in 70 sorties supporting the XIX Corps that was about to attack Magdeburg. The second mission discovered an airdrome near the city and destroyed 69-48. Three morning missions by 32 P-47s to Altengrabow claimed 11-13 including 2-8 Mistels. In three afternoon missions of 36 P-47s the result was 56-27 including 17-6 Me-109s, 28-11 He-111s and 1-0 Me-262. Capt. William Myers, leading the 511th Squadron, claimed 11-0 and 1Lt. Charles Riedel claimed 7-2. Myers 11 ground victories may have been a 9th Air Force daily record.

In air combat that day the 9th Air Force TACs claimed 23-1-2 with the XIX TAC getting 21-0-1

17 April

On 17th the 4th Fighter Group flew a non-eventful support mission to the Karlsbad area destroying three and damaging five on the to show for one KIA by flak.

On his 30th birthday, Lt.Col. Righetti led his 55th Fighter Squadron on an escort mission for the Third Air Division to Dresden where it flew in poor weather and met no Luftwaffe opposition. At 1445 the 343rd Squadron was released from the escort and dipped through the cloud cover to strafe ground targets. Soon FW-190s of 8/SG77 were seen taking off from Kamenz A/D for a fighter-bomber mission against the onrushing Russian armies. The Squadron downed five Folke Wulfs before moving onto Bautzen/Litten A/D where Lt. Lloyd Boring destroyed five aircraft on the ground. Boring spotted about 15 aircraft hidden in a pasture along a hedgerow and among stands of trees. He led his flight in a right hand firing pass and got a compact bullet pattern on a FW-190 and it burst into flamed at once. On his second pass he set fire to a small single engine service aircraft hidden under trees, Boring swung his Mustang around for a third pass and fired on a line up of four or five Fiesler Storch 156s parked along a hedge row and set one on fire. Small caliber AA from two or three positions hidden in some trees at one corner of the runway was harassing the attackers. Boring came around and put the guns out of commission. He made one more pass and exploded a Fi-156 with the last of his ammunition and returned to base. The rest of Boring's flight destroyed four and damaged two.

The Squadron moved onto airdromes near Dresden and destroyed 19 and damaged six aircraft with 2Lt. Howard Mahany accounting for five destroyed and two damaged. The 338th Squadron met the same SG77 FW-190s and got four aerial victories and one damaged south of Dresden. At 1530 Righetti led a flight to strafe the Reiss/Canitz A/D where there were a large number of FW-190s parked on the runway and in the hanger area. Capt. Carroll Henry was flying #2 position off Righetti's wing as the flight flew under the 5/10 cloud base at 5,000 feet and swung a 360 turn descending to 3,000 feet. Righetti instructed two P-51s to circle while he and Henry checked out the flak. As they were crossing the north perimeter of the field at 500 feet a FW-190 was coming in for a landing and Righetti told Henry to attack it. Henry made a pass but missed and flew on deck for three miles to evade the flak before coming around to make another pass on a dispersal area about a half-mile from the main field. After he pulled up to circle the field he saw Righetti's Mustang, *"KATYDID"*, streaming coolant as it was making a firing pass on the field. Henry contacted Righetti who told him that his fighter was badly damaged and that the oil pressure was dropping. He said he wouldn't be able to make it back to base and was going to make one more firing pass with his remaining ammunition. Righetti made the pass destroying another FW-190, his ninth ground victory of the day. While coming to Righetti's aid Henry lost sight of him but received a R/T message from him saying he had crash landed and had broken his nose but was OK and for Henry to tell Righetti's family that he was OK. Henry returned to the area and circled to find Righetti's downed aircraft but was unable to do so. After the war an investigation showed Righetti was possibly killed by either by his civilian or military captors. Five 55th Fighter Group pilots were downed by flak that day, Righetti was one of four KIA and another was made a POW. The group claimed nine aerial victories and 36 on the ground.

Fifty-five fighters of the 339th Fighter Group were assigned to escort bombers and at the target were to break off escort and to attack assigned airfields. The 503rd Squadron attacked several A/Ds and found them to have been previously ravished by USAAF fighters hadfew targets. Another A/D put up intense, accurate light AA that caused them to retreat, scoring only one air victory and five ground victories. The 503rd lost two pilots to unknown causes. One was 2Lt. William Preddy who was the brother of 23.83 victory ace, George Preddy of the 352nd Fighter Group who had been KIA by friendly AA fire on 25 December 1944. The younger Preddy was buried next to his brother at the military cemetery at St. Avold, France. The 504th returned to the fields near Prague that they had attacked on the previous day. At Klatovy they destroyed four Fiesler Storches and four Me-109s and went on to other fields that had already been attacked but they found undamaged aircraft and 15 destroyed more. 1Lt. Leon Orcutt was credited with six Me-109s and two Ju-88s destroyed and Capt. Kirke Everson got two Me-109s, two Storches and a Ju-88 to become ground aces in a day. Thury led six 505th fighters that were to turn south toward Munich 200 miles away to the south of their targets. The plan for the mission was for 12 fighters to fly top cover for the first flight attacking the field. They were to orbit the field looking to pinpoint AA gun positions and to determine if the flak was too heavy to continue the attack. Thury led the first flight in, turning 45 degrees, heading for the left side of the field. He fired on a parked FW-190 and blew it up. There was no flak and the top cover aircraft dove line abreast at 400mph to the attack. A flare exploded over the center of the field and the German AA gunners opened fire and hit several aircraft. Thury didn't think the AA fire looked right and discovered that the Germans had erected platforms in trees. Thury ordered his pilots to again concentrate on the estimated 20 AA positions and put most of them out of action after several passes. The Mustangs then attacked the parked aircraft. Thury got seven and decided to use up his last rounds of ammunition on one last pass. By this time his closing speed had decreased to 300mph and his right wing was hit. He left combat and headed back to England at 130mph trying to gain altitude and eventually nursed his wounded Mustang back to base. The squadron was credited with two air victories, 67 ground victories and nine damaged on the ground and won the Distinguished Unit Citation for their recent work. Thury got five destroyed and one damaged. Thury was awarded the Silver Star and ended the war with the second highest total of ground kills in the ETO with 25.5 (2.5 aerial victories).

The 352nd Fighter Group attacked Platting A/D that was packed with over 75 single and twin-engine aircraft of all types parked in dispersal areas around the field. After the flak suppression flights did their job the 328th (13-9), 486th (18-13) and 487th (24-11) Squadrons left the A/D with 59 aircraft destroyed and 35 damaged with Col. James Mayden scoring 4-2 for HQ. Capt. Raymond Littge was a strafing ace in a day with six victories including two Me-262 jets despite being hit by flak during the initial flak suppression flights. 1Lt. Karl Waldron (487th Fighter Squadron) got five destroyed and two damaged and 1Lt. Joseph Carter (486th Fighter Squadron) got five destroyed and one damaged although his P-51 was hit on his second pass by a 20mm shell through the canopy just behind his head. The group lost one aircraft to flak.

On the 17th fighters of the 8th Air Force destroyed 269 and damaged 128 on the ground and was 12-0-5 in the air. The Eighth lost 18 pilots that day: five POWs, six KIAs and seven MIAs with 15 of the 18 lost when their aircraft was hit by flak. The next day the

Bad Aibling Airdrome. A May 1945 post war photo demonstrates the extensive destruction American fighter-bomber attacks (especially the 350th and 55th Fighter Groups in this airdrome's case) inflicted on the Luftwaffe that was out of fuel and pilots by April 1945. (USAF)

fighters flew bomber support missions to marshaling yards in Germany and only claimed 12-7 on the ground. On the 19th and 20th supporting bombers they got no ground claims and only 18-1-10 in the air.

The four missions of the 10th, 13th, 16th and 17th claimed 1604 destroyed and 941 damaged for a count of 64 fighters. The 4th Fighter Group flew its last mission on 20 April and its rival, the 56th, flew for the last time the following day. The 361st Fighter Group quit on the 20th, the 505th on the 21st and the 78th on the 25th.

April-May Wrap-up

At the end of March the US Sixth Army Group crossed the Rhine at several places in the Worms area and was ready to drive into Germany. The Ruhr had been encircled and the Germans were squeezed by persistent pressure from the VII and XVI Corps until they surrendered 300,000 troops on 18 April. The XIII and XIX Corps of the Ninth Army drove to the east, capturing Hanover on 10 April, Brunswick on the 12th and Magdeburg on the 17th. The Ninth was then ordered to stop and take up defensive positions on the Elbe River. Patton's Third Army duplicating its summer of '44 dash across France; raced across central Germany reaching the Czech border by 18 April. Generally the German withdrawal was disorganized and desperate. Occasionally the Germans mounted local areas of resistance that were either by-passed or overwhelmed by armor fighter-bomber close support. Some large areas, such as Schweinfurt, Wurzburg and Heilbronn put up mass resistance that resulted in the destruction of those cities and their garrisons.

April had only a few non-operational flying days and was a good flying weather month as the 9th Air force flew a record 32,000 sorties. Fighter-bombers mainly flew cover and support missions for the rapidly advancing armored columns and the onrushing armies. Problems arose when the armies moved forward so quickly that the fighter-bomber bases were left so far to the rear that they had only limited time over the battlefield. Armed recce flights were able to rove far behind the lines to attack rail and road transport and in the middle weeks of April to attack Luftwaffe airdromes that were packed with aircraft. The frenzied German retreat furnished the fighter-bombers with abundant targets on the rails, roads and airfields. From 1 April until the end of the war, 8 May, the Germans lost 10,138 motor transport, 531 tanks and armored vehicles, 1,418 locomotives, 6,683 railcars, 1,290 horse-drawn transport and there were 532 rail cuts and 133 road cuts. The Luftwaffe was only able to mount 150 to 200 daily sorties and its aircraft were forced into a small area in west and south Germany, north Czechoslovakia and Austria. These crowded airdromes offered tempting targets for fighter-bombers and the IX destroyed over 1,400 Luftwaffe aircraft on the ground. On 25 April 1945 1Lt. William Hoelscher (334th Fighter Squadron/4th Fighter Group) was the last of many 8th Air Force fighter pilots to be brought down by flak. He was shot down while flying over an airdrome near Prague. He crash-landed and evaded and was returned to base. On 8 May the 9th Air Force lost its last fighter pilot, not by flak but by the other nemesis, hitting the ground. 1Lt. Henry Mohr of the 511th Fighter Squadron of the 405th Fighter Group was flying a scouting mission over a POW camp in Austria his prop hit the water of a lake and he bellied his Thunderbolt onto the water. The heavy fighter sunk immediately with the pilot just able to escape. He floated in his parachute pack until it became waterlogged and he began to sink. Fortunately, a German officer and his girlfriend were on the lake and rescued Mohr before he drown. He was liberated by advancing American troops several hours later ass the war was about to end.

9th Air Force Fighter/Fighter-Bomber Interdiction Operations: Rhine to Victory (8 February-8 May 1945)

	Fighter/Fighter-Bombers		Bombers*	
Targets	**Sorties**	**Bomb Tons**	**Sorties**	**Bomb Tons**
Railways/Bridges	7,570	3,936.3	3,189	5,945.4
Marshaling Yards	8,633	4,596.6	6,888	12,405.7
Roads/Bridges	1,221	756.0	2,301	4,011.5
Motor Transport/Troops	3,817	1,964.1	180	342.8
Military Installations	1,681	962.2	6,333	11,279.1
Shipping	247	134.5	—	—
Totals	23,169	12,355.7	18,891	33,984.5

*Medium and light

8th Air Force Fighter/Fighter-Bomber Interdiction Operations: Rhine to Victory (8 February-8 May 1945)

Bombers flew 21,505 sorties/57,997.7 tons
(Marshaling yards: 16,828sorties/45,253.8 tons)
Fighter-Bombers flew 12 sorties/6 tons against military installations
(Fighter-bombers flew numerous target of opportunity sorties)

First TAF Fighter-Bombers Interdiction Operations: Rhine to Victory (8 February-8 May 1945)

	Fighter/Fighter-Bombers		Bombers*	
Targets	**Sorties**	**Bomb Tons**	**Sorties**	**Bomb Tons**
Railways/Bridges	6,175	2,968.1	707	1,306.5
Marshaling Yards	4,030	1,872.1	296	575.8
Roads/Bridges	384	206.4	6	12.0
Motor Transport/Troops	1,636	724.6	—	—
Military Installations	1,411	712.6	1,424	2,642.7
Shipping	224	100.0	—	—
Totals	13,860	6,583.8	2,433	4,537.0

* Medium

36

Results and Conclusions ETO Tactical Air Campaign

Although this book concerns on the contribution of the American fighter-bomber, the role of the British 2nd Tactical Air Force needs to be addressed. Ranking officers in the British Army and RAF could not agree on a doctrine for the use of their overwhelming air power in the upcoming invasion of France. RAF Bomber Command leader, AM Arthur "Bomber" Harris, had used his influence to demand that strategic bombing take precedent in Allied air power planning. When the 2nd TAF was formed in mid-1943, efforts were focused on its organization, immediate problems and its tactical doctrine in support of the invasion. Thereafter it was left to be developed piecemeal. When the Invasion came there was no general plan in place for tactical level operations. Montgomery's questionable leadership and lack of an air plan early in the campaign, especially during the desperate battles around Caen, put further pressure on the 2nd TAF. It was not used to concentrate its attacks on an operation level to defeat the Germans in Normandy but was dispersed. It was used along the entire front as supplementary fire support for the extensive and effective artillery the Allies possessed. The numerous armed recces were scattered across wide areas and were used to destroy German men and material here and there without concentration and without a real high level tactical and strategic plan.

As America entered the war the higher echelons of her air force were either opposed, uncommitted or uninterested in tactical air support. There was a complete lack of insight as to the concept, there was no air support doctrine in place and thus there was no tactical air experience, training, aircraft or pilots. Finally *Field Manual 31-35* of 9 April 1942 attempted to establish a support doctrine but stated "the most important target at a particular time will usually be that target which constitutes the most serious threat to the operations of the supported ground force" and the "final decision as to priority targets rested with the commander of the supported unit." In North Africa *FM 31-35* was shown to be defective as it divided rather than concentrated air support and did not allow the air commander to take advantage of the flexibility of his forces. After the North African Campaign, enlightened AAF leaders were convinced of the viability of the RAF system of centralizing control of the air force under an air commander who was equal in authority to ground and naval commanders. This concept became doctrine with *FM 100-20* on 21 July 1943 as air and land forces became "co-equal and interdependent forces" and neither was "an auxiliary of the other." By 1944, the junior air commanders learning from experience on the operational level in Sicily and Italy had established the basics of tactical air power; an effective interdiction campaign, armored column cover and put in place a workable coordinated mechanism that delivered the rapid response to air support requests from battlefield to airfield to battlefield. At D-Day the doctrine described by *FM 100-20* was fully formed and took into account the three priorities it developed. However, except for Quesada, most high-level staff commanders concentrated on achieving air superiority for strategic bombing so their opposition or apathy toward tactical air continued until the end of the war and tactical air power's full potential was never realized.

Pilot training in air support was lacking or minimal and the result was revealed on the battlefield and the resultant initial ineptitude to provide support cost the lives of friendly infantry below. The time for air and ground forces to become familiar with each other could have been decreased and the solution to ground/air problems found if a priority would have been given in a training program. Adequate training could have eliminated deficient bomb line discipline and battle line troop and target recognition. Air support was learned through experience, trial and error both on the command level and in the cockpit. The practice of air support depended on a widespread communications system that quickly collected and processed information and then quickly issued orders based on the collected data. The communications systems of the time were relatively primitive, undependable and susceptible to malfunction. There were breakdowns and delays in the handling of the continuous bulk of information incoming and outgoing in the various army and air force echelons. Often by the time the ALOs or GLOs at the fighter-bomber bases briefed the pilots their information was outdated. As time went by tactical became more coordinated and efficient both over the battlefield in close support and armored column cover and in the rear areas in armed recce and interdiction missions.

The primary task of the fighter-bomber was to deliver a large mass of firepower to engulf the target area. Precision attacks, even by experienced pilots were very difficult to realize. The rocket and bomb were inherently inaccurate and targets such as tanks, gun positions troop concentrations were usually unscathed but temporarily neutralized. The problem with temporary neutralization rather than destruction of enemy troops or armor was that it lasted only while the fighter-bombers were overhead or shortly after they had departed. Against German armor, the effectiveness of the fighter-bomber in the close air support role was not the destruction it was unable to obtain but the disruptive and demoralizing effect. In the armed recce role true fighter-bomber effectiveness against armor lay not in its destruction but in the disorder and destruction of the soft-skinned vehicles furnishing them with supplies, fuel and ammunition. Fighter-bombers were particularly effective against rail and road transport. During post war interrogation of Wehrmacht and Luftwaffe officers, the majority categorically attributed the defeat of the German ground forces in the field to Allied air power. Basically they credited air superiority as it allowed the Allies virtually unhindered control of the air and thus of the ground. But in particular they specified continuous air interdiction as the direct cause of their defeat on the ground. Hitler's Blitzkrieg armies had a voracious appetite for supplies and depended on the integral transportation system that fed it and as such was particularly exposed to air interdiction. At every level the transportation system was the most vulnerable part of the German logistics scheme and attacks on it led to the failure of the system and defeat of the Wehrmacht. The enemy was incapable of concentrating his men or supplies at decisive points and times. Repeatedly, when supplies and reinforcements were critically needed, no movement could be risked in daylight. Any movement in daylight became prohibitively expensive in men and materiel. Despite total Allied air supremacy in both the ETO and MTO the German field commanders, soldiers and logistical system coped with difficulties amazingly well. On the other hand, Allied commanders acknowledge that without total air superiority they could have not been as successful in their military strategy and its implementation. Even with air superiority there were a few times when the American battlefield situation was tenuous such as at Anzio and the first hours of D-Day. Attacks on the following supply targets, in order of importance, were found to be the most disruptive:

1) Rail network and the locomotives and rolling stock moving supplies to the armies in the field
2) Road network and traffic moving on it
3) Forward army railheads (which were vulnerable as they were congested and supplies were being trans-shipped from rail to road)
4) Army-level supply convoys (as the supply line was longer and of a larger size it was more exposed than those of divisional and smaller sized units)
5) Division-level supply dumps (because of their proximity to the front and recent arrival were less well dispersed and camouflaged than the army-level dumps farther behind the lines)

The Germans considered the loss, in order, of fuel, ammunition and motor vehicles as most damaging to their tactical ground operations. The Allied strategic bombing campaign against oil production made any loss of fuel to fighter-bombers in the interdiction campaign even more serious. Spaatz "Oil Plan" was the right strategic air plan and should have been implimented on a larger scale earlier.

At the front the simultaneous attacks on rail, road and fuel supplies were decisive. Attacks on the forward railheads increased the need for motor vehicles that increased the demand for fuel that was under attack and had to be brought in by rail. The farther back the railheads were driven the farther motorized traffic had to move, using more fuel and exposing themselves to attack and delay of supply delivery to the front. Even at the time when German fuel reserves were plentiful, that did not mean that it was available at the front. Frontline units could not expect regular fuel shipments and it was that by chance they received any fuel. The Germans had to counter Allied ground attacks by moving reserves and supplies that were fodder for air attacks. The mobility of the German army at the front was reliant on motor transport. Once the personnel and supply left the railheads their local movement was bound to the availability and serviceability of motor transport. The destruction and damage to M/T had a explicit and immediate effect on the front. By the beginning of 1945 regular railway traffic in Germany had closed down and road traffic was responsible for transport.

Allied ground commanders were extravagant in their praise for the contribution of tactical air power but offered a few criticisms particularly the system of calling for air support and the value of mass tactical bombing attacks at the battlefront. Throughout the war the so-called "Pantelleria Effect' often pervaded Allied air power thinking. Strategic air units assigned to support ground armies in a tactical role were unable to do so as the bombing of Cassino, D-Day beach batteries and strong points, Caen and St. Lo demonstrated. The so-called "Transportation Plan", the destruction of the German transportation system in Northwest Europe by strategic air forces, has be deemed unnecessary by post war critics but was also was criticized by many experts at the time. The two factions argue rightly that with uncontested control of the skies, tactical interdiction alone could have achieved the desired disruption of the German transportation system. The strategic bombing of rail centers in France and Belgium failed to accomplish its objective and in the process killed thousands of civilians and smashed many towns and cities. Eisenhower needed to control the strategic air forces to insure the success of the Normandy Invasion and to do so he had to offer them targets suited to heavy bombers, the marshaling yards in towns and cities. Interdiction was not in the scope of heavy bombers and a true interdiction campaign could not be initiated until several days before D-Day. Medium and fighter-bombers took over the interdiction role and were much more successful in that role than heavy bombers. Despite the success of the tactical interdiction campaign, Tedder directed strategic heavy bombers to continue the bombing of rail centers until the end of the war. Tedder believed that heavy bombers would eventually paralyze the German rail system and that, in turn, would eventually collapse the German economy. There were fewer humanitarian protests against killing German civilians who were the enemy. Spaatz continually advocated the bombing of German industry and strategic military targets exclusively. Arthur "Bomber" Harris, Chief of the RAF Bomber Command, had no qualms about bombing civilians in German cities and was sometimes joined by Spaatz such as in the bombing of Dresden. In Italy too, the strategic bombing of large marshaling yards in towns and cities proved to be ineffective and tactical air power was far more effective. The Transportation Plan carried out by the strategic air forces was not necessary or effective and was too damaging to civilian life and property. Tactical interdiction by fighter and medium bombers was to prove more precise and effective.

German officers commented on the lack of an adequate Allied night fighter force that could have made Allied air power a round-the-clock effort which would have made the German supply situation impossible. Fighter-bomber attacks restricted German movement to darkness or periods of bad weather. In the summer of 1944 when there were long hours of daylight, fighter-bombers were especially effective in smashing the German retreat after the Allied armies broke out of the beachheads and Bocage. In December's short hours of daylight and poor weather the Germans were able to amass troops and supplies for the Ardennes Offensive and initiate the attack without having Allied Jabos swooping down on it.

The ETO and MTO were the most anti-aircraft intensive theaters in World War II and fighter-bomber losses were very high. Close air sorties were considerably less hazardous than armed recce sorties. Losses rose in direct proportion to the target distance from the frontlines with deep penetration armed recce sorties suffering the heaviest losses. Also, armed reconnaissance was a continual daylight air offensive that committed more aircraft to achieve its agenda. It was optimistic for US planners to expect armed recce to stop all German road, rail and river traffic, annihilate the Luftwaffe and to prevent all supply and reinforcement of the German battlefront. Again, continual neutralization of this movement through attack and the constant threat of attack was the key to its success. The effort was probably equal to the effect but so were the losses. Every target of vital importance to the Germans was defended by heavy flak concentrations. Close support losses also corresponded to the character of the target. But very little flak was encountered near the battlefront, as the Germans, despite possessing sizable flak resources, simply could not defend every frontline pillbox, gun position and the like.

Gen. Omar Bradley commented on armed reconnaissance:

"One of the outstanding developments of the tactical air forces supporting our armies was their armed reconnaissance missions conducted to the front and flanks of the ground units. Reports from army, corps and division commanders are unanimous in this respect. From the initial beachhead in Normandy, through the breakthrough at St. Lo, the pursuit across France and Belgium, the winter position warfare, the crossing of the Rhine, and the final drive, the fighter-bomber, ranging forward on road and rail-cutting missions, harassing troop concentrations, strafing and bombing of enemy columns on foot or in motor or rail transport, harried the enemy and delayed his shifting of reserves and supplies. This in turn helped army and corps commanders to strike hard at weak spots and exploit advances while limiting the enemy's ability to strike back effectively." (Bradley, *Effect of Air Power on Military Operations*, Western Europe, ibid.)

Close support's contribution to the air offensive was modest and localized in comparison to interdiction and armed recce. Fighter-bombers in ground-controlled front line close support missions were very efficient but the Germans considered them more effective against morale than the actual destruction of men and materiel. After the air attack, ground forces needed to attack immediately to take advantage of the temporary neutralization of the defending troops. The Germans considered fighter-bombers extremely effective in their attacks against forward supply lines than against troops, gun positions and strong points. The reality was that close support and armed recce became paired facets of the TAC air offensive that became more and more flexible and interchangeable. This flexibility permitted the diversion of aircraft from armed recce missions to respond to the immediate, unanticipated requests for close air support that by 1945 became the standard method of calling down close air strikes. When close air targets were absent or over run, close air fighter-bombers were redirected to armed recce sorties. As the Allies swept across France and then after they breached the Rhine and Siegfried Line and rushed into Germany the need for close air support became less and less necessary and fighter-bomber emphasis shifted to interdiction targets. The original IX TAC divided into other TACs and received more pilots and aircraft. Then when the Allies achieved almost total air superiority, the multitude of fighters escorting bombers were released to attack targets on their way home adding to the destruction of the German war effort. The Germans interrogated after the war were struck by the inexhaustibility of the Allied fighter-bomber force.

After its inception the main drawback of armored column cover was that it required a large portion of TAC resources. The post war USAAF Evaluation Board in the ETO determined that a TAC could only cover three armored columns that utilized 30 to 60% of the TAC's available air power, the equivalent of one fighter group per armored division. The later abundance of Allied fighter-bombers allowed Armored Column Cover to develop and flourish. The *Effect of Air Power on Military Operations* written by Gen. Omar Bradley in the post war and the Air Effects Committee of the 12th Army Group both determined that the 9th Air Force's decision to assign significant fighter-bomber resources to armored column cover was a major factor in the various armored breakouts following D-Day through France and into Germany at the end of the war. They went on to credit armored column cover with solving the inherent problems of close air support during various phases of mobile warfare and recognized it as one of the major successes of tactical air warfare.

A highly developed military machine required more supplies and the more complex transportation system to deliver them was vulnerable to tactical air power. Tactical air power was the direct cause of the collapse of the German supply system and a significant cause in the collapse and defeat of the German army. While the TACs could not be credited with winning any ground battle they helped make each victory possible and with fewer casualties. It was the Allied strategic bombing offensive against German in-

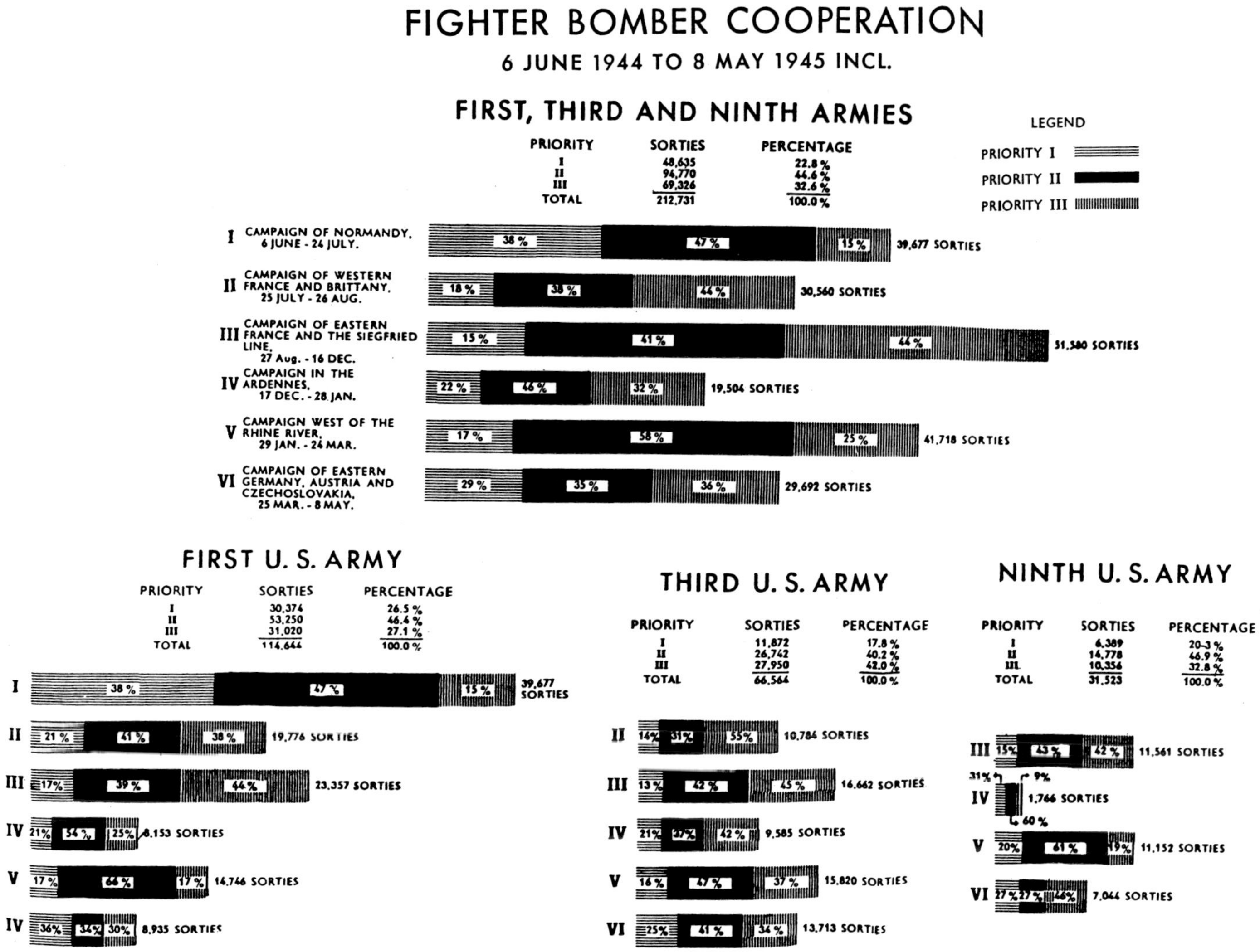

dustry, cities and populace and the armed reconnaissance tactical air offensive behind the battlefront disrupting German movement, supply and harassing the Luftwaffe that was to be the signature effort of Allied air power in World War II. The evolved American tactical air doctrine became the correct one for the situation in Italy and then Northwest Europe and was successful in its application. American fighter-bomber operations were not conducted in the framework of a well developed over all tactical plan and, except for the Argentan-Falaise Pocket, were not concentrated in a defined planned tactical offensive but piecemealed as dictated by situation.

Fighter-Bomber Aircraft in Profile

64 FS/57 FG/9 AF - P-40 K-1 Warhawk s.n. 42-46046 of Lt. R.J. Overcash from the first USAAF outfit assigned to the RAF Desert Air Force, aptly shown here with an RAF type 300-pound centerline ordinance. This premier outfit won two DUCs by the end of April '43, and as of October, took up the first P-47s issued in the MTO and transferred to the 12 AF to win their third DUC in August of '44.

58 FS/33 FG *(NOMADS)* / *12* AF P-40 F-10 Warhawk s.n. 41-14491, a typical Merlin powered P-40 used throughout North Africa. "Joker Sqn" (58 FS) CO Capt. Phil Cochran, armed with a mid-tine 500 pounder as shown, single handedly knocked out the Splendida Hotel German HQ in Kairouan, Tunisia, on 10 January, 1943, setting the pace for tactical sorties to come. Ironically, the "Nomads" earned their DUC in January '43 for downing five enemy bombers in a single interception.

94 FS/1 FG/12 AF P-38 F-1 Lightning s.n. 41-7498 first assigned to Capt. Newell for 50 missions, then reissued as the BAT OUT OF *HELL* to Lt. Hagenback in Sicily, October '43. Two DUCs were gained by "the First to fight" over Italy before taking up escort duty in November with new P-38s in the new 15 AF

346 FS/350 FG/12 AF - P-39 N-1 Airacobra s.n. 42-18309. With a variety of "second team" refit Lightnings, Warhawks and even a few Spitfires, it was the veteran Airacobras on a tactical sweep of the Pisa-Grosseto, Italy, area on 6 April 1944 that warranted a DUC for the many targets destroyed plus five Luftwaffe interceptors shot down.

522 FBS/ 27 FBG/12 AF - A-36 A-1 Invader s.n. 42-83803 of Lt.M.I Russo, sole A-36 ace in the MTO and the only official ace in the three and a half years of the Group's combat history. Ironically, this obscure outfit flew obsolete A-24s in the Philippines campaign of '42, Invaders and Warhawks in North Africa, to VE-Day with P-47s in the 1st TAF, underscored with an unprecedented five Distinguished Unit Citations.

4 FS/52 FG/12 AF - Spitfire Mk Vb s.n. ER 570 of Maj. R. Levine maxed out with two "250's" for sorties in Tunisia in early '43, which sorely proved the "short legged" Spitfire's tactical misuse. In March '44, the 52nd refit with Mustangs for escort missions in the 15 AF where two DUCs were promptly won by summer's end.

87 FS/79 FG/12AF P-47D Thunderbolt , possible D-15-RE s.n. 42-75671; unknown 87 FS "Skeeter" pilot of this veteran T-bott in Late '44. Armed with a variety of ordinance like the clusters of twenty-pound frag bombs shown here, the "Lightning Strike" T-botts remained the Brits' preferred JABO's in Italy, proved by their second DUC in April '45.

527 FS/86 FG/12 AF P-47D Thunderbolt s.n. and pilot unknown for this brightly striped strafer of the "Mustangers" squadron who shared in the first group DUC for May '44. In February '45, the group would join other 12 AF units in France with the new 1 st Tactical Air Force, and win their second DUC for operations in April over northern Germany.

55 FG P-51 D-15 Mustang s.n. 44-14223 *KATYDID; winter* '44-45, the last Mustang of top strafer LtCol. E.G. Righetti. Battle scarred *KATYDID* displays nine aerial victories accrued in the colonel's consequent combat tours with the 20th and the 55th Groups, including a uniquely configured "piggyback" Fw-190/ Ju-88 MISTEL.

84 FS/ 78 FG/8 AF - P-47 D-22 Thunderbolt s.n. 42-25698; the last *OKIE* A/C of Maj. Q. Brown in late March, '44, with 13 aerial victories displayed. Just as with the JABOs of the 9 AF, *OKIE* totes a pair of 500 pounders and a one-hundred gallon belly tank. First to strafe a target in Germany in July '43, Brown's Loss in Aprit'44 to flak and murder by his captors was a dark portent of strafer Righetti's fate a year later.

505 FS/339 FG/8 AF - P-51 D-20 Mustang s.n. 44-72437; last Mustang *PAULINE* of LtC.J.L. Thury as of March '45 with a somewhat cryptic display of 17 kriegsmarine ensigns that neither clarify his strafer total of 25 and one shared, nor his two aerial kills.

434 FS/479 FG/8 AF - P-38 J-10 Lightning s.n. 42-68177 *TARZANA* of pilot Lt. G.D. Hendrix who inherited the field camouflaged A/C from the 20 FG in late June '44. Hendrix used *TARZANA*, named for his California hometown, to knock down a Ju-88 on 12 August, just before the intense five six-week mission era that would yeild the Group's only DUC.

388 FS/365 FG/9 AF - P-47 D-25-RE Thunderbolt s.n. 42-26407 *COFFEY'S POT* of Maj. Bob Coffey, one of the first bubble canopy types issued in the ETO. The POT is maxed out with two 1000 pounders and a one-hundred gallon belly tank. Seven white outlined swastikas tell of ground kilts gained pre-D-Day. The Major bellied in the POT due to flak over Germany in August, hence missing out on the Group's DUCs for October '44 and April '45.

397 FS/368 FG/9 AF - P-47 D-30-RE Thunderbolt s.n. 44-33136 of Lt. C. Price in early '45, well after the Group had won its DUC the previous September over Mons, France. Graced with one of American artist George Petty's most popular "Petty girts," she totes a pair of 500 pounders plus a "fatboy" 175 gallon center line tank.

508 FS/404 FG/9 AF P-47 D-27-RE Thunderbolt s.n. 42-27221 *I'LL GET BY* of CO Col. L.C. Moon totes a pair of 500 pound bombs and is retro fitted with zero-length mounted 60-pound high velocity missiles inboard of the standard wing racks. Thus equipped, their armed reconnaissance in the September '44 offensive resulted in a DUC.

429 FS/474 FG/9 AF - P-38 Lightning purported J-25 s.n. 44-23661 in Belgium in late 44 and flown by several pilots in the squadron. The 474th was the only ETO outfit to fly the P-38 throughout its combat history, inclusive of their 24-hour coverage of the D-Day landings and subsequent DUC for mauling the retreating German army attempting to cross the Seine River west of Paris on 23 August 1944.

Appendices

Enemy Aircraft Destroyed ETO (August 1944 to May 1945)

	Bombers*	Fighters		
Date	Air	Air	Ground	Total
Aug/1942	2	1	0	3
Sept.	16	0	0	16
Oct.	44	5	0	49
Nov.	47	0	0	47
Dec.	53	1	0	54
Total/42	162	7	0	169
Jan/43	45	5	0	50
Feb.	72	2	0	74
March	142	0	0	142
April	146	4	0	150
May	372	8	0	380
June	293	18	0	311
July	533	42	0	575
August	404	53	0	457
Sept.	265	38	0	303
Oct.	794	76	0	870
Nov.	117	105	0	222
Dec.	231	100	0	321
Total/43	3414	451	0	3865
Jan/44	592	203	0	795
Feb.	399	341	1	741
March	365	469	76	910
April	346	418	527	1291
May	382	596	242	1220
June	45	470	148	663
July	101	407	153	661
August	25	551	437	1013
Sept.	65	586	440	1091
Oct.	12	202	139	353
Nov.	29	492	181	702
Dec.	87	867	31	985
Total/44	2448	5602	2375	10425
Jan/45	41	337	87	465
Feb.	2	163	295	460
March	34	395	321	750
April	100	454	3703	4257
May	0	13	15	28
Total/45	177	1362	4421	5960
ETO Total	6201	7422	6796	21419

* Heavy, medium and light

Enemy Aircraft Destroyed in the MTO (July 1942 to May 1945)

	Bombers*		Fighters		
Date	Air	Ground	Air	Ground	Total
July/42	2	0	0	0	2
August	0	0	0	0	0
Sept.	1	0	0	0	1
Oct.	11	10	10	22	43
Nov.	11	0	16	9	36
Dec.	22	9	43	2	76
Total/42	42	24	81	11	158
Jan/43	107	30	56	1	194
Feb.	80	6	57	0	143
March	84	24	103	0	211
April	102	102	319	0	523
May	137	48	132	33	350
June	118	22	115	12	267
July	125	63	125	0	313
August	422	0	117	63	602
Sept.	212	130	102	37	483
Oct.	89	95	81	25	290
Nov.	93	55	21	6	175
Dec.	129	6	42	12	189
Total/43	1698	583	1270	189	3740
Jan/44	150	0	170	0	320
Feb.	244	19	111	3	377
March	107	80	103	17	307
April	429	202	224	103	958
May	242	38	190	62	532
June	226	20	285	31	562
July	337	39	376	120	872
August	122	48	151	277	598
Sept.	13	5	18	215	251
Oct.	2	0	60	197	259
Nov.	10	10	34	32	86
Dec.	51	0	38	28	117
Total/44	1933	461	1760	1085	5239
Jan/45	0	0	8	0	8
Feb.	1	0	8	19	28
March	14	8	105	18	145
April	0	0	68	42	110
May	0	0	0	0	0
Total/45	15	8	189	79	291
MTO Total	3688	1076	3300	1364	9428

*Heavy and light

USAAF Fighter Combat Losses ETO (August 1942-May 1945)

	E/A/C	AA	Other*	Total
Aug/42	8	0	0	8
Sept.	0	0	0	0
Oct.	1	0	0	1
Nov.	1	0	0	1
Dec.	0	0	0	0
Total/42	10	0	0	10
Jan/43	3	0	0	3
Feb.	1	0	0	1
March	1	0	0	1
April	5	0	0	5
May	9	0	3	12
June	8	0	0	8
July	14	0	0	14
August	7	0	3	10
Sept.	10	0	2	12
Oct.	13	0	1	14
Nov.	53	1	0	54
Dec.	37	0	7	44
Total/43	161	1	16	178
Jan/44	57	6	6	69
Feb.	69	13	21	103
March	54	46	91	191
April	201	60	19	280
May	176	98	66	340
June	147	226	167	540
July	65	153	108	326
August	100	294	152	546
Sept.	104	190	63	357
Oct.	99	198	52	349
Nov.	80	164	54	298
Dec.	141	163	62	366
Total/44	1293	1611	861	3765
Jan/45	72	162	40	274
Feb.	38	208	53	299
March	76	244	99	419
April	36	207	100	343
May	5	15	16	36
Total/45	227	837	307	1371
ETO Total	1691	2449	1184	5324

Other and unknown
Note: bombers lost:

Heavy	Light/Medium
2452 lost to E/A/C	131 lost to E/A/C
2439 lost to AA	492 lost to AA
657 lost to other	192 lost to other
5548 total lost	815 total lost

USAAF Fighter Combat Losses MTO (June 1942 to May 1945)

	E/A/C	AA	Other*	Total
June/42	0	0	0	0
July	0	0	0	0
August	3	0	0	0
Sept.	0	0	0	0
Oct.	3	0	0	3
Nov.	10	4	0	14
Dec.	30	4	0	34
Total/42	46	8	0	54
Jan/43	78	6	4	88
Feb.	40	10	2	52
March	55	7	6	68
April	109	4	3	116
May	89	16	11	116
June	58	3	20	81
July	112	12	29	153
August	113	17	27	157
Sept.	56	5	27	88
Oct.	32	6	12	50
Nov.	18	15	6	39
Dec.	56	14	12	80
Total/43	816	115	157	1088
Jan/44	70	17	30	117
Feb.	57	25	22	104
March	38	9	32	89
April	38	17	50	105
May	52	59	69	180
June	67	70	64	201
July	43	42	50	135
August	39	54	104	197
Sept.	18	55	44	117
Oct.	2	55	41	98
Nov.	10	54	56	120
Dec.	7	36	55	108
Total/44	441	493	637	1571
Jan/45	0	33	48	81
Feb.	4	44	59	107
March	13	56	41	110
April	7	72	64	143
May	1	2	3	9
Total/45	24	206	214	444
MTO Total	1327	822	1008	3157

*Other and unknown
Note: Bombers lost to:

Heavy	Light/Medium
837 lost to E/A/C	352 lost to E/A/C
1313 lost to AA	306 lost to AA
606 lost to other	150 lost to other
2766 Total Lost	808 Total Lost

Tons of Bombs Dropped by Fighter-Bombers/MTO (June 1942 to May 1945)

	Bombers*			Fighters		
	HE	Incend.	Total	HE	Incend.	Total
June/42	115	0	115	0	0	0
July	357	0	357	0	0	0
August	414	0	414	0	0	0
Sept.	482	0	482	0	0	0
Oct.	721	0	721	50	0	50
Nov.	1144	0	1144	51	0	51
Dec.	995	0	995	81	0	81
Total/42	4228	0	4228	182	0	182
Jan/43	1940	2	1942	41	0	41
Feb.	1709	0	1709	10	0	10
March	2719	0	2719	54	0	54
April	4712	0	4712	341	0	341
May	6640	1	6641	656	1	657
June	7762	0	7762	1283	0	1283
July	12563	0	12563	1283	0	1283
August	10995	0	10995	1589	0	1589
Sept.	12427	27	12454	1488	0	1488
Oct.	6547	2	6549	1078	0	1078
Nov.	8313	0	8313	1167	0	1167
Dec.	11647	0	11647	1917	0	1917
Total/43	50456	29	50456	10458	1	10459
Jan/44	16998	8	17006	2079	12	2091
Feb.	9989	136	10025	1569	1	1570
March	15299	534	15833	1589	18	1607
April	26256	599	26855	2822	179	3001
May	39514	783	40297	5686	92	5778
June	48103	872	48975	3926	10	3936
July	37659	1653	39312	2454	3	2457
August	37008	246	37254	2954	72	3026
Sept.	27118	261	27379	1900	6	1906
Oct.	19793	593	20386	1710	12	1722
Nov.	22272	1151	23423	3255	17	3272
Dec.	22399	487	22886	3613	7	3620
Total/44	305684	7323	313007	33557	429	33986
Jan/45	10522	57	10579	3836	124	3960
Feb.	29206	245	29451	3054	156	3210
March	37160	152	37312	3621	187	3808
April	38423	181	38604	5334	427	5761
May	88	0	0	39	24	63
Total/45	115399	635	116034	15884	918	16802
MTO Total	513282	7990	521272	60081	1348	61429

HE = High explosive Incendiary = Incendiary

*Heavy and light

Note: MTO totals

Heavy Bombers			Light/Medium Bombers		
HE	Incend.	Total	HE	Incend.	Total
374,941	7,134	382,075	24,668	467	139,197

Tons of Bombs Dropped by Fighter-Bombers/ETO (August 1942 to May 1945)

	Bombers*			Fighters		
	HE	Incend.	Total	HE	Incend.	Total
Aug/42	135	0	135	0	0	0
Sept.	215	0	215	0	0	0
Oct.	334	0	334	0	0	0
Nov.	612	0	612	0	0	0
Dec.	417	0	417	0	0	0
Total/42	1713	0	1713	0	0	0
Jan/43	739	0	739	0	0	0
Feb.	705	0	705	0	0	0
March	1530	0	1530	0	0	0
April	1130	0	1130	0	0	0
May	2665	23	2688	0	0	0
June	2468	0	2468	0	0	0
July	3762	604	4366	0	0	0
August	4737	335	5072	0	0	0
Sept.	8279	240	8519	0	0	0
Oct.	5172	843	6015	0	0	0
Nov.	6496	1796	6851	17	0	17
Dec.	10949	3158	14107	7	0	7
Total/43	48632	6999	55631	24	0	24
Jan/44	11230	2746	13976	39	0	39
Feb.	20067	2476	22543	23	0	23
March	21355	5053	26408	131	0	131
April	32201	4850	37051	1489	0	1489
May	48238	4942	53185	3684	5	3689
June	74073	1253	75326	10321	1	10322
July	49356	7132	56488	6567	7	6574
August	54635	5386	60021	7721	24	7745
Sept.	40564	7310	47874	4300	1	4301
Oct.	36461	11727	48188	4574	98	4672
Nov.	46646	608	47254	4019	140	4159
Dec.	47540	3934	51474	8726	301	9027
Total/44	482371	57417	539786	51594	577	52171
Jan/45	44476	2745	47221	6941	312	7253
Feb.	61108	7780	68888	10955	505	11460
March	89279	13452	102731	13337	1935	15272
April	56119	6514	62633	5689	920	6609
May	301	0	301	67	0	67
Total/45	251283	30491	281774	36989	3672	40661
ETO Total	783999	94907	878906	88607	4249	92856

HE = High Explosive Incend. = Incendiary

* Heavy and light bombers

Note: ETO Totals

Heavy Bombers			Light/Medium Bombers		
HE	Incend.	Total	HE	Incend.	Total
624,141	90,578	714,719	159,858	4,329	164,187

ETO Fighter Sorties Flown
(January 1943 to May 1945)

	Escort	Bombing-Strafing	Recon	Other*	Total
Jan/43	0	0	0	429	429
Feb.	0	0	0	450	450
March	0	0	0	608	608
April	8	0	8	524	540
May	384	0	0	1836	2220
June	169	0	0	1828	1997
July	607	0	0	1679	2286
August	1578	0	0	686	2264
Sept.	2167	0	0	1257	3424
Oct.	2890	0	0	506	3396
Nov.	2638	105	2	1160	3905
Dec.	5095	89	57	500	5741
Total/43	15536	194	67	11463	27260
Jan/44	6080	201	0	886	7167
Feb.	10295	83	0	301	10679
March	14659	887	0	715	16261
April	14072	3803	0	3679	21554
May	26091	6405	0	3714	36210
June	27970	1320	0	16170	55460
July	20577	9098	0	13278	42953
August	23793	4524	0	17510	45827
Sept.	13531	11056	0	9098	33585
Oct.	15659	11731	0	2491	29881
Nov.	19082	7542	0	3496	30120
Dec.	15723	12940	0	6824	35487
Total/44	207532	79590	0	78162	365284
Jan/45	10898	9878	4473	1169	26418
Feb.	13261	13906	8410	649	36226
March	19853	37311	452	5226	62842
April	16654	25420	4452	1530	48056
May	168	729	362	1752	3011
Total/45	60834	87244	18149	10326	176533
ETO Totals	283902	167028	18216	99951	569097

* Others includes sweeps, interceptions, patrols and sea search sorti

MTO Fighter Sorties Flown
(June 1942 to May 1945)

	Escort	Bombing-Strafing	Recon	Other*	Total
Jan/43	1352	286	186	876	2700
Feb.	1093	350	312	266	2021
March	2238	505	68	1698	4509
April	3433	2063	388	3089	8973
May	2889	2393	204	2803	8289
June	3739	1770	94	2894	8527
July	6232	3916	353	5843	16344
August	4486	4011	521	5653	14653
Sept.	2493	4491	210	5127	12321
Oct.	2241	3951	151	2517	8860
Nov.	3036	4161	334	3182	10713
Dec.	3713	6157	291	4104	14265
Total/43	36975	34054	3112	38052	112193
Jan/44	4526	6359	0	8454	19339
Feb.	2628	4014	0	5880	12522
March	4487	4037	0	6137	14661
April	6050	6844	0	3416	16310
May	6746	11759	0	2574	21079
June	5862	8232	0	2672	16766
July	8235	5223	0	2592	16050
August	7887	6461	0	4624	18972
Sept.	4513	4164	0	2624	11301
Oct.	4003	4583	0	977	9563
Nov.	4270	6822	0	893	11985
Dec.	6141	7988	0	851	14980
Total/44	65348	76486	0	41694	183528
Jan/45	2311	7402	1	251	9965
Feb.	6658	6868	0	380	13906
March	0	15062	4	432	15498
April	5340	11749	1400	408	18897
May	0	332	176	37	545
Total/45	14309	41413	1581	1508	58811
MTO Total	116632	151953	4693	81254	354532

*Others includes sweeps, interceptions, patrols and sea search sorties.

Combat Effectiveness VIII Fighter Command

AERIAL			GROUND			COMBINED		
	Avg. Destroyed			Avg. Destroyed			Avg. Destroyed	
Rank	FG	Per Mission	Rank	FG	Per Mission	Rank	FG	Per Mission
1	357	1.903	1	339	1.604	1	339	2.488
2	56	1.488	2	355	1.211	2	358	2.243
3	352	1.200	3	479	1.112	3	56	2.183
4	4	1.038	4	353	0.926	4	355	2.028
5	339	0.884	5	4	0.887	5	4	1.924
6	355	0.817	6	78	0.797	6	352	1.883
7	364	0.769	7	20	0.760	7	479	1.725
8	353	0.744	8	56	0.696	8	353	1.670
9	78	0.738	9	352	0.683	9	78	1.534
10	55	0.735	10	55	0.650	10	20	1.429
11	359	0.694	11	364	0.564	11	55	1.385
12	20	0.671	12	357	0.340	12	364	1.333
13	361	0.648	13	361	0.308	13	359	0.977
14	479	0.614	14	359	0.283	14	361	0.956
15	356	0.487	15	356	0.183	15	356	0.669

Components of the Allied Tactical Air Forces

Italy

RAF Desert Air Force (1945)

Aircraft Type	Number of Squadrons
Fighter/Fighter-Bombers	22 (56.6%) *
Light/Medium Bombers	7 (16.6%)
Night Fighters & Bombers	6 (14.2%)
Air Operations Post	5 (11.9%)
Reconnaissance	2 (4.7%)

* Includes 3 USAAF P-47 Squadrons (attached)

US XII Air Support Command (Jan. 1944)

Aircraft Type	Number of Squadrons
Fighter/Fighter-Bombers	23 (57.5%)
Fighter/Dive-Bombers	6 (15.0%)
Light/Medium Bombers	4 (10.0%)
Night Fighters	3 (7.5%)
Reconnaissance	3 (7.5%)
Radio Counter-Measures	1 (2.5%)

ETO

RAF 2nd Tactical Air Force

Aircraft Type	Numbers of Squadrons
Fighter/Fighter-Bombers	49 (61.2%)
Light/Medium Bombers	13 (16.2%)
Reconnaissance	9 (11.2%)
Air Observation Post	9 (11.2%)

US 9th Air Force (1945)

Aircraft Type	Number of Squadrons
Fighter/Fighter-Bombers	45 (42.8%)
Light/Medium Bombers	45 (42.8%)
Night Fighters	2 (1.9%)
Reconnaissance	13 (12.3%)

US 1st Tactical Air Force (1945)

Aircraft Type	Number of Squadrons
Fighter/Fighter-Bombers	24 (50.0%)
Light/Medium Bombers	14 (29.1%)
Reconnaissance	8 (16.6%)
Night Fighters	2 (4.1%)

Index

Index

A

Adams, John: 349
Albright, Clinton: 356
Albright, Edward: 307
Alexander, Harold: 202, 205, 228, **237,** 237, 242, **245**
Allison, Dixon: 172
Allison, James: 49
Ammon, Robert: 135, 360, 360
Anderson, Carl: 93
Anderson, Frederick: 247, 259
Anderson, Raymond: 310
Anderson, Samuel: 287, 340
Antonides, William: 362
Arnim, Jurgen von: 178
Arnold, Henry "Hap": 13, 22, **32**, 32, 33, 36, 129, **193, 245, 246**, 252, 288, 309
Aulock, Andeas: 301
Avery, Delwin: 172

B

Bacherer, Rudolf: 276
Badoglio, Pietro: 192
Bagian, Philip: 226
Bailey, William: 57, 57,
Barcus, Glenn: 103, **352**
Barger, Clarence: 253, **254**
Barre, George: 173
Baseler, Robert: 212
Bass, Robert: 232
Bates, Earl: 174, 178
Bayerlein, Fritz: 274, 275, 282, 334
Beckham, Walter: 127
Beeson, Duane: 127, 255
Berlichigen, Goetz von: 270
Berlin, Donovan: 44
Bierer, Earl: 310
Billie, Henry: 362
Bjorkman, Henry: 290
Blakeslee, Donald: 158, 158
Blaskowitz, Johannes: 224, 224
Bledsoe, Marvin: 113, 144,**145**
Blickenstaff, Wayne: 88, 89
Blumer. John: 220
Blurock, William: 220
Bohr, T.A.: 315
Boone, Walker: 346
Borek, Chet: 125
Boing, Lloyd: 363
Bostwick, George: 356, 356
Booth, Robert: 272
Bradley, Omar: 22, 28, 30, 95, 249, **266,** 268, 272, 276, 279, 283, 284, 287, 287, 288, 289, 295, 298, 324, 328, 368
Brereton, Lewis: 245, **246,** 246, **253, 266,** 272, 277, 283
Brewer, Philip: 220
Brezas, Michael: 62
Bridges, Lloyd: 214
Broadhurst, Harry: 27, 178, 194, 249, 250, **252,** 252, 279
Brookings, George: 327, 328
Brooks, Edward: 324
Brolich, Frieherr von: 179
Brown, Quince: 32, **33**
Bruelle, Robert: 58
Buelowius, Alfred: 268
Buskley, James: 345
Byers, John: 360

C
Call, Lance: 262, 262
Candee, Robert: 15
Cannon, John: 193, **194,** 205, 222, **236, 239, 257**
Care, Raymond: 256
Carlson, Donald: 126
Carpenter, George: 127
Carr, Vernon: 360
Carson, Leonard "Kit": 168 (a/c)
Carter, Clifford: 34
Carter, James: 356, 362
Carter, Joseph: 364
Case, Harvey: 348
Cassidy, Benjamin: 240
Cassidy, Richard: 328
Chennault, Clair: 33, 44, 130
Chetneky, Steven: 360
Chetwood, Kenneth: 34
Chick, William: 212
Chickering, Edward: 348
Chilton, Robert: 41
Choltitz, Dietrich von: 304
Churchill, Winston: 186, 223, 245, 253, 335
Christian, Thomas: 57, 57, 89
Clark, Lawton: 166 (a/c)
Clark, Mark: 193, 194, 201, 202, 205, 209, **216,** 216, 217, 227, 230, **237**
Clark, William: 360
Cles. Leslie: 58, 80, 117
Cochran, Philip: 175
Cohen, Peter: 184
Colgan, William: 138, 142, 144, 226, 316
Colletti, Anthony: 360
Collins, Frank: 212
Collins, J. Lawton: 117, 253, **266,** 268, 272, 273, 276, 277, 281, 283, 285, **287,** 290, 291, 295, 316, 333
Cole, Charles: 345
Coleman, William: 286
Comstock, Harold: 307
Coningham, Arthur: 14, 15, **26**, 173, 175, 176, 182, 194, 203, 205, 249, 250, **252,** 252, 279, 328
Corlett, Peter: 281
Cowart, William: 102
Craig, Howard: 174
Craig, Malin: 13
Cramer, Darrell: 130
Crockett, James: 130
Crompton, Gordon: 362
Crouch, John: 345
Croy, Capt: 359
Crutchfield, Wilford: 273, 334
Cullerton, William: 7, 7, 61, 129,**131,** 131, 320
Cummings, William: 255, 255
Cunningham, Andrew: 245
Curl, James: 180

D
Dade, Lucien: 307, 358
Darwen, Jackie: 178
Davis, Arthur: 58
Dawley, Ernest: 194
Dean, Frederick: 172, 177
Dean, H.W.: 93, 94
Delashaw, Robert: 285, 285, 286
DeLattre, Jean: 335
Demoulin, Charles: 142
Dempsey, Miles: 249, 283
Devers, Jacob: 222, **225, 324, 335**
DeVilliers, Donald: 360
Dick, Royer: 245
Dietrich, Sepp: 275, 282, 295
Dissette, Lawrence: 256, 362
Dix, Gerald: 255
Donicht, H.L.: 93
Donathan, Lt.: 362
Doolittle, James: 22, 32, 33, 38, 172,175, 176, 194, 205, 241, 246, 250, 253, 288, 322, 341
Doss, Gene: 360
Duncan, Glenn: 33, **127, 130,** 134, **363**
Durant, Charles: 34

E
Eaker, Ira: 12, **205,** 209, **209, 220, 225, 239, 245,** 246, **250,**
Eberbach, Heinrich: 282
Eberhard, Heinz: 295
Edwards, Francis: 34
Edwinson, Clarence: 220
Eiland, John: 180
Einhouse, Merle: 345
Eisenhower, Dwight: 14, **17**, 174, 183, 205, 227, **245, 246,** 249, 250, 253, 259, **266, 277**, 277, 279, 283, 287, 288, 295, 324, 326, 335, 336, 341
Eisenhower, John: 17
Eisenach, Franz: 263
Elder, John: 320, 362
Elster, Eric: 307
Ettleson, Charles: 34
Everson, Kirke: 364

F

Fahringer, John; 356
Fisher, Edwin: 166
Flagg, Capt.: 357
Fortier, Norman: 34
Frank, Walter "Tony": 72
Freyberg, Bernard: 178, 209, 211
Frisch, Robert: 357
Fry, Robert: 327, 328
Fuller, J.F.C.: 28

G

Gabor, Edward: 242
Gabreski, Francis "Gabby": 36, **127**, 127, 128
Galland, Adolf: 322, 333
Gallup, Kenneth: 157
Garland, Blair: 101, 102, 106, 272
Garman, Ralph: 180
Garrod, Guy: 239
Geren, Lloyd: 359
Gerow, Leonard: 266, 281, 283, 301
Gersdorff, Rudolf-Christopher von: 291, 295
Gilbert, Olin: 360
Gilbertson, Merle: 345
Giller, Edward: 355
Godfrey, John: 128, 129
Goff, Robert: 38
Gollob, Gordon: 332
Goodson, James: 127
Grabmann, Walter: 326
Gray, F.C.: 88, 88
Green, Herschel: 212, **232,** 232
Griffin, John: 345
Gutske, Richard: 362

H

Haislip, Wade: 324
Hall, Lance: 139
Halvorson, Harry: 12
Harris, Arthur: 241, 249, 250, 253, **258,** 366, 367
Hatter, Robert: 136
Hausser, Paul: 295, 297, 351
Hawkins, John: 172
Hayden, John: 159
Heilmann, Ludwig: 329
Helfrecht, Kenneth: 362
Heller, Edwin: 361
Hellmich, Heinz: 276
Hendricks, Randall: 285
Hennessey, Lt.: 357
Henry, Arlo: 328
Henry, Carroll: 131, 363
Henry, John: 23, 23
Hewitt, Kent: 191
Heysham, David: 24
Hibbard, H.L.: 39
Hightshoe, Melville: 362
Hitler, Adolf: 343
Hobbs, Luke: 48
Hodges, Courtney: 247, **287,** 287, 289, 290, 305, 322, 328
Hoelscher, William: 365
Hoffman, William: 359
Holle, Alexander: 268
Hollingworth, J.M.: 308
Holmes, Robert: 359
Holt, Harold: 263, 276, 277, 285, 316
Hooe, Roy: **12**
Houston, Byron: 256
Horrocks, Brian: 178
Hough, Cass: 37
Hovde, William: 255
House, E.J.: 194, 196
Howell, John: 263
Huebner, Clarence: 271, 271
Hughes, Richard: 341

I

Ilfrey, Jack: 62, **168, 177,** 177

J

Jackson, Michael: 307
Jackson, Nelson: 336
Jackson, Willie: 361
Jaffe, Abraham: 328
Jenkins, Jack: 40
Jenkins, Ralph: 286
Jennings, Russell: 226
Johnson, Benjamin: 255
Johnson, Gerald: 127, **261,** 261
Johnson, Kelly: 39,
Johnson, Martin: 34,
Johnson, Robert: 36, **59**, 264
Jones, K.R.: 345
Josey, Bradford: 360
Jucheim, Alvin: 127
Junck, Werner: 268

K

Katschke, Kenneth: 214
Keen, Robert: 308
Keitel, Wilhelm: 275
Kelly, Joseph: 34,
Kenney, George: 39,
Kepner, William: 34, 34, 35, **158,** 252, 269
Keppler, Georg: 315
Kesselring, Albert: 107, 190, **192,** 201, 206, **228,** 228, 230, 233, 243, 244, 349
Kincaid, Alvin: 256
Kinnard, Claiborne: 256, 359
Kinne, Frederick: 286
Kluge, Guenther von: 251, 278, 287, 290, 294, **295**, 354
Knerr, Hugh: 72, **312**
Knight, Raymond: 241, 241
Kolb, Herbert: 346, 362
Koldunov, A.I.: 214
Kollar, Karl: 236
Kuhn, Philip: 359
Kulik, Edward: 360
Kuter, Laurence: 14, 173

L

Lake, Joseph: 362
Lander, Richard: 210
Landers, John: 357, 358, 359
Lane, W.J.: 362
Lang, Helmut: 282
Lanoue, Roland: 346
Larkin, Thomas: 222
Lathrop, James: 310
Laughlin, Joseph: 300, 319
Lauritsen, C.C.: 93
Ledington, Dorian: 360
Leigh-Mallory, Trafford: 72, **245**, 245, 249, **250,** 250, 251, 252, 253, 256, 257, 259, 260, 262, **266**, 267, 279, 288, 295
Lewis, Leon: 310
Littge, Raymond: 364
Litton, William: 220
Lloyd, Hugh: 175
Long, Thurman: 362
Loveless, Richard: 360
Lucas, John: 206, 208
Lucini, Guido: 196
Lynch, William: 362

M

Mackensen, Eberhard von: 206, 208
MacNicol, George: 196
Maguire, William: 58
Mahany, Howard: 363
Mahurin, Walker "Bud": 36, 127, 262, 264
Matheson, Charles: 348
Mason, Joe: 89
Marsh, Halbert: 362
Marshall, Bert: 306, 306, 359
Marshall, George: 12,13, **32**, 32, 257
Mayden, James: 364
McAuliffe, Anthony: 330
McClenahan, Robert: 279
McClure, James: 362
McCollom. Francis: 362
McCollum, Loren: 37, **38**, **134**
McColpin, Carroll: 104
McCoy, John: 14
McCreery, Richard: 194, **237**
McDonald, David: 348
McDuffie, Duncan: 360
McGinnis, K.R.: 345
McGoldrick, Peter: 174
McGratten, Bernard: 267
McKee, Seth: 263
McKennon, Pierce: 362
McLachan, Joseph: 290
McLaughlin, Joseph: 285
McMahan, Bruce: 362
McMahan, Darrell: 308
McMillan, Harold: 245
McMinn, Evan: 267
McMullen, Joseph: 362
McNair, Leslie: 285
McNown, William: 177
McTaggart, Elmer: 349
Mellen, Joseph: 359
Mendenhall, Lee: 256
Merony, Virgil: 99
Milburn, Frank: 336, 337
Middleton, Troy: 271, **281**
Miller, Henry: 72
Miller, Gerald: 362
Miller, J.F.: 72
Miller, Roger: 187

Milliken, Robert: 127
Mitchell, Billy: 12, **31**, 31
Model, Walther: 137, 251, 279, 294, **295,** 304, 315, 335, 354
Montgomery, Bernard: 15, 24, 174, 176, 177, 205, **245,** 245, 249, 279, **281,** 294, 304, 328, 366
Moon, Leo: 36(a/c), 295
Morris, John: 310
Motzenbecker, John: 326, 326
Muse, Hugh: 196
Mussolini, Benito: 184
Meyer, John: 332
Meyer, Kurt: 297
Meyers,Gilbert: 263, 277, 305
Mohr, Henry: 365
Morgan, F.A.: 345
Murphy, Randal: 359, 359
Myers, Raymond: 256
Myers, William: 363, 363

N
Naylor, Lt.: 357
Neilson, Melvin: 94
Nichols, Howard: 95
Newman, James: 65, 247
Nolan, Joseph: 290
Norley, Louis "Red": 362
Nugent, Richard: 277, **312**, 312, 326, 328, 331, 345

O
O'Conner, Richard: 282
Oliphint, John: 34
Olson, T.C.: 308
Orcutt, Leon: 364

P
Parcel, Bruce: 286
Parker, James: 359
Patch, Alexander: 247, 324, 335, 352
Pattillo, Charles "Buck": 361
Pattillo, Cuthbert "Bill": 361
Patton, George: 26, 171, 183, 191, 247, 251, 287, 289, 290, **292,** 292, 294, 295, 304, 305, 306, 324, **325**, 328, 329, 330, 347, 348
Peck, George: 328
Pederson, Douglas: 362
Peel, Eugene: 359
Peltz, Dietrich: 268, 326
Penrod, J.C.: 59
Pickering, Harry: 13
Pickert, Wolfgang: 230, 325
Pohl, Erich Ritter von: 219, **234,** 234, 235,
Portal, Arthur: 246, 253, **260,** 260, 341
Preddy, George: 141, 141, 330, 364
Preddy, William: 364
Preston, Rae: 319
Prevost, Herbert: 363
Price, Roy: 328
Priest, Royce: 306, 306

Q
Quesada, Elwood "Pete": 12, 22, **24,** 28, **28, 61, 95, 101, 102, 246, 249, 251,** 252, **252, 253, 256, 257, 262, 268, 276, 277,** 278, **278, 279, 285, 286,** 287,**287**, 312, **316, 317, 322, 327, 328, 329, 331, 333**
Quirk, Michael: 307, 308

R
Ramke, Hermann: 299, **300,** 300
Rentschler, Frederick: 48
Reynolds, Thomas: 131, **132**
Rice, Raymond: 41
Richtofen, Wolfram von: 200, **200,** 234
Riedel, Charles: 363, 363
Righetti, Elwyn: 129, 130, 355, **356**, 361, 363
Rimmerman, Benjamin: 113, **134,** 145, **361,** 361, 362
Robb, J.M.:194
Robinson, David: 290
Robinson, Robert: 328
Rogers, Herbert: 363
Rogers, John: 362
Rommel, Erwin: 21, 176, 177, **178,** 178, **192,** 200, 250, 275, 276, 279, 282
Roosevelt, Franklin: 186, 245
Rose, Maurice: 285
Rotzler, Henry: 307
Royce, Henry: 50
Royce, Ralph: 312, 313, 326, 336
Rudel, Heinz Ulrich: 122
Rudorffer, Erich: 263
Rundstedt, Gerd von: 250, **251,** 282, 315, 322, 331, 333, 344, 348
Russo, Michael: 43
Rush, George: 196
Rutland. Herbert: 126

S

Saied, Kemal: 152
Saunders, Samuel: 328
Schilling, David: 36, 38, 92, 128, 307, **307**
Schlieben, Wilhelm von: 276, **277**, 277
Schmidt, Josef: 326
Schmued, Edgar: 41
Schreiber, Leroy: 127, 256
Seeley, Grant: 362
Seville, Gordon: 336
Shafer, Dale: 357
Sluder, Chet: 232
Shirer, William: 160
Shook, Harry: 295
Simpson, William: 247, 307
Slessor, Arthur: 206, **209,** 209
Slingerland, Chester: 349
Smith. Paul: 168
Smith, Walter Bedell: 245
Smith, T.W.: 357
Smith, V.A.: 357
Smith, Vernon: 359
Smith, Zell: 264
Smoak, Andrew: 362
Solko, Joseph: 196
Spaatz, Carl "Toohey": 12, **33, 72, 139, 173, 175, 176, 183,** 193, **194,** 246, **249, 250, 251, 253,** 259, **259, 260, 287, 288, 309,** 325, **332, 341, 368**
Speer, Albert: 136, 136, **339,** 339, 340, 349
Stauffenberg, Claus von: 179, 283
Starr, Albert: 34
Stecker, Raymond: 256, **305,** 306, **327**, 328
Stegmann, Rudolf: 276
Stewart, Everett: 346
Stewart, Jimmy: 214
Strahm, Victor: 246
Strickland, Abby: 171
Strother, Dean: 232
Stuckey, George: 348
Sturgis, John: 214
Sullivan, John: 34
Swauger, Frederick: 359
Sweat, Dale: 360
Sykes, Henry: 361
Szaniawski, Edward "Jonesy": 255

T

Tacon, Avelin: 22, 22
Taylor, Clyde: 359
Tedder, Arthur: 24, 194, 205, 243, **245,** 245, 249, 252, **258,** 259, 260, 309, 341
Thacker, Robert: 34
Thoman, Robert: 328
Thury, Joseph: 129, **133,** 256, **357,** 358
Tindal, Lorry: 256, 279
Treff, Ernest: 359
Trubenbach, Hannes: 326
Truscott, Lucian: 225, **237**
Twining, Nathan: 39, 206, 241

U

Udet, Ernst: 32
Urton, Thomas: 214

V

Vandenberg, Hoyt: 246, 247, 272, 287, **288,** 288, **312,** 316, **325,** 326, 341, 345
Vickery, Duran: 359
Vietinghoff, Heinrich von: 190, 202, 217, **233,** 233, 241, 242

W

Waldron, Karl: 364
Walton, J.B.: 187
Warlimont, Walter: 287
Watson, Ralph "Doc": 176, 176
Weise, Friedrich: 224, 227
Wells, James: 328
Welch, Robert: 355
Welsh, William: 172
Westlake, G.H.: 240
Westphal, Siegfried: 217
Weyland, Otto,"Opie": 22, 22, 26, 29, 74, 247, 257, 287, **288**, 289, **292**, 292, 307, **325,** 326, 329, 334, 340, 348
Whitley, John: 256
Wigglesworth, H.E.P.: 194, **245**
Wilkerson, William: 356
Williams. Kenneth: 34
Williams. Paul: 175, 176
Williamson, Felix: 362
Wilson, Cy: 167
Wilson, Henry "Jumbo": 205, 205, **237,** 237,
Wittmann, Michael: 122, 122

Wood, Myron: 72, 247
Woods, Sidney: 357, 362
Worley, Neal: 328, 363
Wright. Gilbert: 34,
Wright, Johnny: 34
Wyler, William: 214
Wymond, Gilbert: 214, **214**

Y
Yefimov, A.N.: 122

Z
Zeiss, Richard: 302
Zemke, Hubert: 36, **38, 114, 128,** 158, **158, 290,**
Ziegewald, Edward: 315
Zuckerman, Solly: 110, **257**, 257, 259, 260

Victory Roll:

The American Fighter Pilot and Aircraft in World War II

William Wolf

Well-trained pilots flying superior new fighter aircraft against an enemy, losing its best pilots and unable to afford the luxury of extended training, brought about the inevitable defeat of the Axis air forces. After the war these young men, America's "best and brightest" took a leading place in American society and industry. This is their story.

ISBN: 0764314580

Size: 8 1/2" x 11"

Illustrations: over 670 b/w photographs

Pages: 456

$59.95 hard cover